NEW YORK FIELD CODES SERIES

Volume IV

NEW YORK FIELD CODES SERIES

Volume I. The Code of Civil Procedure of the State of New-York (1850)

Volume II. The Code of Criminal Procedure of the State of New York (1850)

Volume III. The Civil Code of the State of New York (1865)

Volume IV. The Penal Code of the State of New York (1865)

Volume V. The Political Code of the State of New York (1860)

NEW YORK FIELD CODES SERIES

VOLUME IV

THE

PENAL CODE

OF THE

STATE OF NEW YORK

REPORTED COMPLETE

BY THE

COMMISSIONERS OF THE CODE.

General Introduction to the Series
by Michael Weber

THE LAWBOOK EXCHANGE, LTD.
Clark, New Jersey

New York Field Codes Series
ISBN 978-1-886363-40-3

Vol. I. The Code of Civil Procedure of the State of New-York
ISBN 978-1-886363-34-2

Vol. II. The Code of Criminal Procedure of the State of New York
ISBN 978-1-886363-35-9

Vol. III. The Civil Code of the State of New York
ISBN 978-1-886363-38-0

Vol. IV. The Penal Code of the State of New York
ISBN 978-1-886363-36-6

Vol. V. The Political Code of the State of New York
ISBN 978-1-886363-37-3

Lawbook Exchange edition 2011

The quality of this reprint is equivalent to the quality of the original work.

THE LAWBOOK EXCHANGE, LTD.
33 Terminal Avenue
Clark, New Jersey 07066-1321

Please see our website for a selection of our other publications and fine facsimile reprints of classic works of legal history:
www.lawbookexchange.com

Library of Congress Cataloging-in-Publication Data

New York (State). Commissioners of the Code.
The penal code of the State of New-York / reported complete by the Commissioners of the Code.
p. cm. (New York Field codes, 1850-1865)
Originally published: Albany : Weed, Parsons, public printers, 1865.
ISBN 1-886363-36-6 (alk. paper)
1. Criminal law—New York (State) I. Title. II. Series.
KFN6100.A3 1997
345.747—dc21

97-42135
CIP

Printed in the United States of America on acid-free paper

GENERAL INTRODUCTION
TO THE SERIES

These five volumes (of which this is Volume IV) contain the complete texts of the law codes drafted for New York State by David Dudley Field, and his colleagues during the years 1847 to 1865. They include Field's two procedural codes—Civil Procedure and Criminal Procedure—and three substantive codes—Political, Penal, and Civil. The two procedural codes were drafted first, pursuant to Article VI, Section 24, of the 1846 New York State Constitution, which stated:

> The Legislature at its first session after the adoption of the Constitution, shall provide for the appointment of three commissioners, whose duty it shall be to revise, reform, simplify, and abridge the rules and practice, pleadings, forms, and proceedings of the courts of record of this State, and to report thereon to the Legislature, subject to their adoption and modification from time to time.[1]

A separate provision of the Constitution called for commissioners "to reduce into a written and systematic code the whole body of the law of this state, or so much and such parts thereof as to the said commissioners shall seem practicable and expedient." This provision eventually resulted in the substantive political, penal, and civil codes.[2]

Field was perhaps the leading American proponent of codification. He served with both groups of commissioners.

---

[1] Quoted in Mildred V. Coe and Lewis W. Morse, "Chronology of the Development of the David Dudley Field Code," *Cornell Law Quarterly* 27 (1942): 238.

[2] Alison Reppy, "The Field Codification Concept," in *David Dudley Field: Centenary Essays Celebrating One Hundred Years of Legal Reform,* ed. Alison Reppy (New York: New York University School of Law, 1949), 37. Reppy's chapter is very useful for untangling the convoluted history of the commissions, the writing of the codes, and the fates of the codes in the New York legislature.

More than any other individual, Field was responsible for the drafting of all the codes. (He has been called "an inexhaustible one man codifying machine."[3])

New York, however, enacted only three: the Code of Civil Procedure—which is often referred to simply as "the Field Code"—and, after many years, the Code of Criminal Procedure and the Penal Code. But the significance of Field's work extended far beyond New York State. As one legal scholar has observed, Field's efforts changed how lawyers and judges do their work and led to "new ways of understanding the law itself."[4]

The Codification Movement

Field's codes were part of a wider codification movement in the United States in the first half of the nineteenth century.[5] In the 1830s, for example, a few years before Field's work began in New York, U.S. Supreme Court Justice Joseph Story was active in attempting to codify the Massachusetts law. The codification movement was an attempt to clarify the law and remove obsolete rules so that the law could be intelligible to ordinary citizens. Its proponents considered the existing body of law, based as it was on English common law, "inaccessible and uncertain . . . unnecessarily mysterious, complex, and overly technical."[6] Field remarked:

> The common law of New York, like the common law of England, from which it is in great part derived, consists of a vast number of rules of property and of conduct, which have been applied by the judicial tribunals, and which had their origin either in legislative enactments, now forgotten, or in

---

[3] Robert W. Gordon, review of *The American Codification Movement: A Study of Antebellum Legal Reform,* by Charles C. Cook, *Vanderbilt Law Review* 36 (1983): 435.

[4] William P. LaPiana, "Just the Facts: The Field Code and the Case Method," *New York Law School Law Review* 36 (1991): 304.

[5] See Charles C. Cook, *The American Codification Movement: A Study of Antebellum Legal Reform* (Westport, Conn.: Greenwood, 1981).

[6] Ibid., 5.

> traditions from ancient times, or in the consciences of the judges, as the cases came before them.[7]

Proponents of codification took to heart the critical observation of the great English reformer Jeremy Bentham that common law judges made law "as a man makes laws for his dog. When your dog does anything you want to break him of, you wait till he does it, and then you beat him for it."[8] They wanted more system, more precision, and more simplicity in the law. Many were impressed by France's Civil Code, established by Napoleon in 1804, which Edward Livingston had applied to Louisiana in the 1820s.

For some American codifiers, flushed by post-Revolutionary War patriotism, the great weight of the English common law was seen as an alien, un-American presence. A few wanted to go so far as to abolish the common law entirely. Most of the reformers, however, including Field, were not so radical. Their goal was to reduce the common law power of judges and give state legislators the chance to shape the law by reducing to statutory form those parts of the common law that could be plainly stated in a concise book of statutes.

Field's Range of Influence

David Dudley Field (1805–1894) was born in Haddam, Connecticut, into a family of high achievers.[9] Both his father, a minister, and mother were the children of Revolutionary War officers. Among his siblings were Stephen Johnson Field (1816–1899), who was appointed by President Lincoln to the United

---

[7] Introduction to *The Civil Code of the State of New York* (1865), in vol. III of this series, xiv.

[8] Quoted in Lawrence M. Friedman, *American Law* (New York: Norton, 1984), 92.

[9] Useful biographical sources are Helen K. Hoy, "David Dudley Field," in *Great American Lawyers,* ed. William Draper Lewis, vol. 5 (Philadelphia: Winston, 1908; reprint, South Hackensack, N.J.: Rothman, 1971); and the biography written by Field's younger brother, Henry M. Field, *The Life of David Dudley Field* (New York: Scribner's, 1898).

States Supreme Court in 1863, and Cyrus West Field, who laid the first transatlantic cable in 1866. While Field had extra ordinary intelligence, ability, and diligence, he was also competitive, cantankerous, and stubborn. He outlived three wives. (His childhood nurse called him "a most determined fellow."[10]) Not everyone felt affection for him, but very few questioned his legal skill. A colleague, subsequently dean of New York University's Law School, said, "For at least a third of a century, David Dudley Field was the most commanding figure at the American bar."[11]

After attending Williams College, Field studied law in Albany and New York City and was admitted to the New York Bar in 1828. He was active in politics as a Democrat but broke with the party over the Mexican War and slavery and in the 1850s became one of the founders of the Republican Party. Field played an important role in securing Abraham Lincoln's nomination as the Republican candidate for president in 1860. After the Civil War, however, he returned to the Democratic fold and was a close associate of Samuel J. Tilden.

Field was active as a lawyer for 60 years and participated in many notable cases heard by the Supreme Court, including *Ex parte Milligan* (1866), *Cummings* v. *Missouri* (1867), *Ex parte McArdle* (1868), and *United States* v. *Cruikshank* (1876). He provoked considerable controversy in the late 1860s and 1870s by serving as counsel to Jay Gould and James Fisk during the scandal involving the Erie Railroad and by defending New York's notorious William Marcy "Boss" Tweed.

The Origin of the Codes

Field valued precision and clarity. He greatly admired the sciences and mathematics, saying of the latter, "Its superiority over every other department of learning . . . is to be ascribed, I fancy, to the precision of its language."[12] No doubt this penchant

---

[10] Quoted in Stephen N. Subrin, "David Dudley Field and the Field Code: A Historical Analysis of an Earlier Procedural Vision," *Law and History Review* 6 (Fall 1988): 314.
[11] Austin Abbot, quoted in Field, *Life,* vii.
[12] Subrin, "David Dudley Field and the Field Code," 315.

contributed to Field's interest in the movement for codification of the law. He began working for codification in the late 1830s and was instrumental in having the provisions mandating commissions to reform the law of the state written into the 1846 New York Constitution.

Field's goal was to put all of New York's law into written form and to combine in one set of procedures the whole of actions in both law and equity. He wanted to reform the procedural law so that a legal dispute could be started with pleadings that clearly related what happened and settled in one court in one action. In his 1847 essay "What Shall Be Done with the Practice of the Courts?" Field wrote:

> What I propose, then, in respect to cases of legal cognizance, is this: that the present forms of action be abolished, and in their stead a complaint and answer required, each setting forth the real claim and defense of the parties. Such pleadings would be precisely similar to those proposed for equity cases, and we should thus have a uniform course of pleading for all cases, legal and equitable.
>
> . . .
>
> Let the plaintiff set forth his cause of action in his complaint briefly, in ordinary language, and without repetition; and let the defendant make his answer in the same way. Let each party verify his allegation by making oath that he believes it to be true. The complaint will then acquaint the defendant with the real charge, while the answer will inform the plaintiff of the real defense. The disputed facts will be sifted from the undisputed, and the parties will go to trial knowing what they have to answer. The plaintiff will state his case as he believes it, and as he expects to prove it. The defendant, for his part, will set forth what he believes and expects to establish . . . He will not be perplexed with questions of double pleading, nor shackled by ancient technical rules.[13]

---

[13] Quoted in Kermit L. Hall, William M. Wiecek, and Paul Finkelman, eds., *American Legal History: Cases and Materials,* 2nd ed. (New York: Oxford University Press, 1996), 323.

In September 1847 Field became one of the three commissioners—the other two were Arphaxad Loomis and David Graham—appointed by the New York legislature to reform legal procedures as mandated by the Constitution.[14] He replaced Nicholas Hill, who resigned because he was appalled that his colleagues were contemplating changes "so purely experimental, so sudden and general, and so perilous."[15] Field dominated the commission's work, which proceeded swiftly. The commission presented a draft of a Code of Civil Procedure to the legislature on February 29, 1848. The draft was enacted into law on April 12 of that year and has become known as the "Field Code." Subsequently the commission presented additional reports, proposing amendments to the code, some of which the legislature enacted. On December 31, 1849, the commission completed its work by presenting two complete codes: Civil Procedure and Criminal Procedure. Published in 1850, these codes are reprinted as volumes I and II of the present series. Years later, on July 1, 1881, an amended version of the Code of Criminal Procedure was enacted.[16]

Meanwhile, a separate commission also created in 1847 and charged with codifying the substantive law had made little progress, and it was abolished in 1850. But after intense effort Field in 1857 persuaded the legislature to set up a new commission empowered to fulfill the Constitution's mandate "to reduce into a written and systematic code the whole body of the law of the state of New York." Field, William Curtis Noyes, and Alexander W. Bradford were selected as the commissioners.[17] Over the next eight years they labored on three codes: a Political Code, embracing "the laws respecting the government of the state, its civil polity, the functions of its public officers, and the political rights and duties of its citizens"; a Civil Code, covering "the laws of personal rights and relations of property, and of obligations"; and a Penal Code, defining "all the crimes for which persons can be punished and the punishment for the

---

[14] Coe and Morse, "Chronology," 238.

[15] Lawrence M. Friedman, *A History of American Law,* 2nd ed. (New York: Simon & Schuster, 1986), 391.

[16] Reppy, "The Field Codification Concept," 33–8.

[17] Ibid., 38.

crime."[18] Field himself personally prepared the civil code. The entire scheme roughly paralleled the France's Code Napoleon. The Political Code was submitted to the legislature and published in 1860, the final version of the Penal Code was submitted in 1864 and published in 1865, and the final version of the Civil Code was submitted and published in 1865.[19] We reprint them in volumes III-V of the present series.

Field remained devoted to the cause of codification for the rest of his life. His interest even extended to the codification to international law, and in the 1870s he prepared a draft outline for a code of international law. He traveled to both Europe and Asia and was gratified to see the influence his New York codification work was having in Great Britain as well as in India and other British colonies.

When Field died in 1894 at the age of 89, a member of the New York Bar paid him this tribute:

> The magnitude of the results of his labors can scarcely be overestimated. . . . That he exerted a greater influence in modifying and simplifying the judicial systems of the United States and England than any other man of his time will hardly be denied. The world over, wherever the prevailing jurisprudence has had its origin in the English common law, the form and manner of conducting litigations and transacting the business of the courts are due to the influence of David Dudley Field.[20]

The Reception and Significance of the Field Codes

As we have seen, the New York legislature quickly passed Field's Code of Civil Procedure. The legislature later amended the code several times, however, and considerably diluted its concision and weakened the force of Field's reforms.

The other codes encountered much more difficulty in New York. Only two were enacted and both not until 1881: the Code of Criminal Procedure, which had been submitted initially in late

---

[18] Coe and Morse, "Chronology," 244–5.
[19] Ibid., 245.
[20] Quoted in Hoy, "David Dudley Field," 128.

1849, and the Penal Code of 1865. The New York Assembly passed the Civil Code four times, and the entire legislature did so twice—only to have it vetoed each time by the governor.[21] The Civil Code, which the commissioners claimed made important changes in "the rights of married women, the adoption of children, and the assimilation of the laws of real and personal by politicians. James C. Carter, a prominent property,"[22] sparked particularly intense debate. Opposition within the legal profession was intense, and the New York City Bar Association in 1883 unanimously passed a resolution against it.[23]

Opposition to the Civil Code—and to the codification movement in general—centered around two general points. The first was that no code, however skillfully prepared, could encompass all the wealth of experience embodied in the common law. The second was that codification would take control of the law away from the courts, where it belonged, and give it to legislatures run by politicians. James C. Carter. A prominent New York lawyer and a leading opponent of codification—he termed Field's work "grossly defective"[24]—wrote in essays in the 1880s:

> The question is [whether the] growth, development and improvement of the law [should] remain under the guidance of men selected by the people on account of their special qualifications for the work [or] be transferred to a numerous legislative body, disqualified by the nature of their duties for the discharge of this supreme function . . . [Courts apply] "a social standard of justice[,] . . . the product of the combined operation of the thought, the morality, the intellectual and moral culture of the time."[25]

These arguments carried the day in New York.

---

[21] Reppy, "The Field Codification Concept," 46.
[22] *Civil Code,* vol. III of this series, xxxi.
[23] Morton J. Horwitz, *The Transformation of American Law: 1870-1960* (Cambridge: Harvard University Press, 1977), 118.
[24] Quoted in Hoy, "David Dudley Field," 165.
[25] Quoted in Friedman, *A History of American Law,* 404.

But outside New York, especially in the newer western states and territories that did not have an inherited body of law, Field's codes enjoyed considerably more success. The Code of Civil Procedure—the "Field Code"—was adopted in Missouri as early as 1849. California, newly admitted to the Union, followed in 1851 with the help of Field's brother Stephen, who had been elected to the California legislature in 1850 after moving from New York the previous year. By 1862 ten more states and territories had adopted the Code of Civil Procedure, and by 1900 another 12 had done so.[26] In addition several states adopted a procedural criminal code and substantive penal, political, and civil codes based on Field's work. Indeed California enacted adaptations of all five of Field's codes. Portions of these codes are still in effect today.[27]

Ironically Field's attempts through codification to limit the role in America of English-derived common law had consequences for legal reform in Great Britain itself. The authors and proponents of the English Judicature Acts of 1873 and 1875, many of whom knew Field personally, were influenced by his work. Field's codes inspired lawmakers in the British colonies of India, Singapore, and Hong Kong as well.[28]

Field's codes, then, had great impact both in the United States and internationally and clearly are worthy of study today. Scholars agree, however, that Field's outstanding achievement remains the New York Code of Civil Procedure, the "Field Code." That code and the 1938 Federal Rules of Civil Procedure, which it influenced, remain the two most fundamental sets of

---

[26] The states and territories that adopted the Code of Civil Procedure by 1862 were, in addition to Missouri, California, Iowa, Indiana, Kansas, Minnesota, Nebraska, Nevada, Ohio, and Washington. By 1900 they had been joined by Arizona, Colorado, Idaho, Montana, New Mexico, North Carolina, North and South Dakota, Oklahoma, South Carolina, Utah, and Wyoming. Ibid., 394.

[27] See E. Allan Farnsworth, *An Introduction to the Legal System of the United States,* 2nd ed. (New York: Oceana, 1983); Friedman, *A History of American Law,* 405; and Horwitz, *The Transformation of American Law,* 117–8.

[28] Reppy, "The Field Codification Concept," 48.

rules in American civil procedure."[29] Section 554 of the Code of Civil Procedure contained the following revolutionary declaration:

> The distinction between actions at law and suits in equity, and for the forms of all such actions and suits heretofore existing, are abolished; and, there shall be in this state, hereafter, but one form of action, for the enforcement or protection of private rights and the redress or prevention of private wrongs, which shall be denominated a civil action.[30]

As Field intended, the code simplified the pleadings of plaintiff and defendant, limiting the former to a concise factual complaint, demurrer, and reply and the latter to a concise factual answer and demurrer. It adopted the rules of equity for the application of relief.[31] In the words of the great legal scholar Roscoe Pound:

> No treatises on the theory of legislation and no polemical tracts on law reform have led to such far-reaching concrete results. It [the Code of Civil Procedure] stands toward procedure in the world of the common law where Beccaria's treatise on Crimes and Punishments stood toward the nineteenth-century criminal law. It showed the way.[32]

Michael Weber

---

[29] Roscoe Pound, "David Dudley Field: An Appraisal," in *David Dudley Field: Centenary Essays Celebrating One Hundred Years of Legal Reform,* ed. Alison Reppy (New York: New York University School of Law, 1949), 11; Suprin, "David Dudley Field and the Field Code," 312.

[30] See page 225 of volume I of this series.

[31] Reppy, "The Field Codification Concept," 49–51.

[32] Roscoe Pound, "David Dudley Field: An Appraisal," 8.

THE

PENAL CODE

OF THE

STATE OF NEW YORK

REPORTED COMPLETE

BY THE

COMMISSIONERS OF THE CODE.

ALBANY:
WEED, PARSONS & CO., PRINTERS.
1865.

PRELIMINARY NOTE.

This Code, containing a proposed system of Penal Law for the State of New York, has been prepared by the Commissioners of the Code, pursuant to the directions contained in the act of the Legislature by which they were appointed. A draft of the work has been distributed as required by that act,* and many alterations and amendments have been introduced into the present reprint. A title containing a full system of provisions for the management of state prisons and county jails, has been added to the original draft; and the whole is now ready for the consideration of the Legislature.

In compiling the system of Penal Law embodied in this Code, the following have been the leading objects of the Commissioners:

1. To bring within the compass of a single volume the whole body of the law of crimes and punishments in force within this state. The existing statute law of crimes, though comprehensive, does not abrogate rules of the com-

* The act referred to is chapter 266 of the *Laws of* 1857. It directs the Commissioners to prepare three Codes; the POLITICAL CODE, the CIVIL CODE, and the PENAL CODE. It provides that the Penal Code must define all the crimes for which persons can be punished, and the punishment for the same; and that neither of the Codes shall embrace any provisions concerning actions or special proceedings, civil or criminal, or the law of evidence. The act further directs that whenever the Commissioners shall have prepared either Code, they shall cause it to be distributed among judges and other competent persons for examination, after which the Commissioners shall re-examine their work and consider such suggestions as have been made to them; and that they shall then cause the Codes, as finally agreed upon, to be reprinted and again distributed, six months before being presented to the Legislature.

mon law making criminal many acts which are untouched by statute; nor does it, in respect to crimes for which punishment is expressly prescribed, altogether dispense with the necessity of reference to the common law to determine what are the elements which constitute the offense. As long as the criminality of acts is left to depend upon the uncertain definitions or conflicting authorities of the common law, uncertainty must pervade our criminal jurisprudence. The value of the Penal Code must ultimately depend, in great measure, upon its containing provisions which embrace every species of act or omission which is the subject of criminal punishment. That this has been fully accomplished is scarcely to be expected. But it should be understood that this has been the endeavor of the Commissioners; and if any act or neglect of duty, which, upon a sound view of public policy ought to receive criminal punishment, is not made punishable by provisions of the Code, they hope the omission may be detected, and the necessary provision supplied, in the course of the deliberations of the Legislature.

2. To supply deficiencies and correct errors in existing definitions of crimes. The statutory definitions of offenses, found in our existing law, are in many instances incomplete or inaccurate, and in some cases contradictory when compared with each other. They have been revised, and those which bear upon co-related crimes have been collated, in the desire to render each definition, as far as possible, complete in itself and independent, consistent with all definitions of analogous crimes, and accurate in including every grade of the prohibited act, which deserves punishment, and excluding every act which, though partaking some element of the offense, is yet seen to be innocent.

3. To harmonize the provisions of punishment. The system of punishments instituted by the Revised Statutes was carefully devised and was harmonious and well proportioned, but later legislation has introduced many ine-

qualities and disparities. In this Code these have been, to a considerable extent, corrected. In general, however, for the higher crimes, the punishments prescribed by the existing law have been retained, except where special reasons have called for a modification; while in respect to lesser crimes, the limit of power of the courts to impose fines for misdemeanors in general, has been somewhat increased,* and many crimes of inferior grade have been left to be punished as misdemeanors, the particular measure of punishment imposed by the existing law, being omitted.

4. To supply prohibitions of acts deserving of punishment, but not punishable by the present law. The progress of society creates new opportunities and new temptations to crime, which require to be met by new provisions of law. The statutes of other jurisdictions have been extensively consulted for provisions which might meet by anticipation new developments of crime; and the effort has been to adapt the Code as fully as possible to the wants of the present time.

If the views and purposes above mentioned, had been followed without qualification and restriction in the compilation of the Code, the result would have been quite different from that which has been reached. The Commissioners have, however, in a number of instances, felt restrained from framing provisions of the Code in the manner which has appeared absolutely best, by their sense of the dangers and evils attendant upon hasty innovations upon the existing law. They have, in fact, usually considered, in the first place, the existing statute law of the state relative to each crime, and so far as it has appeared correct and consistent, and was believed to have been approved in practical administration, it has been preserved; such modifications in phraseology being made, as were suitable to render the various sections of the Code as a whole, homogeneous. It has only been where alterations

*See section 14 of the Code, and the note thereto.

or additions of the law have been felt to be needed, that they have been introduced. Influenced by these considerations, the Commissioners have, in many instances, refrained from omitting a special prohibition of a particular species of act, even though they thought the provision needless for the reason that all acts of that class were embraced in a more general prohibition found elsewhere. Where a statute forbidding a particular species of acts has for years existed along with a general provision impliedly embracing the same cases, there is danger in omitting the special provision, however needless it may be, lest an inference should be drawn from the omission, that the act was designed to be made no longer punishable. Where provisions of existing statutes have been thought unobjectionable in themselves, but useless because embraced in effect in other provisions of a more general character, they have, therefore, in many cases been retained by the Commissioners, in the belief that the omission of them may more safely be made in the ultimate revision of the work by the Legislature, than at present. And it will be found that the bulk of the Code, in its present shape, may be materially reduced without impairing its clearness and efficiency, by a rigid exclusion of particular provisions which are capable of being combined in general ones, accompanied by some enactment which shall prevent the argument that because a former prohibition of an act was omitted from the Code, therefore it must be deemed the intent of the Legislature that it should no longer be punishable.

It is to be borne in mind, that the subjects of procedure and evidence in criminal cases, are excluded from the scope of the Penal Code; those topics being embraced in the Codes reported by the Commissioners of practice and pleadings. The Penal Code relates chiefly to the enumeration and definition of crimes, and the designation of the kind and measure of punishment to be inflicted for each. The first two titles of the Code, embody some general principles relative to criminal responsibility, which are independent of the distinctions between offenses. The fifteen titles which follow are occupied with provisions relative to the various crimes, separately considered. The eighteenth title contains some general provisions concerning the interpretation and application of the preceding portions of the Code. The nineteenth title treats of prison discipline in its application to our state prisons and county jails.

To aid in the critical examination of the work, the Commissioners have embraced in this volume, several auxiliary papers. The first of them, which is appended to this preliminary note, is a TABLE OF THE PRINCIPAL CRIMES HERETOFORE RECOGNIZED IN THE JURISPRUDENCE OF GREAT BRITAIN OR AMERICA. This table is not precisely an index to the Code, though it will serve as such in a measure. It is intended as a means of testing the completeness of the provisions reported. It mentions the various crimes described in works on penal law, usually considered authorities in this country. If a crime is provided for by the Code, reference is given to the place where the provision may be found. If no provision has been made, the reason for the omission is briefly indicated.

Other papers introduced with the same view, will be found as appendices at the end of the volume.

The Commissioners acknowledge, with thanks, the assistance rendered them in revising their original draft of this Code, by many gentlemen of the profession in this state and elsewhere, who have contributed suggestions towards the perfection of the work. Assistance of this description has been rendered by so many friends that it would be difficult to mention all. The Commissioners may, however, without undervaluing the contributions of others, mention CHARLES SPRENGEL GREAVES, Esq., of London, one of her majesty's counsel, as one to whom they are under especial obligations. Mr. GREAVES' labors and experience in the reform of the criminal law, as one of the commissioners for the amendment of the statute law of Great Britain, and otherwise,—extending over more than a decade of years, and covering nearly all the important topics of the law of crimes,—qualified him in an eminent degree for the task of advising upon the labors of the Commissioners; and a careful and painstaking examination of their draft, made by him, enabled him to make numerous suggestions towards its improvement, a large number of which are embodied in this reprint.

The Commissioners cannot close this note without expressing their obligations to Messrs. BENJAMIN VAUGHAN ABBOTT and AUSTIN ABBOTT, of the bar of New York, who have assisted them in portions of their work on the Political, Civil and Penal Codes, and to whose diligence, ability and accurate learning they have been much indebted.

With these explanations, the Commissioners respectfully submit the Penal Code to the consideration of the Legislature.

DAVID DUDLEY FIELD.
WM. CURTIS NOYES.
ALEXANDER W. BRADFORD.

New York, December, 1864.

A TABLE

OF THE

PRINCIPAL CRIMES,

HERETOFORE RECOGNIZED IN THE

LAW OF GREAT BRITAIN OR AMERICA,

SHOWING

WHERE THEY ARE TREATED IN THE PENAL CODE, OR, WHY THEY ARE OMITTED FROM IT.

Abandonment of children.

This offense is covered by section 332 of the Penal Code.

Abduction.

This term is commonly used to designate taking a woman and compelling her to marry or to be defiled; accomplished by means of force used either at the taking, or at the marriage or defilement. This offense was made felony by *Stat.*, 2 *Hen. VII*, ch. 2, and benefit of clergy was taken away by *Stat.*, 39 *Eliz.*, ch. 9.

This crime is made punishable in part by section 319 of the Code; but chiefly by sections 326 and 327.

Abortion.

Using means to procure abortion is covered by section 334.

Submitting to attempt to procure abortion, by section 335.

Cases where death results are provided for by sections 249 and 250.

Absence from church.

The omission to attend church for one month, was made indictable by statute, in England. See *Stat.*, 23 *Eliz.*, c. 1, § 5; 3 *Jac.* 1, c. 4; 2 *Chitt. Cr. L.*, 20, note d. Similar statutes have at former times existed in this country.

No provisions *enforcing* attendance at church are introduced in the Code; though the right to attend is protected by sections 54, 55 and 56.

Accessories.

Accessories in felony are made punishable by section 28.

Administering poison. See *Poison.*

Adulterations of food, &c.

Are covered by sections 451, 452.

Adultery.

This is not criminally punishable by the English common law, though it is by the law of Scotland, and by the statutes of several of the United States.

In this state it has not been considered a subject of criminal punishment; and the question being a familiar one, and our existing rule well settled, the commissioners have not suggested any change.

Affidavit.

False swearing in an affidavit is made perjury by section 150.

Procuring another to make a false affidavit is subornation of perjury, by section 162.

The refusal of an officer to take and certify an affidavit, in a proper case, is covered by section 215.

Making an affidavit, or taking one in unauthorized cases, is covered by sections 181 and 182.

The refusal of an individual to make an affidavit is not made criminal, except so far as, under peculiar circumstances, it may constitute a criminal contempt of court, under section 201, subdivisions 4, 5 or 6. In general, the duty is left to be enforced by attachment or other appropriate civil remedy.

Affray.

At common law, the fighting together of two or more persons, in some public place, to the terror of the people. It is said to be distinguishable from common assault and battery, in that it must, of necessity, occur in a public place; and from riot, in that two persons may commit an affray, while at least three are required to constitute riot.

In the Code, what would be an affray at common law, is left to be punished as a common assault and battery, under section 307; unless it is attended by circumstances which make it a duel, under section 293 ; or a riot, under section 474.

Animals.

Injuries to property in animals are covered by sections 698 and 699; and see 702.

Cruelty to animals, by section 699; and see 702.

Instigating fights between animals, by sections 700 and 701.

The criminal responsibility of the owner of a mischievous animal which kills a human being, is defined by section 253.

Apostacy.

A total renunciation of Christianity, by one who has once professed it, but afterwards embraces either a false religion or no religion at all. This was made punishable by 9 and 10 *Wm. III*, ch. 32.

It is not treated as a crime by the Code.

Arresting a corpse.

Covered by section 359.

Arson.

Originally, arson was the burning of a human habitation. The term has been, in this state, and in other jurisdictions, extended by statute, to embrace the burning of other descriptions of property not involving danger to human life.

In the Code, the term is used in its original and restricted sense. See sections 521–539.

Other criminal burnings are punishable as malicious mischief; under section 703.

Artisans going abroad.

It was at one time criminal in England for artisans to leave the realm, with an intent to exercise their trade in a foreign country; though the rule is now abrogated.

This is not made punishable by the Code.

Assault and Assault and Battery.

Covered by sections 304–308.

Assault with intent to kill.

Covered by sections 278, 279.

Assault with intent to commit other felony.

Covered by sections 290, 292.

Assignments. See *Fraudulent assignments.*

Attempts.

As respects many crimes, the attempt is declared punishable equally with the commission.

Besides these provisions, attempts in general are covered by sections 745, 746.

Attorneys.

Buying demands to sue, is covered by section 194.

Lending money upon claims received for collection, by section 196.

Renewing application for stay of trial, without leave, by section 202.

Fraudulent practices, by section 209.

Allowing process to be wrongfully sued out in his name, by section 210.

Misconduct relative to criminal prosecutions, by sections 730, 731.

Auctioneers.

Various offenses by, are covered by sections 502–510.

Barratry.

In the sense of misconduct by a ship master, this offense, so far as it is deemed a criminal offense properly cognizable by the law of this state, is covered by section 628. See also sections 630 and 632.

In the sense of stirring up suits and quarrels, barratry—or barretry—is covered by sections 190–193.

Bathing in public. See *Exposure of the person.*

Battery. See *Assault.*

Bawdy houses.

Covered by sections 367, 369.

Begging.

Is not treated as a crime, but left to be dealt with under the provisions reported in the Code of Criminal Procedure, relative to vagrants, so far as they apply.

Bets and wagers.

In conformity with the existing law, these are made criminal in certain cases only. See sections 62, 388, 389, 390, 400, 486, 700.

Bigamy.

Covered by sections 338–340. See also section 341.

Black mailing. See *Extortion.*

Blasphemy.

Covered by sections 31–33.

Body snatching.

Covered by sections 355–357.

Breaking. See *Housebreaking, Pound Breach* and *Prison Breach*; also *Sabbath Breaking.*

Bribery.

Of electors, is covered by sections 61–65.

Of executive officers, by sections 98, 99, 102–109.

Of legislative officers, by sections 120, 121.

Of judicial officers, jurors, &c., by sections 125, 126, 127, 129.

Of witnesses, by sections 162–170.

Of officers or agents of the state employed on the canals, by sections 516, 517.

Buggery.

Is made punishable, though without employing this term, by sections 343, 344.

Bull baiting.

Covered by sections 701, 702.

Burglary.

Covered by sections 540–548.

Burial.

Violations of the right of, are covered by sections 345–362.

Buying.

A corpse for purposes of dissection is covered by section 356.
A public office, by section 106.
Lands in suit, by section 187.
Pretended titles, by section 188.
Demands for suit, by attorneys, &c., by sections 194, 195.
Lottery tickets, by section 374.
Stamped bottles, by section 417.

Carnal abuse of children.

Covered by section 319, subd. 1. See also sections 327–329.

Carrying concealed weapons.

Covered by section 455.

Challenging.

To fight a duel, is covered by section 297.
To engage in a prize fight, by sections 486, 487.

Champerty.

An agreement to assist another in prosecuting a suit, in consideration of receiving a share of the sum or property recovered.

So far as the contracts of this nature are criminal by our existing law, the provisions relating to them have been retained; without being extended. See sections 187, 188, 194–200.

Cheats.

Covered by sections 620–627.

Children.

Abandoning children, is covered by section 332.
Stealing, by section 337.
Fraudulently producing, by section 212.

Substituting one for another, by section 213.
Neglect to provide for, by section 333.
Concealing birth, or death of, by section 336.
Carnal abuse of, by section 319.
Enticing away for illicit purposes, by section 329.

Cockfighting.

Covered by sections 701, 702.

Compassing to kill the king.

This is mentioned as a specific offense by early English writers. Under our elective form of government, no necessity has been felt for guarding the lives of executive officers, by provisions of law additional to those prescribed in favor of citizens; and no such provisions are embodied in the Code.

Compounding crimes.

Covered by section 183.

Compounding prosecutions.

Covered by section 184.

Concealed weapons.

Carrying these, is covered by section 455.

Conjuration, Divination, Fortune-telling, Enchantment, Magic, Prophesying, Sorcery, Witchcraft.

These have formerly been dealt with as crimes, upon the theory that it was possible that truth should be ascertained, or real effects produced, by supernatural means. In this aspect the law of this subject is obsolete.

Practices of pretending to exercise supernatural powers, or make pretended revelations, are left to the operation of the law relative to false pretenses or to vagrants.

Conspiracy.

Covered by sections 224–226, 673.

Contempts.

Such contempts as are deemed proper subjects of indictment, are made indictable, by section 201. See also 202–205.

Contempts generally are left to be punished as such, by the appropriate proceeding for that purpose. See sections 740, 741, 785.

Counterfeiting.

Covered by sections 553–583.

Crime against nature.

Provided for by sections 343, 344.

Cruelty to animals.

Covered by sections 699–702.

Cursing.

Treated under the term "profane swearing," in sections 34–37.

Cutting stamps.

From writings, with intent to use them fraudulently upon other writings. This is made punishable in Eng., by 12 *Geo. III*, ch. 48.

This being a fraud upon the United States revenue, is left to be punished by the laws of the United States.

Dacoity.

This term is used in the recent Indian Penal Code to designate robbery committed by persons going in gangs for that purpose.

Without employing this name, an increased punishment is provided for this form of robbery by section 289.

Defamation.

Criminal penalties are not extended to slander.

Libel is covered by sections 309–318.

Deforcement.

In Scotch criminal law, an attempt to obstruct justice by hindering or resisting officers of the law in the execution of their duty.

The various forms of this offense are covered, without employing this name, by sections 59, 100, 101, 134, 135, 144, 180, 201, subd. 5, 224, subd. 5, 440, 475, subd. 2, 484, 501.

Demembration.

In Scotch law, the separation of any member from the body.

Is treated under the term "maiming" in sections 263–271.

Desertion.

Desertion of soldiers from military service. In England this was formerly a crime cognizable in the common law courts, though it is believed to be so no longer.

It is left by the Code to be dealt with by the military law. See section 785.

Directors of corporations.

Various offenses by, are covered by sections 646–668.

Disorderly houses.

Covered by sections 368, 369. See also section 675.

Disorderly persons.

This Code does not provide for disorderly persons, but leaves them to be dealt with under the system reported in the Code of Criminal Procedure.

Dissection.

Dissection of human bodies is made punishable, except in special cases, by section 349.

Disturbing meetings.

Disturbing religious meetings is covered by sections 55, 56.
Disturbing political meetings, by sections 79–81.
Disturbing funerals, by section 360.
Disturbing other lawful meetings, by section 473.

Divination. See *Conjuration.*

Drunkenness. See *Intoxication.*

Dueling.

Covered by sections 246, 293–303.

Eavesdropping.

At common law, the offense of listening about a dwelling house to hear and repeat what is said therein.

This offense is extended to relate to buildings generally, and made punishable by section 471.

Elections.

Frauds upon the elective franchise, and other infringements of the purity and freedom of elections, are provided for by sections 61–95.

Embezzlement.

The existing law relative to this offense is considerably enlarged and strengthened by sections 601–612.

Embracery.

At common law, the attempt to corrupt a jury.

Without using this term, the offense has been provided for, not only as respects juries, but also as to referees, arbitrators and all persons authorized to hear and determine a controversy, by sections 125, 131. See also sections 128, 129, 133.

Engrossing.

At common law, the buying up of large quantities of provisions with intent to raise the market price by creating a scarcity.

The tendency of our law being towards liberty in matters of trade, the mere purchasing of goods in quantities is not declared punishable by the Code. But the use of any fraudulent means to affect the market price of property is covered by section 469.

Escape.

The allowing a person lawfully in custody to depart from confinement; also the departure of such person from the place of confinement, if accomplished without breaking the same.

Covered by sections 136–146.

Exercising trade.

Exercising a trade without having served apprenticeship, was made indictable by *Stat.*, 5 *Eliz.*, ch. 4.

No such rule is deemed applicable in this state.

Exporting.

Exporting wool, leather, sundry metals, live sheep, &c., was formerly criminal in England. (3 *Co. Inst.*, 95–97, note.)

No such offense is recognized in the Code.

Exposure of the person.

Provided for by section 363.

Extortion.

Covered by sections 613–619.

Falcon stealing.

This was made felony by *Stat.*, 37 *Edw. III*, ch. 19; but that act amounts only, in fact, to declaring falcons, hawks, &c., property, therefore the subject of larceny.

General provisions upon the subject of larceny are given, in sections 584–600; but the question what is to be deemed property, is not within the scope of the Code.

False personation.

Covered by sections 620–622.

False pretenses; False tokens.

Obtaining property by false pretenses or tokens, is covered by sections 623–627.

False weights and measures.

Using them to defraud, is covered by sections 634–640.

Forcible entry and detainer.

Covered by section 492.

Forcible marriage. See *Abduction*.

Forestalling.

As described by *Stat.*, 5 and 6 *Edw. VI*, ch. 44, consists in buying up merchandise on the way to market; or dissuading persons from bringing merchandise to market; or persuading them to enhance the price, when there.

The tendency of our law being towards liberty in matters of trade, these acts are not made punishable unless some false or fraudulent means are employed to affect the market price. That offense is covered by section 469.

Forgery.

Covered by sections 553–583.

Fornication.

This is an indictable offense in Scotland and in several of the United States.

As it is not indictable by our existing law, and no new reasons are perceived for declaring it so, the commissioners have not urged any change.

Fortune-telling. See *Conjuration.*

Frauds.

In fitting out and destroying vessels, are covered by sections 628–630.

In destroying property insured, by sections 632, 633.

In use of false weights and measures, by sections 634–640.

In management of corporations, by 645–668.

In sale of passage tickets, by sections 669–682.

In relation to documents of title to merchandise, by sections 683–691.

To affect market price of merchandise, by section 469.

Fraudulent assignments.

Covered by sections 641–644.

Fraudulent insolvencies.

By individuals, are covered by sections 641–644.

By corporations, by sections 659–660.

Gambling, Gaming.

Covered by sections 385–400.

Gambling or Gaming houses.

Prohibited by section 392, and see 397, 390.

Game.

The existing law for the preservation of game is continued in force, by section 786, subd. 23.

Grand Larceny.

Covered by sections 587, 589, 591, 592.

Hamesucken.

In Scotch law, the felonious seeking and invasion of a person in his dwelling house.

The burning of a dwelling house, is treated under the term "arson;" and breaking or entering a dwelling house, for criminal purposes, under "burglary." Except as provided under these heads, the Code does not, in general, regard the circumstance that a criminal injury was inflicted within the dwelling of the sufferer, as modifying the character of the crime.

Health laws.

Violations of, are provided for by sections 435–441.

Heresy.

Is enumerated among crimes by English authorities; as consisting, not in a total repudiation of Christianity, but in a denial of some of its essential doctrines, publicly and obstinately avowed.

The tendency of our law is so decided towards liberty in matters of religious faith, that provisions against heresy are clearly unsuitably embodied in the Code.

Homicide.

Covered by sections 236–262.

Horse racing.

Racing near a court, is prohibited by section 207.
For a bet or stake, by section 400.
Upon a highway, by section 472.

House breaking.

Covered by section 550.

Illegal voting.

Covered by sections 68–74.

Incest.

Provided for by section 342.

Indecent Exposures.

Provided for by section 363.

Insolvencies.

Fraudulent insolvencies by individuals are covered by sections 641–644.

Those of corporations, by sections 659, 660.

Intoxication.

Intoxication of physicians, is provided for by sections 257, 404.

Intoxication of persons employed on railroad trains, by section 462.

Intoxication in public places, by section 725.

Keeping bawdy and disorderly houses.

Covered by sections 367–369.

Kidnapping.

Covered by sections 272–276.

Larceny.

Covered by sections 584–600.

Leasing making.

In Scotch law, calumny directed against the king.

Under our elective form of government no necessity is perceived for punishing calumny affecting public officers, otherwise than as they share the protection accorded to citizens generally. No provisions on this subject are given in the Code.

Libel.

Covered by sections 309–318.

Lotteries.

Prohibited by sections 370–384.

Magic. See *Conjuration.*

Maiming.

Of persons, is covered by sections 263–271.

Of animals, by section 699.

Maintenance.

Officiously intermeddling in a suit that no way belongs to one; by assisting either party, with money or otherwise, to prosecute or defend it.

In so far as intervening in a single lawsuit in which one is not a party, is criminal by our existing law, the provisions relative to it are retained, without being extended. See sections 187, 188, 194–200.

The *practice* of fomenting lawsuits is made punishable by sections 190–193.

Malicious mischief.

Covered by sections 696–722.

Malpractice.

As to malpractice by attorneys, see sections 194, 196, 202, 209, 210, 730, 731.

By physicians, 257, 404.

Manslaughter.

Covered by sections 248–259.

Masquerades.

Are covered by sections 478, 480.

Mayhem. See *Maiming*.

Mock auctions.

Covered by section 627.

Multiplication of precious metals.

This was formerly considered a crime in England. (3 *Co. Inst.*, 74.)

The impossibility of the act being now understood, the rule by which it was once thought punishable, is, of course, obsolete.

Murder.

Covered by sections 241–257.

Mutilation.

As to mutilations of persons and animals. See *Maiming*.

As to mutilations of written instruments. See sections 147, 148, 715, 716, 721.

Nuisances.

Punishable by sections 430–434.

Obscene books and pictures.

Covered by sections 363–366.

Omitting to bury.

Omitting to bury the body or remains of a dead person, is made punishable by sections 350–353.

Perjury.

Covered by sections 150–161.

Petit larceny.

Covered by sections 586–588, 590.

Prophesying. See *Conjuration.*

Petit treason.

This offense was abolished by the Revised Statutes, and is not restored by the Code. See section 239.

Piracy.

Is left to be dealt with under the laws of the United States. Burning a vessel within this state is, however, made arson, by sections 521 and 522; and destroying or injuring vessels, or their cargoes, with intent to defraud insurers, &c., is punishable by sections 628–630.

Poison.

Administering stupefying drug to facilitate commission of felony, is covered by section 292.

Poisoning food, wells, &c., by section 405.

Selling poison without record and label, by sections 446–448.

Poisoning animals, by section 698.

Posting.

For not fighting a duel, is covered by section 300.

Pound breach.

It is doubted, in English law, whether breaking a pound to rescue cattle therefrom, when unaccompanied by any breach of the peace, should be deemed a criminal offense, or only a civil trespass.

It has not been thought needful to specify it as a crime in the Code. If the circumstances amount to resisting a public officer, or rescuing property from one, the act is punishable by sections 180, 135.

Polygamy.

This offense is included in bigamy, which is covered by sections 338–340.

Prison breach.

Covered by sections 136–146.

Prize fights.

Covered by sections 485–491.

Profane swearing.

Covered by sections 34–37.

Racing. See *Horse Racing*.

Rape.

Provided for by sections 319–324.

Regrating.

As described by *Stat.*, 5 and 6 *Edw. VI*, ch. 14, is the buying up of provisions in any market and selling them again in the same market or within four miles of it.

The rule of the English law, punishing this, is deemed inapplicable at the present day in this state. See *Engrossing*, *Forestalling*.

Receiving stolen goods.

Covered by section 598.

Rescues.

Covered by sections 134, 135; see also 141–144.

Reset of theft.

In Scotch law, is the receiving and keeping of stolen goods, knowing them to be such, and with intent to conceal them from the owner.

This offense is treated in the Code, but not under this name. See section 598.

Resisting officers.

General resistance to a statute is covered by section 59.

Resisting election officers, by sections 83, 84.

Resisting executive and administrative officers generally, by sections 101, 180, 224, subd. 5, 475, subd. 2.

Compelling adjournment of legislature, by section 115.

Retaking goods from custody of officer, by section 135.

Assisting prisoner to escape from officer, by section 144.

Resisting execution of process, by sections 179, 484.

Intimidating officer, by section 185.

Obstructing health officer, by section 440.

Obstructing revenue officer, by section 501.

Returning from transportation.

The provisions of the English statute upon the subject of returning from transportation before discharge are, of course, deemed inapplicable in this state.

Riot.

Covered by sections 474, 475, 481–483.

Robbery.

Covered by sections 280–289.

Rout.

Covered by sections 476, 479.

Sabbath breaking.

Covered by sections 38–52.

Sacrilege.

Provided for, without however employing this term, by sections 550, 704.

Scolds.

It has not been thought needful to continue the rule of the common law specifically punishing common scolds.

Second offenses.

Increased punishment for these is prescribed by sections 748–751.

Seducing.

Artisans to leave the realm, was formerly indictable in England, but is believed to be so there no longer.

No reason is perceived for creating such a crime in this state.

Seducing persons to serve a foreign prince as a soldier, was made felony by 9 *Geo. II*, ch. 30, § 1.

This is left to be dealt with under the laws of the United States.

Seducing soldiers from their duty, was made punishable by *Stat.*, 37 *Geo. III*, ch. 70.

This is not embraced in the Code, but left to be dealt with under the military law, or under the laws of the United States.

Seduction of females.

The provisions of the existing law upon this subject are embodied in sections 328–331.

Selling liquor.

In court houses or prisons, or near election polls, is made punishable by section 208.

Selling in violation of excise laws, by sections 724, 726–728.

Sepulture.

Violations of the right of, are covered by sections 345–362.

Shooting.

Covered by sections 278, 290, 308, 495.

Slander.

Has never been recognized among crimes, in this state; and no reason has been perceived for a change in the law in this respect.

Smuggling.

Is left to be dealt with under the laws of the United States.

Sorcery. See *Conjuration*.

Seconding.

Seconding a duel or prize fight, is covered by sections 296, 485.

Slung shot.

Carrying them, or using them, is covered by section 454.

Slave trade.

Is left to be dealt with by the laws of the United States.

Sodomy

Is made punishable, without employing this term, by sections 343, 344.

Sorning.

The masterful taking of meat and drink without payment. 2 *Hume on Crimes*, 345. In the undisciplined state of society in Scotland, in early times, peculiar temptations to this offense existed, together with peculiar facilities for its commission; and it was therefore made a capital crime.

No reasons are perceived in the present state of society in this state for distinguishing the criminal taking of food or drink, from that of other property. This offense is therefore left to the general provisions relative to robbery, larceny, extortion, &c.

Spies.

Are left to be dealt with under the military law.

Southrief.

This is a general term employed in Scotch law, to designate all forcible thefts or depredations.

The offenses included in it are treated in the Penal Code under the appropriate titles of our law, such as "robbery."

Striking with weapon—in a church or church-yard.

This was made punishable by cutting off an ear, or branding, besides excommunication, by *Stat.*, 5 *Edw. VI*, ch. 4.

No reason is perceived why the law of New York should distinguish assaults in churches or church-yards, from those in other buildings or places.

Subornation.

Subornation of perjury is covered by sections 162, 163, and see 166–169, 170.

Suicide.

Covered by sections 227–235.

Swearing.

Treated under "profane swearing." See sections 34–37.

Theftbute.

In Scotch law, consists in a corrupt compact with a thief, whereby a person having him in his power, barters public justice for profit to himself; whether by taking a ransom from the thief to dismiss him, or by receiving a share of what he has stolen, to protect him.

This is covered by the provisions relative to compounding crimes and prosecutions; sections 183, 184.

Threatening letters.

Covered by section 618.

Threats.

The use of threats is made punishable, in various cases, by sections 53, 54, 80, 81, 82, 100, 116, 131, subd. 3, 280–283, 300, 318, 458, 474, 614, 618, 733, 734.

Trade marks.

Counterfeiting them, is made punishable by sections 410–416.

Treason.

Covered by sections 57–60.

Trespasses—to lands.

So far as these are made punishable by the existing law, they are declared so by the Code, with some additional provisions. See sections 492, 493, 494, 705, 707–714.

Tumultuous petitioning.

By several English statutes, the right of assembling in numbers to present petitions to the king or parliament is restricted, under criminal penalties. See 13 *Car.* 2, c. 5; 57 *Geo. III*, ch. 19, § 23.

The provisions relative to riot, unlawful assemblies, &c., are all that are deemed necessary, in this state, upon this subject.

Unlawful assemblies.

Covered by sections 477–480, 482.

Unlawful oaths.

Taking an oath in any case not authorized by law, is covered by section 181.

Administering such an oath, by section 182.

Usury.

Receiving usury is made punishable by section 426; conformably to the existing law. It has not been thought desirable to extend the penalty to *paying* usury.

Vagrants.

The Code does not provide for vagrants, but leaves them to be dealt with under the system reported in the Code of Criminal Procedure.

Wagers. See *Bets*

Witchcraft. See *Conjuration*.

ANALYSIS OF THE CONTENTS.

PRELIMINARY PROVISIONS.

TITLE I.

OF THE PERSONS LIABLE TO PUNISHMENT FOR CRIME.

TITLE II.

OF PARTIES TO CRIMES.

TITLE III.

OF CRIMES AGAINST RELIGION AND CONSCIENCE.

TITLE IV.

OF TREASON.

TITLE V.

OF CRIMES AGAINST THE ELECTIVE FRANCHISE.

TITLE VI.

OF CRIMES BY AND AGAINST THE EXECUTIVE POWER OF THE STATE.

TITLE VII.

OF CRIMES AGAINST THE LEGISLATIVE POWER.

TITLE VIII.

OF CRIMES AGAINST PUBLIC JUSTICE.

CHAPTER I.

BRIBERY AND CORRUPTION.

CHAPTER II.

RESCUES.

CHAPTER III.

ESCAPES, AND AIDING THEREIN.

CHAPTER IV.

FORGING, STEALING, MUTILATING AND FALSIFYING JUDICIAL AND PUBLIC RECORDS AND DOCUMENTS.

CHAPTER V.

PERJURY AND SUBORNATION OF PERJURY.

CHAPTER VI.

FALSIFYING EVIDENCE.

CHAPTER VII.

OTHER OFFENSES AGAINST PUBLIC JUSTICE.

CHAPTER VIII.

CONSPIRACY.

TITLE IX.

OF CRIMES AGAINST THE PERSON.

CHAPTER I.

SUICIDE.

CHAPTER II.

HOMICIDE.

CHAPTER III.

MAIMING.

CHAPTER IV.

KIDNAPPING.

CHAPTER V.

ATTEMPTS TO KILL.

CHAPTER VI.

ROBBERY.

CHAPTER VII.

ASSAULTS WITH INTENT TO COMMIT FELONY OTHER THAN ASSAULTS WITH INTENT TO KILL.

CHAPTER VIII.

DUELS AND CHALLENGES.

CHAPTER IX.

ASSAULT AND BATTERY.

CHAPTER X.

LIBEL.

TITLE X.

OF CRIMES AGAINST THE PERSON AND AGAINST PUBLIC DECENCY AND GOOD MORALS.

CHAPTER I.

RAPE, ABDUCTION, CARNAL ABUSE OF CHILDREN, AND SEDUCTION.

CHAPTER II.

ABANDONMENT AND NEGLECT OF CHILDREN.

CHAPTER III.

ABORTIONS AND CONCEALING DEATH OF INFANT.

CHAPTER IV.

CHILD STEALING.

CHAPTER V.

BIGAMY, INCEST, AND THE CRIME AGAINST NATURE.

CHAPTER VI.

VIOLATING SEPULTURE AND THE REMAINS OF THE DEAD.

CHAPTER VII.

INDECENT EXPOSURES, OBSCENE EXHIBITIONS, BOOKS AND PRINTS, AND BAWDY AND OTHER DISORDERLY HOUSES.

CHAPTER VIII.

LOTTERIES.

CHAPTER IX.

GAMING.

CHAPTER X.

PAWNBROKERS.

TITLE XI.

OF OTHER INJURIES TO PERSONS.

TITLE XII.

OF CRIMES AGAINST THE PUBLIC HEALTH AND SAFETY.

TITLE XIII.

OF CRIMES AGAINST THE PUBLIC PEACE.

TITLE XIV.

OF CRIMES AGAINST THE REVENUE AND PROPERTY OF THE STATE.

TITLE XV.

OF CRIMES AGAINST PROPERTY.

CHAPTER I.

ARSON.

CHAPTER II.

BURGLARY AND HOUSEBREAKING.

CHAPTER III.

FORGERY AND COUNTERFEITING.

CHAPTER IV.

LARCENY.

CHAPTER V.

EMBEZZLEMENT.

CHAPTER VI.

EXTORTION.

CHAPTER VII.

FALSE PERSONATION, AND CHEATS.

CHAPTER VIII.

FRAUDULENTLY FITTING OUT AND DESTROYING VESSELS.

CHAPTER IX.

FRAUDULENT DESTRUCTION OF PROPERTY INSURED.

CHAPTER X.

FALSE WEIGHTS AND MEASURES.

CHAPTER XI.

FRAUDULENT INSOLVENCIES BY INDIVIDUALS.

CHAPTER XII.

FRAUDULENT INSOLVENCIES BY CORPORATIONS, AND OTHER FRAUDS IN THEIR MANAGEMENT.

CHAPTER XIII.

FRAUDS IN THE SALE OF PASSAGE TICKETS.

CHAPTER XIV.

FRAUDULENT ISSUE OF DOCUMENTS OF TITLE TO MERCHANDISE.

CHAPTER XV.

MALICIOUS INJURIES TO RAILROADS, HIGHWAYS, BRIDGES AND TELEGRAPHS.

TITLE XVI.

OF MALICIOUS MISCHIEF.

TITLE XVII.

OF MISCELLANEOUS CRIMES.

TITLE XVIII.

GENERAL PROVISIONS.

TITLE XIX.

OF THE GOVERNMENT AND DISCIPLINE OF STATE PRISONS AND COUNTY JAILS, AND OF THE CONDUCT AND TREATMENT OF PRISONERS THEREIN.

CHAPTER I.

DESIGNATION OF THE DIFFERENT STATE PRISONS AND COUNTY JAILS, AND GENERAL REGULATIONS RESPECTING THEM, AND THE CUSTODY AND REMOVAL OF PRISONERS.

CHAPTER II.

INSPECTORS OF STATE PRISONS.

CHAPTER III.

GENERAL PROVISIONS RELATIVE TO OFFICERS OF THE VARIOUS STATE PRISONS.

CHAPTER IV.

THE WARDENS.

CHAPTER V.

THE MATRON OF THE FEMALE DEPARTMENT OF THE SING SING PRISON, AND ASSISTANT MATRONS.

CHAPTER VI.

CLERKS.

CHAPTER VII.

THE KEEPERS.

CHAPTER VIII.

THE PHYSICIANS.

CHAPTER IX.

THE CHAPLAINS.

CHAPTER X.

THE INSTRUCTORS AND INSTRUCTRESS.

CHAPTER XI.

THE GUARDS.

CHAPTER XII.

THE MILITARY COMPANIES AT SING SING AND AUBURN.

CHAPTER XIII.

THE FIRE COMPANY AT AUBURN.

CHAPTER XIV.

THE CUSTODY, CONDUCT AND DISCIPLINE OF CONVICTS.

CHAPTER XV.

THE EMPLOYMENT OF CONVICTS.

CHAPTER XVI.

COMMUTATION OF SENTENCES.

CHAPTER XVII.

THE CUSTODY, CONDUCT, DISCIPLINE AND EMPLOYMENT OF PRISONERS IN COUNTY JAILS.

CHAPTER XVIII.

INSPECTION OF COUNTY JAILS.

CHAPTER XIX.

CUSTODY OF INSANE PRISONERS.

CHAPTER XX.

GENERAL PROVISIONS APPLICABLE EQUALLY TO STATE PRISONS AND COUNTY JAILS.

APPENDIX A.

APPENDIX B.

APPENDIX C.

THE

PENAL CODE

OF THE

STATE OF NEW YORK.

AN ACT

TO ESTABLISH A PENAL CODE.

The People of the State of New York, represented in Senate and Assembly, do enact as follows:

PRELIMINARY PROVISIONS.

SECTION 1. This act shall be known as the PENAL CODE OF THE STATE OF NEW YORK. Title of Code.

Its effect. § 2. No act or omission commenced after the day on which this Code shall take effect as a law, shall be deemed criminal or punishable, except as prescribed or authorized by this Code, or by some of the statutes which are specified in section 786 as continuing in force. Any act or omission commenced prior to that day may be inquired of, prosecuted and punished in the same manner as if this Code had not been passed.

Abolition of Common Law Offenses.—This section abolishes all common law offenses. Such appears to have been clearly the intention of the legislature. The act appointing the commissioners prescribes that "the Penal Code must define all the crimes for which persons can be punished."

Effect of the Code upon Anterior Offenses.—In so far as this Code declares acts criminal which heretofore have not been so regarded, or increases the severity or changes the kind of punishment inflicted for a crime defined by our former laws, the familiar provision of the Federal Constitution prohibiting *ex post facto* laws, forbids that it be made applicable to acts committed before it takes effect. (*U. S. Const.*, art. 1, § 10, sub. 1; Calder *v.* Bull, 3 *Dall.*, 386; Fletcher *v.* Peck, 6 *Cr.* 87, 138.) In so far as it *diminishes* the severity of the punishment, by prescribing a less amount or duration of penalty, of the same kind with that inflicted under the former law, there may be no constitutional reason to prevent its being made applicable to all offenses, irrespective of the date of commission. (Hartung *v.* People, 22 *N. Y.*, 95; Commonwealth *v.* Mott, 21 *Pick.*, 492; Keene *v.* State, 3 *Chandl.*, 109.) Ameliorations of punishment introduced by statute are often expressly extended to prior offenses. (See 2 *Rev. Stat.*, 779, § 6; *Laws of* 1861, ch. 303, § 3; *Mass. Gen. Stat.*, 880, § 5; *Rev. Stat. of Wisc.*, 757, § 3.) No natural right arises, however, in behalf of an offender, to claim the benefit of a subsequent statute mitigating the penalty for offenses like his own; though clemency readily awards it to him. Convenience and simplicity in the administration of penal justice should control upon this point. The commissioners are of opinion that any attempt by general words to render such mitigations of punishment as are introduced by the Code, applicable to antecedent offenses, is calculated to raise nice and embarrassing questions as to whether a given modification is a mitigation or not. They observe that it has been held that the judiciary cannot determine whether a provision that no person convicted of a capital offense shall be executed until after a year's confinement, nor then except upon special warrant from the governor — is or is not less severe than a former law imposing absolutely the punishment of death. (Hartung *v.* People, 22 *N. Y.*, 95, 106.) Also that a substitution of imprisonment not exceeding seven years, for whipping, has been held not an increase of punishment. (Strong *v.* State, 1 *Blackf.*, 193; Herber *v.* State, 7 *Tex.*, 69.) They therefore recommend that, as it is necessary to retain the former system of prohibitions and penalties to a great extent, as respects acts already committed, it be retained complete.

Should it be thought desirable to give those whose offenses were committed prior to the Code, the benefit of any ameliorations of punishment introduced, the courts might be relieved of weighing the comparative severity of penalties, by a provision entitling a person convicted, after the Code, of an offense committed before it took effect, the right to elect, at the time of sentence being pronounced, the punishment prescribed by the former law, instead of that authorized by the new. The commissioners, however, deem such a provision inexpedient.

§ 3. A crime or public offense is an act or omission forbidden by law, and to which is annexed, upon conviction, either of the following punishments: "Crime" and "public offense," defined.

1. Death;

2. Imprisonment;

3. Fine;

4. Removal from office; or,

5. Disqualification to hold and enjoy any office of honor, trust, or profit under this state.

Rep. Code Cr. Pro., 2, § 3.

The use of the terms "crime," "felony," "misdemeanor" and "offense," is far from uniform even among legal writers. In addition to the definition given by Mr. Livingston (and referred to *Rep. Code Cr. Pro.*, 2, note), the following may be mentioned:

"A crime, or misdemeanor," says Blackstone, "is an act committed or omitted in violation of a public law, either forbidding or commanding it." "Crimes and misdemeanors, properly speaking, are synonymous terms; though in common usage, the word 'crimes' is made to denote such offenses as are of a deeper and more atrocious dye."

"Misdemeanor," says Christian, "is generally used in contradiction to felony; and misdemeanors comprehend all indictable offenses, which do not amount to felony." (*Note to* 4 *Bl. Comm.*, 5.)

"Misdemeanor," says Chitty, "means every offense inferior to felony, but punishable by indictment, or by particular prescribed proceedings. The term 'offense' is usually understood to be a crime *not indictable*, but *punishable summarily*, or by the forfeiture of a *penalty*." (1 *Gen. Pr.*, 14.)

"A crime," says Bell, "may be defined to be any act done in violation of those duties which an individual owes to the community, and for a breach of which the law has provided that the offender shall make satisfaction to the public." (*Dict. L. of Scot.*, tit. Crime.)

Bishop defines crimes as "those wrongs which the government notices as injurious to the public, and punishes in what is called a criminal proceeding, in its own name." (1 *Cr. L.*, § 43.)

"The word crime," says Chief Justice SAVAGE, of our own State, speaking of the clause in the Federal Constitution which provides for the extradition of persons charged with *treason, felony, or other crime*, "is synonymous with misdemeanor, and includes every offense below felony punished by indictment as an offense against the public." (Matter of Clark, 9 *Wend.*, 212, 222.)

"The term *misdemeanor*," says the same judge, in another case, "is used in contradistinction to *felony*, and comprehends all indictable offenses which do not amount to felony." (Son *v.* People, 12 *Wend.*, 314.)

The Revised Statutes of this State, have employed the terms "crime" and "offense" as equivalent to each other, and as denoting "any offense for which any criminal punishment may by law be inflicted" (2 *Rev. Stat.*, 702, § 22); and have defined "felony" as an offense punishable by death or imprisonment in State prison.

The commissioners have based their definitions upon the usage which has grown up in this State under the Revised Statutes; employing "crime" and "offense" in the extensive signification, and confining "felony" and "misdemeanor" to denote the classes into which crimes are divided. (See also *Rep. Code of Cr. Pro.*, 3, § 5, note.)

Crimes, how divided.

§ 4. Crimes are divided into

1. Felonies;

2. Misdemeanors.

§ 5. A felony is a crime which is, or may be, punishable with death, or by imprisonment in a State prison. Felony defined.

See *Rep. Code Cr. Pro.*, 3, § 5.

§ 6. Every other crime is a misdemeanor. Misdemeanor.

Rep. Code Cr. Pro., 3, § 6.

§ 7. This Code specifies the classes of persons who are deemed capable of crimes, and liable to punishment therefor; and defines the nature of the various crimes; and prescribes the kind and measure of punishment to be inflicted for each. The manner of prosecuting and convicting criminals is regulated by the Code of Criminal Procedure. Objects of the Penal Code.

§ 8. The punishments prescribed by this Code can be inflicted only upon a legal conviction in a court having jurisdiction. Conviction must precede punishment.

A similar provision has already been reported in the Code of Criminal Procedure. (§ 7.) As however the language employed in the various sections of the Penal Code, prescribing punishments, requires some such general restriction to render it accurate, the commissioners have repeated the provision here, in order that each Code may be, as far as possible, complete and independent, and that the legislature may have it in their power to consider either, without being embarrassed by its connection with others. The same consideration has induced them in a number of instances to insert a provision deemed necessary to the completeness of the Code, notwithstanding that it has been embodied in one of the Codes already reported, and now before the Legislature for its consideration.

§ 9. Whenever a crime is distinguished into degrees, the jury, if they convict the prisoner, shall find the degree of the crime, of which he is guilty. Jury are to find degree of crime.

§ 10. The rule of the common law that penal statutes are to be strictly construed, has no application to this Code. All its provisions are to be construed according to the fair import of their terms, with a view to effect its objects and to promote justice. Construction of the Penal Code.

Of sections declaring crimes punishable. § 11. The several sections of this Code which declare certain crimes to be punishable as therein mentioned, devolve a duty upon the court authorized to pass sentence, to determine and impose the punishment prescribed.

Punishments, how determined § 12. Whenever in this Code the punishment for a crime is left undetermined between certain limits, the punishment to be inflicted in a particular case shall be determined by the court authorized to pass sentence, within such limits as may be prescribed by this Code.

Punishment of felonies. § 13. Except in cases where a different punishment is prescribed by this Code or by some existing provision of law, every offense declared to be felony is punishable by a fine not exceeding one thousand dollars or by imprisonment in a state prison not exceeding two years, or by both such fine and imprisonment.

Punishment of misdemeanors. § 14. Except in cases where a different punishment is prescribed by this Code, or by some existing provisions of law, every offense declared to be a misdemeanor, is punishable by imprisonment in a county jail not exceeding one year, or by a fine not exceeding five hundred dollars, or by both such fine and imprisonment.

Based upon 2 *Revised Statutes*, 597, § 40; which provided that misdemeanors for which no punishment was expressly provided, should incur a year's imprisonment, or a fine of two hundred and fifty dollars. In raising the limit of the fine to five hundred dollars, the commissioners do not intend to intimate that cases formerly coming within the operation of the general provision should incur a higher fine; but merely to simplify the provisions of the Code by allowing the general provision to cover misdemeanors of a more aggravated character, than were embraced by the section of the Revised Statutes referred to.

TITLE I.

OF THE PERSONS LIABLE TO PUNISHMENT FOR CRIME.

§ 15. The following persons are liable to punishment under the laws of this State: *Who are liable to punishment.*

1. All persons who commit, in whole or in part, any crime within this State;

2. All who commit theft out of this State, and bring, or are found with the property stolen, in this State;

3. All who, being out of this State, abduct or kidnap, by force or fraud, any person contrary to the laws of the place where such act is committed, and bring, send or convey such person within the limits of this State, and are afterwards found therein;

4. And all who, being out of this State, cause or aid, advise or encourage, another person to commit any act or be guilty of any neglect within this State which is declared criminal by this Code, and who are afterwards found within this State.

The principles embodied in this section are also presented, viewed from a somewhat different point, in the Reported Code of Criminal Procedure (§§ 127–137), coupled with provisions distinguishing the proper county for the trial of various offenses. The question of county jurisdiction belongs wholly to the Code of Procedure But the jurisdiction of the State over offenses planned or in part committed outside its boundaries, ought to be asserted in this Code, unless elsewhere enacted. The principle has therefore been restated; although in language somewhat different from that employed in the Code of Criminal Procedure.

Subd. 2.—Subdivision 2 of this section embodies the rule prescribed by 2 *Rev. Stat.*, 698, § 4. The familiar rule of the English law was that one who committed theft in one county, and carried the stolen goods into another county, might be tried in the latter county; the detaining of the goods there being deemed a continuance of the theft. The former cases in this State held that no such rule was applicable, where property was stolen in another of the United States, and brought into this State. (People *v.* Gardner, 2 *John.*, 477; McCullogh's case, 2 *City H. Rec.*, 45.) The contrary view was, however, adopted by the Supreme Court of Massachusetts, (Commonwealth *v.* Cullins, 1 *Mass.*, 116; Same *v.* Andrews, 2 *Id.*, 14,) which held that there was a sufficient analogy between the different States comprising the Federal Union, and the counties of a single State, to justify the adoption of the English rule. The Revised Statutes following these Massachusetts decisions (see *Revisers' Notes*), prescribed the same rule. The commissioners now propose that it be extended to thefts committed out of the State, whether in another state of the Union, or elsewhere.

Subd. 3. The third subdivision is new; but is suggested as a parallel provision applicable to the case of abduction of the person. It has been held that such abduction furnishes no ground for a *civil action for damages* in the courts of this State. (Malony *v.* Dows, 8 *Abbott's Pr.*, 316.) Conceding this to be so, it is conceived that cases may arise in which the State may be interested to *punish* the act.

Who are capable of committing crimes.

§ 16. All persons are capable of committing crimes, except those belonging to the following classes:

1. Children under the age of seven years;

2. Children of the age of seven years, but under the age of fourteen years, in the absence of proof that at the time of committing the act or neglect charged against them, they knew its wrongfulness;

3. Idiots;

4. Lunatics, insane persons, and all persons of unsound mind, including persons temporarily or partially deprived of reason, upon proof that at the time

of committing the act charged against them, they were incapable of knowing its wrongfulness;

5. Persons who committed the act, or made the omission charged under an ignorance or mistake of fact which disproves any criminal intent. But ignorance of the law does not excuse from punishment for its violation;

6. Persons who committed the act charged without being conscious thereof;

7. Persons who committed the act, or made the omission charged while under involuntary subjection to the power of superiors.

Subd. 4. As drafted, this subdivision expresses the rule of the common law as very uniformly understood and practised, until within a recent period. (McNaughton's case, 1 *Townsend's St. Tr.*, 312, 401.) Within a few years past, some respectable authorities in medical jurisprudence, and some adjudications in cases involving civil rights, have advanced the view that any mental aberration, any monomania however limited in subject, is to be deemed a disease of the mind, as a unit, necessarily involving and embarrassing all the mental action of the individual. That what have been heretofore deemed partial insanities, are in truth special developments of a disease of the mind, which is necessarily so fundamental as to render its soundness, even upon subjects furthest removea .rom the particular hallucination exhibited, wholly uncertain. (Waring *v.* Waring, 12 *Jurist, O. S. C. S.*, 948; *Moore's Privy Co. R.; Ray's Med. Jur. of Insanity*, 2 ed., 27, 29.) If this view shall be deemed sound, and to be a proper element in the criminal jurisprudence of insanity, a question will arise which is now suggested only for the consideration of the Legislature; whether the last clause of the subdivision — the words "upon proof that, &c., they were incapable of knowing its wrongfulness," may be omitted.

§ 17. No act committed by a person while in a state of voluntary intoxication, shall be deemed less criminal by reason of his having been in such condition. But whenever the actual existence of any particular purpose, motive or intent is a necessary element to constitute any particular species or degree of crime, the jury may take into consideration the fact that the Intoxicated persons.

accused was intoxicated at the time, in determining the purpose, motive or intent with which he committed the act.

People *v.* Rogers, 18 *N. Y.* (4 *Smith*), 9; People *v.* Hammill, 2 *Park. Cr.*, 223; People *v.* Robinson, *Id.*, 235; Kenny *v.* People, 27 *How. Pr. R.*, 202.

Morbid criminal propensity.

§ 18. A morbid propensity to commit prohibited acts, existing in the mind of a person who is not shown to have been incapable of knowing the wrongfulness of such acts, forms no defense to a prosecution therefor.

The validity of this defense was thoroughly discussed in the late case of Huntington, in this State; where the earlier authorities will be found collected. See *Trial of Huntington.* See also Milne's Case, 4 *Irvine's Just. Cas.*, 334.

Insane persons, acquitted, how disposed of.

§ 19. When a jury have returned a verdict acquitting a defendant upon the ground of insanity, the court may thereupon, if the defendant be in custody, and they deem his discharge dangerous to the public safety, order him to be committed to the State lunatic asylum till he becomes sane.

Rep. Code Cr. Pro., § 511.

Involuntary subjection.

§ 20. The involuntary subjection to the power of a superior, which exonerates a person charged with a criminal act or omission from punishment therefor, arises either from:

1. Duress; or,
2. Coverture.

Subjection by duress.

§ 21. The duress which excuses a person chargeable with a prohibited act or omission, from punishment, must be actual compulsion by force or fear.

Subjection inferred from coverture.

§ 22. A subjection sufficient to excuse from punishment may be inferred in favor of a wife, from the fact of coverture, whenever she committed the act charged, in the presence of her husband; except where such act is a participation in:

1. Treason;

2. Murder;

3. Manslaughter;

4. Maiming;

5. An attempt to kill;

6. Rape;

7. Abduction;

8. Abuse of children;

9. Seduction;

10. Abortion, either upon herself or another female;

11. Concealing the death of an infant, whether her own or that of another;

12. Fraudulently producing a false child, whether as her own, or as that of another;

13. Bigamy;

14. Incest;

15. The crime against nature;

16. Indecent exposure;

17. Obscene exhibitions of books and prints;

18. Keeping a bawdy or other disorderly house;

19. Misplacing a railway switch; or,

20. Obstructing a railway track.

Treason and murder have long been recognized as exceptions to the rule which exempts a wife from punishment for an act committed in her husband's presence. Other offenses have been considered exceptions by many authorities. The commissioners have deemed it desirable to specify the excepted crimes with precision, and to extend the list to all which are of so grave and clearly marked a character, or relate so closely to the sex, and peculiar duties, privileges, or rights of woman, that a female cannot be supposed to be misled in regard to the character of her act, by the influence of her husband.

That a wife should aid her husband in the commission of a rape, a seduction, or of either of the similar crimes mentioned in the foregoing list, is doubtless improbable. But the supposition of such a case as possible seems justified by the conviction of Lord Audley, for forcibly assisting one of his servants to commit a rape upon his wife. (3 *How. St. Tr.*, 402.)

When not inferred.

§ 23. In case of the crimes enumerated in the last section, the wife is not excused from punishment by reason of her subjection to the power of her husband, unless the facts proved show a case of duress as defined in section 21.

Inference may be rebutted.

§ 24. The inference of subjection arising from the fact of coverture may be rebutted by any facts showing that in committing the act charged the wife acted freely.

The proof of marriage requisite to entitle a woman to the benefit of this exemption, is intended to be left to the operation of the ordinary rules applicable to the proof of that relation in other cases.

Exemption of public ministers.

§ 25. Ambassadors and other public ministers from foreign governments, accredited to the President or Government of the United States, and recognized by it according to the laws of the United States, with their secretaries, messengers, families and servants, are not liable to punishment in this State, but are to be returned to their own country for trial and punishment.

Wheat. Int. L., 264, § 6; 271, § 14; *Vattel*, 470, § 91 and onward; 1 *Bish. Cr. L.*, § 585; *Act of Cong. of Apr.* 30, 1790, ch. 9, § 25.

TITLE II.

OF PARTIES TO CRIMES.

SECTION 26. Classification of parties to crimes.
27. Who are principals.
28. Who are accessories.
29. No accessories in misdemeanor.
30. Punishment of accessories.

Classification of parties to crimes.

§ 26. The parties to crimes are classified as:

1. Principals; and,
2. Accessories.

§ 27. All persons concerned in the commission of a crime, whether it be felony or misdemeanor, and whether they directly commit the act constituting the offense, or aid and abet in its commission, though not present, are principals. Who are principals.

See *Rep. Code Cr. Pro.*, 156, § 310.

§ 28. All persons who, after the commission of any felony, conceal or aid the offender, with knowledge that he has committed a felony, and with intent that he may avoid or escape from arrest, trial, conviction or punishment, are accessories. Who are accessories.

See *Rep. Code Cr. Pro.*, 156, § 311, note, for reasons why the commissioners recommend the abrogation of the distinction between an accessory before the fact, and a principal. That distinction being abrogated, there is no longer a need of retaining the phrase "accessory *after the fact.*"

The above definition of an accessory corresponds with the definition of an accessory after the fact, as given in 2 *Rev. Stat.*, 699, § 7.

§ 29. In misdemeanor there are no accessories. No accessories in misdemeanor.

§ 30. Except in cases where a different punishment is prescribed by law, an accessory to a felony is punishable by imprisonment in a state prison not exceeding five years, or in a county jail not exceeding one year, or by fine not exceeding five hundred dollars, or by both such fine and imprisonment. Punishme't of accessories.

2 *Rev. Stat.*, 699, § 7.

TITLE III.

OF CRIMES AGAINST RELIGION AND CONSCIENCE.

Blasphemy defined.

§ 31. Blasphemy consists in wantonly uttering or publishing words casting contumelious reproach or profane ridicule upon God, Jesus Christ, the Holy Ghost, the Holy Scriptures or the Christian religion.

A variety of definitions of this offense have been given by different authorities, upon a review of which the foregoing definition is based. (Cousult Commonwealth *v.* Kneeland, 20 *Pick.*, 213; S. C., *Thach. Cr. Cas.*, 346; Updegraff *v.* Commonwealth, 11 *Serg. & R.*, 406; People *v.* Ruggles, 8 *Johns.*, 290; State *v.* Chandler, 2 *Harring.*, 553; *Eml. Pref. to St. Tr.*, 8; 2 *Bish. Cr. L.*, § 69; *Starkie, Lib.*, 496; 1 *Hawk. P. C.*, 12; 1 *Hume Cr. L.*, 559.)

It was held in People *v.* Porter (2 *Park. Cr.*, 14), that if no person hears the words complained of, no crime is committed; but that element of the offense seems sufficiently suggested by the words "uttering or publishing."

Words used in serious discussion.

§ 32. If it appears beyond reasonable doubt that the words complained of were used in the course of serious discussion, and with intent to make known or recommend opinions entertained by the accused, such words are not blasphemy.

This is a well settled restriction upon the definitions of blasphemy. (People *v.* Ruggles, 8 *Johns.*, 290; Commonwealth *v.* Kneeland, 20 *Pick.*, 213; S. C., *Thach. Cr. Cas.*, 356; *Starkie Lib.*, 496.) The favor which the law shows towards liberty of speech, and the free discussion of religious opinions, forbids that the sincere expression of belief, however erroneous, should be embarrassed by the penalty of blasphemy.

§ 33. Blasphemy is a misdemeanor. Blasphemy a misdemeanor.

§ 34. Profane swearing consists in any use of the name of God, or Jesus Christ, or the Holy Ghost, either in imprecating divine vengeance upon the utterer or any other person, or in light, trifling or irreverent speech. Profane swearing defined.

§ 35. Every person guilty of profane swearing is punishable by a fine of one dollar for each offense. Punishment of profane swearing.

See 1 *Rev. Stat.*, 664, §§ 61-63.

§ 36. Whenever any profane swearing is committed in the presence and hearing of any justice of the peace, mayor, recorder or alderman of any city, while holding a court, or under any other circumstances such as in the opinion of the magistrate amount to a gross violation of public decency, such magistrate may, in his discretion, immediately convict the offender, without any other proof, and in addition to the fine above prescribed, may impose imprisonment in a county jail not exceeding ten days. Summary conviction for profane swearing.

§ 37. If the offender does not forthwith pay the penalties incurred, with the costs, or give security for their payment within six days, he shall be committed by warrant to the county jail, for every offense or for any number of offenses whereof he was convicted at one and the same time, for not less than one day, nor more than three days; there to be confined in a room separate from all other prisoners. Penalties how collected.

§ 38. The first day of the week being by very general consent set apart for rest and religious uses, the law forbids to be done on that day certain acts deemed useless and serious interruptions of the repose and religious liberty of the community. The Sabbath.

Sabbath breaking. § 39. Any violation of this prohibition is Sabbath breaking.

These sections, and the twelve which follow, are proposed as substitutes for the provisions upon the same subject which are embodied in sections 849 to 851 inclusive, and in section 853 of the Political Code. The Revised Statutes treated the observance of Sunday not among crimes, but as a branch of the internal police management of the State. In order that it might be considered in that connection the Commissioners presented in the Political Code, the provisions contained in the Revised Statutes. They recommend, however, that so far as the *definition* and *punishment* of Sabbath breaking are concerned, the offense should be treated in the Penal Code; while the special provisions found in the Revised Statutes, and incorporated into the Political Code, respecting the *proceedings* to enforce the law, if desired to be preserved, may either be retained in the Political Code, or transferred to the Code of Criminal Procedure.

The sections as now reported present some modifications in the existing law, intended to render it more conformable to public sentiment at the present day.

Day defined. § 40. Under the term "day," as employed in the phrase "first day of the week," in the eight sections following, is included all the time from midnight to midnight.

Sabbath breaking defined. § 41. The following are the acts forbidden to be done on the first day of the week, the doing any of which is Sabbath breaking:

1. Servile labor;

2. Undue travel;

3. Public sports;

4. Trades, manufactures, and mechanical employments;

5. Public traffic;

6. Serving process.

Servile labor. § 42. All manner of servile labor, on the first day of the week, is prohibited, excepting works of necessity or charity.

1 *Rev. Stat.*, 675, § 70.

§ 43. All traveling on the first day of the week is prohibited, excepting such as is performed upon foot or in carrying or in a conveyance carrying the United States mail, or such as is done in cases of charity or necessity, or in going to or returning from some funeral, place of worship, or religious assembly within the distance of twenty miles, or in going for medical aid or for medicines and returning, or in visiting the sick and returning, or in going express by order of some public officer, or in removing one's family or household furniture when such removal was commenced on some other day. Undue travel.

Founded on 1 *Rev. Stat.*, 675, § 70. Exceptions in favor of travel on foot and in a conveyance carrying the U. S. mail, are introduced as harmonizing with the view by which the commissioners have been governed throughout, in preparing these sections, viz.: that whatever does not interrupt the rest and religious observance of others, should be left to private conscience. As the State law cannot interfere with the carrying the mail, no important additional element of disturbance is introduced by excepting travelers accompanying it from these prohibitions.

§ 44. It is a sufficient defense in proceedings for servile labor or undue travel on the first day of the week, to show that the accused uniformly keeps another day of the week as holy time, and does not labor or travel upon that day, and that the labor or travel complained of was done in such manner as not to interrupt or disturb other persons in observing the first day of the week as holy time. Persons observing another day as a Sabbath.

§ 45. All shooting, hunting, fishing, sporting, playing, horse racing, gaming or other public sports, exercises or pastimes, upon the first day of the week, are prohibited. Public sports.

1 *Rev. Stat.*, 675, § 70, modified.

§ 46. All trades, manufactures and mechanical employments upon the first day of the week are prohibited. Trades, manufactures, and mechanical employments.

Public traffic.

§ 47. All manner of public selling, or offering, or exposing for sale publicly, of any commodities upon the first day of the week is prohibited, except that meats, milk and fish may be sold at any time before nine o'clock in the morning, and except that food may be sold to be eaten upon the premises where sold, and drugs and medicines and surgical appliances may be sold at any time of the day.

Founded on 1 *Rev. Stat.*, 676, § 71; the restriction upon restaurants and drug stores being removed.

Serving process.

§ 48. All service of legal process of any description whatever, upon the first day of the week, is prohibited, except in cases of breach of the peace, or apprehended breach of the peace, or when sued out for the apprehension of a person charged with crime; or except where such service shall be specially authorized by law.

Founded on 1 *Rev. Stat.*, 674, § 69.

Punishment of Sabbath breaking.

§ 49. Every person guilty of Sabbath breaking is punishable by a fine of one dollar for each offense.

Forfeiture of commodities exposed for sale.

§ 50. In addition to the fine imposed by the last section, all commodities exposed for sale on the first day of the week in violation of the provisions of this chapter shall be forfeited. Upon conviction of the offender by any justice of the peace of the county, or mayor, recorder or alderman of the city, such officers shall issue a warrant for the seizure of the forfeited articles, which, when seized, shall be sold on one day's notice, and the proceeds shall be paid to the overseers of the poor for the use of the poor of the town or city.

Rep. Pol. Code, § 851.

Proceedings to collect fines imposed by this chapter.

§ 51. The fines prescribed in this chapter for profane swearing and for Sabbath breaking, may be collected by means of the proceedings prescribed by sections 854 to 858 inclusive, of the Political Code.

See note to section 39, *supra*. If the sections of the Political Code relative to the observance of Sunday are stricken out as suggested in the former note, some verbal changes will be required in section 854 and others regulating the procedure peculiar to that offense.

§ 52. Whoever maliciously procures any process in a civil action to be served on Saturday upon any person who keeps Saturday as holy time and does not labor on that day, or serves upon him any process returnable on that day, or maliciously procures any civil action to which such person is a party to be adjourned to that day for trial, is guilty of a misdemeanor. Remedy for maliciously serving process.

Substituted for section 853 of the Political Code. Section 852, belongs appropriately to that Code.

§ 53. Any willful attempt by means of threats or violence, to compel any person to adopt, practice or profess any particular form of religious belief, is a misdemeanor. Compelling adoption of a form of belief.

This section is by no means intended to restrict the authority of parents to instruct their children, or to require them to attend upon public worship or places of religious instruction. It only forbids compelling another to espouse a particular form of belief.

§ 54. Every person who willfully prevents by threats or violence another person from performing any lawful act enjoined upon or recommended to such person by the religion which he professes, is guilty of a misdemeanor. Preventing performance of religious act.

§ 55. Every person who willfully disturbs, interrupts or disquiets any assemblage of people met for religious worship, by any of the acts or things hereinafter enumerated, is guilty of a misdemeanor. Disturbing religious meetings.

§ 56. The following are the acts deemed to constitute disturbance of a religious meeting: Definition of the offense.

1. Uttering any profane discourse, committing any rude or indecent act, or making any unnecessary noise, either within the place where such meeting is held, or so near it as to disturb the order and solemnity of the meeting;

2. Exposing to sale or gift any ardent or distilled liquors, or keeping open any huckster shop within

two miles of the place where any religious society or assembly shall be actually convened for religious worship, and in any other place than such as shall have been duly licensed and in which the person accused shall have usually resided or carried on business;

3. Exhibiting within the like distance, any shows or plays without a license by the proper authority;

4. Engaging in, or aiding or promoting, within the like distance, any racing of animals or gaming of any description;

5. Obstructing in any manner, without authority of law, within the like distance, the free passage along any highway to the place of such meeting.

TITLE IV.

OF TREASON.

Treason defined.

§ 57. The following acts constitute treason against the people of this State:

1. Levying war against the people of this State, within the State; or,

2. A combination of two or more persons, by force to usurp the government of this State, or to overturn the same, evidenced by a forcible attempt made within this State to accomplish such purpose; or,

3. Adhering to the enemies of this State while separately engaged in war with a foreign enemy in the cases prescribed in the Constitution of the United States, and giving to such enemies aid and comfort in this State or elsewhere.

2 *Rev. Stat.*, 656, § 2.

§ 58. To constitute levying war against the people of this State, an actual act of war must be committed. To conspire merely to levy war is not enough. Levying war defined.

Ex parte Bollman, 4 *Cr.*, 75, 126.

§ 59. Where persons rise in insurrection with intent to prevent in general by force and intimidation, the execution of a statute of this State, or to force its repeal, they are guilty of levying war. But an endeavor, although by numbers and force of arms to resist the execution of a law in a single instance, and for a private purpose, is not levying war. Resistance to a statute, when levying war.

Levying war.—The above section is based on the cases of United States *v.* Mitchell, 2 *Dall.*, 348; United States *v.* Hanway, 2 *Wall.*, *Jr.*, 139, 203; United States *v.* Hoxie, 1 *Paine*, 264; United States *v.* Vigol, 2 *Dall.*, 346, These cases (as well as that of ex parte Bollman, *supra*,) were all decided in the federal courts, and involved the question what is to be deemed levying war against the United States, under the constitutional definition of treason. (*U. S. Const.*, *art.* 3, § 3.) They have given a settled construction to the phrase "levying war," which is equally applicable to a definition of treason against a state.

Outlawry for treason.—Proceedings of outlawry for treason are prescribed by *Rep. Code Cr. Pro.*, §§ 884-896.

Number of witnesses.—A provision that in prosecutions for treason, two witnesses to the same overt act shall be required, is already reported. (*Rep. Code Civ. Pro.*, § 1782.)

§ 60. Every person convicted of treason shall suffer death for the same. Punishment.

2 *Rev. Stat.*, 656, § 1. Provisions regulating the manner of inflicting the penalty of death have been already reported. (*Rep. Code Cr. Pro.*, §§ 556–574.)

TITLE V.

OF CRIMES AGAINST THE ELECTIVE FRANCHISE.

Bribery, menace and other corrupt practices, at elections.

§ 61. Every person who by bribery, menace or any other corrupt means, either directly, or indirectly, attempts to influence any elector of this State in giving his vote, or to deter him from giving the same, or to disturb or hinder him in the free exercise of the right of suffrage at any election, is guilty of a misdemeanor.

Laws of 1842, ch. 130, tit. vii, § 4.

Betting upon elections.

§ 62. Every person who makes, offers, or accepts any bet or wager upon the result of any election or upon the success or failure of any person or candidate, or upon the number of votes to be cast either in the aggregate, or for any particular candidate, or upon the vote to be cast by any person or persons; or upon the decision to be made by any inspector, or canvasser, of any question arising in the course of an election, or upon any event whatever depending upon the conduct or result of an election, is guilty of a misdemeanor.

The words "person or candidate" are used in several sections of this chapter in order that it may be clear that the provisions embrace persons who may be voted for as officers to conduct an election—*e. g.*, the presiding officer of a town meeting—yet who are not candidates for the office to fill which the election is held.

Unlawful offers to procure offices for electors.

§ 63. Every person who, being a candidate at any election, offers, or agrees to appoint or procure the appointment of any particular person or persons to office, as an inducement or consideration to any person to vote for, or procure or aid in procuring the election of such candidate, is guilty of a misdemeanor.

Communicating such offer.

§ 64. Every person who, not being a candidate, communicates any offer made in violation of the last section, to any person, with intent to induce him to vote for or to procure or aid in procuring the election of the candidate making the offer, is guilty of a misdemeanor.

Furnishing money for elections, except for specified purposes.

§ 65. Every person, who with intent to promote the election, either of himself or of any other person, or candidate, either

1. Furnishes entertainment at his expense to any meeting of electors previous to or during an election;

2. Pays for, procures or engages to pay for any such entertainment;

3. Furnishes, or engages to pay or deliver any money or property, for the purpose of procuring the attendance of voters at the polls, or for the purpose of compensating any person for procuring attendance of voters at the polls: except for the conveyance of voters who are sick, poor, or infirm; or

4. Furnishes or engages to pay or deliver any money or property, for any purpose intended to promote the election of any candidate, except for the expenses of holding and conducting public meetings for the discussion of public questions, and of printing and circulating ballots, handbills and other papers previous to such election,

Is guilty of a misdemeanor.

See Laws of 1842, ch. 120, tit. vii, § 6. The commissioners have enlarged the existing rule, so far as to allow contributions for the expenses of public meetings as well as those of printing and circulating election documents. The same reasons which justify the second species of expenditure, sustain the first, and the existing rule is known to be stricter than can in practice be enforced.

Defrauding an elector in his vote.

§ 66. Every person who fraudulently alters the ballot of any elector, or substitutes one ballot for another, or furnishes any elector with a ballot containing more than the proper number of names, or who intentionally practices any fraud upon any elector to induce him to deposit a ballot as his vote and to have the same thrown out and not counted, or otherwise to defraud him of his vote, is guilty of a misdemeanor.

Substantially the provision of Laws of 1842, ch. 130, tit. vii, §§ 7 and 8, but extended to embrace any fraud upon an elector whereby he is deprived of his vote.

Obstructing electors attending elections.

§ 67. Every person who willfully and without lawful authority obstructs, hinders, or delays any elector on his way to any poll where an election shall be held, is guilty of a misdemeanor.

See *Laws of* 1842, ch. 130, tit. vii, § 9.

Voting more than once.

§ 68. Every person who votes more than once at the same election, or who offers to vote after having once voted, either in the same or in another election district, is guilty of a misdemeanor.

See *Laws of* 1842, ch. 130, tit. vii, § 10. The language of that section is "who votes or offers to vote more than once," &c. This language is capable of being taken in a sense which prohibits an innocent act. A person who offers his vote in the wrong election district, and being refused then goes to the right one and there offers his vote, may be said to have offered to vote more than once. The commissioners have substituted for the ambiguous expression, the phrase, "who offers to vote after having once voted."

§ 69. Every person who procures or counsels another to give or offer his vote at any election, knowing that such person is not qualified to vote at the place where such vote is given or offered, is guilty of a misdemeanor. Procuring illegal votes.

See Laws of 1842, ch. 130, tit. vii, § 11.

§ 70. Every person who procures or counsels another to enter any town, ward, or election district for the purpose of giving his vote at an election, knowing that such person is not entitled so to vote, is guilty of a misdemeanor. Importing voters who are unqualified.

See Laws of 1842, ch. 130, tit. vii, § 12.

§ 71. Every inhabitant of another state or country who, not being entitled to vote within this State, votes or offers to vote at an election in this State, is guilty of felony. Illegal voting by inhabitant of another state.

See Laws of 1842, ch. 130, tit. vii, § 13.

§ 72. Every inhabitant of this State, who not being entitled to vote, knowingly votes or offers to vote at an election, is guilty of misdemeanor. Illegal voting by inhabitant of this state.

Ib.

§ 73. Every person who, at any election, knowingly votes or offers to vote in any election district in which he does not reside, or in which he is not authorized by law to vote, is guilty of a misdemeanor. Illegal voting by resident of different election district.

See Laws of 1842, ch. 130, tit. vii, § 10.

§ 74. Every person who having been convicted of any bribery or felony, thereafter offers to vote at any election, without having been pardoned and restored to all the rights of a citizen, is guilty of a misdemeanor. Illegal voting by unpardoned convict.

4

Compare *Const. of* 1846, art. 11, § 2; *Laws of* 1847, ch. 240, § 15; *Laws of* 1842, ch. 130, tit. i, § 3 and tit. iv, § 38.

As the definitions of "felony" and "infamous crime" are substantially the same (2 *Rev. Stat.*, 702, §§ 30, 31), the commissioners have employed the word "felony" instead of the phrase "infamous crime deemed by the laws of this State a felony," found in the act of 1842.

Procuring name to be registered improperly.

§ 75. Every person who causes his name to be registered as that of an elector, upon any registry of voters authorized by law to be kept in any town, city or election district of this State, knowing that he is not a qualified voter within the territorial limits covered by such registry, is punishable by imprisonment in a state prison not less than one year.

This section and that next following, are founded on *Laws of* 1859, ch. 380, § 14. That act relates to New York city alone; but the rule is here generalized.

Personating qualified voter.

§ 76. Every person who, at any election, falsely personates another person, and in such personating offers to vote at any election, is punishable by imprisonment in a state prison not less than one year.

The original section applies only to personations of *registered* voters.

False statements upon applying for registry.

§ 77. Every person who, at the time of requesting his name to be registered as that of a qualified voter, upon any registry of voters authorized by law to be kept in any city, town, or election district of this State, or at the time of offering his vote at any election, knowingly makes any false statement or employs any false representation or pretence or token, to procure his name to be registered or his vote to be received, is guilty of a misdemeanor.

See *Laws of* 1859, ch. 380, § 7.

What is deemed a false statement.

§ 78. A false statement, representation or token, made or used in the presence and to the knowledge of a person requesting his name to be registered or offering his vote, is to be deemed made by himself, if it appears that it was made or used in support of his claim to be registered or to vote, that he knew it to be false, and suffered it to pass uncontradicted.

This section is new, but embodies familiar principles, and seems appropriate in order to give the preceding section its full application.

§ 79. Every person who willfully disturbs or breaks up any public meeting of electors and others, lawfully being held for the purpose of considering public questions, is guilty of a misdemeanor. Disturbance of public meetings.

§ 80. Every person who, by threats, intimidations, or unlawful violence willfully hinders or prevents electors from assembling in public meeting for the consideration of public questions, is guilty of a misdemeanor. Preventing public meetings.

§ 81. Every person who makes use of any force or violence, or of any threat to do any unlawful act, as a means of preventing an elector from attending any public meeting lawfully held for the purpose of considering any public questions, is guilty of a misdemeanor. Preventing electors from attending public meetings.

§ 82. Every person who willfully, by unlawful arrest, by force and violence, or by threats or intimidations, prevents an elector from voting at an election, or employs either of such means to hinder him from voting or to cause him to vote for any person or candidate, is guilty of a misdemeanor. Preventing electors from voting.

§ 83. Every person who willfully disobeys a lawful command of an inspector or board of inspectors, given in the execution of their duty as such, at an election, is guilty of a misdemeanor. Disobedience to lawful commands of inspectors.

See *Laws of* 1842, ch. 130, tit. vii, § 9.

§ 84. Every person who is guilty of any riotous conduct, or who causes any disturbance or breach of Riotous conduct or violence which impedes elections. the peace, or uses any disorderly violence, or threats of violence whereby any election is impeded or hindered, or whereby the lawful proceedings of the inspectors or canvassers at such election, in the discharge of their duty, are interfered with, is guilty of a misdemeanor.

Summary arrest therefor. § 85. Whenever at an election any person refuses to obey the lawful command of the inspectors, or by any disorderly conduct in their presence interrupts or disturbs their proceedings, they may make an order directing the sheriff or any constable of the county, or policeman of the town or city, to take the person so offending into custody, and detain him until the final canvass of the votes shall be completed. But such order shall not prohibit the person taken into custody from voting at the election.

See *Laws of* 1842, ch. 130, tit. vii, § 33.

Such arrest no bar to a subsequent prosecution. § 86. The fact that any person, offending against the provisions of the preceding section, was taken into custody and detained, as therein authorized, forms no defense to a prosecution for the offense committed, under any provisions of this Code.

Intended to prevent the possible question, whether the rule that no person shall be twice punished for the same offense should apply in the case contemplated.

Destroying ballots, or ballot-boxes. § 87. Every person who willfully breaks or destroys, on the day of any election, or before the canvass is completed, any ballot-box used or intended to be used at such election, or defaces, injures, destroys or conceals, any ballot which has been deposited in any ballot-box at an election, and has not already been counted, or canvassed, or any poll list used or intended to be used at such election, is guilty of felony.

Keeping false poll lists. § 88. Every clerk of the poll at any election, who willfully keeps a false poll list, or knowingly inserts in his poll list any false statement, is guilty of a misdemeanor.

§ 89. Every inspector of an election who willfully excludes any vote duly tendered, knowing that the person offering the same is lawfully entitled to vote at such election, or who willfully receives a vote from any person who has been duly challenged, in relation to his right to vote at such election, without exacting from such person such oath or other proof of qualification as may be required by law, or who willfully omits to challenge any person offering to vote whom he knows or suspects not to be duly entitled to vote, and who has not been challenged by any other person is guilty of a misdemeanor. Misconduct of inspectors.

§ 90. Every inspector of any election, member of any board of canvassers, messenger or other officer authorized to take part in or perform any duty in relation to any canvass or official statement of the votes cast at any election, who willfully makes any false canvass of such votes, or makes, signs, publishes or delivers any false return of such election, or any false certificate of the result of such election, knowing the same to be false, or willfully defaces, destroys or conceals any statement or certificate entrusted to his care, is guilty of a misdemeanor. Falsely canvassing votes, or certifying result of election.

§ 91. The word "election," as used in this chapter, designates only elections had within this state for the purpose of enabling electors, as such, to choose some public officer or officers under the laws of this state or of the United States. Election defined.

§ 92. Irregularities or defects in the mode of noticing, convening, holding or conducting an election authorized by law, form no defense to a prosecution for a violation of the provisions of this chapter. Irregularities in elections no defense for violations of this chapter.

Decisions in other states raise the question whether the invalidity of an election is an answer to a prosecution for illegally voting at it. For cases in the affirmative, see State *v.* Williams, 25 *Me.*, 561; Commonwealth *v.* Gibbs, 4 *Dall.*, 253: in the negative, State *v.* Bailey, 21 *Me.*, 62; Commonwealth *v.* Shaw, 7 *Metc.*, 52; People *v.* Cook, 8 *N. Y.* (4 *Seld.*), 67. The Commissioners recommend the rule in the text as clearly consonant with justice.

Rights of persons lawfully interfering in elections declared.

§ 93. But nothing in this chapter shall be construed to authorize the punishment of any persons who, by authority of law, may interfere to prevent or regulate an election which has been unlawfully noticed or convened, or is being, or is about to be, unlawfully conducted.

Submission of questions to the people.

§ 94. Every act which by the provisions of this chapter is made criminal when committed with reference to the election of a candidate, is equally criminal when committed with reference to the determination of a question submitted to electors to be decided by votes cast at an election.

Good faith in offering to vote, a defense for alleged illegal voting.

§ 95. Upon any prosecution for procuring, offering or casting an illegal vote, the accused may give in evidence any facts tending to show that he honestly believed upon good reason that the vote complained of was a lawful one; and the jury may take such facts into consideration in determining whether the acts complained of, were knowingly done or not.

This section is intended to enable juries, upon proper proof, to relax in this class of cases, the strict rule that ignorance of the law is no excuse. It has been held that while an elector who votes in ignorance of facts which disqualify him, is not liable to punishment, one who votes with a knowledge of such facts is not excused though he voted in an honest belief that he was entitled to do so. (McGuire *v.* State, 7 *Humph.*, 54; State *v.* Boyett, 10 *Ired.*, 336.) Whether upon given facts a right to vote exists, is frequently a legal question of such difficulty that one claiming it in good faith, though erroneously, ought to be exempt from punishment. See Commonwealth *v.* Aglar, *Thatcher's Crim. Cas.*, 412; Same *v.* Wallace, *Id.*, 592; Same *v.* Bradford, 9 *Metc.*, 268; in support of the rule embodied in the text.

TITLE VI.

OF CRIMES BY AND AGAINST THE EXECUTIVE POWER OF THE STATE.

§ 96. Every person who executes any of the functions of a public office without having taken and duly filed the required oath of office, or without having executed and duly filed the required security, is guilty of a misdemeanor; and in addition to the punishment prescribed therefor, he forfeits his right to the office. Acting in a public office without having qualified.

Corresponds with *Rep. Pol. Code*, § 222.

§ 97. The last section shall not be construed to affect the validity of acts done by a person exercising the functions of a public office in fact, where other persons than himself are interested in maintaining the validity of such acts. Acts of officer *de facto*, not affected.

§ 98. Every person who gives or offers any bribe to any executive officer of this State with intent to influence him in respect to any act, decision, vote, opinion, Giving or offering bribes.

or other proceeding as such officer, is punishable by imprisonment in a state prison not exceeding ten years, or by fine not exceeding five thousand dollars, or both.

2 *Rev. Stat.*, 682, § 9; *Laws of* 1853, ch. 539, § 1.

Asking or receiving bribes.

§ 99. Every executive officer or person elected or appointed to an executive office who asks, receives or agrees to receive any bribe upon any agreement or understanding that his vote, opinion or action upon any matter then pending or which may by law be brought before him in his official capacity, shall be influenced thereby, is punishable by imprisonment in a state prison not exceeding ten years, or by a fine not exceeding five thousand dollars, or both; and in addition thereto forfeits his office and is forever disqualified from holding any public office under this State.

Substantially the provisions of 2 *Rev. Stat.*, 683, § 10, as amended; *Laws of* 1853, ch. 539, § 1; but extended to embrace asking a bribe.

Attempting to prevent officers from performing duty.

§ 100. Every person who attempts, by means of any threat or violence, to deter or prevent an executive officer from performing any duty imposed upon such officer by law, is guilty of a misdemeanor.

Resisting officers.

§ 101. Every person who knowingly resists, by the use of force or violence, any executive officer, in the performance of his duty, is guilty of a misdemeanor.

Taking excessive fees.

§ 102. Every executive officer who asks or receives any emolument, gratuity or reward, or any promise of any emolument, gratuity or reward, excepting such as may be authorized by law, for doing any official act, is guilty of a misdemeanor.

See 2 *Rev. Stat.*, 650, § 5.

Taking reward for omitting or delaying official acts.

§ 103. Every executive officer who asks or receives any emolument. gratuity or reward, or any promise of any emolument, gratuity or reward, for omitting or deferring the performance of any official duty, is guilty of a misdemeanor.

§ 104. Every executive officer who asks or receives any fee or compensation for any official service which has not been actually rendered, except in cases of charges for prospective costs, or of fees demandable in advance in the cases allowed by law, is guilty of a misdemeanor. Taking fees for services not rendered.

§ 105. Every officer of this State who asks or receives any compensation, fee or reward of any kind for any service rendered or expense incurred in procuring from the Governor of this State a demand upon the executive authority of a state or territory of the United States, or of a foreign government, for the surrender of a fugitive from justice; or of any service rendered or expense incurred in procuring the surrender of such fugitive, or of conveying him to this State or for detaining him therein, except upon an employment by the Governor of this State, and upon an account duly audited and paid out of the State treasury, is guilty of a misdemeanor. Taking unlawful reward for services in extradition of fugitives.

This section is suggested to supersede the provisions of *Rep. Code Cr. Pro.*, §§ 907, 908.

§ 106. Every person who gives, or agrees or offers to give any gratuity or reward in consideration that himself or any other person shall be appointed to any public office, or shall be permitted to exercise, perform or discharge the prerogatives or duties of any office, is punishable by imprisonment in the county jail not less than six months nor more than two years, or by a fine of not less than two hundred dollars or more than one thousand dollars, or both. Buying appointments to office.

2 *Rev. Stat.*, 696, § 32, as amended, *Laws of* 1863, ch 51, § 1.

§ 107. Every person who, directly or indirectly, asks or receives or promises to receive any gratuity or reward or any promise of a gratuity or reward, for appointing another person or procuring for another person an appointment to any public office or any Selling appointments to office.

clerkship, deputation or other subordinate position in any public office, is punishable by imprisonment in the county jail not less than six months nor more than two years, and by a fine of not less than two hundred dollars nor more than one thousand dollars, or both.

See 2 *Rev. Stat.*, 696, § 35, as amended *Laws of* 1863, ch. 51, § 1.

Taking rewards for deputation.

§ 108. Every public officer who, for any gratuity or reward, appoints another person to a public office, or permits another person to exercise, perform or discharge any of the prerogatives or duties of his office, is punishable by imprisonment in the county jail not less than six months nor more than two years, and by a fine of not less than two hundred dollars or more than one thousand dollars; and in addition thereto he forfeits his office.

Unlawful grant or deputation void, except as to official acts done before conviction.

§ 109. Every grant or deputation made contrary to the provisions of either of the last two sections is void; but official acts done before a conviction for any offense prohibited by those sections, shall not be deemed invalid, in consequence of the invalidity of such grant or deputation.

Founded on 2 *Rev. Stat.*, 696, § 37.

Exercising functions of office wrongfully.

§ 110. Every person who willfully intrudes himself into any public office to which he has not been duly elected or appointed, and every person who, having been an executive officer, willfully exercises any of the functions of his office after his term of office has expired and a successor has been duly elected or appointed, and has qualified, in his place, and he has notice thereof, is guilty of a misdemeanor.

Refusal to surrender books, &c., of office to successor upon demand.

§ 111. Every person who, having been an executive officer of this State, wrongfully refuses to surrender the official seal or any of the books and papers appertaining to his office, to his successor who has been duly elected or appointed, and has duly qualified, and has demanded the surrender of the seal or books and papers of such office, is guilty of a misdemeanor.

§ 112. The various provisions of this chapter which relate to executive officers apply in relation to administrative officers, in the same manner as if administrative and executive officers were both mentioned. Administrative officers.

TITLE VII.

OF CRIMES AGAINST THE LEGISLATIVE POWER.

§ 113. Every person who willfully and by force or fraud prevents the legislature of this State, or either of the houses composing it, or any of the members thereof, from meeting or organizing, is punishable by imprisonment in a state prison not less than five nor more than ten years, or by a fine of not less than five hundred dollars nor more than two thousand dollars, or both. Preventing the meeting or organization of either branch of the legislature.

See *Liv. Cr. Code*, 381, § 118.

§ 114. Every person who willfully disturbs the legislature of this State, or either of the houses composing it, while in session, or who commits any disorderly conduct in the immediate view and presence Disturbing the legislature while in session.

of either house of the legislature, tending to interrupt its proceedings or impair the respect due to its authority, is guilty of a misdemeanor.

Compelling adjournment.

§ 115. Every person who willfully and by force or fraud compels or attempts to compel the legislature of this State, or either of the houses composing it, to adjourn or disperse, is punishable by imprisonment in a state prison not less than five nor more than ten years, or by fine of not less than five hundred dollars, nor more than two thousand dollars, or both.

Liv. Cr. Code, 381, § 118.

Intimidating a member of the legislature.

§ 116. Every person who willfully, by intimidation or otherwise, prevents any member of the legislature of this State, from attending any session of the house of which he is a member, or of any committee thereof, or from giving his vote upon any question which may come before such house, or from performing any other official act, is guilty of a misdemeanor.

Ib.

Compelling either house to perform or omit any official act.

§ 117. Every person who willfully compels or attempts to compel either of the houses composing the legislature of this State to pass, amend, or reject any bill, or resolution, or to grant or refuse any petition, or to perform or omit to perform any other official act, is punishable by imprisonment in a state prison not less than five nor more than ten years, or by a fine of not less than five hundred dollars nor more than two thousand dollars, or both.

Ib.

Altering draft of bill.

§ 118. Every person who fraudulently alters the draft of any bill or resolution which has been presented to either of the houses composing the legislature, to be passed or adopted, with intent to procure it to be passed or adopted by either house, or certified by the presiding officer of either house, in language different from that intended by such house, is guilty of felony.

§ 119. Every person who fraudulently alters the engrossed copy or enrollment of any bill which has been passed by the legislature of this State, with intent to procure it to be approved by the governor or certified by the secretary of State, or printed or published by the printer of the Statutes in language different from that in which it was passed by the legislature, is guilty of felony. Altering engrossed copy.

§ 120. Every person who gives or offers to give a bribe to any member of the legislature, or attempts directly, or indirectly, by menace, deceit, suppression of truth or any other corrupt means to influence a member in giving or withholding his vote, or in not attending the house of which he is a member, or any committee thereof, is punishable by imprisonment in a state prison not exceeding ten years or by fine not exceeding five thousand dollars, or both. Giving bribes to members of the legisla ture.

§ 121. Every member of either of the houses composing the legislature of this State, who asks, receives, or agrees to receive any bribe upon any understanding that his official vote, opinion, judgment or action shall be influenced thereby, or shall be given in any particular manner or upon any particular side of any question or matter upon which he may be required to act in his official capacity, or who gives or offers or promises to give any official vote in consideration that another member of the legislature shall give any such vote, either upon the same or another question, is punishable by imprisonment in a state prison not exceeding ten years, or by fine not exceeding five thousand dollars, or both. Receiving bribes by members of the legislature.

This section, with the one which precedes, is founded upon the provisions of 2 *Rev. Stat.*, 682, § 9, as amended by *Laws of* 1853, *ch.* 539, § 2. It is extended, however, to embrace what is known as "log rolling," or agreements to exchange votes for or against measures pending before the legislature; and, also, so as to embrace deceits and concealments practised upon members of the legislature to obtain their votes.

In Marshall *v.* Baltimore & Ohio R. R. Co., 16 *How.* (*U. S.*) *R.*, 314, the court (commenting upon the cases of Fuller *v.* Dame, 18 *Pick.*, 470; Hatzfield *v.* Gulden, 7 *Watts*, 152; Clippinger *v.* Hepbaugh, 5 *Watts & S.*, 315; Wood *v.* McCan, 6 *Dana*, 366; Hunt *v.* Test, 8 *Ala.*, 719; The Commonwealth *v.* Callaghan, 2 *Va. Cas.*, 460), say: "The sum of these cases is, 1. All contracts for a contingent compensation for obtaining legislation, or to use personal or any secret or sinister influence on legislators are void by the policy of the law.

2. Secrecy as to the character under which the agent or solicitor acts tends to deception, and is immoral and fraudulent; and where the agent contracts to use secret influences, or voluntarily, without contract with his principal, uses such means, he cannot have the assistance of a court to recover compensation.

3. That what, in the technical vocabulary of politicians, is termed "log rolling" is a misdemeanor at common law, punishable by indictment.

Witnesses refusing to attend before the legislature or legislative committees.

§ 122. Every person who, being duly summoned to attend as a witness before either house of the legislature or any committee thereof, authorized to summon witnesses, refuses or neglects without lawful excuse to attend pursuant to such summons, is guilty of a misdemeanor.

Refusing to testify.

§ 123. Every person who being present before either house of the legislature or any committee thereof authorized to summon witnesses, willfully refuses to be sworn or affirmed, or to answer any material and proper question, or to produce upon reasonable notice any material and proper books, papers, or documents in his possession or under his control, is guilty of a misdemeanor.

Members of the legislature liable to forfeiture of office.

§ 124. The conviction of a member of the legislature of either of the crimes defined in this chapter, involves as a consequence in addition to the punishment prescribed by this Code, a forfeiture of his office; and disqualifies him from ever afterwards holding any office under this State.

TITLE VIII.

OF CRIMES AGAINST PUBLIC JUSTICE.

CHAPTER I.

BRIBERY AND CORRUPTION.

Giving bribes to judges, jurors, referees, &c.

§ 125. Every person who gives or offers to give a bribe, to any judicial officer, juror, referee, arbitrator, umpire or assessor, or to any person who may be authorized by law to hear or determine any question or controversy, with intent to influence his vote, opinion or decision upon any matter or question which is or may be brought before him for decision, is punishable by imprisonment in a state prison not exceeding ten years, or by a fine not exceeding five thousand dollars, or both.

Receiving bribes by judicial officers.

§ 126. Every judicial officer of this State who asks, receives, or agrees to receive any bribe upon any agreement or understanding that his vote, opinion or decision upon any matter or question which is or may be brought before him for decision shall be thereby influenced, is punishable by imprisonment in a state prison not exceeding ten years, or by a fine not exceeding five thousand dollars or both; and in addition thereto forfeits his office and is forever disqualified from holding any public office under this State.

This section, with the preceding, is founded upon 2 *Rev. Stat.*, 683, § 10, as amended, *Laws of* 1853, ch. 539.

Receiving bribes by jurors, referees, &c.

§ 127. Every juror, referee, arbitrator, umpire or assessor, and every person authorized by law to hear or determine any question or controversy, who asks, receives, or agrees to receive any bribe upon any agreement or understanding that his vote, opinion or decision, upon any matter or question which is or may be brought before him for decision shall be thereby influenced, is guilty of felony.

Misconduct by jurors, arbitrators and referees.

§ 128. Every juror, or person drawn or summoned as a juror, or chosen arbitrator, or umpire, or appointed referee, who either:

1. Makes any promise or agreement to give a verdict for or against any party; or,

2. Willfully permits any communication to be made to him, or receives any book, paper, instrument, or information relating to any cause pending before him except according to the regular course of proceeding upon the trial of such cause,

Is guilty of a misdemeanor.

Judicial officer, juror, referee, &c., accepting gifts from parties.

§ 129. Every judicial officer, juror, referee, arbitrator or umpire, who accepts any gift from any person, knowing him to be a party in interest or the attorney or counsel of any party in interest to any action or proceeding then pending or about to be brought before him, is guilty of a misdemeanor.

"Gift" defined.

§ 130. The word "gift" in the foregoing section shall not be taken to include property received by inheritance, by will, or by gift in view of death.

Improper attempts to influence jurors, referees or arbitrators.

§ 131. Every person who attempts to influence a juror, or any person summoned or drawn as a juror, or chosen an arbitrator or appointed a referee, in respect to his verdict, or decision of any cause or matter pending or about to be brought before him, either:

1. By means of any communication oral or written had with him, except in the regular course of proceedings upon the trial of the cause;

2. By means of any book, paper, or instrument exhibited otherwise than in the regular course of proceedings upon the trial of the cause;

3. By means of any threat or intimidation;

4. By means of any assurance or promise of any pecuniary or other advantage; or,

5. By publishing any statement, argument, or observation relating to the cause,

Is guilty of a misdemeanor.

The existing statute declares every person who shall attempt "improperly" to influence a juror, guilty of a misdemeanor (2 *Rev. Stat.*, 693, § 16), but leaves the question, what attempts are improper, to judicial construction. The commissioners deem it desirable that the Code should specify with greater precision the acts intended to be forbidden.

§ 132. Every person authorized by law to assist at the drawing of any jurors to attend any court, who willfully puts or consents to the putting upon any list of jurors as having been drawn, any name which shall not have been drawn for that purpose in the manner prescribed by law; or, who omits to place on such list any name that shall have been drawn in the manner prescribed by law; or, who signs or certifies any list of jurors as having been drawn which was not drawn according to law; or, who is guilty of any other unfair, partial, or improper conduct in the drawing of any such list of jurors, is guilty of a misdemeanor. Drawing jurors fraudulently.

§ 133. Every officer to whose charge any juror is committed by any court or magistrate, who negligently or willfully permits them, or any one of them, either: Misconduct by officer having charge of juries.

1. To receive any communication from any person;

2. To make any communication to any person;

3. To obtain or receive any book or paper, or refreshment; or,

4. To leave the jury room without the leave of such court, or magistrate first obtained,

Is guilty of a misdemeanor.

CHAPTER II.

RESCUES.

Rescuing prisoners.

§ 134. Every person who by force or fraud rescues or attempts to rescue, or aids another person in rescuing or in attempting to rescue any prisoner from any officer or other person having him in lawful custody, is punishable as follows:

1. If such prisoner was in custody upon a charge or conviction of felony, by imprisonment in a state prison for not less than ten years;

2. If such prisoner was in custody otherwise than upon a charge or conviction of felony, by imprisonment in a county jail not exceeding one year, or by fine not exceeding five hundred dollars, or by both such fine and imprisonment.

Retaking goods from custody of officer.

§ 135. Every person who willfully injures or destroys, or takes or attempts to take, or assists any other person in taking or attempting to take from the custody of any officer or person, any personal property which such officer or person has in charge under any process of law, is guilty of a misdemeanor.

CHAPTER III.

ESCAPES, AND AIDING THEREIN.

SECTION 145. "Prison" defined.
146. "Prisoner" defined.

§ 136. Every prisoner confined upon conviction for a criminal offense, who escapes from prison, may be pursued, retaken and imprisoned again notwithstanding the term for which he was sentenced to be imprisoned may have expired at the time when he is retaken and he shall remain so imprisoned, until tried for such escape, or discharged on a failure to prosecute therefor. Re-arrest of escaped prisoner.

2 *Rev. Stat.*, 685, § 20.

§ 137. Every prisoner confined in a state prison for a term less than for life, who by force or fraud escapes therefrom, is punishable by imprisonment in such prison for a term not exceeding five years, to commence from the expiration of the original term of his imprisonment. Escape from state prison.

Compare 2 *Rev. Stat.*, 685, § 21.

§ 138. Every prisoner confined in a state prison for a term less than for life, who attempts by force or fraud, although unsuccessfully, to escape from such prison, is guilty of felony. Attempt to escape from state prison.

Compare 2 *Rev. Stat.*, 685, § 23.

§ 139. Every prisoner confined in any other prison than a state prison, who by force or fraud escapes therefrom, is punishable by imprisonment in a state prison not exceeding two years, or in a county jail not exceeding one year, to commence from the expiration of the original term of his imprisonment. Escape from other than state prison.

Compare 2 *Rev. Stat.*, 685, § 22.

§ 140. Every prisoner confined in any other prison than a state prison, who attempts by force or fraud, although unsuccessfully, to escape therefrom, is punishable by imprisonment in a county jail not exceeding one year, to commence from the expiration of the original term of his imprisonment. Attempt to escape from other than state prison.

Compare 2 *Rev. Stat.*, 685, § 24.

Assisting prisoner to escape from prison.

§ 141. Every person who willfully, by any means whatever, assists any prisoner confined in any prison to escape therefrom, is punishable as follows:

1. If such prisoner was confined upon a charge or conviction of felony, by imprisonment in a state prison not exceeding ten years;

2. If such prisoner was confined otherwise than upon a charge or conviction of felony, by imprisonment in a county jail not exceeding one year, or by fine not exceeding five hundred dollars, or both.

Carrying into prison, things useful to aid an escape.

§ 142. Every person who carries or sends into any prison, anything useful to aid any prisoner in making his escape, with intent thereby to facilitate the escape of any prisoner confined therein, is punishable as follows:

1. If such prisoner was confined upon any charge or conviction of felony, by imprisonment in a state prison not exceeding ten years;

2. If such prisoner was confined otherwise than upon a charge or conviction of felony, by imprisonment in a county jail not exceeding one year, or by a fine of five hundred dollars, or both.

Concealing escaped prisoner.

§ 143. Every person who knowingly and willfully conceals any prisoner, who, having been confined in prison upon a charge or conviction of misdemeanor, has escaped therefrom, is guilty of misdemeanor.

Assisting prisoner to escape from officer.

§ 144. Every person who willfully assists any prisoner in escaping or attempting to escape from the custody of any officer or person having the lawful charge of such prisoner under any process of law or under any lawful arrest, is guilty of a misdemeanor.

"Prison" defined.

§ 145. The term "prison" in this chapter includes state prisons, county jails and every place designated by law for the keeping of persons held in custody under process of law, or under any lawful arrest.

§ 146. The term "prisoner" in this chapter includes every person held in custody under process of law issued from a court of competent jurisdiction whether civil or criminal, or under any lawful arrest. "Prisoner" defined.

CHAPTER IV.

FORGING, STEALING, MUTILATING AND FALSIFYING JUDICIAL AND PUBLIC RECORDS AND DOCUMENTS.

§ 147. Every clerk, register or other officer having the custody of any record, map or book, or of any paper or proceeding of any court of justice filed or deposited in any public office, who is guilty of stealing, willfully destroying, mutilating, defacing, altering or falsifying or fraudulently removing or secreting the whole or any part of such record, map, book, paper or proceeding, or who permits any other person so to do, is punishable by imprisonment in a state prison not exceeding five years, and in addition thereto forfeits his office. Larceny, destruction, &c., of records by officers having them in custody.

§ 148. Every person not an officer such as is mentioned in the last section, who is guilty of any of the acts specified in that section, is punishable by imprisonment in a state prison not exceeding five years, or in a county jail not exceeding one year, or by a fine not exceeding five hundred dollars, or by both such fine and imprisonment. Larceny, destruction, &c., of records, by other persons.

See 2 *Rev. Stat.*, 680, §§ 69, 70.

§ 149. Every person who knowingly procures or offers any false or forged instrument to be filed, registered or recorded in any public office within this State, which instrument, if genuine, might be filed or registered or recorded under any law of this State or of the United States, is guilty of felony. Offering false or forged instruments to be filed or recorded.

CHAPTER V.

PERJURY AND SUBORNATION OF PERJURY.

Perjury defined.

§ 150. Every person who, having taken an oath that he will testify, declare, depose or certify truly before any competent tribunal, officer or person, in any of the cases in which such an oath may by law be administered, willfully and contrary to such oath, states as true any material matter which he knows to be false is guilty of perjury.

Proposed modification of the law.—The definition of perjury given in the Revised Statutes, was as follows:

"Every person who shall willfully and corruptly swear, testify, or affirm falsely, to any material matter, upon any oath, affirmation or declaration, legally administered:

"1. In any matter, cause or proceeding depending in any court of law or equity, or before any officer thereof;

"2. In any case where an oath or affirmation is required by law, or is necessary for the prosecution or defense of any private right, or for the ends of public justice;

"3. In any matter or proceeding before any tribunal or officer created by the constitution or by law, or where any oath may be lawfully required by any judicial, executive or administrative officer."

"Shall upon conviction be adjudged guilty of perjury," &c., 2 *Rev. Stat.*, 681, § 1.

This was a considerable extension of the common law definition, which embraced only cases in which the false testimony was given in a judicial proceeding. But the enlarged definition given by the Revised Statutes appears to have been overlooked by subsequent legislatures. For a practice has grown up of making express provision in statutes authorizing any new mode of investigation or inquiry, that false testimony given under the statute shall be perjury.

The following are the leading instances of such provisions:

Laws of 1829, ch. 368, § 9. This act authorizes the canal board to subpœna witnesses to be examined before them when the interests of the State require it; and section 9 declares willful false swearing before the board to be perjury.

Laws of 1834, ch. 201, § 7. The act authorizes an examination to be instituted by the superintendent of the Onondaga salt springs; and the section cited declares false swearing upon such examination to be perjury.

In the later act concerning the salt springs (*Laws of* 1859, ch. 346), an examination is authorized as in the act of 1834, ch. 201; but the unnecessary provision declaring false swearing perjury, is omitted.

Laws of 1837, ch. 150, § 42. This statute relates to the powers and duties of the commissioners for loaning United States moneys, and directs the manner in which they shall execute their trust. The section cited prescribes that "if any person shall falsely swear or affirm in any of the cases where an oath or affirmation is required to be taken by this act, or shall willfully and knowingly act contrary to any oath or affirmation he has taken in pursuance of this act, such offense shall be deemed to be perjury."

Laws of 1837, ch. 430, § 8, declares a party to the record who swears falsely upon the examination authorized by the usury act, guilty of perjury.

Laws of 1842, ch. 130, tit. VII, § 1. This is the statute regulating elections. After providing that when any person offering to vote is challenged, the inspectors shall tender to him an oath to answer fully and truly, and shall then put certain questions — the act declares false swearing on such examination to be perjury.

Laws of 1839, ch. 389, § 1 (repealed by the act of 1842 above cited), had a provision of the same purport.

Laws of 1843, ch. 57, § 4; *Laws of* 1855, ch. 20, § 4. These acts authorize chairmen of committees of common councils, &c., to administer oaths to witnesses brought before such committee; and declare any false swearing in testimony so taken, to be perjury.

Laws of 1849, ch. 115, § 19. This statute makes it the

duty of clerks of Erie county to render periodical accounts of official fees and disbursements, the correctness of which must be verified by affidavit. Section 19 declares every person who shall willfully swear falsely in verifying any such account, guilty of perjury.

Laws of 1854, ch. 332, § 8. This declares willful false swearing to any oath or affidavit which may be lawfully required by any rules and regulations of certain canal officers, to be perjury.

Laws of 1854, ch. 398, tit. III, § 3. This act provided for an enrollment of the militia; and authorized any person who claimed exemption from duty to file an affidavit of the facts, as the basis of an examination of his claim, to be made by assessors; and the section cited declares that to swear falsely in such affidavit is perjury.

Laws of 1859, ch. 44, tit. IV, § 6. This section authorizes the trustees of the village of Monrovia to examine, on oath, any property owner claiming a reduction of taxes; and declares willful false swearing on such examination to be perjury.

Laws of 1859, ch. 380, §§ 13, 14. This is the registry act for the city of New York. It authorizes certain questions to be put to electors, under oath, by inspectors of election and by the board of registration. The sections cited declare false swearing perjury.

Laws of 1859, ch. 470, § 7. This statute provides for the sale of certain lands belonging to the State, and directs officers therein named to file reports verified by affidavit. Section 7 makes all false swearing under any of the provisions of the act perjury.

Laws of 1860, ch. 259, § 25. The statute is amendatory of the Metropolitan Police Commissioners' act. The twenty-fifth section, after empowering the board of Metropolitan Police Commissioners to subpœna witnesses, &c., declares false swearing by a witness, upon any necessary proceeding under the regulations established by the commissioners, perjury.

Laws of 1860, ch. 465, § 4, declares witnesses testifying falsely before the commissioners appointed to ascertain and collect the damages caused by destruction of property at Quarantine grounds on Staten Island, in Sept., 1858, guilty of perjury.

Laws of 1863, ch. 90, § 15. The act, which is for the protection and improvement of the Tonawanda band of Seneca Indians, authorizes oaths to be administered for several purposes; and provides in section 15 that willful false swearing by any person to whom any oath may be administered, according to the act, shall be deemed perjury.

It is obvious that by force of the definition of perjury contained in the Revised Statutes, false swearing upon the examination or proceeding authorized by either of the above-mentioned statutes would have been punished as perjury, without any express provision to that effect in the statute authorizing the proceeding. Yet, either from a want of clearness in the general definition, or from the fact that under the Revised Statutes there still remained cases in which false swearing was not perjury — *e. g.*, the case of mere voluntary oaths. (See People *v.* Travis, 1 *Park. Cr.*, 213, where it is held that perjury cannot be assigned of a false oath to a protest taken before a notary public as part of the preliminary proofs of loss under a policy of marine insurance.) The penalty of perjury has been declared again and again; of course giving rise to a question in respect to similar statutes in which the express declaration may be omitted, whether perjury can be alleged of a violation of the statute oath. To simplify the existing law and expunge from the statute book these multiplied provisions covering so nearly the same ground, the commissioners propose, by a subsequent section (inserted in the chapter entitled "of other offenses against public justice," to declare it a misdemeanor to administer or to take any oath except in the cases there specified. And they propose by the sections in the text to extend the penalties of perjury to violation of all judicial oaths *authorized* by law, as well as to violations of oaths *required.*

"*Testify, declare, depose or certify.*" It is not intended to confine the definition of perjury to testimony and depositions, properly so called; on the contrary, it is the intention of the commissioners to frame a section which shall embrace every class of statement which, by law, may be attested by an oath applying to the particular statement, in distinction from the general oath taken by public officers. Nearly every mode of oral statement under oath is embraced by the term "testify;" and nearly every written one in the term "depose." But as doubts may arise as to the full extension of these terms, in peculiar cases the commissioners have added "declare" and "certify," in order that all modes of statement may be clearly included.

§ 151. The term "oath," as used in the last section, includes an affirmation, and every other mode of attesting the truth of that which is stated, which is authorized by law. "Oath" defined.

The modes of administering oaths and affirmations in various cases, are prescribed by *Rep. Code Civ. Pro.*, §§ 1873, 1878.

§ 152. So much of an oath of office as relates to the future performance of official duties is not such an oath as is intended by the previous sections. Oath of office

The definition of perjury cannot properly include the violation of an oath of office by misconduct in the office. The official oath serves a valuable purpose in giving point and depth to the sense of the public duty which every person entrusted with the discharge of official responsibilities owes to the community. But it cannot be a convenient mode of punishing official misconduct to treat it as involving a breach of the oath of office, punishable as perjury. The act which violates the official duty should be declared criminal, and the punishment should be affixed to the act itself. The case covered by the provisions of 1 *Rev. Stat.*, 199, 200, §§ 14, 15, which direct that certain surveyors shall take and file the oath required by the constitution — *i. e.*, an oath that they will faithfully discharge the duties of the office — and declare that in case any surveyor shall willfully and knowingly make a false return of the survey by him made, &c., he shall be deemed guilty of perjury — is treated by the commissioners upon this principle. It may be truly said that making a false return is a violation of the duties of the office, and so is a breach of the official oath, yet the commissioners do not extend the penalty of perjury to a false report made in violation of an official oath merely; but reserve that species of offense to be covered by a section declaring it a misdemeanor for any official surveyor to make a report knowing it to be false.

Irregularities in the mode of administering oaths.

§ 153. It is no defense to a prosecution for perjury that the oath was administered or taken in an irregular manner.

Two classes of cases are important to be considered one class is, where an oath is administered in an irregular manner, but the person taking it supposes at the time that all the formalities of law are being complied with. Such were the circumstances in People *v.* Cook (4 *Seld.*, 67), where challenged voters were sworn upon a copy of Watts' Psalms and Hymns; the book being supposed to be the Bible. As to these cases, the decision in People *v.* Cook is, that the oath is valid, and the party is as amenable to the consequences of perjury as if it had been administered in strict conformity to the statute. Another class of cases is, where the person taking the oath evades some formality of the oath with intent to escape its obligation; as where he kisses his thumb instead of the book. In these cases his fraud should not be permitted to secure him against punishment. The section in the text therefore prescribes the same rule for both classes.

§ 154. It is no defense to a prosecution for perjury that the accused was not competent to give the testimony, deposition or certificate of which falsehood is alleged. It is sufficient that he actually was received to give such testimony or make such deposition or certificate.

Incompetency of witness no defense for perjury.

See Van Steenberg *v.* Kortz, 10 *Johns.*, 167.

§ 155. It is no defense to a prosecution for perjury that the accused did not know the materiality of the false statement made by him; or that it did not in fact affect the proceeding in or for which it was made. It is sufficient that it was material, and might have been used to affect such proceeding.

Witness' knowledge of materiality of his testimony not necessary.

§ 156. The making of a deposition or certificate is deemed to be complete, within the provisions of this chapter, from the time when it is delivered by the accused to any other person with intent that it be uttered or published as true.

Making of deposition, &c., when deemed complete.

§ 157. An unqualified statement of that which one does not know to be true is equivalent to a statement of that which one knows to be false.

Statement of that which one does not know to be true.

See, in support of the rule prescribed in this section, People *v.* McKinney, 3 *Park. Cr.*, 511; Bennett *v.* Judson, 21 *N. Y.*, 238; Commonwealth *v.* Cornish, 6 *Binn.*, 249; Steinman *v.* McWilliams, 6 *Penn. St.*, 170; and, opposed to it, United States *v.* Shellmire, *Baldw.*, 370.

§ 158. Perjury is punishable by imprisonment in a state prison as follows:

Punishment of perjury.

1. When committed on the trial of an indictment for felony, by imprisonment not less than ten years;

2. When committed on any other trial or proceeding in a court of justice, by imprisonment for not more than ten years;

3. In all other cases by imprisonment not more than five years.

2 *Rev. Stat.*, 681, § 2, modified. The section of the Revised Statutes cited, prescribed imprisonment for not *less* than ten years as the punishment for perjury com-

mitted on the trial of an indictment for felony, and imprisonment for not *more* than ten years for perjury committed in any other case. As the commissioners have reported a definition of perjury which may embrace some cases of false swearing which were not punishable under the definition given in the Revised Statutes; they have thought it proper to restrict the punishment which may be inflicted for the new offenses, within somewhat narrower limits. They, therefore, prescribe imprisonment for not more than *ten* years for perjury committed before a court of justice, except upon trial for felony, and imprisonment for not more than *five* years for all other cases.

Summary committal of witnesses who have committed perjury.

§ 159. Whenever it appears probable to any court of record that any person who has testified in any action or proceeding in such court has committed perjury, such court may immediately commit such person by an order or process for that purpose to prison, or take a recognizance with sureties for his appearing and answering to an indictment for perjury.

Compare 2 *Rev. Stat.*, 681, § 5.

Witnesses necessary to prove the perjury may be bound over to appear.

§ 160. Such court shall thereupon bind over the witnesses to establish such perjury to appear at the proper court to testify before the grand jury, and upon the trial in case an indictment is found for such perjury; and shall also cause immediate notice of such commitment or recognizance, with the names of the witnesses so bound over, to be given to the district attorney of the county.

2 *Rev. Stat.*, 681, § 6.

Documents necessary to prove such perjury may be detained.

§ 161. If, upon the hearing of such action or proceeding in which such perjury has probably been committed, any papers or documents produced by either party shall be deemed necessary to be used on the prosecution for such perjury, the court may by order detain such papers or documents from the party producing them, and direct them to be delivered to the district attorney.

2 *Rev. Stat.*, 682, § 7.

§ 162. Every person who willfully procures another person to commit any perjury is guilty of subornation of perjury. Subornation of perjury defined

2 *Rev. Stat.*, 681, § 3.

§ 163. Every person guilty of subornation of perjury is punishable in the same manner as he would be if personally guilty of the perjury so procured. Punishment of subornation.

2 *Rev. Stat.*, 681, § 4.

§ 164. No person who has been convicted of perjury, or of subornation of perjury, shall thereafter be received as a witness in any action, proceeding or matter whatever upon his own behalf; nor in any action or proceeding between adverse parties, against any person who shall object thereto, until the judgment against him has been reversed. But where such person has been actually received as a witness contrary to the provisions of this section, his incompetency shall not prejudice the rights, innocently acquired, of any other person claiming under the proceeding in which such person was so received. Convict of perjury declared incompetent as a witness.

Modification of the existing rule.—As the statute defining the powers of the commissioners of the Code expressly excludes from their consideration the law of evidence; and as the commissioners of practice and pleading have already (*Rep. Code Civ. Pro.*, § 1708) recommended the adoption of a general rule that those who have been convicted of crime shall not be excluded as witnesses, the commissioners would not suggest the above section, were the rule which it embodies a new one in our jurisprudence. But a rule even broader than that here stated, has been so long established, and seems so just and reasonable an exception to the general principle enunciated in the Code of Civil Procedure, that it appears proper to recall it to the attention of the legislature.

The section in the text is suggested as a substitute for the provision of 2 *Rev. Stat.*, 681, § 1, which forbade a convicted perjurer from being received as a witness "in any matter or cause whatever." This latter language seems broad enough to disqualify a convicted perjurer from proving the execution of a deed, or testifying upon any similar *ex parte* proceeding. It is obvious that the rule of exclusion, if pressed to this extent, in cases where the interests of third persons are affected, cannot fail to result in injustice; inasmuch as the only method of enforcing it, where the testimony is taken *ex parte*, is by declaring the proceeding taken, to be null and void for the incompetency of the witness afterwards proved. In the case of a convict produced as a witness by another person, the party who produces him cannot be regarded as any more chargeable with his previous perjury, or even with notice of it, than the person to be affected by his testimony. The rule should therefore be limited to contested proceedings, and the party against whom the convict is called, should be required to interpose objection, seasonably, to the examination. Where the convict comes forward as a witness in his own behalf—*e. g.*, to verify a petition for his own discharge in insolvency, the above reason for limiting the rule does not apply.

Constitutionality of the rule.—The commissioners have noticed that the language in which the pardoning power vested in the Governor is defined by the constitution of 1846, suggests a possible objection to the rule of disqualification, in so far as it applies to exclude a convict of perjury who has been pardoned. By the Revised Statutes, such person remains disqualified notwithstanding the pardon; and this has been the familiar rule in this State from the earliest period. The provision is borrowed from the Stat., 5 *Eliz.*, ch. 9. It was enacted in this State in 1788 (2 *Greenl. L.*, 36, § 1; 2 *Jones & V.*, 207, § 1), and was reënacted in 1801 (1 *Kent & R.*, 313, § 1; 1 *Webst. & S.*, 313, § 1; 1 *Laws of* 1813, 171, § 1), and again in the Revised Statutes; and the commissioners are not aware that it was ever questioned as an unconstitutional restriction upon the pardoning power. The constitution of 1846, however, confers the pardoning power upon the Governor in these words: "The Governor shall have the power to grant reprieves, commutations and pardons after conviction for all offenses except treason and cases of impeachment, *upon such conditions and with such restrictions and limitations as he may think proper, subject to such regulation as may be provided by law relative to the manner of applying for pardons*" (art. IV, § 5). The words in italic are new in the constitution, though the legislature conferred upon the Governor the power to impose conditions, in substantially the same language, by a very early statute. (Act of March 12, 1794; 3 *Greenl.*, 113; 1 *Kent & R.*, 158; 1 *Laws of* 1813, 126; 2 *Rev. Stat.*, 745, § 21.) And the objection anticipated is that these words exclude any power on the part of the legislature to impose any restriction or limitation upon pardons except such as relates to the manner of applying for them, and that the rule which disqualifies a convicted perjurer, notwithstanding pardon, is in effect a restriction or limitation upon the effect of the pardon.

The commissioners are of opinion, however, that in

view of the long-established and unquestioned practice in this State, the rule is not to be regarded as a restriction upon the pardon, but rather as an incompetency or disqualification based upon public policy, and which it is in the power of the legislature to impose or remove. It is analogous in this respect to the rule prohibiting the disclosure by physicians, clergymen, &c., of communications made to them in professional confidence. The provision that no pardon of a person sentenced to imprisonment for life shall restore him to the rights of a previous marriage, &c. (2 *Rev. Stat.*, 139, § 7), trenches even more closely upon the executive power than the rule retaining the disqualification to testify. Certainly, no innovation upon the existing rule could have been intended by the framers of the constitution of 1846. In introducing the clause relating to conditions, the intention was to express in the constitution the power already long established by statute, whereby the Governor might impose a condition or grant a qualified pardon in cases where he considered the offender undeserving of an unconditional one. And the clause respecting regulations relative to the manner of applying for pardons, was intended to enable the legislature to protect the community by requiring such modes of obtaining pardons to be pursued as should ensure full information of all relevant facts being brought before the Governor. Neither clause was designed to curtail the well-established legislative rule which retained the disqualification of a convict of perjury, notwithstanding a pardon granted.

CHAPTER VI.

FALSIFYING EVIDENCE.

§ 165. Every person who, upon any trial, proceeding, inquiry or investigation whatever, authorized by law, offers in evidence, as genuine, any book, paper, document, record, or other instrument in writing, knowing the same to have been forged, or fraudulently altered, is punishable in the same manner as [Offering false evidence.]

the forging or false alteration of such instrument is made punishable by the provisions of this Code.

Deceiving a witness.

§ 166. Every person who practices any fraud or deceit, or knowingly makes or exhibits any false statement, representation, token or writing, to any witness or person about to be called as a witness, upon any trial, proceeding, inquiry or investigation whatever, proceeding by authority of law, with intent to affect the testimony of such witness, is guilty of misdemeanor.

Preparing false evidence.

§ 167. Every person guilty of preparing any false book, paper, record, instrument in writing, or other matter or thing, with intent to produce it, or allow it to be produced for any fraudulent or deceitful purpose, as genuine, upon any trial, proceeding or inquiry whatever, authorized by law, is guilty of felony.

The Tracy Peerage case (10 *Cl. & F.*, 154), though involving no points of criminal law, supplies an illustration relevant to this subject. In that case a claimant to a peerage produced manuscript entries in a prayer book, alleged to be of ancient date; and, at a very late stage of the proceeding, called witnesses to testify to an inscription upon a tombstone, tending to make out the pedigree necessary to the claimant's case. The tombstone itself could not be produced; and, the circumstances of the case involving suspicion, the claim was dismissed; Lord CAMPBELL expressing his conviction that the case was founded on fraud and forgery.

Destroying evidence.

§ 168. Every person who, knowing that any book, paper, record, instrument in writing, or other matter or thing, is about to be produced in evidence upon any trial, proceeding, inquiry or investigation whatever, authorized by law, willfully destroys the same, with intent thereby to prevent the same from being produced, is guilty of misdemeanor.

Compare a statute of New Jersey upon this subject; *Elmer's Digest*, 113, § 60; *Nixon's Digest*, 188, § 69.

Preventing or dissuading witness from attending.

§ 169. Every person who willfully prevents or dissuades any person who has been duly summoned or subpenaed as a witness from attending, pursuant to the summons or subpœna, is guilty of a misdemeanor.

§ 170. Every person who gives or offers or promises to give, to any witness or person about to be called as a witness, any bribe, upon any understanding or agreement that the testimony of such witness shall be thereby influenced, or who attempts by any other means fraudulently to induce any witness to give false testimony or to withhold true testimony, is guilty of a misdemeanor. Bribing witnesses.

CHAPTER VII.

OTHER OFFENSES AGAINST PUBLIC JUSTICE.

Injury to records and embezzlement committed by ministerial officers.

§ 171. Every sheriff, coroner, clerk of a court, constable or other ministerial officer, and every deputy or subordinate of any ministerial officer, who either:

1. Mutilates, destroys, conceals, erases, obliterates or falsifies any record or paper appertaining to his office; or,

2. Fraudulently appropriates to his own use or to the use of another person, or secretes with intent to appropriate to such use, any money, evidence of debt or other property entrusted to him in virtue of his office,

Is guilty of felony.

Permitting escapes and other unlawful acts committed by ministerial officers.

§ 172. Every sheriff, coroner, clerk of a court, constable, or other ministerial officer, and every deputy or subordinate of any ministerial officer, who either:

1. Allows any person lawfully held by him in custody to escape or go at large, except as may be permitted by law; or,

2. Receives any gratuity or reward, or any security or promise of one, to procure, assist, connive at or permit any prisoner in his custody to escape, whether such escape is attempted or not; or,

3. Commits any unlawful act tending to hinder justice,

Is guilty of misdemeanor.

See 2 *Rev. Stat.*, 684, § 18.

§ 173. Every officer who, in violation of a duty imposed upon him by law as such officer to receive into his custody any person, as a prisoner, willfully neglects or refuses so to receive such person into his custody, is guilty of a misdemeanor. Officer refusing to receive prisoner into his custody.

See 2 *Rev. Stat.*, 684, § 18.

§ 174. Every public officer or other person having arrested any person upon any criminal charge, who willfully and wrongfully delays to take such person before a magistrate having jurisdiction to take his examination, is guilty of a misdemeanor. Delaying to take person arrested before a magistrate.

This section is intended to enforce the well understood duty of officers or private persons who have made arrests. The arrested person is entitled to a speedy hearing upon the charge preferred against him. The subject might indeed be considered covered so far as public officers are concerned, by the general provision elsewhere reported (§ 215), making it a misdemeanor for an officer willfully to omit an official duty. But there would still remain cases in which a private person is authorized to make an arrest. The commissioners deem it the safer course to make express provision upon the subject.

§ 175. Every public officer or person pretending to be a public officer, who, under the pretense or color of any process or other legal authority, arrests any person, or detains him against his will, or seizes or levies upon any property, or dispossesses any one of any lands or tenements, without a regular process Making arrests, &c., without lawful authority.

or other lawful authority therefor, is guilty of a mis demeanor.

2 *Rev Stat.*, 692, § 11.

Misconduct in executing search warrant.

§ 176. Every peace officer, who, in executing a search warrant, willfully exceeds his authority, or exercises it with unnecessary severity is guilty of a misdemeanor.

Rep. Code Cr. Pro., § 882.

Refusing to aid officer in making an arrest.

§ 177. Every person, who, after having been lawfully commanded to aid any officer in arresting any person, or in retaking any person who has escaped from legal custody, or in executing any legal process, willfully neglects or refuses to aid such officer is guilty of a misdemeanor.

This section is suggested as a substitute for sections 86 and 981 of the *Rep. Code Cr. Pro.* For the various cases in which a private citizen may lawfully be called upon to aid in an arrest, &c., see *Rep. Code Cr. Pro.*, §§ 64, 84, 92, 167, 180, 868, 980, 982.

Refusing to make an arrest.

§ 178. Every person, who, after having been lawfully commanded by any magistrate to arrest another person, willfully neglects or refuses so to do, is guilty of a misdemeanor.

Resisting execution of process; aiding escapes, &c., in county which has been proclaimed in insurrection.

§ 179. Every person, who, after proclamation issued by the governor declaring any county to be in a state of insurrection, resists or aids in resisting the execution of process in the county declared to be in a state of insurrection, or who aids or attempts the rescue or escape of another from lawful custody or confinement, or who resists or aids in resisting a force ordered out by the governor to quell or suppress an insurrection, is punishable by imprisonment in the state prison for not less than two years.

Rep. Code Cr. Pro., § 99.

Obstructing public officer in the discharge of his duty.

§ 180. Every person who willfully delays or obstructs any public officer in the discharge or attempt to discharge any duty of his office is guilty of a misdemeanor.

§ 181. Every person who takes an oath before an officer or person authorized to administer judicial oaths, except when such oath is required or authorized by law, or is required by the provisions of some contract as the basis of or in proof of a claim, or when the same has been agreed to be received by some person as proof of any fact, in the performance of any contract, obligation or duty, instead of other evidence, is guilty of a misdemeanor. Taking extra judicial oaths.

§ 182. Every officer or other person who administers an oath to another person, or who makes and delivers any certificate that another person has taken an oath, except when such oath is required or authorized by law, or is required by the provisions of some contract as a basis of or in proof of a claim, or when the same has been agreed to be received by some person as proof of any fact in the performance of any contract, obligation or duty, instead of other evidence, is guilty of a misdemeanor. Administering extra judicial oaths.

It is known that, in many cases, persons employ the sanctity of a judicial oath to gain credence for their statements, yet escape punishment for falsity in those statements because the penalties of perjury do not extend to mere voluntary oaths. Sworn statements are frequently published to advance the sales of a particular article; or to support one side in a public controversy. The commissioners intend, by the two sections above, to restrict the practice of taking or administering these voluntary oaths. The provisions reported will allow affidavits to be made in proof of loss under policies of insurance; in proof of facts necessary to show title, between vendor and purchaser of real property; and in all the other cases where thore is an agreement to receive them instead of pursuing the ordinary methods of legal investigation. And by antecedent provisions of this Code, the penalties of perjury are extended to willful false swearing in these cases, as well as in cases where the oath is required by law. (See § 150, and note.)

§ 183. Every person who, having knowledge of the actual commission of a crime or violation of statute, takes any money or property of another, or any gratuity or reward, or any engagement or pro- Compounding crimes.

mise therefor, upon any agreement or understanding, express or implied, to compound or conceal such crime, or violation of statute, or to abstain from any prosecution therefor, or to withhold any evidence thereof, is punishable as follows:

1. By imprisonment in a state prison, not exceeding five years, or in a county jail, not exceeding one year, where the crime compounded is one punishable either by death or by imprisonment in a state prison for life;

2. By imprisonment in a state prison, not exceeding three years, or in a county jail, not exceeding six months, where the crime compounded was punishable by imprisonment in a state prison for any other term than for life;

3. By imprisonment in a county jail, not exceeding one year, or by fine, not exceeding two hundred and fifty dollars, or by both such fine and imprisonment, where the crime or violation of statute compounded is a crime punishable by imprisonment in a county jail or by fine, or is a misdemeanor, or violation of statute for which a pecuniary or other penalty or forfeiture is prescribed.

Embodies 2 *Rev. Stat.*, 689, §§ 17, 18; *Id.*, 692, § 12; *Id.*, 897, § 40.

That the offense of compounding may extend as well to misdemeanors as to felonies, see Jones *v.* Rice, 18 *Pick.*, 440.

Compounding prosecutions.

§ 184. Every person who takes any money or property of another, or any gratuity or reward, or any engagement or promise therefor, upon any agreement or understanding, express or implied, to compound, discontinue or delay any prosecution then pending for any crime or violation of statute, or to withhold any evidence, in aid thereof, is guilty of a misdemeanor.

Attempting to intimidate judicial or ministerial

§ 185. Every person who, directly or indirectly, utters or addresses any threat or intimidation to any judicial or ministerial officer, or to any juror, referee, arbitrator, umpire or assessor, or other person authorized by law to hear or determine any controversy, with intent to induce him, contrary to his duty, either to do, or omit or delay any act, is guilty of a misdemeanor.

officers, jurors, &c.

§ 186. Every person who maliciously practices any deceit or fraud, or uses any threat, menace or violence, with intent to prevent any party to an action or proceeding from obtaining or producing therein any book, paper, or other matter or thing which might be evidence, or from procuring the attendance or testimony of any witness therein, or with intent to prevent any person having in his possession any book, paper, or other matter or thing which might be evidence in such suit or proceeding, or to prevent any person being cognizant of any fact material thereto from producing or disclosing the same, is guilty of a misdemeanor.

Suppressing evidence.

§ 187. Every person who takes any conveyance of any lands or tenements, or of any interest or estate therein, from any person not being in the possession thereof, while such lands or tenements are the subject of controversy, by suit in any court, knowing the pendency of such suit and that the grantor was not in possession of such lands or tenements, is guilty of a misdemeanor.

Buying lands in suit.

See 2 *Rev. Stat.*, 691, § 5; also. Wolcott *v.* Knight, 6 *Mass.*, 418; Everden *v.* Beaumont, 7 *Id.*, 76; Sweet *v.* Poor, 11 *Id.*, 549; Bringly *v.* Whitney, 5 *Pick.*, 349; to the effect that the purchase of a dormant title to lands from a party not seised, by a stranger out of possession, when made with intent to disturb the tenant in possession, constitutes the offense of maintenance and is indictable at common law.

§ 188. Every person who buys or sells, or in any manner procures, or makes or takes any promise or covenant to convey any pretended right or title to any lands or tenements, unless the grantor thereof

Buying pretended titles.

or the person making such promise or covenant has been in possession, or he and those by whom he claims, have been in possession of the same or of the reversion and remainder thereof, or have taken the rents and profits thereof for the space of one year before such grant, conveyance, sale, promise or covenant made, is guilty of a misdemeanor.

2 *Rev. Stat.*, 691, § 6.

Mortgage of lands under adverse possession not prohibited.

§ 189. The two last sections shall not be construed to prevent any person having a just title to lands, upon which there shall be an adverse possession, from executing a mortgage upon such lands.

2 *Rev. Stat.*, 691, § 7; 1 *Id.*, 739, § 148.

Common barratry defined.

§ 190. Common barratry is the practice of exciting groundless judicial proceedings.

Declared a misdemeanor.

§ 191. Common barratry is a misdemeanor.

What proof is required.

§ 192. No person can be convicted of common barratry, except upon proof that he has excited suits or proceedings at law, in at least three instances, and with a corrupt or malicious intent to vex and annoy.

Interest.

§ 193. Upon a prosecution for common barratry, the fact that the accused was himself a party in interest or upon the record to any proceedings at law, complained of, is not a defense.

Buying demands or suit by an attorney.

§ 194. Every attorney who, either directly or indirectly, buys or is interested in buying any evidence of debt or thing in action with intent to bring suit thereon is guilty of a misdemeanor

Buying demands by a justice or constable for suit before a justice.

§ 195. Every justice of the peace and every constable who, directly or indirectly, buys or is interested in buying any evidence of debt or thing in action for the purpose of commencing any suit thereon before a justice, is guilty of a misdemeanor.

Lending money upon claims delivered for collection.

§ 196. Every attorney, justice of the peace or constable, who, directly or indirectly, lends or advances any money or property, or agrees for or procures any loan or advance, to any person as a consideration for or inducement towards committing any evidence of debt or thing in action to such attorney, justice, constable, or any other person, for collection, is guilty of a misdemeanor.

§ 197. Every person convicted of a violation of either of the three preceding sections, in addition to the punishment, by fine and imprisonment, prescribed therefor by this Code, forfeits his office. Forfeiture of office.

§ 198. Nothing in the four preceding sections shall be construed to prohibit the receiving in payment of any evidence of debt or thing in action for any estate, real or personal, or for any services of an attorney actually rendered, or for a debt antecedently contracted; or the buying or receiving any evidence of debt or thing in action for the purpose of remittance, and without any intent to violate the preceding section. Receiving claims, in what cases allowable.

The four sections preceding are founded upon the provisions of 2 *Rev. Stat.*, 267, §§ 235, 236; *Id.*, 288, §§ 71–74.

The words "counsellor or solicitor" (2 *Rev. Stat.*, 288, §§ 71–74, are omitted; because, under the existing law, those offices are, for all purposes, within the purview of these sections, merged in that of the attorney. The other changes made are intended merely to attain greater clearness, and conciseness of expression.

§ 199. The provisions of sections 194, 196, and 198, relative to the buying of claims by an attorney, with intent to prosecute them, or to the lending or advancing of money by an attorney in consideration of a claim being delivered for collection, shall apply to every case of such buying a claim, or lending or advancing money, by any person prosecuting a suit or demand in person. Application of previous sections to persons prosecuting in person.

Laws of 1847, ch. 470, § 47.

§ 200. No person shall be excused from testifying, in any civil action, to any facts showing that an evi- Witness' privilege restricted dence of debt or thing in action has been bought, sold or received contrary to law, upon the ground that his testimony might tend to convict him of a crime. But no evidence derived from the examination of such person shall be received against him upon any criminal prosecution.

Compare 2 *Rev. Stat.*, 288, §§ 75–82. The sections of the Revised Statutes contain provisions, in detail, enabling a defendant to procure the testimony of the guilty party in aid of a defense setting up that the purchase of the demand in suit was contrary to law. Since the statute enabling either party to a suit to call his adversary as a witness these special provisions are no longer necessary to be retained.

Witness' privilege. It may here be remarked that section 1854, of *Rep. Code Civ. Pro.*, prescribes the general rule that a witness "need not give an answer which will have a tendency to subject him to punishment for felony; nor need he give an answer which will have a direct tendency to degrade his character, unless it be to the very fact in issue, or to a fact from which the fact in issue would be presumed."

The Commissioners have retained in the Penal Code the various provisions of the existing law whereby, in respect to particular crimes, the privilege to refuse to testify is removed; *e. g.*, in respect to buying demands for suit; duelling, &c. But they have added no new provisions of this character. The chapter of general provisions and explanations, at the close of this Code, contains a section prescribing that the various provisions of the Code, which declare that evidence obtained upon the examination of a person as a witness shall not be received against him in any criminal proceeding, shall not be construed to forbid such evidence being proved against such person upon a proceeding for perjury committed in such examination.

Criminal contempts. § 201. Every person guilty of any contempt of court of either of the following kinds, is guilty of misdemeanor:

1. Disorderly, contemptuous, or insolent behavior, committed during the sitting of any court of justice, in immediate view and presence of the court, and directly tending to interrupt its proceedings, or to impair the respect due to its authority;

2. Behavior of the like character, committed in the

presence of any referee or referees, while actually engaged in any trial or hearing, pursuant to the order of any court, or in the presence of any jury while actually sitting for the trial of a cause, or upon any inquest or other proceeding authorized by law;

3. Any breach of the peace, noise or other disturbance directly tending to interrupt the proceedings of any court;

4. Willful disobedience of any process or order lawfully issued by any court;

5. Resistance willfully offered by any person to the lawful order or process of any court;

6. The contumacious and unlawful refusal of any person to be sworn as a witness; or, when so sworn, the like refusal to answer any material question;

7. The publication of a false or grossly inaccurate report of the proceedings of any court. But no person can be punished, as for a contempt, in publishing a true, full, and fair report of any trial, argument, decision, or proceeding had in court;

8. Presenting to any court having power to pass sentence upon any prisoner under conviction, or to any member of such court, any affidavit or testimony or representation of any kind, verbal or written, in aggravation or mitigation of the punishment to be imposed upon such prisoner, except as provided by sections 544 and 545 of the Code of Criminal Procedure.

Subd. 1, 2, 3, 4, 5, 6, and 7, of the above section, are framed upon the existing provisions of 2 *Rev. Stat.*, 278, § 10. *Id.*, 692, § 14, modified to extend to all courts, instead of to courts of record only.

Subd. 2, is designed to extend the principles embodied in subdivision 1, to embrace contempts committed before referees and sheriffs and other juries. This enlargement of the present rule is demanded by the extension of the practice of referring causes.

Subd. 7. It has been decided that a publication, pending a suit, reflecting upon the court, the parties, witnesses, jurors or counsel, or intended to prejudice the public mind in regard to the cause, is a contempt. Bayard *v.* Passmore, 3 *Leak's Penn.*, 438; Van Hook's case, 3 *City H. Rec.*, 64; Noah's case, *Id.*, 31; Respublica *v.*

Oswald, 1 *Dall.*, 319; Hollingsworth *v.* Duane, *Wall.*, 77, 102. But no reason is perceived for enlarging the restricted provision of the Revised Statutes on the subject. The last clause of this subdivision is, however, deemed unnecessary by the Commissioners; inasmuch as section 2 of this Code provides that no person can be punished criminally except as prescribed by this Code, or by some of the statutes which it specifies as continuing in force; and neither the Code nor any of those acts contain any provision authorizing the punishment of a person for publishing a true account of judicial proceedings. As, however, the clause is found in the existing law, the Commissioners retain it lest the omission should give rise to the inference that a change in the law was intended.

Subd. 8, conforms to the provisions of sections 546 and 547 of the *Rep. Code Cr. Pro.*

Renewing application to stay trial of an indictment without leave.

§ 202. Every attorney or counselor-at-law who, knowing that an application has been made for an order staying the trial of an indictment to a judge, authorized to grant the same, and has been denied, without leave reserved to renew it, makes an application to another judge to stay the same trial, is guilty of misdemeanor.

Rep. Code Cr. Pro., § 369.

Grand juror acting after challenge has been allowed.

§ 203. Every grand juror who, with knowledge that a challenge, interposed against him by a defendant, has been allowed, is present at or takes part or attempts to take part in the consideration of the charge against the defendant who interposed the challenge, or the deliberations of the grand jury thereon, is guilty of a misdemeanor.

Rep. Code Cr. Pro., § 244.

Disclosure of depositions taken by a magistrate.

§ 204. Every magistrate or clerk of any magistrate who willfully permits any deposition taken on an information or examination of a defendant before such magistrate, and remaining in the custody of such magistrate or clerk, to be inspected by any person, except a judge of a court having jurisdiction of the offense, the attorney-general, the district-attorney of the county and his assistants, and the defendant and his counsel, is guilty of a misdemeanor.

§ 205. Every clerk of any court who willfully permits any deposition returned by any grand jury with a presentment made by them, and filed with such clerk, to be inspected by any person, except the court, the deputies or assistants of such clerk, and the district attorney and his assistants, until after the arrest of the defendant, is guilty of a misdemeanor. **Disclosure of depositions returned by grand jury with presentment**

This section and the one preceding it are designed to carry into effect the provisions of *Rep. Code Cr. Pro.*, §§ 204, 205, and §§ 273 and 274. Both sections have been so modified as to permit depositions to be examined by the *assistants* of district attorneys.

§ 206. Every insolvent debtor who, having applied to any court for a discharge from an imprisonment on execution, under the provisions of Part III of the Code of Civil Procedure, Title X, Chapter I, or for a discharge from his debts, under the provisions of Chapter II, of the same Title, either: **Fraud in applying for insolvent's discharge.**

1. Willfully conceals any part of his estate or effects, or any books or writings relative thereto, either before or after making any transfer and delivery of his property to a receiver appointed under said provisions; or,

2. Willfully omits to disclose to the court, before whom his application may be pending, any debts or demands which he has collected, or any transfer of his property which he has made, after presenting to such court his application for a discharge, is guilty of a misdemeanor.

The substance of the foregoing provisions is taken from those of 2 *Rev. Stat.*, 691, § 4. They are, however, adapted to the modifications in the method of obtaining insolvents' discharges proposed in *Rep. Code of Civ. Pro.*, §§ 1595–1606.

§ 207. Every person concerned in any racing, running, or other trial of speed between any horses or other animals, within one mile of the place where any court is actually sitting, is guilty of a misdemeanor. **Racing near a court.**

2 *Rev. Stat.*, 692, § 13.

Selling liquor in court houses or prisons or near election polls.

§ 208. Every person who sells any spirituous or intoxicating liquor within, or brings with intent to sell, or offer or expose for sale therein, any such liquor into, either:

1. Any building established as a court house for the holding of courts of record while any session of such court is being held therein, except in such part of such building not appropriated to the use of courts or of juries attending them, in which such sale has been authorized by a resolution of the board of supervisors of the county; or,

2. Any building established as a jail or prison; or,

3. Any building or shed, outhouse, porch, yard or curtilage appertaining to any building which, or any part of which, is at the time occupied or used for holding the polls at an election of any public officer of this state or of the United States, or for canvassing votes cast at such election,

Is guilty of misdemeanor.

Embraces provisions of 2 *Rev. Stat.*, 291, § 95 *Id.*, 431, § 29.

Misconduct by attorneys.

§ 209. Every attorney who, whether as attorney or as counselor, either:

1. Is guilty of any deceit or collusion, or consents to any deceit or collusion, with intent to deceive the court or any party; or,

2. Willfully delays his client's suit with a view to his own gain; or,

3. Willfully receives any money or allowance for or on account of any money which he has not laid out or become answerable for,

Is guilty of misdemeanor, and in addition to the punishment prescribed therefor by this Code, he forfeits to the party injured treble damages, to be recovered in a civil action.

See 2 *Rev. Stat.*, 287, §§ 69, 70.

"*As attorney or as counselor.*" In general throughout the Code, the Commissioners have used the word "attorney," as embracing all classes of legal practitioners, conformably to the existing law by which both the functions of the attorney and those of the counselor-at-law are united in the same person. (See note to section 198, above.) But it has been held that although candidates for admission to the bar are now admitted as attorneys and as counselors at the same time, yet the offices are still distinct. (Easton *v.* Smith, 1 *E. D. Smith*, 318; Brady *v.* Mayor, &c., of N. Y., 1 *Sandf.*, 559.) As some of the acts prohibited in the above section might be committed by one acting only as a counselor, and who, though in fact also an attorney, had no retainer as such in the cause to which the misconduct related, the Commissioners have declared the acts punishable in which ever capacity the defendant acts.

Permitting attorneys' names to be used.

§ 210. If any attorney knowingly permits any person, not being his general law partner or a clerk in his office, to sue out any process or to prosecute or defend any action in his name, except as authorized by the next section, such attorney, and every person who shall so use his name, is guilty of a misdemeanor.

The existing law imposes a forfeiture of fifty dollars, instead of a criminal punishment, for this species of misconduct. (2 *Rev. Stat.*, 287, § 70.) The Commissioners recommend that the prohibition be restricted by allowing an attorney to permit his name to be used in the cases specified in the following section; and that, except as therein permitted, such use of the name be made a misdemeanor.

In what cases lawful.

§ 211. Whenever an action or proceeding is authorized by law to be prosecuted or defended in the name of the people, or of any public officer, board of officers, or municipal corporation, on behalf of another party, the attorney-general, or district attorney, or attorney of such public officer or board or corporation may permit any proceeding therein to be taken in his name by an attorney to be chosen by the party in interest.

Fraudulent pretenses relative to birth of infant.

§ 212. Every person who fraudulently produces an infant, falsely pretending it to have been born of any parent whose child would be entitled to inherit any real estate or to receive a share of any personal estate, with intent to intercept the inheritance of any such real estate, or the distribution of any such personal estate from any person lawfully entitled thereto, is punishable by imprisonment in a state prison not exceeding ten years.

This is substantially the provision of 2 *Rev. Stat.*, 676, § 51. The Commissioners would have recommended the enactment of a more extended provision, which should forbid the holding out of a child as born of other than its true parents, were it not that such an enactment would render necessary a system of provisions regulating and legalizing the adoption of children. The subject of adoptions is one which the Commissioners have under consideration, and some systematic provisions relative to it may perhaps be reported, but the topic does not come within the Penal Code.

Substituting one child for another.

§ 213. Every person to whom an infant has been confided for nursing, education, or any other purpose, who, with intent to deceive any parent or guardian of such child, substitutes or produces to such parent or guardian another child in the place of the one so confided, is punishable by imprisonment in a state prison not exceeding seven years.

Founded upon 2 *Rev. Stat.*, 677, § 52. The changes introduced are two. The provisions of the Revised Statutes is limited to cases where the infant confided to the accused is under six years. The Commissioners are of opinion that while the substitution may become less and less feasible with the advancing age of the child, it is not the less criminal, if perpetrated, because the child has passed the age of six; and they therefore omit the restriction. They also use the words "substitutes *or* produces," in place of "substitutes *and* produces;" in order to embrace cases in which the child may not be exhibited in person to the parent or guardian.

Importing foreign convicts.

§ 214. Every owner, master or commander of any vessel arriving from a foreign country who knowingly lands or permits to land at any port, city, harbor, or place within this state, any passenger or hand who is a foreign convict of any crime which, if committed within this state, would be punishable therein, without giving notice thereof to the mayor of such city, or other principal municipal officer of such port or place, is guilty of a misdemeanor.

Founded upon *Laws of* 1833, ch. 230, § 1. That act renders the bringing within this state of any foreign convict of felony, a misdemeanor, if done with intent to land him or to permit him to land. The objection to this form of the provision is that if the character of the felon is not known to the master until after the ship has left the foreign port, upon her voyage home, the master may have no option but to bring him within this state. The provision might be relieved of injustice in its operation in this class of cases by specifying the taking on board of a foreign convict, with intent to bring him to this country, as the criminal act. But this would be to declare punishable an act committed without this state, which ought only to be done in cases involving a special necessity. The Commissioners have, therefore, allowed masters to relieve themselves of criminal responsibility by giving notice of the character of the passenger to the public authorities of the place where he is landed.

The Commissioners have also substituted the word "crime" for "felony," in view of the increasing evils suffered by our people from the influx of foreign criminals.

§ 215. Where any duty is or shall be enjoined by law upon any public officer, or upon any person holding any public trust or employment, every willful omission to perform such duty, where no special provision shall have been made for the punishment of such delinquency, is punishable as a misdemeanor. Omission of duty by public officer.

See 2 *Rev. Stat.*, 696, §§ 38, 40. The enactment of this provision will render it unnecessary to embrace section 91 of the *Rep. Code Cr. Pro.* in this Code. That section is as follows. "Every magistrate or officer, authorized to keep the peace, having notice of an unlawful or riotous assembly, who neglects to proceed to the place of the assembly, or as near thereto as he can with safety, and to exercise the authority with which he is invested for suppressing the same and arresting the offenders, is guilty of a misdemeanor."

§ 216. Where the performance of any act is prohibited by any statute, and no penalty for the violation of such statute is imposed in any statute, the doing such act is a misdemeanor. Commission of prohibited acts.

See 2 *Rev. Stat.*, 696, § 39.

Disclosing fact of indictment having been found.

§ 217. Every grand juror, district attorney, clerk, judge, or other officer, who, excepting by issuing or in executing a warrant to arrest the defendant, willfully discloses the fact of a presentment or indictment having been made for a felony, until the defendant has been arrested, is guilty of a misdemeanor.

See *Rep. Code Cr. Pro.*, §§ 276, 277.

Grand juror disclosing what transpired before the grand jury.

§ 218. Every grand juror who, except when required by a court, willfully discloses any evidence adduced before the grand jury or anything which he himself or any other member of the grand jury may have said, or in what manner he or any other grand juror may have voted on a matter before them, is guilty of a misdemeanor.

See *Rep. Code Cr. Pro.*, §§ 267–269.

Instituting suit in false name.

§ 219. Every person who maliciously institutes or prosecutes any action or legal proceeding, or makes or procures any arrest, in the name of a person who does not exist or has not consented that it be instituted or made, is guilty of a misdemeanor.

This provision has been prepared as a substitute for 2 *Rev. Stat.*, 550, § 1.

Maliciously procuring search warrant.

§ 220. Every person who maliciously, and without probable cause, procures a search warrant to be issued and executed, is guilty of a misdemeanor.

Rep. Code Cr. Pro., § 881.

Unauthorized communications with convict in state prison

§ 221. Every person who, not being authorized by law, or by a written permission from an inspector, or by the consent of the warden, communicates with any convict in any state prison, or brings into or conveys out of any state prison any letter or writing to or from any convict, is guilty of a misdemeanor.

See *Laws of* 1847, ch. 460, § 7.

Neglect to return names of constables.

§ 222. Every town clerk who willfully omits to return to the county clerk the name of any person who has qualified as constable, as required by subdivision

4 of section 1021 of the Political Code, is punishable by a fine not exceeding ten dollars.

Rep. Pol. Code, § 1022.

§ 223. Every public officer who being authorized by law to make or give any certificate or other writing, knowingly makes and delivers as true any such certificate or writing containing any statement which he knows to be false, is guilty of a misdemeanor. False certificates by public officers.

CHAPTER VIII.

CONSPIRACY.

§ 224. If two or more persons conspire, either: Criminal conspiracies defined

1. To commit any crime; or,

2. Falsely and maliciously to indict another for any crime, or to procure another to be charged or arrested for any crime; or,

3. Falsely to move or maintain any suit, action or proceeding; or,

4. To cheat and defraud any person of any property by any means which are in themselves criminal or by any means which, if executed, would amount to a cheat or to obtaining money or property by false pretenses; or,

5. To commit any act injurious to the public health, to public morals, or to trade or commerce, or for the perversion or obstruction of justice or the due administration of the laws,

They are guilty of a misdemeanor.

See 2 *Rev. Stat.*, 691, § 8. Instead of the word "offense," employed in the Revised Statutes, in subdivisions 1 and 2, the Commissioners have used "crime." In section 3 of this Code the Commissioners have defined "public offense" as synonymous with "crime;" leaving the word "offense" to be used in a broader signification, including the graver wrongs towards individuals which are not cognizable by the criminal law. In the section of the Revised Statutes "offense" is plainly used as synonymous with "crime," and the Commissioners, in substituting the latter, have intended no change in the law, but merely to secure a consistent use of terms throughout the Code.

The common law definitions of conspiracy are broader than that given in our Revised Statutes.

Hawkins says that it is a consultation and agreement between two or more persons either falsely to charge another with a crime, punishable by law; or wrongfully to injure or prejudice a third person, or any body of men in any other manner; or to commit any punishable offense by law; or to do any act with intent to prevent the course of justice; or to effect a legal purpose with a corrupt intent or by improper means. (*Hawk. P. C.*, ch. 72, § 2.)

Archbold defines conspiracy to be "an agreement between two or more persons:

1. Falsely to charge another with a crime punishable by law.

2. Wrongfully to injure or prejudice a third person, or any body of men in any manner.

3. To commit any offense punishable by law.

4. To do any act with intent to prevent the course of justice.

5. To effect a legal purpose with a corrupt intent, or by improper means.

6. Combination by journeymen to raise their wages. (*Arch. Cr. Pl.*, 390, 1.) See section 733, *infra*.

In the State *v.* Buchanan (5 *Har. & J.*, 317, 351), it is said that, by a course of decisions running through a space of more than four hundred years, from the reign of Edw. III to the 59 Geo. III, without a single conflicting adjudication, these points are clearly settled.

That a conspiracy to do any act that is criminal *per se* is an indictable offense at common law.

That an indictment will lie at common law: 1. For a conspiracy to do an act not illegal, nor punishable if done by an individual, but immoral only. 2. For a conspiracy to do an act neither illegal, nor immoral in an individual, but to effect a purpose which has a tendency to prejudice the public; *e. g.*, a combination by workmen to raise their wages. 3. For a conspiracy to extort money from another or to injure his reputation by means not indictable, if practised by an individual, as by verbal defamation, and that whether it be to charge him with an indictable offense or not. 4. For a conspiracy to cheat and defraud a third person, accomplished by means of an act which would not in law amount to an indictable cheat, if effected by an individual. 5. For a malicious conspiracy to impoverish, or ruin a third person in his trade, or profession. 6. For a conspiracy to defraud a third person by means of an act *not per se* unlawful, and though no person be thereby injured. 7. For a bare conspiracy to cheat or defraud a third person, though the means of effecting it could not be determined on at the time.

The Revisers, in their note to the section of the Revised Statutes, which is embodied in the section in the text, assign the following reason for restricting the definition of conspiracy within narrower limits than those of the common law. "The great difficulty in enlarging the definition of this offense consists in the inevitable result of depriving the courts of equity of the most effectual means of detecting fraud by compelling a discovery on oath. It is a sacred principle of our institutions that no man shall be compelled to accuse himself of any crime, which ought not to be violated in any case. Yet such must be the result, or the ordinary jurisdiction of courts of equity must be destroyed by declaring any private fraud when committed by two, or any concert to commit it, criminal. Frauds and combinations to defraud constitute the mass of equity business, and seldom is a case presented when there are not at least two parties to a fraud."

This was said in 1828, before the passage of the statute authorizing the unrestricted examination of a defendant to a bill in chancery charging fraud. That statute was passed in 1833. It provided in substance that a defendant might be compelled to answer any bill in chancery, charging the defendant with being a party to any conveyance made with intent to defraud; or when the defendant shall be charged with any fraud whatever; but no such answer should be read in evidence against any party thereto on any complaint or on the trial of any indictment for the fraud charged in such bill. (*Laws of* 1833, ch. 14.) To some extent the adoption of this principle obviates the objection urged by the revisers to a full recognition of the common law definition of conspiracy. But as the provisions of the Revised Statutes have stood without objection for a long period, and are believed to be satisfactory, in practical operation, the Commissioners have not thought it best to enlarge them; except that they suggest the addition of the section next following, which is new. Their reason for refraining from reporting new exceptions to the general rule that a witness shall not be compelled to criminate himself, are stated in their note to section 200 of this Code.

Other conspiracies. The Revised Statutes also contain a section (2 *Rev. Stat.*, 692, § 9,) declaring that no conspiracies other than such as are enumerated in the statute are punishable criminally. This provision is here omitted, as unnecessary, in view of the general one to like effect, embodied in section 2.

Conspiracies against the peace of the state.

§ 225. If two or more persons, being out of this state, conspire to commit any act against the peace of this state, the commission or attempted commission of which, within this state, would be treason against the state, they are punishable by imprisonment in a state prison not exceeding ten years.

Overt act, when necessary.

§ 226. No agreement except to commit a felony upon the person of another, or to commit arson or burglary, amounts to a conspiracy, unless some act beside such agreement be done to effect the object thereof, by one or more of the parties to such agreement.

2 *Rev. Stat.*, 692, § 10.

This rule is also a restriction of the rule of the common law. By that rule the gist of conspiracy is the unlawful confederating; and the act is complete when the confederacy is made. Any act done in pursuance of it is no constituent part of the offense, but merely an aggravation of it. See Commonwealth *v.* Judd, 2 *Mass.*, 329; State *v.* Rikey, 4 *Halst.*, 293; State *v.* Buchanan, 5 *Har. & J.*, 317, 352.

So, also, it is said that where an indictment charges an ordinary conspiracy, it is not necessary to prove a common design between the defendants before proving the acts of each defendant; for the acts of each defendant are only evidence against himself, and may be the only means of establishing the conspiracy. In high treason, the overt act of one is the overt act of all; and therefore a common design must, in such cases, precede the proof of individual acts. Reg. *v.* Brittain, 11 *L. T.*, 48; 3 *Cox Cr. Cas.*, 77.

As to whether the misdemeanor of conspiracy to commit a felony is to be deemed merged in the felony when subsequently committed, see Commonwealth *v.* Fisher, 5 *Mass.*, 106; Lambert *v.* People, 9 *Cow.*, 620; Rey *v.* Button, 3 *Cox Cr. Cas.*, 229; and 18 *L. J. M. C.*, 19

TITLE IX.

OF CRIMES AGAINST THE PERSON.

CHAPTER I.

SUICIDE.

§ 227. Suicide is the intentional taking of one's own life. Suicide defined.

§ 228. Although suicide is deemed a grave public wrong, yet from the impossibility of reaching the successful perpetrator, no forfeiture is imposed. No forfeiture imposed for suicide.

See 2 *Rev. Stat.*, 701, § 22.

§ 229. But every person who, with intent to take his own life, commits upon himself any act dangerous to human life, or which if committed upon or towards another person and followed by death as a conse- Attempting suicide.

quence, would render the perpetrator chargeable with homicide, is guilty of attempting suicide.

An attempt to commit suicide is a misdemeanor at common law. And in this, as in other cases, the mere fact of drunkenness is no excuse, if there was an actual intent on the part of the accused to take his own life. The fact is, however, material as bearing on the question of intent. Rey *v.* Doody, 6 *Cox Cr. Cas.*, 463.

Aiding suicide.

§ 230. Every person who willfully, in any manner, advises, encourages, abets or assists another person in taking his own life, is guilty of aiding suicide.

Furnishing weapon or drug to commit suicide.

§ 231. Every person who willfully furnishes another person with any deadly weapon or poisonous drug, knowing that such person intends to use such weapon or drug in taking his own life, is guilty of aiding suicide, if such person thereafter employs such instrument or drug in taking his own life.

Aiding attempt at suicide.

§ 232. Every person who willfully aids another in attempting to take his own life, in any manner which by the preceding sections would have amounted to aiding suicide if the person assisted had actually taken his own life, is guilty of aiding an attempt at suicide.

Mental incapacity of person aided, no defense.

§ 233. It is no defense to a prosecution for aiding suicide, or aiding an attempt at suicide, that the person who committed or attempted the suicide was not a person deemed capable of committing crime.

Intended to meet the possible argument in defense of one who assists the suicide of an insane person, &c., that as the principal was incapable of crime, no crime was committed by him, and therefore the abettor cannot be deemed to have assisted a crime.

Punishment of aiding suicide.

§ 234. Every person guilty of aiding suicide is punishable by imprisonment in a state prison for not less than seven years.

Corresponds with 2 *Rev. Stat.*, 661, § 7; and *Id.*, 662, § 20.

Punishment of attempting

§ 235. Every person guilty of attempting suicide, or of aiding an attempt at suicide, is punishable by imprisonment in a state prison not exceeding two years, or by a fine not exceeding one thousand dollars, or both. suicide or aiding an attempt.

CHAPTER II.

HOMICIDE.

SECTION 236. Homicide defined.
237. Different kinds of homicide.
238. What proof of death is required.
239. Petit treason abolished.
240. Effect of proof of a domestic or confidential relation.
241. Murder defined.
242. Design to effect death when inferred.
243. Premeditation.
244. Anger or intoxication no defense.
245. Act eminently dangerous, and evincing a depraved mind.
246. Duel fought out of this state.
247. Punishment of murder.
248. Manslaughter in first degree defined.
249. Killing unborn quick child by injury to person of mother.
250. By administering drugs, &c.
251. Punishment of manslaughter in first degree.
252. Manslaughter in second degree defined.
253. Liability of owner of mischievous animal.
254. Liability of persons navigating vessels.
255. Liability of persons in charge of steamboats.
256. Liability of persons in charge of steam engines.
257. Liability of physicians.
258. Liability of persons making or keeping gunpowder contrary to law.
259. Punishment of manslaughter in second degree.
260. Excusable homicide defined.
261. Justifiable homicide by public officers.
262. Justifiable homicide by other persons.

§ 236. Homicide is the killing of one human being by another. Homicide defined.

§ 237. Homicide is either: Different kinds of homicide.

1. Murder;

2. Manslaughter;

3. Excusable homicide; or,

Justifiable homicide.

What proof of death is required.

§ 238. No person can be convicted of murder or manslaughter, or of aiding suicide, unless the death of the person alleged to have been killed and the fact of killing by the accused, are each established as independent facts beyond a reasonable doubt.

To this extent the strict rule of the common law requiring the finding of the body as an invariable condition to a conviction for homicide has, by the latter cases, been relaxed. See Ruloff *v.* People, 18 *N. Y.* (4 *Smith*), 179; compare also State of Vermont *v.* Davidson, 30 *Vt.*, 377.

Petit treason abolished.

§ 239. The rules of the common law, distinguishing the killing of a master by his servant, and of a husband by his wife as petit treason, are abolished, and these offenses are deemed homicides, punishable in the manner prescribed by this chapter.

See 2 *Rev. Stat.*, 657, § 8. In modifying the language of the Revised Statutes upon this subject, the Commissioners have not intended any change in the law, but have simply designed to introduce such a reference to the common law as should serve to explain why any legislation upon the point was demanded.

Effect of proof of a domestic or confidential relation.

§ 240. Whenever the grade or punishment of homicide is made to depend upon its having been committed under circumstances evincing a depraved mind or unusual cruelty, or in a cruel manner, the jury may take into consideration the fact that any domestic or confidential relation existed between the accused and the person killed, in determining the moral quality of the acts proved.

Murder defined.

§ 241. Homicide is murder in the following cases:

1. When perpetrated without authority of law, and with a premeditated design to effect the death, of the person killed or of any other human being;

2. When perpetrated by any act imminently dangerous to others and evincing a depraved mind, regardless of human life, although without any premeditated design to effect the death of any particular individual;

3. When perpetrated without any design to effect death, by a person engaged in the commission of any felony.

The former definition. This section is founded on 2 *Rev. Stat.*, 657, § 5. The definitions of the four grades of homicide given in the Revised Statutes, though drawn with care, and resulting, when attentively considered, in an accurate demarcation, are yet obscured and embarrassed with references to each other, and to the rules of the common law. The Commissioners have, in subsequent sections, recommended a modification of the law of manslaughter, distinguishing it into two degrees only, instead of four. In other respects, whenever they have departed, in these definitions of homicide, from the phraseology of the Revised Statutes, it has chiefly been in order to render each definition independent and sufficient in itself.

Degrees in Murder. By recent statutes (*Laws of* 1860, 712, ch. 410, § 2, and 1862, 369, ch. 197, § 5), murder was divided into two degrees, the first degree only being punishable with death. The practical result of introducing such a distinction will be that jurors influenced by unwillingness to unite in a capital conviction, will always find the prisoner guilty of the second degree only. The Commissioners are of opinion that the simplicity of the definition of murder in the Revised Statutes should be restored.

§ 242. A design to effect death is inferred from the fact of killing, unless the circumstances raise a reasonable doubt whether such design existed. **Design to effect death when inferred.**

§ 243. A design to effect death sufficient to constitute murder, may be formed instantly before committing the act by which it is carried into execution. **Premeditation.**

People *v.* Clark, 7 *N. Y.* (3 *Seld.*), 385.
People *v.* Austin, 1 *Park. Cr.*, 154.

§ 244. Homicide committed with a design to effect death is not the less murder because the perpetrator was in a state of anger or voluntary intoxication at the time. **Anger or intoxication no defense.**

People *v.* Johnson, 1 *Park. Cr.*, 291.
People *v.* Sullivan, 7 *N. Y.* (3 *Seld.*), 396.
People *v.* Austin, 1 *Park. Cr.*, 154, 167.
People *v.* Vinegar, 2 *Id.*, 24.

Act eminently dangerous and evincing a depraved mind.

§ 245. Homicide perpetrated by an act eminently dangerous to others and evincing a depraved mind, regardless of human life, is not the less murder because there was no actual intent to injure others.

Intended to correct the rules deemed incorrect, laid down in People *v.* Sheriff of Westchester Co., 1 *Park. Cr.*, 659; Darry *v.* People, 10 *N. Y.* (6 Seld.), 120.

Duel fought out of this state.

§ 246. Every person who, by previous appointment within this state, fights a duel without this state, and in so doing inflicts a wound upon his antagonist or any other person, whereof the person injured dies, and every second engaged in such duel, is guilty of murder, and may be indicted, tried and convicted in any county of the state.

See 2 *Rev. Stat.*, 657, § 6.

Punishment of murder.

§ 247. Every person convicted of murder shall suffer death for the same.

Corresponds with 2 *Rev. Stat.*, 656, § 1. See notes to sections 60 and 241, above.

Manslaughter in first degree defined.

§ 248. Homicide is manslaughter in the first degree in the following cases:

1. When perpetrated without a design to effect death by a person while engaged in the commission of a misdemeanor;

2. When perpetrated without a design to effect death, and in a heat of passion, but in a cruel and unusual manner or by means of a dangerous weapon; unless it is committed under such circumstances as constitute excusable or justifiable homicide;

3. When perpetrated unnecessarily either while resisting an attempt by the person killed to commit a crime, or after such attempt shall have failed.

Subd. 1. This clause is intended to embody the provisions of 2 *Rev. Stat.*, 661, § 6.

The words "by the act, procurement or culpable negligence of another," used in that statute, are omitted. They are not found in the corresponding clause in the definition of murder. (2 *Rev. Stat.*, 657, § 5, *subd.* 3.

See also section 241, *supra.*) If the accused was committing *felony* when he perpetrated the homicide, it is murder, though unintentional. If he was committing a *misdemeanor*, the homicide is manslaughter in the first degree. The sections embodying these two ideas should correspond in language. Homicide by culpable negligence is made manslaughter in the second degree, by section 252 of this Code.

The word "misdemeanor" is substituted for the phrase "crime or misdemeanor, not amounting to felony," that being the exact meaning expressed by the term misdemeanor under the definition already given in this Code.

The restriction "in cases where such killing would be murder at the common law," is omitted because it is deemed essential to the usefulness of the Code that its definitions should not be dependent upon a recourse to the common law to render them intelligible.

Subd. 2. This provision embodies two sections of the existing law; 2 *Rev. Stat.*, 661, §§ 10 and 12. Both species of homicide there respectively defined as manslaughter in the second and third degrees, are here brought within the first degree, in harmony with the design of the Commissioners to simplify the law of manslaughter by reducing the number of its degrees.

Subd. 3. This embodies the provision of 2 *Rev. Stat.*, 661, § 11. The phrase "to commit a crime" is substituted for "to commit any felony or to do any unlawful act," because the words "unlawful act" might be deemed to embrace trespass; yet the case of homicide of a person committing a trespass, is specifically declared manslaughter in the third degree by 2 *Rev. Stat.*, 661, § 13.

§ 249. The willful killing of an unborn quick child by any injury committed upon the person of the mother of such child, and not prohibited in the next following section, is manslaughter in the first degree. Killing unborn quick child by injury to person of mother.

Substituted for 2 *Rev. Stat.*, 661, § 8, the language of which is obscure. Whether an injury to the mother resulting in death would be murder depends wholly on the intent, and not at all on the description of the injury.

§ 250. Every person who provides, supplies or administers to any woman, whether pregnant or not, or who prescribes for such woman, or advises or procures any such woman to take any medicine, drug or substance whatever, or who uses or employs any instrument or other means, with intent thereby to procure the miscarriage of such woman, unless the same shall By administering drugs, &c.

have been necessary to preserve the life of such woman, is guilty, in case the death of such woman, or of any quick child with which she may be pregnant, is thereby produced, of manslaughter in the first degree.

See *Laws of* 1846, ch. 22, § 1.

Punishment of manslaughter in first degree.

§ 251. Every person guilty of manslaughter in the first degree is punishable by imprisonment in a state prison for not less than four years.

Founded upon 2 *Rev. Stat.*, 662, § 20; but modified to correspond with the reduction in the number of degrees in manslaughter, introduced by the preceding provisions.

Manslaughter in second degree defined

§ 252. Every killing of one human being by the act, procurement or culpable negligence of another, which under the provisions of this chapter is not murder, nor manslaughter in the first degree, nor excusable nor justifiable homicide, is manslaughter in the second degree.

Liability of owner of mischievous animal.

§ 253. If the owner of a mischievous animal, knowing its propensities, willfully suffers it to go at large, or keeps it without ordinary care, and such animal, while so at large or not confined, kills any human being who has taken all the precautions which the circumstances permitted, to avoid such animal, the owner is deemed guilty of manslaughter in the second degree.

See 2 *Rev. Stat.*, 662, § 14.

Liability of persons navigating vessels.

§ 254. Every person navigating any vessel for gain, who willfully or negligently receives so many passengers or such a quantity of other lading on board such vessel, that by means thereof such vessel sinks or is overset or injured, and thereby any human being is drowned or otherwise killed, is guilty of manslaughter in the second degree.

See 2 *Rev. Stat.*, 662, § 15.

Liability of persons in charge of steamboats.

§ 255. Every captain or other person having charge of any steamboat used for the conveyance of passengers, or of the boilers and engines thereof, who, from ignorance or gross neglect, or for the purpose of excelling any other boat in speed, creates, or allows to be created, such an undue quantity of steam as to burst or break the boiler or other apparatus in which it shall be generated, or any apparatus or machinery connected therewith, by which bursting or breaking any person is killed, is deemed guilty of manslaughter in the second degree.

See 2 *Rev. Stat.*, 662, § 16.

Liability of persons in charge of steam engines.

§ 256. Every engineer, or other person having charge of any steam boiler, steam engine or other apparatus for generating or employing steam, employed in any manufactory, railway or other mechanical works, who willfully or from ignorance or gross neglect creates, or allows to be created, such an undue quantity of steam as to burst or break the boiler, engine or apparatus, or to cause any other accident whereby the death of a human being is produced, is guilty of manslaughter in the second degree.

Liability of physicians.

§ 257. Every physician who, being in a state of intoxication, without a design to effect death, administers any poison drug or medicine, or does any other act as such physician, to another person, which produces the death of such other, is guilty of manslaughter in the second degree.

See 2 *Rev. Stat.*, 442, § 17.

Liability of persons making or keeping gunpowder contrary to law.

§ 258. Every person guilty of making or keeping gunpowder or saltpetre within any city or village, in any quantity or manner such as is prohibited by law or by any ordinance of said city or village, in case any explosion thereof occurs whereby any human being is killed, is guilty of manslaughter in the second degree.

Punishment of manslaugh-

§ 259. Every person guilty of manslaughter in the second degree is punishable by imprisonment in a ter in second degree.

state prison not more than four years, and not less than two years, or by imprisonment in a county jail not exceeding one year, or by a fine not exceeding one thousand dollars, or by both such fine and imprisonment.

Founded on 2 *Rev. Stat.*, 662, § 20; but modified to correspond with the reduction in the number of degrees in manslaughter, introduced by the preceding provisions.

Excusable homicide defined.

§ 260. Homicide is excusable in the following cases:

1. When committed by accident and misfortune, in lawfully correcting a child or servant, or in doing any other lawful act, by lawful means, with usual and ordinary caution, and without any unlawful intent;

2. When committed by accident and misfortune in the heat of passion, upon any sudden and sufficient provocation, or upon a sudden combat; provided that no undue advantage is taken, nor any dangerous weapon used, and that the killing is not done in a cruel or unusual manner.

2 *Rev. Stat.*, 660, § 4. The verbal alterations introduced are intended only to attain greater clearness of expression; and not to introduce any substantive changes.

Justifiable homicide by public officers.

§ 261. Homicide is justifiable when committed by public officers and those acting by their command in their aid and assistance, either:

1. In obedience to any judgment of a competent court; or,

2. When necessarily committed in overcoming actual resistance to the execution of some legal process, or to the discharge of any other legal duty; or,

3. When necessarily committed in retaking felons who have been rescued, or who have escaped, or when necessarily committed in arresting felons fleeing from justice.

Justifiable homicide by other persons.

§ 262. Homicide is also justifiable when committed by any person in either of the following cases:

1. When resisting any attempt to murder any

person, or to commit any felony upon him or her, or upon or in any dwelling house in which such person is; or,

2. When committed in the lawful defense of such person, or of his or her husband, wife, parent, child, master, mistress or servant, when there is a reasonable ground to apprehend a design to commit a felony, or to do some great personal injury, and imminent danger of such design being accomplished; or,

3. When necessarily committed in attempting, by lawful ways and means, to apprehend any person for any felony committed; or in lawfully suppressing any riot; or in lawfully keeping and preserving the peace.

2 *Rev. Stat.*, 660, § 3; substituting "*any* person," for "*such* person," in subdivision 1.

CHAPTER III.

MAIMING.

§ 263. Every person who, with premeditated design to injure another, inflicts upon his person any injury which disfigures his personal appearance, or disables any member or organ of his body, or seriously diminishes his physical vigor, is guilty of maiming. Maiming another person defined.

Definitions of mayhem found in several of the more familiar English authorities confine the offense to such wounds as impair the powers of attack or defense; the gravamen of the offense being deemed to consist in the disability for self protection which it creates. (Consult 4 *Blackst. Comm.*, 205, 150; 1 *Coke, Inst.*, § 502.)

Earlier authorities, however, are to be found giving the word a more extended signification. Thus, Pulton (*De Pace Regis*, 1609, fol. 15, §§ 58 and 59) says: "Mai-

"heming is when one member of the commonweale shall "take from another member of the same a natural mem-"ber of his bodie, or the use and benefit thereof, and "thereby disable him to serve the commonweale by his "weapons in the time of warre, or by his labor in the "time of peace; and also diminisheth the strength of "his bodie, and weaken him thereby to get his own "lyving, and by that means the commonweale is in a "sort deprived of the use of one of her members.' Wounds which merely disfigured the person without impairing the general strength or the powers of some particular member seem to have been excluded by all the common law definitions of mayhem; though made the subject of several stringent enactments. In this country, however, many of the statutes, punishing maims, embrace also wounds, deemed aggravated from the personal disfigurement involved, merely. Thus, our own statute (2 *Rev. Stat.*, 664, § 27), without defining the term "mayhem," imposes one and the same punishment on any person who "shall cut out or disable the tongue; put out an eye; *slit the lip or nose;* cut off or disable any limb," &c. So the Revised Statutes of Ohio embrace biting the nose, lip or ear. (1 *Rev. Stat.* of Ohio, 1860, 411, § 23.) The act of congress of 1790 (1 *U. S. Stat. at L.*, 115, § 13), specifies cutting off an ear. So in Illinois, mayhem is expressly defined to consist in unlawfully depriving a human being of a member of his or her body, or disfiguring or rendering it useless. (1 *Purple's Stat. of Ill.*, 365, § 47.) And there are many other statutes substantially like these, in this respect. (Compare 2 *Gavin & H. Stat. of Ind.*, 1862, 440, § 12; 2 *Rev. Stat. of Miss.*, 565, § 34; *Pen. Code of La.*, 141, art. 235; 1 *Md. Code*, 235, § 121; *Rev. Stat. of Maine*, 667, § 15; *Rev. Code, D. C.*, 517, § 20; *Code of Iowa*, 350, § 2577; *Code of Ala.*, 563, § 3105; *Stat. of Conn., Comp. of* 1854, 307, § 12; 1 *Rev. Stat. of Ky.*, 382, art. 6, § 1.) Following the example of these enactments, the Commissioners have extended the penalty of maiming to embrace wounding which either disables or disfigures.

Maiming one's self to escape the performance of a duty.

§ 264. Every person who, with design to disable himself from performing any legal duty, existing or anticipated, inflicts upon himself any injury whereby he is so disabled, is guilty of maiming.

In countries burdened with a severe military conscription, self inflicted injuries, to escape the service, are not uncommon.

"It is curious to observe," says Foderé (*Tr. de Med. Leg.*, vol. 2, p. 480, cited in 1 *Beck's Med. Jur.*, 37) "how many young men have, during the last twenty years, worn convex glasses, in order to acquire *myopia* or near-sightedness."

"Ulcers," says Beck (1 *Med. Jur.*, 50), "are frequently induced by the use of acetate of copper quicklime, &c. * * * Frauds of this description are frequently attempted in hospitals or to avoid the performance of labor of every kind." And he narrates several striking instances of this species of imposture.

The military law of France declares any individual drafted to perform military duty who incapacitates himself, either temporarily or permanently, punishable by imprisonment.

The extent to which practices of this sort have been carried in modern Egypt is very remarkable. Mr. Edward Lane, writing in 1834, says: "There is seldom to be found, in any of the villages, an ablebodied youth or young man who has not had one or more of his teeth broken out (that he may not be able to bite a cartridge), or a finger cut off, or an eye pulled out or blinded, to prevent his being taken for a recruit. Old women and others make a regular trade of going about from village to village to perform these operations upon the boys, and the parents themselves are sometimes the operators." (1 *Lane's Mod. Egyptians*, 3d ed., 294.)

St. John, writing in 1851 (*Village Life in Egypt*), and Warburton (*The Crescent and the Cross*), give similar accounts.

During the present war similar means are known to have been resorted to, in some instances, to avoid military service; and this suggests the insertion of the section.

§ 265. Every person who inflicts upon himself any injury such as if inflicted upon another would constitute maiming, with intent to avail himself of such injury, to excite sympathy, or to obtain alms, or any charitable relief, is guilty of maiming. *Maiming one's self to obtain alms.*

§ 266. To constitute maiming it is immaterial by what means or instrument, or in what manner, the injury was inflicted. *What injury may constitute maiming.*

U. S. *v.* Scroggins, 1 *Hempst.*, 478.
Baker *v.* State, 4 Ark., 56, 63.

§ 267. To constitute maiming by disfigurement the injury must be such as is calculated, after healing, to attract observation. A disfigurement which can only *What disfigurement may constitute maiming.*

be discovered by close inspection does not constitute maiming.

State *v.* Girkin, 1 *Ired. L.*, 121.
State *v.* Abram, 10 *Ala.*, 928.

Designing to maim, &c.

§ 268. A design to injure, disfigure or disable, is inferred from the fact of inflicting an injury which is calculated to disfigure or disable, unless the circumstances raise a reasonable doubt whether such design existed.

State *v.* Girkin, 1 *Ired. L.*, 121.
State *v.* Evans, 1 *Hayw.*, 281.
State *v.* Crawford, 2 *Dev.*, 425.

Premeditated design.

§ 269. A premeditated design to injure, disfigure or disable, sufficient to constitute maiming, may be formed instantly before inflicting the wound.

The Revised Statutes required "a premeditated design evinced, lying in wait for the purpose, or in any other manner;" or an intent to kill or commit a felony. (2 *Rev. Stat.*, 664, § 27.) As, however, the words "premeditated design," as used in the Revised Statutes, relative to murder, have been construed to embrace a design formed at the instant of the act, the Commissioners suggest the employment of them in the same sense in reference to maiming. That rule has been laid down in State *v.* Simmons, 3 *Ala.*, 497.

Subsequent recovery of injured person, when a defense.

§ 270. Where it appears, upon a trial for maiming another person, that the person injured has, before the time of trial, so far recovered from the wound that he is no longer by it disfigured in personal appearance, or disabled in any member or organ of his body, or affected in physical vigor, no conviction for maiming shall be had; but the accused may be convicted of assault and battery, with or without a special intent, according to the proof.

To constitute maiming the injury should be permanent. Where, however, the prosecution have proved a wound inflicted by the prisoner, and effective at the time to disable the person injured, it is for the prisoner to show that the injury was only temporary. (Baker *v.* State, 4 *Ark.*, 56, 64.)

Punishment.

§ 271. Every person guilty of maiming is punishable by imprisonment in a state prison not exceeding seven years, or by imprisonment in a county jail not exceeding one year, or by fine not exceeding one thousand dollars, or by both such fine and imprisonment.

The punishment prescribed by the Revised Statutes, for maiming, is imprisonment in a state prison, not exceeding seven years. (2 *Rev. Stat.*, 664, § 27.) As the Commissioners have extended their definition to embrace self-inflicted injuries, they have provided for a broader range of judicial discretion, in respect to the punishment.

CHAPTER IV.

KIDNAPPING.

§ 272. Every person who, without lawful authority, forcibly seizes and confines another, or inveigles or kidnaps another, with intent, either: Kidnapping defined.

1. To cause such other person to be secretly confined or imprisoned in this state against his will; or,

2. To cause such other person to be sent out of this state against his will; or,

3. To cause such person to be sold as a slave, or in any way held to service against his will,

Is punishable by imprisonment in a state prison not exceeding ten years.

2 *Rev. Stat.*, 664, § 28.

The above section embraces substantially the provisions of 2 *Rev. Stat.*, 664, § 30, and is somewhat broader than the term "kidnapping," in the caption of the chapter, would imply. That term is, by earlier writers, used to denote the abduction of children only; and this seems its etymological meaning. (See *Philip's World of Words; Webst. Dict.; Johns. Dict.*) Many accurate authorities employ it without respect to the age of the subject; but confine it to an abduction committed with intent to export the person injured out from his own home, state or country, to another.

(See *Bell's Dict. Law of Scot.; Bouvier's Law Dict.; Jacob's Law Dict.*) Thus, the Revised Statutes of Illinois (vol. 1, p. 366, §§ 54 and 55,) make false imprisonment to consist in a confinement or detention without legal authority, and confine kidnapping to the offense of abducting and sending to another country. The existing provisions of our own Revised Statutes draw no such distinction. The Commissioners have thought it best to preserve them as they now stand. In employing the term kidnapping as a caption to the chapter, they use it only as a convenient title for purposes of reference, and not as restrictive upon the definitions given of offenses prohibited.

Particular offenses, analogous to kidnapping, *e. g.*, abduction of females, and child stealing, are the subject of some special provisions in other chapters of this Code.

In Hadden *v.* The People, 25 *N. Y.*, 372, it has been lately held that procuring the intoxication of a sailor with the design of getting him on shipboard, without his consent, and taking him on board in that condition is kidnapping under the Revised Statutes; and that it is immaterial whether the offender did the acts, or any of them, in person or caused them to be done.

Where the intent and expectation, in such a case, is that the seaman will be carried out of this state, the offense is complete, although the ship be not in fact, destined to leave the state.

Effect of consent of injured person.

§ 273. Upon any trial for a violation of the preceding section the consent of the person kidnapped or confined thereto shall not be a defense, unless it appear satisfactorily to the jury that such person was above the age of twelve years, and that such consent was not extorted by threats or by duress.

See 2 *Rev. Stat.*, 664, § 30. The above section is deemed by the Commissioners unnecessary; but as it is found in the existing law, and embodies a principle clearly correct, they have hesitated to omit it, lest a change in the law should seem to have been intended. They have inserted the words "that such person was above the age of twelve years;" believing that the consent of a child under that age, however freely given, should not operate as a defense.

Punishment of accessaries. Section 31, of 2 *Rev. Stat.*, 665, providing that every person convicted as an accessary to any kidnapping or confinement hereinbefore prohibited is punishable by imprisonment in a state prison, not exceeding six years, or in a county jail, not exceeding one year, or by a fine, not exceeding five hundred dollars, or by both such fine and imprisonment, is omitted. The Commissioners have preferred to leave the punishment of accessaries in kidnapping to the operation of the general provision relative to accessaries, in section 30.

§ 274. Every person who, within this state or elsewhere, sells or in any manner transfers, for any term, the services or labor of any black, mulatto, or other person of color, who has been forcibly taken or inveigled, or kidnapped from this state, is punishable by imprisonment in a state prison not exceeding ten years. Selling services of person of color.

See 2 *Rev. Stat.*, 665, § 32. The words "within this state or elsewhere" are added. It was held in People *v.* Merrill, 2 *Park. Cr.*, 590, that, under the Revised Statutes, no prosecution could be maintained where the sale was effected out of the state. The Commisioners are of opinion that in conformity to the views relative to the jurisdiction of the state over offenders who being out of the state, co-operate in the commission of an offense within it, which have been embodied in section 15 of this Code, one who, in another state, consummates the kidnapping of a person from this state, by selling him as a slave, may be held amenable to the penal justice of this state, if afterwards found within the jurisdiction of our courts.

Limit of punishment. The Revised Statutes contain an additional clause, allowing imprisonment in a county jail, or fine, to be imposed. The commissioners have omitted this clause; considering the offense deserving of imprisonment in a state prison, in all cases.

§ 275. Every person claiming that he or another is entitled to the services of a person alleged to be held to labor or service in a state or territory of the United States who, except as authorized by Title V, of the Code of Criminal Procedure, takes or removes or willfully does any act tending towards removing from this state any such person, is guilty of felony, punishable by imprisonment in the state prison not exceeding ten years, and by a penalty of five hundred dollars, recoverable in a civil action by the party aggrieved. Removing from this state persons held to service in another state.

§ 276. Every judge, or other public officer of this state who grants or issues any warrant, certificate or Penalty imposed on judicial officers.

other process in any proceeding for the removal from this state of any person claimed as held to labor or service in a state or territory of the United States, except in pursuance of the provisions of Part VI, Title V, of the Code of Criminal Procedure, is guilty of a misdemeanor; and in addition to the punishment therefor prescribed by law, he forfeits five hundred dollars to the party aggrieved, recoverable in a civil action.

Embodies the provisions of *Rep. Code Cr. Pro.*, §§ 910, 923. On comparing the provisions reported by the commissioners of practice and pleadings and which were founded on former provisions of the Revised Statutes, it will be observed that while a *judge or other public officer* who issues process for the removal of a fugitive, except as permitted by the Code of Criminal Procedure, is punishable by the penalties of *misdemeanor* the *claimant* of the fugitive who does any act towards his removal is guilty of felony, and may be punished by imprisonment extending to ten years. The commissioners do not consider this one of those extreme cases which justify the infliction of a penalty upon a judicial officer for an act in the nature of a judicial decision. They are of opinion that the above section should be omitted and the offenses specified, if flagrant enough to demand punishment should be left to the remedy by impeachment. If, however, a criminal penalty is to be inflicted upon the judge at all, the propriety of making so marked a distinction between the punishment to be inflicted upon the claimant and that prescribed for the judge is doubtful.

CHAPTER V.

ATTEMPTS TO KILL.

Shooting, and assault and battery with deadly weapons.

§ 277. Every person who with intent to kill, administers or causes or procures to be administered to another any poison which is actually taken by such other, but by which death is not caused, is punishable by imprisonment in a state prison not less than ten years.

Founded on 2 *Rev. Stat.*, 666, § 37.

§ 278. Every person who shoots or attempts to shoot at another, with any kind of fire arms, air gun or other means whatever, with intent to kill any person, or who commits any assault and battery upon another by means of any deadly weapon, or by such other means or force as was likely to produce death, with intent to kill any other person, is punishable by imprisonment in a state prison not exceeding ten years. **Administering poison.**

This section embraces so much of 2 *Rev. Stat.*, 665, § 36, as relates to attempts to kill; assaults, &c., in attempt to commit other felonies are embraced by a subsequent chapter.

Intent to kill a third person. The language of section 36 of 2 *Rev. Stat.*, 655, above cited,—"any person who shall be convicted * * * of any assault and battery upon another * * * with the intent to kill, &c., *such other person*,"—seems to require, in order to warrant a conviction, that the accused should have intended a felony on the very individual assaulted. A broader rule is recommended by the commissioners in view of the following adjudications. The person was indicted for wounding Y, with intent to murder him. It appeared that he shot at Y supposing him to be M, and intending to murder M; *held* he was properly convicted of wounding Y, with intent to murder him. He intended to murder the man at whom he shot. Reg. *v* Smith, 1 *Jur.*, *N. S.*, 1116; 25 *Law J.* (*M. C.*), 29.

On a trial for assault and battery with intent to kill, it appeared that the prisoner being pursued by two officers, attempting to arrest him, fired a pistol in the direction of both, and so near as to endanger both. He intended to harm at least one; but was regardless which he might harm, his object being to prevent an arrest. *Held*, that he might be convicted on an indictment charging him with an assault on two. Commonwealth *v.* McLaughlin, 12 *Cush.*, 615.

The defendant fired into a crowd with intent to kill some one, and A was wounded. *Held*, that this was enough to establish an assault and battery upon A, with intent to kill. Walker *v.* State, 8 *Ind.*, 290.

And where a woman jumped out of a window for the purpose of avoiding violence threatened by her husband, and sustained a dangerous bodily injury, it was held that the husband could not be convicted of an attempt to murder, unless he intended, by his conduct, to make her jump from the window. Reg. *v.* Donovan, 4 *Cox Cr. Cas.*, 400.

Other assaults with intent to kill.

§ 279. Every person who is guilty of an assault with intent to kill any person, the punishment for which is not prescribed by the foregoing section, is punishable by imprisonment in a state prison for a term not exceeding five years, or in a county jail not exceeding one year, or by a fine not exceeding five hundred dollars, or by both such fine and im prisonment.

Embraces so much of 2 *Rev. Stat.*, 666, § 39, as relates to assaults with intent to kill.

CHAPTER VI.

ROBBERY.

Robbery defined.

§ 280. Robbery is a wrongful taking of personal property in the possession of another, from his person or immediate presence, and against his will, accomplished by means of force or fear.

This definition embodies substantially the elements suggested by 2 *Rev. Stat.*, 677, §§ 55, 56; the word "wrongfully" being substituted for "feloniously." Three elements are necessary to constitute the offense of robbery, as it is generally understood. 1. A taking of property from the person or presence of its possessor. 2. A wrongful intent to appropriate it. 3. The use of violence or fear to accomplish the purpose. The first and second of these elements, the third being wanting, constitute simple larceny. The first and third, without the second, amount at most to a trespass. The second and third, without the first, constitute an attempt to rob. These elements are kept in view in the provisions upon robbery; and offenses not presenting all are excluded from this chapter, and covered by other provisions of the Code.

For the distinctions between robbery, larceny, extortion, embezzlement, and those cases of taking of personal property which amount only to trespass, see notes upon the subjects of larceny and extortion.

§ 281. To constitute robbery the force or fear must be employed either to obtain or retain possession of the property or to prevent or overcome resistance to the taking. If employed merely as a means of escape it does not constitute robbery. How force or fear must be employed.

This provision conforms to the existing law, as established by the Revised Statutes. It has been held, indeed, that violence employed to get possession of the property does not constitute robbery; to have this effect the force must be employed to prevent or overpower resistance. State *v.* John., 5 *Jones N. C. Law Rep.*, 163; Rex *v.* Gnosil, 1 *Carr. & P.*, 304; Rex *v.* Baker, *Leach.*, 290; R. *v.* Homer, *Leach*, 291, n. The Commissioners believe, however, it will be found the safer rule to punish the taking as robbery where it is accomplished by force, against an actual dissent of the owner's will. This will exclude secret stealing from the person; such as picking the pocket, and other cases in which, though an indefinitely small force is used in removing the property, it is done without the owner's knowledge.

§ 282. When force is employed in either of the ways specified in the last section, the degree of force employed is immaterial. Degree of force immaterial.

In an English case, it appeared that the prisoner struck the prosecutor's hand so as to cause money in it to fall to the ground, and then picked up the money himself, using threatening violence to prevent the prosecutor from doing so. *Held*, robbery if the taking by the prisoner was committed while the owner of the money still remained present. Rex *v.* Francis, 2 *Strange*, 1015.

In a case in Rhode Island it appeared that the prisoner put one of his hands through the arm of the prosecutor, and with the other seized the latter's watch; saying, "I will have your watch;" and, breaking the watch guard, fled with the watch. *Held*, robbery, on the ground, the taking was by *force*. The expressed determination made the case one of *open* violence, as distinguished from a secret taking or mere snatching by surprise. State *v.* McCune, 5 *R. I.*, 60.

§ 283. The fear which constitutes robbery may be either: What fear may be an element in robbery.

1. The fear of an unlawful injury, immediate or future, to the person or property of the person robbed, or of any relative, of his, or member of his family; or,

2. The fear of an immediate and unlawful injury to the person or property of any one in the company of the person robbed, at the time of the robbery.

Founded upon the provisions of 2 *Rev. Stat.*, 677, §§ 55, 56; but extended to embrace the case of a theft accomplished by means of a threat of immediate violence towards a *companion* of the person deprived of property, who is not, however, a relative or member of his family; and, also, the case of theft accomplished by means of a threat of a future injury to the *property* of a relative of the person robbed, or of a member of his family.

Value of property taken immaterial.

§ 284. When property is taken under the circumstances required to constitute robbery, the fact that the property was of trifling value does not qualify the offense.

In Rex *v.* Bingley, 5 *Carr. & P.*, 602, the property taken was a slip of paper containing a memorandum of a debt due to the person robbed. It was held that the offense was robbery notwithstanding the small value of the paper. That the prosecutor showed, by carrying the memorandum in his pocket, he considered it of some value.

Taking of property secretly not robbery.

§ 285. The taking of property from the person of another is not robbery, when it clearly appears that the taking was fully completed without his knowledge, unless such knowledge was prevented by the use of force or fear.

Two degrees of robbery.

§ 286. Robbery when accomplished by the use of force or of putting the person robbed in fear of some immediate injury to his person, is robbery in the first degree. When accomplished in any other manner it is robbery in the second degree.

Corresponds with the distinction established by 2 *Rev. Stat.*, 677 and 678, §§ 55, 56.

Punishment of robbery in first degree.

§ 287. Every person guilty of robbery in the first degree is punishable by imprisonment in a state prison not less than ten years.

2 *Rev. Stat.*, 678, § 57.

§ 288. Every person guilty of robbery in the second degree is punishable by imprisonment in a state prison not exceeding ten years. Punishment of robbery in second degree.

2 *Rev. Stat.*, 678, § 57.

§ 289. Whenever two or more persons conjointly commit a robbery, or where the whole number of persons conjointly committing a robbery, and persons present and aiding such robbery amount to two or more, each and either of such persons is punishable by imprisonment for life. Punishment of robbery committed by two or more persons.

Intended as a stringent provision against "garroting" and other forms of robbery by gangs. The language of the section is framed upon that of section 391 of the *Indian Penal Code.*

CHAPTER VII.

ASSAULTS WITH INTENT TO COMMIT FELONY OTHER THAN ASSAULTS WITH INTENT TO KILL.

§ 290. Every person who shoots or attempts to shoot at another with any kind of fire-arms, air-gun, or other means whatever, or commits any assault and battery upon another by means of any deadly weapon or by such other means or force as was likely to produce death, with intent to commit any felony other than an assault with intent to kill, or in resisting the execution of any legal process, is punishable by imprisonment in a state prison not exceeding ten years. Shooting and assaults with deadly weapons.

Embraces so much of 2 *Rev. Stat.*, 665, § 36, as is not already covered by the provisions of sections 278, *supra*, relative to attempts to kill.

§ 291. Every person who is guilty of an assault with intent to commit any felony, except an assault with intent to kill, the punishment for which assault is not prescribed by the preceding section, is punish- Other assaults.

able by imprisonment in a state prison not exceeding five years, or in a county jail not exceeding one year, or by a fine not exceeding five hundred dollars, or by both such fine and imprisonment.

Embraces so much of 2 *Rev. Stat.*, 666, § 39, as is not embraced by the provisions of section 279, *supra*, relative to attempts to kill.

Administering stupefying drugs.

§ 292. Every person guilty of administering to another any chloroform, ether, laudanum or other intoxicating, narcotic or anesthetic agent, with intent thereby to enable or assist himself or any other person to commit any felony, is guilty of felony.

See *Consol. Stat. of Canada*, 955, § 13.

CHAPTER VIII.

DUELS AND CHALLENGES.

Duel defined.

§ 293. A duel is any combat, with deadly weapons, fought between two persons by previous agreement or upon a previous quarrel.

Punishment for fighting a duel.

§ 294. Every person guilty of fighting any duel, although no death or wound ensues, is punishable by imprisonment in a state prison not exceeding ten years.

Founded on 2 *Rev. Stat.*, 686, § 1.

Incapacity to hold office.

§ 295. Every person convicted of fighting a duel is thereafter incapable of holding or being elected or appointed to any office, place or post of trust or emolument, civil or military, under this state.

2 *Rev. Stat.*, 686, § 4.

§ 296. Every person who is present at the time when any duel is fought, either as second, aid or surgeon, or who advises or gives any countenance to any duel, is punishable by imprisonment in a state prison not exceeding seven years. Punishment of seconds, aids, and surgeons.

2 *Rev. Stat.*, 686, § 2.

§ 297. Every person who challenges another to fight a duel; every person who accepts any such challenge; and every person who knowingly forwards, carries or delivers any such challenge, is punishable by imprisonment in a state prison not exceeding seven years. Punishment for challenges.

Founded on 2 *Rev. Stat.*, 686, § 2.

§ 298. Any words, spoken or written, or any signs, uttered or made to any person, expressing or implying or intended to express or imply a desire, request, invitation or demand, to fight a duel, or to meet for the purpose of fighting a duel, are deemed a challenge. Challenge defined.

See State *v.* Perkins, 6 *Blackf.*, 20; Commonwealth *v.* Tibbs, 1 *Dana*, 524.

§ 299. Every person guilty of sending, uttering or making to another any words or signs whatever, with intent to provoke or induce such person to give or receive any challenge to fight a duel, is guilty of a misdemeanor. Attempts to induce a challenge.

So held in King *v.* Philips, 6 *East.*, 464; upon the ground that as sending a challenge is a misdemeanor (as to which see Rex *v.* Rice, 3 East., 581,) any act done with intent to cause one to be sent is a misdemeanor.

§ 300. Every person who posts or publishes another for not fighting a duel, or for not sending or accepting a challenge to fight a duel, or who uses any reproachful or contemptuous language, verbal, written or printed, to or concerning another, for not sending or Posting for not fighting.

accepting a challenge to fight a duel, or with intent to provoke a duel, is guilty of a misdemeanor.

Founded upon 2 *Rev. Stat.*, 694, § 20.

Leaving the state with intent to evade laws against dueling.

§ 301. Every person who leaves this state with intent to elude any of the provisions of this chapter, and to commit any act out of this state, such as is prohibited by this chapter, and who does any act, although out of this state, which would be punishable by said provisions, if committed within this state, is punishable in the same manner as he would have been, in case such act had been committed within this state.

Founded upon 2 *Rev. Stat.*, 686, § 5. Under that provision the prosecution might be required to prove the sending a challenge in order to warrant a conviction. The Commissioners have extended the provision so that proof of any act, in aid of a duel, will be sufficient.

Where such person may be indicted and tried.

§ 302. Such person may be indicted and tried in any county within this state

Witness's privilege.

§ 303. No person shall be excused from testifying or answering any question upon any investigation or trial for a violation of either of the provisions of this chapter, upon the ground that his testimony might tend to convict him of a crime. But no evidence given upon any examination of a person so testifying shall be received against him in any criminal prosecution or proceeding.

Intended as a substitute for 2 *Rev. Stat.*, 686, § 3.

CHAPTER IX.

ASSAULT AND BATTERY.

§ 304. An assault is any willful and unlawful attempt or offer, with force or violence, to do a corporal hurt to another. Assault defined.

See Hays *v.* People, 1 *Hill*, 351; 2 *Bish. Cr. L.*, § 32; 3 *Blackst. Comm.*, 120.

Intent to strike. An assault has also been said to be an intentional attempt, by violence, to do an injury to the person of another. It must be *intentional.* If there is no present purpose to do an injury, there is no assault. There must also be an *attempt.* A purpose not accompanied by an effort to carry it into immediate execution falls short of an assault. Thus no words can amount to an assault. But rushing towards another with menacing gestures and with a *purpose to strike* is an assault, though the accused is prevented from striking before he comes near enough to do so. State *v.* Davis, 1 *Ired.* (*N. C.*), 121.

But mere threatening gestures unaccompanied by such a purpose, although sufficient to cause a man of ordinary firmness to believe he was about to be struck, do not constitute an assault. Thus, when the defendant shook his whip at the prosecutor, saying, at the same time: "if you were not an old man I would knock you down." *Held*, no assault, unless the jury should be satisfied that there was a present purpose to strike. State *v.* Crow, 1 *Ired.* (*N. C.*), 375. To the same effect is Commonwealth *v.* Eyre, 1 *Serg. & R.*, 347.

So where an ambassador exhibited a painting in the window of his house which gave offense to the crowd without, and defendant, among the crowd, fired a pistol at the painting at the very time when the ambassador and his servants were in the window to remove it, but did not intend to hurt any of them, and in fact did not. *Held*, that there being no intent to injure the person there could be no conviction for an assault. U. S. v. Hand, 2 *Wash. C. C.*, 435.

But threatening another with a weapon, as a means of coercing him to yield to a demand, intending to strike if he refuses, but not to strike if he complies, is an assault, although the other party negotiates and no blow is finally given. It makes no difference that the purpose to commit violence is not absolute but only conditional. State *v.* Morgan, 3 *Ired.* (*N. C.*), 186.

And, in general, it is an assault to present a pistol which purports to be loaded at another person, so near as would endanger life if it were fired, although the pistol is not, in fact, loaded. State *v.* Smith, 2 *Humph.*, 457. Rex *v.* Parfait, *Lach.*, 23; *East. P. C.*, 416; Rex *v.* Thomas, *Lach.*, 272; *East. P. C.*, 417; also, Morgan *v.* State, 33 *Ala.*, 413, where it is held that the presenting a pistol loaded and cocked, although with the finger on the trigger, and in an angry manner, does not of itself raise a presumption of an intent to murder, but is a common assault.

Consent. In general, if the party suffering the violence has consented to it, there is no assault. Thus, although a child of tender years cannot legally consent to a rape upon her, yet she may consent to an attempt to commit it; and such an attempt, if committed with her consent, is not an assault. Rey *v.* Cockburn, 3 *Cox Cr. Cas.*, 543; Rey *v.* Read, 2 *Carr. & K.*, 957; 3 *Cox Cr. Cas.*, 266; 1 *Den. C. C.*, 377; Rex *v.* Wehegan, 7 *Cox Cr. Cas.*, 145.

But there must be actual consent. Mere omission to resist is not enough. Reg. *v.* McGavaran, 6 *Cox Cr. Cas.*, 64.

And where a medical man to whom a girl of fourteen years of age was sent for professional advice had criminal connection with her, she making no resistance, from a *bona fide* belief that the defendant was treating her medically, as he represented he was doing. *Held*, he was properly convicted of an assault, and might have been of rape. Reg. *v.* Case, 4 *Cox Cr. Cas.*, 220; 1 *Den. C. C.*, 580.

Battery defined.

§ 305. A battery is any willful and unlawful use of force or violence upon the person of another.

Use of force or violence declared not unlawful in certain cases.

§ 306. To use or attempt or offer to use force or violence upon or towards the person of another is not unlawful in the following cases:

1. When necessarily committed by a public officer in the performance of any legal duty; or by any other person assisting him or acting by his direction

2. When necessarily committed by any person in arresting one who has committed any felony, and delivering him to a public officer competent to receive him in custody;

3. When committed either by the party about to be injured or by any other person in his aid or defense, in preventing or attempting to prevent an offense against his person, or any trespass or other unlawful interference with real or personal property in his lawful possession; provided the force or violence used is not more than sufficient to prevent such offense;

4. When committed by a parent or the authorized agent of any parent, or by any guardian, master, or

teacher, in the exercise of a lawful authority to restrain or correct his child, ward, apprentice or scholar; provided restraint or correction has been rendered necessary by the misconduct of such child, ward, apprentice or scholar, or by his refusal to obey the lawful command of such parent, or authorized agent or guardian, master or teacher, and the force or violence used is reasonable in manner and moderate in degree;

5. When committed by a carrier of passengers, or the authorized agents or servants of such carrier, or by any person assisting them, at their request, in expelling from any carriage, railroad car, vessel or other vehicle, any passenger who refuses to obey a lawful and reasonable regulation prescribed for the conduct of passengers; if such vehicle has first been stopped and the force or violence used is not more than is sufficient to expel the offending passenger, with a reasonable regard to his personal safety;

6. When committed by any person in preventing an idiot, lunatic, insane person or other person of unsound mind, including persons temporarily or partially deprived of reason, from committing an act dangerous to himself or to another, or in enforcing such restraint as is necessary for the protection of his person or for his restoration to health; during such period only as shall be necessary to obtain legal authority for the restraint or custody of his person.

Subd. 2. Supported by People *v.* Adler, 3 *Park. Cr.*, 249; People *v.* Wolven. 7 *N. Y. Leg. Obs.*, 89; People *v.* McArdle, 1 *Wheel. Cr.*, 101.

Subd. 3. Corresponds with the provisions relative to resistance to prevent offenses, reported in *Rep. Code Cr. Pro.*, §§ 60–62; except that the provision has been enlarged to embrace resistance to trespasses upon real property.

Subd. 4. It was held in Hernandez *v.* Carnobeli (4 *Duer*, 642; S. C., 10 *How. Pr.*, 433), that the authorized agent of a father was not liable to a civil action for assault and battery for force necessarily used in conveying a son from this country back to his father in Cuba. But, in People *v.* Philips (1 *Wheel. Cr.*, 155), it was held that the right of a master to chastise his apprentice is strictly personal, the master cannot direct or permit another person to chastise the apprentice for any offense whatever. In the light of these cases the Commissioners have drafted the section in the text in such a form as to recognize the right of a parent, whether father or mother, to delegate the power to restrain, and also the power to chastise, if indeed it is considered that any distinction exists between the two, while the similar power of a guardian or teacher is placed upon the same ground with that of the master of an apprentice. Upon this subject the general rule is that when a teacher, inflicting punishment upon his pupil, goes beyond the limit of moderate castigation, and either in mode or degree is guilty of unreasonable or disproportionate violence, he is liable to a prosecution for assault and battery. And it is not necessary to show actual passion or vindictive feeling. The criminal intent is inferred from the nature of the act. Commonwealth *v.* Randall, 4 *Gray*, 36.

Subd. 5. See People *v.* Jillson, 3 *Park. Cr.*, 234; Hibbard *v.* New York & Erie R. R. Co., 15 *N. Y.*, 455. In Sanford *v.* Eighth Avenue R. R. Co. (23 *N. Y.*, 243), it was said that the right to expel a passenger from a railroad car cannot be exercised without first stopping the car. Though the language used in the opinion seems more directly applicable to cars propelled by steam, yet as the car, in the particular case before the court, was a city railroad car, drawn by horses, the Commissioners have regarded the condition that the vehicle or carriage must be stopped before the offending passenger can be ejected as applicable in all cases.

As to whether, after the refusal of a passenger to produce his ticket or pay his fare, on alighting from a railway carriage, he can be compelled to proceed by train to the principal station on the line, to be there dealt with by the authorities of the company, see Reg. *v.* Mann, 6 *Cox Cr. Cas.*, 461; S. C., 23 *L. T.*, 12.

Punishment of assault or assault and battery.

§ 307. Assault or assault and battery is punishable by imprisonment in a county jail not exceeding one year, or by fine not exceeding one thousand dollars, or both.

This is an increase in severity of punishment as compared with that inflicted under the existing laws. The frequency and aggravation of instances of violence to the person which have been observed during the past few years require that a more stringent punishment be affixed to the offense.

Assaults with dangerous weapons, &c.

§ 308. Every person who, with intent to do bodily harm, and without just cause or excuse commits any assault upon the person of another with any sharp or dangerous weapon, or who without such cause shoots or attempts to shoot at another with any kind of fire-arms, or air-gun, or other means whatever, with intent to injure any person, although without intent to kill such person or to commit any felony, is punishable by imprisonment in a state prison not exceeding five years, or by imprisonment in a county jail not exceeding one year.

See *Laws of* 1854, ch. 74, § 1.

CHAPTER X.

LIBEL.

§ 309. Any malicious publication, by writing, printing, picture, effigy, sign or otherwise, which exposes any person, or the memory of any person deceased, to hatred, contempt, ridicule or obloquy, or which causes any person to be shunned or avoided, or which has a tendency to injure any person or corporation or association of persons, in their occupation or business, is a libel. Libel defined.

This definition the commissioners think is broad enough to embrace all the particulars of a definition of libel at common law. 4 *Bl. Com.*, 150; 1 *Fost & F.*, 149; 2 *Id.*, 524; *Indian Penal Code*, § 499, *et seq;* 2 *Kent's Com.*, 16; *Whart Cr. L.*, *2d ed.*, 735.

§ 310. Every person who willfully, and with a malicious intent to injure another, publishes any libel, is guilty of a misdemeanor. Libel a misdemeanor.

Malice presumed. § 311. An injurious publication is presumed to have been malicious if no justifiable motive for making it is shown.

Truth may be given in evidence. § 312. In all criminal prosecutions or indictments for libel, the truth may be given in evidence to the jury, and if it shall appear to the jury, that the matter charged as libelous is true and was published with good motives and for justifiable ends, the party shall be acquitted.

Const. of 1846, art. 1, § 8.

Publication defined. § 313. To sustain a charge of publishing a libel it is not needful that the words complained of should have been read by another. It is enough that the accused knowingly parted with the immediate custody of the libel under circumstances which exposed it to be read by any other person than himself.

Giles *v.* The State, 6 *Ga.*, 276.

Liability of editors and others. § 314. Each author, editor and proprietor of any book, newspaper or serial publication, and each member of any partnership or incorporated association, by which any book, newspaper or serial publication is issued, is chargeable with the publication of any words contained in any part of such book, or number of such newspaper or serial.

Compare Rex *v.* Gutch, 1 *Moo. & M.*, 433; Commonwealth *v.* Kneeland, *Thach. Cr. C.*, 346.

Publishing a true report of public official proceedings privileged. § 315. No reporter, editor or proprietor of any newspaper, is liable to any prosecution for a fair and true report of any judicial, legislative, or other public official proceedings, or of any statement, speech, argument, or debate in the course of the same, except upon proof of malice in making such report, which shall in no case be implied from the mere fact of publication.

Laws of 1854, ch. 130, § 1.

In Sanford *v.* Bennett (24 *N. Y.*, 20), the question was whether a speech made by a convict at the place of execution was a speech made in the course of a judicial or public official proceeding, within the meaning of the statute, so that one publishing it was protected by the statute from a civil action for injurious words contained in it, concerning other persons. The court decided the question in the negative. They held that the statute applies only to judicial and legislative proceedings, and to transactions resembling them, and not to an executive act to be performed by a single person and admitting of no deliberation; and it protects only the publication of speeches which form properly a part of the proceeding. The act having thus received a judicial construction, the Commissioners have substantially followed its language.

§ 316. Libelous remarks or comments connected with matter privileged by the last section receive no privilege by reason of their being so connected. Extent of the privilege.

See *Laws of* 1854, ch. 130, § 2.

§ 317. A communication made to a person interested in the communication by one who was also interested or who stood in such a relation to the former as to afford a reasonable ground for supposing his motive innocent, is not presumed to be malicious, and is called a privileged communication. Other privileged communications

Dr. Civ. Code, § 25; See also 15 *Law. Mag. N. S.*, 216, 241; 1 *Cr. M. & W.*, 193; Eastwood *v.* Holmes, 1 *Fost. & F.*, 347; Turnbull *v.* Bird, 2 *Id.*, 524; *Indian Penal Code*, 443.

§ 318. Every person who threatens to another to publish a libel concerning him or any parent, husband, wife or child of such person or member of his family, and every person who offers to prevent the publication of any libel upon another person with intent to extort any money or other valuable consideration from any person, is guilty of a misdemeanor. Threatening to publish a libel.

Intentionally confined to threats uttered directly to the person about to be libeled. The gronnd upon which the criminal remedy for libel is allowed, is the tendency of a libel to provoke a breach of the peace. A threat to publish one uttered to third persons, and only reaching the injured party through indirect repetition, is no more calculated to create disturbance of the peace than other forms of slander; and should not be distinguished from slander in the remedy allowed.

See also *Stat.* 6 and 7 *Vict.*, ch. 96, § 3, as to offers to *prevent* publication of libel.

TITLE X.

OF CRIMES AGAINST THE PERSON AND AGAINST PUBLIC DECENCY AND GOOD MORALS.

CHAPTER I.

RAPE, ABDUCTION, CARNAL ABUSE OF CHILDREN, AND SEDUCTION.

Rape defined.

§ 319. Rape is an act of sexual intercourse accomplished with a female not the wife of the perpetrator, under either of the following circumstances:

1. Where the female is under the age of ten years;

2. Where she is incapable, through lunacy or any

other unsoundness of mind, whether temporary or permanent, of giving legal consent;

3. Where she resists, but her resistance is overcome by force or violence;

4. Where she is prevented from resisting by threats of immediate and great bodily harm, accompanied by apparent power of execution;

5. Where she is prevented from resisting by any intoxicating, narcotic or anesthetic agent administered by or with the privity of the accused;

6. Where she is at the time unconscious of the nature of the act, and this is known to the accused;

7. Where she submits under a belief that the person committing the act is her husband; and this belief is induced by any artifice, pretense or concealment, practised by the accused, with intent to induce such belief.

This section is an extension of the generally received definition of rape. East defines this offense to be "the unlawful carnal knowledge of a woman by force and against her will." (1 *East. P. C.*, 434.) Blackstone defines it in the same language, omitting the word "unlawful." (4 *Blackst. Comm.*, 210.) And this is believed to be substantially the definition given by the leading writers on criminal law, except that some of the later decisions indicate a disposition to substitute the idea "without her consent" for "against her will." (See Reg. *v.* Camplin, 1 *Cox Cr. Cas.*, 220; 1 *Den. C. C.*, 89; 1 *Carr. & K.*, 746; Reg. v. Sweenie, 8 *Cox Cr. Cas.*, 223; 3 *Irvine*, 159.)

Our own Revised Statutes, in lieu of any formal definition of the crime, provide that: "Every person who shall be convicted of rape, either: 1. By carnally and unlawfully knowing any female child under the age of ten years; or, 2. By forcibly ravishing any woman of the age of ten years or upwards; shall be punished," &c. (2 *Rev. Stat.*, 663, § 22.)

*The Commissioners have designed to present a definition which should expressly include the various instances which have been adjudged to constitute the offense, with some others which have been held not to fall within the limited definition of the common law authorities, but to which the same penalties ought to be extended.

Subd. 1. This provision embodies the well settled rule of the existing law; that a girl under ten years of age is incapable of giving any consent to an act of intercourse which can reduce it below the grade of rape. Consult 2 *Rev. Stat.*, 663, § 22, subd. 1; quoted, *supra*, Stephen *v.* State, 11 *Ga.*, 225; State *v.* Farmer, 4 *Ired.*, 224; 4 *Blackst. Comm.*, 212.

Subd. 2. It is probable that an act of intercourse with a woman above the age of ten years, but mentally incapable of giving legal consent would be held to be "forcibly ravishing," within the meaning of subdivision 2 of 2 *Rev. Stat.*, 663, § 22, quoted *supra*. The question is not known to have arisen in the courts of our state. In England it has been held that under the statute, 13 *Edw. I, c.* 34,—which provides that if a man * * do ravish a woman * * when she did not consent, neither before nor after, he shall, &c.,—forcible intercourse with a female incapable, through imbecility of mind, of giving legal consent, is rape; although she was above ten years of age, and offered no resistance. (Reg. *v.* Fletcher, 8 *Cox Cr. Cas.*, 131; 5 *Jur., N. S.*, 179.) See, also, in support of the same principle, Rex *v.* Ryan, 2 *Cox Cr. Cas.*, 115; State *v.* Cron, 10 *West. L. J.*, 501; McNamara's case, *Oakley*, 521. Believing that, under the existing law, an insane female stands in the same position, in respect to this offense, with a child under ten, the Commissioners have embodied a statement of that rule in the section.

Subd. 3 *and* 4. These embrace the ordinary cases of the offense, and require no special remark. As to resistance overcome by force, see Charles *v.* State, 6 *Engl.*, 389; State *v.* Jim, 1 *Den.*, 142; Pollard *v.* State, 2 *Clarke*, 567; Myatt *v.* State, 2 *Swan.*, 394; Lewis *v.* State, 30 *Ala.*, 54; State *v.* Blake, 39 *Me.*, 322; Barney *v.* People, 22 *Ill.*, 160. As to resistance overcome by fear, see Pleasant *v.* State, 8 *Engl.*, 360; Reg. *v.* Hallett, 9 *Carr. & P.*, 748; Reg. *v.* Day, *Id.*, 722; Wright *v.* State, 4 *Humph.*, 194.

Subd. 5. This provision is intended to cover cases where the female is rendered temporarily incapable of giving consent by means of liquors or drugs; and embraces the cases now covered, though not under the name of rape, by the provisions of 2 *Rev. Stat.*, 663, § 23.

In Reg. *v.* Camplin, 1 *Cox Cr. Cas.*, 220; 1 *Den. C. C.*, 89; 1 *Carr. & K.*, 746; the jury found that the prisoner gave liquor to the female for the purpose of exciting her passions and inducing her consent; it had, however, the effect of rendering her drunk and insensible; in which condition he violated her. This was held to be rape; on the ground that the connection was accomplished *without* the consent and against the will of the female, which was all that was necessary to constitute the offense. Actual resistance on her part was not necessary to be shown.

A number of similar instances of the commission of

the offense are referred to in *Wharton & St. Med. Jur.*, §§ 441–443.

The Commissioners do not limit this provision to cases in which the stupefying drug is administered with intent to facilitate a rape. Cases in which the drug is administered from proper motives, but the accused afterwards avails himself of the helplessness of the subject to commit the offense are designed to be included. It is indeed doubtful whether, in the case of Reg. *v.* Camplin, above cited, a conviction would have been sustained independent of the circumstances, upon which some stress is laid by members of the court, that the liquor was given with an unlawful intent, and that the prosecutrix indicated dissent by refusing the prisoner's solicitations as long as she had the power. But a comparatively recent and familiar trial in which it was charged that advantage was taken of helplessness induced by the administration of chloroform, shows the possibility of a case arising in which the stupefying drug may have been originally given for a lawful purpose, and no indication of dissent given by the female for the reason that there was no previous solicitation, nor was any violence apprehended by her; and the offense may be an afterthought, suggested by the opportunity. Such a case ought to be embraced within the law.

Subd. 6. It can but rarely happen that the subject of the offense consciously submits to the act uncompelled, without being aware of its nature; yet some cases of this sort are reported.

In Reg. *v.* Case (4 *Cox Cr. Cas.*, 220), the defendant was a medical practitioner, and the prosecutrix was a young girl placed under his care for medical treatment. She made no resistance to the connection owing to a belief, from representations of defendant, that she was submitting to medical treatment for the ailment under which she labored. *Held*, upon an indictment for assault, that the accused was rightly convicted. Her submission to the act under an impression that it was something necessary to her case was not such a consent as relieved the defendant from criminal responsibilty.

Whether it is to be regarded as possible that a connection should be accomplished during the unconsciousness of natural sleep, without arousing the female, is said to be an open question in medical jurisprudence. (See *Beck's Med. Jur.*, 7th ed., 117; *Tayl. Med. Jur.*, 5th ed., 654; *Whart. & St. Med. Jur.*, 336, §§ 440, 441; *Montgomery on Pregnancy*, 2d ed., p. 361; *Bundelius*, 96, 99.) Whether an unlawful connection so accomplished should be deemed, if proved, to amount to rape has been differently decided by the courts. (See Reg. *v.* Sweenie, 8 *Cox Cr. Cas*, 223; 3 *Irvine*, 159, in the affirmative, and Fields case, 4 *Leigh*, 648; Charles *v.* State, 6 *Engl.*, 389, in the negative. It has not been thought best on a review of the authorities to specify this as one of the cases embraced. The danger of giving rise to unjust prosecutions in cases where the sleep was merely simulated, is to be weighed against that of the commission of the offense where the sleep is genuine.

Subd. 7. Several cases are to be found in the reports, in which a criminal connection has been accomplished by means of personating the husband of the female. In England this is held not to be rape. (Reg. *v.* Clarke, *Dearsly*, 397; 6 *Cox. Cr. Cas.*, 412; 18 *Jur.*, 1059; 29 *Eng. L. & Eq.*, 542; Rex *v.* Jackson, *Russ & Ry.*, 487; Reg. *v.* Williams, 8 *Carr & P.*, 286; Reg. *v.* Saunders, *id.*, 265. In Scotland it has been held to be rape. Fraser's case, *Arkley*, 329; Reg. *v.* Sweenie, 8 *Cox Cr. Cas.*, 223. In this country the question has been differently decided in the different states. See Wyatt *v.* State, 2 *Swan*, 394; Lewis *v.* State, 30 *Ala.*, 54; People *v.* Bartow, 1 *Wheel. Cr. Cas.*, 378; following the English view; and State *v.* Shepard, 7 *Conn.*, 54; Anon., 1 *Wheel. Cr. Cas.*, 381, note adopting the contrary.

Without reviewing the reasoning of these cases, or questioning the soundness of the English decisions considered as exposition of the existing law, the commissioners think that this offense fully partakes of the guilt of rape, and should share its punishment in all instances in which any means are used by the accused to create a belief that he is the husbaud.

When physical ability must be proved.

§ 320. No conviction for rape can be had against one who was under the age of fourteen years at the time of the act alleged; unless his physical ability to accomplish penetration is proved as an independent fact, and beyond a reasonable doubt.

Many of the authorities lay down the rule as conclusive that incapacity is to be presumed when the accused is under 14 years of age (See 2 *Bish. Cr. L.*, § 936). In People *v.* Randolph, 2 *Park. Cr.*, 174; and Williams *v.* State, 14 *Ohio*, 222, the presumption has been held capable of being rebutted by proof of actual capacity in the individual.

As by our existing law, penetration is declared sufficient to constitute the offense (2 *Rev. Stat.*, 735, § 18), it seems consistent that the special proof of power to commit the crime, required in the case of a boy under 14, should be adduced to that point though this is probably a severer rule than is contemplated by the decisions above cited.

Penetration sufficient.

§ 321. The essential guilt of rape consists in the outrage to the person and feelings of the female

Any sexual penetration, however slight, is sufficient to complete the crime.

See 2 *Rev. Stat.*, 735, § 18; Robertson's Case, 1 *Swint.*, 98.

§ 322. Rape committed upon a female under the age of ten years, or incapable through lunacy or any other unsoundness of mind of giving legal consent, or accomplished by means of force overcoming her resistance, is rape in the first degree. Rape in the first degree defined.

§ 323. In all other cases rape is of the second degree. Rape in the second degree defined

§ 324. Rape in the first degree is punishable by imprisonment in a state prison not less than ten years. Punishment of rape in the first degree

See 2 *Rev. Stat.*, 663, §§ 22, 23.

§ 325. Rape in the second degree is punishable by imprisonment in a state prison not less than five years. Punishment of rape in the second degree.

Ibid.

§ 326. Every person who, by force, menace or duress, compels any woman, against her will, to marry him or to marry any other person, is punishable by imprisonment in a state prison not less than ten years. Compelling woman to marry.

See 2 *Rev. Stat.*, 663, § 24. The language of the Revised Statutes is, "Every person who shall take any woman *unlawfully*, against her will, and by force menace or duress compel her to marry him or to marry any other person, *or to be defiled*," &c. The commissioners have omitted the words "or to be defiled," because the offense of taking a woman and by force compelling her to be defiled is covered by the provisions of section 319, defining rape, taken in connection with section 27, which abrogates the distinction between principals and accessories before the fact, and declares persons who aid and abet in the commission of a crime, principals. And they have omitted the word "unlawfully," because there is no case in which a woman can be lawfully taken and compelled to marry. But in the next section the language of the Revised Statutes is retained because the taking of a woman *with intent* to cause her to be defiled, is not embraced in the crime of rape; which requires an act of penetration.

Taking a woman with intent to compel her to marry or to be defiled.

§ 327. Every person who takes any woman unlawfully against her will, with the intent to compel her by force, menace or duress to marry him, or to marry any other person, or to be defiled, is punishable by imprisonment in a state prison not exceeding ten years.

"Not *exceeding* ten years" is substituted for "not *less* than ten years."

Seduction for purposes of prostitution.

§ 328. Every person who inveigles or entices any unmarried female of previous chaste character under the age of twenty-five years, into any house of ill-fame or of assignation, or elsewhere, for the purpose of prostitution; and every person who aids or assists in such abduction for such purpose; and every person who, by any false pretenses, false representations or other fraudulent means, procures any female to have illicit carnal connection with any man; is punishable by imprisonment in a state prison not exceeding five years, or by imprisonment in a county jail not exceeding one year, or by a fine not exceeding one thousand dollars, or by both such fine and imprisonment.

Founded upon *Laws of* 1848, ch. 105; and *Stat.* 24 and 25 *Vict.*, ch. 100, § 49.

Omitted provisions. The further provision of the act of 1848, that no conviction shall be had upon the unsupported testimony of the female enticed away, is here omitted for the reason that it belongs to the subject of evidence. See the provisions already reported upon that subject. *Rep. Code Civ. Pro.*, Part IV.

So much of the act of 1848, above cited, as provides that indictments for the offense of enticing away females for the purpose of prostitution, must be found within two years after the commission of the offense, is already embodied in *Rep. Code Cr. Pro.*, § 141.

Abduction.

§ 329. Every person who takes away any female under the age of sixteen years, from her father, mother, guardian or other person having the legal charge of her person, without their consent, either for the purpose of marriage, concubinage or prostitution is punishable by imprisonment in a state prison not exceeding five years, or by imprisonment in a county jail not exceeding one year, or by a fine not exceeding one thousand dollars, or by both such fine and imprisonment.

Founded upon 2 *Rev. Stat.*, 664, § 26. The limit of age being varied from 14 years to 16.

Under the analogous English statute, 9 Geo. IV, ch. 31, § 20, it has been held not to be necessary that the girl should be taken by force, either actual or constructive, or be taken out of the actual possession of the parent or guardian. It is enough if she be persuaded by the prisoner to leave her home, and the control of the parent continues down to the time of the taking. Where, therefore, the prisoner persuaded a girl under sixteen to meet him at a place two miles from her father's house, where she lived, for the purpose of going with him to America, and did so voluntarily, leaving her home alone, then meeting the prisoner at the place appointed, and afterwards traveling with him to London: *Held*, that he was guilty of abduction. Reg. *v.* Monktelow, 6 *Cox Crim. Cas.*, 143; 22 *L. J. M. C.*, 115, *S. P.*, Reg. *v.* Kipps, 4 *Cox Cr. Cas.*, 167; Reg. *v.* Frazer, 8 *id.*, 446.

So it has been held that the statute was satisfied, though the prisoner and the female quitted the house together in consequence of a proposition which emanated from the girl herself to that effect, and a statement by her to the prisoner that she intended to leave her father's house. Reg. *v.* Biswell, 2 *Cox Cr. Cas.*, 279.

So where it was proved that the prisoner (with whom the girl had previously stayed out for a night), met her by arrangement, and stayed with her away from her father's house for three days, sleeping with her at night, that he took her away without the father's consent in order to gratify his passions, and then allow her to return home, but not with a view of keeping her away from her home permanently, it was held that the evidence justified a conviction under the above enactment. Reg. *v.* Timmons, 8 *Cox Cr. Cas.*, 401.

But where it did not appear that the prisoner had any improper motive, the jury were directed that if they thought the prisoner merely wished to have the child to live with him, and honestly believed that he had a right to the custody of the child although he had no such right, they ought to acquit him. Reg. *v.* Tinkler, 1 *Fost. & F.*, 513.

As to what is to be deemed a person "having the legal charge of her person," in the case of an orphan child, over whom no guardian has been appointed, see State *v.* Ruhl, 8 *Clarke*, 447.

Seduction under promise of marriage.

§ 330. Every person who, under promise of marriage, seduces and has illicit connection with any unmarried female of previous chaste character, is punishable by imprisonment in a state prison not exceeding five years, or by imprisonment in a county jail not exceeding one year, or by a fine not exceeding one thousand dollars, or by both such fine and imprisonment.

Founded upon *Laws of* 1848, ch. 111, § 1; the punishment being modified to correspond with that prescribed for the analogous offenses specified in the two sections preceding.

Omitted provisions. The further provision of the statute cited that no conviction shall be had upon the unsupported testimony of the female seduced is here omitted for reason that it belongs to the subject of evidence. See the provisions already reported upon that subject. *Rep. Code Civ. Pro.*, Part IV.

So much of the act of 1848, above cited as provides that indictments for seduction must be found within two years after the commission of the offense, is already embodied in *Rep. Code Cr. Pro.*, § 141.

"*Promise of Marriage.*" As to what promise is sufficient. See People *v.* Alger, 1 *Park. Cr.*, 333; Crozier *v.* People, *Id.*. 453; State *v.* Bierce, 27 *Conn.*, 319.

"*Seduced,*" &c. The words "and has illicit connection with," are retained for the reason they are found in the existing statute; and it is desired to avoid implying any change in the law in this respect. But the words quoted are probably unnecessary. The word "seduce," when used in such a statute and with reference to conduct of a man towards a woman, has been held to describe the offense sufficiently. State *v.* Bierce, 27 *Conn.*, 319.

"*Unmarried Female.*" That the condition of the female as unmarried, is an element of the offense, under statutes of this description, and must be proved by the government. See West *v.* State, 1 *Wisc.*, 209.

"*Previous Chaste Character.*" Character here is to be distinguished from reputation; in which sense the word is often used, even in our statutes (*e. g.*, *Code of Pro.*, § 179, subd. 1 and 5). Character consists of the qualities which constitute the individual; reputation the sum of opinions entertained concerning him. Character is interior; reputation external. Character is the substance of the individual; reputation is the shadow. The word is used in this statute, and in the similar provisions embodied in section 328, in its strict and proper sense; and requires that the female should actually *be*, not merely that she should have been *reputed* to be of personal virtue up to the time of the seduction by defendant. Carpenter *v.* People, 8 *Barb.*, 603; Safford *v.* People, 1 *Park. Cr.*, 474; See also Andre *v.* State, 5 *Clarke*, 389; Boak *v.* State, *Id.*, 430.

§ 331. The subsequent marriage of the parties is a defense to a prosecution for a violation of the last section. Subsequent marriage a defense.

See *Laws of* 1848, ch. 111.

CHAPTER II.

ABANDONMENT AND NEGLECT OF CHILDREN.

§ 332. Every parent of any child under the age of six years, and every person to whom any such child has been confided for nurture or education, who deserts such child in any place whatever, with intent wholly to abandon it, is punishable by imprisonment in a state prison not exceeding seven years, or in a county jail not exceeding one year. Deserting child.

See 2 *Rev. Stat.*, 665, § 35.

§ 333. Every parent of any child who willfully omits, without lawful excuse, to perform any duty imposed upon him by law to furnish necessary food, clothing, shelter, or medical attendance for such child, is guilty of misdemeanor. Omitting to provide child with necessaries.

Consult the Civil Code for the provisions reported defining the duty of parental support. As to the criminality of a willful omission to perform this duty. See Reg. *v.* Chandler, 1 *Jur. N. S.*, 429; 25 *Law T.*, 133; Reg. *v.* Gray, 7 *Cox Cr. Cas.*, 326; 3 *Jur. N. S.*, 988; Reg. *v.* S——, 5 *Cox Cr. Cas.*, 279; Reg. *v* Philpot, 6 *Id.*, 140.

CHAPTER III.

ABORTIONS AND CONCEALING DEATH OF INFANT.

Administering drugs with intent to procure miscarriage.

§ 334. Every person who provides, supplies or administers to any woman, whether pregnant or not, or prescribes for any such woman, or advises or procures any such woman to take any medicine, drug or substance, or uses or employs any instrument, or other means whatever, with intent thereby to procure the miscarriage of such woman, unless the same is necessary to preserve her life, is punishable by imprisonment in a state prison not exceeding three years or in a county jail not exceeding one year.

See *Laws of* 1845, ch. 260, § 2.

That it is not necessary to prove that the medicine was actually taken, see State *v.* Murphy, 3 *Dutch.*, 112. Nor that the prisoner was present when it was taken. Reg *v.* Wilson, 1 *Dears. & B.* 127; 37 *Eng. L. & Eq.*, 605; Reg *v.* Farrow, 40 *Eng. L. & Eq.*, 550. Compare also Reg *v.* Fretwell, 9 *Cox Cr. Cas.*, 152.

Submitting to attempt to procure miscarriage

§ 335. Every woman who solicits of any person any medicine, drug or substance whatever, and takes the same, or who submits to any operation or to the use of any means whatever, with intent thereby to procure a miscarriage, unless the same is necessary to preserve her life, is punishable by imprisonment in a county jail not exceeding one year, or by a fine not exceeding one thousand dollars, or by both.

See *Laws of* 1845, ch. 260, § 3. The offense of wilfully killing an unborn quick child is covered by provisions in the chapter upon HOMICIDE.

The exception "unless the same is necessary to preserve her life," is found in *Laws of* 1846, ch. 22, § 1. See section 250, *supra*. And is introduced in this and the preceding section in order that the analogous provisions may correspond.

§ 336. Every person who endeavors either alone or by the aid of others to conceal the still birth of any child, which if born alive would be a bastard, or the death of any such child under the age of two years, whether such person be the mother of such child or not, is punishable by imprisonment in a county jail not exceeding one year, or by a fine not exceeding one thousand dollars, or by both. *Concealing still birth or death of infant.*

See *Laws of* 1845, ch. 260, § 4; *Stat.* 24 and 25 *Vict.*, ch. 100, § 60.

As to the evidence requisite to support an indictment for concealing the birth of a child, see Reg. *v.* Bird, 2 *Carr. & K.*, 817; Reg. *v.* Goode, 6 *Id*, 318; Reg. *v* Berriman, *Id.*, 388; Reg. *v.* ———, *Id.*, 391; Reg. *v.* Perry, *Id.*, 531; 24 *L. J.* (2. *B.*), 137; Reg. *v.* Opie, 8 *Cox Cr. Cas.*, 332.

CHAPTER IV.

CHILD STEALING.

SECTION 337. Definition and punishment of child stealing.

§ 337. Every person who maliciously, forcibly or fraudulently takes or entices away any child under the age of twelve years, with intent to detain and conceal such child from its parent, guardian or other person having the lawful charge of such child, is punishable by imprisonment in a state prison not exceeding ten years or by imprisonment in a county jail not exceeding one year, or by fine not exceeding five hundred dollars, or by both such fine and imprisonment. *Definition and punishment of child stealing.*

2 *Rev. Stat.*, 665, § 34. The words "takes or entices," away are substituted for "leads, takes or carries away, or decoys or entices away," merely for greater conciseness, and not to introduce any change in the law.

CHAPTER V.

BIGAMY, INCEST AND THE CRIME AGAINST NATURE

Bigamy defined.

§ 338. Every person who, having been married to another who remains living, marries any other person, except in the cases specified in the next section, is guilty of bigamy.

See 2 *Rev. Stat.*, 687, § 8. *Modification of the law.* The language of the Revised Statutes is: "Every person having a husband or wife living, who shall marry any other person," &c. Under this phraseology it was held that notwithstanding the exception in next section, which provided that the previous section should not extend to any person by reason of any former marriage which had been dissolved for some cause other than the adultery of such person, a person who married again after a divorce pronounced for his or her own adultery, was not guilty of bigamy. A divorced person, it was held could not be said to have a "husband or wife living" within the meaning of section 8, of 2 *Rev. Stat.*, 687; People *v.* Hovey, 5 *Barb.*, 117.

On viewing together all the provisions of the existing law of marriage, divorce and bigamy the Commissioners believe it to be the clear intention of the legislature that where a divorce is granted for adultery, the innocent party only should be set free to marry again, and that the guilty one should remain incapable of marrying and liable to punishment for bigamy if he assumes so to do. They have, therefore modified the language of the provision so as to avoid the possibility of the rule laid down in People *v.* Hovey, being applied.

It may be added that the reasoning in People *v.* Hovey which was decided in the supreme court in 1849, is shaken by the decision of the court of appeals in 1850, in Wait *v.* Wait, 4 *Comst.*, 95. In that case it was held that a woman who had been granted a divorce from her husband for his adultery is entitled, notwithstanding, to dower on his estate, after his death; under the language of 1 *Rev. Stat.*, 740, § 1, viz.: "*A widow* shall be endowed," &c.

Except perhaps for the rule that penal statutes are to be strictly construed it would seem indisputable that if a woman so divorced were to be deemed to become the *widow* of her former husband at his death so as to entitle her to dower, she must be held to have remained his *wife*, notwithstanding the divorce, during his lifetime, so as to render his subsequent marriage bigamy. But the language employed in the text, will, it is believed, avoid all question upon the subject.

What is proof of marriage. What is to be deemed a marriage is left to the operation of the rules of law governing that relation. It is generally understood that a marriage in fact must be proved, and that mere proof of reputation is not enough. In a recent case in the court of Appeals this rule and its limit, were carefully considered. In that case the prosecution to establish the fact of a recent marriage, called a witness who testified in substance that the prisoner conducted her to a house where he had taken rooms. The prisoner went out and returned with a person represented to be a minister. He was dressed like one, and had on a white-neck-tie. She did not ask his name. The marriage ceremony was then performed by this person. He used the form of marriage of the Protestant Episcopal Church. He inquired of the witness if she would take the prisoner for her husband, and she replied in the affirmative; and the prisoner was asked if he would have her for his wife, and upon his replying affirmatively, the minister declared them man and wife. The person officiating gave her a certificate, using a partly printed form, and filling in the blanks by writing. The certificate was taken by the prisoner, and put in his trunk, and was afterwards seen by a sister of the witness, when the parties were living together as man and wife. This marriage ceremony was followed by cohabitation, which continued for about a year. *Held*, that even if to constitute a valid marriage, it must be solemnized by a minister or magistrate, the evidence was sufficient *prima facie*, to prove a marriage in fact. A person appeared in the character of a clergyman, performed the ceremony, and it was followed by cohabitation. If the person officiating was not a clergyman, it was for the prisoner to show that fact. 12 *Vt.*, 396; 10 *East*, 282. But in this state there may be a valid marriage, though not formally solemnized by a clergyman or consent declared before a magistrate. If parties competent to contract, in the presence of witnesses, agree together to be husband and wife, and afterwards cohabit and recognize each other as such, it is a sufficient marriage to sustain an indictment for bigamy in the event of one of the parties having before that time married another, who is still living. It was not an error therefore for the judge to instruct the jury, that if the prisoner and the witness agreed, in the presence of the man represented to be a minister, to be man and wife, and afterwards lived together as such, that was, in the eye of the law, a sufficient marriage to sustain an indictment for bigamy; the fact that the prisoner had, before that time, married Sarah E. Blair, and she was then living, being admitted; and that it was of no consequence whether the man represented to be a minister was such or not. Marriage in this state is a civil contract, and does not require the intervention of a minister or magistrate to make it legal. Hayes *v.* People, 25 *N. Y.*, 390.

Whether the prisoner's confession that his first wife was living when he contracted the second marriage is sufficient evidence, see Reg. *v.* Flaherty, 2 *Carr. & K.*, 782; Laugtry *v.* State, 30 *Ala.*, 536; Gorman *v.* State, 23 *Tex.*, 646.

Exceptions. § 339. The last section does not extend:

1. To any person by reason of any former marriage, whose husband or wife by such marriage has been absent for five successive years without being known to such person within that time to be living; nor,

2. To any person by reason of any former marriage whose husband or wife by such marriage has absented himself or herself from his wife or her husband and has been continually remaining without the United States for the space of five years together; nor,

3. To any person by reason of any former marriage which has been pronounced void, annulled or dissolved by the judgment of a competent court, unless such marriage was dissolved upon the ground of adultery committed by such person; nor,

4. To any person by reason of any former marriage with a husband or wife who has been sentenced to imprisonment for life.

Founded upon 2 *Rev. Stat.*, 687, § 9.

Subd. 1. What proof of the defendant's *knowledge* that the former husband or wife was living when the second marriage was contracted, is proper, depends upon the facts of each case. Reg. *v.* Ellis, 1 *Fost. & F.*, 309.

Where the prisoner was indicted for bigamy, and no evidence was given on either side as to the prisoner's knowledge that his wife was alive, but it was proved that they had separated by agreement in 1843, and that in 1857 the prisoner produced her at a trial in which he was interested; *Held*, that it was for the jury to say whether there was an absence of knowledge on the part of the prisoner that his wife was alive in 1855, the date of the second marriage. Reg. *v.* Cross, 1 *Fost. & F.*, 510.

Upon a trial for bigamy, where it appeared that the first husband had been continually absent from the prisoner for the space of seven years next preceding the second marriage, the jury being asked to consider whether she knew her husband to be alive at the time of the second marriage; and, if not, whether she had had the means of acquiring the knowledge: found that they had no evidence of her knowledge, but were of opinion that she had the means of acquiring knowledge, if she had chosen to make use of them: *Held*, that upon that finding the conviction could not be sustained, inasmuch as it left it uncertain whether, in fact, she had or had not the knowledge. Reg. *v.* Briggs, 7 *Cox Crim. Cas.*, 175.

That express proof that the former husband or wife was living is not always required, but strong presumption of continued life may suffice. See Gorman *v.* State, 23 *Tex.*, 646.

Subd. 3 In order to attain greater conciseness, and to render the provisions of the text conformable to the nomenclature respecting proceedings in courts of justice introduced by the Code of Procedure, subdivision 3 in the text is substituted for the following subdivisions of the section as it stands in the Revised Statutes:

"3. To any person by reason of any former marriage which shall have been dissolved by the decree of a competent court for some cause other than the adultery of such person; nor,

"4. To any person by reason of any former marriage which shall have been pronounced void by the sentence or decree of any competent court on the ground of nullity of the marriage contract; nor,

"5. To any person by reason of any former marriage contracted by such person, within the age of legal consents, and which shall have been annulled by the decree of a competent court."

Place of trial. The substance of the provisions of 2 *Rev. Stat.*, 688, § 10, declaring bigamists triable in the county where apprehended as well as in the county where the offense was committed has been embodied in *Rep. Code Cr. Pro.*, § 135.

§ 340. Every person guilty of bigamy is punishable by imprisonment in a state prison not exceeding five years. Punishment of bigamy.

See 2 *Rev. Stat.*, 687, § 8.

Other unlawful marriages.

§ 341. Every person who knowingly marries the husband or wife of another, in any case in which such husband or wife would be punishable according to the foregoing provisions, is punishable by imprisonment in a state prison not exceeding five years or in a county jail not exceeding one year, or by a fine not exceeding five hundred dollars, or by both such fine and imprisonment.

See 2 *Rev. Stat.*, 688, § 11. That provision, as now in force, applies only to *unmarried* persons; the idea being, doubtless, that a married person who knowingly marries the husband or wife of another, is punishable for the higher offense of bigamy, by reason of his or her own previous marriage. But to sustain a prosecution for bigamy the people must be prepared to prove the first marriage of the accused. A case might arise in which a married person contracting a marriage with a husband or wife of another might escape an indictment for bigamy for want of evidence of an earlier marriage, and yet, if indicted under section 11 of 2 *Rev. Stat.*, 688, defeat the prosecution by proof of such earlier marriage. The Commissioners have, therefore, omitted the word "unmarried." It may be remarked that by a subsequent section it is provided that where an act or omission is made punishable in different ways by different provisions of this Code, it may be punished under either of said provisions, but not under more than one. Therefore, under the above sections, as reported by the Commissioners, a person supposed to be married, and charged with marrying the husband or wife of another may be indicted either for bigamy under section 338, or for the felony prohibited by section 341, according as it may be easiest to prove the former marriage of the accused or that of the person with whom the accused has now intermarried.

Incest.

§ 342. Persons who, being within the degrees of consanguinity within which marriages are, by section 30 of the Civil Code, declared incestuous and void, intermarry with each other, or commit adultery or fornication with each other, are punishable by imprisonment in a state prison not exceeding ten years.

2 *Rev. Stat.*, 688, § 12.

Crime against nature.

§ 343. Every person who is guilty of the detestable and abominable crime against nature, committed with mankind or with any animal, is punishable by imprisonment in a state prison not exceeding ten years.

Ibid, § 20; 24 and 25 *Vict.*, ch. 100, § 61.

§ 344. Any sexual penetration, however slight, is sufficient to complete the crime against nature. Crime against nature.

See 2 *Rev. Stat.*, 735, § 18.

CHAPTER VI.

VIOLATING SEPULTURE AND THE REMAINS OF THE DEAD.

§ 345. Every person has the right to direct the manner in which his body shall be disposed of after his death; and to direct the manner in which any part of his body which becomes separated therefrom during his lifetime shall be disposed of. The provisions of this chapter do not apply where such person has given directions for the disposal of his body or any part thereof inconsistent with those provisions. Right to direct disposal of one's own body after death.

§ 346. Except in the cases in which a right to dissect a dead body is expressly conferred by law, every Duty of burial.

dead body of a human being lying within this state must be decently buried within a reasonable time after the death.

Burial in other states

§ 347. The last section does not affect the right to carry the dead body of a human being through this state, or to remove from this state the body of a person dying within it, for the purpose of burying the same in another state.

Dissection, when allowed.

§ 348. The right to dissect the dead body of a human being exists in the following cases:

1. In the cases defined in section 845 of the Political Code;

2. Whenever a coroner is authorized by law to hold an inquest upon the body, so far as such coroner authorizes dissection for the purposes of the inquest and no further;

3. Whenever and so far as the husband or next of kin of the deceased, being charged by law with the duty of burial, authorizes dissection for the purpose of ascertaining the cause of death, and no further.

Unlawful dissection a misdemeanor.

§ 349. Every person who makes or causes or procures to be made any dissection of the body of a human being, except by authority of law, or in pursuance of a permission given by the deceased, is guilty of a misdemeanor.

Remains after dissection must be buried.

§ 350. In all cases in which a dissection has been made, the provisions of this chapter, requiring the burial of a dead body, and punishing interference with or injuries to a dead body, apply equally to the remains of the body dissected, as soon as the lawful purposes of such dissection have been accomplished.

Dead limb or member of a human body.

§ 351. All provisions of this chapter requiring the burial of a dead body, or punishing interference with or injuries to a dead body, apply equally to any dead limb or member of a human body, separated therefrom during lifetime.

§ 352. The duty of burying the body of a deceased person devolves upon the persons hereinafter specified: Who are charged with duty of burial.

1. If the deceased were a married woman the duty of burial devolves upon her husband;

2. If the deceased were not a married woman, but left any kindred, the duty of burial devolves upon the person or persons in the same degree nearest of kin to the deceased, being of adult age, and within this state, and possessed of sufficient means to defray the necessary expenses;

3. If the deceased left no husband, nor kindred, answering the foregoing description, the duty of burial devolves upon the coroner conducting an inquest upon the body of the deceased, if any such inquest is held, if none, then upon the persons charged with the support of the poor in the locality in which the death occurs;

4. In case the person upon whom the duty of burial is cast by the foregoing provisions omits to make such burial within a reasonable time, the duty devolves upon the person next specified; and if all omit to act, it devolves upon the tenant, or, if there is no tenant, upon the owner of the premises, or master, or, if there is no master, upon the owner of the vessel in which the death occurs or the body is found.

§ 353. Every person upon whom the duty of making burial of the remains of a deceased person is imposed by law, who omits to perform that duty within a reasonable time, is guilty of a misdemeanor; and, in addition to the punishment prescribed therefor, is liable to pay to the person performing the duty in his stead, treble the expenses incurred by the latter in making the burial, to be recovered in a civil action. Punishment for omitting to bury.

§ 354. The person charged by law with the duty of burying the body of a deceased person is entitled to the custody of such body for the purpose of burying it; except that in the cases in which an inquest is required by law to be held upon a dead body, by a Who entitled to custody of a body.

coroner, such coroner is entitled to its custody until such inquest has been completed.

Unlawful removal of or interference with the bodies of the dead.

§ 355. Every person who removes any part of the dead body of a human being from any grave or other place where the same has been buried or from any place where the same is deposited while awaiting burial, with intent to sell the same, or to dissect it without authority of law, or from malice or wantonness, is punishable by imprisonment in a state prison not exceeding five years, or in a county jail not exceeding one year, or by a fine not exceeding five hundred dollars, or by both such fine and imprisonment.

This section embraces the provisions of 2 *Rev. Stat.*, 688, § 13, extended so as to embrace the case of removing a part only of the remains of a deceased person, and also to embrace the case of removal of remains while yet unburied. In Reg. *v.* Sharpe (40 *Eng. L. & Eq.*, 581), it appeared that the prisoner had, without leave, entered a burying ground, and without authority from the custodians, had disinterred a corpse, and removed it. The removal was conducted in a proper manner, the corpse was that of the prisoner's mother, and his motive for the removal was to bury her remains in a church-yard with the body of his father, then recently deceased. *Held*, that the disinterment was a misdemeanor. The mere fact that the defendant acted from praiseworthy motives, was no defense. Neither does the English law recognize the right of any one child to the corpse of its parent. It recognizes no property in a corpse. Nor will relationship justify the taking of a corpse away from the grave where it has been buried.

The present statute of this state, however, from which the section in the text is taken, has regard to the motives from which the act is done. The Commissioners have adhered to this principle; leaving a disinterment to pass without criminal punishment if the unworthy motives specified in the section are not proved to have actuated the defendant, and if there was nothing in the manner of performing it, amounting to an offense under other provisions of the Code.

Purchasing corpses forbidden.

§ 356. Every person who purchases, or who receives, except for the purpose of burial, any dead body of a human being, knowing that the same has been removed contrary to the last section, is punishable by imprisonment in a state prison not exceeding five years, or in a county jail not exceeding one year, or by a fine not exceeding five hundred dollars, or by both such fine and imprisonment.

See 2 *Rev. Stat.*, 688, § 14.

§ 357. Every person who opens any grave or other place of burial, temporary or otherwise, or who breaks open any building wherein any dead body of a human being is deposited while awaiting burial, with intent, either: Unlawful interference with places of burial.

1. To remove any dead body of a human being for the purpose of selling the same, or for the purpose of dissection; or,

2. To steal the coffin, or any part thereof, or anything attached thereto, or connected therewith, or the vestments or other articles buried with the same,

Is punishable by imprisonment in a state prison not exceeding two years, or in a county jail not exceeding six months, or by a fine not exceeding two hundred and fifty dollars, or by both such fine and imprisonment.

2 *Rev. Stat.*, 688, § 15.

§ 358. Whenever a cemetery or other place cf burial is lawfully authorized to be removed from one place to another, the right and duty to disinter, remove and rebury the remains of bodies there lying buried, devolves upon the persons named in section 352, in the order in which they are there named; and, if they all fail to act, then upon the lawful custodians of the place of burial so removed. Every omission of such duty is punishable in the same manner as other omissions to perform the duty of making burial are made punishable by section 353. Remova from one burial place to another.

§ 359. Every person who arrests or attaches any dead body of a human being upon any debt or demand whatever, or detains or claims to detain it for any debt or demand, or upon any pretended lien or charge, is guilty of a misdemeanor. Arresting or attaching a dead body.

Disturbing funerals.

§ 360. Every person who willfully disturbs, interrupts or disquiets any assemblage of people met for the purpose of any funeral; or who, without authority of law, obstructs or detains any persons engaged in carrying or accompanying any dead body of a human being to a place of burial, is guilty of a misdemeanor.

Defacing tombs, monuments, &c.

§ 361. Every person who willfully defaces, breaks, destroys or removes any tomb, monument or gravestone erected to any deceased person, or any memento or memorial, or any ornamental plant, tree or shrub appertaining to the place of burial of a human being, without authority from the owner of the soil, and husband or wife, or if there be no husband or wife, then from the next of kin of the deceased, is guilty of a misdemeanor.

Unlawful dissection.

§ 362. Every person who violates any of the provisions of sections 845, 846, or 847 of the Political Code, relative to dissection, is guilty of a misdemeanor.

CHAPTER VII.

INDECENT EXPOSURES, OBSCENE EXHIBITIONS, BOOKS AND PRINTS, AND BAWDY AND OTHER DISORDERLY HOUSES.

Indecent exposures, exhibitions, pictures, &c

§ 363. Every person who, willfully and lewdly, either:

1. Exposes his person, or the private parts thereof, in any public place, or in any place where there are present other persons to be offended or annoyed thereby; or,

2. Procures, counsels or assists any person so to expose himself, or to take part in any model artist exhibition, or to make any other exhibition of himself to public view, or to the view of any number of persons, such as is offensive to decency, or is adapted to excite to vicious or lewd thoughts or acts; or,

3. Writes or composes, stereotypes, prints, publishes, sells, distributes, or keeps for sale, or exhibits any obscene or indecent writing, paper or book, or designs or copies, draws or engraves, paints, or otherwise prepares any obscene or indecent picture or print, or moulds, cuts, casts, or otherwise makes any obscene or indecent figure; or,

4. Writes, composes or publishes any notice or advertisement of any such writing, paper, book, picture, print or figure; or any notice or advertisement of any cure, specific or medicine for venereal or other kindred diseases, or for producing or facilitating menstruation, or for producing or facilitating a miscarriage in females; or,

5. Sings any lewd or obscene song, ballad or other words, in any public place or in any place where there are persons present to be annoyed thereby,

Is guilty of a misdemeanor.

See Reg. *v.* Holmes, 22 *Law & J.* (*M. C.*), 122; Reg. *v.* Watson, 2 *Cox Cr. Cas.*, 376; Reg. *v.* Webb, 3 *Id.*, 183; Reg. *v.* Orchard, *Id.*, 248; Dugdale *v.* Queen, 1 *El. & B.*, 435.

Seizure of indecent articles authorized.

§ 364. Every person who is authorized or enjoined to arrest any person for a violation of subdivision 3 of the last section, is equally authorized and enjoined to seize any obscene or indecent writing, paper, book, picture, print or figure found in possession or under the control of the person so arrested, and to deliver the same to the magistrate before whom the person so arrested is required to be taken.

Provisions regulating the issuing and execution of search warrants, applicable to cases, among others, where it is desired to discover property which is in possession of any person with intent to use it as the means of committing a public offense, are reported, *Code Cr. Pr.*, §§ 862, 883.

Their character to be summarily determined.

§ 365. The magistrate to whom any obscene or indecent writing, paper, book, picture, print or figure, is delivered pursuant to the foregoing section, shall, upon the examination of the accused, or, if the examination is delayed or prevented, without awaiting such examination, determine the character of such writing, paper, book, picture, print or figure, and if he finds it to be obscene or indecent he shall cause the same to be destroyed, or to be delivered to the district attorney of the county in which the accused is liable to indictment or trial, as the interests of justice in his judgment require. But not more than two copies of any one writing, paper, book, picture, print or figure, shall be delivered to the district attorney.

Their destruction.

§ 366. Upon the conviction of the accused such district attorney shall cause any writing, paper, book, picture, print or figure, in respect whereof the accused stands convicted and which remains in the possession or under the control of such district attorney, to be destroyed.

Keeping bawdy house.

§ 367. Every person who keeps any bawdy house, house of ill-fame, of assignation, or of prostitution, or any other house or place for persons to visit for unlawful sexual intercourse or for any other lewd, obscene or indecent purpose, is guilty of a misdemeanor.

Keeping disorderly house.

§ 368. Every person who keeps any disorderly house, or any house of public resort by which the peace, comfort or decency of the immediate neighborhood is habitually disturbed, or who keeps any inn in a disorderly manner, is guilty of a misdemeanor.

See 2 *Bish. Cr. L.*, § 251.

Letting building for unlawful purposes.

§ 369. Every person who lets any building or portion of any building knowing that it is intended to be used for any purpose declared punishable by this chapter, or who otherwise permits any building or portion of any building to be so used, is guilty of a misdemeanor.

See 2 *Rev. Stat.*, 702, § 29; Abrahams *v.* State, 4 *Iowa*, 541; State *v.* Abrahams, 6 *Clarke*, 117.

CHAPTER VIII.

LOTTERIES.

§ 370. A lottery is any scheme for the disposal or distribution of property by chance among persons who have paid or promised or agreed to pay any valuable consideration for the chance of obtaining such property or a portion of it, or for any share of, or interest in such property, upon any agreement, understanding or expectation that it is to be distributed or disposed of by lot or chance; whether called a lottery, a raffle, or a gift enterprise, or by whatever name the same may be known. "Lottery" defined.

See 1 *Rev. Stat.*, 665, § 22; Governor of Alms House *v.* American Art Union, 7 *N. Y.*, 228; *Bouvier's Law Dict.*, tit. Lottery; *Mass. Gen. Stat.*, 823, § 1. In the popular use of the above mentioned terms a lottery is a distribution by chance of *several* prizes among purchasers of separate chances: a raffle is a disposal by chance of a *single* prize among purchasers of separate chances; and a gift enterprise is a disposal of property in mass to a body of shareholders, upon an understanding or expectation that they will decide it among themselves by chance.

But as all schemes of this description are involved in a common condemnation and punishment, the retaining of these distinctions in the statute book will serve no important purpose in defining the offense, while it will embarrass prosecutions by suggesting questions as to the requisite averments in the indictment. The Commissioners have, therefore, defined the word "lottery" broadly enough to cover all these homogeneous devices, in order that that word may be intelligibly used as including all.

As to unlawfulness of "gift enterprises," see Wooden *v.* Shotwell, 4 *Zabr.*, 789; Bell *v.* State, 5 *Sneed*, 507.

Lottery declared a public nuisance.

§ 371. Every lottery is unlawful and a common and public nuisance.

See 1 *Rev. Stat.*, 665, § 26; *Const. of* 1846, art. 1, § 10. This provision of the Constitution, viz.: "Nor shall any lottery hereafter be authorized, or any sale of lottery tickets allowed within this state;" has rendered obsolete many of the distinctions of our former laws relative to lotteries, and has enabled the Commissioners to present provisions much more brief and simple than those of the Revised Statutes and subsequent enactments, while they are also in reality more stringent.

It may here be remarked that, in view of the modification of the law, since the enactment of the Revised Statutes, by which all lotteries are made unlawful, the Commissioners have regarded lottery tickets as no longer the subject of property which the law will be sedulous to protect; and they have omitted those provisions of the Revised Statutes which made forgery and larceny of such tickets punishable. The reasons upon which the forgery of foreign bank notes of a particular denomination has been held criminal notwithstanding the circulation of bills of such denomination has been made unlawful, are not considered fully applicable to the case of lottery tickets.

Setting up lotteries.

§ 372. Every person who contrives, prepares, sets up, proposes or draws any lottery, is punishable by a fine equal to double the amount of the whole sum or value for which such lottery was made; and if such amount cannot be ascertained, then by imprisonment in a state prison not exceeding two years, or by imprisonment in a county jail not exceeding one year, or by a fine of two thousand five hundred dollars, or by both such fine and imprisonment.

See 1 *Rev. Stat.*, 665, § 27.

§ 373. Every person who sells, gives, or in any manner whatever furnishes or transfers to or for any other person, any ticket, chance, share or interest, or any paper, certificate or instrument, purporting or represented or understood to be, or to represent any ticket, chance, share or interest in or depending upon the event of any lottery, is guilty of a misdemeanor. Selling lottery tickets.

1 *Rev. Stat.*, 666, § 29.

§ 374. Every person who buys, or in any manner whatever accepts or receives for himself or another, any ticket, chance, share or interest, or any paper, certificate, or instrument, purporting or represented or understood to be, or to represent any ticket, chance, share or interest in or depending upon the event of any lottery, forfeits ten dollars, to be recovered by the persons charged with the support of the poor in the locality where the offense was committed. Buying lottery tickets.

§ 375. Every person who, by writing or printing, by circulars or letters, or in any other way, advertises or publishes any account of any lottery, stating when or where the same is to be or has been drawn, or what are the prizes or any of them therein, or the price of a ticket or of any share or interest, or where it may be obtained, or in any way aiding or assisting the same, or adapted to induce persons to adventure therein, is guilty of a misdemeanor. Advertising lotteries.

Founded upon 1 *Rev. Stat.*, 665, § 28; the punishment being modified to correspond with other provisions of the Code.

§ 376. Every person who offers for sale, distribution or disposition in any way, any real or personal property, or things in action, or any interest therein, to be determined by lot or chance that shall be dependent upon the drawing of any lottery, within or out of this state; and every person who sells, furnishes or procures, or causes to be sold, furnished or procured in any manner whatsoever, any chance or share, or any interest whatever, in any property Offering property for disposal dependent upon the drawing of any lottery.

offered for sale, distribution or disposition in violation of this section, or any ticket or other evidence of any chance, share or interest in such property, is guilty of a misdemeanor.

See 1 *Rev. Stat.*, 666, § 30.

Lottery offices.

§ 377. Every person who opens, sets up or keeps, by himself, or by any other person or persons, any office or other place for registering the numbers of any ticket in any lottery, or for making, receiving or registering any bets or wagers upon the drawing, determination or result of any lottery, is punishable by imprisonment in a county jail not exceeding one year, or by a fine not exceeding one thousand dollars.

1 *Rev. Stat.*, 667, §§ 34, 37.

Advertising lottery offices.

§ 378. Every person who by writing or printing, by circulars or letters, or in any other way, advertises or publishes any account of the opening, setting up or keeping of any office or other place for either of the purposes prohibited by the last section, is guilty of a misdemeanor.

See 1 *Rev. Stat.*, 667, § 37; *Id.*, 665, § 28.

Insuring lottery tickets, &c.

§ 379. Every person who insures or receives any consideration for insuring for or against the drawing of any ticket, share or interest in any lottery, or for or against the drawing of any number, or ticket, or number of any ticket in any lottery; and every person who receives any valuable consideration upon any agreement to pay any sum, or to deliver any property or thing in action in the event that any ticket, share or interest in any lottery, or any number, or ticket, or number of any ticket in any lottery shall prove fortunate or unfortunate, or shall be drawn or not drawn on any particular day, or in any particular order; and every person who promises, agrees or offers to pay any sum of money or to deliver any property or thing in action, or to do, or forbear to do anything for the benefit of any other person, with or without consideration, upon any event whatever connected with any lottery, is guilty of a misdemeanor.

See 1 *Rev. Stat.*, 667, §§ 36, 37.

§ 380. Every person who by writing or printing, by circulars or letters, or in any other way, advertises or publishes any offer, notice, or proposal for any violation of the last section, is guilty of a misdemeanor.

Advertising offers to insure lottery tickets.

§ 381. All property offered for sale, distribution or disposition, in violation of the provisions of this chapter, is forfeited to the people of this state, as well before as after the determination of the chance on which the same was dependent. And it is the duty of the respective district attorneys, to demand, sue for and recover, in behalf of this state, all property so forfeited, and to cause the same to be sold when recovered, and to pay the proceeds of the sale of such property, and any moneys that may be collected in any such suit, into the county treasury, for the benefit of the poor.

Property offered for disposal in lotteries forfeited.

See 1 *Rev. Stat.*, 666, § 31.

§ 382. Every person who lets, or permits to be used any building or portion of any building, knowing that it is intended to be used for any of the purposes declared punishable by this chapter, is guilty of a misdemeanor.

Letting building for lottery purposes.

§ 383. The provisions of this chapter apply in respect to lotteries drawn or to be drawn out of this state, whether authorized or not by the laws of the state where they are drawn or to be drawn, in the same manner as to lotteries drawn or to be drawn within this state.

Lotteries out of this state.

§ 384. The provisions of sections 375 and 378 are applicable wherever the advertisement was published, or the letter or circular sent or delivered through or in this state, notwithstanding the person causing or procuring the same to be published, sent or delivered, was out of this state at the time of so doing.

Advertisements by persons out of this state.

CHAPTER IX.

GAMING.

Keeping gambling apparatus in certain places.

§ 385. It is unlawful to maintain or keep any table, cards, dice or any other article or apparatus whatever, useful or intended to be used in playing any game of cards or faro, or other game of chance, upon which money is usually wagered, at either of the following places:

1. Within any building, or the appurtenances or grounds connected with any building in which any court of justice usually holds its sessions; or any building, any part of which is usually occupied by any religious corporation, or any incorporated benevolent, charitable, scientific or missionary society, or any incorporated academy, high school, college or other institution of learning, or any library company, or building and mutual loan company;

2. Within any building or the appurtenances or grounds connected with any building, while votes are being received or canvassed therein at any election

for any officer of this state, or of the United States; or while any public meeting is being held therein;

3. Within the distance of one mile from any grounds upon which any training, review, drill or exercise of any military organization created or permitted by the laws of this state, is proceeding, or upon which any public fair, exhibition, exercise or meeting is being held or conducted, in the open air;

4. Within any vessel lying in, or navigating any of the waters of this state; or owned, or navigated by, or for account of any corporation created by the laws of this state.

§ 386. Every person who knowingly violates the last section is guilty of a misdemeanor. Punishment.

§ 387. Every article or apparatus maintained or kept in violation of section 385, is a common and public nuisance. Gambling apparatus declared a nuisance.

§ 388. Every person who, by any fraud, cheat, or false pretense whatsoever, while playing at any game, or while bearing a share in any wagers played for, or while betting on the sides or hands of such as play, wins or acquires to himself, or to any other, any sum of money or other valuable thing, is guilty of a misdemeanor. Winning at play by fraudulent means.

See 1 *Rev. Stat.*, 662, § 11. The words, "and on conviction shall be deemed infamous," at the close of this section, in the Revised Statutes, are omitted.

§ 389. Every person who exacts or receives from another, directly or indirectly, any valuable consideration, by reason of the same having been won by playing at cards, faro, or any other game of chance, or any bet or wager whatever upon the hands or sides of players, forfeits five times the value of the consideration so exacted or received, to be recovered in a civil action, by the persons charged with the support of the poor in the locality Exacting payment of money won at play.

in which the offense was committed, for the benefit of the poor.

See 1 *Rev. Stat.*, 662, § 12.

Recommended as a substitute for 1 *Rev. Stat.*, 662, § 12, which is as follows:

"Every person who shall, at any one time or sitting, win, by playing at any game, of any one or more persons, any sum or value, shall forfeit five times the value of the money or other things so won, to be recovered by and in the name of the overseers of the poor of the town for the use of the poor."

The offense consists, when carefully considered, not so much in winning the money as in exacting or receiving payment of the money when won.

Winning or losing upwards of $25.

§ 390. Every person who wins or loses at play or by betting, at any time, the sum or value of twenty-five dollars or upwards, within the space of twenty-four hours, is punishable by a fine not less than five times the value or sum so lost or won, to be recovered in a civil action, by the persons charged with the support of the poor in the place where the offense was committed, for the benefit of the poor.

1 *Rev. Stat.*, 662, § 13.

Witness' privilege.

§ 391. No person shall be excused from giving any testimony or evidence upon any investigation or proceeding for a violation of this chapter, upon the ground that such testimony would tend to convict him of a crime; but such testimony or evidence shall not be received against him upon any criminal investigation or proceeding.

Omitted provisions. The following provision of the Revised Statutes is omitted for the reason that it pertains to evidence in civil causes, and if retained at all should be transferred to the Code of Civil Procedure:

"No person, other than the parties in the cause, shall be incapacitated or excused from testifying, touching any offense committed against any of the foregoing provisions relating to gaming, by reason of his having played, betted or staked, at any game, as herein prohibited; but the testimony of any such person shall not be used against him in any suit or prosecution hereby authorized." 1 *Rev. Stat.*, 663, § 18.

The following provision of the Revised Statutes is

omitted because it is anomalous, and amounts to conferring a pardoning power upon the court:

"Any person offending against any of the provisions contained in this article, who shall be admitted and examined as a witness in any court of record, to sustain any suit or prosecution herein authorized, may, by rule of the court, be discharged from all penalties by reason of such offense, if such person hath not been before convicted thereof, or of a similar offense, and if it appear to the court satisfactorily that such person was duped or enticed into the commission of the offense by those against whom he shall testify." 1 *Rev. Stat.*, 664, § 21.

As to witness' privilege, see note to section 200.

Keeping gambling establishment or letting places for gambling purposes.

§ 392. Every person who keeps any building or part of any building, or any vessel or float to be used or occupied for gambling, and every owner, agent or superintendent of any such place who knowingly lets the same or allows it to be used or occupied for gambling, is guilty of a misdemeanor.

See *Laws of* 1851, ch. 504, § 1.

Keeping gambling tables, promoting prohibited games, &c., prohibited.

§ 393. Every person who, for gambling purposes, keeps or exhibits any gambling table, establishment, device or apparatus, or is guilty of dealing "faro" or banking for others to deal "faro," or acting as "look-out" or game-keeper for the game of "faro," or any other banking game where money or property is dependent upon the result, or who sells or vends what are commonly called lottery policies, or any writing, card, paper or document in the nature of a bet, wager, or insurance upon the drawing or drawn numbers of any public or private lottery, or indorses a book or any other document for the purpose of enabling others to sell or vend lottery policies, is deemed a common gambler, and is punishable as for a misdemeanor.

Laws of 1851, ch. 504, § 2, as amended *Laws of* 1855, ch. 214, the punishment being modified. By the existing laws the punishment prescribed is that the accused shall be sentenced "to not less than ten days' hard labor in the penitentiary, or not more than two years' hard labor in the state prison, and be fined in any sum not more than one thousand dollars, to be paid into the county treasury where such conviction shall take place, for the use of the common schools therein, to be divided among the school districts in that county, in the same manner as the school money of the state is divided among said districts, and in default thereof shall remain imprisoned until such fine be remitted or paid." This punishment is anomalous, and the offense has, therefore, been declared a misdemeanor, in order to harmonize the penalties throughout the Code.

Seizure of gambling implements authorized.

§ 394. Every person who is authorized or enjoined to arrest any person for a violation of the provisions of this chapter, is equally authorized and enjoined to seize any table, cards, dice or other article or apparatus, suitable to be used for gambling purposes, found in the possession or under the control of the person so arrested, and to deliver the same to the magistrate before whom the person so arrested is required to be taken.

Provisions regulating the issuing and execution of search warrants, applicable to cases, among others, where it is desired to discover property which is in possession of any person with intent to use it as the means of committing a public offense, are reported, *Code Cr. Pro.*, §§ 861–883.

Such implements to be destroyed or delivered to district attorney.

§ 395. The magistrate to whom any thing suitable to be used for gambling purposes is delivered pursuant to the foregoing section, shall, upon the examination of the accused, or if such examination is delayed or prevented, without awaiting such examination, determine the character of the thing so delivered to him, and whether it was actually employed by the accused in violation of the provisions of this chapter; and if he finds that it is of a character suitable to be used for gambling purposes, and that it has been used by the accused in violation of this chapter, he shall cause it to be destroyed or to be delivered to the district attorney of the county in which the accused is liable to indictment or trial, as the interests of justice, in his judgment, require.

Such implement to be destroyed

§ 396. Upon the conviction of the accused such district attorney shall cause any such thing suitable to be used for gambling purposes, in respect whereof the accused stands convicted, and which remains in the possession or under the control of such district attorney, to be destroyed. upon conviction.

§ 397. Every person who persuades another to visit any building or part of a building, or any vessel or float used or occupied for the purpose of gambling, in consequence whereof such other person gambles therein, is guilty of a misdemeanor; and in addition to the punishment prescribed therefor, is liable to such other person in an amount equal to any money or property lost by him at play at such place, to be recovered in a civil action. Persuading another person to visit gambling places.

Founded on *Laws of* 1851, ch. 504, § 2.

§ 398. It is the duty of all sheriffs, police officers, constables, and prosecuting or district attorneys to inform against and prosecute all persons whom they have credible reason to believe are offenders against the provisions of this chapter; and any omission so to do is punishable by a fine not exceeding five hundred dollars. Certain officers directed to prosecute offenses under this chapter.

See *Laws of* 1851, ch. 504, § 6.

§ 399. If any commander, owner or lessee of any vessel or float, knowingly permits any gambling for money or property on board such vessel or float, and does not, upon his knowledge of the fact, immediately prevent the same, he is punishable by a fine not exceeding five hundred dollars; and in addition thereto is liable to any party losing any money or property by means of any gambling permitted in violation of this section, in a sum equal to the money or property, to be recovered in a civil action. Duty of masters to suppress gambling on board their vessels.

See *Laws of* 1851, ch. 504, § 7.

§ 400. All racing or trial of speed between horses or other animals for any bet, stake or reward, except such as is allowed by special laws, is a common nuisance; and every person acting or aiding therein, or making or being interested in any such bet, stake or Racing of animals for a stake.

reward is guilty of a misdemeanor; and in addition to the penalty prescribed therefor he forfeits all title or interest in any animal used with his privity in such race or trial of speed, and in any sum of money or other property betted or staked upon the result thereof.

See *Rep. Pol. Code*, §§ 775, 777, 778.

CHAPTER X.

PAWNBROKERS.

Pawnbroking without a license.

§ 401. Every person who carries on the business of a pawnbroker, by receiving goods in pledge for loans at any rate of interest above that allowed by law, except by authority of a license from a municipal corporation empowered to grant licenses to pawnbrokers, is guilty of a misdemeanor.

See 1 *Rev. Stat.*, 711, § 9.

Refusal to exhibit stolen goods to owner.

§ 402. Every pawnbroker or person carrying on the business of a pawnbroker, and every junk dealer, who having received any goods which have been embezzled or stolen, refuses or omits to exhibit them, upon demand, during the usual business hours, to the owner of said goods or his agent authorized to demand an inspection thereof, is guilty of a misdemeanor.

Selling before time to redeem has expired and refusing to disclose particulars of sale.

§ 403. Every pawnbroker who sells any article received by him in pledge, before the time to redeem the same has expired, and every pawnbroker who willfully refuses to disclose the name of the purchaser and the price received by him for any article received by him in pledge, and subsequently sold, is guilty of a misdemeanor.

TITLE XI.

OF OTHER INJURIES TO PERSONS.

§ 404. Every physician, who, being in a state of intoxication, administers any poison, drug or medicine, or does any other act as such physician, to another person, by which the life of such other is endangered, is guilty of misdemeanor. Acts of intoxicated physicians.

See 2 *Rev. Stat.*, 694, § 22; and *supra*, § 257.

§ 405. Every person who willfully mingles any poison with any food, drink or medicine, with intent that the same shall be taken by any human being to his injury, and every person who willfully poisons any spring, well or reservoir of water, is punishable by imprisonment in a state prison not exceeding ten years, or in a county jail not exceeding one year, or Willfully poisoning food, &c.

by a fine not exceeding five hundred dollars, or by both such fine and imprisonment.

2 *Rev. Stat.*, 666, § 38.

Overloading passenger vessel.

§ 406. Every person navigating any vessel for gain, who willfully or negligently receives so many passengers or such a quantity of other lading on board such vessel, that by means thereof such vessel sinks or is overset or injured, and thereby the life of any human being is endangered, is guilty of a misdemeanor.

See 2 *Rev Stat.*, 694, § 24.

Mismanagement of steamboats

§ 407. Every captain or other person having charge of any steamboat used for the conveyance of passengers, or of the boilers and engines thereof, who, from ignorance or gross neglect, or for the purpose of excelling any other boat in speed, creates or allows to be created such an undue quantity of steam as to burst or break the boiler or other apparatus in which it shall be generated, or any apparatus or machinery connected therewith, by which bursting or breaking human life is endangered, is guilty of a misdemeanor.

Embodies the provision of 2 *Rev. Stat.*, 694, § 25; modified in expression to correspond with the analogous provision of § 255 of this Code.

Mismanagement of steam boilers.

§ 408. Every engineer or other person having charge of any steam boiler, steam engine, or other apparatus for generating or employing steam, employed in any manufactory, railway or other mechanical works, who, willfully or from ignorance or gross neglect, creates or allows to be created such an undue quantity of steam as to burst or break the boiler or engine or apparatus, or cause any other accident whereby human life is endangered, is guilty of a misdemeanor.

Compare section 256 of this Code.

Fictitious copartnership names.

§ 409. Every person transacting any business in the name of a person as a partner who is not interested in his firm, or transacting business under a firm name in which the designation "and company" or "& Co." is used without representing an actual partner, except in the cases in which the continued use of a copartnership name is authorized by law, is guilty of a misdemeanor.

Laws of 1833, ch. 281. Compare, also, *Laws of* 1849, ch. 347; *Laws of* 1854, ch. 400; *Laws of* 1863, ch. 144; which regulate the continued use of copartnership names.

§ 410. Every person who willfully forges, counterfeits or procures to be forged or counterfeited any trade mark usually affixed by any person to any goods of such person, with intent to pass off any goods to which such forged or counterfeit trade mark is affixed or intended to be affixed, as the goods of such person, is guilty of a misdemeanor. Counterfeiting trade marks

Founded upon *Laws of* 1862, ch. 306, § 1, the phraseology being rendered more concise, and the punishment being reduced from an imprisonment not less than six months and not more than twelve or a fine not exceeding five thousand dollars to that of a misdemeanor.

The subject of counterfeiting trade marks, including the kindred topic of refilling and selling stamped mineral water bottles, has very recently received the careful attention of the Legislature. In 1845 an act was passed (*Laws of* 1845, ch. 279,) punishing the forgery of stamps or labels. In 1850, the provisions of this act were somewhat enlarged. In 1862, both these acts were repealed; and a more comprehensive and stringent statute was passed (*Laws of* 1862, ch. 306), which, with an amendment enacted in 1863 (*Laws of* 1863, ch. 209), giving the party aggrieved a civil remedy, in addition to the fine and imprisonment prescribed by the act of 1862, embodies the law existing at the present time, upon the general subject of counterfeiting trade marks. The kindred offense of selling mineral waters, water-bottles, and others bearing the stamp of a particular manufacturer was made punishable by *Laws of* 1847, ch. 207; which was amended by *Laws of* 1860, ch. 117.

In the sections in the text upon these subjects the Commissioners have embodied the provisions of these statutes, omitting some provisions not within the scope of the Penal Code, and retrenching the phraseology and modifying the measure of punishment to correspond with the forms of expression used and penalties prescribed throughout the Code. They have also adopted some of the provisions of a very stringent English statute on this subject, passed in 1862; the 25th & 26th *Vict.*, ch. 88.

Keeping dies, &c., with intent to counterfeit trade marks.

§ 411. Every person who, with intent to defraud, has in his possession any die, plate or brand, or any imitation of the trade mark of any person, for the purpose of making any counterfeit or imitation of any description whatever of such trade mark, or of selling the same when made, or of affixing the same to any goods, and selling or offering the same for sale or disposal as the original goods of any other person; and every person who so uses or sells the same, or who fraudulently uses the genuine trade mark of another with intent to sell or offer for sale or disposal any goods not the goods of the person to whom such trade mark properly belongs, as genuine and original, is guilty of a misdemeanor.

Founded on *Laws of* 1862, ch. 306, § 2.

Selling goods which bear counterfeit trade marks.

§ 412. Every person who sells or keeps for sale any goods upon or to which any counterfeited trade mark has been affixed, intended to represent such goods as the genuine goods of another, knowing the same to be counterfeited, is guilty of a misdemeanor.

Founded upon *Laws of* 1862, ch. 306, § 3; as amended *Laws of* 1863, ch. 209, § 1.

Colorable imitations of trade marks.

§ 413. Every person who, with intent to defraud, affixes or causes to be affixed to any goods, any description of label, stamp, brand, imprint, printed wrapper, label or mark, which designates such goods by any word or token which is wholly or so far the same as to deceive or be calculated to deceive the eye or the ear, as the word or any of the words or tokens used by any other person as his trade mark, and every person who knowingly sells, or keeps or offers for sale any goods, or any box, bale, barrel, bottle, case, cask, wrapper, or other package, with any such label, stamp, brand, imprint, printed wrapper, ticket or mark, affixed to it, in case the person affixing such mark, or selling, or keeping, or offering for sale such goods, or box, bale, barrel, bottle, case, cask, wrapper, or other package, was not the first to employ such words as his trade mark, is guilty of a misdemeanor; and in addition to the punishment prescribed therefor is also liable to the party aggrieved in the penal sum of one hundred dollars for each and every offense, to be recovered by him in a civil action.

Laws of 1862, ch. 306, § 4; as amended *Laws of* 1863, ch. 209, § 2.

§ 414. The word "trade mark," as used in the sections preceding, includes every description of word, letter, device, emblem, stamp, imprint, brand, printed ticket, label or wrapper, usually affixed by any mechanic, manufacturer, druggist, merchant or tradesman, to denote any goods to be goods imported, manufactured, produced, compounded or sold by him; other than any name, word or expression generally denoting any goods to be of some particular class or description. "Trade mark" defined.

See *Stat.*, 25 and 26 *Vict.*, ch. 88, § 1.

§ 415. The word "goods," as used in the sections preceding, includes every kind of goods, wares, merchandise, compound or preparation, which may be lawfully kept or offered for sale. "Goods" defined.

§ 416. The offense of affixing a false trade mark to goods is equally complete within the meaning of sections 410, 412, and 413, whether such mark is affixed to the goods themselves, or to any box, bale, barrel, bottle, case, cask, wrapper, or other package or vessel, or any cover or stopper thereof, in which such goods are put up. "Affixing" defined.

See *Stat.*, 25 and 26 *Vict.*, ch. 88.

§ 417. Whenever any person engaged in manufacturing, bottling, or selling in bottles, soda, mineral waters, porter, ale, cider or small beer, has filed and published, in the manner authorized by law, a description of a name, mark, or label, usually stamped by him in the bottles containing such beverage, every other person who, without the written consent of such manufacturer or dealer, refills with any Refilling or selling stamped mineral water bottles, &c.

beverage, whether genuine or otherwise, with intent to sell the same, any bottles stamped with such name, mark, or label; and every person who sells, disposes of, purchases or traffics in such bottles, is liable to a penalty of fifty cents for each and every bottle so filled, sold, bought, disposed of, or trafficked in, for the first offense, and five dollars for each and every bottle so filled, sold, bought, disposed of, or trafficked in, for every subsequent offense.

Laws of 1860, ch. 117, § 1; modified to correct the defect pointed out in Mullins *v.* People (24 *N. Y.*, 398; S. C., 23 *How. Pr.*, 289); that the keeping of bottles secreted upon the premises of the defendant subjects him, under the language of the act of 1860, to a search warrant to discover them, but not to any criminal penalty.

Keeping such bottles with intent to refill or sell them.

§ 418. Every person who keeps any bottles such as are designated in the last section, without the written consent of the manufacturer so to do, unless it appears that they were not kept with intent to refill or use or sell them in violation of the last section, is liable to the penalty therein prescribed.

Search for bottles kept in violation of law, authorized.

§ 419. Whenever any manufacturer or dealer designated by section 417, or his agent, shall make oath or affirmation before any magistrate that he has reason to believe, and does believe, that any of his bottles stamped and registered as mentioned in said section are being unlawfully used by any person or persons selling or manufacturing mineral water or other beverages, or that any junk dealer, or vender of bottles, has any of such bottles secreted in any place, such magistrate shall thereupon issue a search warrant to discover and obtain the same under the provisions of the Code of Criminal Procedure, which are hereby declared to fully relate to the purposes of this chapter; and the magistrate may summarily bring or cause to be brought before him the person in whose possession the bottles are found, to examine into the circumstances of his possession, and if such magistrate, on summary examination, finds that such person has been guilty of a violation of section 417, such magistrate shall proceed to impose the fine therein prescribed, and, if the same be not paid, to commit such person to prison for a term not exceeding fifteen days.

See *Laws of* 1860, ch. 117, § 2.

§ 420. Every person who defaces or obliterates the marks upon wrecked property, or in any manner disguises the appearance thereof with intent to prevent the owner from discovering its identity, or who destroys or suppresses any invoice, bill of lading or other document tending to show the ownership, is guilty of a misdemeanor. Defacing marks upon wrecked property.

Rep. Pol. Code, § 305.

§ 421. Every person who cuts out, alters or defaces any mark made upon any log or lumber, whether such mark be recorded or not, or puts a false mark upon any log or lumber floating in any of the waters of this state or lying upon land, is guilty of a misdemeanor. Defacing marks upon logs or lumber.

Rep. Pol. Code, § 295.

§ 422. Every officer who, without authority of law detains any wrecked property or the proceeds thereof, after the salvage and expenses chargeable thereon have been paid or offered to him, or who is guilty of any fraud, embezzlement or extortion in the discharge of his duties, or who violates any provision of Article IV of Chapter I of Title III of the Political Code, is guilty of a misdemeanor. Officer unlawfully detaining wrecked property

Rep. Pol. Code, § 303.

§ 423. Every member of a limited partnership who is guilty of any fraud in the affairs of the partnership, is guilty of a misdemeanor. Fraud in affairs of limited partnership

See 1 *Rev. Stat.*, 766, § 19.

§ 424. Every minister, or magistrate who solemnizes any marriage where either of the parties is Solemnizing unlawful marriages.

known to him to be within the age of legal consent, or to be an idiot or an insane person, or any marriage to which within his knowledge any legal impediment exists, is guilty of a misdemeanor.

Corresponds with 2 *Rev. Stat.*, 140, § 12; substituting "insane person" for "lunatic."

Unlawful confinement of idiots, insane persons, &c.

§ 425. Every person who confines any idiot, lunatic or insane person in any other manner or in any other place than is authorized or allowed by law, and every person guilty of any harsh, cruel or unkind treatment of, or any neglect of duty towards any idiot, lunatic or insane person under confinement, whether lawfully or not, is guilty of a misdemeanor.

See 1 *Rev. Stat.*, 625, § 11.

Taking usury.

§ 426. Every person who directly or indirectly receives any interest, discount, or consideration upon the loan or forbearance of any money, goods or things in action, greater than is allowed by law, is guilty of a misdemeanor.

See 1 *Rev. Stat.*, 773, § 15.

Reconfining persons discharged upon writ of deliverance.

§ 427. Every person who either solely or as a member of a court, in the execution of a judgment, order or process, knowingly recommits, imprisons or restrains of his liberty, for the same cause, any person who has been discharged from imprisonment upon a writ of deliverance, is guilty of a misdemeanor; and in addition to the punishment prescribed therefor, he forfeits to the party aggrieved, one thousand dollars to be recovered in a civil action.

Corresponds with *Rep. Code Civ. Pro.*, § 1339.

Concealing persons entitled to writ of deliverance.

§ 428. Every person having in his custody or power or under his restraint a party who, by the provisions of Chapter V of Title II of Part III of the Code of Civil Procedure, would be entitled to a writ of deliverance or for whose relief a writ of deliverance has been issued, who, with intent to elude the service of such writ, or to avoid the effect thereof, transfers the party to the custody, or places him under the power or control of another, or conceals or changes the place of his confinement, or who without lawful excuse refuses to produce him, is guilty of a misdemeanor.

Rep. Code Civ. Pro. § 1340.

The provision of *Ibid.*, § 1341, is substantially covered by section 27 of this Code. The provision of 2 *Rev. Stat.*, 149, § 7, is omitted, as being merged in the preceding provisions.

§ 429. Every person, and every agent or officer of any corporation, carrying on business as an innkeeper, or as a common carrier of passengers, who refuses, without just cause or excuse, to receive and entertain any guest, or to receive and carry any passenger, is guilty of a misdemeanor. **Innkeepers and carriers refusing to receive guests and passengers.**

TITLE XII.

OF CRIMES AGAINST THE PUBLIC HEALTH AND SAFETY.

"Public nuisance" defined.

§ 430. A public nuisance is a crime against the order and economy of the state; and consists in unlawfully doing any act or omitting to perform any duty which act or omission either:

1. Annoys, injures or endangers the comfort, repose, health or safety of any considerable number of persons; or,

2. Offends public decency; or,

3. Unlawfully interferes with, obstructs, or tends to obstruct, or renders dangerous for passage, any lake, or any navigable river, bay, stream, canal or basin, or any public park, square, street or highway; or,

4. In any way renders any considerable number of persons insecure in life, or the use of property.

Suggested as more appropriate for this Code than the definitions given in the Draft Civil Code, sections 1571, 1572, which are as follows:

"§ 1571. That is a nuisance which wrongfully causes loss, harm, annoyance, or great apprehension of danger, by:

1. Creating public alarm;
2. Disturbing public order;
3. Endangering the public health;
4. Offending public decency;
5. Obstructing a right of way;
6. Disgusting the senses; or,
7. In any way rendering life or the use of property uncomfortable."

"§ 1572. A public nuisance is one which affects equally the rights of the whole community or neighborhood, although the extent of the damage may be unequal."

The reasons for the change are chiefly: 1. That, while the definition in the Civil Code properly embraced both private and public nuisances, it is unnecessary for the purposes of the Penal Code to include private nuisances in the definition; and, 2. That the specific prohibition in other chapters of the Code, of some acts which have formerly been classed under the general term "public nuisance," has rendered it practicable to restrict the definition of that term, in this Code, to some extent.

The following are the leading decisions which support the several clauses of the definition in the text.

Subd. 1. Rex *v.* Wigg, *Salk.*, 460; 2 *Ld. Raym.*, 1163; Rex *v.* Pierce, 2 *Show.*, 327; Rex *v.* Wharton, 12 *Mod.*, 510; Rex *v.* Smith, 1 *Stra.*, 704; Rex *v.* Moore, 3 *Barn. & Ad.*, 184; Rex *v.* White, 1 *Burr.*, 333; Rex *v.* Davey, 5 *Esp.*, 217; Rex *v.* Lloyd, 4 *Id.*, 200; Rex *v.* Neil, 2 *Carr. & P.*, 485; Putnam *v.* Payne, 13 *Johns.*, 312; Hinckley *v.* Emerson, 4 *Cow.*, 351; State *v.* Baldwin, 1 *Dev. & B.*, 195; Commonwealth *v.* Brown, 13 *Metc.*, 365; Reg. *v.* Lester, 3 *Jur.* (*N. S.*), 570; Douglass *v.* State, 4 *Wisc.*, 387.

Subd. 2. State *v.* Bertheol, 6 *Blackf.*, 474; State *v.* Purse, 4 *McCord*, 472; Crane *v.* State, 3 *Ind.*, 193.

Subd. 3. Hall's case, *Vent.*, 196; 1 *Mod.*, 76; 2 *Keb.*, 846; Rex *v.* Leach, 6 *Mod.*, 145; *Id.*, 155; Rex *v.* Grosvenor, 2 *Stark.*, 511; Rex *v.* Hollis, *Id.*, 536; Rex *v.* Webb, 1 *Ld. Raym.*, 737; Rex *v.* Russell, 6 *Barn. & C.*, 566; Rex *v.* Trafford, 1 *Barn. & Ad.*, 874; Rex *v.* Watts, 2 *Esp.*, 675; Rex *v.* Tindall, 1 *Nev. & P.*, 719; 6 *Ad. & E.*, 143; *W. W. & D.*, 316; Rex *v.* Ward, 4 *Ad. & E.*, 384; 1 *Har. & W.*, 703; Rex *v.* Pease, 4 *Barn. & Ad.*,

30; Rex *v.* Morris, 1 *Barn. & Ad.*, 441; Reg. *v.* Botfield, 1 *Carr. & M.*, 151; Rex *v.* Smith, 4 *Esp.*, 109; Rex *v.* Canfield, 6 *Esp.*, 136; Rex *v.* Sarmon, 1 *Burr.*, 516; Rex *v.* Cross, 3 *Camp.*, 224; Rex *v.* Russel, 6 *East.*, 427; 2 *Smith*, 424; Rex *v.* Jones, 3 *Camp.*, 230; Rex *v.* Carlile, 6 *Carr. & P.*, 637; Rex *v.* Gregory, 2 *Nev. & M.*, 478; 5 *Barn. & Ad.*, 555; Reg. *v.* Scott, 2 *Gale & D.*, 729; 3 *Ad. & E. (N. S.)*, 543; 3 *Railw. Cas.*, 187; Reg. *v.* Betts, 22 *Eng. L. & Eq.*, 240; People *v.* Lawson, 17 *Johns.*, 276; People *v.* Cunningham, 1 *Den.*, 524; Renwick *v.* Morris, 7 *Hill*, 575; Harlon *v.* Humiston, 6 *Cow.*, 189; Lansing *v.* Smith, 8 *Id.*, 146; Dygert *v.* Schenck, 23 *Wend.*, 446; Drake *v.* Rogers, 3 *Hill*, 604; People *v.* Lambier, 5 *Den.*, 9; Moshier *v.* Utica & Schenectady R. R. Co., 8 *Barb.*, 427; Hart *v.* Mayor, &c., of Albany, 9 *Wend.*, 571; Hecker *v.* N. Y. Balance Dry Dock Co., 13 *How. Pr.*, 549; and see Same *v.* Same, 24 *Barb.*, 215; Peckham *v.* Henderson, 27 *Barb.*, 207; People *v.* Vanderbilt, 24 *How. Pr.*, 301; Wetmore *v.* Atlantic White Lead Co., 37 *Barb.*, 70; Commonwealth *v.* Wright, *Thach. Cr. Cas.*, 211; Commonwealth *v.* Gowen, 7 *Mass.*, 378; State *v.* Spainhour, 2 *Dev. & B.*, 547; Commonwealth *v.* Tucker, 2 *Pick.*, 44; Commonwealth *v.* Webb, 6 *Rand.*, 726; State *v.* Godfrey, 3 *Fairf.*, 361; Commonwealth *v.* Ruggles, 10 *Mass.*, 391; State *v.* Mobley, 1 *McMullan*, 44; State *v.* Brown, 16 *Conn.*, 54; Elkins *v.* State, 2 *Humph.*, 543; Simpson *v.* State, 10 *Yerg.*, 525; State *v.* Miskimmons, 2 *Carter*, 440; Commonwealth *v.* Rush, 14 *Penn. St.*, 186; State *v.* Morris & Essex R. R. Co., 3 *Zabr.*, 360; Commonwealth *v.* Bowman, 3 *Barr*, 202; Commonwealth *v.* Milliman, 13 *Serg. & R.*, 403; Commonwealth *v.* Chapin, 5 *Pick.*, 199; State *v.* Hunter, 5 *Ired.*, 369; State *v.* Commissioners, 3 *Hill (So. Car.)*, 149; State *v.* Yarrell, 12 *Ired.*, 130; State *v.* Duncan, 1 *McCord*, 404; State *v.* Thompson, 2 *Strobh.*, 12; Commonwealth *v.* Elburger, 1 *Whart.*, 469; State *v.* Atkinson, 24 *Vt.*, 448; Newark Plankroad Co. *v.* Elmer, 1 *Strockt.*, 754; Attorney General *v.* Hudson River R. R. Co., *Id.*, 526; Works *v.* Junction R. R. Co., 5 *McLean*, 425; State *v.* Phipps, 4 *Ind.*, 515; State *v.* Freeport, 43 *Me.*, 193.

Subd. 4. Rex *v.* White, *Burr.*, 333; Rex *v.* Smith, *Stra.*, 703; White *v.* Cohen, 19 *Eng. L. & Eq.*, 146; Catlin *v.* Valentine, 9 *Paige*, 575; Brady *v.* Weeks, 3 *Barb.*, 157; Prescott's case, 2 *City Hall Rec.*, 161; Prout's case, 4 *Id.*, 481; Lynch's case, 6 *Id.*, 61; People *v.* Townsend, 3 *Hill*, 479; Hackney *v.* State, 8 *Ind.*, 494; State *v.* Wetherall, 5 *Harring.*, 487; 3 *Blackst. Comm.*, 216; *Bell's Sc. Law Dict.*, tit. *Nuisance.*

The following are intended to be excluded from the definition, because they have been decided not to be nuisances, upon grounds deemed to be sufficient by the Commissioners:

Exercising banking privileges without authority. Attorney General *v.* Bank of Niagara, *Hopk.*, 354.

An immigrant depot, if not kept in an improper manner. Phœnix *v.* Commissioners of Emigration, 1 *Abbott's Pr.*, 466.

A person sick of a contagious disease, if not needlessly exposed so as to endanger the public. Boom *v.* City of Utica, 2 *Barb.*, 104.

Several offenses which in this Code are made the subject of specific provisions have been held indictable under the common law definition of nuisance.

See as to throwing gas tar into public streams. Rex *v.* Meadley, 6 *Carr. & P.*, 292.

As to obstructing railways. Reg. *v.* Holroyd, 2 *M. & Rob.*, 339.

As to keeping gunpowder. Rex *v.* Taylor, 2 *Stra.*, 1167• People *v.* Sands, 1 *Johns.*, 78; Myers *v.* Malcolm, 6 *Hill* 292.

As to establishments for gaming and other useless sports. Tanner *v.* Trustees of Albion, 5 *Hill*, 121; Updike *v.* Campbell, 4 *E. D. Smith*, 570; State *v.* Doon, *R. M. Charlt.*, 1; State *v.* Haines, 30 *Maine*, 65.

As to other disorderly houses. Smith *v.* Commonwealth, 6 *B. Monr.*, 21; Bloomhuff *v.* State, 8 *Blackf.*, 205; State *v.* Bailey, 1 *Fost.*, 343; Rex *v.* Williams, 1 *Salk.*, 384; Hackney *v.* State, 8 *Ind.*, 494.

As to dangerous driving through public streets. U. S. *v.* Hart, *Pet. C. C.*, 390.

As to exposure of the person. Reg. *v.* Webb, 1 *Den. C. C. R.*, 338; 13 *Jur.*, 42; 18 *Law J.* (*M. C.*), 39.

As to digging up or injuring highways. Reg. *v.* Sheffield Gas Consumers' Co., 22 *Eng. L. & Eq.*, 200; State *v.* Peckhard, 5 *Harring.*, 500.

As to neglect to keep ferry in repair. State *v.* Willis, *Busb.*, 223.

As to profane swearing. State *v.* Graham, 3 Sneed., 134.

Consult, also, upon other branches of the criminal law relative to what are nuisances, the following: Rex *v.* Wigg, 1 *Ld. Raym.*, 737; Rex *v.* Village of Hornsey, 1 *Ro.*, 406; Anon., 12 *Mod.*, 342; Rex *v.* Record, 2 *Show.*, 216; Rex *v.* Dunraven, *W. W. & D.*, 577; Rex *v.* Cross, 2 *Carr. & P.*, 483; Rex *v.* Neville, *Peake*, 93; Rex *v.* Watts, *Mood. & M.*, 281; Wetmore *v.* Tracy, 14 *Wend.*, 250; Harris *v.* Thompson, 9 Barb., 350; Plant *v.* Long Island R. R. Co., 10 *Id.*, 26; Leigh *v.* Westervelt, 2 *Duer*, 618; Williams *v.* N. Y. Central R. R. Co., 18 *Barb.*, 222; Lynch's case, 6 *City Hall Rec.*, 61; Dygert *v.* Schenck, 23 *Wend.*, 446; People *v.* Cunningham, 1 *Den.*, 424; Renwick *v.* Morris, 7 *Hill*, 575; Peckham *v.* Henderson,

27 *Barb.*, 207; State *v.* Commissioners, *Riley*, 146; Ellis *v.* State, 7 *Blackf.*, 534; Works *v.* Junction Railroad, 5 *McLean*, 425; Douglass *v.* State, 4 *Wisc.*, 387; Commonwealth *v.* Upton, 6 *Gray*, 473.

Unequal damage.

§ 431. An act which affects a considerable number of persons, in either of the ways specified in the last section, is not less a nuisance because the extent of the damage is unequal.

Embodies a part of section 1572 of the Draft Civil Code; the words "a considerable number of persons" being substituted for "the whole community or neighborhood," to avoid uncertainty. It may be doubtful in some cases, whether the persons affected by an obstruction in a navigable stream, for instance, form what can be called a neighborhood.

Maintaining a nuisance a misdemeanor.

§ 432. Every person who maintains or commits any public nuisance, the punishment for which is not otherwise prescribed, or who willfully omits to perform any legal duty relating to the removal of a public nuisance, is guilty of a misdemeanor.

Keeping gunpowder unlawfully.

§ 433. Every person who makes or keeps gunpowder or saltpeter within any city or village, and every person who carries gunpowder through the streets thereof, in any quantity or manner such as is prohibited by law, or by any ordinance of such city or village, is guilty of a misdemeanor.

See *Laws of* 1846, ch. 291, § 19. It is not intended to confine this provision to cases in which an explosion occurs. Keeping powder in violation of law should be punishable, irrespective of any mischief in the particular case.

Throwing gas tar into public waters.

§ 434. Every person who throws or deposits any gas tar, or refuse of any gas house or factory, or any offal, refuse, or other noxious or poisonous ingredients, into any public waters, river or stream, or into any sewer or stream running or emptying into any such public waters, river or stream, is guilty of a misdemeanor.

Founded upon *Laws of* 1845, ch. 201. That act applies only to the counties of New York, Kings and Queens.

In view of the extension of gas manufactories to almost all towns of considerable size throughout the state, the Commissioners think the provision should be made general.

§ 435. Every master of a vessel subject to quarantine or visitation by the health officer, arriving in the port of New York, who refuses or omits, either: Violations of quarantine laws by master of vessel.

1. To proceed with and anchor his vessel at the place assigned for quarantine, at the time of his arrival; or,

2. To submit his vessel, cargo and passengers, to the examination of the health officer, and to furnish all necessary information to enable that officer to determine to what length of quarantine and other regulations they ought respectively to be subject; or,

3. To remain with his vessel at quarantine during the period assigned for her quarantine, and while at quarantine to comply with the directions and regulations prescribed by law, and with such as any of the officers of health, by virtue of the authority given to them by law, shall prescribe in relation to his vessel, his cargo, himself, his passengers or crew, is punishable by imprisonment in a county jail not exceeding one year, or by a fine not exceeding two thousand dollars, or both.

Laws of 1856, ch. 147, § 28.

§ 436. Every master of a vessel hailed by a pilot who, either: Giving false information relative to vessel, or permitting persons to land before visit of health officers.

1. Gives false information to such pilot, relative to the condition of his vessel, crew or passengers, or the health of the place or places from whence he came, or refuses to give such information as shall be lawfully required; or,

2. Lands any person from his vessel, or permits any person, except a pilot, to come on board of his vessel, or unlades or tranships any portion of his cargo before his vessel has been visited and examined by the health officers; or,

3. Approaches with his vessel nearer the city of New York than the place of quarantine to which he may be directed, is punishable by imprisonment in a county jail not exceeding one year, or by a fine not exceeding two thousand dollars, or both.

Laws of 1856, ch. 147, § 29.

Landing from vessel before visit of health officers.

§ 437. Every person who, being on board any vessel at the time of her arrival at the port of New York, lands from such vessel, or unlades, or tranships, or assists in unlading or transhipping any portion of her cargo, before such vessel has been visited and examined by the health officers, is punishable by imprisonment in a county jail not exceeding one year, or by a fine not exceeding two thousand dollars, or both.

See *Laws of* 1856, ch. 147, § 29.

Going on board vessel at quarantine grounds, or entering quarantine grounds without leave.

§ 438. Every person who goes on board of or has any communication, intercourse or dealing with any vessel at quarantine, or with any of the crew or passengers of such vessel, without the permission of the health officer, and every person who, without such authority enters the quarantine grounds or anchorage, is punishable by imprisonment in a county jail not exceeding one year, or by a fine not exceeding two thousand dollars, or both; and in addition thereto he may be detained at quarantine so long as the health officers shall direct, not exceeding twenty days. And in case such person shall be taken sick of any infectious, contagious or pestilential disease, during such twenty days, he may be detained for such further time at the marine hospital, as the health officer shall direct.

Laws of 1856, ch. 147, § 32.

Violating quarantine regulations

§ 439. Every person who, having been lawfully ordered by any health officer to be detained in quarantine, and not having been discharged, leaves the quarantine grounds or anchorage, or willfully violates any quarantine law or regulation, is guilty of a misdemeanor.

See *Laws of* 1856, ch. 147, § 13.

§ 440. Every person who willfully opposes or obstructs any health officer or physician charged with the enforcement of the health laws, in performing any legal duty, is guilty of misdemeanor.

Obstructing health officer in performance of his duty.

See *Laws of* 1856, ch. 147, § 31.

§ 441. Every person who willfully violates any provision of the health laws, the punishment for violating which is not otherwise prescribed by those laws, or by this Code; and every person who willfully violates or refuses or omits to comply with any lawful order, direction, prohibition or regulation prescribed by any board of health or health officer, or any regulation lawfully made or established by any public officer under authority of the health laws, is punishable by imprisonment in a county jail not exceeding one year, or by a fine not exceeding two thousand dollars, or both.

Willful violation of health laws.

See *Laws of* 1856, ch. 147, §§ 30, 31, 33; *Ibid.*, § 28, subd. 3.

§ 442. Every person not holding a license as pilot under Article V of Chap. I of Title III of the Political Code, or under the laws of the state of New Jersey, who pilots, or offers to pilot any vessel to or from the port of New York, by the way of Sandy Hook, except such as are exempt; and every person not being a Hellgate pilot, or one of the crew of the vessel who pilots or offers to pilot any vessel through Hellgate; and every master or person in command of any steam tug or tow boat who tows any vessel through Hellgate without having a licensed pilot on board, is guilty of misdemeanor.

Unlicensed piloting.

See *Rep. Pol. Code,* §§ 329, 345.

§ 443. The last section does not apply to vessels propelled wholly or in part by steam, owned or belonging to citizens of the United States, and licensed and engaged in the coasting trade.

Coasting steamers excepted.

See *Rep. Pol. Code,* § 329.

§ 444. Every person who not being a port-warden, assumes or undertakes to act as such, or undertakes the

Acting as portwarden without authority.

performance of any of the duties prescribed in Article VII of Chap. I of Title III of the Political Code, as pertaining to the office of port-warden; and every person who knowingly employs any other than the wardens for the performance of such duties; and every person who issues any certificate of a survey on vessels, materials or goods damaged, with the intent to avoid the provisions of that article, is guilty of a misdemeanor.

Rep. Pol. Code, § 355.

Apothecary omitting to label drugs, or labeling them wrongly, &c.

§ 445. Every apothecary, or druggist, and every person employed as clerk or salesman by any apothecary or druggist, or otherwise carrying on business as a dealer in drugs or medicines, who, in putting up any drugs or medicines, or making up any prescription, or filling any order for drugs or medicines, willfully, negligently or ignorantly omits to label the same, or puts any untrue label, stamp or other designation of contents upon any box, bottle or other package containing any drugs or medicines, or substitutes a different article for any article prescribed or ordered, or puts up a greater or less quantity of any article than that prescribed or ordered, or otherwise deviates from the terms of the prescription or order which he undertakes to follow, in consequence of which human life or health is endangered, is guilty of misdemeanor.

The frequent occurrence of accidents, involving, often, even the loss of human life, through mistakes in the putting up of prescriptions, render necessary some legislation to enforce care and caution on the part of dealers in drugs. The recent case of Thomas *v.* Winchester, 2 *Seld.*, 397, illustrates the danger arising in a different class of cases, also embraced by the section in the text; viz.: cases in which a manufacturer or dealer in drugs sends them into the market under an untrue label; in consequence of which, retail dealers are innocently led to supply dangerous articles without intending it. In that case it appeared that defendants, who were manufacturing druggists, sold to a dealer a jar labeled, "extract of dandelion;" but which really contained extract of belladonna. The dealer, relying on the label, sold the jar to a retailer; and the latter, in turn, used a part of the contents of the jar, supposing them to be extract of dandelion, in putting up a prescription in which that article was required. A dangerous illness was the result to the person taking the prescription. The court of appeals, in the case cited, held the manufacturers liable in damages to the injured person, notwithstanding the article had passed through intermediate sales, in reaching such person. This liability is founded upon the duty which the law imposes upon the dealer, to avoid acts dangerous to other persons; and not upon any contract, or privity between him and the consumer. Obvious considerations make it proper that this duty should be enforced by criminal penalty as by a remedy in damages.

§ 446. Every apothecary or druggist, and every person employed as clerk or salesman by any apothecary or druggist, or otherwise carrying on business as a dealer in drugs or medicines, who sells or gives any poison or poisonous substance, without first recording in a book to be kept for that purpose, the name and residence of the person receiving such poison, together with the kind and quantity of such poison received and the name and residence of some person known to such dealer, as a witness to the transaction, excepting upon the written order or prescription of some practising physician whose name is attached to such order, is guilty of a misdemeanor.

Apothecary selling poison without recording the sale.

Founded on *Laws of* 1860, ch. 442, § 1, as amended. *Laws of* 1862, ch. 273, § 1.

Restriction to dealers. The Commissioners have restricted the provision to sales or gifts made by persons dealing in drugs. The statute of 1860, is stringent enough to prohibit any individual from selling or giving an article of a poisonous character to another without opening a book and making a record of what is perhaps his only transaction of the kind for years. Such record cannot be expected to be kept, and serves no important purpose if kept, excepting when maintained in connection with an establishment of somewhat permanent and public character, carrying on a business of dealing in articles of the kind to be specified in the record.

Contents of the record. The act of 1860, as amended in 1862, requires the seller to record in a book "the name of the person receiving said poison, and his or her residence together with the name of some person as witness to such sale. The Commissioners have substitued for this language the words "the name and residence of the person receiving such poison, together with *the kind and quantity of such poison received*, and the name and residence of some person *known to such dealer*, as a witness to the *transaction*." Unless the kind and quantity of the poison sold are inserted, the record is a mere list of persons who have bought poisons, and lacks the very element necessary to render it of service in any subsequent legal investigation. If the purchaser may bring his own witness with him, fictitious names and residences of witnesses will be imposed upon the dealer whenever the purchaser wishes to evade the law. And the word "transaction" is more appropriate than "sale" because by the antecedent provisions gifts are to be recorded equally with sales.

The punishment. For the sake of greater harmony in the system of penalties, this offense has been declared a misdemeanor, simply, instead of retaining the special penalty of fifty dollars affixed by the present statutes.

Refusing to exhibit record.

§ 447. Every person whose duty it is by the last section to keep any book for recording the sale or gift of poisons, and who willfully refuses to permit any person to inspect said book upon reasonable demand made during ordinary business hours, is punishable by a fine not exceeding fifty dollars.

See *Laws of* 1860, ch. 442, § 1, as amended by *Laws of* 1862, ch. 273, § 1.

Selling poison without label.

§ 448. Every person who sells, gives or disposes of any poison or poisonous substance, except upon the order or prescription of a regularly authorized practising physician, without attaching to the vial, box or parcel containing such poisonous substance, a label with the name and residence of such person, the word "poison" and the name of such poison all written or printed thereon in plain and legible characters, is guilty of a misdemeanor.

Laws of 1860, ch. 442, § 2. The reasons which influenced the commissioners to recommend that the provision requiring a record of transactions in poisons be restricted to the case of persons habitually dealing in kindred articles, (see note to section 446 *supra*) do not apply in all their force to the provision requiring the package to be labeled. But they do forbid preserving the exact provision of the present statute, which requires that the word "poison" be *printed* in *red ink;* while the particular name of the poison may be printed or written at the dealer's option. Unless the furnishing of such articles as laudanum, corrosive sublimate, and the stronger acids by one neighbor to another, upon a casual necessity for their use is to be absolutely prevented, the requirement of a printed label will be inapplicable in a variety of cases arising under the statute. The Commissioners have thought it necessary, therefore, either to restrict this section as they have that relating to the record book to the case of dealers, or else to modify it by recognizing a label wholly in manuscript as a compliance with the law. This conforms to our former statute. 2 *Rev. Stat.*, 694, § 23.

What are poisons. As the section enumerating the articles deemed poisonous, within the meaning of the act of 1860 (*Laws of* 1860, ch. 442, § 3), was deliberately repealed in 1862 (*Laws of* 1862, ch. 273, § 2), without any recognition of the propriety of a statutory enumeration, the Commissioners have not restored it.

Restriction as to locality. In view of the more guarded manner in which the provisions of sections 446 and 448 are expressed, they are deemed proper to be generally enforced throughout the state; therefore the provision of *Laws of* 1860, ch. 442, § 5, restricting the application of that act to incorporated cities and villages having a population of one thousand inhabitants and upwards, is omitted.

§ 449. Every person, who, in putting up or pressing any bundle or bale of hay for market, omits to mark or brand, in a legible manner, the initials of his name on some wood or metal securely attached to such bundle or bale of hay, is punishable by a fine of twenty-five dollars for each offense.

Omitting to mark name upon package of hay.

Laws of 1860, 155, §§ 1, 4.

§ 450. Every person, who, in putting up in any bag, bale, box, barrel or other package, any hops, cotton, hay or other goods usually sold in bags, bales, boxes, barrels or packages, by weight, puts in or conceals therein any thing whatever, for the purpose of increasing the weight of such bag, bale, box, barrel or package, is punishable by a fine of twenty-five dollars for each offense.

Putting extraneous substances in packages of goods usually sold by weight, with intent to increase weight.

See *Laws of* 1860, ch. 155, §§ 2, 4.

§ 451. Every person who adulterates or dilutes any article of food, drink, drug, medicine, strong, spiritu-

Adulterating food, drugs, liquors, &c.

ous or malt liquor, or wine, or any article useful in compounding either of them, whether one useful for mankind or for animals, with a fraudulent intent to offer the same, or cause or permit it to be offered for sale as unadulterated or undiluted; and every person who fraudulently sells, or keeps or offers for sale the same as unadulterated or undiluted, knowing it to have been adulterated or diluted, is guilty of a misdemeanor.

Disposing of tainted food, &c.

§ 452. Every person who knowingly sells, or keeps, or offers for sale or otherwise disposes of any article of food, drink, drug or medicine knowing that the same has become tainted, decayed, spoiled or otherwise unwholesome or unfit to be eaten or drank, with intent to permit the same to be eaten or drank by any person or animal, is guilty of a misdemeanor.

Making or keeping slung shot.

§ 453. Every person who manufactures or causes to be manufactured, or sells, or offers or keeps for sale, or gives or disposes of any instrument or weapon of the kind usually known as slung shot, or of any similar kind, is guilty of a misdemeanor.

See *Laws of* 1849, ch. 278, § 1.

Carrying upon the person, or using or attempting to use slung shot.

§ 454. Every person who carries upon his person, whether concealed or not, or uses or attempts to use against another, any instrument or weapon of the kind usually known as slung shot or of any similar kind, is guilty of felony.

See *Laws of* 1849, ch. 278, § 2. So much of this section as makes it felony to "be found in possession of" a slung shot is omitted because many cases of possession are covered by section 1 of that act; embodied in section 453, *supra*.

Carrying concealed weapons.

§ 455. Every person who carries concealed about his person any description of fire-arms, being loaded or partly loaded, or any sharp or dangerous weapon such as is usually employed in attack or defense of the person, is guilty of a misdemeanor.

Such a provision as the above does not infringe the provision of the United States constitution (Amendments art. 2,) which declares that the right of the people to keep and bear arms, shall not be infringed; inasmuch as it is a measure of police, prohibiting only a *particular mode* of carrying arms, which is found dangerous to the peace of society. State *v.* Zumel, 13 *La. Ann.*, 399.

§ 456. Every person who negligently sets fire to his own woods, or negligently suffers any fire upon his own land to extend beyond the limits thereof, is guilty of a misdemeanor. Negligence in respect to fires.

See *Rep. Pol. Code*, § 763.

§ 457. Every person who, having been lawfully ordered, as provided by section 764 of the Political Code, to repair to the place of a fire in the woods and assist in extinguishing it, omits without lawful excuse to comply with such order, is guilty of a misdemeanor. Refusing to assist in extinguishing fire in the woods.

§ 458. Every person who, at any burning of a building is guilty of any disobedience to lawful orders of any public officer or fireman, or of any resistance to or interference with the lawful efforts of any fireman or company of firemen, to extinguish the same, or of any disorderly conduct calculated to prevent the same from being extinguished, or who forbids, prevents or dissuades others from assisting to extinguish the same, is guilty of a misdemeanor. Obstructing attempts to extinguish fires.

§ 459. Every person who maintains any ferry for profit or hire upon any waters within this state, without authority of law, is punishable by a fine not exceeding twenty-five dollars for each time of crossing or running such ferry. Where such ferry is upon waters dividing two counties, the offender may be prosecuted in either. Maintaining ferry without authority of law.

Suggested as a substitute for *Rep. Pol. Code*, § 661.

§ 460. Every person who, having entered into a recognizance, as provided by section 659 of the Political Code, to keep and attend a ferry, violates the condition of such recognizance, is guilty of a misdemeanor. Violating condition of recognizance to keep a ferry

See *Rep. Pol. Code*, § 660.

Engineer omitting to ring bell or sound whistle when locomotive crosses highway.

§ 461. Every person in charge, as engineer, of a locomotive engine, who omits to cause a bell to ring or a steam whistle to sound at the distance of at least eighty rods from the place where the track crosses, on the same level, any traveled public way, is punishable by a fine not exceeding fifty dollars, or by imprisonment in the county jail not exceeding sixty days.

See *Rep. Pol. Code*, § 557.

Intoxication of engineers, conductors and drivers upon railroads.

§ 462. Every person who, while in charge, as engineer, of a locomotive engine or while acting as conductor or driver upon any railroad train or car, whether propelled by steam or drawn by horses, is intoxicated, is guilty of a misdemeanor.

Substituted for *Rep. Pol. Code*, § 588.

Violations of duty by officers, agents or servants of railroad companies.

§ 463. Every engineer, conductor, brakeman, switchtender or other officer, agent or servant of any railroad company, who is guilty of any willful violation or omission of his duty as such officer, agent or servant by which human life or safety is endangered, the punishment for which is not otherwise prescribed, is guilty of a misdemeanor.

Duty of guarding ice cuttings

§ 464. All persons and incorporated companies cutting ice in or upon any waters within the boundaries of this state, for the purpose of removing such ice for sale, shall surround the cuttings and openings made, with fences of bushes or other guards sufficient to warn all persons of such cuttings and openings.

See *Laws of* 1860, ch. 20, § 1.

How long such guards must be maintained.

§ 465. Such fences or guards must be erected at or before the time of commencing such cuttings or openings, and must be maintained until ice has again formed in such openings to the thickness of at least six inches.

Ibid.

Violation of duty to maintain guards around ice cuttings a misdemeanor.

§ 466. Every person who violates the provisions of the last two sections, is guilty of a misdemeanor.

Ibid., § 2.

The act of 1860, ch. 20, § , on which the three sections in the text are founded, applies only to ice cuttings in the waters of the Hudson river and the tide waters of the Rondout and Catskill creeks; and it requires the fence to be at least four feet high. The Commissioners deem the principle upon which the act is founded, one which should be extended to other waters than those specified in the act. In many localities, however, a less expensive fencing than the act referred to requires, would give ample protection to the public. The Commissioners have, therefore, defined the duty in general terms, leaving the sufficiency of guards erected in any particular locality to be judged when occasion arises.

§ 467. Every person who uses any net or weir or sets any pole or other fixture in any part of the Hudson river, except as permitted by section 266 of the Political Code, is guilty of a misdemeanor. *Using net or weir un lawfully in Hudson river.*

Rep. Pol. Code, § 266.

§ 468. Every person who willfully exposes himself or another, affected with any contagious or infectious disease, in any public place or thoroughfare, except in his necessary removal in a manner not dangerous to the public health, is guilty of a misdemeanor. *Exposing person infected with a contagious disease in a public place*

§ 469. Every person who willfully makes or publishes any false statement, spreads any false rumor, or employs any other false or fraudulent means or device, with intent to affect the market price of any kind of property, is guilty of a misdemeanor. *Frauds practised to affect the market price.*

§ 470. Every editor or proprietor of any newspaper who willfully publishes in such newspaper as true, any statement which he has not good reason to believe to be true, with intent to increase thereby the sales of copies of such paper, is guilty of a misdemeanor. *Publishing false statements in newspapers.*

§ 471. Every person guilty of secretly loitering about any building, with intent to overhear discourse therein, and to repeat or publish the same to vex or annoy or injure others, is guilty of a misdemeanor. *Eavesdropping.*

The common law definition of this offense, which is known as "eavesdropping," seems to have confined it to loitering about dwelling houses (2 *Bish. Cr. L.*, § 274; 1 *Russ. on Cr.*, 327; 4 *Blackst. Comm.*, 168). The reasons which render the act obnoxious to punishment when committed with reference to dwellings, apply, however, with nearly equal force, to buildings occupied for other purposes.

Racing upon highways.

§ 472. Every person driving any conveyance drawn by horses upon any public road or way, who causes or suffers his horses to run, with intent to pass another conveyance or to prevent such other from passing his own, is guilty of a misdemeanor.

Suggested as a substitute for *Rep. Pol. Code*, § 669.

TITLE XIII.

OF CRIMES AGAINST THE PUBLIC PEACE.

§ 473. Every person who, without authority of law, willfully disturbs or breaks up any assembly or meeting, not unlawful in its character, other than such as are mentioned in sections 55, 79, and 360 of this Code, is guilty of a misdemeanor. Disturbing lawful meetings.

The assemblies specified in the sections referred to are religious meetings, meetings of electors held for discussion of public questions, and funerals.

§ 474. Any use of force or violence, disturbing the public peace, or any threat to use such force or violence if accompanied by immediate power of execution, by three or more persons acting together and without authority of law, is riot. "Riot" defined.

Consult State *v.* Conolly, 3 *Rich.*, 337; State *v.* Snow, 6 *Shep.*, 346; Dougherty *v.* People, 4 *Scamm.*, 180; Rex *v.* Langford, 1 *Car. & M.*, 604; State *v.* Cole, 2 *McCord*, 117; State *v.* Brooks, 1 *Hill* (*So. Car.*), 361; State *v.* Brazil, 1 *Rice*, 258; 4 *Blackst. Comm.*, 146; 4 *Burn's Just.*, tit. *Riot*; *Bouv. Law Dict.*, *Id.*; 1 *Hawk. P. C.*, ch. 65, § 1; *Whart. Cr. L.*, 722; *Chitty's Cr. L.*, 274.

§ 475. Every person guilty of participating in any riot is punishable as follows: Punishment of riot.

1. If any murder, maiming, robbery, rape or arson, was committed in the course of such riot, such person is punishable in the same manner as a principal in such crime.

2. If the purpose of the riotous assembly was to resist the execution of any statute of this state or of the United States, or to obstruct any public officer of this state or of the United States in the performance of any legal duty, or in serving or executing any legal process, such person is punishable by imprisonment in a state prison not exceeding ten years and not less than two.

3. If such person carried, at the time of such riot, any species of fire-arms, or other deadly or dangerous weapon, or was disguised, he is punishable by imprisonment in a state prison not exceeding ten years and not less than two.

4. If such person directed, advised, encouraged, or solicited other persons, who participated in the riot, to acts of force or violence, he is punishable by imprisonment in a state prison for not less than three years.

5. In all other cases such person is punishable as for a misdemeanor.

Rout" defined.

§ 476. Whenever three or more persons, acting together, make any attempt or do any act towards the commission of an act which would be riot if actually committed, such assembly is a rout.

Unlawful assembly.

§ 477. Whenever three or more persons assemble with intent or with means and preparations to do an unlawful act which would be riot if actually committed, but do no act towards the commission thereof; or whenever such persons assemble without authority of law, and in such a manner as is adapted to disturb the public peace, or excite public alarm, such assembly is an unlawful assembly.

Consult upon the first branch of this section 4 *Blackst. Comm.*, 147; Rex *v.* Birt, 5 *Carr. & P.*, 154; Rex *v.* Heass, 2 *Salk.*, 594.

Upon the second, 1 *Hawk. P. C.*, ch. 65, § 9; 1 *Russ. Cr.*, 272; *Whart. Cr. L.*, 722; Rex *v.* Hunt, 1 *Russ. C. & M.*, 254; 3 *Cox Cr. Cas.*, 215; Reg. *v.* Vincent, 9 *Carr. & P.*, 91; Reg. *v.* Neale, 9 *Carr. & P.*, 431; Reg. *v.* Soley, 11 *Mod.*, 116; Gagarty *v.* Queen, 3 *Cox Cr. Cas.*, 306.

Assembly of persons disguised.

§ 478. Every assembly of three or more persons having their faces painted, discolored, colored or concealed, or being otherwise disguised in a manner adapted to prevent them from being identified, is an unlawful assembly.

Laws of 1845, ch. 3, § 6.

Punishment of rout and unlawful assembly

§ 479. Every person who participates in any rout or unlawful assembly, is guilty of a misdemeanor.

Allowing masquerades to be

§ 480. Every person being a proprietor, manager or keeper of any theater, circus, public garden, public hall or premises, or other place of public meeting, resort or amusement whatever, for admission to which any price or payment is demanded, who permits therein any masquerade, or masked ball, or any assemblage of persons masked, is guilty of a misdemeanor, punishable by imprisonment in a state prison not exceeding two years, or in a county jail not exceeding one year, or by a fine not exceeding five thousand dollars and not less than two thousand five hundred dollars, or by both such fine and imprisonment.

held in places of public resort.

Laws of 1829, ch. 270; as amended *Laws of* 1858, ch. 359.

§ 481. Every person remaining present at the place of any riot, rout or unlawful assembly, after the same has been lawfully warned to disperse, except public officers and persons assisting them in attempting to disperse the same, is guilty of a misdemeanor.

Remaining present at place of riot, &c., after warning to disperse.

§ 482. Where three or more persons assemble for a lawful purpose, and afterwards proceed to commit an act that would amount to riot if it had been the original purpose of the meeting, every person who does not retire when the change of purpose is made known, except public officers and persons assisting them in attempting to disperse the same, is guilty of a misdemeanor.

Remaining present at place of a meeting, originally lawful, after it has adopted an unlawful purpose.

§ 483. Every person present at any riot, and lawfully commanded to aid the magistrates or officers in arresting any rioter, who neglects or refuses to obey such command, is deemed one of the rioters, and punishable accordingly.

Refusing to obey a lawful command to assist in arresting rioter.

See *Rep. Code Cr. Pro.*, § 90.

§ 484. Every person who resists, or enters into a combination with any other person to resist the execution of any legal process, under circumstances not amounting to a riot, is punishable by imprisonment in a county jail not exceeding one year, or by a fine not exceeding one thousand dollars, or both.

Combinations to resist execution of process.

Laws of 1845, ch. 69, § 17.

Prize fights. § 485. Every person who engages in, instigates, encourages or promotes, any ring or prize fight, or any other premeditated fight or contention, whether as principal, aid, second, umpire, surgeon, or otherwise, although no death or personal injury ensues, is guilty of a misdemeanor.

Challenges to engage in prize fights. § 486. Every person who challenges another to engage in any such fight as is specified in the last section; every person who accepts any such challenge; every person who knowingly forwards, carries or delivers any such challenge; and every person who bets, stakes or wagers any money or property upon the result of any such fight, or who undertakes to hold any money or property so betted, staked or wagered, to be delivered to or for the benefit of the winner thereof, is guilty of a misdemeanor.

What is a challenge. § 487. Any words spoken or written, or any signs uttered or made to any person, expressing or implying, or intended to express or imply a desire, request, invitation or demand to engage in any fight, such as is mentioned in section 485, are deemed a challenge within the meaning of the last section.

Corresponds with § 298 of this Code.

Leaving the state to engage in prize fights. § 488. Every person who leaves this state with intent to elude any of the provisions of the last three sections, and to commit any act out of this state, such as is prohibited by them, and who does any act which would be punishable under these provisions if committed within this state, is punishable in the same manner as he would have been in case such act had been committed within this state.

Corresponds with § 301 of this Code.

Place of trial. § 489. Such person may be indicted and tried in any county within this state.

Corresponds with § 302 of this Code.

§ 490. It is the duty of all sheriffs, constables, policemen, and watchmen, who have reasonable grounds to believe that any offense specified in section 485 is about to be committed within their jurisdiction, to make complaint under the provisions of this act to some magistrate within their jurisdiction. Special duty of peace officers with respect to prize fights.

Laws of 1859, ch. 37, § 4.

§ 491. Every sheriff, constable, policeman or watchman, who willfully neglects the duty prescribed by the last section, is guilty of a misdemeanor; and in addition to the punishment prescribed therefor, he forfeits his office. Neglect of duty by peace officers a misdemeanor.

Laws of 1859, ch. 37, § 4.

§ 492. Every person guilty of using, or of procuring, encouraging or assisting another to use, any force or violence in entering upon or detaining any lands or other possessions of another, except in the cases and manner allowed by law, is guilty of misdemeanor. Forcible entry and detainer.

§ 493. Every person who has been removed from any lands by process of law, or who has removed from any lands pursuant to the lawful adjudication or direction of any court, tribunal or officer, and who afterwards, without authority of law, returns to settle or reside upon such lands, is guilty of a misdemeanor. Returning to take possession of lands after being removed by legal process.

Founded upon 1 *Rev. Stat.*, 206, § 54, but made more general.

§ 494. Every person who intrudes or squats upon any lot or piece of land within the bounds of any incorporated city or village, without license or authority from the owner thereof, or who erects or occupies thereon any hut, hovel, shanty or other structure whatever without such license or authority; and every person who places, erects, or occupies within the bounds of any street or avenue of such city or village, any hut, hovel, shanty, or other structure whatever, is guilty of a misdemeanor. Unlawful intrusions upon lands of another.

See *Laws of* 1857, ch. 396, § 1.

Discharging fire-arms in public places. § 495. Every person who willfully discharges any species of fire-arms, air-gun or other weapon, or throws any other missile in any public place, or in any place where there is any person to be endangered thereby, although no injury to any person shall ensue, is guilty of a misdemeanor.

Witness' privilege. § 496. No person shall be excused from giving any evidence upon any investigation or prosecution for any of the offenses specified in this chapter, upon the ground that such testimony or evidence might tend to convict him of a crime. But such answer or evidence shall not be received against him upon any criminal proceeding or prosecution.

See *Laws of* 1860, ch. 141. That act applies only to prosecutions for prize fighting; but the reasons which render it proper in connection with that offense apply equally in the case of other crimes committed by numbers acting in concert, such as are specified in this chapter.

TITLE XIV.

OF CRIMES AGAINST THE REVENUE AND PROPERTY OF THE STATE.

§ 497. Every public officer, and every deputy, or clerk of any such officer, and every other person receiving any moneys on behalf of, or for account of the people of this state, or of any department of the government of this state, or of any bureau or fund created by law, and in which the people of this state, are directly or indirectly interested, who either: Embezzlements and falsification of accounts by public officers.

1. Appropriates to his own use, or to the use of any person not entitled thereto, without authority of law, any money received by him as such officer, clerk or deputy, or otherwise, on behalf of the people of this state or in which they are interested; or,

2. Knowingly keeps any false account or makes any false entry or erasure in any account of or relating to any moneys so received by him, on behalf of the people of this state, or in which they are interested; or,

3. Fraudulently alters, falsifies, conceals, destroys or obliterates any such account; or,

4. Willfully omits or refuses to pay over to the people of this state or their officer or agent authorized by law to receive the same, any money received by him under any duty imposed by law so to pay over the same,

Is guilty of felony.

Other violations of law.

§ 498. Every officer or other person mentioned in the last section who willfully disobeys any provisions of law regulating his official conduct, in cases other than those specified in that section, is guilty of a misdemeanor.

Officer authorized to make any sale, lease or contract, becoming interested under it.

§ 499. Every public officer, being authorized to sell or lease any property, or make any contract in his official capacity, who voluntarily becomes interested individually in such sale, lease or contract, directly or indirectly, is guilty of a misdemeanor.

See *Laws of* 1860, ch. 488, § 19; *Laws of* 1861, ch. 340, § 18; *Laws of* 1862, ch 285, § 2; also Howell *v.* Barker, 4 *Johns. Ch.*, 118.

County clerks omitting to publish statement required by law.

§ 500. Any county clerk who willfully omits to publish the annual statement required by section 905 of the Political Code, within the time therein prescribed, is guilty of a misdemeanor.

Rep. Pol. Code, § 906.

Obstructing officer in collecting revenue.

§ 501. Every person who willfully obstructs or hinders any public officer from collecting any revenue, taxes or other sums of money in which, or in any part of which the people of this state are directly or indirectly interested, and which such officer is by law empowered to collect, is guilty of a misdemeanor.

Selling goods by auction without filing bond required by the Political Code.

§ 502. Every person who acts as auctioneer in selling any goods liable to auction duties, or in selling in the cities of New York, Brooklyn, Albany, Troy or Buffalo, any personal property whatsoever, except such as is sold under authority of the United States, without having filed the bond required by the provisions of Article II of Chapter IV of Title IV of Part III of the Political Code, or being authorized as assistant to one who has filed such bond, as provided by section 723 of that Code, is guilty of a misdemeanor; and in addition to the punishment prescribed therefor, he forfeits one hundred and twenty-five dollars, for each article so exposed by him to sale, to be recovered by a civil action in the name of the people.

Rep. Pol. Code, § 723.

§ 503. Every auctioneer who accepts an appointment as auctioneer from any other state or is concerned as principal or partner in selling any property in any other state by public auction, or who knowingly receives any benefit on account of any such sale, is guilty of a misdemeanor; and in addition to the punishment prescribed therefor by law, is forever disqualified after his conviction therefor, from being licensed to act as an auctioneer within this state.

Auctioneer accepting appointment as auctioneer in another state, or selling in another state.

§ 504. No auctioneer, in any city of this state shall at one time have more than one place for carrying on the general business of an auctioneer; and every such auctioneer, before acting as such, shall file with the clerk of such city a writing, signed by him, designating such place and naming therein the partners, if any, engaged with him in business.

Auctioneer having two places of business.

See Rep. Pol. Code, § 727.

§ 505. No such auctioneer shall expose to sale by public auction any articles liable to auction duties at any other place than that so designated, except goods sold in original packages as imported, pictures, household furniture, libraries, stationery and such bulky articles as have usually been sold in warehouses, or in the public streets or on the wharves.

Auctioneer selling goods at other than his regular place of business

Rep. Pol. Code, § 728.

§ 506. A violation of either of the last two sections is punishable by a fine not exceeding two hundred and fifty dollars for each offense.

Punishment for violating last two sections.

Rep. Pol. Code, § 729.

§ 507. Every person carrying on, interested in or employed about, the business of selling property by auction in the city of New York, who sells any property by auction without having first advertised the same in the manner required by law, or is concerned in any sale by auction not so advertised, is guilty of a misdemeanor.

Selling goods without due advertisement.

See *Rep. Pol. Code*, § 731. The mode of advertising auction sales is more particularly prescribed by that section.

What sales must be made by day.

§ 508. All sales of goods by public auction in the cities of New York, Brooklyn, Albany, Buffalo, Oswego, Syracuse, Troy, Poughkeepsie and Rochester, shall be made in the day-time between sunrise and sunset, excepting:

1. Books, prints, pictures or stationery.

2. Goods sold in the original packages as imported, according to a printed catalogue, of which samples shall have been opened and exposed to public view at least one day previous to the sale. Every person who violates the provisions of this section is guilty of misdemeanor; and in addition to the punishment prescribed therefor by law, is forever disqualified after his conviction therefor, from being licensed to act as an auctioneer within this state.

This provision has been reported in substantially the above form in *Rep. Pol. Code,* § 732, being there restricted to the cities of New York and Albany. In view of the extension of auction business in the larger towns of the state, the Commissioners are of opinion that the section should be extended to embrace the other cities named in the text.

Auctioneer omitting to render account.

§ 509. Every auctioneer, and every partner or clerk of an auctioneer, and every person whatever in any way connected in business with an auctioneer, who willfully omits to render any semi-annual or other account, by law required to be rendered, at the time or in the manner prescribed by law, or who willfully omits to pay over any duties legally payable by him at the time and in the manner prescribed by law, is guilty of a misdemeanor.

See *Rep. Pol. Code,* §§ 738–748.

Auctioneer committing fraud or attempting to evade the provisions of the Political Code.

§ 510. Every auctioneer, and every partner or clerk of any auctioneer, and every person whatever in any way connected in business with an auctioneer, who commits any fraud or deceit, or by any fraudulent means whatever seeks to evade or defeat the provisions of Chapter IV of Title IV of Part III of the Political Code, entitled AUCTIONS, is guilty of misdemeanor, and in addition to the punishment prescribed therefor is liable in treble damages to any party injured thereby.

Rep. Pol. Code, § 750.

§ 511. Every person whose duty it may be to deliver to any collector of tolls upon any of the canals belonging to this state, a bill of lading of any property transported upon any such canal, who delivers a false bill of lading as true, or makes or signs a false bill of lading intending it to be delivered as true, knowing such bill to be false, is punishable by imprisonment in a state prison not exceeding two years, or by a fine not exceeding three times the value of any property omitted in such bill, or both.

Delivering false bill of lading to canal collector.

Suggested as a substitute for *Rep. Pol. Code*, § 570
See 1 *Rev. Stat.*, 241, § 125.

§ 512. Every weighmaster upon any of the canals belonging to this state, and every clerk of such weighmaster, who makes a false entry of the weight of any boat, or cargo of any boat, navigating such canal, or who makes a false certificate of the light weight of any boat, knowing such entry or certificate to be false, is guilty of misdemeanor.

Weighmaster making false entry of weight of canal boat.

See *Laws of* 1861, ch. 124, § 4.

§ 513. Every public officer or agent employed by the people of this state in relation to the canals belonging to this state, who knows, or has good reason to believe that any fraud upon the revenues of the canals has been committed or attempted, and who omits to disclose the same, and enforce the penalties therefor, if within his power, is guilty of a misdemeanor.

Canal officer concealing frauds upon the revenue.

See *Laws of* 1855, ch. 534, § 4.

§ 514. Every person who, without authority of law willfully inflicts any injury upon any of the canals belonging to this state, or disturbs or injures any of the boats, locks, bridges, buildings, machinery or

Willful injuries to the canals.

other works or erections connected with any such canal, and in which the people of this state have an interest, is guilty of felony.

See 1 *Rev. Stat.*, 248, §§ 179, 180.

Drawing off water from canals.

§ 515. Every person who draws water from any canal in this state, or from any feeder or reservoir of any canal, during the navigation season of the canal, and to the detriment or injury of the navigation thereof, without authority of law, is punishable by imprisonment in a county jail not less than one year, and by a fine not less than one thousand dollars.

Founded upon *Laws of* 1860, ch. 213, § 5, and intended to cover the provisions of *Laws of* 1861, ch. 124, § 5, and of 1 *Rev. Stat.*, 235, §§ 94, 95.

Canal officer accepting bribe to allow water to be drawn off from canals.

§ 516. Every public officer or agent employed by the people of this state in relation to the canals belonging to this state, or contractor for canal repairs, or person having any charge of any canal, or of any part thereof, or of any lock, waste weir, feeder or other work belonging thereto, or being employed thereon, who asks, or accepts or promises to accept any bribe as an inducement to permit any water to be drawn from any canal, feeder or reservoir in violation of the last section; and every person who gives, or offers or promises to give to any officer or person above mentioned, any bribe as an inducement to him to permit any water to be drawn from any canal, feeder or reservoir in violation of this section, is guilty of a misdemeanor.

Founded upon *Laws of* 1860, ch. 213, § 5.

Fraudulent appropriation of lost treasure, &c.

§ 517. Every person who fraudulently conceals or appropriates to his own use any lost treasure or any waived property belonging to the state as sovereign, is guilty of a misdemeanor.

1 *Black. Com.*, 295–297; 4 *Id.*, 121; 9 *Cox Cr. Cas.*, 376.

§ 518. Every person who willfully burns, destroys, or injures any salt manufactory connected with the Onondaga salt springs, or any building appurtenant to such manufactory, or any part of such manufactory, or any of the buildings, reservoirs, pumps, conductors or water conduits, belonging to the state, used in the raising of salt water for the use of the manufacturers of salt, without authority of law, is punishable by imprisonment in a state prison not exceeding five years. Injuries to the salt works.

Founded on *Laws of* 1859, ch. 346, § 62. That act requires that the injury to the works should be shown to have been inflicted "with intent to retard the pumping, &c., of salt water for the use of manufacturers." The words "without authority of law" are substituted for this clause, as equally consonant with justice, and imposing a less onerous burden of proof upon the prosecution.

§ 519. Every person who enters any fort, magazine, arsenal, armory, arsenal yard or encampment, and seizes or takes away any arms, ammunition, military stores or supplies belonging to the people of this state; and every person who enters any such place with intent so to do, is punishable by imprisonment in a state prison not exceeding ten years. Seizing military stores belonging to the state.

§ 520. Every person, who, in making any statement, oral or written, which is required or authorized by law to be made as the basis of imposing any tax or assessment, or of an application to reduce any tax or assessment, willfully makes, as to any material matter, any statement which he knows to be false, is guilty of a misdemeanor. Making false statements in reference to taxes.

See *Stat.*, 50 *Geo.* III, ch. 105, § 9.

TITLE XV.

OF CRIMES AGAINST PROPERTY.

CHAPTER I.

ARSON.

§ 521. Arson is the willful and malicious burning of a building, with intent to destroy it. "Arson" defined.

This definition is substantially that of the common law authorities. They, nearly all, restrict the offense to the burning of a dwelling house, or some edifice adapted for or connected with human occupation; making the gravity of the offense to consist in the peril to the person which such burning involves. (4 *Blackst. Comm.*, 220; 2 *East P. C.*, 1015; *Barb. Cr. L.*, 53; *Whart. Am. Cr. L.*, 534; *Coke Ch.*, 15, 66; State *v.* Roe, 12 *Verm.*, 93; People *v.* Cotteral, 18 *Johns.*, 115. See also *Laws of Ga.*, 712; 4 *U. S. Stat at L.*, 115; *Rep. Cr. Code, Mass.*) The statutes of this state have enlarged the use of the term to include many acts of burning not involving special danger to the person. Thus, burning a carding machine, a stack of grain or hay, a bridge, a crop of grain, &c., &c., is arson in the fourth degree. (2 *Rev. Stat.*, 667, §§ 7, 8.) The Commissioners recommend that the term "arson" be confined to the offense of setting on fire buildings or edifices (including ships and vessels, see § 521, *infra*). Other criminal acts of burning should be classed under other titles; *e. g.*, malicious mischief. See section 703.

§ 522. Any house, edifice, structure, vessel, or other erection, capable of affording shelter for human beings, or appurtenant to, or connected with an erection so adapted, is a "building" within the meaning of the last section. "Building" defined.

§ 523. Any building is deemed an "inhabited building" within the meaning of this chapter, any part of which has usually been occupied by any person lodging therein at night. "Inhabited building" defined.

People *v.* Orcutt, 1 *Park. Cr.*, 252; See also Hooker *v.* Commonwealth, 13 *Gratt.*, 763; Commonwealth *v.* Barney, 10 *Cush.*, 478; Rex *v.* Donovan, *Leach C. C.*, 81; Reg. *v.* Connor, 2 *Cox Cr. Cas.*, 65.

§ 524. The words "night time" in this chapter include the period between sunset and sunrise. "Night time" defined.

§ 525. To constitute a burning within the meaning of section 521, it is not necessary that the building set on fire should be destroyed. It is sufficient that "Burning" defined.

fire is applied so as to take effect upon any part of the substance of the building.

People *v.* Butler, 16 *Johns.*, 203: Commonwealth *v.* Van Schaack, 16 *Mass.*, 105; State *v.* Sandy, 5 *Ired.*, 570; Reg. *v.* Parker, 9 *Carr. & P.*, 45; Reg. *v.* Russel, 1 *Carr. & M.*, 541. See also, Hester *v.* State, 17 *Geo.*, 130; State *v.* De Bruhl, 10 *Rich. Law*, 23.

Ownership of the building. § 526. To constitute arson it is not necessary that another person than the accused should have had ownership in the building set on fire. It is sufficient that at the time of the burning another person was rightfully in the possession of, or was actually occupying, such building, or any part thereof.

People *v.* Van Blarcum, 2 *Johns.*; 105; Shepherd *v.* People, 19 *N. Y.* (5 *Smith*), 537; State *v.* Taylor, 45 *Me.*, 322. At common law arson was the maliciously burning the house of *another*. *East P. C.*, 1015. And one could not be convicted of arson in burning his own house. Rex *v.* Pealey, *Leach C. C.*, 277; Rex *v.* Breeme, *Id.*, 261; Rex *v.* Spalding, *Leach C. C.*, 248.

The offense of burning insured property with intent to defraud the insurers, is provided for in chapter IX. of this title.

Variance in proof of ownership. § 527. An omission to designate, or error in designating in an indictment for arson, the owner or occupant of a building, shall not prejudice the proceedings thereupon, if it appears that upon the whole description given of the building, it is sufficiently identified to enable the prisoner to prepare his defense.

Compare Martha *v.* State, 26 *Ala.*, 72; State *v.* Fish, 3 *Dutch.*, 323.

What constitutes malice. § 528. Malice sufficient to constitute arson is inferred from proof that the prisoner committed an act of burning a building, and that some other person was rightfully in possession of, or actually occupying any part thereof. It is not necessary that the accused should have had actual knowledge of such possession or occupancy, or should have intended to injure another person.

Rex *v.* Farrington, *Russ. & Ry. C. C.*, 207; People *v.* Van Blarcum, 2 *Johns.*. 105; People *v.* Orcutt, 1 *Park. Cr.*, 252; People *v.* Henderson, *Id.*, 563; Jesse *v.* State,

28 *Miss.*, 100. In Reg. *v.* Regan (4 *Cox Cr. Cas.*, 335), it appeared that the prisoner's intent in setting fire to the building was to obtain a reward offered for giving the earliest intimation of a fire, at the engine station. *Held,* he was guilty of arson.

§ 529. But the burning of a building under circumstances which shows beyond a reasonable doubt that there was no intent to destroy it, is not arson. Intent to destroy the building requisite.

People *v.* Cotteral, 18 *Johns.*, 115.
State *v.* Mitchell, 5 *Ired.*, 350.

§ 530. Where any appurtenance to any building is so situated with reference to such building, or where any building is so situated with reference to another building that the burning of the one will manifestly endanger the other, a burning of the one is deemed a burning of the other, within the foregoing definition of arson, and as against any person actually participating in the original setting fire, as of the moment when the fire from the one shall communicate to and burn the other. Contiguous buildings.

Robert's case, 2 *East P. C.*, 1030; Isaac's case, *Id.*, 1031; Reg. *v.* Fletcher, 2 *Carr. & K.*, 215; Reg. *v.* Price, 1 *Id.*, 73; Rex *v.* Petley, *Leach C. C.*, 277.

§ 531. Arson is distinguished into four degrees. Degrees of arson.

§ 532. Maliciously burning in the night time an inhabited building, in which there is at the time some human being, is arson in the first degree. First degre defined.

Founded upon 2 *Rev. Stat.*, 657, § 9. Taken in connection with the definition of "building," and "inhabited," given in sections 522 and 523 of this Code, the foregoing section would embrace as arson in the first degree, the burning of a ship or vessel while lying within this state. This is, by the Revised Statutes (2 *Rev. Stat.*, 667, § 4), only arson in the third degree; but it is an offense of as grave a character as burning an inhabited dwelling.

§ 533. No warehouse, barn, shed, or other outhouse, is a subject of arson in the first degree, unless Appurtenances to buildings.

it is immediately connected with, and forms part of, an inhabited building.

Founded upon 2 *Rev. Stat.*, 657, § 10.

Burning in day time, when arson in second degree.

§ 534. Maliciously burning in the day time an inhabited building, in which there is at the time some human being, is arson in the second degree.

Substituted for 2 *Rev. Stat.*, 666, § 1.

Burning in night time, when arson in second degree.

§ 535. Maliciously burning in the night time a building, not an inhabited building, but adjoining to or within the curtilage of an inhabited building in which there is at the time some human being, so that such inhabited building is endangered, even though it be not in fact injured by such burning, is arson in the second degree.

See Peverelly *v.* People, 3 *Park. Cr.*, 59.

Burning in day time, when arson in third degree.

§ 536. Maliciously burning in the day time a building, the burning of which in the night time would be arson in the second degree, is arson in the third degree.

Burning in night time, when arson in third degree.

§ 537. Maliciously burning in the night time any building, not the subject of arson in the first or second degree, including any house for public worship, school house, or public building belonging to the people of this state, or to any county, city, town or village, any building in which have usually been deposited the papers of any public officer, and any barn, mill or manufactory, is arson in the third degree.

Founded on 2 *Rev. Stat.*, 667, § 4.

Fourth degree defined.

§ 538. Maliciously burning in the day time any building, the burning of which in the night time would be arson in the third degree, is arson in the fourth degree.

Founded on 2 *Rev. Stat.*, 667, § 7.

Punishment of arson.

§ 539. Arson is punishable by imprisonment in a state prison, as follows:

1. Arson in the first degree, for any term not less than ten years;

2. Arson in the second degree, not exceeding ten years and not less than seven years;

3. Arson in the third degree, not exceeding seven years and not less than four years;

4. Arson in the fourth degree, not exceeding four years and not less than one year; or by imprisonment in a county jail not exceeding one year.

The above are the grades of punishment recently prescribed by statute, (*Laws of* 1862, ch. 197, §§ 7, 8,) as a substitute for the provisions of the Revised Statutes. Under those provisions arson was punishable, in the first degree, by death (2 *Rev. Stat.*, 656, § 1); in the second degree by imprisonment in a state prison not less than ten years; in the third degree by like imprisonment not more than ten years and not less than seven; and in the fourth degree by like imprisonment not more than seven years and not less than two, or by imprisonment in a county jail not exceeding one year. (2 *Rev. Stat.*, 667, § 9.) In view of the many and aggravated instances of this crime which have recently occurred, there seems reason to favor a return to the more stringent system of punishment prescribed by the former law. The commissioners have, however, presented the existing rules in the text, leaving the question of a restoration of those formerly in force, to the consideration of the legislation.

CHAPTER II.

BURGLARY AND HOUSEBREAKING.

Burglary in first degree defined.

§ 540. Every person who, with intent to commit some crime therein, breaks into and enters in the night time the dwelling house of another, in which there is at the time some human being, either:

1. By forcibly bursting or breaking the wall, or an outer door, window, or shutter of a window of such house, or the lock or bolt of such door, or the fastening of such window or shutter; or,

2. By any other means, being armed with any dangerous weapon, or being assisted or aided by one or more confederates, then actually present; or,

3. By unlocking an outer door by means of false keys, or by picking the lock thereof;

Is guilty of burglary in the first degree.

2 *Rev. Stat.*, 668, § 10. It has not been thought best to insert any definition of "breaking" or of "entering," but rather to leave the meanings of those words, now quite well settled, to adjudication. For cases on the subject, see Rex *v.* Cornwall, 2 *Stra.*, 880; Rex *v.* Gray, 1 *Id.*, 481; Rex *v.* Gibbons, *Fost.*, 107; Rex *v.* Hughes, *Leach C. C.*, 452; Reg. *v.* Davis, 6 *Cox Cr. Cas.*, 367; Reg. *v.* O'Brien, 4 *Id.*, 398; Reg. *v.* Meal, 3 *Id.*, 70; Reg. *v.* Wenmouth, 8 *Cox Cr. Cas.*, 483; Reg. *v.* Wheeldon, 8 *Carr. & P.*, 747; Rex *v.* Paine, 7 *Id.*, 135; Rex *v.* Jordan, 7 *Id.*, 432; Reg. *v.* Bird, 9 *Id.*, 44; Rex *v.* Hughes, 1 *Leach C. C.*, 406; 2 *East P. C.*, 491; Rex *v.* Lewis, 2 *Carr. & P.*, 628; Rex *v.* Brown, 2 *East P. C.*, 487; 2 *Leach C. C.*, 1016; Rex *v.* Johnson, 2 *East P. C.*, 488; Rex *v.* Bailey, *Russ. & R. C. C.*, 341; 2 *Russ. C. & M.*, 12; 1 *R. & M. C. C*, 23; Rex *v.* Perkes, 1 *Carr. & P.*, 300; Rex *v.* Lawrence, 4 *Carr. & P.*, 231; Rex *v.* Russell, 1 *M. C. C. R.*, 377; State *v.* McCall, 4 *Ala.*, 643; State *v.* Wilson, *Coxe*, 439; Commonwealth *v.* Steward, 7 *Dane's Ab.*, 136; Com. *v.* Stephenson, 8 *Pick.*, 354; People *v.* Boujet, 2 *Park. Cr. Rep.*, 11; Commonwealth *v.* Trimmer, 1 *Mass.*, 476; Finch's case, 14 *Gratt.*, 643; Guche's case, 6 *City Hall Rec.*, 1: Robertson's case, 4 *Id.*, 63; Smith's case, *Id.*, 62; People *v.* Tralick, *Hill & D.*, 63; People *v.* Bush, 3 *Park. Cr.*, 552.

§ 541. Every person who breaks into any dwelling house in the day time under such circumstances as would have constituted the crime of burglary in the first degree, if committed in the night time, is guilty of burglary in the second degree.

Breaking into dwelling house in the day time burglary in second degree.

2 *Rev. Stat.*, 668, § 11.

§ 542. Every person who, having entered the dwelling house of another in the night time, through an open outer door or window, or other aperture not made by such person, breaks any inner door, window, partition, or other part of such house, with intent to commit any crime, is guilty of burglary in the second degree.

Breaking inner door in night time, burglary in second degree.

Founded upon 2 *Rev. Stat.*, 668, § 14.

§ 543. Every person who, being lawfully in any dwelling house, breaks in the night time any inner door of the same house, with intent to commit any crime, is guilty of burglary in the second degree.

Such breaking by person lawfully in the house burglary in second degree.

Founded upon 2 *Rev. Stat.*, 669, § 15. The language of that section is: "Every person who, being admitted into any dwelling house with the consent of the occupant thereof, or who being lawfully in such house," &c. The Commissioners in omitting the words, "being admitted into any dwelling house with the consent of the occupant thereof," do not intend any substantial change in the law, but deem those words fully covered by the clause in the text; "being lawfully in any dwelling house."

§ 544. Every person who breaks into any dwelling house in the night time, with intent to commit a crime, but under such circumstances as do not constitute the offense of burglary in the first degree, is guilty of burglary in the third degree.

Breaking into dwelling house when burglary in third degree.

2 *Rev. Stat.*, 668, § 12; modified by reducing the offense to the third degree.

§ 545. Every person who breaks and enters, in the day or in the night time, either:

Other burglaries of the third degree.

1. Any building within the curtilage of a dwelling house, but not forming a part thereof; or

2. Any building or part of any building, booth, tent, railroad car, vessel, or other structure or erection in which any property is kept, with intent to steal therein or to commit any felony,

Is guilty of burglary in the third degree.

Compare 2 *Rev. Stat.*, 669, § 17, as amended, *Laws of* 1863, ch. 244.

Breaking and entering dwelling, when burglary in fourth degree.

§ 546. Every person who breaks and enters the dwelling house of another, by day or by night, in such manner as not to constitute any burglary specified in the preceding section, with intent to commit a crime, is guilty of burglary in the fourth degree.

See 2 *Rev. Stat.*, 668, § 13, which declares this species of offense to be burglary in the second degree. The section in the text also merges 2 *Rev. Stat.*, 669, § 18.

Breaking out of dwelling house burglary in fourth degree.

§ 547. Every person who, having committed any crime in the dwelling house of another, breaks in the night time, any outer door, window shutter, or other part of such house, to get out of the same, is guilty of burglary in the fourth degree.

See 2 *Rev. Stat.*, 668, § 13.

The following provisions of 2 *Rev. Stat.*, 669, are here omitted, not with intention to change the existing law, but because they are embraced in the general provision of § 2 of this Code.

§ 19. The breaking out of any dwelling house by any person being therein, shall not be deemed such a breaking of a dwelling house as to constitute burglary, in any case other than such as are herein particularly specified.

§ 20. The breaking of the inner door of any house by any person being therein, shall not be deemed such a breaking of a dwelling house as to constitute burglary, in any case other than such as are herein particularly specified.

Punishment of burglary.

§ 548. Burglary is punishable by imprisonment in a state prison as follows:

1. Burglary in the first degree, for any term not less than ten years;

2. Burglary in the second degree, not exceeding ten years, and not less than five;

3. Burglary in the third degree, not exceeding five years;

4. Burglary in the fourth degree, not exceeding three years.

Compare 2 *Rev. Stat.*, 669, § 21. A lesser punishment for burglary in the fourth degree, is here added to those prescribed for the higher degrees by the Revised Statutes.

Having possession of burglar's implements

§ 549. Every person who, under circumstances not amounting to any felony, has in his possession in the night time any dangerous, offensive weapon or instrument whatever, or any picklock, crow, key, bit, jack, jimmy, nippers, pick, betty or other implement of burglary, with intent to break and enter any building or part of any building, booth, tent, railroad car, vessel or other structure or erection and to commit any felony therein, is guilty of a misdemeanor.

See *Laws of* 1862, ch. 374, § 1.

Entering buildings other than dwelling houses.

§ 550. Every person who, under circumstances not amounting to any burglary, enters any building or part of any building, booth, tent, warehouse, railroad car, vessel or other structure or erection with intent to commit any felony, larceny or malicious mischief, is guilty of a misdemeanor.

See *Laws of* 1862, ch. 374, § 1.

"Dwelling house" defined.

§ 551. The term "dwelling house," as used in this chapter, includes every house or edifice any part of which has usually been occupied by any person lodging therein at night, and any structure joined to and immediately connected with such a house or edifice.

The only attempt at a definition of "dwelling house" in our existing statute law of burglary, is that found in 2 *Rev. Stat.*, 669, § 16, viz.: "No building shall be deemed a dwelling house, or any part of a dwelling house within the meaning of the foregoing provisions, unless the same be joined to, immediately connected with, and part of a dwelling house." While this provision may have served a useful purpose in excluding from the provisions of the statutes relative to burglary a class of buildings wholly disconnected from dwelling houses, it is wholly useless as a definition. It entirely fails to designate what is to be considered a dwelling house; and indeed, if literally taken, excludes all habitations standing alone. The Commissioners have given in the text a distinct definition of the term.

"Night time" defined.

§ 552. The words "night time," in this chapter, include the period between sunset and sunrise.

Corresponds with § 524 of this Code, relative to arson.

CHAPTER III.

FORGERY AND COUNTERFEITING.

§ 553. Every person who, with intent to defraud, forges, counterfeits or falsely alters: Forgery of wills, conveyances, certificates of acknowledgment, &c.

1. Any will or codicil of real or personal property, or any deed or other instrument being or purporting to be the act of another, by which any right or interest in real property is or purports to be transferred, conveyed or in any way charged or affected; or,

2. Any certificate or indorsement of the acknowledgment by any person of any deed or other instrument which by law may be recorded or given in evidence, made or purporting to have been made by any officer duly authorized to make such certificate or indorsement; or,

3. Any certificate of the proof of any deed, will, codicil or other instrument which by law may be recorded or given in evidence, made or purporting to have been made by any court or officer duly authorized to make such certificate,

Is guilty of forgery in the first degree.

2 *Rev. Stat.*, 670, § 22.

§ 554. Every person who, with intent to defraud, forges, counterfeits or falsely alters: Forgery of public securities.

1. Any certificate or other public security, issued or purporting to have been issued under the authority of this state, by virtue of any law thereof, by which certificate or other public security, the payment of any money absolutely or upon any contingency is promised, or the receipt of any money or property acknowledged; or,

2. Any certificate of any share, right or interest in any public stock created by virtue of any law of this state, issued or purporting to have been issued by any public officer, or any other evidence of any debt or liability of the people of this state, either absolute or contingent, issued or purporting to have been issued by any public officer; or,

3. Any indorsement or other instrument transferring or purporting to transfer the right or interest of

any holder of any such certificate, public security, certificate of stock, evidence of debt or liability, or of any person entitled to such right or interest,

Is guilty of forgery in the first degree.

2 *Rev. Stat.*, 670, § 23. That section contained a clause in subd. 1, punishing also the forgery of any bill of credit heretofore issued by or under the authority of the legislature of this state, or purporting to have been so issued. As the Constitution of the United States (art. 1, § 10, subd. 1), prohibits the state from emitting any bills of credit, it seems unnecessary to continue this provision longer.

Forgery of public and corporate seals.

§ 555. Every person who, with intent to defraud, forges or counterfeits the great or privy seal of this state, the seal of any public office authorized by law, the seal of any court of record, including surrogates' seals, or the seal of any corporation created by the laws of this state or of any other state, government or country, or any other public seal authorized or recognized by the laws of this state, or of any other state, government or country, or who falsely makes, forges or counterfeits any impression purporting to be the impression of any such seal, is guilty of forgery in the second degree.

2 *Rev. Stat.*, 671, § 24; extended to protect seals of foreign corporations.

Forgery of records and official returns.

§ 556. Every person who, with intent to defraud, falsely alters, destroys, corrupts or falsifies:

1. Any record of any will, codicil, conveyance or other instrument, the record of which is, by law, evidence; or,

2. Any record of any judgment in a court of record, or any enrollment of any decree of a court of equity; or,

3. The return of any officer, court or tribunal to any process of any court,

Is guilty of forgery in the second degree.

2 *Rev. Stat.*, 671, § 25.

§ 557. Every person who, with intent to defraud, falsely makes, forges or alters any entry in any book of records, or any instrument purporting to be any record or return, specified in the last section, is guilty of forgery in the second degree. Making false entries in records or returns.

See 2 *Rev. Stat.*, 671, § 26.

§ 558. If any officer authorized to take the acknowledgment or proof of any conveyance of real estate, or of any other instrument which by law may be recorded, knowingly and falsely certifies that any such conveyance or instrument was acknowledged by any party thereto, or was proved by any subscribing witness, when in truth such conveyance or instrument was not acknowledged or proved as certified, he is guilty of forgery in the second degree. False certificates of acknowledgment or proof.

See 2 *Rev. Stat.*, 671, § 27.

§ 559. Every person who makes or engraves, or causes or procures to be made or engraved, any plate in the form or similitude of any promissory note, bill of exchange, draft, check, certificate of deposit or other evidence of debt, issued by any banking corporation or association, or individual banker, incorporated or carrying on business under the laws of this state, or of any other state, government or country, without the authority of such bank; or has or keeps in his custody or possession any such plate, without the authority of such bank, with intent to use or permit the same to be used for the purpose of taking therefrom any impression, to be passed, sold or altered; or has or keeps in his custody or possession, without the authority of such bank, any impression taken from any such plate, with intent to have the same filled up and completed for the purpose of being passed, sold or altered; or makes or causes to be made, or has in his custody or possession, any plate upon which are engraved any figures, or words, which may be used for the purpose of falsely altering any evidence of debt issued by any such bank, with the intent to use the same, or to permit them to be used Making false bank note plates, &c.

26

for such purpose, is guilty of forgery in the second degree.

Founded upon 2 *Rev. Stat.*, 672, § 30.

What plate may be deemed an imitation of a genuine plate.

§ 560. Every plate specified in the last section shall be deemed to be in the form and similitude of the genuine instrument imitated, in either of the following cases:

1. When the engraving on such plate resembles and conforms to such parts of the genuine instrument as are engraved; or,

2. When such plate is partly finished, and the part so finished resembles and conforms to similar parts of the genuine instrument.

2 *Rev. Stat.*, 672, § 31.

Uttering forged evidences of debt.

§ 561. Every person who sells, exchanges or delivers any forged or counterfeited promissory note, check, bill, draft, or other evidence of debt, or engagement for the payment of money absolutely, or upon any contingency, knowing the same to be forged or counterfeited, with the intent to have the same uttered or passed; or who offers any such note or other instrument for sale, exchange or delivery, with the like knowledge and intent; or who receives any such note or other instrument upon a sale, exchange or delivery, with the like knowledge and intent; whether the same be done for or without any consideration, is guilty of forgery in the second degree.

2 *Rev. Stat.*, 673, § 32. The original section is limited to cases where the uttering is "for any consideration."

Having possession of certain forged evidences of debt with intent to utter them.

§ 562. Every person who, with intent to defraud, has in his possession any forged, altered or counterfeited negotiable note, bill, draft, or other evidence of debt, issued or purporting to have been issued by any corporation or company duly authorized for that purpose by the laws of this state, or of any other state, government or country, the forgery of which is hereinbefore declared to be punishable, knowing the same to be forged, altered or counterfeited, with intent to utter the same as true, or as false, or to cause the same to be so uttered, is guilty of forgery in the second degree.

2 *Rev. Stat.*, 674, § 36.

Having possession of other forged instruments.

§ 563. Every person who has in his possession any forged or counterfeited instrument, the forgery of which is hereinbefore declared to be punishable, other than such as are enumerated in the last section, knowing the same to be forged, counterfeited or falsely altered, with intent to injure or defraud by uttering the same as true, or as false, or by causing the same to be so uttered, is guilty of forgery in the fourth degree.

2 *Rev. Stat.*, 674, § 37.

Issuing spurious certificates of stock in corporations

§ 564. Every officer, and every agent of any corporation or joint stock association formed or existing under or by virtue of the laws of this state, or of any other state, government or country, who, within this state, willfully signs or procures to be signed, with intent to issue, sell or pledge, or to cause to be issued, sold or pledged, or who willfully issues, sells or pledges or causes to be issued, sold or pledged, any false or fraudulent certificate or other evidence of the ownership or transfer of any share or shares of the capital stock of such corporation or association, whether of full paid shares or otherwise, or of any interest in its property or profits, or any certificate or other evidence of such ownership, transfer or interest, or any instrument purporting to be a certificate or other evidence of such ownership, transfer or interest, the signing, issuing, selling or pledging of which has not been duly authorized by the board of directors or other managing body of such corporation or association having authority to issue the same, is guilty of forgery in the second degree.

Reissuing canceled certificates of stock.

§ 565. Every officer, and every agent of any corporation or joint stock association formed or existing under or by virtue of the laws of this state, or of any other state, government or country, who within this state willfully reissues, sells or pledges, or causes to be reissued, sold or pledged, any surrendered or canceled certificate, or other evidence of the ownership or transfer of any share or shares of the capital stock of such corporation or association, or of an interest in its property or profits, with intent to defraud, is guilty of forgery in the second degree.

Issuing false evidences of debt of corporation.

§ 566. Every officer, and every agent of any corporation, municipal or otherwise, or of any joint stock association formed or existing under or by virtue of the laws of this state, or of any other state, government or country, who, within this state, willfully signs or procures to be signed with intent to issue, sell or pledge, or to cause to be issued, sold or pledged, or who willfully issues, sells or pledges, or causes to be issued, sold or pledged any false or fraudulent bond or other evidence of debt against such corporation or association, or any instrument purporting to be a bond or other evidence of debt against such corporation or association, the signing, issuing, selling or pledging of which has not been duly authorized by the board of directors or common council or other managing body or officers of such corporation having authority to issue the same, is guilty of forgery in the second degree.

The three preceding sections embody 2 *Rev. Stat.*, 676, § 49, and *Laws of* 1855, ch. 155, §§ 1, 2.

Counterfeiting coin to be circulated within this state.

§ 567. Every person who counterfeits any gold or silver coin, whether of the United States or of any foreign government or country, with intent to sell, utter, use or circulate the same as genuine, within this state, is guilty of forgery in the second degree.

Substituted for 2 *Rev. Stat.*, 671, § 28: "Every person who shall be convicted of having counterfeited any of the gold or silver coins which shall be at the time current by custom or usage within this state, shall be adjudged guilty of forgery in the second degree."

§ 568. Every person who counterfeits any gold or silver coin, whether of the United States or of any foreign country or government, with intent to export the same, or permit the same to be exported, and to injure or defraud any foreign government, or the subjects thereof, is guilty of forgery in the third degree. Counterfeiting coin to be exported

Proposed as a substitute for 2 *Rev. Stat.*, 672, § 29.

§ 569. Every person who, with intent to defraud, falsely makes, alters, forges or counterfeits: Forging process of court, and other instruments.

1. Any instrument in writing, being or purporting to be any process issued by any competent court, magistrate or officer; or being, or purporting to be, any pleading, proceeding, bond or undertaking filed or entered in any court; or being, or purporting to be, any certificate, order or allowance by any competent court or officer; or being, or purporting to be, any license or authority authorized by any statute; or,

2. Any instrument or writing by which any pecuniary demand or obligation is, or purports to be, or to have been, created, increased, discharged or diminished, or by which any rights or property whatever, are or purport to be, or to have been, transferred, conveyed, discharged, diminished, or in any manner affected, the punishment of which is not hereinbefore prescribed, by which false making, altering, forging or counterfeiting, any person may be affected, bound, or in any way injured in his person or property,

Is guilty of forgery in the third degree.

2 *Rev. Stat.*, 673, § 33; modified to embrace such cases as the alteration of a paid check, by the maker, to defraud the bank in final settlement of accounts. See Britton *v.* Bank of London, 3 *Fost. & F.*, 465; 11 *Weekly R.*, 569; 8 *Law T.* (*N. S.*), 382; also, People *v.* Fitch, 1 *Wend.*, 148.

§ 570. Every person who, with intent to defraud, makes any false entry or falsely alters any entry made in any book of accounts kept in the office of the Making false entries in accounts of certain public officers.

comptroller of this state, or in the office of the treasurer, or of the state engineer and surveyor, or of any county treasurer, by which any demand or obligation, claim, right or interest, either against or in favor of the people of this state, or any county or town, or any individual, is, or purports to be, discharged, diminished, increased, created, or in any manner affected, is guilty of forgery in the third degree.

2 *Rev. Stat.*, 673, § 34.

Forging passage tickets.

§ 571. Every person who, with intent to defraud, forges, counterfeits, or falsely alters any ticket, check or other paper or writing, entitling or purporting to entitle the holder or proprietor thereof to a passage upon any railroad, or in any vessel or other public conveyance; and every person who, with like intent, sells, exchanges or delivers, or keeps or offers for sale, exchange or delivery, or receives upon any purchase, exchange or delivery, any such ticket, knowing the same to have been forged, counterfeited or falsely altered, is guilty of forgery in the third degree.

See *Laws of* 1855, ch. 499, § 4.

Forging U. S. stamps.

§ 572. Every person who forges, counterfeits or alters any postage or revenue stamp of the United States, or who sells, or offers, or keeps for sale, as genuine or as forged, any such stamp, knowing it to be forged, counterfeited or falsely altered, is guilty of forgery in the third degree.

This section is new and adapted to the recent introduction of stamps under the laws of the United States. It has not been intended to draft the section so as to render punishable frauds upon the *revenue of the United States* by *using* forged stamps. That crime is left to the legislation of congress. The object of the section is solely to protect inhabitants of this state from fraudulent sales of forged stamps.

Making false entries in books of account, of corporations.

§ 573. Every person who, with intent to defraud, makes any false entry, or falsely alters any entry made in any book of accounts kept by any corporation within this state, or in any book of accounts kept by any such corporation or its officers, and delivered, or intended to be delivered, to any person dealing with such corporation, by which any pecuniary obligation, claim or credit is, or purports to be, discharged, diminished, increased, created, or in any manner affected, is guilty of forgery in the third degree.

Founded upon 2 *Rev. Stat.*, 673, § 35. That section is limited to books kept by "moneyed" corporations, The Commissioners have omitted the word "moneyed," recommending that the provision be made general.

§ 574. Every person who, being a member or officer, or in the employment of any corporation, association, partnership or individual, falsifies, alters, erases, obliterates or destroys any account or book of accounts or records belonging to such corporation, association, partnership or individual, or appertaining to their business, or makes any false entries in such account or book, or keeps any false account in such business, with intent to defraud any person or to conceal any embezzlement of any money or property, or any defalcation, or other misconduct, committed by any person in the management of their business, is guilty of forgery in the fourth degree. Clerks and others making false entries in employers' books.

§ 575. Every person who has in his possession any counterfeit of any gold or silver coin, whether of the United States or of any foreign country or government, knowing the same to be counterfeited, with intent to sell, utter, use, circulate or export the same, as true or as false, or to cause the same to be so uttered or passed, is guilty of forgery in the fourth degree. Having possession of counterfeit coin, with intent to utter.

Founded upon 2 *Rev. Stat.*, 674, § 38. The words "whether of the United States or of any foreign country or government," are substituted instead of the words "which shall be at the time current in this state," to correspond with the language employed in sections 567 and 568.

§ 576. Forgery is punishable by imprisonment in a state prison as follows: Punishment of forgery.

1. Forgery in the first degree, by imprisonment not less than ten years;

2. Forgery in the second degree, not exceeding ten years, and not less than five;

3. Forgery in the third degree, not exceeding five years;

4. Forgery in the fourth degree, by imprisonment in a state prison not exceeding two years, or by imprisonment in a county jail not exceeding one year.

2 *Rev. Stat.*, 675, § 42.

Uttering forged instrument, or coin, forgery in same degree as making it.

§ 577. Every person who, with intent to defraud, utters or publishes as true any forged, altered or counterfeited instrument, or any counterfeit gold or silver coin, the forging, altering or counterfeiting of which is hereinbefore declared to be punishable, knowing such instrument or coin to be forged, altered or counterfeited, is guilty of forgery in the same degree as if he had forged, altered or counterfeited the instrument or coin so uttered, except as in the next section specified.

Exception, when such instrument or coin was received in good faith.

§ 578. If it appears on the trial of the indictment, that the accused received such forged or counterfeited instrument or coin from another, in good faith, and for a good and valuable consideration, without any circumstances to justify a suspicion of its being forged or counterfeited, the jury may find the defendant guilty of forgery in the fourth degree.

2 *Rev. Stat.*, 674, §§ 39, 40.

Fraudulently signing one's own name as that of another.

§ 579. Every person who, with intent to defraud, makes or subscribes any instrument in his own name, intended to create, increase, discharge, defeat or diminish any pecuniary obligation, right or interest, or to transfer or affect any property whatever, and utters or passes such instrument, under the pretense that it is the act of another who bears the same name, or that it is the act of a person who does not exist, is guilty of forgery in the same degree as if he had forged the instrument of a person bearing a different name from his own.

2 *Rev. Stat.*, 674, § 41.

§ 580. Every person who, with intent to defraud, indorses any negotiable instrument in his own name, and utters or passes such instrument, under the fraudulent pretense that it is indorsed by another person who bears the same name, or does not exist, is guilty of forgery in the same degree as if he had forged the indorsement of a person bearing a different name from his own. **Fraudulently indorsing one's own name.**

§ 581. The total or partial erasure, or obliteration of any instrument or writing, with intent to defraud, by which any pecuniary obligation, or any right, interest or claim to property is or is intended to be created, increased, discharged, diminished or in any manner affected, is forgery in the same degree as the false alteration of any part of such instrument or writing. **Erasures and obliterations.**

6 *Rev. Stat.*, 675, § 43

§ 582. Every instrument partly printed and partly written, or wholly printed with a written signature thereto, and every signature of an individual, firm or corporation, or of any officer of such body, and every writing purporting to be such signature, is a writing or a written instrument, within the meaning of the provisions of this chapter. **"Writing" and "written instrument" defined.**

2 *Rev. Stat.*, 675, § 45.

§ 583. The false making or forging of an evidence of debt purporting to have been issued by any corporation and bearing the pretended signature of any person as an agent or officer of such corporation, is forgery in the same degree as if such person was at the time an officer or agent of such corporation; notwithstanding such person may never have been an officer or agent of such corporation, or notwithstanding there never was any such person in existence. **Fictitious names of officers and of corporations.**

2 *Rev. Stat.* 675, § 47.

CHAPTER IV.

LARCENY.

Larceny defined.

§ 584. Larceny is the taking of personal property accomplished by fraud or stealth, or without color of right thereto, and with intent to deprive another thereof.

Four of the crimes affecting property, require to be somewhat carefully distinguished; robbery, larceny, extortion and embezzlement. The leading distinctions between these, in the view taken by the Commissioners, may be briefly stated thus: All four include the criminal acquisition of the property of another. In robbery this is accomplished by means of force or fear, and by overcoming or disregarding the will of the rightful possessor. There is a taking of property from another against his consent; the physical power to resist being overcome by force, or what is equivalent in law, the moral power to refuse being prostrated by fear. In larceny there is still a taking: but it is accomplished by fraud or stealth; the property is taken, not *against* the consent of the owner, but *without* it. In extortion there is again a taking. Now it is *with* the consent of the party injured; but this is a consent induced by threats, or under color of some official right. In embezzlement there is no taking, in the technical sense; that is, no taking from the possession of another. The offender being in possession of the property in virtue of some trust, which the law deems worthy of special sanction, applies it by fraud or stealth to his own use. Thus extortion partakes in an inferior degree of the nature of robbery, and embezzlement shares that of larceny.

In larceny it is not necessary that the property taken should be strictly the property of another person. A man may be guilty of stealing his own property, when done with intent to charge another person with the value of it; *e. g.*, where property which has been levied upon is stolen from the officer by the general owner. Palmer *v.* People, 10 *Wend.*, 165; see also People *v.* Call, 1 *Den.*, 120.

As to what property may be the subject of larceny, see Rex *v.* Westbee, *Leach*, 15; Rex *v.* Hedge, *Id.*, 240; Rex *v.* Martin, *Id.*, 205; Rex *v.* Cheafor, 2 *Den. & P.*, 361; 5 *Cox Cr.*, 367; Reg. *v.* White, 6 *Cox Cr. Cas.*, 213; 7 *Id.*, 183; Reg. *v.* Smith, *Id.*, 93; Reg. *v.* Jones, *Id.*, 498; Reg. *v.* Morrison, 8 *Cox Cr. Cas.*, 194; Linenden's Case, 1 *City H. Rec.*, 30; Ward *v.* People, 6 *Hill*, 144; People *v.* Caryl, 12 *Wend.*, 547; Johnson *v.* People, 4 *Den.*, 364; Low *v.* People, 2 *Park. Cr.*, 37; People *v.* Loomis, 4 *Den.*, 380; Payne *v.* People, 6 *Johns.*, 103; People *v.* Campbell, 4 *Park. Cr.*, 386; People *v.* Bradley, *Id.*, 245; Corbett *v.* State, 31 *Ala.*, 329; State *v.* Hall, 5 *Harring.*, 492; State *v.* Bond, 8 *Clarke*, 540; Commonwealth *v.* Rourke, 10 *Cush.*, 397; State *v.* Taylor, 3 *Dutch.*, 117.

As to what constitutes a sufficient removal or asportation of the property to constitute larceny, see Rex *v.* Coslet, *Leach*, 271; Rex *v.* Lapier, *Id*, 360; Rex *v.* Farrell, *Id.*, 362, n.; Rex *v.* Simpson, *Id.*, 362, n.; Tobias' Case, 1 *City Hall Rec.*, 30; Philips' Case, 4 *Id.*, 177; McDowel's Case, 5 *Id.*, 94; Scott's Case, *Id.*, 169; Reg. *v.* Hall, 3 *Cox Cr. Cas.*, 245; Reg. *v.* Wallis, *Id.*, 67; 10 *Law T.*, 49; Reg. *v.* Lawrence, 4 *Cox Cr. Cas.*, 438; Reg. *v.* Simpson, 6 *Id.*, 422; 24 *Law J.* (m. c.), 7.

As to what is an intent to deprive another of his interest in the property taken, within the meaning of the law of larceny, see Reg. *v.* Wynn, 3 *Cox Cr. Cas.*, 269; 1 *Den. C. C. R.*, 365; Reg. *v.* Holloway, 3 *Cox Cr. Cas.*, 241; 1 *Den. C. C. R.*, 370; Reg. *v.* Beecham, 5 *Cox Cr. Cas.*, 181; Reg. *v.* O'Donnell, 7 *Id.*, 337; Reg. *v.* Poole, *Id.*, 373; Reg. *v.* Guernsey, 1 *Fost. & F.*, 394; Crocheron's Case, 1 *City Hall Rec.*, 177; Ellis *v.* People, 21 *How. Pr.*, 356; State *v.* Bond, 8 *Clarke*, 540; Hamilton *v.* State, 35 *Miss.*, 214; State *v.* Gresser, 19 *Mis.*, 247; U. S. *v.* Durkee, 1 *McAll. C. C.*, 196; Alexander *v.* State, 12 *Tex.*, 540; Dignowitty *v.* State, 17 *Tex.*, 521.

For cases upon the distinction between a taking originally felonious, and which is therefore larceny, and a possession acquired without intent to steal, and followed by a wrongful appropriation, see Rex *v.* Bass, *Leach*,

285; Rex *v.* Chipchase, *Id.*, 805; Rex *v.* Palmer, *Id.*. 782; Rex *v.* Sharpless, *Id.*, 108; Rex *v.* Aickles, *Id.*, 330; Rex *v.* Harvey, *Id.*, 528; Rex *v.* Charlewood, *Id.*, 756; Rex *v.* Pear, *Id.*, 253; Rex *v.* Tunnard, *Id.* 255. n.; Rex *v.* Semple, *Leach*, 470; Rex *v.* Wi'kins, *Id.*, 586; Reg. *v.* Cole, 2 *Cox Cr. Cas.*, 340; Reg. *v.* Thistle, 3 *Id.*, 573; Reg. *v.* Hey, 3 *Id.*, 582; Reg. *v.* Roberts, *Id.*, 74; Reg. *v.* Janson, *Id.*, 82; Reg. *v.* Brockett, 4 *Id.*, 274; Reg. *v.* Mattheson, 5 *Id.*, 276; Reg. *v.* Webb, *Id.*, 154; Reg. *v.* Medland, *Id.*, 292; Reg. *v.* Jones, *Id.*, 156; Reg. *v.* Peyser, *Id.*, 241; Reg. *v.* Johnson, *Id.*, 372; Reg. *v.* Saward, *Id.*, 295; Reg. *v.* Riley, 6 *Id.*, 88; Reg. *v.* Featherstone, *Id.*, 376; Reg. *v.* Cornish, *Id.*, 432; 33 *Eng. L. & Eq.*, 527; Reg. *v.* Fitch, 7 *Cox Cr. Cas.*, 269; Reg. *v.* Davis, 2 *Jur.* (*N. S*), 478; 36 *Eng. L. & Eq.*, 607; Reg. *v.* Wright, 7 *Cox Cr. Cas.*, 413; 4 *Jur.* (*N. S.*), 313; Reg. *v.* Brown, 36 *Eng. L. & Eq.*, 610; 2 *Jur.* (*N. S.*), 192; Reg. *v.* Poole, 7 *Cox Cr. Cas.*, 373; Reg. *v.* Williams, *Id.*, 355; Reg. *v.* North, 8 *Id.*, 433; Reg. *v.* Bramley, *Id.*, 468; Reg. *v.* Thompson, 15 *Law T.*, 101; Reg. *v.* Guernsey, 1 *Fost. & F.*, 394; Reg. *v.* Gillings, *Id.*, 36; Reg. *v.* Hooper, *Id.*, 85; Mourey *v.* Walsh, 8 *Cow.*, 238; Ross *v.* People, 5 *Hill.*, 294; Dayton's Case, 2 *City H. Rec.*, 167; Dow's Case, *Id.*, 129; Lloyd's Case, *Id.*, 132; McClure's Case, *Id.*, 154; O'Terre's Case, *Id.*, 154; Valentine's Case, 4 *Id.*, 33; Bowen's Case, *Id.*, 46; Langley's Case, *Id.*, 159; Bartrons' Case, 6 *Id.*, 56; Cochran's Case, *Id.*, 62; People *v.* Jackson, 3 *Park. Cr.*, 590; People *v.* Wood, 2 *Id.*, 22; People *v.* Call, 1 *Den.*, 120; Nichols *v.* People, 17 *N. Y.*, 114; People *v.* Schuyler, 6 *Cow.*, 572; Ennis *v.* State, 3 *Iowa*, 67; Spivey *v.* State, 26 *Ala.*, 79; Commonwealth *v.* King, 9 *Cush.*, 284; Commonwealth *v.* White, 11 *Id.*, 483; Richards *v.* Commonwealth, 13 *Gratt.*, 803; Welsh *v.* People, 17 *Ill.*, 339; Farrell *v.* People, 16 *Id.*, 506; White *v.* State, 11 *Tex.*, 469; Watson *v.* State, 36 *Miss.*, 593.

Larceny of lost property.

§ 585. One who finds lost property under circumstances which give him knowledge or means of inquiry as to the true owner, and who appropriates such property to his own use, or to the use of another person who is not entitled thereto, without having first made such effort to find the owner and restore the property to him as the circumstances render reasonable and just, is guilty of larceny.

See Reg. *v.* Dixon, 36 *Eng. L. & Eq.*, 597: Reg. *v.* York, 3 *Cox Cr. Cas.*, 181; 18 L. J. (M. C.), 38; Reg. *v.* Thorburn, 3 *Cox Cr. Cas.*, 453; Reg. *v.* Preston, 5 *Id.*, 390

Reg. *v.* Pierce, 6 *Id.*, 117; Reg. *v.* West, *Id.*, 415; Reg. *v.* Shea, 7 *Id.*, 147; Reg. *v.* Dixon, *Id.*, 35; Reg. *v.* Christopher, 8 *Id.*, 91; Reg. *v.* Moore, *Id.*, 416; Reg. *v.* Vincent, 11 *Law T.*, 374; People *v.* Anderson, 14 *Johns.*, 294; People *v.* McGarren, 17 *Wend.*, 460; People *v.* Swan, 1 *Park. Cr.*, 9; People *v.* Cogdell, 1 *Hill*, 94; People *v.* Kaatz, 3 *Park. Cr.*, 129; State *v.* McCann, 19 *Mis.*, 249; State *v.* Martin, 28 *Mis.*, 530; Pritchett *v.* State, 2 *Sneed*, 285; Tanner's Case, 14 *Gratt.*, 635.

Grand and petit larceny.

§ 586. Larceny is divided into two degrees; the first of which is termed grand larceny, the second petit larceny.

The use of the terms "grand" and "petit" larceny is so interwoven with the law of this subject, that it is expedient to retain them; but a provision describing them as "degrees" of the offense, is necessary to render the provisions of section 9 of this Code applicable to this crime.

Grand larceny defined

§ 587. Grand larceny is larceny committed in either of the following cases:

1. When the property taken is of value exceeding twenty-five dollars;

2. When such property, although not of value exceeding twenty-five dollars in value, is taken from the person of another.

See 2 *Rev. Stat.*, 679, § 63; *Laws of* 1860, ch. 508, § 33; *Laws of* 1862, ch. 374, § 2. The provision of section 3 of the latter statute, that "every person who shall lay hand upon the person of another, or upon the clothing upon the person of another, with intent to steal under such circumstances as shall not amount to an attempt to rob, or an attempt to commit larceny, shall be deemed guilty of an assault with intent to steal, and shall be punished as now provided by law for the punishment of misdemeanors," is omitted as unnecessary, as section 307 of this Code makes the assault itself punishable, and no case can well arise in which the evidence requisite to support an indictment for an assault with intent to steal under the act of 1862 would not be enough to sustain a prosecution for an assault under the provisions of the Code.

Petit larceny.

§ 588. Larceny in other cases is petit larceny.

Punishment of grand larceny.

§ 589. Grand larceny is punishable by imprisonment in a state prison not exceeding five years.

See 2 *Rev. Stat.*, 679, § 63; and 2 *Rev. Stat.*, 690, § 1.

Punishment of petit larceny.

§ 590. Petit larceny is punishable as a misdemeanor.

By the present law (2 *Rev. Stat.*, 690, § 1), the punishment prescribed for petit larceny, is imprisonment in a county jail not exceeding six months, or by a fine not exceeding one hundred dollars, or both. The above section involves, therefore, a discretionary power, in the court, to impose an increased punishment. The change is suggested with a view to render the system of punishment prescribed by this Code, as a whole, more simple and harmonious.

Of grand larceny committed in dwelling house or vessel.

§ 591. When it appears upon the trial of an indictment for grand larceny that the larceny alleged was committed in any dwelling house or vessel, the offender may be punished by imprisonment in a state prison not exceeding eight years.

See 2 *Rev. Stat.*, 679, § 64.

Of grand larceny committed in the night time from the person.

§ 592. When it appears upon such trial, that such larceny was committed by stealing in the night time, from the person of another, the offender may be punished by imprisonment in a state prison not exceeding ten years.

2 *Rev. Stat.*, 679, § 65.

Larceny of written instrument.

§ 593. If the thing stolen consists of any evidence of debt, or other written instrument, the amount of money due thereupon, or secured to be paid thereby, and remaining unsatisfied, or which in any contingency might be collected thereon, or the value of the property, the title to which is shown thereby, or the sum which might be recovered in the absence thereof, as the case may be, shall be deemed the value of the thing stolen.

The language of our present statute on this subject is as follows: "If the property stolen consist of any bond, covenant, note, bill of exchange, draft, order or receipt, or any other evidence of debt, or of any public security issued by the United States, or by this state, or of any instrument whereby any demand, right or obligation shall be created, increased, released, extinguished or diminished" (except, &c.), "the money due thereon or secured thereby, and remaining unsatisfied, or which in any event or contingency might be collected thereon, or the value of the property transferred or affected thereby, as the case may be, shall be deemed the value of the article so stolen." 2 *Rev. Stat.*, 679, § 66. The commissioners consider the principle proper to be extended to all writings affecting rights of property.

Omitted provisions. The provisions of 2 *Rev. Stat.*, 680, §§ 69 and 70, relative to stealing documents from file or record in public offices, are omitted here, for the reason that they are embraced in sections 147 and 148 of this Code.

§ 594. If the thing stolen is any ticket, or other paper or writing entitling or purporting to entitle the holder or proprietor thereof to a passage upon any railroad, or in any vessel or other public conveyance, the price at which tickets entitling a person to a like passage, are usually sold by the proprietors of such conveyance, shall be deemed the value of such ticket. Value of passage ticket.

See *Laws of* 1855, ch. 499, §§ 1 and 2.

Lottery Tickets. The Revised Statutes contain a provision, in substance, that if the property stolen consist of a ticket in any lottery authorized by the laws of this state, and is stolen *before* the drawing of the lottery, the price paid for the ticket shall be deemed its value; if stolen *after* the drawing the amount due and payable to the holder shall be deemed the value. 2 *Rev. Stat.*, 679, § 67. This was proper while the law of the state authorized some kinds of lotteries. But as provisions are elsewhere reported prohibiting all lotteries (see sections 370–384), and all dealing in lottery tickets within the state, it seems proper that such tickets should no longer be recognized as property which can be the subject of larceny. The provision of the Revised Statutes above referred to is therefore omitted.

§ 595. All the provisions of this chapter shall apply where the property taken is an instrument for the payment of money, evidence of debt, public security or passage ticket, completed and ready to be issued or delivered, although the same has never been issued or delivered by the makers thereof to any person as a purchaser or owner. Securities completed, but not yet issued, declared property.

See *Laws of* 1855, ch. 499, § 3.

§ 596. All the provisions of this chapter shall apply where the thing taken is any fixture or part of the realty, and is severed at the time of the taking, Severing and removing a part of the realty, declared larceny.

in the same manner as if such thing had been severed by another person at some previous time.

Substituted for 2 *Rev. Stat.*, 679, § 68, which is as follows: "If any person shall sever from the soil of another any produce growing thereon of the value of more than twenty-five dollars, or shall sever from any building, or from any gate, fence, or other railing or enclosure, any part thereof, or any material of which it is formed, of the like value, and shall take and convert the same to his own use, with the intent to steal the same, he shall be deemed guilty of larceny in the same manner, and of the same degree as if the articles so taken had been severed at some previous and different time."

Stealing wrecked goods, &c.

§ 597. Every person who takes away any goods from any stranded vessel, or any goods cast by the sea upon the land, or found in any bay or creek, or who knowingly becomes possessed of any such, and does not deliver the same, within forty-eight hours thereafter, to the sheriff or one of the coroners or wreck masters of the county where the same were found, is guilty of a misdemeanor.

Rep. Pol. Code, § 304.

Receiving stolen property.

§ 598. Every person who buys or receives, in any manner, whether upon any consideration or not, any personal property of any value whatsoever, that has been stolen from any other, knowing the same to have been stolen, is punishable by imprisonment in a state prison not exceeding five years, or in the county jail not exceeding six months, or by a fine not exceeding two hundred and fifty dollars, or by both such fine and imprisonment.

2 *Rev. Stat.*, 680, § 71. This provision of the Revised Statutes is immediately followed by a section as follows: "In any indictment for any offense specified in the last section, it shall not be necessary to aver, nor on the trial thereof to prove, that the principal who stole such property has been convicted." 2 *Rev. Stat.*, 680, § 72. This provision is here omitted merely as not being within the scope of the Penal Code. The principle embodied is unquestionable, and the section should be transferred to the Code of Criminal Procedure, to follow section 312.

Fraudulent consumption of illu-

§ 599. Every person who, with intent to defraud, makes or causes to be made any pipe or other instrument or contrivance, and connects the same, or causes it to be connected with any pipe laid for conducting illuminating gas, so as to conduct gas to a point where the same may be consumed without its passing through the meter provided for registering the quantity consumed, or in any other manner so as to evade paying therefor, and every person who with like intent injures or alters any gas meter, or obstructs its action, is guilty of a misdemeanor. minating gas.

See *Laws of* 1854, ch. 109, § 1; *Laws of* 1859, ch. 311, § 11; Reg. *v.* White, 6 *Cox. Cr. Cas.*, 213.

§ 600. Every person who, in any other state or country, steals the property of another or receives such property knowing it to have been stolen, and brings the same into this state, may be convicted and punished in the same manner as if such larceny or receiving had been committed in this state; and such offense may be charged to have been committed in any town or city into or through which such stolen property has been brought. Larceny committed out of this state.

2 *Rev. Stat.*, 698, § 4; *Stat.* 24 and 26 *Vict.*, ch. 96, § 114.

CHAPTER V.

EMBEZZLEMENT.

"Embezzlement" defined.

§ 601. Embezzlement is the fraudulent appropriation of property by a person to whom it has been entrusted.

As to the distinctions between robbery, larceny, embezzlement and extortion, see notes to sections 280 and 584.

When officer, &c., of any association, guilty of embezzlement.

§ 602. If any person, being an officer, director, trustee, clerk, servant or agent of any association, society or corporation (public or private), fraudulently appropriates to any use or purpose not in the due and lawful execution of his trust, any property which he has in his possession or under his control in virtue of his trust, or secretes it with a fraudulent intent to appropriate it to such use or purpose, he is guilty of embezzlement.

This chapter embodies a considerable extension of our existing law relative to embezzlement. Several of the provisions reported are founded upon, or suggested by those of the recent English statutes, 24 and 25 *Vict.*, ch. 96.

When carrier, or other person, having property for transportation for hire, guilty of embezzlement.

§ 603. If any carrier or other person having under his control personal property for the purpose of transportation for hire, fraudulently appropriates it to any use or purpose inconsistent with the safe keeping of such property and its transportation according to his trust, he is guilty of embezzlement, whether he has broken the package in which such property is contained, or has otherwise separated the items thereof, or not.

When trustee, banker, &c. &c., guilty of embezzlement.

§ 604. If any person, being a trustee, banker, merchant, broker, attorney, agent, assignee in trust, executor, administrator or collector, or being otherwise entrusted with or having in his control property for the use of any other person, or for any public or benevolent purpose, fraudulently appropriates it to any use or purpose not in the due and lawful execution of his trust, or secretes it with a fraudulent intent to appropriate it to such use or purpose, he is guilty of embezzlement.

When bailee guilty of

§ 605. If any person being entrusted with any property as bailee, or with any power of attorney for the sale or transfer thereof, fraudulently converts the same or the proceeds thereof to his own use, or secretes it or them with a fraudulent intent to convert to his own use, he is guilty of embezzlement, whether he has broken the package or otherwise determined the bailment or not.

embezzlement.

§ 606. If any clerk or servant of any private person or copartnership or corporation (except apprentices and persons within the age of eighteen years), fraudulently appropriates to his own use, or secretes with a fraudulent intent to appropriate to his own use, any property of any other person which has come into his control or care by virtue of his employment as such clerk or servant, he is guilty of embezzlement.

When clerk, or servant guilty of embezzlement.

See 2 *Rev. Stat.*, 678, § 59.

§ 607. A distinct act of taking is not necessary to constitute embezzlement; but any fraudulent appropriation, conversion or use of the property, coming within the above prohibitions, is sufficient.

Distinct act of taking, not necessary to constitute embezzlement

People *v.* Dalton, 15 *Wend.*, 581.

§ 608. Any evidence of debt, negotiable by delivery only, and actually executed, is equally the subject of embezzlement, whether it has been delivered or issued as a valid instrument or not.

Evidence of debt, undelivered, may be subject of embezzlement.

2 *Rev. Stat.*, 678, § 60.

§ 609. Upon any indictment for embezzlement it is a sufficient defense that the property was appropriated openly and avowedly, and under a claim of title preferred in good faith, even though such claim is untenable. But this provision shall not excuse the retention of the property of another to offset or pay demands held against him.

Claim of title a ground of defense.

§ 610. The fact that the accused intended to restore the property embezzled, is no ground of defense, or of mitigation of punishment, if it has not been restored before an information has been laid before a magistrate, charging the commission of the offense.

Intent to restore the property, is no defense.

But actual restoration is a ground for mitigation of punishment.

§ 611. Whenever it is made to appear that prior to any information laid before a magistrate, charging the commission of embezzlement, the person accused voluntarily and actually restored or tendered restoration of the property alleged to have been embezzled, or any part thereof, such fact is not a ground of defense to the indictment, but it authorizes the court to mitigate punishment in its discretion.

Punishment for embezzlement.

§ 612. Every person guilty of embezzlement is punishable in the manner prescribed for feloniously stealing property of the value of that embezzled. And where the property embezzled is an evidence of debt or right in action, the sum due upon it, or secured to be paid by it, shall be taken as its value.

Founded upon 2 *Rev. Stat.*, 678, § 59.

CHAPTER VI.

EXTORTION.

"Extortion" defined.

§ 613. Extortion is the obtaining of property from another, with his consent, induced by a wrongful use of force or fear, or under color of official right.

See note to section 584; also, as to extortion under color of official right, People *v.* Whaley, 6 *Cow.*, 661.

What threats may constitute extortion.

§ 614. Fear, such as will constitute extortion, may be induced by a threat, either:

1. To do an unlawful injury to the person or property of the individual threatened, or to any relative of his or member of his family; or,

2. To accuse him, or any relative of his or member of his family, of any crime; or,

3. To expose, or impute to him, or them, any deformity or disgrace; or,

4. To expose any secret affecting him or them.

§ 615. Every person who extorts any money or other property from another, under circumstances not amounting to robbery, by means of force or any threat such as is mentioned in the last section, is punishable by imprisonment in a state prison not exceeding five years.

Punishment of extortion in certain cases.

§ 616. Every person who commits any extortion under color of official right, in cases for which a different punishment is not prescribed by this Code or by some of the statutes which it specifies as continuing in force, is guilty of a misdemeanor.

Punishment of extortion committed under color of official right.

§ 617. Every person, who, by any extortionate means, obtains from another his signature to any paper or instrument, whereby, if such signature were freely given, any property would be transferred, or any debt, demand, charge or right of action created, is punishable in the same manner as if the actual delivery of such property or payment of the amount of such debt, demand, charge or right of action, were obtained.

Obtaining signature by means of threats

§ 618. Every person who, with intent to extort any money or other property from another, sends to any person any letter or other writing, whether subscribed or not, expressing or implying, or adapted to imply, any threat, such as is specified in section 614, is punishable in the same manner as if such money or property were actually obtained by means of such threat.

Sending threatening letters.

Suggested as a substitute for the provisions of 2 *Rev. Stat.*, 678, § 58, which are as follows: "Every person who shall knowingly send or deliver, or shall make, and for the purpose of being delivered or sent, shall part with the possession of any letter or writing, with or without a name subscribed thereto, or signed with a fictitious name, or with any letter, mark or other designation, threatening therein to accuse any person of any crime, or to do any injury to the person or property of any one, with a view or intent to extort or gain any money or property of any description belonging to another, shall, upon conviction, be adjudged guilty of an attempt to rob, and shall be punished by imprisonment in a state prison not exceeding five years."

Attempts to extort money, or property, by verbal threats.

§ 619. Every person who unsuccessfully attempts by means of any verbal threat, such as is specified in section 614, to extort money or other property from another, is guilty of a misdemeanor.

Compare 2 *Rev. Stat.*, 690, § 2.

CHAPTER VII.

FALSE PERSONATION, AND CHEATS.

Falsely personating another.

§ 620. Every person who falsely personates another and in such assumed character, either

1. Marries or pretends to marry, or to sustain the marriage relation towards another, with or without the connivance of such other person; or,

2. Becomes bail or surety for any party in any proceeding whatever, before any court or officer authorized to take such bail or surety; or,

3. Subscribes, verifies, publishes, acknowledges or proves, in the name of another person, any written instrument, with intent that the same may be delivered or used as true; or,

4. Does any other act, whereby if it were done by the person falsely personated, he might in any event

become liable to any suit or prosecution, or to pay any sum of money, or to incur any charge, forfeiture or penalty, or whereby any benefit might accrue to the party personating, or to any other person,

Is punishable by imprisonment in a state prison not exceeding ten years.

See 2 *Rev. Stat.*, 676, § 48.

§ 621. Every person who falsely personates another, and in such assumed character receives any money or property, knowing that it is intended to be delivered to the individual so personated, with intent to convert the same to his own use, or to that of another person who is not entitled thereto, is punishable in the same manner and to the same extent as for larceny of the money or property so received. **Receiving property in false character.**

See 2 *Rev. Stat.*, 676, § 50.

§ 622. Every person who falsely personates any public officer, civil or military, or any fireman, or any private individual having special authority by law to perform any act affecting the rights or interests of another, or assumes, without authority, any uniform or badge by which such are usually distinguished, and in such assumed character does any act whereby another person is injured, defrauded, vexed or annoyed, is guilty of a misdemeanor. **Personating officers, firemen and other persons.**

§ 623. Every person who, with intent to cheat or defraud another, designedly, by color or aid of any false token or writing, or other false pretense, obtains the signature of any person to any written instrument, or obtains from any person any money or property, is punishable by imprisonment in a state prison not exceeding three years, or in a county jail not exceeding one year, or by a fine not exceeding three times the value of the money or property so obtained, or by both such fine and imprisonment. **Obtaining property by false pretenses.**

See 2 *Rev. Stat.*, 677, § 53.

The words by "color *or aid* of any false token," &c., are employed in this and the next section instead of the words "by color of," &c., used in our existing statutes, in order that it may be clear that cases are embraced in which a false pretense is used in aid of the fraud, but such pretense is not the controlling inducement operative upon the mind of the party defrauded. At present, it is well settled that a mere assertion may be a "false pretense;" but it must be an untrue assertion of an existing fact, not a representation or promise as to the future (People *v.* Tompkins, 1 *Park. Cr.*, 224; State *v.* Magee, 11 *Ind.*, 154; Dillingham *v.* State, 5 *Ohio* (*N. S.*), 280); and it must be one adapted under the circumstances to deceive, notwithstanding the use of ordinary care and caution in giving credence to it (People *v.* Williams, 4 *Hill*, 9; People *v.* Wood, 10 *N. Y. Leg. Obs.*, 61; People *v.* Stetson, 4 *Barb.*, 151); and it must have actually influenced the defrauded person to part with his property; for if the prosecutor knew the representation to be false at the time of parting with the property (Reg. *v.* Mills, 7 *Cox Cr. Cas.*, 263; 40 *Eng. L. & Eq.*, 562); or if he disregarded the pretense and relied on his own examination as to the fact in question (Reg. *v.* Roebuck, 7 *Cox Cr. Cas.*, 126; 2 *Jur.* (*N. S.*), 597; 36 *Eng. L. & Eq.*, 631), the indictment cannot be sustained. These rules the Commissioners do not propose to disturb. But it is further held that though the false pretense need not be the *only* inducement influential with the injured party, it must be the *controlling* one. (People *v.* Crissie, 4 *Denio*, 525; see also People *v.* Haynes, 11 *Wend.*, 557; People *v.* Herrick, 13 *Id.*, 87.) This rule sometimes leads to a failure of justice; as, for instance, in the late case of Ranney *v.* People (22 *N. Y.*, 413). In that case the accused represented to one Hock that he had employment for him at a distance in traveling to collect money and do other business; and he promised to give him certain wages therefor, upon condition that Hock should deposit with the accused one hundred dollars as security for his faithful performance of duty. It was held that, although the representation and promise were false and fraudulent, an indictment could not be sustained. "There must be," say the court, "a direct and positive false assertion as to some existing matter by which the victim is induced to part with his money or property. In this case the material thing was the promise of the accused to employ the person defrauded and to pay him for his services. There was a statement, it is true, that the prisoner had employment which he could give to Hock; but this was obviously of no importance without the contract which was made. The false representation complained of was, therefore, essentially promissory in its nature, and this has never been held to be the foundation of a criminal charge.

The Commissioners doubt the soundness of this decision, even under the existing law. See Reg. *v.* Bates (3 *Cox Cr. Cas.*, 201), where it is held that an indictment which charges a false pretense of an existing fact calculated to induce the confidence which led to the prosecutor's parting with his property, though mixed up with false pretenses as to the prisoner's future conduct, is sufficient. Where the false pretense is as to the *status* of the party at the time, or as to any collateral fact supposed to be then existing, it will equally support an indictment under the statute. See also Reg. *v.* Burnsides (8 *Cox Cr. Cas.*, 370), where the indictment charged that the prisoner falsely pretended to the prosecutor that a certain person who lived in a large house down the street, and had had a daughter married some time back, had been at him, the prisoner, about some carpet, to wit, about twelve yards, by which, &c.; whereas no such person had been at the prisoner about any carpet, nor had any such person asked the prisoner to procure any piece of woolen carpet; and the evidence was, that the prisoner stated to the prosecutor that he wanted some carpeting for a family in a large house in the village, who had a daughter lately married, and thereby obtained twenty yards of carpet from him; and it was held that there was a sufficient false pretense alleged.

But conceding the decision in Ranney *v.* People to be a correct exposition of the Revised Statutes, it calls for a modification of the law. Under the language employed in the text, it will be sufficient that the false assertion cooperated with other influences to induce the prosecutor to act; that it aided the prisoner to perpetrate the fraud.

The words "money or property" are substituted in this and the preceding sections for the words "money, personal property or other valuable thing," employed in the existing statutes, as being a briefer expression of equivalent import; and without intent to change the law.

Obtaining property for charitable purposes.

§ 624. Every person who designedly, by color or aid of any false token or writing, or other false pretense, obtains the signature of any person to any written instrument, or obtains from any person any money or property for any alleged charitable or benevolent purpose whatever, is punishable by imprisonment in a state prison not exceeding three years, or in a county jail not exceeding one year, or by a fine not exceeding the value of the money or property so obtained, or by both such fine and imprisonment.

See *Laws of* 1851, ch. 144.

Obtaining negotiable evidence of debt by false pretenses.

§ 625. If the false token by which any money or property is obtained in violation of sections 623 and 624 is a promissory note or other negotiable evidence of debt purporting to be issued by or under the authority of any banking company or corporation not in existence, the person guilty of such cheat is punishable by imprisonment in a state prison not exceeding seven years, instead of by the punishments prescribed by those sections.

See 2 *Rev. Stat.*, 677, § 54.

Using false check or order for payment of money.

§ 626. The use of a matured check, or other order for the payment of money, as a means of obtaining any signature, money or property, such as is specified in the last two sections, by a person who knows that the drawer thereof is not entitled to draw for the sum specified therein, upon the drawee, is the use of a false token within the meaning of those sections, although no representation is made in respect thereto.

As to the necessity of such a provision see Allen's case, 3 *City H. Rec.*, 118; Conger's case, 4 *Id.*, 65; 1 *Wheel. Cr.*, 448; Van Pelt's case, 1 *City H. Rec.*, 137; People *v.* Tompkins, 1 *Park. Cr.*, 224.

Mock auctions.

§ 627. Every person who obtains any money or property from another, or obtains the signature of another to any written instrument, the false making of which would be forgery, by means of any false or fraudulent sale of property or pretended property by auction, or by any of the practices known as mock auctions, is punishable by imprisonment in a state prison not exceeding three years, or in the county jail not exceeding one year, or by a fine not exceeding one thousand dollars, or by both such fine and imprisonment; and in addition thereto he forfeits any license he may hold to act as an auctioneer, and is forever disqualified from receiving a license to act as auctioneer within this state.

See *Laws of* 1853, ch. 138.

CHAPTER VIII.

FRAUDULENTLY FITTING OUT AND DESTROYING VESSELS.

§ 628. Every captain or other officer or person in command or charge of any vessel, who within this state willfully wrecks, sinks, or otherwise injures or destroys such vessel, or any cargo in such vessel, or willfully permits the same to be wrecked, sunk, or otherwise injured or destroyed, with intent to prejudice or defraud an insurer or any other person, is punishable by imprisonment in a state prison for life. Captain, or other officer willfully destroying vessel, &c.

Injuring or destroying vessels upon the high seas, is provided for by various acts of Congress. See the acts collected, Brightly's Dig., 209–211. The above section is therefore limited to acts committed within this state.

§ 629. Every person other than such as are embraced within the last section, who is guilty of any act therein prohibited, is punishable by imprisonment in a state prison not exceeding ten years and not less than three. Other persons willfully destroying vessel, &c.

§ 630. Every person guilty of fitting out any vessel, or of lading any cargo on board of any vessel, with intent to cause or permit the same to be wrecked, sunk or otherwise injured or destroyed, and thereby to prejudice or defraud an insurer or any other person, is punishable by imprisonment in a state prison not exceeding ten years, and not less than three. Fitting out, or lading any vessel with intent to wreck the same.

§ 631. Every person guilty of preparing, making or subscribing, any false or fraudulent manifest, invoice, bill of lading, ship's register or protest, with intent to defraud another, is punishable by imprison- Making false manifest, &c.

ment in a state prison not exceeding three years, or by a fine not exceeding one thousand dollars, or both.

The offense of making false evidence to be used in legal trials or investigations, is covered by sections 165–170.

CHAPTER IX.

FRAUDULENT DESTRUCTION OF PROPERTY INSURED.

Destroying property insured.

§ 632. Every person who willfully burns, or in any other manner injures or destroys any property whatever which is at the time insured against loss or damage by fire, or by any other casualty, with intent to defraud or prejudice the insurer, whether the same be the property or in the possession of such person or of any other, is punishable by imprisonment in the state prison not exceeding seven years, and not less than four.

Corresponds with the punishment for arson in the third degree, reported in section 539. See also note to sections 521 and 526.

Presenting false proofs of loss in support of claim upon policy of insurance.

§ 633. Every person who presents or causes to be presented any false or fraudulent claim, or any proof in support of any such claim, upon any contract of insurance, for the payment of any loss, or who prepares, makes or subscribes any account, certificate, survey, affidavit, proof of loss, or other book, paper or writing, with intent to present or use the same, or to allow it to be presented or used in support of any such claim, is punishable by imprisonment in a state prison not exceeding three years, or by a fine not exceeding one thousand dollars, or both.

CHAPTER X.

FALSE WEIGHTS AND MEASURES.

§ 634. Every person who uses any weight or measure, knowing it to be false, by which use another is defrauded or otherwise injured, is guilty of a misdemeanor. Using false weights or measures.

See 2 *Rev. Stat.*, 5, § 32.

§ 635. When the property sold by false weight or measure consists of any description of provisions, the offense is felony. Selling provisions by false weight or measure.

By "provisions" are intended bread, meat, milk and other articles which form ordinary food.

§ 636. Every person who retains in his possession any weight or measure, knowing it to be false, unless it appears beyond a reasonable doubt that it was so retained without intent to use it, or permit it to be used in violation of the last section, is guilty of a misdemeanor. Keeping false weights.

§ 637. Every person who is authorized or enjoined by law to arrest another person for a violation of sections 634, 635 and 636, is equally authorized and enjoined to seize any false weights or measures found in the possession of the person so arrested, and to deliver the same to the magistrate before whom the person so arrested is required to be taken. False weights and measures authorized to be seized

§ 638. The magistrate to whom any weight or measure is delivered pursuant to the last section, May be tested by committing magistrate, and destroyed, or delivered to district attorney.

shall, upon the examination of the accused, or if the examination is delayed or prevented, without awaiting such examination, cause the same to be tested by comparison with standards conformable to law; and if he finds it to be false, he shall cause it to be destroyed, or to be delivered to the district attorney of the county in which the accused is liable to indictment or trial, as the interests of justice in his judgment require.

Shall be destroyed after conviction of offender.

§ 639. Upon the conviction of the accused, such district attorney shall cause any weight or measure in respect whereof the accused stands convicted, and which remains in the possession or under the control of such district attorney, to be destroyed.

Stamping false weight or tare, on casks or packages.

§ 640. Every person who knowingly marks or stamps false or short weight, or false tare on any cask or package, or knowingly sells or offers for sale any cask or package so marked, is guilty of a misdemeanor.

Rep. Pol. Code, § 704.

CHAPTER XI.

FRAUDULENT INSOLVENCIES BY INDIVIDUALS.

Fraudulent conveyances.

§ 641. Every person who, being a party to any conveyance or assignment of any real or personal property, or of any interest therein, made or created with intent to defraud prior or subsequent purchasers, or to hinder, delay or defraud creditors or other persons, and every person being privy to or knowing of such conveyance, assignment or charge, who willfully puts the same in use as having been made in good faith, is guilty of a misdemeanor.

See 2 *Rev. Stat.*, 690, § 3.

§ 642. Every person who removes any of his property out of any county, with intent to prevent the same from being levied upon by any execution or attachment, or who secretes, assigns, conveys or otherwise disposes of any of his property, with intent to defraud any creditor, or to prevent such property being made liable for the payment of his debts, and every person who receives any such property with such intent, is guilty of a misdemeanor.

Fraudulent removal of property to prevent levy.

See 2 *Rev. Stat.*, 51, § 26.

§ 643. Every person who, knowing that his property is insufficient for the payment of all his lawful debts, assigns, transfers or delivers any property for the benefit of any creditor, or creditors, upon any trust or condition, that any creditor shall receive a preference or priority over any other, except in the cases in which such preference is expressly allowed to be given by law, or with intent to create such preference or priority, is guilty of a misdemeanor.

Making assignments with preferences by insolvents prohibited.

The adoption of the above section involves, of course, the abrogation of the right, so long recognized in this state, of making preferential assignments. At the time when the provisions of the Draft Civil Code, upon assignments for the benefit of creditors, were in course of compilation, the commissioners were not prepared to recommend so great a change in the existing law, without further deliberation and a fuller examination of the evils of the existing practice of assignments, than the time then at their command admitted. They, therefore, at that time presented a system of sections adapted to express the existing law of this state upon the subject, and suitable for enactment in case the legislature considered it best to adhere to the present system. They now, however, recommend that the right of a confessed insolvent debtor to make an assignment with preferences be abrogated, and that an order of priority in the payment of debts in cases of insolvency, suited as far as possible to the common sense of justice of the community, and independent of the choice of the individual debtor, be substituted.

The details of the system proper to be adopted for the distribution of an insolvent's property, if this recommendation should be approved, would be out of place in the Penal Code. The revision of the Civil Code will afford the proper opportunity for considering those details. In general, the rule of *pro rata* distribution, receives the common approval, on the principle that "equality is equity." The custom of merchants to recognize certain descriptions of debts, cash loans, trust funds, &c., as confidential debts entitled to a preference over those arising upon ordinary business transactions, ought not, however, to be overlooked. Debts resting in judgment may perhaps be properly preferred to open demands. Debts infected with usury, or otherwise invalid, may, with even greater propriety, be postponed to all other classes. The act of congress of 1799 (ch. 128, § 65), requires that a priority shall be given to the United States, in cases where an insolvent has made an assignment for the benefit of his creditors. Reserving these details for future consideration, it is only necessary here to suggest a penal provision for an attempt to create unlawful preferences in an assignment, and to call the attention of the legislature to the steady and remarkable progress of the jurisprudence of this state, in a direction tending always towards restriction of the privilege of preferential assignments within narrower and narrower bounds; and to the evidence to be derived from the whole course of our decisions and legislation upon the subject, that the privilege itself, as usually exercised, creates opportunities for fraud and temptations to litigation which form a sufficient reason why it should be abrogated.

The earlier adjudications of our courts abound in recognitions of the right of a debtor, although insolvent, to prefer lawful debts at discretion. Jackson *v.* Brownell, 3 *Cai.*, 222; McMenomy *v.* Ferrers, 3 *Johns.*, 71; Wilkes *v.* Ferris, 5 *Id.*, 335; Hyslop *v.* Clarke, 14 *Id.*, 458; Murray *v.* Riggs, 15 *Id.*, 571; Hendricks *v.* Robinson, 2 *Johns. Ch.*, 283, aff'd, 17 *Johns*, 438; McMenomy *v.* Roosevelt, 3 *Johns. Ch.*, 446; Nicoll *v.* Mumford, 4 *Id.*, 522; Williams *v.* Brown, 4 *Id.*, 682; Wilder *v.* Winne, 6 *Cow.*, 284; Wintringham *v.* La Foy, 7 *Id.*, 735; Jackson *v.* Cornell, 1 *Sand. Ch.*, 438; Cunningham *v.* Freeborn, 11 *Wend.*, 241.

The later periods of our legal history abound in decisions pointing out and endeavoring to remedy frauds to which this privilege has given rise. The following is a brief review of the leading restrictions which have been imposed:

1. Moneyed corporations and limited partnerships have been prohibited by statute from making assignments with preferences. 1 *Rev. Stat.*, 591, § 9; *Id.*, 766, §§ 20, 21. This prohibition is held to apply to associations organized under the general banking law, and to forbid even an assignment to a single creditor in payment of his particular demand. Robinson *v.* Bank of Attica, 21 *N. Y.*, 406. Whether corporations are left at liberty to make

assignments *without* preference, is disputed. See De Ruyter *v.* St. Peter's Church, 3 *N. Y.*, 238; Hurlbert *v.* Carter, 21 *Barb.*, 221; Bowery Bank case, 5 *Abb. Pr.*, 415; Loring *v.* U. S. Vulcanized Gutta Percha & B. Co., 36 *Barb.*, 329, though the better opinion, probably, is that they are. An infant is incompetent to assign; because an assignment must be absolute, while an infant's act is defeasible on becoming of age. Fox *v.* Heath, 21 *How. Pr.*, 384.

2. Under the former bankrupt laws an assignment with preferences was held to be a fraud upon creditors, if made in contemplation of proceedings for a discharge in bankruptcy. Ogden *v.* Jackson, 1 *Johns.*, 370; Phœnix *v.* Ingraham, 5 *Id.*, 412; Hastings *v.* Belknap, 1 *Den.*, 190; Freeman *v.* Denning, 3 *Sandf. Ch.*, 327. A similar rule has obtained with respect to assignments—although without preferences—made pending proceedings to compel the debtor to make an assignment, instituted under the non-imprisonment act of 1831. Spear *v.* Wardell, 1 *Comst.*, 144; Hall *v.* Kellogg, 2 *Kern*, 325; Wood *v.* Boland, 8 *Paige*, 556. And one who has made an assignment with preferences is debarred from a discharge under the insolvent act. 2 *Rev. Stat.*, 20, § 24.

3. After some dispute it has been settled that a general assignee for the benefit of creditors stands in no better position, and has no higher rights in respect to enforcing choses in action transferred by the assignment, than those of his assignor. He is not to be regarded as a purchaser for a valuable consideration. Matter of Howe, 1 *Paige*, 125; Mead *v.* Phillips, 1 *Sandf. Ch.*, 83; Marine and Fire Ins. Bank of Georgia *v.* Jauncey, 1 *Barb.*, 486; Leger *v.* Bonaffe, 2 *Barb.*, 475; Warren *v.* Fenn, 28 *Id.*, 333; Van Heusen *v.* Radcliff, 17 *Id.*, 580; Bliss *v.* Cottle, 32 *Barb.*, 322; Reed *v.* Sands, 37 *Id.*, 185; Maas *v.* Goodman, 2 *Hill*, 275; Schieffelin *v.* Hawkins, 14 *Abbott's Pr.*, 112. Thus he takes evidences of debt subject to any offset which existed against his assignor (Chance *v.* Isaacs, 5 *Paige*, 592; Maas *v.* Goodman, 2 *Hilt.*, 275) and merchandise subject to any right of stoppage in transit (Harris *v.* Hunt, 6 *Duer*, 606; Harris *v.* Pratt, 17 *N. Y.*, 249), or to any vendor's lien (Haggerty *v.* Palmer, 6 *Johns. Ch.*, 437), which might have been enforced against his assignor. And he cannot impeach previous transfers of property made by his assignor which were binding upon the latter, although they may be voidable for fraud at the instance of creditors. Van Heusen *v.* Radcliff, 17 *N. Y.*, 580; Brownell *v.* Curtis, 10 Paige, 210; Storm *v.* Davenport, 1 *Sandf. Ch.*, 135; Osborne *v.* Moss, 7 *Johns.*, 161; Averill *v.* Loucks, 6 Barb., 470; Mills *v* Argall, 6 *Paige*, 577, with which compare Bayard *v.* Hoffman, 4 *Johns. Ch.*, 450.

4. Any clauses in an assignment which confer any power or privilege upon the assignee inconsistent with the simple duty of converting the assets promptly into cash, and distributing it among the creditors, or which give him a compensation or advantage therein not allowed by law, operate to defraud creditors, and are therefore held to render the assignment void. Upon this ground assignments have been condemned in several cases;—for instance, for giving the assignee power to name his successor (Planch *v.* Schermerhorn, 3 *Barb. Ch.*, 644); for giving him an extended time within which to perform his duty of sale and payment (Woodburne *v.* Mosher, 9 *Barb.*, 255; D'Ivernois *v.* Leavitt, 23 *Barb.*, 63; compare Bellows *v.* Partridge, 19 *Barb.*, 176); for providing in effect that he should not be personally liable for losses resulting from a mere want of ordinary diligence (Litchfield *v.* White, 3 *Seld.*, 438; Olmstead *v.* Herrick, 1 *E. D. Smith*, 310; with which compare Van Nest *v.* Yoe, 1 *Sandf. Ch.*, 4; Jacobs *v.* Allen, 18 *Barb.*, 549); for providing a compensation beyond that allowed by law (Nichols *v.* McEwen, 17 *N. Y.*, 22); and for enabling him to vary the order of preferences. Barnum *v.* Hempstead, 7 *Paige*, 568; Boardman *v.* Halliday, 10 *Id.*, 223; Strong v. Skinner, 4 *Barb.*, 546.

But clauses which merely express in terms, powers or rights which the law would confer upon the assignee, were they not expressed;—such as a provision that he may employ agents (Mann *v.* Whitbeck, 17 *Barb.*, 388; Van Dine *v.* Willett, 24 *How. Pr.*, 206); that he may advertise for demands, and pay those presented within a certain time (Ward *v.* Tingley, 4 *Sandf. Ch.*, 476); that he may pay insurance premiums, and mortgage interest upon the property (Whitney *v.* Krows, 11 *Barb.*, 198); or rent and taxes (Van Dine *v.* Willett, 24 *How. Pr.*, 206, and 38 *Barb.*, 319); or a provision for his compensation which allows of its being adjusted at a sum within his legal commissions (Keteltas *v.* Wilson, 36 *Barb.*, 298; 23 *How. Pr.*, 69; Halstead *v.* Gordon, 34 *Barb.*, 422; Campbell *v.* Woodworth, 33 *Barb.*, 425; 24 *N. Y.*, 304); or directions as to sale or distribution which leave him at liberty to comply with the requirements of the law (Wilson *v.* Robertson, 21 *N. Y.*, 589; 19 *How. Pr.*, 350; Ogden *v.* Peters, *Id.*, 23; Griffin *v.* Marquadt, *Id.*, 221; Jessup *v.* Hulse, *Id.*, 168; Stern *v.* Fisher, 32 *Barb.*, 198; Halstead *v.* Gordon, 34 *Barb.*, 422);—are unobjectionable. See also, Brigham *v.* Tillinghast, 15 *Barb.*, 618; Dow *v.* Platner, 16 *N. Y.*, 562; Bellows *v.* Partridge, 19 *Barb.*, 176.

5. Ingenuity has been frequently exerted to prepare assignments in such a form as should secure some ultimate surplus, or other benefit or advantage, to the assignor. Assignments upon any trust which operates in this man-

ner have been, from an early period, declared void by statute. 1 *Rev. Stat.*, 135, § 1. The application of this statute has been often invoked to defeat endeavors of insolvents to place property out of the reach of their creditors, with a view to their own ultimate benefit. The case of Goodrich *v.* Downs (6 *Hill*, 438,) was upon this subject. The assignment drawn in question in that case directed the assignees to pay certain specified creditors, making no provision for others, and to pay the surplus, if any, to the assignor. It was held that such an assignment was void upon its face; as operating to put a part of the debtor's property out of the reach of creditors for his own benefit; and that as the statute declares that in such a case the *conveyance* shall be void, the void trust as to the surplus avoided the whole deed. And it could not be aided by extrinsic proof that there would be no surplus. The parties having expressly provided for a surplus, were not at liberty to say they did not contemplate one. To the same effect is Strong *v.* Skinner, 4 *Barb.*, 456. See, however, a disapproval of the grounds of decision in Goodrich *v.* Downs, in Curtis *v.* Leavitt, 15 *N. Y.*, 9, 114.

In Goodrich *v.* Downs the property assigned was *personal;* in Barney *v.* Griffin, decided in the court of appeals in 1849 (2 *Comst.*, 365), similar principles were established with reference to assignments of *real* property. It was there determined that an assignment of a debtor's entire property, in trust to pay certain specified creditors, and, without making any provision for others, to repay the residue to the assignor, is void, for fraud upon creditors not provided for; inasmuch as the property is placed beyond the reach of their executions, in the hands of men not accountable to them, and upon a trust in part for the benefit of the debtor. And the defect cannot be aided by proof there will be no surplus. Substantially the same view is taken in Leitch *v.* Hollister (4 *Comst.*, 211), Lansing *v.* Woodruff (1 *Sandf.* ch. 43), and Clark *v.* Dowlings (1 *Hill & D. Supp.*, 105); and the rule has even been applied in a case where it was thought that the resulting trust was not intended, but arose from an inadvertent omission in drawing the assignment Hooper *v.* Tuckerman (3 *Sandf.*, 311); and in cases where the assignment was of partnership property, and the resulting trust arose only indirectly through the individual interest of partners in the residue of the firm assets. (Johnson *v.* Gardner, 4 *N. Y. Leg. Obs.*, 424; Collomb *v.* Caldwell, 16 *N. Y.*, 484; Wilson *v.* Robertson, 21 *N. Y.*, 387; 19 *How. Pr.*, 350; Smith *v.* Howard, 20 *How. Pr.*, 121); with which compare Collumb *v.* Read (24 *N. Y.*, 405); compare, however, upon this subject, Wilkes *v.* Tenis (5 *Johns.*, 335), and remarks upon Barney *v.* Griffin (cited *supra*), in Curtis *v.* Leavitt (15 *N. Y.*, 118, 176).

Some cases, indeed, are recognized as not within the rule avoiding an assignment for expressing a trust to pay a surplus to the assignor. One class is, cases in which property is assigned direct to a particular creditor, as a means of securing payment of his demand. Such an assignment being in the nature of a mortgage for the particular demand, a trust to pay the surplus to the assignor, is held to result from the nature of the instrument; and whether it is stated in the instrument or left to implication, is immaterial. (Leitch *v.* Hollister, 4 *Comst.*, 24; Hendricks *v.* Robinson, 3 *Johns. Ch.*, 284, affirmed 17 *Johns.*, 438; Dunham *v.* Whitehead, 21 *N. Y.*, 131; McLelland *v.* Remsen, 36 *Barb.*, 622; 14 *Abbott's Pr.*, 381; 23 *How. Pr.*, 175.)

Another class embraces cases in which the surplus directed to be returned is only such as may remain after paying *all* creditors in full. Where a surplus results under such circumstances, the law implies a trust to repay it to the assignor. Hence a direction to repay a surplus in an assignment will not avoid it, if the instrument in effect empowers the assignor first to pay all creditors in full, in case assets are sufficient. (Wintringham *v.* Lafroy, 7 *Cow.*, 735; Van Rossum *v.* Walker, 11 *Barb.*, 237; Ely *v.* Cook, 18 *Id.*, 612; Taylor *v.* Stevens, 7 *How. Pr.*, 415.)

A third class comprises cases in which particular items of property are excepted from the assignment. As these remain open to the reach of creditors in the same manner as they were before the assignment was made, the reservation does not operate to delay them. (Carpenter *v.* Underwood, 19 *N. Y.*, 520.)

A reservation of a specific sum to the assignor for the support of his family, was thought, in an early case, to constitute no objection to the instrument, as to the residue. (Murray *v.* Riggs, 15 *Johns.*, 535.) Later, it has been held to render the whole assignment void, as operating to put property of the assignor out of the reach of his creditors, and for his own enjoyment. (Mackie *v.* Cairns, 5 *Cow.*, 547.) The same principle has been held applicable where an assignment provided for payment of a sum which the assignor had applied for as a loan, and had reason to believe was upon the way to him, but which he had not yet received. As such sum would not belong to the assigned assets, but must be repaid from them, the effect was an indirect reservation of the sum, from the estate, for the individual benefit of the assignor. (Sheldon *v.* Dodge, 4 *Den.*, 217; see, also, to nearly the same effect, Barnum *v.* Hempstead, 7 *Paige*, 568.)

6. Provisions have often been inserted in assignments tending to enable the debtor to exercise a future preference between his creditors. These are held to avoid the instrument. Examples are, where the assignment pre.

ferred the creditors who should be named in a schedule to be thereafter made out and affixed (Averill *v.* Loucks, 6 *Barb.*, 470); where it directed that, in a certain contingency, debts enumerated in a later class should be preferred to those mentioned in an earlier one (Sheldon *v.* Dodge, 4 *Den.*, 217); and where it directed that if certain creditors should refuse to release the assignor then such creditors should be preferred to them as the assignors should appoint. (Hyslop *v.* Clarke, 14 *Johns.*, 458.)

7. The endeavor to empower an assignee to impose conditions upon creditors, before paying their demands, has frequently been held ground for avoiding the assignment; as where certain creditors are directed to be preferred upon the condition that they execute releases of their demands (Hyslop *v.* Clarke, 14 *Johns.*, 458; Austin *v.* Bell, 20 *Id.*, 442; Grover *v.* Wakeman, 11 *Wend.*, 187; Armstrong *v.* Byrne, 1 *Edw.*, 79; Lentilhon *v.* Moffat, 1 *Edw. Ch.*, 451; Searing *v.* Brincherhoff, 5 *Johns. Ch.*, 329; Hone *v.* Henriquez, 13 *Wend.*, 240; Gasherie *v.* Apple, 14 *Abbott's Pr.*, 64); or where the assignment authorizes a surplus to be divided among those who will execute a release. (Grover *v.* Wakeman, 11 *Wend.*, 187; Mills *v.* Levy, 2 *Edw.*, 183; but see De Caters *v.* De Chaumont, 2 *Paige*, 490; Hastings *v.* Belknap, 1 *Den.*, 190. See also, upon the same general principle, Berry *v.* Riley, 2 *Barb.*, 307; Bellows *v.* Partridge, 19 *Barb.*, 176; Oliver Lee & Co's. Bank *v.* Talcott, 19 *N. Y.*, 146; Bank of Silver Creek *v.* Talcott, 22 *Barb.*, 550; Jewett *v.* Woodward, 1 *Edw.*, 195; Van Nest *v.* Yoe, 1 *Sandf. Ch.*, 4; Spaulding *v.* Strong, 36 *Barb.*, 310.)

8. Directions to an assignee to deal with the estate in a given way, in order to increase the amount to be realized from it, are another class of frauds upon creditors; that is, they are held to be fraudulent and to avoid the assignment wherever they operate to *delay* a sale. At one period their tendency was not fully perceived. Therefore, where in an assignment made by proprietors of a foundry, the trustee was directed to conduct and carry on the establishment for the benefit of the creditors, to sell the manufactured articles, to work up and sell those unmanufactured, and, in general, to sell all the property as soon as it could conveniently be done without a sacrifice, it was held that these directions were not necessarily fraudulent. But this view has been disapproved by the later cases; which go upon the general ground that the creditors have a right to a prompt sale and distribution of proceeds, whether a sacrifice is the result or not. Without their consent the debtor cannot carry on his business through the medium of an assignee, for the purpose of increasing the ultimate fund. He may direct, in general terms, a sale of the property, and to what debts and in what order the proceeds shall be

applied; but beyond this he can prescribe no condition whatever as to the management or disposal of the estate. (Dunham *v.* Waterman, 17 *N. Y.*, 9. To the same effect are Van Nest *v.* Yoe, 1 *Sandf. Ch.*, 4; 2 *N. Y. Leg. Obs.*, 70; Schlussel *v.* Willett, 34 *Barb.*, 615; 12 *Abb. Pr.*, 397; 22 *How. Pr.*, 15.)

9. Akin to the last mentioned provisions are clauses which empower the assignee to sell upon credit, with a view thereby to realize a larger price for the assets. As this necessarily protracts the ultimate distribution until the term of credit expires, such a sale is held a fraud upon the right of the creditors to have the assets converted into money, and the money divided without delay. (Rogers *v.* De Forest, 7 *Paige*, 272; Barney *v.* Griffin, 2 *Comst.*, 365; 8 *N. Y. Leg. Obs.*, 68; and 9 *Id.*, 106; Nicholson *v.* Leavitt, 2 *Seld.*, 510; and 6 *Id.*, 591; Burdick *v.* Post, 2 *Id.*, 522; Houghton *v.* Westervelt, *Seld. notes*, No. 1, 32; Porter *v.* Williams, 5 *Seld.*, 142; and 12 *How. Pr.*, 107; Lyons *v.* Platner, 11 *N. Y. Leg. Obs.*, 87.) As in the case of clauses conferring other powers on the assignee, so in respect to the terms in which the power to sell is expressed, if they do not necessarily import discretionary power to sell upon credit, inconsistent with the legal duty of his trust, but may be construed as consistent with an immediate conversion into money, the assignment is not rendered invalid. (Kellogg *v.* Slauson, 1 *Kern.*, 302; Whitney *v.* Krows, 11 *Barb.*, 198; Southworth *v.* Sheldon, 7 *How. Pr.*, 414; Bellows *v.* Partridge, 19 *Barb.*, 176; 12 *N. Y. Leg. Obs.*, 219; Clark *v.* Fuller, 21 *Barb.*, 128; Nichols *v.* McEwen, *Id.*, 65; Wilson *v.* Ferguson, 10 *How. Pr.*, 175; Clapp *v.* Utley, 16 *Id.*, 384; Meacham *v.* Stearns, 9 *Paige*, 398; Wilson *v.* Robertson, 21 *N. Y.*, 589; 19 *How. Pr.*, 350; Ogden *v.* Peters, *Id.*, 23; Griffin *v.* Marquadt, *Id.*, 121; Schufeldt *v.* Abernethy, 2 *Duer*, 533; 12 *N. Y. Leg. Obs.*, 173; Murphy *v.* Bell, 8 *How. Pr.*, 468.) And a clause forbidding the assignee to sell upon credit, though superfluous, does not affect the assignment. (Carpenter *v.* Underwood, 19 *N. Y.*, 520; Van Rossum *v.* Walker, 11 *Barb.*, 237; Stern *v.* Fisher, 32 *Barb.*, 198.)

10. In addition to the protection thrown around the rights of creditors by the principles embodied in the adjudications abovementioned, it was found necessary, in 1860, for the legislature to interpose in their behalf; and to enact that assignments shall be in writing and acknowledged and recorded; that the assignor shall deliver to the county judge a sworn schedule containing an account of the creditors, stating their residences, the sums due them respectively, the consideration of each debt, and any collateral security held for it, and containing also an inventory of all the debtor's estate, stating incumbrances upon it, vouchers and securities appertaining to

it and its value; that the assignee must file a bond with sureties for the faithful performance of his duty, and that an accounting may be compelled, in due season, by legal proceedings for that purpose. (*Laws of* 1860, ch. 348.) This act has been deemed directory merely (Evans *v.* Chapin, 12 *Abbott's Pr.*, 161; 20 *How. Pr.*, 289; Fairchild *v.* Gwynne, 14 *Abbott's Pr.*, 121), at least in so far as it requires an inventory and bond (Juliand *v.* Rathbone, 39 *Barb.*, 97); but it appears to be the better opinion that a compliance by the assignor with the prerequisites imposed by the statute to be performed upon his part is essential to the validity of the instrument. (Fairchild *v.* Gwynne, 16 *Abbott's Pr.*, 23, rev'g s. c., *supra;* Cook *v.* Kelley, 14 *Id.*, 466.)

This brief review of the leading authorities in our state upon the restrictions imposed upon the right of preferential assignments, indicates what is much more clear upon a careful perusal of the decisions and statutes, viz.: that the strong tendency of the rule recognizing a discretionary power in debtors to give preferences, is towards fraud, and that the whole course of our jurisprudence and legislation has been steadily to restrict this power within narrower limits, and give creditors new means of protection.

The system of restrictions which has thus grown up may be briefly stated thus: A debtor, if not a moneyed corporation, nor a member of a limited partnership, nor an infant, nor a person contemplating proceedings for an insolvent's discharge, may make an assignment indicating preferences among his creditors, if the demands preferred are actual, valid, and honest;—provided that he confers no right or privilege upon his assignee inconsistent with the simple duty to sell and divide, nor any compensation exceeding that awarded by law; that he withholds nothing directly or indirectly, intentionally or inadvertently, immediately, or remotely, for himself; that he denotes the preferences to be made absolutely and finally, neither reserving to himself, nor giving his assignee a power to modify them, nor making them dependent upon contingencies; that he abstains from any attempt to exact or empower his assignee to exact favor from his creditors, as a condition of the payment of their dividends; that he authorizes an immediate conversion of the property into cash, neither permitting the sale to be deferred to allow the assets to be nursed into greater value, nor credit to be given in hope of obtaining a higher price; and lastly (which provision opens a wide field of litigation not touched by the decisions above reviewed), that there are not in all the attendant circumstances under which the act is done, indications of an actual intent to hinder, delay or defraud his creditors;—the privilege being moreover allowed to be exercised only by means of an instrument in writing, acknowledged and recorded, and accompanied by a full disclosure of both the debit and credit sides of the assignor's affairs,—and even then only upon the condition that the assignee shall give bonds for the discharge of his duty, and stand liable to render account of his proceedings to a legal tribunal. Stated in the books, viewed as a theory, the privilege seems reasonable, and the guards against abuse sufficient. But as actually administered, a system better adapted to tempt the designing and corrupt, to fraud, and to provoke litigation against the well disposed and the honest, could not easily be devised.

The Commissioners are of opinion that the policy of permitting insolvents to regulate the distribution of their estates among their creditors should be abandoned, and that the order of preference should be prescribed by law, upon general considerations of justice and sound policy, instead of being left to be determined by the irresponsible and often capricious or prejudiced judgment, or fraudulent purposes of the insolvent, or influenced by the undue solicitation of particular creditors.

The effect of the provision in the text, unless modified by such provisions as have been above suggested, would be that the property of an insolvent would become a trust fund to be administered in equity for the equal benefit of all his (if needed) creditors, as in the case of insolvent limited partnerships. (Inness *v.* Lansing, 7 *Paige*, 583.)

Frauds in procuring discharge in insolvency.

§ 644. Every person who, upon making or prosecuting any application for a discharge as an insolvent debtor, either:

1. Fraudulently presents, or authorizes to be presented on his behalf, such application, in a case in which it is not authorized by law; or,

2. Makes or presents to any court or officer, in support of such application, any petition, schedule, book, account, voucher, or other paper or document, knowing the same to contain any false statement; or,

3. Fraudulently makes and exhibits, or alters, obliterates or destroys any account or voucher relating to the condition of his affairs, or any entry or statement in such account or voucher; or,

4. Practices any fraud upon any creditor, with intent to induce him to petition for, or consent to such discharge; or,

5. Conspires with or induces any person fraudu-

lently to unite as creditor in any petition for such discharge, or to practice any fraud in aid thereof,

Is guilty of a misdemeanor.

CHAPTER XII.

FRAUDULENT INSOLVENCIES BY CORPORATIONS, AND OTHER FRAUDS IN THEIR MANAGEMENT.

§ 645. Every person who signs the name of a fictitious person to any subscription for, or agreement to take stock in any corporation, existing or proposed; and every person who signs, to any subscription or Frauds in subscriptions for stock of corporations.

agreement, the name of any person, knowing that such person has not means or does not intend in good faith to comply with all the terms thereof, or under any understanding or agreement that the terms of such subscription or agreement are not to be complied with or enforced, is guilty of a misdemeanor.

This section, which is new, is intended to reach a species of fraud frequently practised in the organization of corporations. See Palmer *v.* Lawrence, 3 *Sandf.*, 161; 1 *Seld.*, 389.

Frauds in procuring organization of corporation, or increase its capital.

§ 646. Every officer, agent or clerk, of any corporation, or of any persons proposing to organize a corporation, or to increase the capital stock of any corporation, who knowingly exhibits any false, forged or altered book, paper, voucher, security or other instrument of evidence to any public officer or board authorized by law to examine the organization of such corporation, or to investigate its affairs, or to allow an increase of its capital, with intent to deceive such officer or board in respect thereto, is punishable by imprisonment in a state prison not exceeding ten years and not less than three.

See *Laws of* 1829, ch. 94, § 29.

Unauthorized use of names in prospectuses, &c.

§ 647. Every person who, without being authorized so to do, subscribes the name of another to, or inserts the name of another in any prospectus, circular or other advertisement or announcement of any corporation or joint stock association existing or intended to be formed, with intent to permit the same to be published and thereby to lead persons to believe that the person whose name is so subscribed is an officer, agent, member or promoter of such corporation or association, is guilty of a misdemeanor.

Misconduct of directors of stock corporations.

§ 648. Every director of any stock corporation, who concurs in any vote or act of the directors of such corporation, or any of them, by which it is intended, either:

1. To make any dividend, except from the surplus

profits arising from the business of the corporation, and in the cases and manner allowed by law; or,

2. To divide, withdraw, or in any manner pay to the stockholders, or any of them, any part of the capital stock of the corporation; or to reduce such capital stock without the consent of the legislature; or,

3. To discount or receive any note or other evidence of debt in payment of any installment actually called in, and required to be paid, or with the intent to provide the means of making such payment; or,

4. To receive or discount any note or other evidence of debt with the intent to enable any stockholder to withdraw any part of the money paid in by him, or his stock; or,

5. To apply any portion of the funds of such corporation, except surplus profits, directly or indirectly, to the purchase of shares of its own stock; or,

6. To receive any such shares in payment or satisfaction of any debt due to such corporation; or,

7. To receive from any other stock corporation, in exchange for the shares, notes, bonds, or other evidences of debt of their own corporation, shares of the capital stock of such other corporation, or notes, bonds or other evidences of debt issued by such other corporation,

Is guilty of a misdemeanor.

§ 649. Every director of any corporation having banking powers, who concurs in any vote or act of the directors of such corporation, or any of them, by which it is intended, either: **Misconduct of directors of banking corporations.**

1. To make any loan, or discount, by which the whole amount of the loans and discounts of the corporation is made to exceed three times its capital stock then paid in and actually possessed; or,

2. To make any loan or discount to any director of such corporation, or upon paper upon which any such director is responsible, to an amount exceeding

in the aggregate one-third of the capital stock of such corporation, then paid in and actually possessed,

Is guilty of a misdemeanor.

The provisions of this and the preceding section are founded on 1 *Rev. Stat.*, 589, § 1. That section embodies nine subdivisions, the first seven of which correspond with those of section 648 in the text, while the eighth and ninth correspond with those of section 649. The whole section is, however, as it appears in the Revised Statutes, limited to *moneyed* corporations; while the last two subdivisions are restricted to corporations having banking powers. In the opinion of the commissioners, the provisions of the first seven subdivisions should be extended to all *stock* corporations; and they have so framed them; placing in a separate section, confined to banking corporations, the provisions of subdivisions 8 and 9.

The word "corporation" is substituted for "company," in one or two instances, merely for the sake of greater uniformity of expression.

Loans made in violation of last section, not invalid.

§ 650. Nothing in the last section shall render any loan made by the directors of any such corporation, in violation thereof, invalid.

See 2 *Rev. Stat.*, 590, § 1, *subd.* 9.

Sale, or hypothecation of bank notes, by officer, &c.

§ 651. Every officer or agent of any corporation having banking powers, who sells, or causes or permits to be sold, any bank notes of such corporation, or pledges or hypothecates, or causes or permits to be pledged or hypothecated, with any other corporation, association or individual, any such notes, as a security for a loan or for any liability of such corporation, is punishable by imprisonment in a county jail not exceeding one year, or by a fine not exceeding five thousand dollars, or both.

See *Laws of* 1842 ch. 247, § 10.

Officer of bank putting excessive number of its notes in circulation.

§ 652. Every officer or agent of any corporation having banking powers, who issues or puts in circulation, or causes or permits to be issued or put in circulation, the bank notes of such corporation to an amount, which, together with previous issues, leaves in circulation or outstanding a greater amount of notes than such corporation is allowed by law to issue and circulate, is punishable by imprisonment in a county jail not exceeding one year, or by a fine not exceeding five thousand dollars, or both.

See *Laws of* 1842, ch. 247, § 11.

§ 653. Every officer or agent of any banking corporation, who makes or delivers any guarantee or indorsement upon behalf of such corporation, whereby it may become liable upon any of its discounted notes, bills or obligations, in any sum beyond the amount of loans and discounts which such corporation may legally make, is guilty of a misdemeanor. **Officer or agent of banking corporation, making guarantee or indorsement in its behalf in certain cases.**

See *Laws of* 1841, ch. 292, § 2.

§ 654. Every officer, agent, teller or clerk of any bank, banking association or savings bank, who knowingly overdraws his account with such bank, and thereby wrongfully obtains the money, notes or funds of such bank, is guilty of a misdemeanor. **Bank officer overdrawing his account.**

See *Nixon's Dig., L. of N. J.*, 372, § 4; State *v.* Stimson, 4 *Zabr.*, 478.

§ 655. Every officer, agent, teller or clerk of any bank, banking association or savings bank, and every individual banker, or agent, teller or clerk of any individual banker, who receives any deposits knowing that such bank, or association, or banker is insolvent, is guilty of a misdemeanor. **Receiving deposits in insolvent banks.**

§ 656. Every director, officer or agent of any corporation or joint stock association, who knowingly receives or possesses himself of any property of such corporation or association, otherwise than in payment of a just demand, and who, with intent to defraud, omits to make, or to cause or direct to be made, a full and true entry thereof, in the books or accounts of such corporation or association; and every director, officer, agent or member of any corporation or joint stock association, who, with intent to defraud, destroys, alters, mutilates or falsifies any of the **Frauds in keeping accounts in books of corporations.**

books, papers, writings or securities belonging to such corporation or association, or makes or concurs in making any false entry, or omits or concurs in omitting to make any material entry in any book of accounts, or other record or document kept by such corporation or association, is punishable by imprisonment in a state prison not exceeding ten years, and not less than three, or by imprisonment in a county jail not exceeding one year, or by a fine not exceeding five hundred dollars, or by both such fine and imprisonment.

See *Laws of* 1829, ch. 94, § 29; and *Stat.* 24 and 25 *Vict*, ch. 96, § 82.

Officer of corporation publishing false reports of its condition.

§ 657. Every director, officer or agent of any corporation or joint stock association, who knowingly concurs in making or publishing any written report, exhibit or statement of its affairs or pecuniary condition, containing any material statement which is false, other than such as are mentioned in sections 646 and 647, is guilty of a misdemeanor.

See Cross *v.* Sackett, 6 *Abbott's Pr. R.*, 247, and numerous cases there cited; also, Harper *v.* Chamberlain, 11 *Abbott's Pr.*, 234.

Officer of corporation to permit an inspection of its books

§ 658. Every officer or agent of any corporation having or keeping an office within this state, who has in his custody or control any book, paper or document of such corporation, and who refuses to give to a stockholder or member of such corporation, lawfully demanding, during office hours, to inspect or take a copy of the same, or of any part thereof, a reasonable opportunity so to do, is guilty of a misdemeanor.

See *Laws of* 1825, ch. 325, § 1; Cotheal *v.* Brouwer, 1 *Seld.*, 562.

Insolvencies of corporations deemed fraudulent, when.

§ 659. Every insolvency of a moneyed corporation is deemed fraudulent unless its affairs appear, upon investigation, to have been administered fairly and legally, and generally with the same care and diligence that agents receiving a compensation for their services are bound by law to observe.

2 *Rev. Stat.*, 592, § 14.

§ 660. In every case of a fraudulent insolvency of a moneyed corporation, every director thereof who participated in such fraud, if no other punishment is prescribed therefor by this Code, or any of the acts which are specified as continuing in force, is guilty of a misdemeanor.

Directors participating in fraudulent insolvency, how punishable.

§ 661. Every director of any moneyed corporation, who willfully does any act, as such director, which is expressly forbidden by law, or willfully omits to perform any duty expressly imposed upon him as such director, by law, the punishment for which act or omission is not otherwise prescribed by this Code, or by some of the acts which it specifies as continuing in force, is guilty of a misdemeanor.

Violation of duty of directors of moneyed corporations.

§ 662. Every officer, agent or stockholder of any railroad company who knowingly assents to or has any agency in contracting any debt, by or on behalf of such company, unauthorized by a special law for the purpose, the amount of which debt, with other debts of the company, exceeds its available means for the payment of its debts, in its possession, under its control, and belonging to it, at the time such debt is contracted, including its bona fide and available stock subscriptions, and exclusive of its real estate, is guilty of a misdemeanor.

Officer of railroad company contracting debt in its behalf, exceeding its available means.

Founded on *Laws of* 1845, ch. 230; the language of that act being modified with a view to attain greater clearness.

§ 663. The last section does not affect the validity of a debt created in violation of its provisions, as against the company.

Debt contracted in violation of last section not invalid.

Laws of 1845, ch. 230.

§ 664. Every director of a corporation, or joint stock association, is deemed to possess such a know-

Director of corporation presumed to have knowledge of its affairs.

ledge of the affairs of his corporation, as to enable him to determine whether any act, proceeding or omission of its directors, is a violation of this chapter.

See 2 *Rev. Stat.*, 592, § 12.

Director present at meeting, when presumed to have assented to proceedings.

§ 665. Every director of a corporation, or joint stock association, who is present at a meeting of the directors at which any act, proceeding or omission of such directors, in violation of this chapter occurs, is deemed to have concurred therein, unless he at the time causes, or in writing requires, his dissent therefrom to be entered in the minutes of the directors.

See 2 *Rev. Stat.*, 592, § 12.

Director absent from meeting, when presumed to have assented to proceedings.

§ 666. Every director of a corporation, or joint stock association, although not present at a meeting of the directors at which any act, proceeding, or omission of such directors, in violation of this chapter, occurs, is deemed to have concurred therein, if the facts constituting such violation appear on the record or minutes of the proceedings of the board of directors, and he remains a director of the same company for six months thereafter, and does not, within that time, cause, or in writing require his dissent from such illegality to be entered in the minutes of the directors.

See 2 *Rev. Stat.*, 592, § 13.

Foreign corporations.

§ 667. It is no defense to a prosecution for a violation of the provisions of this chapter, that the corporation was one created by the laws of another state, government or country, if it was one carrying on business, or keeping an office therefor, within this state.

"Director" defined.

§ 668. The term "director," as used in this chapter, embraces any of the persons having by law the direction or management of the affairs of a corporation, by whatever name such persons are described in its charter, or known by law.

See 2 *Rev. Stat.*, 599, § 53.

CHAPTER XIII.

FRAUDS IN THE SALE OF PASSAGE TICKETS.

Sale of passage tickets on vessels and railroads forbidden, except by agents specially authorized.

§ 669. No person except the persons designated in section 676 shall issue or sell or offer to sell, within this state, any passage ticket, or any instrument giving or purporting to give any right, either absolutely or upon any condition or contingency, to any passage or conveyance upon any vessel or railroad train, unless he is an authorized agent of the owners or consignees of such vessel, or of the company running such train; and no person is deemed an authorized agent of such owners, consignees or company, within the meaning of this chapter, unless he has been by them duly appointed by an authority in writing, and which designates the name of the company, line, vessel or railroad for which such person is authorized to act as agent, together with the street and number of the street, and the city, town or village in which his office shall be kept, for the sale of passage tickets.

Founded upon *Laws of* 1860, ch. 103, § 1. The provisions of this chapter are substantially a re-enactment of the act of 1860, with such modifications of language as are deemed suitable to incorporate the sections of the act of 1860, with those of the Penal Code. The provisions are extended to railroad tickets, the sale of which offers opportunities for frauds, corresponding with those in the sale of tickets on vessels. The regulations comprised in the act are new in our law; and the subject has been recently and fully treated by the legislature. The Commissioners have, therefore, not thought it necessary to propose any other substantial changes.

Sales by authorized agents, restricted.

§ 670. No person except the persons designated in section 676 shall, within this state, ask, take or receive any money or valuable thing as a consideration for any passage or conveyance upon any vessel or railroad train, or for the procurement of any ticket or instrument giving or purporting to give any right, either absolutely or upon any condition or contingency, to any passage or conveyance upon any vessel or railroad train, unless he is an authorized agent within the provisions of the last section; nor shall any person, as such agent, sell any such ticket or instrument, or ask, take or receive any consideration for any such passage or conveyance, excepting at the office designated in his appointment, nor until he has been authorized to act as such agent according to the provisions of the preceding section, nor for a sum exceeding the price charged at the time of such sale, by the company, owners or consignees of the vessel or railroad referred to in such ticket. Nor shall any such ticket or instrument be issued or sold, which purports to entitle a person to a passage by any mode of conveyance, or to any place of destination, or by any route, vessel or train, other than the one bargained for.

Founded upon *Laws of* 1860, ch. 103, § 2.

Unauthorized persons forbidden to sell certificates, receipts,

§ 671. No person other than an agent appointed, as provided in section 669, shall sell, or offer to sell, or in any way attempt to dispose of any order, cer-

&c., for the purpose of procuring tickets.

tificate, receipt or other instrument for the purpose, or under the pretense of procuring any ticket, or instrument mentioned in section 669, upon any company or line, vessel or railroad train therein mentioned. And every such order sold or offered for sale by any agent, must be directed to the company, owners or consignees at their office.

Ibid., § 3.

Punishment for violation of the preceding sections.

§ 672. Every person guilty of a violation of any of the provisions of the preceding sections of this chapter, is punishable by imprisonment in a state prison not exceeding two years, or by imprisonment in a county jail not less than six months.

Ibid., § 4.

Conspiring to sell passage tickets in violation of law.

§ 673. All persons who conspire together to sell or attempt to sell, to any person, any passage ticket, or other instrument mentioned in sections 669 and 671, in violation of those sections, and all persons, who, by means of any such conspiracy obtain, or attempt to obtain any money or other property, under the pretense of procuring or securing any passage or right of passage in violation of this chapter, are punishable by imprisonment in a state prison not exceeding five years.

Ibid., § 5.

Conspirators may be indicted, notwithstanding object of conspiracy has been accomplished.

§ 674. Persons guilty of violating the last section, may be indicted and convicted for a conspiracy, notwithstanding the object of such conspiracy has been executed.

Ibid., § 6.

Office kept for unlawful sale of passage tickets declared disorderly houses.

§ 675. All offices kept for the purpose of selling passage tickets in violation of any of the provisions of this chapter, and all offices where any such sale is made, are deemed disorderly houses; and all persons keeping any such office, and all persons associating together for the purpose of violating any of the provisions of this chapter, are punishable by imprisonment in a county jail for a period not exceeding six months, and not less than three months.

Ibid., § 7.

Section 8 of the act is omitted for the reason that it is of doubtful expediency; and if desirable to be retained, it appertains to the Code of Criminal Procedure. It is as follows: "All complaints regarding the violation of this act shall be presented by the district attorney of the district where such complaint was made, to the grand jury, for indictment, in preference to all other complaints. And it shall be the duty of judges of the court of general sessions of the peace, and of the courts of oyer and terminer, in the counties of Erie, Albany and New York, to call the attention of the several grand juries to the provisions of this act."

Owners, pursers, &c., allowed to sell tickets.

§ 676. The provisions of this chapter do not prevent the actual owners or consignees of any vessel, from selling passage tickets thereon; nor do they prevent the purser or clerk of any vessel from selling in his office on board of such vessel, any passage tickets upon such vessel.

Laws of 1860, ch. 103, § 9,

Station masters, conductors, &c., allowed to sell tickets.

§ 677. The provisions of this chapter do not prevent the station master or other ticket agent upon any railroad, from selling in his office in any station on such railroad, any passage tickets upon such railroad; nor do they prevent any conductor upon any railroad from selling such tickets upon the trains of such road.

What must be stated in passage ticket.

§ 678. Every ticket or instrument issued as evidence of a right of passage upon the high seas, from any port in this state, to any port of any other state or nation, and every certificate or order issued for the purpose, or under pretense of procuring any such ticket or instrument, and every receipt for money paid for any such ticket or instrument, must state the name of the vessel on board of which the passage is to be made, the name of the owners or consignees of such vessel, the name of the company, or line, if any, to which such vessel belongs, the place from which such passage is to commence, the place where such passage is to terminate, the day of the month and year upon which the voyage is to commence, the name of the person or persons purchasing such ticket or instrument, or receiving such order, certificate or receipt, and the amount paid therefor; and such ticket or instrument, order, certificate or receipt, unless sold or issued by the owners or consignees of such vessel, must be signed by their authorized agent.

Ibid., § 11.

§ 679. Every person who issues, sells or delivers to another, any ticket, instrument, certificate, order or receipt, which is not made or filled out as prescribed in the last section, is guilty of felony. Sale of tickets not filled out as required in last section a felony.

Ibid., § 11.

§ 680. No indictment or conviction under any provision of the preceding sections of this chapter, for the sale, attempted sale, issuing or delivering of any ticket, instrument, certificate, order or receipt, is defective because such ticket, instrument, certificate, order or receipt is not made or filled out according to the requirements of the last section. Requisites of indictment.

Ibid., § 11.

Section 12 of the act, which defines the words "ship" and "steamship," is omitted. A definition of the word "vessel" is given, among other definitions of terms, in section 769.

§ 681. The term "company," as used in this chapter, includes all corporations, whether created under the laws of this state, or of those of any other state or nation. "Company" defined.

Laws of 1860, ch. 103, § 13.

§ 682. The provisions of this chapter do not permit railroad companies incorporated in any other state to sell passage tickets under this chapter in this state; nor do they permit the owners or agents of any Foreign railroad companies.

vessel to sell tickets for or on behalf of any such railroad company.

Ibid., § 14.

CHAPTER XIV.

FRAUDULENT ISSUE OF DOCUMENTS OF TITLE TO MERCHANDISE.

Issuing fictitious bills of lading &c.

§ 683. Every person being the master, owner or agent of any vessel, or officer or agent of any railroad, express or transportation company, or otherwise being or representing any carrier, who delivers any bill of lading, receipt or other voucher, by which it appears that any merchandise of any description has been shipped on board any vessel, or delivered to any railroad, express or transportation company, or other carrier, unless the same has been so shipped or delivered and is at the time actually under the control of such carrier, or the master, owner or agent of such vessel, or of some officer or agent of such company, to be forwarded as expressed in such bill of lading, receipt or voucher, is punishable by imprisonment in a state prison not exceeding five years, or by a fine not exceeding one thousand dollars, or both.

See *Laws of* 1858, ch. 326, § 5.

Issuing fictitious warehouse receipts.

§ 684. Every person carrying on the business of a warehouseman, wharfinger, or other depositary of property, who issues any receipt, bill of lading or other voucher for any merchandise of any description which has not been actually received upon the premises of such person, and is not under his actual control at the time of issuing such instrument, whether such instrument is issued to a person as being the owner of such merchandise, or as security for any indebtedness, is punishable by imprisonment in a state prison not exceeding five years, or by a fine not exceeding one thousand dollars, or both.

See *Laws of* 1858, ch. 326, §§ 1, 2.

§ 685. No person can be convicted of an offense under the last two sections by reason that the contents of any barrel, box, case, cask or other vessel or package mentioned in the bill of lading, receipt or other voucher did not correspond with the description given in such instrument of the merchandise received, if such description corresponded substantially with the marks, labels or brands upon the outside of such vessel or package, unless it appears that the accused knew that such marks, labels or brands were untrue. Erroneous bills of lading or receipts, issued in good faith, excepted.

§ 686. Every person mentioned in sections 683 and 684, who issues any second or duplicate receipt or voucher, of a kind specified in those sections, at a time while any former receipt or voucher for the merchandise specified in such second receipt is outstanding and uncanceled, without writing across the face of the same the word "duplicate," in a plain and legible manner, is punishable by imprisonment in a state prison not exceeding five years, or by a fine not exceeding one thousand dollars, or both. Duplicate receipts must be marked "Duplicate."

See *Laws of* 1858, ch. 326, § 3. The words "bill of lading" are not inserted in this section, as suggested by *Laws of* 1859, ch. 353, because by the settled commercial form of that instrument, a different mode of indicating that the parts of the bill are duplicates, is in use, and no advantage is anticipated from insisting on the word "duplicate."

§ 687. Every person mentioned in sections 683 and 684, who sells, hypothecates or pledges any merchan- Selling, hypothecating or pledging property received for transportation or storage. dise for which any bill of lading, receipt or voucher has been issued by him, without the consent in writing thereto of the person holding such bill, receipt or voucher, is punishable by imprisonment in a state prison not exceeding five years, or by a fine not exceeding one thousand dollars, or both.

See *Laws of* 1858, ch. 326, § 4.

Bill of lading or receipt issued by warehouseman must be canceled on redelivery of the property.

§ 688. Every person mentioned in section 684, who delivers to another any merchandise for which any bill of lading, receipt or voucher has been issued, unless such receipt or voucher bore upon its face the words "not negotiable," plainly written or stamped, or unless such receipt is surrendered to be canceled at the time of such delivery, or unless, in the case of a partial delivery, a memorandum thereof is indorsed upon such receipt or voucher, is punishable by imprisonment in a state prison not exceeding five years, or by a fine not exceeding one thousand dollars, or both.

See *Laws of* 1858, ch. 326, § 6; *Laws of* 1859, ch. 353. The latter seems to have been intended to amend the former by adding the words "bill of lading" to the words "receipt or voucher," whenever they occur, and the word "forwarder" to the words "warehouseman, wharfinger, &c." The commissioners have inserted the words "bill of lading" in the sections in the text, wherever they are appropriate; but to insert the word "forwarder" is thought unnecessary in the present form of the provision, and in some of the sections unsuitable.

Property demanded by process of law.

§ 689. The last two sections do not apply where property is demanded by virtue of process of law.

See *Laws of* 1858, ch. 326, § 8.

CHAPTER XV.

MALICIOUS INJURIES TO RAILROADS, HIGHWAYS, BRIDGES AND TELEGRAPHS.

§ 690. Every person who maliciously either: Injuries to railroads.

1. Removes, displaces, injures or destroys any part of any railroad, whether for steam or horse cars, or any track of any railroad, or any branch or branchway, switch, turnout, bridge, viaduct, culvert, embankment, station house, or other structure or fixture, or any part thereof, attached to or connected with any railroad; or,

2. Places any obstruction upon the rails or track of any railroad, or of any branch, branchway or turnout connected with any railroad,

Is punishable by imprisonment in a state prison not exceeding four years, or in a county jail not less than six months.

See 2 *Rev. Stat.*, 689, § 21.

§ 691. Whenever any offense specified in the last section results in the death of any human being, the offender is punishable by imprisonment in a state prison for not less than four years. Cases where death ensues.

§ 692. Every person who maliciously digs up, removes, displaces, breaks or otherwise injures or destroys any public highway or bridge, or any private way laid out by authority of law, or bridge upon such way, is guilty of felony. Injuries to highways, private ways and bridges.

§ 693. Every person who maliciously injures or destroys any toll house or turnpike gate, is guilty of felony. Injuries to toll houses and turnpike gates.

See 2 *Rev. Stat.*, 695, § 30.

§ 694. Every person who removes or injures any mile board, mile stone or guide post, or any inscription on such, erected upon any highway, is guilty of a misdemeanor. Injuries to mile boards and guide posts.

Rep. Pol. Code, § 518.

Injuring telegraph line, or intercepting message, a misdemeanor.

§ 695. Every person who maliciously takes down, removes, injures or obstructs any line of telegraph or any part thereof, or appurtenance or apparatus therewith connected, or severs any wire thereof, or fraudulently intercepts any message in its passsge over such wire, is guilty of a misdemeanor.

TITLE XVI.

OF MALICIOUS MISCHIEF.

§ 696. Every person who maliciously injures, defaces or destroys any real or personal property not his own, in cases other than such as are specified in the following sections, is guilty of a misdemeanor; and in addition to the punishment prescribed therefor, he is liable in treble damages for the injury done, to be recovered in a civil action by the owner of such property or public officer having charge thereof. Malicious mischief, in general, defined.

See *Rep. Pol. Code*, 860.

§ 697. The specification of the acts enumerated in the following sections of this chapter, is not intended to restrict or qualify the interpretation of the last section. Specifications in following sections, not restrictive of last section.

§ 698. Every person who maliciously administers any poison to any animal, the property of another, and every person who maliciously exposes any poisonous substance with intent that the same shall be taken by any such animal, is punishable by imprisonment in a state prison not exceeding three years, or in a county jail not exceeding one year, or by a fine not exceeding two hundred and fifty dollars, or by both such fine and imprisonment. Poisoning cattle.

2 *Rev. Stat.*, 689, § 16.

§ 699. Every person who maliciously kills, maims or wounds any animal, the property of another, or who maliciously and cruelly beats, tortures or injures any animal, whether belonging to himself or another, is guilty of a misdemeanor. Killing, maiming or torturing animals.

2 *Rev. Stat.*, 695, § 26.

§ 700. Every person who maliciously, or for any bet, stake or reward, instigates, encourages or promotes any fight between animals, or instigates or encourages any animal to attack, bite, wound or worry another, is guilty of a misdemeanor. Instigating fights between animals.

§ 701. Every person who keeps any house, pit or other place to be used in permitting any fight between Keeping houses, pits, &c., for fights between animals.

animals, or in any other violation of the last section, is guilty of a misdemeanor.

Wounding or trapping birds, or destroying birds' nests in cemeteries.

§ 702. Every person who, within any public cemetery or burying ground, wounds or traps any bird or destroys any bird's nest, or removes any eggs or young birds from any nest; and every person who buys or sells, or offers or keeps for sale, any bird which has been killed or trapped in violation of this section, is punishable by a fine of five dollars for each offense, recoverable by a civil action in any justice's court within the county where the offense is committed, brought in the name of any person making a complaint. Such fine shall be applied to the support of the poor of such county.

See *Laws of* 1853, ch. 629; *Laws of* 1855, ch. 564.

Burning buildings and other property not the subject of arson.

§ 703. Every person who willfully burns any building not the subject of arson, any stack of grain of any kind, or of hay, any growing or standing grain, grass, trees or fence, not the property of such person, is punishable by imprisonment in a state prison not exceeding four years and not less than one year, or by imprisonment in a county jail not exceeding one year.

This species of offense is by the existing law denominated arson in the fourth degree. 2 *Rev. Stat.*, 667, §§ 7, 8. The Commissioners have transferred it to this chapter for the reasons specified in the note to section 521, applying to it the punishment prescribed for arson in the fourth degree by *Laws of* 1862, ch. 197, § 9.

Breaking or injuring property in houses of worship.

§ 704. Every person who willfully breaks, defaces or otherwise injures any house of worship, or any part thereof, or any appurtenance thereto, or any book, furniture, ornament, musical instrument, article of silver or plated ware, or other chattel kept therein for use in connection with religious worship, is guilty of felony.

Using gunpowder, &c., in destroying or

§ 705. Every person who maliciously, by the explosion of gunpowder or other explosive substance, destroys, throws down or injures the whole or any part of any building, by means of which the life or safety of any human being is endangered, is punishable by imprisonment in a state prison not exceeding ten years, and not less than three. Injuring any building.

See *Stat.*, *24th* and *25th Vict.*, ch. 97, § 9.

§ 706. Every person who places in, upon, under, against or near to any building, any gunpowder or other explosive substance, with intent to destroy, throw down or injure the whole or any part thereof, under circumstances, that if such intent were accomplished, human life or safety would be endangered thereby, although no damage is done, is guilty of felony. Endangering human life by placing gunpowder, &c., near building.

Ibid, § 20.

§ 707. Every person who willfully commits any trespass, by either: Malicious injuries to freeholds.

1. Cutting down or destroying any kind of wood or timber, standing or growing upon the lands of another; or,

2. Carrying away any kind of wood or timber that has been cut down, and is lying on such lands; or

3. Maliciously severing from the freehold any produce thereof, or anything attached thereto; or,

4. Digging, taking or carrying away from any lot situated within the bounds of any incorporated city, without the license of the owner, or legal occupant thereof, any earth, soil or stone, severed from the freehold at some previous time, under such circumstances as would render the trespass a larceny, if the thing so severed or carried away were personal property; or,

5. Digging, taking or carrying away from any land in any of the cities of the state, laid down on the map or plan of said city as a street or avenue, or otherwise established or recognized as a street or

avenue, without the license of the mayor and common council or other governing body of such city, or of the owner of the fee thereof, any earth, soil or stone, under such circumstances as would render the trespass a larceny, if the thing so severed or carried away were personal property; or,

6. Putting up, affixing, fastening, printing or painting, without authority of law, upon any real property belonging to the state, or to any city, town or village, or dedicated to the public, or upon any real property of any person, association or corporation, without license from the owner thereof, any notice, advertisement or designation of, or any name for any commodity, whether for sale or otherwise, or any picture, word, sign or device, intended to call attention thereto;

Is guilty of a misdemeanor.

Embraces such of the provisions of 2 *Rev. Stat.*, 693, § 15, as amended *Laws of* 1851, ch. 182, as are not already covered by other sections of the Code. See section 596.

Subd. 6. This provision is rendered necessary by the practice, unfortunately, common, of affixing to any picturesque rock or point of land, some advertisement of a current nostrum, or other notice, without permission from any competent authority. This is now only a simple trespass; but it should be a misdemeanor.

Injuries to standing crops, &c.

§ 708. Every person who maliciously injures or destroys any standing crops, grain, cultivated fruits or vegetables, the property of another, in any case for which a punishment is not otherwise prescribed by this Code, or by some of the statutes which it specifies as continuing in force, is guilty of a misdemeanor.

See *Stat.*, 24*th* and 25*th Vict.*, ch. 97, §§ 23, 24.

Removing, defacing or altering landmarks.

§ 709. Every person who either:

1. Maliciously removes any monuments of stone, wood or other material, erected for the purpose of designating any point in the boundary of any lot or tract of land; or,

2. Maliciously defaces or alters the marks upon any tree, post or other monument, made for the purpose of designating any point, course or line in any such boundary; or,

3. Maliciously cuts down or removes any tree upon which any such marks have been made for such purpose, with intent to destroy such marks,

Is guilty of a misdemeanor.

See 2 *Rev. Stat.*, 695, § 32.

§ 710. Every person who, without authority of law, interferes with any pier, booms or dams, lawfully erected or maintained upon any waters within this state, or hoists any gate in or about said dams, is guilty of a misdemeanor. Interfering with piers, dams, &c.

Founded upon *Laws of* 1859, ch. 350, § 2, but made general. That act applies only to booms and dams in Salmon river.

§ 711. Every person who maliciously destroys any dam or structure erected to create hydraulic power, or any embankment necessary for the support thereof, or maliciously makes, or causes to be made, any aperture in such dam or embankment, with intent to destroy the same, is guilty of a misdemeanor. Destroying or injuring dams, &c.

2 *Rev. Stat.*, 695, § 31.

§ 712. Every person who maliciously draws up or removes, or cuts or otherwise injures, any piles fixed in the ground and used for securing any sea bank or sea walls, or the bank or dam of any river, canal, drain, aqueduct, marsh, reservoir, pool, port, harbor, dock, quay, jetty or lock, is punishable by imprisonment in a state prison not exceeding five years and not less than two, or by imprisonment in a county jail not exceeding one year, or by a fine not exceeding five hundred dollars, or by both such fine and imprisonment. Removing or injuring piles used in sea or river embankments, &c.

See *Stat.*, 24*th* and 15*th Vict.*, ch. 97, § 31.

Removing any beacon in New York harbor.

§ 713. Every person who willfully removes any buoy or beacon placed in the harbor of New York by the United States light house board, or any other lawful authority, is guilty of a misdemeanor.

Rep. Pol. Code, § 331.

Masking or removing signal lights.

§ 714. Every person who unlawfully masks, alters or removes any light or signal, or willfully exhibits any false light or signal, with intent to bring any vessel into danger, is punishable by imprisonment in a state prison not exceeding ten years, and not less than three.

See *Stat.*, *24th* and *25th Vict.*, ch. 97, § 47.

Injuring or destroying written instruments.

§ 715. Every person who maliciously mutilates, tears, defaces, obliterates or destroys any written instrument being the property of another, the false making of which would be forgery, is punishable in the same manner as the forgery of such instrument is made punishable.

See *Nixon's Dig. Laws of N. J.*, 188, § 69.

Destroying or delaying election returns.

§ 716. Every messenger appointed by authority of law to receive and carry any report, certificate or certified copy of any statement relating to the result of any election, who willfully mutilates, tears, defaces, obliterates or destroys the same, or does any other act which prevents the delivery of it as required by law; and every person who takes away from such messenger any such report, certificate or certified copy, with intent to prevent its delivery, or who willfully does any injury or other act such as is above specified, is punishable by imprisonment in a state prison not exceeding five years, and not less than two.

See *Laws of* 1842, ch. 130, tit. vi., § 18.

Opening or publishing sealed letters.

§ 717. Every person who willfully opens or reads, or causes to be read any sealed letter not addressed to himself, without being authorized so to do, either by the writer of such letter, or by the person to whom it is addressed; and every person who without the like authority publishes any letter, knowing it to have been opened in violation of this section or any part, is guilty of a misdemeanor.

§ 718. Every person who discloses the contents of any telegraphic dispatch, or any part thereof, addressed to another person, without the permission of such person, to his loss, injury or disgrace, is guilty of a misdemeanor.

Disclosing contents of telegraphic dispatch.

§ 719. Every person who, having in his possession any telegraphic dispatch addressed to another, maliciously secretes, conceals or suppresses the same, is guilty of a misdemeanor.

Concealing telegraphic dispatch.

§ 720. Every person who willfully injures, disfigures or destroys, not being the owner thereof, any monument, work of art, or useful or ornamental improvement, within the limits of any village, town or city, or any shade tree or ornamental plant growing therein, whether situated upon private ground, or on any street, sidewalk or public park or place, is guilty of a misdemeanor.

Injuring works of art or improvements in any city or village.

See *Laws of* 1853, ch. 573. *Laws of* 1860, ch. 98, § 3.

§ 721. Every person who maliciously cuts, tears, defaces, disfigures, soils, obliterates, breaks or destroys any book, map, chart, picture, engraving, statue, coin, model, apparatus, specimen or other work of literature or art, or object of curiosity deposited in any public library, gallery, museum, collection, fair or exhibition, is punishable by imprisonment in a state prison for not exceeding three years, or in a county jail not exceeding one year.

Destroying works of literature or art, or objects of curiosity in public libraries, museums, &c.

§ 722. Every person who willfully breaks, digs up or obstructs, any pipe or main for conducting gas or water, or any works erected for supplying buildings with gas or water, or any appurtenances or appen-

Breaking or obstructing gas or water pipes or appurtenances.

dages therewith connected, is punishable by imprisonment in a state prison not exceeding three years, or in a county jail not exceeding one year.

See *Laws of* 1860, ch. 172, § 7.

TITLE XVII.

OF MISCELLANEOUS CRIMES.

Commissioner of excise granting license wrongfully.

§ 723. Every commissioner of excise who concurs in granting any license to sell strong or spirituous liquors, or wines, contrary to the provisions of Chapter II of Title IV of Part III of the Political Code, is guilty of a misdemeanor.

See *Rep. Pol. Code*, § 792.

Selling liquor to Indians.

§ 724. Every person who sells or gives away any strong or spirituous liquor, or wine, to any Indian in this state, is guilty of a misdemeanor.

See *Rep. Pol. Code*, § 797.

Being intoxicated in public places.

§ 725. Every person being intoxicated in any public place, is punishable, upon conviction, in the manner specified in section 799 of the Political Code, by a fine of ten dollars and costs of the proceedings at the same rate as in courts of special sessions, and by imprisonment in the county jail, workhouse or penitentiary until such fine is paid, not, however, exceeding ten days.

See *Rep. Pol. Code*, § 799.

§ 726. Every person guilty of selling any strong or spirituous liquor, or wine, to any person guilty of habitual drunkenness, or to any person to whom the seller has been requested by the parent, guardian, husband or wife of such person not to sell any strong or spirituous liquor, or wine, is punishable by a fine not exceeding fifty dollars and not less than twenty, for each offense; and in addition thereto he forfeits any license he may have received to sell strong or spirituous liquors, or wines, and is forever after incapable of receiving such license. **Selling liquor to habitual drunkards.**

See *Rep. Pol. Code*, § 801.

§ 727. Every person who sells or gives to any person, knowing him to be a pauper or inmate of any poor house or alms house, any strong or spirituous liquor, or wine, without authority from the superintendent or physician of such poor house or alms house, is punishable by a fine of twenty-five dollars. **Selling liquor to paupers.**

Rep. Pol. Code, § 802.

§ 728. Every innkeeper, or person licensed to sell liquors, who sells or gives away any strong or spirituous liquor, or wine, upon Sunday, or upon any election day, in violation of section 803 of the Political Code, is guilty of a misdemeanor. **Selling liquor upon Sundays.**

See *Rep. Pol. Code*, § 803.

§ 729. Every master or other person engaged in navigating any steamboat, who violates any of the provisions of sections 268, 269, 270, 271, 272, 273, 274, 275 or 282 of the Political Code, is guilty of a misdemeanor; and in addition to the punishment prescribed therefor, is liable to a penalty of two hundred and fifty dollars. **Violation of laws relative to navigation.**

See *Rep. Pol. Code*, §§ 276, 283. Sections 285 is not included in the above enumeration of sections, for the reason that its provisions are substantially embraced in other provisions of this Code.

Attorneys forbidden to defend criminal prosecutions carried on by their partners or formerly by themselves.

§ 730. Every attorney who directly or indirectly advises in relation to, or aids or promotes the defense of any action or proceeding in any court, the prosecution of which is carried on, aided or promoted by any person as district attorney or other public prosecutor, with whom such person is directly or indirectly connected as a partner; or who, having himself prosecuted or in any manner aided or promoted any action or proceeding in any court, as district attorney or other public prosecutor, afterwards directly or indirectly advises in relation to, or takes any part in, the defense thereof, as attorney or otherwise; or who takes or receives any valuable consideration from or on behalf of any defendant in any such action, upon any understanding or agreement whatever, express or implied, having relation to the defense thereof, is guilty of a misdemeanor; and in addition to the punishment prescribed therefor, he forfeits his license to practice.

This section and the next are founded on the provisions of *Laws of* 1846, ch. 120. The verbal changes made are chiefly to secure greater conciseness of expression.

Attorneys may defend themselves.

§ 731. The last section does not prohibit an attorney from defending himself in person, as attorney or as counsel, when prosecuted either civilly or criminally.

Fraudulently presenting bills or claims to public officers for payment.

§ 732. Every person who, with intent to defraud, presents for allowance or for payment to any state board or officer, or to any county, town, city, ward or village board or officer, who would be authorized to allow or pay the same, if genuine, any false or fraudulent claim, bill, account, voucher or writing, is guilty of felony.

The latter part of the section is founded upon the act of Congress of March 3, 1823, under which Kohnstamm was lately convicted. See also act of March 2, 1863. Some such provision is rendered necessary by practices unhappily too notorious to need to be specified.

§ 733. Every person who, by any use of force, threats or intimidation, prevents or endeavors to prevent any hired foreman, journeyman, apprentice, workman, laborer, servant or other person employed by another, from continuing or performing his work, or from accepting any new work or employment, or in like manner endeavors to induce such hired person to relinquish his work or employment, or to return any work he has in hand, before it is finished; and every person who, by any use of force, threats or intimidation, prevents or endeavors to prevent another from employing any person, or, in like manner, endeavors to compel another to employ any person, or to force or induce another to alter his mode of carrying on business, or to limit or increase the number of his hired foremen, journeymen, apprentices, workmen, laborers, servants or other persons employed by him, or their rate of wages or time of service, is guilty of a misdemeanor. Intimidating laborers or employers.

See *Stat.*, 6 *Geo.* IV., ch. 129, § 3. As to what constitutes a "threat," within such a provision, see O'Neill *v.* Layman, 11 *Weekly R.*, 947: 8 *Law T.* (*N. S.*), 657. It is there held that under the English statute already cited, it is not necessary to show a threat of actual violence; but a threat to follow out an unlawful purpose is sufficient. Thus where L., being at the time in the employ of K., was summoned to attend a meeting of a club to which he belonged, and was asked by the chairman, "whether he intended to continue an honorable member of the club and leave K.'s employ, or remain where he was and be despised by the club, and have his name sent round all over the country, and be put to all sorts of unpleasantness;" it was held that this was a threat within the statute.

§ 734. Every person who votes at any annual town meeting, in a town in which he does not reside, or Voting unlawfully at annual town meeting. who offers to vote at any annual town meeting after having voted at an annual town meeting held in another town, within the same year, is guilty of a misdemeanor.

Suggested as a substitute for *Rep. Pol. Code*, § 986. See note to section 68 of this Code, for reasons for change of phraseology.

Publishing false messages, &c., of Federal or State executive.

§ 735. Every person who prints, publishes or circulates, as true, any message, order or proclamation purporting to be the message, order or proclamation of the executive of the United States or of this state, or of any other state of the United States now or hereafter admitted, or of any territory of the United States, knowing the same not to be genuine, is punishable, in any county in which the same is printed, published or circulated, by imprisonment in a state prison not exceeding five years, or by fine not exceeding one thousand dollars, or both.

This section is rendered necessary by the recent publication, by one Howard, of a proclamation purporting to be the act of the president of the United States, in effect announcing the defeat of the Union armies, appointing a day of fasting, and calling for additional troops. If this be regarded as the act of two or more in combination, it would have been punishable at common law as a conspiracy to affect the price of stocks. (See Cochrane's case, 2 *Townsh. St. Tr.*, 1), and also under section 244, subd. 5, of this code; and if considered as the act of an individual, it is made punishable by section 469. But the magnitude of the offense, especially in times of great public excitement like the present, demands that such an act should be punished with more severity than a simple misdemeanor.

The section in the text is extended to messages, &c., of the executive of the United States, because the greatest evil lies in such publications, and they are most likely to be made in our commercial metropolis, as a center of influence and information. Besides, there being no common law of the United States, the offense cannot be punished as a conspiracy, in the Federal courts. Nor is there any statute of the United States making it punishable at all, unless it may be treated as a military offense, which is doubtful. Indeed, it is understood that

Howard has been discharged, there being no law of the United States to which he is amenable.

The reasons which require the section to be extended so as to include messages of the executive of this state, justify its enlargement to include those of the executive officers of other states and territories.

§ 736. Every person who willfully and wrongfully commits any act which grossly injures the person or property of another, or which grossly disturbs or endangers the public peace or health, or which openly outrages public decency and is injurious to public morals, for which no other punishment is expressly prescribed therefor by this Code, is guilty of a misdemeanor. Acts not expressly forbidden.

See *Barb. Cr. L.*, 220, 222; Commonwealth *v.* Sharpless, 2 *Serg. & R.*, 91; 1 *Russ. Cr.*, 45; *Bish. Cr. L.*, § 394.

TITLE XVIII.

GENERAL PROVISIONS.

Acts made punishable by different provisions of this Code

§ 737. An act or omission which is made punishable in different ways by different provisions of this Code, may be punished under either of such provisions (except that in the cases specified in sections 748 to 751, inclusive, the punishment therein prescribed are substituted for those prescribed for a first offense), but in no case can it be punished under more than one; and an acquittal or conviction and sentence under either one, bars a prosecution for the same act or omission under any other.

§ 738. An act or omission declared punishable by this Code, is not less so because it is also punishable under the laws of another state, government or country, unless the contrary is expressly declared in this Code, Acts punishable under foreign law.

§ 739. But whenever it appears upon the trial of an indictment that the accused has already been acquitted or convicted upon any criminal prosecution under the laws of another state, government or country, founded upon the act or omission in respect to which he is upon trial, this is a sufficient defense Foreign conviction or acquittal.

This section is intended to apply in cases where the foreign acquittal or conviction took place in respect to the particular *act or omission* charged against the accused upon the trial in this state, and is not restricted to cases where the accused was tried abroad under the same *charge*.

§ 740. A criminal act is not the less punishable as a crime, because it is also declared to be punishable as a contempt. Contempts, how punishable.

§ 741. But where it is made to appear at the time of passing sentence upon a person convicted upon indictment, that such person has already paid a fine or suffered an imprisonment for the act of which he stands convicted, under an order adjudging it a contempt, the court authorized to pass sentence may mitigate the punishment to be imposed, in its discretion. Mitigation of punishment in certain cases.

Founded upon 2 *Rev. Stat.*, 278, § 15.

§ 742. Whenever an act is declared a misdemeanor, and no punishment for counseling or aiding in the commission of such act is expressly prescribed by law, every person who counsels or aids another in the commission of such act, is guilty of a misdemeanor, Aiding in misdemeanor.

The punishment of accessories in cases of felony, is provided for by section 30 of this Code.

Sending letter, when deemed complete.

§ 743. In the various cases in which the sending of a letter is made criminal by this Code, the offense is deemed complete from the time when such letter is deposited in any post office or any other place, or delivered to any person with intent that it shall be forwarded. And the party may be indicted and tried in any county wherein such letter is so deposited or delivered, or in which it shall be received by the person to whom it is addressed.

See Rex *v.* Williams, 2 *Campb.*, 506.

Omission to perform duty, when punishable able.

§ 744. No person is punishable for an omission to perform an act, where such act has been performed by another person acting in his behalf, and competent by law to perform it.

Attempts to commit crimes, when punishable.

§ 745. Any person may be convicted of an attempt to commit a crime although it appears on the trial that the crime intended or attempted was perpetrated by such person in pursuance of such attempt, unless the court, in its discretion, shall discharge the jury and direct such person to be tried for such crime.

See 2 *Rev. Stat.*, 702, § 26; *Stat.* 14 and 15 *Vict.*, ch. 100, § 9.

Attempts to commit crimes, how punishable.

§ 746. Every person who attempts to commit any crime, but fails, or is prevented or intercepted in the perpetration thereof, is punishable, where no provision is made by law for the punishment of such attempt, as follows:

1. If the offense so attempted be punishable by imprisonment in a state prison for four years or more, or by imprisonment in a county jail, the person guilty of such attempt is punishable by imprisonment in a state prison, or in a county jail, as the case may be, for a term not exceeding one-half the longest term of imprisonment prescribed upon a conviction for the offense so attempted;

2. If the offense so attempted be punishable by imprisonment in a state prison for any time less than

four years, the person guilty of such attempt is punishable by imprisonment in a county jail for not more than one year;

3. If the offense so attempted be punishable by a fine, the offender convicted of such attempt is punishable by a fine not exceeding one-half the largest fine which may be imposed upon a conviction of the offense so attempted;

4. If the offense so attempted be punishable by imprisonment and by a fine, the offender convicted of such attempt may be punished by both imprisonment and fine, not exceeding one-half the longest term of imprisonment, and one-half the largest fine which may be imposed upon a conviction for the offense so attempted.

2 *Rev. Stat.*, 698, § 3.

Omitted provisions. In the corresponding provision in the Revised Statutes the first subdivision is: "If the offense so attempted to be committed was such as is punishable by the death of the offender, the person convicted of such attempt shall be punished by imprisonment in a state prison not exceeding ten years." As arson is not punishable, according to the provisions of this Code, by death, there only remain attempts to commit murder and treason, to which this provision can possibly apply. Attempts to murder are the subject of specific provisions. See sections 277, 278, 279. If there can be recognized an attempt to commit treason, which might be the subject of punishment under the above provision, such act will generally be found embraced under provisions of the Code relative to conspiracy, riot, &c. It has therefore not been thought important to retain the provision.

§ 747. The last two sections do not protect a person who, in attempting unsuccessfully to commit a crime, accomplishes the commission of another and different crime, whether greater or less in guilt, from suffering the punishment prescribed by law for the crime committed. **Restriction upon the preceding sections.**

§ 748. Every person who, having been convicted of any offense punishable by imprisonment in a state prison, commits any crime after such conviction, is punishable therefor as follows: **Second offenses, how punished, after conviction of former offense.**

1. If the offense of which such person is subsequently convicted is such that, upon a first conviction an offender would be punishable by imprisonment in a state prison for any term exceeding five years, such person is punishable by imprisonment in a state prison for a term not less than ten years;

2. If such subsequent offense is such that, upon a first conviction, the offender would be punishable by imprisonment in a state prison for five years, or any less term, then the person convicted of such subsequent offense is punishable by imprisonment in a state prison for a term not exceeding ten years;

3. If such subsequent conviction is for petit larceny, or for any attempt to commit an offense which, if committed, would be punishable by imprisonment in a state prison, then the person convicted of such subsequent offense is punishable by imprisonment in a state prison for a term not exceeding five years.

Founded upon 2 *Rev. Stat.*, 699, § 8, the provision being extended to embrace cases of offenders who, upon a first conviction of a crime punishable in the discretion of the court by imprisonment in a state prison or otherwise, received sentence for the alternative punishment; instead of being confined to those who have been actually discharged from imprisonment upon the first conviction.

Attempts to conceal death of child, how punished after conviction of former attempt.

§ 749. Every woman who, having been convicted of endeavoring to conceal the still birth of any issue of her body, which, if born alive, would be a bastard, or the death of any such issue under the age of two years, subsequently to such conviction endeavors to conceal any such birth or death of issue of her body, is punishable by imprisonment in a state prison not exceeding five years, and not less than two.

Laws of 1845, ch. 260, § 4, modified as stated in note to preceding section.

Second offenses, how punished, after conviction of

§ 750. Every person who, having been convicted of petit larceny, or of an attempt to commit an offense which, if perpetrated, would be punishable by imprisonment in a state prison, commits any crime after such conviction, is punishable as follows: petit larceny, or of attempt to commit a state prison offense.

1. If such subsequent offense is such that upon a first conviction the offender would be punishable by imprisonment in a state prison for life, at the discretion of the court, such person is punishable by imprisonment in such prison during life;

2. If such subsequent offense is such that upon a first conviction the offender would be punishable by imprisonment in a state prison for any term less than for life, such person is punishable by imprisonment in such prison for the longest term prescribed, upon a conviction for such first offense.

3. If such subsequent conviction is for petit larceny or for any attempt to commit an offense which, if perpetrated, would be punishable by imprisonment in a state prison, then such person is punishable by imprisonment in such prison for a term not exceeding five years.

2 *Rev. Stat.*, 699, § 9, modified as stated in note to section 748.

Foreign conviction for former offense.

§ 751. Every person who has been convicted in any other state, government or country of an offense which, if committed within this state, would be punishable by the laws of this state by imprisonment in a state prison, is punishable for any subsequent crime committed within this state, in the manner prescribed in the last three sections, and to the same extent as if such first conviction had taken place in a court of this state.

2 *Rev. Stat.*, 700 § 10.

Second term of imprisonment, when to commence.

§ 752. When any person is convicted of two or more crimes before sentence has been pronounced upon him for either, the imprisonment to which he is sentenced upon the second or other subsequent conviction, must commence at the termination of the first term of imprisonment to which he shall be adjudged, or at the termination of the second or other subsequent term of imprisonment, as the case may be.

2 *Rev. Stat.*, 700, § 11.

Imprisonment for life.

§ 753. Whenever any person is declared punishable for a crime by imprisonment in a state prison for a term not less than any specified number of years, and no limit to the duration of such imprisonment is declared, the court authorized to pronounce judgment upon such conviction may, in its discretion, sentence such offender to imprisonment during his natural life, or for any number of years, not less than such as are prescribed. But no person can in any case be sentenced to imprisonment in a state prison for any term less than one year.

2 *Rev. Stat.*, 700, § 12, as amended by *Laws of* 1862, ch. 417. Section 12 is evidently the one intended to be amended by the act of 1862, though by a clerical error the reference made is to section 13.

Sentence to state prison, how to be limited.

§ 754. In cases where convicts sentenced to be imprisoned in a state prison for a longer period than one year, it is the duty of the court before which the conviction is had to limit the time of the sentence so that it will expire between the month of March and the month of November, unless the exact period of the sentence is fixed by law.

Laws of 1836, ch. 171, § 6; "one year" being substituted for "two years," to correspond with the change introduced by *Laws of* 1862, ch. 417.

Juvenile offenders may be sent to penitentiary.

§ 755. Whenever any person under the age of twenty-one and above the age of sixteen years is convicted of an offense punishable by imprisonment in a state prison, in either of the judicial districts of this state within which is a penitentiary, the court before whom such conviction is had may, in its discretion, sentence the person so convicted to imprisonment in the penitentiary situated in that judicial district.

See *Laws of* 1856, ch. 158, § 1.

§ 756. Upon a conviction for any crime punishable by imprisonment in any jail or prison, in relation to which no fine is herein prescribed, the court may impose a fine on the offender not exceeding two hundred dollars, in addition to the imprisonment prescribed. Fine may be added to imprisonment.

2 *Rev. Stat.*, 700, § 13.

§ 757. A sentence of imprisonment in a state prison for any term less than for life, suspends all the civil rights of the person so sentenced, and forfeits all public offices, and all private trusts, authority or power during the term of such imprisonment. Civil rights of convict suspended.

2 *Rev. Stat.*, 700, § 19.

§ 758. A person sentenced to imprisonment in a state prison for life, is thereafter deemed civilly dead. Civil death.

2 *Rev. Stat.*, 700, § 20.

§ 759. The person of a convict sentenced to imprisonment in a state prison is under the protection of the law, and any injury to his person, not authorized by law, is punishable in the same manner as if he was not convicted or sentenced. Person of convict protected.

2 *Rev. Stat.*, 700, § 21.

§ 760. No conviction of any person for crime works any forfeiture of any property, except in the cases of an outlawry for treason, as provided by Title III of Part VI of the Code of Criminal Procedure, and other cases in which a forfeiture is expressly imposed by law; and all forfeitures to the people of this state in the nature of a doedand, or where any person shall flee from justice, are abolished. Forfeitures.

See 2 *Rev. Stat.*, 700, § 22. That no forfeiture is imposed for suicide, see section 228.

§ 761. The various sections of this Code which declare that evidence obtained upon the examination of a person as a witness shall not be received against Witness' testimony may be read against him on prosecution for perjury.

him in any criminal proceeding, do not forbid such evidence being proved against such person upon any proceedings founded upon a charge of perjury committed in such examination.

Certain terms defined, in the senses in which they are used in this Code.

§ 762. Wherever the terms mentioned in the following sections are employed in this Code, they are deemed to be employed in the senses hereafter affixed to them, except where a different sense plainly appears.

"Willfully" defined.

§ 763. The term "willfully," when applied to the intent with which an act is done or omitted, implies simply a purpose or willingness to commit the act or the omission referred to. It does not require any intent to violate law, or to injure another, or to acquire any advantage.

"Neglect," "negligence," &c., defined.

§ 764. The terms "neglect," "negligence," "negligent" and "negligently," when so employed, import a want of such attention to the nature or probable consequences of the act or omission as a prudent man ordinarily bestows in acting in his own concerns.

"Corruptly" defined.

§ 765. The term "corruptly," when so employed, imports a wrongful design to acquire or cause some pecuniary or other advantage to the person guilty of the act or omission referred to, or to some other person.

"Malice" and "Maliciously" defined.

§ 766. The terms "malice" and "maliciously," when so employed, import a wish to vex, annoy or injure another person; established either by proof or presumption of law.

"Knowingly" defined.

§ 767. The term "knowingly," when so applied, imports only a knowledge that the facts exist which bring the act or omission within the provisions of this Code. It does not require any knowledge of the unlawfulness of such act or omission.

§ 768. The term "bribe" signifies any money, goods, right in action, property, thing of value or advantage, present or prospective, or any promise or undertaking to give any, asked, given or accepted with a corrupt intent to influence, unlawfully, the person to whom it is given, in his action, vote or opinion in any public or official capacity. "Bribe" defined.

§ 769. The word "vessel" when used with reference to shipping, includes ships of all kinds, steamboats and steamships, canal boats, and every structure adapted to be navigated from place to place. "Vessel" defined.

§ 770. The term "peace officer" signifies any one of the officers mentioned in section 154 of the Code of Criminal Procedure. "Peace officer" defined.

§ 771. The term "magistrate" signifies any one of the officers mentioned in section 147 of the Code of Criminal Procedure. "Magistrate" defined.

§ 772. The term "signature" includes any name, mark or sign, written with intent to authenticate any instrument or writing. "Signature" defined.

§ 773. The term "writing" includes both printing and writing. "Writing" defined.

§ 774. The term "real property" includes every estate, interest and right in lands, tenements and hereditaments. "Real property" defined.

§ 775. The term "personal property" includes every description of money, goods, chattels, effects, evidences of rights in action, and all written instruments by which any pecuniary obligation, right or title to property, real or personal, is created, acknowledged, transferred, increased, defeated, discharged or diminished, and every right and interest therein. "Personal property" defined.

"Property" defined.

§ 776. The term "property" includes both real and personal property.

See, as to the three sections above, 2 *Rev. Stat.*, 702, §§ 33, 34.

"Person" defined.

§ 777. The word "person" includes corporations, as well as natural persons.

"Person" when used to denote owner of property.

§ 778. Where the term "person" is used in this Code to designate the party whose property may be the subject of any offense, it includes this state, any other state, government or country which may lawfully own any property within this state, and all public and private corporations, or joint associations, as well as individuals.

2 *Rev. Stat.*, 703, § 35.

Singular includes plural.

§ 779. The singular number includes the plural, and the plural the singular.

Masculine word includes feminine, &c.

§ 780. Words used in the masculine gender, comprehend as well the feminine and neuter.

Present tense, how used.

§ 781. Words used in the present tense include the future, but exclude the past.

What intent to defraud is sufficient.

§ 782. Whenever, by any of the provisions of this Code chapter, an intent to defraud is required, in order to constitute any offense, it is sufficient if an intent appears to defraud any person, association or body politic or corporate whatever.

Suggested as a substitute for 2 *Rev. Stat.*, 703, § 36, which is as follows: Where any intent to injure, defraud or cheat is required by law to be shown in order to constitute any offense, it shall be sufficient, if such intent be to injure, defraud or cheat the United States, this state or any other state or country, or the government or any public officer thereof, or any county, city or town, or any corporation, body politic or private individual.

The section in the text will also include the provision of 2 *Rev. Stat.*, 675, § 46, which is as follows: "Whenever by any of the foregoing provisions an intent to defraud is required to constitute forgery, it is sufficient if an intent appears to defraud the United States, any state, or territory, any body corporate, any county, city, town or village or any public officer in his official capacity, any copartnership, or any one of such partners or any real person what.

ever." It may be doubted whether this language includes a joint stock association, though doubtless intended so to do. And aside from this, the language is needlessly verbose.

§ 783. The omission to specify or affirm in this Code any liability to any damages, penalty, forfeiture or other remedy, imposed by law, and allowed to be recovered or enforced in any civil action or proceeding, for any act or omission declared punishable herein, does not affect any right to recover or enforce the same.

Civil remedies preserved.

§ 784. The omission to specify or affirm in this Code any ground or forfeiture of a public office or other trust or special authority conferred by law, or any power conferred by law to impeach, remove, depose or suspend any public officer or other person holding any trust, appointment or other special authority conferred by law, does not affect such forfeiture or power, or any proceeding authorized by law to carry into effect such impeachment, removal, deposition or suspension.

Proceedings to impeach or remove officers and others preserved.

§ 785. This Code does not affect any power conferred by law upon any court martial or other military authority or officer, to impose or inflict punishment upon offenders; nor any power conferred by law upon any public body, tribunal or officer, to impose or inflict punishment for a contempt; nor any provisions of the laws relating to apprentices, bastards, disorderly persons, Indians and vagrants.

Military punishments and punishments for contempt and certain special proceedings preserved.

§ 786. Nothing in this Code affects any of the provisions of the following statutes; but such statutes are recognized as continuing in force, notwithstanding the provisions of this Code; except so far as they have been repealed or affected by any subsequent laws.

Certain statutes specified as continuing in force.

1. All acts incorporating municipal corporations, and acts amending acts of incorporation or charters of such corporations, or providing for the election or

appointment of officers therein, or defining the powers and duties of such officers.

2. All acts relating to emigrants or other passengers in vessels coming from foreign countries.

3. An act concerning foreign bank notes. Passed May, 1839.

Laws of 1839, ch. 355.

4. An act to amend the act entitled "an act to authorize the business of banking." Passed May 14, 1840.

Laws of 1840, ch. 363.

5. An act to amend the act entitled "an act to amend the act entitled an act to authorize the business of banking," passed May 14, 1840. Passed April 10, 1850.

Laws of 1850, ch. 251.

6. An act requiring the police justices in the city of New York to file records of all convictions of vagrancy. Passed April 12, 1853.

Laws of 1853, ch. 183.

7. An act to provide for the care and instruction of idle and truant children. Passed April 12, 1853.

Laws of 1853, ch. 185.

8. An act to amend an act entitled "an act concerning foreign bank notes." Passed April 13, 1853.

Laws of 1853, ch. 223.

9. An act in relation to the property and money taken from persons arrested and accused of crimes in the city of New York and Brooklyn. Passed April 9, 1855.

Laws of 1855, ch. 199.

10. An act to regulate the business of purchasing rags, rope and metals in the city of Albany. Passed March 28, 1857.

Laws of 1857, ch. 193.

11. An act to establish a metropolitan police district and provide for the government thereof. Passed April 15, 1857.

Laws of 1857, ch. 569.

12. An act to provide for the preservation of timber and stone on the lands of Onondaga Indian Reservation. Passed April 16, 1857.

Laws of 1857, ch. 659.

13. An act to establish regulations for the port of New York. Passed April 16, 1857.

Laws of 1857, ch. 671.

14. An act in relation to jurors and to the appointment and the duties of a commissioner of jurors in the county of Kings. Passed April 17, 1858.

Laws of 1858, ch. 322.

15. An act to provide for the organization and government of the police force of the city of Albany. Passed March 31, 1859.

Laws of 1859, ch. 82.

16. An act to amend an act entitled "an act for the regulation and government of the central park in the city of New York," passed April 17, 1857, and further to provide for the maintenance and government of said park. Passed April 15, 1859.

Laws of 1859, ch. 349.

17. An act in relation to the court of special sessions in the city and county of New York, and the powers of police justices. Passed April 19, 1859.

Laws of 1859, ch. 491.

18. An act to amend an act entitled "an act to establish a metropolitan police district, and to provide for the government thereof," passed April 15, 1857. Passed April 10, 1860.

Laws of 1860, ch. 259.

19. An act to lay out a public park and a parade ground for the city of Brooklyn, and to alter the commissioner's map of said city. Passed April 17, 1860.

Laws of 1860, ch. 488.

20. An act to preserve the public peace and order on the first day of the week commonly called Sunday. Passed April 17, 1860.

Laws of 1860, ch. 501.

21. An act to amend an act entitled "an act to lay out a public park and a parade ground in the city

of Brooklyn, and to alter the commissioner's map of said city," passed April 17, 1860. Passed May 2, 1861.

Laws of 1861, ch. 340.

22. An act to regulate places of public amusement in the cities and incorporated villages of this state. Passed April 17, 1862.

Laws of 1862, ch. 281.

23. An act for the preservation of moose, wild deer, birds and fresh water fish. Passed April 23, 1862.

Laws of 1862, ch. 474.

24. An act for the better regulation and discipline of the New York State Inebriate Asylum. Passed April 14, 1864.

Laws of 1864, ch. 196.

25. An act in relation to the sale, use and disposition of butts, hogsheads, barrels, casks or kegs, used by the manufacturers of malt liquors. Passed April 22, 1864.

Laws of 1864, ch. 276.

26. An act to amend an act entitled "an act to amend an act entitled 'an act to establish a metropolitan police district and to provide for the government thereof,' passed April 15, 1857," passed April 10, 1860. Passed April 25, 1864.

Laws of 1864, ch. 403.

27. An act to revise and consolidate the general acts relating to public instruction. Passed May 2, 1864.

Laws of 1861, ch. 555.

28. All acts passed since the first day of January, 1864, to declare, protect or enforce any right of persons in the military or naval service of the United States or to redress or punish wrongs sustained by such persons.

See *Laws of* 1864, ch. 2; *Ibid.*, ch. 253; *Ibid.*, ch. 390; *Ibid.*, ch. 391.

It will be observed that no statutes whatever, are *repealed* by the foregoing provisions. The various provisions of our statute law declaring crimes or imposing criminal punishments, are in numerous instances so interwoven with provisions relative to civil rights and remedies, that a repealing act which should exhibit the proposed changes in the law in the form of designating the acts or parts of acts *repealed*, would be almost impracticable. A mere provision in general terms that all inconsistent provisions should be deemed repealed, leaves the whole effect and operation of the Code open to judicial construction. The particular operation of the Code, upon the existing statutes, might doubtless be exhibited in detail, by a chapter enumerating acts or parts of acts which are repealed, in full, and *amending* sections of existing statutes which contain provisions relative to criminal law, combined with others. The great difficulty of doing this without disturbing civil rights founded upon the existing statutes, and the amount of space required in the printed Code, for such a chapter, are the objections to this method, The Commissioners have, therefore, made no provision in the Penal Code for *repeal* of laws defining crimes; though some acts relative to prisons are repealed by section 1070. They have provided by section 2, that, from the time when the Code takes effect, no person shall be punished criminally, except as provided by this Code, or by some of the statutes which it specifies as continuing in force. In the section in the text they enumerate the statutes which are intended to be continued. The effect is that while other statutes will remain unrepealed, and in full effect, so far as past transactions or civil rights or remedies are concerned, courts of criminal jurisdiction will be forbidden to enforce them, in so far as before the adoption of the Code they authorized criminal punishments.

The acts enumerated in the above section are for the most part either local or special in their character, and proper to be continued as separate laws, rather than to be incorporated in either of the proposed Codes, or acts which have been passed since the other Codes now before the legislature were reported, but which relate to subjects embraced within the scope of some one of the Codes, and the valuable provisions of which should be incorporated with the Code to which they belong wherever it is finally reviewed by the legislature. In addition to the above mentioned statutes there are laws relative to special subjects, which it is designed to retain in a separate form and which will contain some provisions of a penal nature but not of general interest or application. These are the Health Laws, the School Laws, the Poor Laws, the Fiscal Laws, the Laws relative to the Inspection of Merchandise, &c.

TITLE XIX.

OF THE GOVERNMENT AND DISCIPLINE OF STATE PRISONS AND COUNTY JAILS, AND OF THE CONDUCT AND TREATMENT OF PRISONERS THEREIN.

CHAPTER I.

DESIGNATION OF THE DIFFERENT STATE PRISONS AND COUNTY JAILS, AND GENERAL REGULATIONS RESPECTING THEM, AND THE CUSTODY AND REMOVAL OF PRISONERS.

§ 787. There are maintained for the security and reformation of convicts, in this state, three state prisons; one at Sing Sing, in Westchester county, at which is established a separate department for female convicts; one at Auburn, in the county of Cayuga; and one at Dannemora, in the county of Clinton; which prisons are respectively denominated the Sing Sing prison, the Auburn prison, and the Clinton prison. Designation of the state prisons.

See *Laws of* 1847, ch. 460, § 29.

§ 788. The common jails in the several counties of this state are kept by the sheriffs of the counties in which they are respectively situated, and are used as prisons: Designation of the county jails

1. For the detention of persons, duly committed, in order to secure their attendance as witnesses in any criminal case;

2. For the detention of persons charged with crime, and committed for trial;

3. For the confinement of persons duly committed for any contempt or upon civil process or by other authority of law; and,

4. For the confinement of persons sentenced to imprisonment therein, upon conviction for crime.

Laws of 1847, ch. 460, § 1.

Convicts, how to be sentenced.

§ 789. All male convicts sentenced in the first and second judicial districts to an imprisonment in a state prison shall be confined in the state prison at Sing Sing, and all so sentenced in the fifth, sixth, seventh and eighth judicial districts, in the state prison at Auburn, and all so sentenced in the other judicial districts, in the Clinton state prison.

See *Laws of* 1847, ch. 460, § 84. The latter part of this section, providing for the removal of convicts from one state prison to another, is omitted; for the reason that regulations upon that subject are contained in subsequent sections.

Female convicts.

§ 790. All female convicts sentenced in any county in the state to imprisonment in a state prison, must be confined in the female department of the Sing Sing prison.

Laws of 1847, ch. 460, § 85.

Reports of male and female departments.

§ 791. The annual and all other reports and estimates of earnings and expenditures of the male and female departments of the state prisons, must be made out separately and distinctly, the one from the other.

Laws of 1860, ch. 283, § 1.

Compensation for transportation.

§ 792. The compensation allowed to sheriffs for transporting convicts to the state prisons, shall not exceed the following rates:

For conveying a single convict, for each mile from

the county prison from which such convict shall be conveyed, thirty-five cents.

For conveying two convicts, for each such mile, forty-five cents;

For conveying three convicts, fifty cents;

For conveying four convicts, fifty-five cents;

For conveying five convicts, sixty cents;

For all additional convicts, such reasonable allowance as the comptroller may think just.

The above allowance, with one dollar per day for the maintenance of each convict whilst on the way to the state prison, but not exceeding one dollar for every thirty miles travel, shall be in full of all charges and expenses in the premises.

See *Laws of* 1849, ch. 123, § 1. Section 2 repeals section 2 of *Laws of* 1847, ch. 497.

Account to be rendered on delivering convicts.

§ 793. On the delivery of any convict to the keeper of a state prison, the sheriff or other person having charge of such convict must make and render to the warden, keeper or clerk of the prison, an account of the number of miles necessarily traveled in coming, estimated by the shortest practicable route, and of the sums actually expended for the maintenance of the convicts, while coming.

See *Laws of* 1847, ch. 497, § 3. The commissioners suggest that instead of the existing mode of transporting convicts, the sheriff be required to notify the proper warden, and that it be made a part of his official duty to send for the convicts.

How it is to be certified.

§ 794. The account required by the last section must be certified under oath by the sheriff or other person rendering the same to be correct. And there must be added to such account the certificate of either the warden, keeper or clerk of such prison, setting forth the number of convicts so delivered, and the distance from such prison to the place of their conviction.

Taken from *Laws of* 1847, ch. 497, § 3. So much of this section as provides that the "keeper of the respective prison * * * are hereby authorized to administer the oath above required"—is omitted; for the reason that the powers conferred on inspectors by section 843 and on clerks and wardens by section 920 of this Code, to administer oaths, are deemed amply sufficient for the purposes required.

And how paid.

§ 795. The account, certified and attested as provided in the last section, shall be paid by the warden, or certified by him to be paid by the comptroller, according to the provisions of section 881.

Substituted for *Laws of* 1847, ch. 497, § 4.

What convicts must be transported together.

§ 796. All the convicts who are sentenced to imprisonment in the same state prison, at one session of a criminal court, must be transported thither at the same time, unless there are more than five and the court expressly direct otherwise.

Ibid.

Removal of convicts where number is excessive.

§ 797. Whenever, in the opinion of the inspectors of state prisons, it appears that there is a greater number of convicts in any state prison that can well be accommodated therein, or that such convicts cannot be employed profitably to the state, the inspectors may cause as many of such convicts as they deem proper to be removed, by the warden of such prison, to either of the other state prisons which the inspectors may designate. But the inspectors must not, in such case, reduce the number of convicts in any prison below one hundred.

See *Laws of* 1849, ch. 132, § 1. This provision is considered sufficient to provide for all cases of overstocking the state prisons; and the more restricted provision of *Laws of* 1860, ch. 399, § 15, is therefore omitted. That provision is as follows:

"Whenever there shall be more convicts in any state prison than there are separate cells for the accommodation of each, and there are vacant cells in either of the other prisons, the inspectors of state prisons may order the agent and warden of the prison in which such convicts are confined to order the transfer of such number of convicts as there shall be vacant cells in the prison to which they are transferred. In selecting convicts so to be transferred the agent and warden shall take those convicts last received at the prison."

§ 798. All necessary expenses of any removal of convicts authorized by the last section, or by sections 804, 805, or 806, form a part of the incidental expenses of the prison from which such convicts are removed. They must be audited by the comptroller, and paid by the warden of such prison out of any moneys in his hands belonging to the state and applicable to the expenses of the prison. Expenses of such removal.

See *Laws of* 1847, ch. 460, § 90; *Laws of* 1849, ch. 132, § 2.

§ 799. Whenever a removal of convicts from one state prison to another shall be ordered, the warden must cause the convicts so to be removed to be sufficiently chained in pairs, and transported to the prison to which they shall be sent, and must deliver such convicts, with the certified copies of their sentences, to the warden of the prison to which they shall be removed, the warden of which prison must receive and keep them according to their sentences, as if they had been originally committed to such prison. Manner of removal.

Laws of 1847, ch. 460, § 88.

§ 800. The persons so employed to conduct such convicts, must prohibit all intercourse between them and other persons, and may inflict any reasonable and necessary correction upon the convicts for disobedience or misconduct in any respect. Intercourse with other persons prohibited.

Laws of 1847, ch. 460, § 89.

§ 801. The inspectors may, by warrant, under their hands, direct any convict, under the age of seventeen years, who is confined in the Sing Sing prison, to be removed to the House of Refuge in the city of New York; and any like convict who is confined in the Auburn or Clinton prisons to be removed to the Western House of Refuge in the city of Rochester. Removal of convicts under seventeen.

See *Laws of* 1847, ch. 460, § 91; *Laws of* 1850, ch. 24, § 2.

Manner of such removal.

§ 802. Whenever the inspectors of state prisons shall, pursuant to the last section, direct the removal of any convict to a house of refuge, the wardens of the prison in which such convict is confined must cause him to be conveyed to the house of refuge designated in the warrant, to be there confined, according to the rules and regulations of such house of refuge, until the expiration of the term for which such convict was sentenced.

See Ibid.

Expenses of such removal.

§ 803. The expenses of any removal authorized by the last section may be the same as are allowed to sheriffs for like services; and form a part of the incidental expenses of the prison from which such convict is removed. The expenses of such removal must be first paid out of any funds of the prison not otherwise appropriated, and must be certified by the warden. It is also the duty of the warden of the prison to make out a certificate of such expenses, and transmit the same, or a counterpart thereof, to the sheriff in each county in which any such convicts were sentenced; and the sheriffs receiving such certificate must present the same to the board of supervisors of the county, at the first annual meeting thereof. The board of supervisors must raise the amount specified in such certificate, as a county charge, and the treasurer of the county, within ten days after receiving the amount, must remit the same to the warden of the prison.

See *Laws of* 1847, ch. 460, §§ 91, 92, 93.

Removal of convicts in case of fire.

§ 804. Whenever, by reason of any state prison being on fire, or any building contiguous or near to any state prison being on fire, there is reason to apprehend that the convicts confined in such prison may be injured or endangered by such fire, or may escape, the warden may, in his discretion, remove such convicts to some safe and convenient place, and there confine them so long as may be necessary to avoid such danger; and such removal shall not be deemed an escape of such convicts.

§ 805. Whenever any pestilence or contagious disease breaks out among the convicts in either of the state prisons, or in the vicinity of either, of which the certificate of the physician shall be conclusive evidence, the inspector in charge of such prison may cause the convicts confined therein to be removed to some suitable place of security, where such of them as may be sick shall receive all necessary care and medical assistance. Such convicts must be returned as soon as may be to the prison from which they were taken, to be confined until the expiration of their respective sentences.

Removal of convicts in case of pestilence.

See *Laws of* 1847, ch. 460, §§ 94, 95.

§ 806. Whenever, from any riot or civil commotion, from any insecurity of any state prison, or from any other cause, it becomes absolutely necessary for the safe keeping of the convicts confined in any state prison, that they should be removed therefrom, the inspector in charge of such prison may remove such convicts to some safe and convenient place, and there confine them so long as the necessity continues; and such removal and confinement shall not be deemed an escape of such prisoners.

Removal of convicts in case of riot, &c.

§ 807. It is the duty of the inspectors to cause to be erected, at as early a period as practicable, in each of the state prisons of this state, separate rooms or cells, not less in their dimensions, in the clear, than nine hundred and ninety-six cubic feet, as follows: such number, not exceeding twenty, as the said inspectors shall deem necessary and expedient, at the Sing Sing prison; and, under like restrictions, not exceeding ten at the Auburn prison, and not exceeding five at the Clinton prison. Such cells must be constructed of stone, in a manner that shall render

Solitary cells to be erected.

them secure, for the purposes mentioned in section 980.

Laws of 1847, ch. 460, § 44. The duty is here rendered imperative instead of being left to depend on the amount of the prison funds, as under the existing law.

Lands at Clinton prison.

§ 808. All uncultivated lands now or hereafter belonging to this state, situated within ten miles of the Clinton prison, shall be withdrawn from sale, and retained by the state for the purpose of furnishing fuel for the manufacture of iron by the convicts in such prison.

Taken from *Laws of* 1847, ch. 460, § 138, substituting *ten* miles for *twenty*. This appears to be what was intended by the act of 1851, ch. 259, § 4.

The original act authorizing the establishment of the Clinton prison (*Laws of* 1844, ch. 245), contained no provision reserving lands around it.

On April 16, 1845, however, an act was passed entitled "an act to amend an act in relation to state prisons, passed May 1, 1844," which contained the following provision:

"All uncultivated lands belonging to the state of New York, or which may hereafter become the property of said state, and which shall be situated within twenty miles of said prison, shall be withdrawn from sale and shall be retained by the state for the purpose of furnishing fuel for the manufacture of iron by the convicts of said prison."

Laws of 1845, ch. 70, § 6.

This section, with other parts of the acts of 1845, was repealed by the general repealing section (160) of the act of 1847, ch. 460 (as will appear by consulting that section, which is reprinted in the note to section 1070 of this Code). A provision in words identically the same (except one wholly unimportant variation) with section six of the act of 1845, was inserted as section 138 of the act of 1847.

In 1851, an act was passed "amendatory of section six of chapter 70 of the *Laws of* 1845,"—the section previously repealed. It provided that:

"The sixth section of the act entitled, 'An act to amend an act in relation to state prisons, passed May 1st, 1844,' passed April 16, 1845, is hereby amended so as to read as follows:

"'All uncultivated lands belonging to the state of New York, or which may hereafter become the property of said state, and which shall be situated within ten miles of the Clinton prison, shall be withdrawn from sale, and shall be retained by the state for the purpose of furnishing fuel for the manufacture of iron by the convicts in said prison.'"

Laws of 1851, ch. 259, § 4.

The reference should have been to section 138 of chapter 460 of the *Laws of* 1847, as the section amended.

§ 809. Each county jail must contain a sufficient number of rooms to allow all persons belonging to either one of the following classes to be confined separately and distinctly from persons belonging to either of the other classes: Rooms required in county jails.

1. Persons committed on criminal process, and detained for trial;

2. Persons already convicted of crime and held under sentence;

3. Persons detained as witnesses, or held under civil process, or under an order imposing punishment for a contempt;

4. Males separately from females.

Substituted for *Laws of* 1847, ch. 460, § 2, which is as follows: "Each county prison shall contain:

"1. A sufficient number of rooms for the confinement of persons committed on criminal process and detained for trial, separately and distinct from prisoners under sentence.

"2. A sufficient number of rooms for the confinement of prisoners under sentence.

"3. A sufficient number of rooms for the separate confinement of persons committed on civil process, for contempt, or as witnesses."

This language is obscure, in several respects. In particular it will be noticed that unless the word "or" may be supplied by way of construction between the words "on civil process," and the words "for contempt," no provision is made for the confinement of a person held under civil process, separately from persons confined under sentence upon conviction. And if the word "or" be so supplied there is room for a question whether, upon the literal language of the section, a person who is held under sentence upon a conviction on *indictment* for contempt must not be confined separately from other convicts.

In existing laws, the phrase "county *prison*" is usually employed in statutes relating to prison discipline; but "county *jail*" is most frequently used in sections defining crimes and their punishment. For the sake of uniformity in phraseology, the words "county jail" have been used throughout this Code.

Sheriff may remove prisoners in county jails.

§ 810. The sheriff of any county of this state in which there is or shall be established more than one jail may confine the prisoners in his custody in either of such jails, and may remove them from one jail to another, within the county, whenever he deems it necessary for their safe keeping, or for their appearance at any court.

This section, and the two which follow, are founded upon the provisions of 2 *Rev. Stat.*, 430, §§ 24, 25 and 26; which by *Laws of* 1847, ch. 460, § 12, are extended to criminal prisoners.

Removal in case of fire.

§ 811. Whenever, by reason of any jail being on fire, or any building contiguous or near to a jail being on fire, there is reason to apprehend that the prisoners confined in such jail may be injured or endangered by such fire, or may escape, the sheriff or keeper of such jail may, in his discretion, remove such prisoners to some safe and convenient place, and there confine them, so long as may be necessary to avoid such danger; and such removal and confinement shall not be deemed an escape of such prisoners.

2 *Rev. Stat.*, 430, § 25.

Removal in case of pestilence.

§ 812. Whenever any pestilence or contagious disease breaks out in any jail, or in its vicinity, and the physician to such jail certifies that such pestilence or disease is likely to endanger the health of the prisoners confined therein, the county judge of the county in which such jail is situated, or in the city and county of New York, the mayor or recorder, and any alderman of that city, and in the city and county of Albany, the mayor or recorder, and any alderman of the city of Albany, shall, in writing designate some safe and convenient place within such county, or the jail of some contiguous county, as a place of confinement for such prisoners, which designation shall be filed in the office of the clerk of the county. The sheriff of such county is thereupon authorized to remove such prisoners to the place or jail so designated, and there confine them, until they can be safely returned to the jail from which they were taken.

See *Rev. Stat.*, 430, § 26, as modified by *Laws of* 1847, ch. 280, § 29.

§ 813. Whenever, from any riot or civil commotion, from any insecurity of any county jail, or from any other cause, it becomes actually necessary for the safe keeping of the prisoners confined in any county jail that they should be removed therefrom, the sheriff or keeper of such jail may remove such prisoners to some safe and convenient place, and there confine them, so long as the necessity continues; and such removal and confinement shall not be deemed an escape of such prisoners. Removal in case of riot, &c.

This provision is new.

§ 814. Any place to which the prisoners in any jail shall be removed, pursuant to the last four sections, shall, during the time of the confinement of such prisoners therein, be deemed the jail of the county. Place of removal declared the county jail for the time being.

2 *Rev. Stat.*, 430, § 27.

§ 815. All provisions of this title relative to the mode of confining prisoners and convicts, apply to persons committed by any court or officer of the United States, in the same manner as if they were committed by a court or officer of this state. This title applicable to United States prisoners.

See *Laws of* 1847, ch. 460, § 16.

§ 816. It is the duty of the keeper of each county jail to receive into the jail every person duly committed thereto, upon charge of an offense against the United States, by the president of the United States, or by any court or officer of the United States, and to confine such person in the jail until he is duly discharged; the United States supporting such person during his confinement. United States prisoners to be received into county jails.

See *Laws of* 1847, ch. 460, § 16. The commissioners have inserted the words "by the president of the United States," which are not found in the existing law, in order that the section may conform to the corresponding provision of section 818. They recommend that the legislation of this state, relative to imprisonment, be adapted to carry into effect the extraordinary powers of arrest recently conferred upon the president by act of congress; in the full belief that those powers will be modified or withdrawn, whenever it is perceived that a necessity for them no longer exists.

United States convicts to be received into state prisons and county jails.

§ 817. It is the duty of the respective wardens and keepers of each of the state prisons and county jails, to receive into their respective prisons and jails, and safely to keep therein, subject to the discipline of such prison or jail, any criminal convicted of any offense against the United States, sentenced to imprisonment therein by any court of the United States, sitting within this state, until such sentence be executed, or until such convict shall be discharged by due course of law; the United States supporting such convict, and paying the expenses attendant upon the execution of such sentence.

Laws of 1847, ch. 460, § 145.

Punishment for escapes.

§ 818. In case any prisoner committed to either of the prisons by the president of the United States, or by any court or officer of the United States, shall escape from the custody of any warden or keeper to whom such convict may have been so committed, he shall be liable to the like punishment as if he had been committed by virtue of a commitment or conviction under the authority of this state; and any expenses incurred in searching for, or apprehending such convict shall be a proper charge against the government of the United States.

Taken from *Laws of* 1860, ch. 399, § 14, where it is stated as an amendment to section 156 of the act of 1847, ch. 460. By an examination of that act it will be obvious that the reference to section 156 is an error; and that section 146 is the one intended to be amended. That section is as follows:

"In case any such prisoner shall escape or attempt to escape out of the custody of any keeper to whom such prisoner may have been so committed, he shall be liable to the like punishment as if he had been committed by virtue of a commitment or conviction under the authority of this state."

The commissioners present the above enactment that they may not be supposed to intend a change in the law by omitting it; but they consider the provision for punishing the escape unnecessary under the provisions rendering escapes punishable, reported in chapter iii of title IX of this Code; and if it were desirable to be retained, it should be transferred to that chapter.

§ 819. Every warden or keeper or other officer of any prison or jail, to whom such prisoner may have been committed, shall be liable to the like penalties and punishment, for any neglect or violation of duty in respect to the custody of such prisoner, as if such prisoner had been committed by virtue of a commitment or conviction under the authority of this state. Punishment of officers for violating duty.

See *Laws of* 1847, ch. 460, § 147.

CHAPTER II.

INSPECTORS OF STATE PRISONS.

Inspectors, how chosen.

§ 820. The state prisons are under the charge and superintendence of three inspectors, chosen at a general election, according to the provisions of the fourth section of the fifth article of the constitution of this state.

See *Laws of* 1847, ch. 460, § 30.

How removed.

§ 821. The governor has power to remove any inspector, so elected, for misconduct or malversation in office; but must first give to such inspector a copy of the charge against him, and an opportunity of being heard in his defense.

Laws of 1847, ch. 460, § 31.

When to enter upon their duties.

§ 822. Each inspector shall enter upon the duties of his office on the first day of January next following his election.

Recommended as a substitute for *Laws of* 1847, ch. 460, § 32, which is as follows:

"The inspectors elected at the last general election shall enter upon the duties of their office on the first day of January, eighteen hundred and forty-eight, and each inspector to be hereafter chosen shall enter on the duties of his office on the first day of January next following his election."

To take oath of office.

§ 823. Each inspector, before entering upon the duties of his office, must take and subscribe the oath of office, prescribed by the constitution of this state. Such oath may be taken and subscribed before any officer authorized by law to take and administer oaths, and must be filed in the office of the secretary of state.

This provision is taken from *Laws of* 1847, ch. 460, § 2, and is reported only in order that an intention to change the existing law may not be inferred from its being omitted. No special provision on the subject of the official oath of the inspectors seems necessary. The constitution itself provides (*Const. of* 1846, art. xii), that "members of the legislature and all officers, executive and judicial, except such inferior officers as may be by law exempted, shall, before they enter on the duties of their respective offices, take and subscribe the following oath," &c. In the absence of any provision of law exempting inspectors from taking the oath of office, the obligation imposed upon them to do so is clear. The proper place for *filing* the oath seems pointed out with sufficient certainty by the provisions of 1 *Rev. Stat.*, 119, § 24; which are substantially embodied in *Rep. Pol. Code*, § 215.

§ 824. The inspectors must hold a joint meeting on the first Wednesday in each year, at the state prison at Sing Sing; and at such meeting must choose one of their number as president of the board for the ensuing year. In case of the absence of such president from any meeting of the board, one of the other members shall preside at such meeting, and shall have all the powers of president. Election of president.

§ 825. The inspectors must, at the meeting prescribed in the last section, assign to each inspector the special charge and supervision of one of the state prisons, to be designated, for the ensuing four months; and they must make a similar designation at the commencement of each four months' term thereafter. But no inspector can be assigned to, or have the special charge of the same prison during the next eight months. Each inspector to take special charge of one prison.

This and the last section are founded on *Laws of* 1854, ch. 240, § 1, as amended *Laws of* 1860, ch. 399, § 5; which is as follows:

"The inspectors shall hold their first joint meeting on the first Wednesday of January in each and every year, at the state prison at Sing Sing, and at such meeting, shall choose one of their number as president of the board for the ensuing year, and shall assign to each inspector the special charge and supervision of one of the state prisons, to be designated, for the ensuing four months of the year; and they shall make a similar assignment and designation at the commencement of each four months' term thereafter; but no inspector shall be re-assigned to, or have the special charge of the same prison for the next eight succeeding months."

Visitation of prisons.

§ 826. The inspectors must visit jointly each of the state prisons that now are, or hereafter may be, established in this state, at least four times in the year.

See *Laws of* 1847, ch. 460, § 34, subd. 1. This and several sections following are founded on the various subdivisions of the section referred to. In that section the powers and duties of the inspectors are stated in a series of subdivisions, introduced by the general words, "the inspectors, &c., shall have the power, and it shall be their duty." As some of the powers conferred are discretionary, and are not coupled with an absolute duty, the commissioners have preferred to distinguish these from duties imperatively imposed. They have accordingly stated the powers and duties of inspectors in distinct sections; introducing each by the words "the inspectors *must*," or "the inspectors *may*," according as they understand the intent of the law to be, to impose an absolute, imperative duty, or to vest a discretionary power.

What matters must be inquired of by the inspectors.

§ 827. The inspectors must examine and inquire into all matters connected with the government, discipline and police of each prison, the punishment and employment of the convicts therein confined, the money concerns and contracts for work, and the purchases and sales of the articles provided for each prison, or sold on account thereof.

Ibid., subd. 2.

They may require reports.

§ 828. The inspectors may, from time to time, require reports from the warden or other officers of the prison in relation to any or all of the matters mentioned in the last section.

Ibid., subd. 3.

They may make regulations for the prisons.

§ 829. The inspectors may make such general regulations for the government and discipline of each prison, as they deem expedient, not inconsistent with the laws of this state, and may, from time to time, alter and amend the same; and, in making such regulations, it is their duty to adopt such as in their judgment, while consistent with the discipline of the prison, shall best conduce to the reformation of the convicts.

Ibid. subd. 4.

§ 830. The inspectors may make like regulations, and alter and amend the same, for the government and discipline of all female convicts in the female department of the Sing Sing prison, and may cause them to be employed as shall conduce to their support and reformation. They may, by order, from time to time, prescribe the kind of labor in which such convicts shall be employed, having due regard in making such order, to the mechanical interests of the citizens of the state. **And for the female department of the Sing Sing prison.**

See *Ibid.*, subd. 12; and *Laws of* 1847, ch. 460, § 73.

§ 831. The inspectors may inquire into any improper conduct which may be alleged to have been committed by any officer or agent of, or other person employed in either of the prisons of this state. **They must inquire into alleged improper conduct.**

See *Ibid.*, subd. 5, as amended *Laws of* 1855, ch. 552 § 1. Power to send for persons and papers is conferred by section 842.

§ 832. The inspectors must keep regular minutes of their meetings and proceedings at each prison which they shall visit; which minutes must be entered by the clerk in a book kept for that purpose, in each of said prisons, and signed by the inspectors. **They must keep minutes of their proceedings.**

See *Ibid.*, subd. 6.

§ 833. The inspectors must make an annual report on or before the fifteenth day of January, in each year, of the state and condition of each of said prisons, the convicts confined therein, of the money expended and received, and generally of all the proceedings during the past year. **They must make an annual report.**

Ibid., subd. 7.

They must furnish abstracts of returns made to them.

§ 834. The inspectors must furnish to the legislature, with their respective annual reports, summary abstracts of all the returns which shall have been made to them, during the past year, by the warden or any other officer of each prison; and also a list of all contracts entered into during the past year for the employment of convicts, stating what portion of each contract may have been finished during the year, any sums of money received thereon, the probable time of its completion, and the amount which will then remain and become due.

Ibid., subd. 8.

They must cause orders, &c., adopted by them to be recorded.

§ 835. The inspectors must cause all orders, rules and regulations adopted by them, and the entries of their proceedings at each meeting, to be recorded by the clerk of the prison then visited, and furnish to each officer of the prison, on his appointment, a printed copy of the general rules and regulations of the prison.

Ibid., subd. 9.

They may employ artisans from abroad.

§ 836. The inspectors may employ artisans from abroad for the purpose of teaching such new branches of business in the state prisons as are not pursued in the state.

Ibid., subd. 10.

They must prescribe the provisions for the convicts.

§ 837. The inspectors must prescribe the kinds of provisions, and the quantities of each kind, that shall be inserted in each contract for the supply of provisions to each state prison, and may authorize each contract to be made for the term of one year, or for any less term, in their discretion, or may cause such provisions to be furnished by the warden, in their discretion.

Ibid., subd, 11. Subdivision 12 is omitted for the reason that its provisions appear fully embraced by the various sections of this title.

They must transmit wardens'

§ 838. The inspectors must transmit to the comptroller of the state, on or before the first day of

January in each year, the account and inventory rendered to them by the warden of each state prison, with such observations and remarks thereon, as they may deem necessary to enable the comptroller to understand the same, and to correct any errors that may be discovered therein. account to comptroller.

Ibid., subd, 13.

§ 839. The inspectors must cause an estimate to be made of the value of the goods, and other property of the state, of which an inventory has been rendered to them, by the warden of each prison, which estimate must be made under oath by two or more competent and disinterested persons to be appointed for that purpose by the inspectors, and must be transmitted by the inspectors to the comptroller, with the inventory to which it relates. They must cause the property of the state to be valued.

Ibid., subd. 14.

§ 840. The inspectors must select, as far as practicable, such persons, in appointing keepers to each prison where manufacturing is carried on by the state, as are qualified to instruct the convicts in the trades and manufactures thus prosecuted in such prison. Their duty in appointments.

Ibid., subd. 15.

§ 841. The inspectors must keep in repair the armories hereafter erected or used at Sing Sing or Auburn for the use and convenience of the company of guards attached to the prison; and the expense attending such repairs shall be paid out of the funds of the prison. They must keep armories in repair

Laws of 1847, ch. 460, § 126.

§ 842. In any investigation or inquiry lawfully made by the board of inspectors, the president of such board may issue subpœnas to compel witnesses to attend and testify, or to produce books and papers or other instruments of evidence, before such board, in the same manner, and with like effect, and with the same power to punish for disobedience, as is or Power of president to summon witnesses.

may be authorized by law in respect to trials before justices of the peace.

Power of inspectors to administer oaths.

§ 843. Either inspector may administer an oath or affirmation to, or take an affidavit of any person voluntarily consenting thereto, in or relating to any matter connected with the affairs of any prison. And in any investigation or inquiry lawfully made by any inspector, he may issue subpœnas to compel witnesses to attend and testify, or to produce books and papers or other instruments of evidence before him, in the same manner, and with like effect, and with the same power to punish for disobedience, as is, or may be authorized by law in respect to trials before justices of the peace.

This and the preceding section are recommended as substitutes for the existing provisions of *Laws of* 1847, ch. 460, § 34, subd. 5, as amended *Laws of* 1855, ch. 552, § 1; *Laws of* 1849, ch. 133, § 1, and *Laws of* 1849, ch. 133, § 2, as amended *Laws of* 1854, ch. 240, § 10. Those provisions are as follows:

"The inspectors shall have power to inquire into any improper conduct," &c., "and for that purpose to issue subpœnas to compel the attendance of witnesses, and the production before them of books, writings and papers, in the same manner, and with like effect, and subject to the same penalties for disobedience, as in cases of trial before justices of the peace, and to examine any person or persons who may be brought before them as such witnesses."

Laws of 1847, ch. 460, § 34, as amended *Laws of* 1855, ch. 552, § 1.

"The president of the board of inspectors of state prisons shall have power to administer oaths and to take affidavits in all matters pertaining to the fiscal affairs, business transactions, discipline or government of said state prisons."

Laws of 1849, ch. 133, § 1.

"In like manner, any inspector of state prisons may administer oaths, and take affidavits in all matters relating to the affairs of the state prison under his charge, and for that purpose shall have power to issue subpœnas to compel the attendance of witnesses, and the production before him of books, papers and writings, in the same manner, with the like effect, and subject to the same penalties for disobedience, as in cases of trial before justices of the peace, and to examine any person or persons who may be brought before him as such witnesses."

Laws of 1849, ch. 133, § 2, as amended *Laws of* 1854, ch. 240, § 10.

These provisions, it will be seen, in effect, vest the power to issue subpœnas to witnesses to attend before the *board*, in the board as a body. The commissioners propose that it be vested in the *president*, as the proper person actually to exercise it. The existing law confines the power of an inspector in taking voluntary oaths, to those which relate to the prison under his charge. No reason is perceived why a voluntary oath relative to the affairs of any prison may not be taken before any inspector.

§ 844. Each inspector must spend at least one week at the prison assigned him, at least once in each month, which shall be within the first fifteen days of the month, except in the months when the quarterly meetings occur; and at that time must diligently examine and inquire into the condition of such prison and give such instructions in writing, for its government and discipline, being consistent with the laws of this state and the general regulations established by the inspectors, as he deems necessary and expedient. No inspector can draw his salary, until he has made and filed with the comptroller an affidavit that he has performed such duty. He must keep a journal of his proceedings at each monthly or other visitation, and report the same to the board of inspectors at their first joint meeting thereafter. Such journal shall also be entered by the clerk in the book of the proceedings of the board of inspectors kept in the prison to which the journal relates.

Duties of individual inspectors.

Laws of 1847, ch. 460, § 35, as amended *Laws of* 1860, ch. 399, § 1.

§ 845. The inspector in charge at each prison must examine the books of the store keeper or kitchen keeper, and compare the books kept by him with the original bills taken by the warden at the time of purchasing the goods, and as they agree or disagree, must certify on the books accordingly.

Examination of books of store keeper.

See *Laws of* 1855, ch. 552, § 4.

Inspector can hold no other prison office or contract.

§ 846. No inspector can hold any other appointment connected with any prison, be interested directly or indirectly in any contract for the employment of any convicts, or the supply of provisions, or the purchase of materials, for any prison.

Laws of 1847, ch. 460, § 39.

CHAPTER III.

GENERAL PROVISIONS RELATIVE TO OFFICERS OF THE VARIOUS STATE PRISONS.

Designation of officers of the state prisons.

§ 847. The inspectors shall appoint the following officers of the state prisons:

1. One warden of each prison;

2. One principal keeper of each prison;

3. One matron of the female department of the Sing Sing prison;

4. One clerk of each prison;

5. One chaplain of each prison;

6. Two instructors for each of the prisons at Auburn and Sing Sing, and one for the Clinton prison;

7. One instructor for the female department of the Sing Sing prison;

8. One physician of each prison, who must also perform the duties of surgeon;

9. One store keeper at Sing Sing prison:

10. One kitchen keeper at Sing Sing prison;

11. One kitchen keeper at each of the Auburn and Clinton prisons, who must also perform the duties of storekeeper;

12. So many keepers at each prison as the inspectors deem it expedient to employ; but not exceeding the proportion of one keeper to twenty-four male convicts;

13. So many assistant matrons of the female department of the Sing Sing prison as the inspectors deem it expedient to employ, but not exceeding the proportion of one assistant matron to twenty-four female convicts.

See *Laws of* 1847, ch. 460, § 40, as amended *Laws of* 1860, ch. 399, § 9.

The act of 1847, authorized the appointment at each state prison, of an "agent" whose duties were to be confined exclusively to the financial concerns of the prison, and of a principal keeper to be denominated a warden, whose duties were to be exclusively confined to the government, discipline and police regulation of the prison. (*Laws of* 1847, ch. 460, §§ 40, 47, 52.)

In 1854, it was enacted that "the office of warden and agent of the Auburn and Sing Sing prisons is abolished, and the duties of agent and warden of each of the said state prisons, as now prescribed by law, shall be performed by one person, who shall be known as the agent and warden, and shall receive, in consideration of the increase of duties prescribed by this act, an additional compensation of two hundred and fifty dollars per annum, payable monthly; there shall also be appointed by the inspector of state prisons for each of the prisons at Auburn and Sing Sing, some suitable person who shall be designated and known as principal keeper, and whose duty it shall be to obey and carry into effect all such orders and directions as he may receive from the agent and warden, as to the management and discipline of the prison, not inconsistent," &c., &c. (*Laws of* 1854, ch. 240, § 3.)

The commissioners have not observed any statute abolishing the distinction between the officers of agent and warden at *Clinton* prison. It appears, however, by the report of the prison association of New York, covering the year 1863, that the distinction is not kept up at that prison. The committee of the association who inspected the Clinton prison say, "the officers who are concerned in the administration of the government and discipline of the Clinton state prison are the agent and warden, the principal keeper, seventeen subordinate keepers and twenty-five guards.

"The agent and warden is the responsible head of the institution, both in respect of its financial affairs and its government.

"To the principal keeper are committed the immediate superintendence of the industries of the prison, and the exercise of its discipline." (*Nineteenth Annual Report of the Prison Assoc. of N. Y., Albany*, 1864, p. 151.)

It would seem, therefore, that no practical reasons exist requiring the fiscal affairs of either prison to be directed by a different person from the one entrusted with the management and discipline of the convicts. The commissioners have, therefore, provided in the text for the appointment of a single officer for the performance of both classes of duties.

No good reason is perceived for retaining the double name, "agent and warden," to designate the principal officer of the state prison. This name was employed in the act of 1854 (ch. 240, § 3), undoubtedly, in order that the then existing provisions of law in which the separate duties of the agent and of the warden were separately stated, might more clearly apply to the newly created officer whom it was intended to charge with both. The name *warden* alone is, however, appropriate to designate the officer to whom the general charge of a public institution is committed. Jacobs defines the term to mean "he that hath the keeping or charge of any persons or things by office." (*Law Dict.*) And an examination of the statutes of other states shows that the term is frequently used as applicable to a single person charged with the financial management as well as with the government of a prison. Thus, in Maryland, the governor biennially appoints a warden of the Maryland penitentiary, who, in addition to the government and discipline of the convicts, is charged with a part of the duties heretofore, in this state, assigned to the agent. (*Md. Code, Pub. Gen. L.*, 487, and *seq.*) In Rhode Island the "warden" of the state prison appoints subordinate officers, is purveyor of supplies, purchases materials for convict labor and sells the products thereof, keeps accounts of all expenses, &c., &c. (*Rev. Stat. of R. I.*, 1857, 583, 584.) In Massachusetts the "warden" has charge and custody of all convicts in the state prison, and is required to employ them for the benefit of the state. He also has the charge and custody of the prison, with every species of property pertaining thereto, is treasurer of the prison, receives and pays out all money granted by the legislature for the support thereof, and is required to keep accounts of all the property, expenses, income, business and concerns of the establishment. And all contracts on account of the prison are made by him, subject to approval by the inspectors. (*Rev. Stat. of Mass.*, 1860, 872–874.) In Canada all dealings and transactions on account of the provincial penitentiary of Canada, and all purchases and contracts necessary for maintaining and carrying on the establishment are, by law, to be entered into, conducted and executed by and in the name of the "warden." He may sue and be sued in matters relating to the penitentiary by his name of office of "the warden of the provincial penitentiary." He has entire executive control and management of all the concerns of the penitentiary; and, among other duties, designates the employment of convicts, makes all purchases, sales and contracts, under the advice and instructions of the board of inspectors, keeps accounts of the financial and other transactions of the prison, &c., &c. (*Consol. Stat. of Canada*, 1859, 1181–1184.)

Believing that both usage and convenience recommend the use of the name "warden" instead of "agent and warden," now employed in the statute book, the former has been employed throughout the sections in the text. This change in the law renders it proper to omit several provisions found in the present statutes. See note to section 862.

Who are not eligible to office at the state prisons.

§ 848. No person can be appointed to any office in a state prison, who is under the age of twenty-one years, or who is related to either of the inspectors holding office as such at the time of his appointment, by consanguinity or affinity within the third degree.

See *Laws of* 1847, ch. 460, § 38; and *Laws of* 1863, ch. 465, § 4.

Inspectors may make temporary appointments to fill vacancies.

§ 849. Each inspector may suspend any officer appointed by the board for cause, and may make temporary appointments to supply any vacancies in office at the prison under his special charge. Such appointments shall be in force until the next meeting of the board of inspectors. During such suspension the officer suspended shall not receive any remuneration whatever. Whenever any inspector has suspended any officer he must immediately notify the other inspectors of such suspension, and of the causes for which such suspension is made, and request a meeting of the board to be held within ten days after such notice is given, for the purpose of considering the same. Two of the inspectors attending such meeting shall have power to confirm or disapprove such suspension.

Laws of 1847, ch. 460, § 36, as amended *Laws of* 1860, ch. 399, § 2.

Such appointments must be entered in journal.

§ 850. Every appointment to office made by an inspector must be by him immediately entered in the journal of his proceedings kept at the prison where such appointment is made, and must specify the particular vacancy which the same is intended to fill; and written notice thereof must be by him immediately given to the warden of such prison. Every appointment or removal made by the inspectors must be by them entered in the regular minutes of the meeting at which the same is made, and like notice thereof given to the warden of the prison affected thereby; and if such appointment or removal relates to a prison other than that at which such meeting shall be held, a copy of the entry of such appointment or removal, signed by them or a majority of them, must be immediately transmitted to the warden of the prison affected thereby, and entered by the clerk in the book of record of inspectors' meetings kept at such prison. The warden of each prison, in every account rendered to the comptroller, must note all changes in the officers of such prison made since rendering his account next previous thereunto.

Laws of 1847, ch. 460, § 37, as amended *Laws of* 1860, ch. 399, § 3.

Oath of office.

§ 851. Each of the officers mentioned in section 847, before entering upon the duties of his office, must take and subscribe the oath of office prescribed by the constitution of this state. Such oath may be taken and subscribed before any officer authorized by law to take and administer an oath, and must be filed in the office of the clerk of the county in which the prison for which such officer is appointed is situated.

See *Laws of* 1847, ch. 460, § 42.

§ 852. Each of the following officers of the state prisons, before entering upon the duties of his office, must execute a bond to the people of this state, with sufficient sureties to be approved by the inspector in charge, in the penal sum mentioned below, for the faithful performance of his duties according to law: Official bond.

1. Each warden must execute such a bond in the penal sum of twenty-five thousand dollars;

2. The store keeper of the Sing Sing prison, and the kitchen keepers of Auburn and Clinton prisons must execute such a bond in the penal sum of six thousand dollars;

3. Each principal keeper must execute such a bond in the penal sum of five thousand dollars;

4. Each clerk must execute such a bond in the penal sum of four thousand dollars;

5. The matron of the female department of the Sing Sing prison, must execute such a bond in the penal sum of three thousand dollars;

6. The kitchen keeper of the Sing Sing prison, must execute such a bond in the penal sum of three thousand dollars.

See *Laws of* 1847, ch. 460, § 43; *Ibid.*, § 56; *Ibid.*, § 66. subd. 3, as amended *Laws of* 1855, ch. 522, § 4, subd. 10, and § 5.

§ 853. The various bonds required by the last section must be filed in the office of the comptroller of this state. Bond where to be filed.

§ 854. The annual salaries of the different officers, teachers and guards at the various state prisons, are as follows: Salaries.

1. That of each of the wardens, eighteen hundred dollars;

2. That of each of the principal keepers, twelve hundred dollars;

3. That of each of the clerks, twelve hundred dollars;

4. That of each of the physicians, twelve hundred dollars;

5. That of each of the chaplains, one thousand dollars;

6. That of each of the keepers whose salaries are not otherwise prescribed by this section, seven hundred and twenty dollars;

7. That of each of the instructors, one hundred and fifty dollars;

8. That of the guards at each prison, five hundred and fifty dollars;

9. That of the store keeper at the Sing Sing prison, one thousand dollars;

10. That of the kitchen keeper at the Sing Sing prison, one thousand dollars;

11. That of each of the kitchen keepers at the Auburn and Clinton prisons, one thousand dollars;

12. That of the matron at the female department of the Sing Sing prison, six hundred and sixty dollars;

13. That of each of the assistant matrons at the female department of the Sing Sing prison, five hundred and forty dollars;

14. That of the instructress at the female department of the Sing Sing prison, one hundred and fifty dollars.

The commissioners have intended to continue the rates of compensation prescribed by the existing law, and are not to be understood as making any recommendation upon the subject. All questions as to the proper amount of the various salaries are proper to be left to the consideration of the legislature at the time when the Code shall come before them for examination. The above salaries correspond with those prescribed by *Laws of* 1864, ch. 300. All are, however, reduced to annual rates; and the phraseology and arrangement of the statute of 1864, is also modified, to harmonize it more perfectly with the other parts of the Code.

The previous laws on the subject of salaries of prison officers, are chiefly *Laws of* 1847, ch. 460, § 66; *Laws of* 1849, ch. 141, § 6; and *Laws of* 1862, ch. 403, § 2.

§ 855. The salaries of the officers and guards of the state prisons are payable monthly at the end of each month. The warden of each prison must pay the salaries of the officers and guards at his prison out of the funds thereof. **How paid.**

See *Laws of* 1847, ch. 460, §§ 66, 67.

§ 856. The comptroller is hereby authorized to audit and allow, from time to time, all necessary traveling expenses and subsistence of the warden of each state prison, when necessarily traveling on official business, or when the attendance of such warden is required at the seat of government; the necessity of such travel and attendance to be decided by the comptroller, and the accounts when audited to be paid by the treasurer on the warrant of the comptroller. **Traveling expenses to be audited and allowed.**

Laws of 1847, ch. 460, § 68.

§ 857. The wardens and other officers, and the guards of the respective prisons must support themselves from their own salaries and resources, and shall not receive any perquisites or emoluments for their services other than the compensation provided in this chapter, except that the wardens, physicians and chaplains shall keep their offices at the respective prisons, and that the warden shall reside therein and they shall all be furnished with the fuel for their offices, and those who are required to reside in the prison, for themselves and families, from the stock provided for the use of the state; and from the same stock the warden shall furnish fuel for the barracks of the guards. **Officers to support themselves.**

Laws of 1847, ch. 460, § 69.

§ 858. No warden or other officer of either of the state prisons of this state shall give any note, draft **Officers cannot give evidence of debt.**

or other evidence of debt, except a check on the bank selected as the depository of the prison funds, as prescribed by section 874, and such drafts as are authorized by law, in payment for any article purchased for either of the prisons, and signed by him or them individually or in their official capacity; nor shall any such warden, or other officer, sign any paper as warded for the purpose or with the intent of putting or having the same put in circulation for any purpose whatever, nor give any credit to any contractor for money due to any of the prisons.

Laws of 1854, ch. 240, § 11.

Official reports must be verified.

§ 859. Every officer of a prison who is required by law to make any report or render any statement of account in writing, for which no particular form of attestation or verification is prescribed by law, must verify every such report or account by his affidavit that the same is just and true.

Suggested as a substitute for *Laws of* 1855, ch. 552, § 8, which is as follows:

"All officers of either of the prisons, who, under any section of this act, or of any act of which this is amendatory, whose duty it is to report annually, quarterly or monthly to the governor, secretary of state, comptroller, inspector or inspectors of state prisons, or to the agent and warden of either of the prisons, will hereafter be required to attest the same by his or her affidavit that such report is just and true."

Time of making reports.

§ 860. All reports required by law to be made annually to the inspectors of state prisons, or to the secretary of state, by any officer of the prisons must be made up to and including the thirtieth day of September of each year, and must be delivered on or before the first day of December in each year.

Laws of 1857, ch. 94, § 3.

Officers not to be interested in contracts.

§ 861. No inspector or officer employed at either of the prisons shall be directly or indirectly interested in any contract, purchase or sale for, by or on account of such prison, nor shall any inspector, officer, keeper or guard, or other person employed at such prison, accept any present from any contractor or contractor's agent, either directly or indirectly, nor shall any person whatever, convey into either of the prisons of this state, any article for the use of the convicts prohibited by the rules of the inspectors or by the laws of the state.

Laws of 1847, ch. 460, § 83, as amended *Laws of* 1855, ch. 552, § 10. The clause "any person violating this section shall be deemed guilty of a misdemeanor and punishable as such," found at the end of the original section, is omitted as unnecessary in view of the provisions of sections 215 and 216 of this Code.

CHAPTER IV.

THE WARDENS.

Warden must reside at the prison.

§ 862. The warden of each prison must reside in the prison to which he is appointed, and attend it constantly, except when absent while performing some necessary duties connected with his office.

The sections of this chapter which define the duties of the warden have been framed so as to present at a single view the duties now imposed, by several distinct provisions of statute, upon the agents, or wardens, of the state prisons; prescribing them, in conformity with the change of phraseology recommended in earlier sections (see section 847 and note), as the duties of the *warden.* The provisions are chiefly founded on *Laws of* 1847, ch. 460, § 48; *Ibid.*, § 53; *Laws of* 1854, ch. 240, § 4; *Ibid.*, § 5; *Laws of* 1860, ch. 399, § 6; *Ibid.*, § 10. The following provisions of existing laws are omitted, as superseded by the measure proposed of uniting the powers and duties of agent and warden, in one officer to be denominated "warden:"

"Whenever any number of convicts in any state prison shall be less than three hundred, the warden of the prison shall have all the powers and perform all the duties herein imposed upon the agent."

Laws of 1847, ch. 460, § 41.

"The duties of the agent of each of the state prisons shall be confined exclusively to the financial concerns thereof. He shall have the exclusive disposal of the services, and shall designate the employment of all the convicts, but shall exercise no control over their discipline or government, nor shall he interfere in the government of, or exercise any control over the officers of such prison, other than to require them to keep a correct daily account of the labor of the convicts under their charge, and to report the same to him at such periods as he shall require."

Ibid., § 47.

"The duties of the wardens of each of the state prisons shall be exclusively confined to the government, discipline and police regulation of the same."

Ibid., § 52.

"Whenever there shall exist a vacancy in the office of agent of either of the prisons, all the powers and duties of such agent shall devolve upon, and be executed by the warden of said prison, until such vacancy shall be filled."

Ibid., § 54.

"The agent of each prison shall possess all the powers, and discharge all the duties of the warden of the prison, during a vacancy in the office of warden, or disability in the warden from any cause to act."

Ibid., § 55.

"The person holding the office of agent and warden herein before mentioned shall perform all the duties heretofore by law imposed upon the person holding the office of agent of either of the state prisons of this state, and also all the duties heretofore by law imposed upon the person holding the office of warden of either of the state prisons; and such agent and warden shall in all cases be appointed by the inspectors of state prisons, to hold the office under the same restrictions and qualifications as are by law imposed in the appointment of an agent of a state prison."

Laws of 1854, ch. 240, § 15.

Must attend to fiscal concerns of prison.

§ 863. The warden must attend to the fiscal and business concerns of the prison, and use his best endeavors to defray all the expenses of the prison by the labor of the convicts. All the fiscal and business concerns of each prison shall be conducted by and in the name of the warden thereof, who has control over all matters of finance relating to the prison, subject to the directions and supervision of the board of inspectors. Each warden has capacity to sue in any court, and institute and prosecute any legal proceedings, in all matters concerning his prison, by his name of office, and by that name may recover all sums of money due from any person to any former agent or warden, or agent and warden of the prison, or due to the state on account of such prison. But it shall not be lawful in any such suit or action, for any defendant to plead or give in evidence any offset or matter by way of recoupment (except for payments made and not credited to such defendant) or to recover any judgment against such warden in such suit or action, other than for the costs and disbursements therein.

See *Laws of* 1847, ch. 460, § 48; *Laws of* 1854, ch. 58, as amended *Laws of* 1860, ch. 399, § 8.

May make contracts.

§ 864. The warden may make, under the direction of the inspectors, in the manner hereinafter provided, contracts for the employment of the convicts, and for furnishing the necessary supplies for their support; but no contract can be entered into by the warden of either of the state prisons, for the hire or labor of the convicts, or for supplies for their support, or for any purpose whatever, unless the same shall have been approved by a majority of the inspectors, who must be present in all cases at such lettings.

Laws of 1847, ch. 460, § 48, subd. 3, as amended *Laws of* 1854, ch. 240, § 4.

Must superintend manufactures, &c.

§ 865. The warden must superintend all manufacturing and mechanical business that may be carried on in the prison, receive the articles to be manufactured, and sell and dispose of the same for the benefit of the state.

Laws of 1847, ch. 460, § 48, subd. 4.

Must purchase requisite materials.

§ 866. The warden must purchase such raw materials as may be necessary to be manufactured by the convicts.

Laws of 1847, ch. 460, § 48, subd. 5.

Must take bills and affidavits of all purchases made for the prison.

§ 867. The warden must take bills and receipts in duplicate for all supplies and materials for the prison, purchased by or for him, at the time of such purchase, and take bills and receipts for all services that shall be rendered for either of the prisons, at the time of making payment therefor. The person to whom any bill shall be paid by any warden must in all cases make and subscribe an affidavit, to be sworn to before some person duly authorized by law to take the same, stating that such accounts and the articles therein specified were actually furnished as charged; that neither the warden, nor any person for him or in his behalf, had any pecuniary or other interest in the articles sold, or in the profits thereof; that no commissions, presents or profits were paid, or agreed or promised to be paid in the future to him or to any person for him; that the receipt signed represents the correct amount due; that the articles included in such account were sold at fair cash market prices, and that the person deposing has actually received the full amount in cash from the warden. And no articles purchased for the use of either prison shall be accepted, or a receipt given therefor, unless accompanied by a proper bill of the same, verified as above stated, and ascertained to be correct. The original bills must be delivered to the clerk and the duplicate bills for supplies or materials furnished must be marked "duplicate," and delivered to the store keeper or kitchen keeper.

See *Laws of* 1854, ch. 240, § 5, as amended *Laws of* 1860, ch. 399, § 10; also *Laws of* 1855, ch. 552, § 4.

§ 868. The warden must enforce the payment of all debts due to the prison as soon and with as little delay as possible. But with the approbation of the inspector having at the time charge of the prison, he may accept any security from any debtor, on granting him time, that he deems conducive to the interest of the state. Must collect debts due the prison.

See *Laws of* 1847, ch. 460, § 48, subd. 7. Subdivision 8 of this section was repealed by *Laws of* 1854, ch. 240, § 12.

§ 869. The warden must take charge of all moneys and other articles which may be brought to the prison by convicts, and cause the same immediately on the receipt thereof, to be entered by the clerk among the receipts of the prison. Such moneys and other articles, whenever the convict from whom the same Must take charge of moneys and effects of convicts.

were received is discharged from prison, or the same are otherwise legally demanded, must be returned by the warden to such convict or other person legally entitled to the same, and proper vouchers taken therefor. And for such money as any convict or any other person for him may have so deposited, he shall be entitled to receive interest at the rate of six per cent from the time of such deposit until payment.

See *Laws of* 1847, ch. 460, § 48, subd. 9, as amended *Laws of* 1860, ch. 399, § 6.

Must provide discharged convicts with certain sums of money.

§ 870. The warden must furnish to each convict who shall be discharged from prison by pardon or otherwise, necessary clothing, not exceeding ten dollars in value, and such sum of money, not exceeding upon an average three dollars to each convict, as he deems proper and necessary, and the sum of three cents for each mile for which it may be necessary for such convict to travel to reach the place of his residence, and if he has no residence within the state, to the place of his conviction; and also any sum which shall stand to the credit of the convict for any extra work which he may have performed; of which an account shall be kept, under such regulations as the inspectors shall prescribe. But the allowance of any such additional sum may be made dependent on the good behavior of the convict.

See *Laws of* 1847, ch. 460, § 48, subd. 10; also *Laws of* 1862, ch. 417, § 5, as amended *Laws of* 1863, ch. 415.

May draw money from the treasury

§ 871. The warden may draw from the treasurer of the state, by a warrant of the comptroller upon the treasurer, in favor of the warden, all moneys appropriated to the use of the prison under his charge. But he shall not draw at any one time, or have in his hands unaccounted for at any one time, of moneys so appropriated, a greater sum than five thousand dollars.

Laws of 1847, ch. 48, § 48, subd. 11.

May draw money from the literature fund.

§ 872. The warden may draw, each and every year, from the income of the literature fund, the sum of one hundred dollars, to be expended in the purchase of books, maps and stationery, for the use of the convicts. And he must append to his annual report a catalogue of such prison library.

Laws of 1847, ch. 460, § 48, subd. 12.

§ 873. The warden must furnish, at the expense of the state, a bible and hymn book to each convict. Must furnish bibles and hymn books.

See *Laws of* 1847, ch. 460, § 60, subd. 3.

§ 874. The warden must deposit all moneys received by him as such warden, once in each week, to the credit of the treasurer of the state, in a bank located in the city or village most adjacent to the prison; and he must send to the comptroller, weekly, a statement showing the amount so received, and from whom and when and for what received, and the days on which the deposits were made. This statement of deposits must be certified to by the proper officer of the bank receiving such deposit. The warden must also verify by his affidavit that the sum so deposited is all the money received by him, from whatever source of prison income, during the week, and up to the time of deposit. All moneys so deposited by the warden of any prison shall be subject to the quarterly drafts of the treasurer of the state. Any bank in which deposits are made under the provisions of this act must, before receiving any such deposits, file a bond with the comptroller of the state, subject to his approval, for such sum as he shall deem necessary. Must deposit moneys received, in bank.

See *Laws of* 1854, ch. 58, as amended *Laws of* 1860, ch. 399, § 8. This provision is regarded as superseding *Laws of* 1854, ch. 240, § 6, subd. 2, as amended *Laws of* 1855, ch. 552, § 11; which declares it the duty of the warden "to deposit, at least once in a week, to the credit of the treasurer of the state, in such bank or banks as may be designated by the comptroller, all the moneys received by him as such warden, and send to the comptroller weekly a statement showing the amount so received, and from whom and when and for what received and deposited, and the days on which such deposits were made; the statements of deposits to be certified to by the proper officers of the bank receiving such deposit or deposits; the agent and warden must also verify by his affidavit that the sum so deposited is all the money received by him, from whatever source of prison income, during the week, and up to the time of deposit.

Must keep regular accounts.

§ 875. The warden must keep a regular and correct account of all moneys received by him from any source whatever, by virtue of his office, including all moneys taken from convicts or received as the proceeds of property taken from them, and all sums paid by him, and the persons to whom and purposes for which the same were paid. He must keep in his office regular books of entries, in which all his accounts and transactions must be entered. Such books and the accounts entered therein must be open for the examination of the inspector or inspectors, the comptroller, or any person authorized by him for that purpose, during office hours.

See *Laws of* 1847, ch. 460, § 48, subd. 14; *Laws of* 1854, ch. 240, § 6, subd. 1.

Must report estimates in advance of incurring expenses.

§ 876. The warden must, monthly, and before any expenses are incurred by him, make an estimate, in minute detail, of the necessary expenses for the support and maintenance of the prison under his charge, including the number of rations or kind of property to be delivered during the coming month, upon any contract made under section 864, and present the same to the comptroller; who, if satisfied that the expenditures are necessary and proper, shall thereupon authorize the warden to make his draft on the treasury for the sum thus estimated, or any part thereof; which amount shall be paid, on the warrant of the comptroller. It is not lawful for such warden to make purchases on behalf of the state, unless such purchases have been included in the estimate presented to and approved by the comptroller. The estimate required from the warden by this section must first be submitted to the inspector in charge of the prison, and his approval written thereon, certifying that he has carefully examined the same, and that the articles contained in such estimate are actually required for the use of the prison. Such estimate must be accompanied by the report of the store keeper, or of the kitchen keeper when the duties of store keeper are performed by the kitchen keeper, under oath, giving the amount of each article consumed for the last month, and the amount of each article then on hand.

Laws of 1854, ch. 240, § 6, subd. 3, as amended *Laws of* 1855, ch. 552, § 12.

§ 877. The warden must close his account, annually, on the last day of September of each year; and, on or before the first day of December thereafter, must render to the inspectors a full and true account, accompanied by copies of the necessary vouchers, of all moneys received by him on account of the prison under his charge, and all the moneys expended by him for the use thereof, and also an inventory of the goods, raw materials and other property of the state then on hand, exhibiting, in detail, all the transactions of the prison for the year.

Must render account to the inspectors.

See *Laws of* 1847, ch. 460, § 48, subd. 15.

§ 878. The warden must, on the first day of every month, make to the comptroller a full and perfect statement of the receipts and expenditures, specifying the items thereof for the prison under his charge for the past month, which must be accompanied by the necessary vouchers, regularly rendered according to their respective dates, with some short designation thereon of the consideration of the payment evidenced by the vouchers, and the amount of the vouchers carried out in figures; if the vouchers are objectionable, the comptroller must enter his dissent on the particular voucher, and return it to the warden reporting the same, who must cause it to be immediately corrected and returned. Every such statement must be verified by an affidavit of the warden thereunto annexed, as follows: I,

Must make monthly report to the comptroller of receipts and expenditures.

warden of the prison, do solemnly swear that I have deposited in the bank, being the bank designated by law for such purpose, all the moneys received by me, belonging to the state, during the last month; and I do further swear that the foregoing is a true abstract of all the moneys received and expenditures made by me as such warden, during the month ending on the day of 18 , and that the goods and other articles therein specified, were purchased and received by me at the prison of which I am in charge, and that the goods were purchased at fair cash market prices, and that the same were paid for in cash; that I had no pecuniary or other interest in the articles purchased, or any person in my behalf; that I receive no pecuniary or other benefit therefrom in the way of commissions, per centage, deductions or presents, or in any other manner whatever, either directly or indirectly, nor any promise of future payments, presents or benefits or to any other person for me, either directly or indirectly; and further, that all the receipts were filled up as they now appear, and were read or the amount distinctly stated to the signer of each before they were signed. The affidavit of the clerk must likewise be appended thereto, certifying that the articles contained in such bill were received at the prison, and that they conformed in all respects to the invoice of the goods received and entered by him, both in quantity and quality.

Laws of 1854, ch. 240, § 6, subd. 4, as amended *Laws of* 1860, ch. 399, § 11. These acts are regarded as superseding subdivision 13 of Laws of 1847, ch. 460, § 48, which is therefore omitted. It requires the "agent" to account monthly with the comptroller for all moneys so drawn by him from the treasurer of the state, and for all other moneys received by him as such agent, from whatever source the same may be derived.

Must file copies of contracts.

§ 879. The warden must file or cause to be filed, in the office of the comptroller, a copy of each and every contract made and executed by him, as such warden, within thirty days after the execution thereof. He must also, monthly, report to the comptroller a detailed account of the number of days' labor performed on such contracts, which account must be verified by the affidavit of such warden and the clerk of the prison where such labor was performed, to the effect that such account correctly states the whole number of days' labor performed on such contracts.

Laws of 1854, ch. 240, § 6.

§ 880. The warden must, as often as the inspectors deem necessary, advertise, in one or more newspapers in the county where the prison is situated, all personal property of the prison then on hand, which may have become useless, or which is no longer required for prison purposes, and sell the same at a public sale to the highest bidder, and deposit the amount received from such sale to the credit of the treasurer, as now required by law. **Must advertise useless property for sale.**

Laws of 1855, ch. 552, § 6.

§ 881. The warden must pay to the sheriffs or their deputies for transporting convicts to the prison the fees to which such sheriffs or their deputies are by law entitled, provided there are funds belonging to such prison sufficient to warrant such expenditure and meet the current demands for its support; if not, the warden shall so certify, and in that case such fees shall be paid from the treasury, upon the warrant of the comptroller. **Must pay sheriffs for transporting convicts.**

Laws of 1847, ch. 460, § 87.

§ 882. The warden must exercise a general supervision over the government, discipline and police regulation of the prison. **Must superintend the prisons.**

See *Laws of* 1847, ch. 460, § 53, subd. 1.

§ 883. The warden must keep a time-book, in which must be inserted the names of all the officers, keepers or guards belonging to the prison, and opposite to each name he must daily mark whether **Must keep a time-book.**

such officer, keeper or guard was "absent or present;" and if absent, he must give the alleged reasons for such absence; and at the end of each month he must add up the absences appearing in the time book, and forward a full statement thereof to the comptroller with such warden's monthly report.

See *Laws of* 1855, ch. 552, § 7.

Must instruct the keepers.

§ 884. The warden must give the necessary instructions to the keepers, and examine whether they have been careful and diligent in the discharge of their several duties.

See *Laws of* 1847, ch. 460, § 53, subd. 2.

Must daily examine the prison.

§ 885. The warden must examine daily into the state of the prison, and into the health, condition and safe keeping of the convicts, and inquire into the justice of any complaints made by the convicts relative to their provisions, clothing and treatment by the keepers.

Laws of 1847, ch. 460, § 53, subd. 3.

Must make rules for the subordinate officers.

§ 886. The warden may make such general orders or rules for the government of the subordinate officers of the prison as he deems proper, and are approved by the board of inspectors. Such rules and orders must be entered in writing, in a book to be kept by the warden for that purpose, and are subject to any alteration or amendment by the inspectors.

Laws of 1847, ch. 460, § 53, subd. 4.

Must keep a daily journal.

§ 887. The warden must keep a daily journal of the proceedings of the prison, in which must be entered a note of every infraction of the rules and regulations of the prisons by any officer thereof, which comes to his knowledge; and of every punishment inflicted on a convict, the nature and amount thereof, and by whom it was inflicted; and, also, a memorandum of every well founded complaint, made by any convict, of bad or insufficient food, want of clothing, or cruel and unjust treatment by a keeper. This journal must be kept open at all times to the examination of the inspector in charge of the prison, and of the board of inspectors.

Laws of 1847, ch. 460, § 53, subd. 5.

May suspend subordinate officers.

§ 888. The warden may suspend, for cause, any officer, keeper or guard in said prison, and employ another in his stead, until the pleasure of the inspector in charge shall be known; whom he must immediately notify of such suspension and the reasons thereof.

Taken from *Laws of* 1847, ch. 460, § 65, as amended *Laws of* 1857, ch. 94, § 1.

Must receive certain convicts.

§ 889. The warden must receive into the prison under his charge, on the order of the governor, any person convicted of any crime punishable with death, or who shall be pardoned on condition of being confined either for life or a term of years in the state prison, and confine such prisoner according to the terms of such condition.

Laws of 1847, ch. 460, § 53, subd. 6.

Must admit the inspectors to visit the prison.

§ 890. The warden must admit the inspectors, or any one of them, or any agent or committee of the Prison Association of New York, into every part of the prison, and exhibit to them, on demand, all the books, papers, warrants and writings, pertaining to the prison or to the business, management, discipline or government thereof, and render to them every other facility in his power to enable them to discharge their duties.

Laws of 1847, ch. 460, § 53, subd. 7.

Must make a monthly report to the inspectors.

§ 891. The warden must make a monthly report, through the inspector having charge of the prison, to the inspectors, stating the names of all convicts received into the prison during the preceding month, the counties in which they were tried, the crimes of which they were convicted, the nature and duration of their sentences, their former trade, employment or occupation, the nature of their employment in prison, their habits, color, age, place of nativity, degree of instruction, and a description of their persons, and also stating whether such convicts have ever before been confined in any state prison or county jail, and if so, stating the offense for which they were confined, and the duration of their punishment, and also stating in such report the names of all the convicts pardoned or discharged during the past month, and all other particulars in relation to the parties so pardoned or discharged, that are required to be stated in relation to the convicts received in the prison.

Laws of 1847, ch. 460, § 53, subd. 8.

Must communicate discovery of insanity of offenders to the governor.

§ 892. Whenever the warden of a prison has reason to believe that any convict in the prison was insane at the time he committed the offense for which he was sentenced, such warden must communicate, in writing, to the governor, his reason for such opinion, and must refer the governor to all the sources of information with which he may be acquainted, in relation to the insanity of such convict.

Laws of 1847, ch. 460, § 98.

Requisites of the warden's monthly accounts.

§ 893. The monthly accounts to be rendered by the warden of each prison to the comptroller, must embrace a general current account of the receipts and expenditures at his prison for the month, and an abstract of the expenditures in detail, which must be accompanied by the necessary vouchers regularly numbered, according to their respective dates, with some short designation thereon of the consideration of the payment, evidenced by the vouchers, and the amount of the voucher carried out in figures; such account must be attested by the affidavit of the warden and clerk thereto annexed.

Laws of 1847, ch. 460, § 49.

His accounts must be audited by the comptroller.

§ 894. It is the duty of the comptroller of the state to examine and audit the accounts of the respective wardens, and annually to lay a statement thereof before the legislature.

Laws of 1847, ch. 460, § 51.

§ 895. If the warden of a state prison willfully neglects or refuses to make any weekly or monthly return, estimate or statement, or to transmit any statement and certificate of deposits, to the comptroller, directed by any provision of this title, it shall be the duty of the comptroller to notify the inspectors of such omission, and to order the bond of the warden to be put in suit, for the recovery of any moneys which may be in his hands belonging to the state. Penalty for neglect to make statement.

Laws of 1854, ch. 240, § 13.

§ 896 Each warden of a state prison is liable to indictment and punishment, as for a misdemeanor, for any willful neglect of duty, or for any malpractice in the discharge of the duties of his office. Warden liable to punishment for neglect or breach of duty.

Laws of 1854, ch. 240, § 14.

§ 897. The warden of the Sing Sing prison shall continue to have charge of the farm and premises on which the same is situated, and it is his duty to rent or otherwise use or improve the same to the best advantage for the benefit of the state; but no lease shall be made by him for a longer term than three years. Farm at Sing Sing

Laws of 1847, ch. 460, § 143.

§ 898. The moneys which may, from time to time, be in the hands of the warden of the Sing Sing prison, and which are not required for the current expenses of the prison, must be paid into the treasury of this state, and the comptroller must keep an account with the prison, in which the sums so paid into the treasury, with the annual interest thereon, must be credited to the prison; the sums thus credited must be set apart for the use of the prison, and whenever the same may be required for the ordinary expenses of the prison, or for any expenses authorized by law, connected with the prison, they may be drawn from the treasury by the warden of the prison on the written direction of the inspectors. All sums Receipts of of warden at Sing Sing.

thus drawn from the treasury must be charged to the prison, in the account kept by the comptroller.

Laws of 1847, ch. 460, § 111.

Warden at Clinton may draw arms from state arsenal.

§ 899. The warden of the Clinton prison may draw, from time to time, from the state arsenal, in the city of Albany, such arms and ammunitions as he deems necessary for the use of the keepers and guards of the prison.

Laws of 1847, ch. 460, § 135.

May sell ore.

§ 900. The warden of the Clinton prison may sell the ores raised at that prison, at the common market price, on time, not exceeding six months, receiving therefor such indorsed paper as shall be approved by the warden and clerk of the prison. The proceeds of such sales must be applied to the support of the prison.

Laws of 1847, ch. 460, § 136; *Laws of* 1850, ch. 306, § 3.

May appropriate waters upon the prison lands.

§ 901. The warden of the Clinton prison may appropriate to the use thereof, all waters upon the tract purchased for the establishment of said prison; and any person claiming damages in consequence of such appropriation of water. shall, within six months thereafter, make application to the county judge of the county of Clinton, who shall appoint three commissioners, not interested in lands through which the stream or streams of water so appropriated may have previously run. Such commissioners must personally examine the lands of the applicant, and make an estimate of the damages he has sustained by reason of such appropriation of water, which estimate must be reduced to writing, subscribed and sworn to by such commissioners, and then transmitted to the comptroller. The comptroller must thereupon pay the estimated damages of the applicant out of the funds appropriated for the prison.

Laws of 1847, ch. 460, § 137.

CHAPTER V.

THE MATRON OF THE FEMALE DEPARTMENT OF THE SING SING PRISON, AND ASSISTANT MATRONS.

§ 902. The matron of the female department of the Sing Sing prison must exercise a general supervision over the government, discipline and police regulation of the department. Matron of the female department at Sing Sing must superintend the department.

The existing provision relative to the duties of the matron is as follows: "The matron of the female convict prison at Sing Sing shall have the same powers, and perform the same duties, in relation to that prison, as are herein given and imposed upon the wardens of prisons, and the powers and duties of assistant matron shall be the same as those of the keepers of the prison; but such matron and assistant matron shall, in all cases, be bound to obey such regulations and instructions as the inspectors shall, from time to time, prescribe." *Laws of* 1847, ch. 460, § 59.

This method of defining her powers and duties becomes inappropriate if the office of warden is extended to embrace that of agent. The provisions in the text are therefore recommended instead.

§ 903. The matron must give the necessary instructions to the assistant matrons, and examine whether they have been careful and diligent in the discharge of their several duties. Must instruct the assistant matrons.

§ 904. The matron must examine, daily, into the state of the female department of the prison, and into the health, condition and safe keeping of the female convicts, and inquire into the justice of any complaints made by such convicts relative to their Must examine, daily, the state of the department.

provisions, clothing and treatment by the assistant matrons.

Must make rules for the assistant matrons.

§ 905. The matron may make such general orders or rules, for the government of the assistant matrons, as she deems proper, and are not inconsistent with those prescribed for the general government of the prison by the inspectors or warden. Such orders and rules must be reduced to writing and furnished to the warden to be entered by him in the book required to be kept by section 886, and are subject to any alteration or amendment by the inspectors.

Must keep a daily journal of the department.

§ 906. The matron must keep a daily journal of the proceedings of the female department of the prison, in which must be entered a note of every infraction of the rules and regulations of the prison or of the female department, by any officer thereof, and occurring within or affecting the female department, which comes to her knowledge; and of every punishment inflicted on a female convict, the nature and amount thereof, and by whom it was inflicted; and also a memorandum of every well founded complaint made by any female convict, of bad or insufficient food, want of clothing, or cruel or unjust treatment. This journal must be kept open at all times to the examination of the warden and of the inspector in charge of the prison, and of the board of inspectors; and shall be deemed a part of the record required to be kept by the warden, by section 887.

Must furnish a monthly account to the inspector in charge.

§ 907. The matron must furnish, at the end of each month, to the inspector in charge, an account containing a true statement of all the articles drawn on her requisition or received during the month then ended, with the amount of each article remaining on hand.

See *Laws of* 1847, ch. 460, § 66, as amended *Laws of* 1855, ch. 522, § 5. The verification of the account is sufficiently provided for by section 859.

CHAPTER VI.

THE CLERKS.

§ 908. The clerk of each prison must attend daily at the prison during the proper business hours; unless by the direction of an inspector, or of the warden, he is otherwise engaged in transacting business on account of the prison.

Clerk must attend daily at prison.

Laws of 1847, ch. 460, § 57, subd. 1.

§ 909. The clerk must act as clerk of the inspectors at their meetings held at the prison.

Must act as clerk of the inspectors.

Laws of 1847, ch. 460, § 56.

§ 910. The clerk must keep a register of convicts, in which the names of the convicts shall be alphabetically arranged, and in which shall be entered, under appropriate columns, the date of conviction, where born, age, occupation, complexion, stature, crime, court and county where convicted, term of sentence, number of previous convictions, to what prison or prisons previously sent, when discharged, and how discharged. The inspectors may require such additional facts to be stated on the register as they may deem proper.

Must keep a register of convicts.

Laws of 1847, ch. 460, § 57, subd. 2.

Must keep all the books and accounts.

§ 911. The clerk must keep all the books and accounts of the financial transactions of the prison, and annually report to the inspectors, on the thirty-first day of December, the number of convicts remaining in prison at the commencement of the year, the number received during the year, the number discharged and how, the number of deaths and escapes, and the number removed to the house of refuge and lunatic asylum, and the number then remaining in prison.

Ibid., subd. 3.

Must keep a separate account of articles received from convicts.

§ 912. The clerk must keep a separate account in a book, provided for that purpose, of all money and other articles received by the warden from the convicts, in which account each convict must be credited with the money and other articles so received from him.

See *Laws of* 1847, ch. 460, § 48, subd. 9, as amended *Laws of* 1860, ch. 399, § 6.

Must enter bills received by warden.

§ 913. The clerk must enter each bill taken by the warden of the prison, for any supplies or materials purchased for, or services rendered to the prison, in the books of the prison, immediately upon the receiving such bill.

Taken from *Laws of* 1847, ch. 460, § 57, subd. 5, as amended *Laws of* 1854, ch. 240, § 7.

Must examine articles purchased by the warden and compare them with the bill.

§ 914. The clerk must examine, at the time of their delivery, all articles purchased by the warden for the use of the prison, and compare them with the bills rendered thereof, and examine all materials or supplies furnished to the prison under contract, so as to ascertain whether such articles, materials or supplies correspond in weight, quantity or quality, with the description given in the bill, or called for by the contract; and in case they do not, he must immediately note the discrepancy in the books of the prison, and also notify the warden thereof.

See *Laws of* 1847, ch. 460, § 57, subd. 4; *Ibid.*, subd. 5, as amended *Laws of* 1854, ch. 240, § 7.

§ 915. The clerk must do such writing as may be required of him by the inspectors, or inspector having charge of the prison, or warden, relating to the affairs of the prison. Must write for the warden and inspectors.

Laws of 1847, ch. 460, § 57, subd. 5.

§ 916. The clerk must take the charge and custody, under the direction of the inspectors, of all the books of account, registers, returns, and other documents and papers relating to the affairs of the prison; all of which must be preserved and remain in the prison as public property, and be open at all times to the examination of each inspector and of every other person authorized by law to examine the same. Must have the custody of books and papers.

Ibid, subd. 6.

§ 917. The clerk must preserve, in the prison, a set of all official reports made to the legislature, respecting the same, and a set of similar reports in relation to each of the other state prisons, and of prisons in other states as far as practicable; for which purpose a suitable number of such reports, when printed, shall be supplied to him by the secretary of state. Must preserve a set of all official reports.

See *Ibid*, subd. 7.

§ 918. The clerk must make an annual report to the secretary of state, on or before the first Tuesday of February in each year, stating the names of convicts discharged or pardoned, during the preceding year, from the prison, and all the particulars in relation to such convicts required to be stated in the warden's monthly report to the inspectors, and stating also, in cases of pardon, how much of the term of sentence was unexpired when the pardon was granted, the conditions, if any, on which it was granted, and the state of health of each convict so pardoned, at the time of his discharge. Must make an annual report to secretary of state.

See *Ibid*, subd. 8.

§ 919. The clerk must make an annual report to the inspectors, on or before the first day of December Must make an annual report to inspectors.

in each year, exhibiting the number of convicts then confined therein, the various branches of business in which they are employed, and the number employed in each branch.

Ibid., subd. 9.

May take affidavits. § 920. The clerks of the several prisons in this state, or in their absence, the wardens are hereby authorized and required to take affidavits, in all matters of accounts against their respective prisons, and also in relation to fees of sheriffs in bringing convicts to either of the prisons.

See *Laws of* 1854, ch. 240, § 8, as amended *Laws of* 1855, ch. 552, § 13.

CHAPTER VII.

THE KEEPERS.

Keepers must obey directions of warden. § 921. The principal keeper and assistant keepers of each prison must obey and carry into effect all such orders and directions as they may receive from the warden, as to the management and discipline of the prison, not inconsistent with the laws of this state, and the general regulations prescribed by the inspectors.

See *Laws of* 1854, ch. 240, § 3; *Laws of* 1855, ch. 552, § 9. The substance of the former of these statutes is stated in the note to section 847. The latter statute is as follows:

"Whenever the number of convicts in the Clinton prison shall exceed three hundred, a principal keeper shall be appointed for such prison, and from the time

such appointment is made, the salary of the agent and warden and of such principal keeper shall be the same as now allowed by law to the agents and wardens and principal keepers of the Sing Sing and Auburn prisons, and the duties of the said agent and warden and of such principal keeper, the same as required by chapter two hundred and forty of the Laws of eighteen hundred and fifty-four, or of the acts of which that was amendatory."
Laws of 1855, ch. 552, § 9.

§ 922. The principal keeper and assistant keepers, in each prison, must preserve proper order and discipline among the convicts under their respective charge; and take care that they are diligently employed in the labor or business assigned them. They must also, when having the charge of convicts employed upon contracts or otherwise, keep a correct, daily, account of the labor of each convict so employed, in the manner that shall be prescribed by the warden, and make reports to him of the same, at such periods as he shall require; which reports must, in all cases, be attested by the affidavit of the keeper, that the account fairly and justly sets forth the labor performed on such contract or otherwise, during the period charged in such account.

Must preserve proper discipline.

Laws of 1847, ch. 460, § 58, as amended *Laws of* 1855, ch. 552, § 2.

§ 923. The store keeper at Sing Sing must take charge of all goods, provisions, and other articles, purchased or designed for the use of the prison, and enter the same in books to be kept by him for that purpose, and note all discrepancies, if any, which arise between the goods received and the bill accompanying such articles. Such goods, when received, must be kept in some safe place under his charge, and no goods shall be delivered by him, except on a requisition from the kitchen keeper, or warden, or principal keeper, or, at the Sing Sing prison, from the matron of the female department, or in his, her, or their absence, the person acting as such. Such requisition must, in all cases, be in writing, and by him placed on file, and in addition thereto, the articles named in

Store keeper at Sing Sing must take charge of goods purchased.

such requisition must be entered in his books, which books must state what the articles were, the quantity delivered, and on whose order they were delivered, and to what shop or place sent.

This and the next three sections are taken from *Laws of* 1855, ch. 552, § 4.

Must make out monthly statement for inspector in charge.

§ 924. The store keeper must, at the end of each month, make out a correct statement, giving the amount and kind of each article received, the amounts and kinds of goods delivered on requisitions, and to whom delivered, and the quantity of each kind of property then on hand, with the value thereof at that time; which statement, when made up, must be delivered to the inspector in charge, and by him examined; and if found correct, he shall so certify thereon. Such statement and certificate must then be delivered to the warden, and by him forwarded to the comptroller, with his monthly estimate and shall form a part thereof.

Must compare bills taken for goods purchased.

§ 925. The store keeper must take the duplicate bills for all goods and other articles purchased by the warden for the use of the prison, and compare them carefully with the originals. If he finds that they agree and that the goods delivered to him also agree with the bills, he must enter them in a book to be furnished by the warden for that purpose.

Must keep account of goods sold by the warden, &c.

§ 926. The store keeper must keep a perfect, just and true account of all goods sold by the warden or other officers of the prison, belonging to the prison.

General duties of kitchen keeper.

§ 927. The kitchen keeper, at each prison, must take the charge and care of the kitchen of the prison, and of the preparation of food for the convicts. He must enter in a book to be kept for the purpose, all articles received to be cooked, and must, at the end of each month, state, in a report which he must submit to the inspectors, what amount has been received, what amount has been consumed, whether any of such articles remain on hand, and what they are.

See *Laws of* 1855, ch. 552, § 4.

Kitchen keepers at Auburn and Clinton must act as store keepers.

§ 928. The kitchen keepers at the Auburn and Clinton prisons must also perform, at their respective prisons, the duties imposed upon the store keeper of the Sing Sing prison. All provisions of law which treat of the duties of store keeper at Sing Sing, apply in the same manner to the kitchen keepers of Auburn and Clinton prisons, in all respects.

Duties of hospital and hall keepers.

§ 929. Such of the keepers as may be designated by the warden, to act as hospital and hall keepers, must examine and enter all goods coming into the hospital, and to the halls or galleries; make requisitions for all goods required by them, through the warden or principal keeper; and enter in books, to be kept for that purpose, all articles so received or sent away from their respective departments.

Laws of 1847, ch. 460, § 66, subd. 3, as amended *Laws of* 1855, ch. 522, § 4.

CHAPTER VIII.

THE PHYSICIANS.

Physician must attend constantly at the prison.

§ 930. The physician must attend daily, during the proper business hours, at the prison, and hold himself, at all times, in readiness to discharge his duties as such physician, unless, by the direction of an inspector, or of the warden of the prison, he is otherwise engaged in transacting business on account of the prison.

See *Laws of* 1862, ch. 403, § 1.

Must take charge of hospital. § 931. The physician of each prison must take charge of the hospital of the prison.

This section and the seven which follow are taken from *Laws of* 1847, ch. 460, § 63.

Must attend the sick. § 932. The physician must attend, at all times, to the wants of the sick convicts, whether in the hospital or in their cells.

Must examine the cells of convicts weekly. § 933. The physician must examine, weekly, the cells of the convicts for the purpose of ascertaining whether they are kept in a proper state of cleanliness and ventilation, and report the same, weekly, to the warden.

Must make a monthly report to the inspectors of patients in hospital. § 934. The physician must report, monthly, to the inspectors the number of patients received into the hospital during the month, stating their respective ages, color, disease, and occupations in prison, the quality and kind of medicines administered during the month, the number of those discharged, their condition when discharged, the time they shall have remained in the hospital, and the number of deaths, stating the cause of such deaths.

And of sick convicts not received into hospital. § 935. The physician must report, in like manner, the number of sick convicts not received into the hospital, for whom he shall have prescribed during the last month, and the quantity and kind of the medicines so prescribed, and the number of days during which such convicts, in consequence of sickness, shall have been relieved from labor.

Must examine the provisions furnished. § 936. The physician must examine, daily, into the quality and state of the provisions delivered to the prisoners. And whenever he has reason to believe that any of such provisions are prejudicial to the health of the prisoners, he must immediately make a report thereof to the warden of the prison. He must also prescribe the diet of sick convicts, whether in the hospital or in their cells or elsewhere, and his directions in relation thereto must be followed by the warden.

§ 937. The physician must keep a daily record of all admissions to the hospital, indicating the sex, color, nativity, age, occupations, habits of life, crime, period of entrance and discharge from the hospital, date of admission to the prison, time in county prison before conviction, disease, if afflicted with scrofula before admission, scrofula during the first, second and third six months after admission to prison, and of the prescriptions and treatment of each case. Must keep a daily record of admissions to the hospital.

§ 938. The physician must make a yearly report to the inspectors, of the sanitary condition of the prison for the past year, in which all the information contained in his daily record and his monthly reports shall be condensed. Must make a yearly report to the inspectors.

§ 939. If the inspectors deem it necessary, they may require the physicians at Sing Sing and Clinton prisons, respectively, to reside in the prison, and in that case they may, in their discretion, add, not exceeding one hundred dollars, to the salary of each of the said physicians respectively. Inspectors may require physicians at Sing Sing and Clinton to reside in the prison.

Laws of 1847, ch. 460, § 63.

CHAPTER IX.

THE CHAPLAINS.

Chaplain must perform religious services.

§ 940. The chaplain of each prison must perform religious services in the prison, under such regulations as the inspectors may prescribe, and attend to the spiritual wants of the convicts.

Laws of 1847, ch. 460, § 60, subd. 1.

Must visit convicts in their cells.

§ 941. The chaplain must visit the convicts in their cells for the purpose of giving them religious and moral instruction, and devote at least one hour in each week day, and the afternoon of each Sunday, to such instruction.

Ibid., subd. 2.

Must see that books are furnished.

§ 942. The chaplain must see that a bible and hymn book is furnished, by the warden, to each convict.

See *Ibid.*, subd. 3.

Must take charge of library.

§ 943. The chaplain must take charge of the library, and take care that no improper books are introduced into the cells of the convicts, and if any such books are found, either in the cells or in the possession of a convict, he must take away and return the same to the warden; and for the purpose of properly discharging these duties, he must visit, weekly, each cell in the prison.

Ibid., subd. 4.

Must visit the sick.

§ 944. The chaplain must visit, daily, the sick in the hospital.

Ibid., subd. 5.

Must make an annual report to the inspectors.

§ 945. The chaplain must make an annual report, to the inspectors, up to the first day of December, relative to the religious and moral conduct of the prisoners during the past year, stating therein what services he has himself performed, and the fruits, if any, of his instructions. He must append thereto, as far as practicable, in tabular form, a statement exhibiting the number of convicts then in prison, the number of white males between the ages of twenty and thirty, thirty and forty, forty and fifty,

fifty and over, and, in like manner, of colored males, white females, and colored females, the number born in the United States, foreigners and of what country, the number that cannot read, that can read only, or can read and write, are well educated, classically educated, temperate, intemperate, health, whether scrofulous, whether employed at the time of the commission of the crime, counties where convicted, occupation, sentence, how many times recommitted, and whether married or unmarried.

See *Ibid.*, subd. 6.

§ 946. The chaplain must make a quarterly report to the inspectors, stating the number of convicts that shall have been instructed during the last quarter by the instructors or instructress, the branches of education in which they have been instructed, the text books used in such instruction, and the progress made by the convicts, and must note, especially, any cases in which an unusual progress has been made by a convict. Must make a quarterly report.

Laws of 1847, ch. 460, § 62.

CHAPTER X.

THE INSTRUCTORS AND INSTRUCTRESS.

§ 947. The instructors at the several state prisons, and the instructress at the female department of the Sing Sing prison, in conjunction with and under the supervision of the chaplain, must give instruction in the useful branches of an English education to such convicts as, in the judgment of the warden or the chaplain, may require the same and be benefited by it. Duty of instructors and instructress.

This section and the next are suggested as substitutes for *Laws of* 1847, ch. 460, § 61, and *Laws of* 1849, ch. 141, § 5, which are as follows:

"Two instructors shall be appointed by the board of inspectors for each of the prisons at Sing Sing and

Auburn, and one for the Clinton state prison; it shall be the duty of such instructors, in conjunction with and under the supervision of the chaplain, to give instruction in the useful branches of an English education to such convicts as, in the judgment of the warden or the chaplain, may require the same and be benefited by it; such instruction shall be given for not less than one hour and a half daily, Sunday excepted, between the hours of six and nine in the evening."

Laws of 1847, ch. 460, § 64.

"The inspectors of state prisons shall appoint one instructress for the female convict prison at Sing Sing, whose duty it shall be, in conjunction with and under the supervision of the chaplain, to give instructions in the useful branches of learning to such convicts as, in the judgment of the matron or the chaplain, may require the same and be benefited by it; such instruction to be given for not less than one hour and a half daily (Sundays excepted), between the hours of four and six in the afternoon.

Laws of 1849, ch. 141, § 5.

Instruction, when to be given. § 948. Such instruction must be given for not less than one hour and a half daily, Sunday excepted, between the hours of six and nine in the evening.

CHAPTER XI.

THE GUARDS.

SECTION 949. A guard to be maintained at each prison.
950. Guards to be furnished with arms, &c.

A guard to be maintained at each prison. § 949. There shall be maintained at each state prison a guard, to be employed by the inspectors, to consist of one sergeant and so many privates as the inspectors may, from time to time, direct; but the guard at Sing Sing, including the sergeant, shall not exceed thirty in number; the guard at Auburn shall not exceed the number of twenty, and that at Clinton shall not exceed the number of twenty-five.

Laws of 1847, ch. 460, § 64.

Guards to be furnished with arms, &c. § 950. The guards of the respective prisons shall be furnished from the arsenals of this state with sufficient arms, ammunition and accoutrements, and are subject to the command and direction of the warden of the prison.

Taken from *Laws of* 1847, ch. 460, § 65.

CHAPTER XII.

THE MILITARY COMPANIES AT SING SING AND AUBURN.

§ 951. For the safety of the Sing Sing prison, a military company shall continue to be organized in the village of Sing Sing; and for the safety of the Auburn prison, a similar company shall continue to be organized in the village of Auburn. Two military companies to be organized.

Laws of 1847, ch. 460, § 112.

The commissioners simply continue the existing law, upon this subject. They make no provision for a military company at the Clinton prison, because the present law does not provide for one, and no new necessity requiring one is known.

§ 952. Each of these companies shall be formed from the persons liable to militia duty residing in the vicinity of the prison to which it is attached, and shall consist of one captain, one first and second lieutenant, four sergeants, four corporals, two drummers, two fifers, and forty-five privates, who shall, from time to time, as may be necessary, receive Their organization prescribed arms, accoutrements, and ammunition, from the state arsenal at Albany, upon the order of the warden of the prison.

Laws of 1847, ch. 460, § 113.

Arms, &c., to be kept in good order.

§ 953. The arms, accoutrements, and ammunition, received by the members of each company, must be kept by them, in good order, for their use, when called upon, in defense of the prison; and, whenever such arms, accoutrements, and ammunition, are delivered, the person receiving the same must execute a receipt therefor, stating the purpose to which the same are to be applied.

Laws of 1847, ch. 460, § 114.

Companies to be always ready for service.

§ 954. Each of said companies must always be ready for immediate service, and must repair, with their arms, on the first alarm or notice from the warden or principal officer of the prison, to the prison, and there aid and assist, under his direction, in defense of the prison, and in preventing the escape of the convicts, or the execution of any injury threatened or premeditated by them; and shall be under his sole control.

Laws of 1847, ch. 460, § 115.

Companies, how formed, and officers, how appointed.

§ 955. Each of these companies must be formed and organized by the commander-in-chief, and the officers thereof designated, appointed and commissioned, as in the case of uniform companies. The persons composing them are exempt from all other militia duty, and from serving on any grand or petit jury so long as they respectively continue to be members of such companies.

Laws of 1847, ch. 460, § 116.

Restriction as to serving as firemen, &c.

§ 956. No person, duly enlisted into either of these companies, shall, without the written consent of the commanding officers of the company to which he belongs, leave the same to serve as fireman in any fire company, or to enlist into any other company of militia, except in case of a removal from out of the beat of said company.

Laws of 1847, ch. 460, § 117.

§ 957. These companies are respectively known, the first by the name of the Sing Sing Guards, and the other by the name of the Auburn Guards. They shall be ordered out for drill and exercise by the commanding officer thereof not less than six nor more than ten times in any one year. **Companies named "Sing Sing Guards" & "Auburn Guards."**

See *Laws of* 1847, ch. 460, § 118.

§ 958. Whenever the office of captain or subaltern in either of these companies becomes vacant, the same shall be filled in the manner now provided by law for filling vacancies in the companies of the militia of this state, except that the warden of the prison to which the company in which any such vacancy happens shall be attached, must cause the necessary notices of an election to fill vacancies, to be served on the members of the company. **Vacancies, how to be filled.**

Laws of 1847, ch. 460, § 119.

§ 959. The commanding officer of each company must return as a delinquent, to the inspector having charge of the prison, any non-commissioned officer, musician or private of the company, who does not appear on parade in the complete uniform of the company, or who is guilty of any neglect of duty or improper conduct on parade. **Return of delinquents to be made.**

Laws of 1847, ch. 460, § 120.

§ 960. The inspectors of the prison may summon any person so returned as a delinquent, to appear before them, at such time and place as they shall appoint, to answer to such alleged delinquency, and upon proof of such summons having been served, may proceed, at the time and place therein specified, to impose upon such delinquent such fine, not exceeding five dollars for each offense, as in their judgment the case may require. **Delinquents may be fined.**

Laws of 1847, ch. 460, § 121.

Fines, how to be collected.

§ 961. The president of the board of inspectors shall make out his warrant for the collection of such fines, in like manner, and with like effect, as a president of a court martial; the warrant shall be directed to any constable in the county in which the fine shall be imposed, commanding him to levy and collect such fine; and such constable shall collect such fine in like manner as other militia fines are now directed by law to be collected.

Laws of 1847, ch. 460, § 122.

Fines, how to be applied.

§ 962. All moneys collected by virtue of such warrant shall be paid over to the commanding officer of the company to which the delinquent upon whom such fine may be imposed shall belong, and may be applied, by a vote of the company, to any beneficial purpose that the company may direct.

Laws of 1847, ch. 460, § 123.

Officers may be dismissed for neglect of duty.

§ 963. If any officer of either of the said compa nies neglects to perform any duty enjoined upon him by law, it is the duty of the commander-in-chief, upon such neglect being reported by the inspectors, to dismiss such officer from the company; and if any non-commissioned officer or private refuses or neglects to perform his duties, such delinquent, in addition to the fine herein before prescribed, may be discharged by the commanding officer of the company to which he shall belong, and another person may be enrolled in his stead.

Laws of 1847, ch. 460, § 124.

Service for ten years to exempt from future military duty.

§ 964. Every non-commissioned officer, musician or private of either of said companies who shall serve faithfully therein for the period of ten years, shall thereafter be exempt from militia duty in this state, except in cases of insurrection or invasion.

See *Laws of* 1847, ch. 460, § 125.

CHAPTER XIII.

THE FIRE COMPANY AT AUBURN.

§ 965. There shall continue to be organized, in the vicinity of the prison at Auburn, one fire company, to consist of one foreman and thirty-six men residing in that vicinity. Fire company at Auburn prison.

Laws of 1847, ch. 460, § 127. The commissioners simply continue the existing law upon this subject. They make no provision for fire companies at Sing Sing and Clinton prisons, because the present law does not authorize them, and no new necessity for requiring them is known.

§ 966. It is the duty of such company, on the first alarm or notice of a fire in the prison, or in any of the adjacent buildings, to repair to the prison, and there to use and manage, under the direction of the warden, the engine belonging to the prison, and to aid by all means in their power, in the preservation of the prison, and of the persons confined therein. To attend on alarm of fire.

Laws of 1847, ch. 460, § 128.

§ 967. It is also the duty of such company to attend to the engine, and to exercise and try it at such stated times as the inspectors or warden shall prescribe; and the inspectors may, in their discretion, remove any member of the company and appoint another person in his stead. To attend to the fire engine.

Laws of 1847, ch. 460, § 129.

§ 968. The members of the fire company shall, upon the certificate of the board of inspectors, be exempt from serving on juries, and from serving in Privileges of members of the company.

the militia, except in cases of invasion, or insurrection, so long as they continue such members.

Laws of 1847, ch. 460, § 130.

When entitled to discharge. § 969. The members of the fire company, after service of nine years therein, shall be exempt from militia duty, except in time of war or insurrection, and shall be entitled to a discharge from the company.

Laws of 1847, ch. 460, § 131.

CHAPTER XIV.

THE CUSTODY, CONDUCT AND DISCIPLINE OF CONVICTS.

Certificate of conviction to be delivered with convict. § 970. Whenever any convict is delivered to the warden of either state prison, the officer having such convict in his charge, must deliver to such warden the certified copy of the sentence received by such officer from the clerk of the court by which such convict shall have been sentenced, and take from the warden a certificate of the delivery of such convict.

Laws of 1847, ch. 460, § 86.

§ 971. Whenever there are a sufficient number of cells in the prison, it is the duty of the warden to keep each convict single in his cell at night, and also in the day time when not employed. Convicts to be kept single in cells at night, &c.

Laws of 1847, ch. 460, § 104.

§ 972. Convicts confined in the state prisons are entitled to be provided, at the expense of the state, with a sufficient quantity of inferior but wholesome food, and with inferior but comfortable clothing and bedding. Such clothing must be manufactured, as far as practicable, in the prison. Convicts to be provided with food, clothing and bedding.

Laws of 1847, ch. 460, § 105.

§ 973. The convicts in each prison shall be supplied with provisions by contract, to be made by the warden, under the direction of the inspectors, with such person and for such a term, not exceeding one year, as the inspectors may determine to be most advantageous to the state, at a fixed price per day for each convict, or they may, at their option, require the warden of the prison to furnish the rations by purchase. Provisions to be furnished by contract.

Laws of 1847, ch. 460, § 78.

§ 974. The kinds of provisions and the quantities of each kind, shall be prescribed by the inspectors and inserted in the contract; and so many rations shall be delivered at the prison daily, or at such other times as may be agreed on, as there are convicts confined therein. The articles of food to be prescribed by inspectors.

Laws of 1847, ch. 460, § 79.

§ 975. For the purpose of ascertaining who will furnish supplies on the lowest terms, the warden must cause a notice to be published in a newspaper printed in the county in which the prison is situated, and in such other newspapers, and for such time as the inspectors may direct, stating the particular supplies wanted, the manner in which they are to be delivered, and the time during which proposals will be received by such agent for furnishing the same. Notice of supplies wanted, to be published.

Laws of 1847, ch. 460, § 80.

Proposals must specify the lowest price.

§ 976. The proposals to be offered pursuant to such notice, must specify the lowest price per ration per day, and the contracts must be made with those persons whose terms shall be most advantageous to the state, and who shall give satisfactory security for the performance of their contracts, unless the inspectors shall deem it expedient to decline all pro posals and advertise anew.

Laws of 1847, ch. 460, § 96.

Contracts must be in writing.

§ 977. All contracts to be made under last four sections, must be reduced to writing and signed by the parties; a duplicate, so signed, of every such contract shall be filed with the clerk of the prison, and a copy thereof shall be delivered to the inspector. Unless these provisions are complied with, the contractor shall have no right to recover for any articles supplied under such contract.

See *Laws of* 1847, ch. 460, § 82. The last sentence is added by the commissioners to protect the state against frauds by contractors.

Provision in case of violence being offered by convicts.

§ 978. When any convict offers violence to any officer of the state prison or to any other convict, or does or attempts to do any injury to the building or any work shop, or to any appurtenances thereof, or property therein, or attempts to escape, or resists or disobeys any lawful command, the officers of the prison shall use all suitable means to defend themselves, or to enforce the observance of discipline, to secure the persons of the offenders, and to prevent any such attempt or escape.

Laws of 1847, ch. 460, § 106.

Restrictions as to inflicting blows on convicts.

§ 979. No officer in any state prison shall inflict any blows whatever upon any convict, unless in self-defense, or to suppress a revolt or insurrection. If in the opinion of the warden of such prison, it is necessary in any case to inflict unusual punishment in order to produce the entire submission or obedience of any convict, it is the duty of such warden to confine such convict immediately in a cell, upon a short allowance, and to retain him therein until he shall be reduced to submission and obedience. The short allowance to each convict so confined shall be prescribed by the physician, whose duty it shall be to visit such convict and examine daily into the state of his health, until the convict be released from solitary confinement and returned to his labor.

Laws of 1847, ch. 460, § 108.

Certain convicts may be confined in solitary cells.

§ 980. Whenever any convict is found incorrigibly disobedient to the rules of either of the state prisons, the warden must confine him in one of the solitary cells provided for in section 807, at hard labor, and when practicable, he must, when so confined, be employed at the same trade or business he was employed in immediately previous to such solitary confinement.

Laws of 1847, ch, 460, § 45.

Inspector to visit such cells.

§ 981. It is the duty of the inspector having charge, at the time, of each prison, to visit such cells from time to time, and examine into the causes of confinement of each convict thus confined, and he may designate the length of time during which such solitary confinement, in each individual case, shall continue, subject to the approval of the board of inspectors at each meeting thereof, held at such prison. It is the duty of the inspectors to regulate and control such solitary confinement; and to prescribe the fare and treatment of all convicts so confined, and they may adopt such rules and regulations in réference thereto as they deem proper, not inconsistent with the existing laws.

Laws of 1847, ch. 460, § 46. The commissioners think it better to vest the power to designate the length of time during which solitary confinement shall continue, wholly in the inspector, instead of allowing him, as in the existing law, to designate it "if the warden ,shall concur." To make the power of the inspector dependent on the concurrence of the warden, deprives the convict of efficient protection in case he has excited unreasonable prejudice or ill will on the part of the warden.

Apprehension of escaped convicts.

§ 982. Whenever any convict confined in a state prison escapes therefrom, it is the duty of the warden to take all proper measures for the apprehension of such convict; and in his discretion he may offer a reward not exceeding fifty dollars, for the apprehension and delivery of every such convict, and with the consent of the inspector in charge of the prison, such reward may be increased to a sum not exceeding two hundred and fifty dollars.

Laws of 1847. ch. 460, § 109, as amended *Laws* of 1860, ch. 399, § 7.

Rewards, how to be paid.

§ 983. All rewards and other sums of money necessarily paid for advertising and apprehending any convict who may escape from a state prison, must be paid by the warden out of the funds of the prison.

Laws of 1847, ch. 460, § 110.

Letters, &c., to convicts must be examined.

§ 984. No letter, writing, picture or sign can be delivered to any convict, nor can any, written or made by a convict, be sent from the prison, until the same has been examined and read by the warden, or by some other officer of the prison authorized by the warden.

Taken from *Laws of* 1847, ch. 460, § 107. Other provisions of that section are omitted here, because they have already been embraced in section 221 of this Code, deemed a more appropriate place.

In certain cases of death, a coroner's inquest may be held..

§ 985. Whenever a convict shall die in any state prison, it is the duty of the inspector having charge of the prison, and of the warden, physician and chaplain of the prison, if they or either of them have reason to believe that the death of the convict arose from any other than ordinary sickness, to call upon the coroner having jurisdiction, to hold an inquest upon the body of such deceased convict.

Laws of 1847, ch, 460, § 102.

§ 986. Whenever a convict shall die in the Sing Sing prison, it is the duty of the warden, unless the body of such convict be taken away for interment by the relatives or friends of the deceased within twenty-four hours after his death, to deliver on demand, such dead body to the agent of the college of physicians and surgeons in the city of New York, or to the agent of the medical faculty of the university of the city of New York, so that one-half of the number of such dead bodies shall be delivered to each institution.

Bodies of convicts dying at Sing Sing, when to be given for dissection.

Laws of 1847, ch. 460, § 132.

§ 987. It is in like manner the duty of the warden of the Auburn state prison, whenever a convict dies in that prison, whose body shall not be taken away for interment by his relatives or friends within twenty-four hours after his death, to deliver on demand, such dead body to the agent of the medical faculty of the university of Buffalo, or to the agent of the medical faculty of Geneva college, so that one-half of the number of such dead bodies shall be delivered to each institution.

The like at Auburn prison.

Laws of 1847, ch. 460, § 133.

§ 988. All children born of female convicts in the female department of the Sing Sing prison, may, by an order of the warden of the prison, be sent to the poor house in the county of Westchester, to be there supported upon such terms as may be agreed upon between the warden and the superintendent of the poor of the county; and all expenses incurred thereby shall be paid by the warden out of the funds of the prison. But no child under the age of two years shall be so sent away, if its mother be able and willing to nurse it.

Children of female convicts.

See *Laws of* 1847, ch. 460, § 134. The last sentence of the section is added in view of the necessity that the child should be in the care of its mother during early infancy.

Restriction as to sale of liquors near Clinton prison.

§ 989. No license shall hereafter be granted for the sale of intoxicating liquors within three miles of the Clinton prison; and every person who shall, directly or indirectly, sell or dispose of any alcoholic drinks within the distance of three miles from that prison, shall, upon conviction thereof, before any justice of the peace of the county of Clinton, be subject to a penalty of fifty dollars; one-half thereof to be paid to the person prosecuting for the same, and the other half to be paid to the persons charged with the support of the poor of the town in which the offense was committed.

See *Laws of* 1847, ch. 460, § 144.

CHAPTER XV.

THE EMPLOYMENT OF CONVICTS.

§ 990. All convicts in a state prison must not be allowed to converse with each other and must be kept constantly employed at hard labor during the daytime, not exceeding twelve hours, except when incapable of laboring by reason of sickness or bodily infirmity. Convicts to be kept at hard labor.

Laws of 1847, ch. 460, § 103. The prohibition on conversing, and limit of time, are new.

§ 991. It is the duty of the court in which any person shall be convicted of an offense punishable in a state prison, before passing the sentence, to ascertain by the examination of such convict on oath, and in addition to such oath, by such evidence as can be obtained, whether such convict has learned and practiced any mechanical trade. The clerk of the court must enter the facts as ascertained and decided by the court, on the minutes thereof, and deliver a certificate stating the facts as ascertained, to the sheriff of the county, who must cause the same to be delivered to the warden of the proper prison at the same time that such convict is delivered to the warden pursuant to his sentence. Courts to examine convicts as to their having learned a trade.

Laws of 1847, ch. 460, § 70. This provision should be transferred to the Code of Criminal Procedure, Part II, tit. ix, ch. 1.

§ 992. No convict sentenced to imprisonment in either of the state prisons shall be permitted to work therein at any other mechanical trade than that which, as shall appear by the certificate of the clerk of the court in which he was convicted, such convict had learned and practiced previous to his conviction, except in the making or manufacture of articles of which the chief supply for the consumption of this state is imported from other countries or states, and except that the convicts at Sing Sing prison may be employed Convicts not to be permitted to work at any other trade.

in the cutting and manufacture of stone, and the convicts at Clinton prison in the manufacture of iron.

See laws of 1847, ch. 460, § 71.

Trade of convicts who were previously in state prison.

§ 993. If the warden of the prison in which any convict is detained shall ascertain that such convict has been previously in a state prison or penitentiary, he may in his discretion, direct such convict to be employed in the same kind of labor in which he had been employed during such former imprisonment, notwithstanding it may appear from the certificate of the clerk of the court that a different trade had been learned or practiced by him. And if the warden of either prison shall ascertain to his entire satisfaction, that any convict so certified, had not in fact learned and practiced previous to his conviction, the trade mentioned in the certificate, he may, with the approbation of the inspector then having charge of such prison, direct such convict to be employed in the trade or kind of labor which he shall have ascertained by competent proof that such convict had previously learned and practiced.

See *Laws of* 1847, ch. 460, § 72.

Officers not to employ convicts.

§ 994. No inspector, or officer of either prison shall employ the labor of any convict or other person employed in such prison on any work in which such inspector, or officer shall be interested.

Laws of 1847, ch. 460, § 74.

Penalty for hiring convicts contrary to law.

§ 995. Every inspector or warden of either of the state prisons who knowingly lets or hires, or consents to the letting or hiring of the labor or services of a convict contrary to law, and every officer of either prison who knowingly causes a convict to be employed at work prohibited by law, is punishable by imprisonment in a county jail not exceeding one year or by a fine not exceeding one thousand dollars.

See *Laws of* 1847, ch. 460, § 75.

§ 996. Whenever a complaint is made to the attorney-general, accompanied by satisfactory information that any of the provisions of the two last preceding sections have been violated by an inspector, or by any officer of either of the prisons, it is his duty to cause the offender to be prosecuted; and any indictment for such an offence may be found or tried in any county in which the offense was committed, or in an adjoining county.

Attorney-General to prosecute in certain cases.

Laws of 1847, ch. 460, § 76.

§ 997. Whenever the board of inspectors deem it expedient for the warden of either of the prisons to enter into any contract for the labor and services of convicts for a term of more than one year, they shall pass a resolution to that effect, specifying the number of convicts whose labor and services are to be let, the prison in which they are confined, the business at which they are to be employed, the number of years for which their labor and services are to be let, the time the contract shall commence, the shop room, yard room, store room, hydraulic or steam power, machinery and other facilities, if any there be, for the business which will be furnished with the labor and services to be let, and directing the warden to advertise for sealed proposals therefor in the state paper, in one newspaper published in the county where said prison is located, and in one newspaper published in each of the cities of this state.

The warden to let the services of convicts under directions from board of inspectors.

This section and the nine which follow, are taken from *Laws of* 1847, ch. 460, § 77, as amended *Laws of* 1854, ch. 240, § 9, and further amended *Laws of* 1860, ch. 399, § 12.

§ 998. Upon the passage of any such resolution and the serving a copy thereof upon the warden, that officer must proceed at once to execute it, by preparing and publishing, for the period of thirty days next preceding the time fixed for opening such proposals, the notice required in the manner above provided, and by preparing a duplicate form of the contract to be en-

Warden must advertise for proposals and prepare form of contract.

tered into, with the date, amount of compensation per day, and the names of contractors, and their sureties, in blank, to be approved by the inspectors or a majority of them. A copy of such contract must be deposited with the clerk of the prison at which such convict labor is to be let, for the inspection of all persons desirous of proposing therefor, for at least the period of twenty days prior to the time fixed in such notice for opening such proposals.

Sureties of contractor must justify.

§ 999. To every proposal for convict labor, shall be annexed a justification of the sureties, in an amount in the aggregate not less than the sum of five thousand dollars, over and above all debts and liabilities and property exempt from execution.

Warden must submit proposals to inspectors.

§ 1000. The warden must receive and preserve unopened all the sealed proposals for such labor and services which shall be delivered to or received by him up to the day and hour mentioned in his published notice, and no longer; and must thereupon, or as soon thereafter as the board of inspectors shall convene, lay the proposals before the board of inspectors.

Inspectors to award contract.

§ 1001. The inspectors must proceed at once publicly to open and canvass such of the proposals as are substantially in the form prescribed in the published notice of the warden, and are accompanied by an offer to enter into the contract for the labor of such convicts which has been prepared and deposited with the clerk, with the name of the bidder and the price per day for the labor and services of the convicts which he proposes to pay, and with the names of at least two sufficient sureties accompanied by their written consent to become sureties in such contract; and they shall award the contract for such labor and services to the person or persons who shall be found to be, by such canvass, the highest bidder or bidders therefor; and shall thereupon direct the warden to fill up the blanks in such contract pursuant to such proposal, and execute the same with such bidder.

§ 1002. Such contract when so filled up and signed, and approved by the inspectors or a majority of them, as to the sufficiency of the sureties therein, shall be a valid contract in law with the parties thereto and their sureties. Effect of the contract.

§ 1003. No such contract shall be executed by the warden or be valid in law, which contains any stipulation on the part of the warden to accept any less than the full contract price (which shall be the price per day only) for the labor and services of any of the convicts referred to in the contract, or that the convicts shall execute any specific amount of labor per day, per month or year, or that they shall have or possess any particular degree of skill in the trade or business at which they are to be employed, or that the contractor or contractors shall have any accommodations or facilities for business or privileges which were not specified in the contract prepared and deposited with the clerk as provided by section 998 or that the warden shall maintain any particular kind, standard, or quality of discipline in said prison over the convicts, during the time they shall be employed under such contract. What the contract must not contain.

§ 1004. No such contract shall be executed by the warden, or be valid in law, if it runs for a longer time than five years from the time when it is by its terms to commence; nor unless it contains a stipulation on the part of the contractor, to pay the contract price for the labor and services therein specified, monthly, on the first day of each month, to the warden, at his office at the prison; and a stipulation that the warden may, by and with the consent of the board of inspectors, or a majority of them, annul the contract and declare it void, if the contractor at any time neglects or refuses to make the monthly payments within ten days from the time they shall respectively fall due; and a stipulation that the state will not be held re- What it must contain.

sponsible for any loss sustained by fire on the part of any contractor.

Penalty for bidder's refusal to complete the contract.

§ 1005. In case any bidder to whom any contract may be awarded, refuses, or for twenty-four hours after award made to him neglects to execute such contract, with at least two sufficient sureties, to be approved by the inspectors, or a majority of them; he shall pay to the warden as stipulated damages for such refusal or neglect, a sum equal to the difference between the aggregate of earnings of the number of convicts specified in such contract, at the price per day named in the proposal of such bidder, for the term of such contract, and the aggregate of earnings of such number of convicts at the price per day at which the same shall be finally awarded; and the warden shall have an immediate right of action against such bidder so neglecting or refusing, and his proposed sureties, for the recovery of such damages; and unless the same shall be paid within thirty days after personal demand thereof of such bidder, the warden shall forthwith bring suit for the recovery thereof.

Inspectors may advertise anew.

§ 1006. If upon opening such proposals, the inspectors with the assent of the warden, deem it for the interest of the state not to award the contract to any of the bidders, they may reject all of the proposals, and re-advertise the contract, and if after awarding the contract to any bidder or bidders, who refuse or neglect to enter into such contract, the inspectors do not deem it for the interest of the state to award the same to any person bidding a lower rate of compensation, they may reject all lower bids, and re-advertise; and any bidder whose proposal has been accepted by the inspectors and who has refused or neglected to enter into such contract, shall be liable to the warden for the expenses of such re-advertisement, in addition to the damages by reason of such refusal or neglect, to be computed as hereinbefore provided.

§ 1007. Whenever the board of inspectors deem it expedient and proper for the warden of either prison to enter into any contract for the labor and services of convicts for a term not exceeding one year, it shall be the duty of the board to pass a resolution to that effect, specifying the number of convicts whose labor and services are to be let, the prison in which they are confined, the business at which they may be employed, if contracted for, the time when a contract therefor may commence, and the shop or yard room, store room, and the accommodations and facilities for carrying on the proposed business or labor which will be furnished with such labor and services, directing the warden to ascertain what price per day he can obtain for such labor and services and report the same to the board; and if upon advisement the board shall consider it for the interest of the state to accept the highest price thus offered and reported, they shall pass a resolution to that effect, directing the warden to enter into a contract in the form prescribed in the preceding sections with the party making the proposal and his sureties. **Contract for labor of convicts for one year or less.**

Laws of 1860, ch. 399, § 13.

§ 1008. In all contracts let or awarded for convict labor at any state prison, a clause must be inserted that any debt which may be or become due from any contractor upon such contract shall be a lien, in favor of the prison, upon the machinery and tools used or owned by such contractor in operating such contract upon the prison premises. Such lien commences with such contract, and continues during the existence of the contract, and until the claim or debt has been satisfied or canceled. And the warden of the prison, under the direction of the inspectors or a majority of them, whenever any sum becomes due from a contractor, may proceed to satisfy such lien by a sale of the property affected by it in the same manner as by a sale upon a chattel mortgage. **Debt of contractor a lien upon his tools, &c.**

See *Laws of* 1863, ch. 465, § 1.

Contractor to deposit money with comptroller, as security.

§ 1009. In all contracts let or awarded for convict labor, at any state prison, a clause must be inserted requiring the contractor to deposit with the comptroller of the state a sum of money not less than five hundred dollars, and not greater than two thousand dollars, as the inspectors may determine, according to the nature of the contract; and no contract shall be valid until such deposit has been made. Such money shall remain on deposit with the comptroller as security for the payment of any debt which may arise on the contract during the continuance thereof, and until such debt be adjusted. The comptroller may apply such money upon and towards the liquidation of any such debt which may become due. When ever the sum so to be applied does not suffice to meet such debt, it becomes the duty of the inspectors forthwith to annul such contract, and the same shall be and become immediately annulled. The labor and services of the convicts provided for in such contract may thereupon be relet and contracted anew, but not to such defaulting contractor. Nor shall any other contract for convict labor be awarded to any person who shall have been a defaulting contractor. But the annulment of such contract does not cancel any lien existing thereby upon machinery and tools, for any indebtedness then existing.

Laws of 1863, ch. 465, § 2.

Citizen labor not to be employed except, &c.

§ 1010. It is not lawful for any person holding a contract for convict labor at any state prison to employ in the shops or grounds of such prison, upon the ordinary work of convicts as carried on at such prison, any other persons than convicts, without the permission of the board of inspectors, as foremen, superintendents, teamsters or otherwise.

See *Laws of* 1863, ch. 465, § 3.

Clothing for convicts in Clinton prison.

§ 1011. All necessary clothing for the use of the convicts in the Clinton prison shall be manufactured by the convicts in the Auburn and Sing Sing prisons, whenever a written order for that purpose shall be made by the inspectors and be delivered to the respective wardens of those prisons.

Laws of 1847, ch. 460, § 139.

§ 1012. The Sing Sing and Auburn prisons shall respectively have credit on the books of the comptroller for the value of any cloth or clothing manufactured in such prisons in conformity to law, for the use of the Clinton prison, on making specific returns thereof, verified as to quantity and value by the affidavit of the agent of the prison manufacturing the same. The sum so to be credited must be paid by the treasurer, on the warrant of the comptroller, out of any moneys in the treasury not otherwise appropriated, to the order of the inspectors, whenever such payment becomes necessary to defray the expenses of the prison entitled to the credit. **The Sing Sing and Auburn prisons to be credited for clothing.**

Laws of 1847, ch. 460, § 140.

§ 1013. The warden of the Clinton prison must not deposit or pledge any article produced by the labor of the convicts, by way of security for moneys borrowed on the credit thereof or otherwise; and all articles purchased by him for the use of the prison or to be employed in conducting any of its operations, must be purchased for cash, and not upon credit, unless the inspector having charge of the prison shall otherwise direct. The warden must make sale of the articles produced by the labor of the convicts, in such manner and on such terms as shall be prescribed by the rules and regulations established from time to time by the board of inspectors. **Purchases made for the Clinton prison to be for cash.**

Laws of 1847, ch. 460, § 141.

§ 1014. The warden of the Clinton prison, must, under the direction of the comptroller, deposit to the credit of the state, all moneys he may receive from the sale of any manufactures produced in the prison, whenever the same exceeds the sum of one thousand **Warden must deposit moneys to the credit of the state.**

dollars, and are not required, within fifteen days after the receipt thereof, to defray the expenses of the prison.

Laws of 1847, ch. 460, § 142.

Warden of Sing Sing prison may let services of convicts for a term of years.

§ 1015. The warden of the Sing Sing prison is authorized to let, by contract, the services of such number of convicts in that prison as he may have at his disposal from time to time, to any such person or persons as shall conform to the terms hereinafter contained, to be employed in the business of quarrying, splitting, sawing and removing stone from the quarries on the state lands adjacent to the prison. for fifteen years from the date thereof.

Laws of 1855, ch. 334, § 1.

The contract must be in writing.

§ 1016. Such contract must be in writing and approved by the inspectors of state prisons, and the comptroller of this state, and shall guarantee to such contractor the exclusive use of the quarries on the state land at Sing Sing, and the right to get out and quarry stone therefrom (reserving the right in the warden to get out and quarry from any quarries now opened, all necessary stone for building and improving in and about the prison), and the services of at least one hundred convicts to be employed as mentioned in the last section, and all such other convicts in the prison as are at the disposal of the warden at any time during such term, without interfering with the right of the warden, to re-advertise and let such other contracts as may expire during such term.

Laws of 1855, ch. 334, § 2.

Services of convicts, how to be paid for.

§ 1017. Such contractor must covenant and agree in the contract, to pay such warden for the services of the convicts at the rate of not less than fifty cents for each day's labor of each convict employed, without reference to their skill; payment to be made on the last day of each month after the contract takes effect, and such payment to be secured in such manner as shall be satisfactory to the warden and inspectors, and the comptroller of this state; and the contractor must further covenant and agree in the contract, to build and construct, at his expense, all such additional shops, buildings and docks, and put up all necessary machinery for the purpose of carrying on the business; and must further covenant and agree in the contract, to take from the warden, and employ under the contract all the convicts which such warden shall tender to him under the same, not to exceed one thousand convicts at any one time. No such contract shall be assignable without the consent of the inspectors.

See *Laws of* 1855, ch. 334, § 3.

CHAPTER XVI.

COMMUTATION OF SENTENCES.

§ 1018. Every convict confined in any state prison in this state, may earn for himself a commutation or diminution of the term of his sentence, subject to the provisions of section 1023, and in the manner following: If he shall diligently work the number of hours prescribed by the rules of the prison, during each day that he is ordered to work, for the space of one month, and if he shall obey the rules and quietly submit to the discipline of the prison, for the space of one month, he shall be entitled, for every period of one month for which he shall so work, obey and submit, to a commutation or deduction from the term for which he has been sentenced, of one day, unless he shall subsequently forfeit the same by an assault upon any officer, or any foreman or convict, or other- Convicts may earn commutation of sentence.

wise endanger life, or by other flagrant disregard of the rules of the prison, in which case all previous commutations earned by him shall be wholly for feited; but such shall not be the effect in cases where, without any violence whatever, a rule or rules shall be broken by him, and it is clear that no willfulness or malice was intended. If he shall so work and obey, as above, and submit, for the space of six or more successive months, he shall be entitled, for every one of those six or more successive months, to a commutation or deduction from the term for which he was sentenced, of two days, instead of the commutation already mentioned. If he shall so work and obey, for the space of two years or more, he shall be entitled, instead of the commutation already mentioned, to a commutation of one month on each of the first two years; of two months on each succeeding year to the tenth year; and of four months on each remaining year of the time of his imprisonment.

This section and the two which follow, are taken from the *Laws of* 1862, ch. 417, § 2, as amended, *Laws of* 1863, ch. 415, and *Laws of* 1864, ch. 321, § 1. The last mentioned act is obscurely framed, but the commissioners have followed what they believe to be the intent of the Legislature. See note to section 1023, *infra.*

The original act applies not only to state prisons, but also to penitentiaries. It will be noticed that the last section of this Code, which repeals the existing statutes relative to prisons, repeals them only so far as they apply to state prisons and county jails; and leaves their provisions in force, in so far as they govern the discipline of penitentiaries and other institutions of special character.

Convicts in the hospitals.

§ 1019. During the period that any convict is confined to the prison hospitals, if he is dutiful to the rules thereof, time, as contemplated by this section, shall not be counted either for or against the convict; and a period of consecutive time before confinement in hospital, and an additional period of consecutive time after discharge therefrom, may be added together and counted as six successive months, the same as if no time had been passed in hospital, if the convict, during the entire period, shall have fulfilled all the requirements of the last section.

§ 1020. The provisions of the last two sections apply to convicts serving as waiters and cooks in and about any prison, and to female convicts, and to convicts for whom the warden has no work at which to put them, under any contract for the labor of convicts. But they do not apply to any convict under sentence of imprisonment for the term of his natural life, nor to any convict confined under a sentence by a court of the United States.

To whom the provisions apply.

The exception of United States prisoners is new, but seems plainly necessary, as the governor of the State of New York has no power to remit any part of the sentences of such prisoners.

§ 1021. It is the duty of every warden of a state prison whenever a convict to whom the provisions of this chapter can apply, is delivered to him for confinement in the prison, to make such provisions known to him.

Warden must notify convicts of the provisions of this chapter.

Laws of 1862, ch. 417, § 3.

§ 1022. It is the duty of the keepers and matrons of each state prison, to keep such record, day by day, of the manner of working of each convict therein to whom the provisions of this chapter are applicable, and of his or her conduct therein, as shall show what convicts have fulfilled the requirements of the section 1018, and to report such record at the end of each month to the warden of the prison, and it is the duty of the warden to preserve such record, and not more than thirty days before the term of each convict expires, as diminished by said record, to transmit to the governor a certificate and report, showing that it appears from the record kept by the keepers of the prison of the manner of working and of the daily conduct of each convict confined therein, duly preserved by him as required by law, that the convict has diligently worked the number of hours prescribed

Keepers and matrons must keep record of work, and of manner of doing it, and report the same.

by the rules of the prison, during each day that he or she has been ordered to work, for the space of six or more successive months, or otherwise, as the case may be, and that he or she has well obeyed the rules and strictly submitted to the discipline of the prison for the space of six or more successive months, or otherwise, as the case may be, and that the convict has fulfilled all the requirements of this chapter. Such certificate and report must give the name of the convict, the county where convicted, the crime, the date of conviction, at what court, by whom held, the date of sentence, the term of sentence, and the time the convict was received at the prison.

See *Laws of* 1862, ch. 417, § 4, as amended *Laws of* 1863, ch. 415.

Governor may direct deduction from term of imprisonment.

§ 1023. The governor may thereupon in his discretion, direct the abatement or deduction of the term of the sentence of such convict of the number of days of commutation or diminution thereof which such convict shall have earned.

Taken from *Laws of* 1862, ch. 417, § 4, as amended *Laws of* 1863, ch. 415.

The following remarks, extracted from the Nineteenth Annual Report of the Prison Association of New York, will be read with interest in connection with this chapter:

"THE COMMUTATION SYSTEM.—On the 22d of April, 1862, an act was passed by the Legislature, containing, among others, the following provision: 'If he (a convict in any state prison or penitentiary) shall diligently work the number of hours prescribed by the rules of the prison or penitentiary during each day that he is so ordered to work, for the space of one month, and if he shall well obey the rules and quietly submit to the discipline of the penitentiary for the space of one month, he shall be entitled, for every period of one month, for which he shall so work, obey and submit, to a commutation or deduction from the term for which he has been sentenced, of one day. If he shall so work and obey and submit for the space of six or more successive months, he shall be entitled, for every one of said six or more successive months, to a commutation or deduction from the term for which he was sentenced of two days, which two days shall be in addition to the deduction of one day for each month hereinbefore provided for.'

"Two interpretations have been given to this provision, by one of which the maximum of commutation for any space of six months is eight days; by the other, eighteen. This alleged obscurity of the law, and some other circumstances, caused Gov. Morgan to decline all action under it. Accordingly, no commutations were granted by him during the nine months of his administration after the passage of the law.

"A year later, an amendatory act was passed, in which, after providing, as in the original act, for a commutation of one day for each several month, it is enacted as follows: 'If he (the convict) shall so work and obey as above, and submit for the space of six or more successive months, he shall be entitled, for every one of said six or more successive months, to a commutation or deduction from the term for which he was sentenced, of two days.'

"Under this provision, it is evident that twelve days are the maximum of commutation that can be earned in any space of six months. It would, therefore, be unnecessary to discuss the meaning of the prior act, if there were not a class of cases to which its provisions are still rightfully applicable. If that be the true construction of the act of 1862, which assigns eight days as the maximum for any space of six or more successive months, then from any such period during which commutation may have been earned under the said act, four days less must be allowed than for an equal period under the act of 1863. But if, according to the true intent and meaning of the law, eighteen days constitute the maximum, then the convict, on his discharge, will be entitled to six days for each space of six successive months *additional* to the time allowed by the law as it now stands, and one day more for each month in excess of six.

"The question of the true interpretation of the original act, which was in operation a full year, is, therefore, of no little interest to the convicts who were in prison during that period.

"The interpreters who contend for eight days as the maximum for six or more successive months, affirm that, in using that language, the Legislature meant every *space* of six or more successive months, and not every *one* of said months. To this it is enough to reply, that the whole statute must be taken together. Every word in it must be supposed to have a purpose, and the whole must be so construed as to render each part effective. But, on the construction given above, the words 'or more,' in connection with the words 'six successive months,' cannot be shown to have a purpose, nor can they be interpreted consistently with good sense or good morals. They must be entirely ignored or they lead to absurdity. Ignore them, and the construction alleged may be made to appear plausible at least. But take the words as they stand, give them life, and mark the consequence. Five years of continued good conduct constitute but one *space* of 'six or MORE successive months,' and entitle the convict to only one additional allowance of two days, and to only sixty-two days in the whole five years, whereas the allowances for five years, with a regular outbreak of disorder every seventh month, would be for eight spaces of six months, and the convict would be entitled to a commutation of sixteen days instead of two. And this shortening of his imprisonment by fourteen days would not simply be in spite of his insubordination, but because of it. That is to say, the state would not reward good conduct in proportion to its uninterrupted continuance, but her choicest acts of grace would be reserved for alternations of virtue and vice. Such a law might be an encouragement to good conduct for six months, but it would be an equal encouragement to bad conduct the seventh. It cannot for a moment be supposed that the Legislature ever intended such a combination of absurdity and immorality.

"It may be remarked in passing, that since the phraseology of the original act and the amended act is the same in those parts which designate the amount of commutation that may be earned, if the construction combatted be the true one, it would follow that the sum total of commutation capable of being earned during any number of years of uninterrupted good conduct under the amended act would be just two days, for the whole would be but one *space* of 'six or more successive months.'

"We must, then, have recourse to the construction which regards the additional allowance of two days as intended, not for the *term* of six or more successive months, but for each *month* in the term, thus giving three days as the maximum per month, when the good conduct of the convict is maintained for six months or more without interruption. This construction avoids all the absurdities and difficulties of the other. Moreover, it is the obvious construction—that which lies upon the very surface of the statute—that which would first occur to every reader. It takes the words 'every one' in their natural sense, as meaning every one of the six months, and not in the forced signification of every space of six months. It discloses a purpose in the words 'or more.' It makes those significant and effective, requiring the deduction of three days per month to be continued for as many successive months in excess of six as the conditions of the law are met by the convict. The only rational conclusion is, that this construction of the law is the true one and correctly sets forth the intent of the legislature in its enactment.

"The establishment of this construction, if it has been established by the foregoing argument or can be by any other, draws after it, by inevitable sequence, the obligation on the part of the executive, to abide by it in determining the amount of commutation to be granted to any convict, so far as the commutation earned by him is covered by the period during which the law was in operation. For instance, since the maximum under the original statute was three days per month, while under the statute as amended it is only two, if the convict behaved unexceptionably for twelve successive months while the former law was in force, then on his discharge he will be entitled to a deduction from his term of sentence of twelve days, in addition to the twenty-four days to be remitted, if the provisions of the existing law are allowed to exert their force over the whole period of his imprisonment. This is a material consideration to all convicts holding the relations to the old law indicated above, and is, we have reason to know, felt by them to be so; but, what is still more important, if our construction of the law be correct, it is essential to the maintenance of the honor of the state and the interests of justice, that practical effect be given to the said interpretation.

"The principle of this law is believed by this association to be founded in reason and justice. The policy established by it, we are no less firmly persuaded, is wise in itself, and, supposing it to be permanently incorporated into our system of prison discipline, its operation will be fruitful of good results. The effect of this policy will be to change materially, in some respects, the aspect and condition of prison life. In keeping before the prisoner a permanent inducement to good conduct, it will fortify the resolutions of many a feeble mind, and in others it will counteract the tendency to feelings of despondency, recklessness, and revenge, which their situation is apt to engender, and in which many of them are prone to indulge. In encouraging them to perform their work cheerfully, it will.

so far, have the good effect of converting coerced into voluntary labor, while, as a means of discipline, appealing to the better feelings of all in whom such feelings still have a place, and substituting rewards in place of punishments, and moral instead of mere brute force, we feel confident that, properly administered, its effect will be all that its most ardent advocates can reasonably desire. A law of which all this can be said with truth, and we believe it can be so said of the act under consideration, needs no farther vindication.

"But the interesting inquiry arises here: what has been the actual operation and effect of this law during the twenty months of its existence on our statute books? In answering this question we have the following remarks to submit:

"*First.* Twenty months are hardly a sufficient length of time whereon to found an intelligent, reliable judgment, as to the permanent results of a great innovation upon long established usage, such as that which has been introduced into our penal system by the law in question.

"*Second.* The history of the law and its treatment at the hands of the public authorities, have been such as greatly to obstruct its natural operation, and hinder the good effects which it was designed and (as we believe) adapted to produce. For nine months after its passage, Governor Morgan refused to act upon it at all. This was a severe blow at the start. On its announcement in our state prisons, the resolution was very generally formed by the convicts to deserve and obtain its full benefit. There is reason to believe, so at least we have been assured, that at Sing Sing there were scarcely ten prisoners whose minds were not made up to put forth every effort to secure the desired result. But for those nine weary months, this thing, so seeming fair, proved an utter delusion. Man after man, whose conduct had been irreproachable, was seen discharged without any benefit from the law. It was felt by the prisoners, and many of them loudly declared that they were 'humbugged,' 'tricked,' 'cheated' out of their due and legal reward. That they were wronged out of it, unjustly denied it, must be admitted even by those who are most fastidious in their use of language. What was to have been expected as the result? In the natural course of things, when just and reasonable hopes were disappointed, when this law, so big with promise, was seen to produce nothing, the pendulum swung as far in the opposite direction as it had been drawn in the other; and feelings of satisfaction and encouragement gave way to the contrary sentiments of discontent and despondency. Despair took the place of hope.

"But this was not the only revulsion reserved for these unhappy men. The interpretation put upon the law by the convicts was that which would occur to every man, on its first perusal, viz., that by good behavior for six or more successive months they might earn a commutation of three days per month, and to that extent shorten the term of their imprisonment. When the law, within a year after its enactment, was so amended as to make the maximum deduction from the term of sentence two days instead of three, and especially when the amended law was made practically retroactive in its operation, and only two days were allowed for the period during which three, as they felt and believed, had been earned, a general feeling of disappointment was produced, which gave rise to a sort of chronic dissatisfaction—an impression that, after all, the law was but little better than a delusion and a mockery. In effect, it looked, to convict apprehension at least, very much like trifling with expectations, which the parties themselves had voluntarily raised. How fatal to the normal operation of the law the reaction in such a case must have proved, any reflecting mind can judge. It would not be strange if its effect was disastrous in precisely those cases in which the healthful stimulus of the law was most needed. To many of these men the law is now, perhaps, a dead letter; to some it may possibly be worse, for human feelings are subject to reactions, and unjust disappointments often induce recklessness, and sometimes even drive to desperation. But by a just and generous conduct on the part of the authorities in the future, and especially by a return to the old maximum—perchance, even, if it should be judged expedient, by a still broader application of the principle—these sores may be healed, and the law may yet produce, without stint, all the good fruits, which it is capable of yielding. But,

"*Third.* Despite the serious drawbacks enumerated above, there is abundant evidence that the law has already borne excellent fruit, and that its direct and active tendency is to promote good order, quietness, industry and obedience to prison rules on the part of convicts. To this effect is the concurrent testimony of all the reports made by the special committees appointed to 'visit, inspect and examine' the three great penal institutions established and conducted by state authority. The association unhesitatingly accepts this testimony as decisive of the question—at least until the same is disproved and rebutted by contrary testimony, resting on results developed by future observation and experience. Indeed, upon the evidence before us, we are prepared to second a suggestion made by the committee who inspected Clinton prison, to the effect that, if the time has not come yet, it soon may, when the principle of the commutation law may be judiciously extended.*

"A member of the abovenamed committee, and one of our vice-presidents,—the Hon. John Stanton Gould,—who has since visited the state prison at Columbus, Ohio, in a letter addressed to the corresponding secretary of the association, says: 'I have recently visited the Ohio state prison, at Columbus, and find that the [commutation] law works, as well there as it does in New York. It is thought that no law ever passed by the legislature has been so marked in its influence for good since Ohio has been a state. The excellent working of the law, enabling prisoners to earn the remission of part of their sentence by good conduct, should be commented on [meaning in the annual report] in emphatic terms.'

"That provision of the present commutation law, which exacts the forfeiture of all previously earned commutations for fresh acts of misconduct, ought in the judgment of this association, to be repealed. We consider it unwise to place the time of a convict, once earned, at the mercy of any man.

---

* Since the date of this report, the executive of the state, in his annual message to the legislature, has recommended the same thing. The passage relating to this subject is appended, and is as follows:

"By recent acts of the legislature, convicts can, by good behavior, shorten the terms of their imprisonment twenty-four days in each year. I advise an extension of this system. It should be so graduated that it will give more encouragement to convicts sentenced for long terms. Those who behave well for many years give stronger evidences of reformation than can be shown by those confined for shorter periods. An allowance for good conduct should be made of one month on each of the first two years; of two months on each succeeding year to the fifth year; of three months on each following year to the tenth year; and of four months on each remaining year of the terms of their imprisonment. Under this system, a person sentenced for five years can reduce his term to four years and four months; those for ten years to eight years and one month; those for fifteen years to eleven years and five months." [*Note to Report of the Prison Association.*]

This recommendation appears to have suggested the enactment of *Laws of* 1864, ch. 321; which the commissioners have embodied in section 1018 in the text. [*Note by the commissioners.*]

We would have each man feel that he is striving not for *chances* but for *certainties*. If offenses are committed after time is earned, let them be punished independently, each according to its own desert, and not by forfeiture of time. Let time once earned be held sacred. It will then seem to the convict trebly worth striving for; while the loss of such time, under a contrary rule, would be extremely disheartening, and the possibility of such loss must diminish proportionately the effort to earn it.

"Any possibility of forfeiture, or provision to that effect in the law, we consider highly objectionable, as tainting the whole matter with uncertainty, which it should be a main object, as far as possible, to avoid. Certainty, good faith, a scrupulous respect for every hour of time earned, we regard as of incalculable importance to the beneficial operation of the law.

"And this should be placed, as far as practicable, beyond contingency; more especially in view of the frequent changes in the executive administration of our prisons, which must ever occur under our existing prison system. The confidence felt by convicts in one set of officers may not be extended to their successors, and may not, in point of fact, be deserved by them. We are, therefore, opposed to placing time earned at the mercy of we know not who; and no one we think will seriously advise it, who justly estimates what must be its effect upon the operation of the law. We would have legislation of this sort, whose whole design and operation is to bestow grace upon the fallen, conducted, not in a reluctant and grudging, but a free, generous, whole-souled spirit; that is, in a manner worthy of a great and magnanimous state, and calculated to inspire the respect and confidence, as well as the gratitude, of those whom it is designed to affect."

The commissioners would add, that they fully appreciate the importance of assuring to every convict who complies with the provisions of the law, the full and reliable right to the commutation earned. No fluctuations in policy should frustrate the promise of the statute. They have been held back from suggesting an imperative provision of law, in the place of the section in the text, only by the doubt whether such a provision would not be held to infringe the constitution, as amounting to an attempt by the legislature to exercise the pardoning power.

CHAPTER XVII.

THE CUSTODY, CONDUCT, DISCIPLINE AND EMPLOYMENT OF PRISONERS IN COUNTY JAILS.

Application of this chapter.

§ 1024. The provisions of this chapter relate exclusively to the county jails.

Keepers must receive persons duly committed.

§ 1025. The keepers of the several county jails, must receive and safely keep every person duly committed to their custody; and they must not, without lawful authority, let out of jail, on bail or otherwise, any such person.

Suggested as a substitute for *Laws of* 1847, ch. 460, § 3, which is as follows:

"The keepers of the several county prisons shall receive and safely keep every person duly committed to their custody for safe keeping, examination or trial, or duly sentenced for imprisonment in such prison upon conviction for any contempt or misconduct, or for any criminal offense; and shall not, without lawful authority, let out of prison, on bail or otherwise, any such person.

The commissioners do not intend any change in the law by omitting the clause designating the classes of persons who may be committed. That clause is stricken out as superfluous; since it is the duty of the prison keeper to detain *all* persons duly committed.

For the reason for substituting the phrase "county *jail*," for "county *prisons*," see note to section 809.

§ 1026. All prisoners committed on criminal process and detained for trial, or committed for contempts or upon civil process, and all persons detained as witnesses, must at all times be kept in rooms separate and distinct from those in which convicts are confined. What prisoners must be kept separate.

Suggested as a substitute for *Laws of* 1847, ch. 460, § 4: which contains no provision to protect persons detained as witnesses from being confined with convicts. It is as follows:

"Prisoners committed on criminal process, and detained for trial, and persons committed for contempts, or upon civil process, shall be kept in rooms separate and distinct from those in which persons convicted and under sentence shall be confined; and on no pretense whatever shall prisoners be detained for trial, or persons committed for contempt, or upon civil process, be kept or put in the same room with convicts under sentence."

§ 1027. Male and female prisoners (except husband and wife) must not be kept or put in the same room. Male and female prisoners.

Laws of 1847, ch. 460, § 5.

§ 1028. It is the duty of the keepers of the several county jails to keep the prisoners committed to their charge, so far as practicable, separate and distinct from each other, and to prevent all conversation between such prisoners. Conversation to be prevented.

Laws of 1847, ch. 460, § 6.

§ 1029. Prisoners detained for trial may converse with their counsel, and with such other persons as the keeper, in his discretion, may allow; prisoners under sentence must not be permitted to hold any conversation with any person, except the keeper or the inspectors of state prisons, unless in the presence of a keeper or inspector. Prisoners may converse with counsel, &c.

See *Laws of* 1847, ch. 460, § 7.

§ 1030. All persons confined in county jails are entitled to be provided at the expense of the county, with a sufficient quantity of inferior but wholesome food, and with inferior but comfortable clothing and Prisoners to be provided with food, clothing and bedding.

bedding; and persons detained as witnesses and prisoners detained for trial, or held upon civil process or for contempts, may, at their own expense, and under the direction of the keeper, be supplied with any other proper article of food.

Suggested as a substitute for *Laws of* 1847, ch. 460, § 8; which omits to recognise the right of persons held under civil process, or as witnesses, to be fed at the expense of the county. The section is as follows:

"Prisoners detained for trial and those under sentence, shall be provided with a sufficient quantity of inferior but wholesome food, at the expense of the county; but prisoners detained for trial, may, at their own expense, and under the direction of the keeper, be supplied with any other proper article of food."

The right to be supplied with suitable clothing and bedding, seems also proper to be recognized in connection with the right to be fed.

To be employed at hard labor.

§ 1031. It is the duty of the keeper of each county jail to cause each prisoner under sentence, except such as are under sentence of death, to be constantly employed at hard labor, when practicable, during every day except Sunday, and it is the duty of the inspectors, or if they fail to act, of the keeper of the prison, to prescribe the kind of labor at which the prisoners shall be employed. The keeper must account at least annually, with the board of supervisors of the county for the proceeds of such labor.

See *Laws of* 1847, ch 460, § 9.

Convicts may be employed on highways, streets, &c.

§ 1032. The keeper of each county jail may, with the consent of the supervisors of the county, from time to time cause such of the convicts under his charge as are capable of hard labor, to be employed upon any of the public avenues, highways, streets, or other works, in the county in which such prisoners shall be confined, or in any of the adjoining counties, upon such terms as may be agreed upon between such keeper and the officers or other persons under whose direction such convicts are employed.

Laws of 1847, ch. 460, § 10.

§ 1033. Whenever any convicts are employed under the last section, they must be well chained and secured; and shall be subject to such regulations as the keeper legally charged with their custody shall, from time to time, prescribe.

When so employed to be chained.

Laws of 1847, ch. 460, § 11.

Section 12 of the act of 1847—which declares that: "The provisions contained in the twenty-fourth, twenty-fifth, twenty-sixth and twenty-seventh sections in the second article of the sixth title of the seventh chapter of the third part of the Revised Statutes, shall extend to prisoners confined upon any criminal process, or for a contempt, or under sentence, in like manner as for prisoners confined in civil cases"—is omitted here. These sections relate to the removal of the prisoners in county jails, in certain specified cases, and are substantially embraced by sections 810, 811, 812 and 814 of this Code. The provision of *Laws of* 1847, ch. 280, § 29, modifying section 26 of 2 Rev. Stat., 430, above mentioned, is also presented in section 812.

§ 1034. It is the duty of the keeper of each county jail to provide a bible for each room in the prison, to be kept therein; and he shall, if practicable, cause divine service to be performed for the benefit of the prisoners, at least once each Sunday, provided there is a room in the prison that can be safely used for that purpose.

Keepers must provide a bible for each room.

Laws of 1847, ch. 460, § 13.

Section 14 of the act of 1847—which provides that: "The provisions in relation to insane persons contained in the thirty-second section of the act entitled 'an act to organize the state lunatic asylum and more effectually to provide for the care, maintenance and recovery of the insane,' passed April 7th, 1842, shall be construed to apply to all prisoners in a county jail other than those who are committed for contempt or on civil process"—is omitted here. Provisions for the care of insane convicts are presented in chapter XIX of this title.

§ 1035. The keeper of each county jail must keep a daily record, in a book which must be furnished by the county and remain in the jail as county property, of the commitments and discharges of all prisoners delivered to his charge; which must contain the infor-

Keepers must keep daily record.

mation indicated in the headings to the following table; and may be kept substantially in that form:

186 .

COUNTY JAIL.

Date of entrance.	Name.	Offense.	Term of sentence.	Fine.	Age.	Sex.	Country.	Color.	Social relations.	Parents.	Habits of life.	Cannot read. Read only. Read and write. Well educated. Classically educated.

186 .

RECORD OF COMMITMENTS AND DISCHARGES.

Religious instruction.	How committed.	By whom committed.	State of health when committed.	How discharged.	Date of discharge.	Trade or occupation.	Whether so employed when arrested.	Number of previous convictions.	Value of articles stolen.

The section and form of table given in the text are a substitute for *Laws of* 1847, ch. 460, § 15, as follows:

"It is the duty of the keeper of each county prison to keep a daily record of the commitments and discharges of all prisoners delivered to his charge, which record shall exhibit the date of entrance, name, offense, term of sentence, fine, age, sex, county, color, social relations, parents, habits of life, cannot read, read only, read and write, well educated, classically educated, religious instruction, how committed, by whom committed, state of health when committed, how discharged, trade or occupation, whether so employed when arrested, value of articles stolen."

§ 1036. It is the duty of the keeper of every county jail to present to every court of oyer and terminer, and to every court of sessions held in his county, at the opening of such court, a calendar, stating: Keepers must present a calendar to courts.

1. The name of every prisoner then detained in such jail;

2. The time when such prisoner was committed, and by virtue of what process or precept; and,

3. The cause of the detention of every such prisoner.

See *Laws of* 1847, ch. 460, § 25.

§ 1037. It is the duty of each court, within twenty-four hours after the discharge of any grand jury by any court of oyer and terminer or court of sessions, to cause every person so confined in such prison upon any criminal charge, who shall not have been indicted, to be discharged without bail, unless satisfactory cause is shown to such court for detaining such person in custody, or upon bail, as the case may require, until the meeting of the next grand jury in such county. Persons confined but not indicted, when to be discharged.

Laws of 1847, ch. 460, § 26.

§ 1038. After the court of oyer and terminer has commenced its sittings in any county, no prisoner detained in the common jail of any such county, upon any criminal charge, can be removed therefrom by any writ of habeas corpus, except one issued by Prisoners, when not to be removed.

such court of oyer and terminer, or made returnable before it.

See *Laws of* 1847, ch. 460, § 27. The words "deliverance from imprisonment" should be substituted for "habeas corpus" if the provisions of the *Rep. Code of Civil Pro.* relative to that writ, are enacted.

Prisoners unable to pay fine, how discharged.

§ 1039. Upon satisfactory proof being made to the county court of any county that any person confined in the county jail of such county for non-payment of a fine not exceeding two hundred and fifty dollars, imposed for any crime, and against whom no other cause of detention exists, is, and ever since his conviction has been unable to pay such fine, such court may, in its discretion, order the discharge of such person.

Recommended as a substitute for *Laws of* 1847, ch. 460, § 28, which is as follows:

"When any person shall be confined in any county prison for the non-payment of any fine not exceeding two hundred and fifty dollars, imposed for any criminal offense, and against whom no other cause of detention exists, on satisfactory proof being made to the county court of the county in which such prisoner may be confined, that he is unable, and has been ever since his conviction unable to pay such fine, the court may, in its discretion, order his discharge,"

CHAPTER XVIII.

INSPECTION OF COUNTY JAILS.

§ 1040. It is the duty of the inspectors of state prisons to visit and inspect, separately or collectively, at least once in each year, all the county jails in this state.

Inspectors of state prisons to inspect county jails.

Section 17 of the act of 1847 (ch. 460), provided that it should be the duty of the inspectors to inspect "*all the jails or other county prisons, penitentiaries and houses of detention* in this state." By *Laws of* 1849, ch, 331, § 1, so much of the act of 1847 as required the inspectors of state prisons to visit and examine *county jails*, was repealed. This left the provisions relative to inspection of other inferior prisons, in force. No new provision for the official inspection of county jails was substituted by the repealing act; though the charter of the Prison Association of New York makes it the duty of the Association to visit, inspect and examine all the prisons in the state, and annually to report their state and condition and all such other things in regard to them, as may enable the Legislature to perfect their government and discipline. In the performance of this duty, the Association has organized a system of visitation of the county jails which nearly, though not quite, secures the visit of a committee of the Association to each county jail, once in each year.

The commissioners have, however, restated in the text the provisions of the act of 1847, requiring an inspection of county jails by the inspectors of state prisons, notwithstanding its repeal in 1849. This is done for the purpose of calling the attention of the Legislature to the question whether some system of inspection of county jails by public officers of the state, is not desirable, in addition to that conducted by the Prison Association. The salaries of inspectors should doubtless be increased if this duty is reimposed upon them. The commissioners also suggest the question whether *two* annual visits are not desirable, one in summer and one in winter; as a management suitable for one season might be improper at another; and whether there should not be an official inspection of poor houses and insane, inebriate and idiot asylums, whether public or private.

§ 1041. For the purpose of carrying into effect the provisions of the last section, the inspectors must, as soon as practicable, after entering upon their official duties, designate and set apart to each of their number the counties to be so visited by them, respectively, during the current year, for the purpose of such inspection; and at the same time adopt such plan and

Counties to be divided among the inspectors.

regulations, not inconsistent with the laws of this state, as they deem expedient and necessary to carry into effect a uniform system for the government and regulation of all the county jails of this state, and the modification and improvement of the structure of such jails, with a view to such uniformity.

Laws of 1847, ch. 460, § 18.

Plan to be submitted to governor, comptroller and attorney-general.

§ 1042. Such plan and regulations, when agreed upon and adopted by the inspectors, shall be by them immediately submitted to the governor, comptroller and attorney-general for their approval, but shall subsequently be subject to such modifications as the inspectors may deem expedient and proper. A copy of such plan and any modifications shall be furnished to the county judge and sheriff of each county, and to the keepers of each of the county jails of this state, whose duty it shall be to observe and carry the same into effect.

Laws of 1847, ch. 460, § 19.

Sheriff and keepers to admit inspectors into every part, &c.

§ 1043. It is the duty of the sheriff and keeper of each of the jails to admit the inspectors, or any one of them, into every part of such jail; to exhibit to them, on demand, all the books, papers, documents and accounts pertaining to such jail, or to the detention of persons confined therein; and to render them every other facility in their power to enable them to discharge the duties above prescribed, and to enable them to obtain any necessary information. And the inspectors are empowered to examine on oath, to be administered by any one of them, any of the keepers or officers of such jail, and any person not under sentence confined therein, and to converse with any of the prisoners so confined, without the presence of the keeper thereof, or any of them.

Laws of 1847, ch. 460, § 20.

Inspector must make report of

§ 1044. Such inspector or inspectors, after a careful and thorough examination and inspection of each jail or other prison, must immediately make a detailed report of the same, stating the condition of the same at the time of such inspection, the number of persons confined therein for the year ending at the date of such report, the causes of such confinement, the manner in which convicts confined in such jail or prison during that period have been employed, the number of persons usually confined together in one room, the distinction, if any, usually observed in the treatment of persons therein confined, the evils and abuses, if any, found to exist, and particularly whether any of the rules and regulations prescribed by the inspectors or any of the provisions of this title have been violated, so far as the information required in this section can be obtained from the records of said jail or prison or otherwise. his examination.

Laws of 1847, ch. 460, § 21.

§ 1045. Such inspector or inspectors must note and include in such report, or append thereto, any defect or defects he or they may deem to exist in the structure and arrangements of such jail, and suggest such improvements in the same as he may deem to be necessary to carry into successful operation and to ensure uniformity in the system by them adopted; and he or they shall then immediately leave with the county judge of such county a duplicate copy of such report and suggestion. Such judge must file the same with the clerk of the county, and cause a copy thereof, together with, if he approves the same, or any part thereof, such approval indorsed thereon, to be delivered to the clerk of the board of supervisors of the county. Must report defects in the jail.

See *Laws of* 1847, ch. 460, § 22.

§ 1046. The clerk of the board of supervisors must present such report and suggestions (with any approval indorsed thereon by the county judge) to the board of supervisors at their next meeting, who are authorized and required to cause such alterations Alterations in plans of county jails, how to be made.

to be made in the plan and construction of the jail of such county, and such additional rooms to be constructed as shall have been so suggested and approved by the county judge, and as shall be necessary to remedy such deficiencies, and to levy, and cause the expenses so to be incurred to be assessed upon the county as other county expenses are levied and assessed. And in all cases where there exists any deficiency in room or arrangement of apartments in any county jail which prevents such classification of prisoners as is prescribed in section 809, it is the duty of the supervisors to cause such deficiency to be supplied without unnecessary delay.

Laws of 1847, ch. 460, § 23, as amended, *Laws of* 1849, ch. 331, § 2.

Annual report to be made to legislature.

§ 1047. The inspectors must annually, on or before the fifteenth day of January in each year, make an abstract report of their inspections of such county jails and prisons, to the legislature, in which report shall be included, in tabular form, a summary of the record required by section 1035 to be kept by the keepers of such county jails.

Laws of 1847, ch. 460, § 24.

CHAPTER XIX.

CUSTODY OF INSANE PRISONERS.

§ 1048. Whenever the physician of either state prison has certified to the board of inspectors or to the inspector in charge of such prison that any convict confined therein is insane, it is the duty of such board or inspector in charge, to make, immediately, a full examination into the condition of such convict, and if satisfied that he is insane, such board, or inspector in charge, may order the warden of such prison, forthwith to convey such convict to the state lunatic asylum for insane convicts, and to deliver him to the superintendent thereof.

Inspectors may order removal of insane convicts from state prisons.

Taken from *Laws of* 1858, ch. 130, § 8, as amended *Laws of* 1863, ch. 139, § 1.

The provisions of this chapter, except the last section, are all taken from this act, which is entitled "An act to organize the State Lunatic Asylum for Insane Convicts." The act provides for the custody of all persons, who, having been sent to state prison under sentence, are there discovered to be insane. Two other classes exist. *First.* Persons put upon trial for crime, but acquitted on the ground of insanity. Provision is made for these by section 19 of this Code. *Second.* Persons who are found insane while under confinement in a county jail. These cases are embraced by section 1058. And an additional provision is made in favor of persons who were insane when their offense was committed, but whose insanity was not discovered at their trial, by section 892.

In so far as the act of 1858 provides for the organization and management of the state lunatic asylum for insane convicts, considered as an independent institution (though situated upon the Auburn prison grounds), it is left unaffected by this Code.

The following provisions of former laws, upon the subject of the disposition to be made of insane convicts, are considered to be superseded by the act of 1858, as amended.

"Section ninety-six of the act for the better regulation of the county and state prisons of the state, and consolidating and amending the existing laws in relation thereto, passed December fourteenth, eighteen hundred and forty-seven, is hereby amended so as to read as follows: The inspectors of the prisons of this state are hereby authorized and required, without delay, to make the necessary and suitable provisions in one of the state prisons of this state, and the removal to such place for safe keeping and proper care, all the insane convicts now in the state lunatic asylum at Utica, and whenever the physician of a state prison shall duly report to the warden of such prison that any convict confined therein, is so far insane as to render him dangerous, or an improper subject of prison discipline, it shall be the duty of said warden to remove such convict to the place so provided, and the officers having charge of such place shall receive such convict and retain him there, at the expense of the state, so long as he or she shall continue insane."

Laws of 1855, ch. 456, § 1.

"The words 'lunatic asylum,' 'state lunatic asylum,' or 'asylum at Utica,' whenever the same occur in the act hereby amended, shall be construed to apply to the place for safe keeping and proper care of insane convicts, provided for in the first section of this act."

Ibid., § 2.

"If such insane person shall recover from his insanity before the expiration of the term for which he was sentenced, the officer having the principal charge of the asylum shall give notice of such recovery to the agent of the prison from which such convict was sent, as soon as in his judgment such convict may be safely removed; and it shall then be the duty of the agent to cause the convict to be returned to such prison."

Laws of 1847, ch. 460, § 97.

"The ninety-ninth section of the aforesaid act—*Laws of* 1847, ch. 460—is hereby repealed, and the following substituted therefor:

"'§ 99. When any convict sent to the state lunatic asylum under and by virtue of the provisions of this act, shall have remained in the asylum until the term of his sentence has expired, the managers of said asylum may cause such insane convict to be removed at the expense of the state from the asylum to the county of which he is a resident, to be placed under the care and charge of the superintendents of the poor of such county, in case the superintendent of the asylum shall certify that such insane convict will not be benefited by longer remaining in the asylum, and that he can probably be made comfortable in the county poor house. The managers of said asylum shall be authorized to give, at the expense of the state, to any patient sent to the asylum under the provisions of this act, and who shall, after the expiration of the term of his sentence, be discharged from the asylum recovered, such sum, not exceeding ten dollars, as will defray his necessary traveling expenses from the asylum to the county in which he last resided.'"

Laws of 1848, ch. 294, § 2.

"So much of chapter four hundred and fifty-six, of the Laws of eighteen hundred and fifty-five, entitled 'An act to provide for insane criminals,' as requires that female insane convicts shall be removed from the state lunatic asylums, to the place provided for in said act, is hereby repealed, and the female insane convicts shall continue to be sent to the state lunatic asylums as heretofore.' *Laws of* 1857, ch. 144, § 3.

"The preceding six sections shall all be construed to apply to the convicts in the female convict prison at Sing Sing." *Laws of* 1847, ch. 460, § 100.

"The expense of removing insane convicts to the lunatic asylum, and returning them to the prison from which they were sent, shall be paid by the agent of said prison, out of any funds belonging to the prison, in his hands." *Ibid.*, § 101.

§ 1049. The superintendent of the asylum must receive such convict into the asylum, and retain him there until he is legally discharged.

Superintendent of asylum must receive them.

Taken from *Laws of* 1858, ch. 130, § 8, as amended *Laws of* 1863, ch. 139, § 1.

§ 1050. Whenever any convict placed in the state lunatic asylum for insane convicts, under the provisions of this chapter, shall continue to be insane at the expiration of the term for which he was sentenced, the board of inspectors, upon the superintendent's certificate that he is harmless and will probably continue so, and that he is not likely to be improved by further treatment in the asylum, or upon a like certificate that he is manifestly incurable and can probably be rendered comfortable at the county alms house, may cause such insane convict to be removed at the expense of the state, from the asylum to the county wherein he was convicted, or to the county of his former residence, and delivered to and placed under the care of the persons charged with the support of the poor of such county.

When insane convict may be removed to the county of his residence.

Taken from *Laws of* 1858, ch. 130, § 9, as amended *Laws of* 1863, ch. 139, § 2.

§ 1051. The persons charged with the support of the poor of such county, must receive such insane convict under their charge.

Poor officers must receive such convict.

Taken from *Ibid.*

When insane convict may be delivered to relatives.

§ 1052. The board of inspectors may also deliver any convict whose sentence has expired, and who is still insane, to his relatives or friends, who will undertake, with good sureties to be approved by the superintendent of the state lunatic asylum for insane convicts, for his peaceful behavior, safe custody and comfortable maintenance without further public charge.

Taken from *Ibid.*

Convicts not to be retained in asylum after expiration of sentence.

§ 1053. No convict shall be retained in the asylum after the expiration of his sentence to the state prison, unless by the order of the county judge of the county in which the asylum is situated.

Taken from *Ibid.*

Except upon examination and order by county judge.

§ 1054. In case any convict cannot be removed from the asylum upon the expiration of his term of sentence under the preceding sections, it is the duty of the county judge, upon the application of the said superintendent, to proceed to investigate the question of the insanity of such convict, and cause two respectable physicians to be designated by him to examine the convict; and upon their evidence under oath, and upon such other testimony as he shall require, he shall decide the case as to his insanity, and if he is satisfied that such convict is insane, he shall make an order that such convict shall be retained in the asylum until he is recovered of his insanity, or is otherwise discharged according to law. The fees of such physicians and witnesses shall be audited by the state prison inspector in charge, and shall be a charge against the state, to be paid by the comptroller out of the general fund; but such fees shall not in any one case exceed the sum of ten dollars.

Taken from *Ibid.*

Convicts when restored to reason must be transferred to Auburn prison.

§ 1055. Whenever any convict placed in the asylum under the provisions of this chapter, has become restored to reason, and the medical superintendent of the asylum shall so certify in writing, such convict shall be forthwith transferred to the Auburn state prison; and the warden of that prison must receive such convict into the prison, and must in all respects treat such convict as if he had been originally sentenced to imprisonment in that prison, though he may have been conveyed to the asylum from either of the other prisons.

Founded on *Laws of* 1858, ch. 130, § 10.

§ 1056. Whenever the board of inspectors or an inspector shall order any convict to be transferred to the asylum, the warden of the prison from which such convict is transferred, must cause a correct copy of the original certificate of conviction of such convict to be filed in his office, and deliver the original certificate to the superintendent of the asylum; and when any such convict shall be transferred to the Auburn prison from such asylum, as hereinbefore provided, the superintendent must deliver to the warden of that prison such original certificate, which shall be filed in the clerk's office in that prison. Transfer of certificate.

Founded on *Ibid.*, § 11.

§ 1057. Every physician who attends any meeting of the board of inspectors, or who makes any examination of any convict, as provided by this chapter, shall be paid his actual and reasonable traveling expenses in going to and returning from such meeting or examination, on the certificate of the president of the board of inspectors, that he has attended such meeting or examination. Pay of physicians.

Founded on *Ibid.*, § 12.

§ 1058. Whenever any prisoner confined in a county jail, other than such as are committed for contempt or upon civil process, appears to be insane, the county judge of the county shall institute a careful investigation, shall call two respectable physicians and other credible witnesses, and invite the district Inquiry into insanity of prisoners in county jails.

attorney to aid in the examination; and may, if he deem it necessary, call a jury; and for the purposes of such examination such judge is fully empowered to compel the attendance of witnesses and jurors. If it be satisfactorily proved that such prisoner is insane, such judge may discharge him from imprisonment and order him to be removed to the state lunatic asylum, to remain until restored to his right mind; and then, if such judge shall have so directed, the superintendent shall give notice of such restoration to such judge, and the county clerk and district attorney of the county, so that such prisoner may, within sixty days thereafter, be remanded to prison, and criminal proceedings be resumed, or otherwise discharged; or if the period of his imprisonment has expired, he shall be discharged. The expense of the removal and support of any prisoner, under this section, shall be defrayed by the county in which the jail from which he is removed is situated.

See *Laws of* 1842, ch. 135, § 32; and *Laws of* 1847, ch. 460, § 14.

CHAPTER XX.

GENERAL PROVISIONS APPLICABLE EQUALLY TO STATE PRISONS AND COUNTY JAILS.

§ 1059. The officers and persons employed in every county jail or state prison shall be exempted during their continuance in office, from serving on juries and from militia duty. Exemption of officers, &c., from militia and jury duty.

Laws of 1847, ch. 460, § 148. The exemptions from military duty granted in this and several other sections of the prison laws already cited, are retained in this Code, notwithstanding they are not recognized in the act for the enrollment of the militia (*Laws of* 1862, ch. 477, as amended *Laws of* 1863, ch. 425), as it is thought probable the omission of them in the militia law may have been inadvertent.

§ 1060. No person confined in any prison can be punished by whipping. The following punishments and no others may be inflicted upon convicts for incorrigible disobedience to the rules of the prison or jail, or for wanton destruction of or injury to clothing, bedding or other property within the jail: What punishments are allowed.

1. Confinement by chains or shackles;

2. Privation of food or bedding;

3. Confinement in solitary cells;

4. In a state prison, showering; but only in the presence and under the direction of the physician of the prison.

As to the first clause, see *Laws of* 1847, ch. 460, § 149. The word "person" is substituted for "female."

§ 1061. No spirituous or fermented liquors shall, on any pretense whatever, be sold within any county jail or state prison, nor shall any kind of spirituous or fermented liquor be brought into any county jail for the use of any convict confined therein, without a written permit, signed by the physician to such prison, specifying the quantity and quality of the liquor which may be furnished to any convict, the name of the prisoner for whom, and the time when the same may be furnished, which permit shall be delivered to and kept by the keeper of the prison. But this section shall not prevent the purchase of supplies of such liquor for the ordinary hospital supply of the state prisons. Spirituous and fermented liquors not to be sold or brought into prison.

See *Laws of* 1847, ch. 460, § 152.

When permits may be granted.

§ 1062. No permit shall be granted unless it shall satisfactorily appear to such physician that the liquor allowed to be furnished is necessary for the health of the prisoner for whose use it is permitted, which shall be stated in such permit.

Laws of 1847, ch. 460, § 153. Section 154 of that act is omitted for the reason that its provisions are substantially embraced in section 208 of this Code, except that portion which imposes a forfeiture of office. That subject may well be left to the operation of the power of removal of the various officers, for official misconduct.

Persons authorized to visit county and state prisons.

§ 1063. The following persons are authorized to visit at pleasure all county jails and state prisons: the governor and all persons authorized by him in writing, the lieutenant-governor, secretary of state, comptroller and attorney-general, members of the legislature, judges of the court of appeals, supreme court and county judges, district attorneys, the officers and committees of the New York prison association, and every minister of the gospel having charge of a congregation in the town wherein any such prison is situated. No other person not otherwise authorized by law shall be permitted to enter the rooms of a county jail in which convicts are confined, unless under such regulations as the sheriff of the county shall prescribe, nor to enter a state prison except under such regulations as the inspectors shall prescribe. But no fees shall be charged for any admission.

See *Laws of* 1847, ch. 460, § 159.

Convicts may be called as witnesses in certain trials.

§ 1064. Whenever any convict confined in any county jail or state prison shall be considered an important witness in behalf of the people of this state, upon any criminal prosecution against any other convict, by the district attorney conducting the same, it shall be the duty of any officer authorized by law to allow writs of habeas corpus, upon the affidavit of such district attorney, to grant a habeas corpus for the purpose of bringing such prisoner before the proper court to testify upon such prosecution.

Laws of 1847, ch. 460, § 150. The words "writ of deliverance from imprisonment" should probably be substituted for "habeas corpus" in this and following sections, if the provisions of the Code of Civil Procedure are to be enacted; though the name, writ of deliverance from imprisonment, seems inappropriate where the proceeding has no purpose to review the imprisonment from which the person brought up is taken.

§ 1065. Such convict may be examined on such trial, and shall be considered a competent witness against any fellow prisoner, for any offense actually committed whilst in prison, and whilst the witness so offered shall have been confined in the prison in which such offense shall have been committed. And may testify.

Laws of 1847, ch. 460, § 151.

§ 1066. Whenever it shall appear to the court in which an indictment is pending and to be tried against any person for any offense committed by him while imprisoned in any county jail, or any one of the state prisons, on the person of any other individual confined in such jail or state prison, that any other person confined in any county jail, or in any of the state prisons, is an important witness in behalf of the person so indicted, such court is hereby authorized to grant a writ of habeas corpus for the purpose of bringing such prisoner before such court to testify, upon the trial of such indictment, in behalf of the party making the application. Prisoners may be brought before courts as witnesses.

Laws of 1847, ch. 460, § 155.

§ 1067. Every person, when brought up on such writ, may be examined as a witness on such trial, and shall be competent to testify thereon in behalf of the defendant or the people, notwithstanding his conviction and imprisonment. And may testify.

Laws of 1847, ch. 460, § 156. The amendment designated to this section by *Laws of* 1860, ch. 399, § 14, is obviously intended for section 146, instead of 156; and is therefore disregarded here. See note to section 818.

Prisoners indicted may be brought before court for trial.

§ 1068. The court in which any indictment is pending against any person imprisoned on conviction of a crime in any county jail or state prison, for an offense committed during such imprisonment, is hereby authorized to issue a writ of habeas corpus for the purpose of bringing the individual so indicted before the court, for arraignment or trial on such indictment.

Laws of 1847, ch. 460, § 170.

In cases of indictment for felony.

§ 1069. The court in which any indictment is pending for a felony, against any person imprisoned on conviction of a crime in any county jail or state prison, is hereby authorized to issue a writ of habeas corpus for the purpose of bringing the individual so indicted before such court for arraignment or trial on such indictment.

Laws of 1847, ch. 460, § 158.

Repeal of former laws.

§ 1070. From the time at which this Code shall take effect as a law, the following acts, except as to such provisions therein as are temporary in their nature, and have not been wholly executed, are repealed, in so far as they apply to state prisons and county jails, and no farther. But such repeal shall not revive any act or part of any act repealed by either of such laws.

1. An act for the better regulation of the county and state prisons of the state, and consolidating and amending the existing laws in relation thereto. Passed December 14, 1847.

Laws of 1847, ch. 460.

2. An act in relation to the transportation of convicts to the state prisons and houses of refuge. Passed December 15, 1847.

Laws of 1847, ch. 497.

3. An act to amend the act for the better regulation of the county and state prisons of this state. Passed April 12, 1848.

Laws of 1848, ch. 294.

4. An act fixing the fees of sheriffs for transporting convicts to the state prisons. Passed March 22, 1849.

Laws of 1849, ch. 123.

5. An act in relation to the removal of convicts from one state prison to another. Passed March 26, 1849.

Laws of 1849, ch. 132.

6. An act authorizing the inspectors of state prisons to administer oaths and take affidavits in certain cases. Passed March 26, 1849.

Laws of 1849, ch. 133.

7. An act in relation to Sing Sing prison. Passed March 27, 1849.

Laws of 1849, ch. 141.

8. An act to amend "an act for the better regulation of the county and state prisons of the state, and consolidating and amending the existing laws in relation thereto." Passed April 14, 1849.

Laws of 1849, ch. 331.

9. Section two of an act in relation to juvenile delinquents. Passed February 26, 1850.

Laws of 1850, ch. 21.

10. An act to amend the Revised Statutes in relation to agents of state prisons. Passed March 13, 1854.

Laws of 1854, ch. 58.

11. An act to amend several acts in relation to state prisons, and making appropriations for the Clinton, Auburn and Sing Sing prisons. Passed April 15, 1854.

Laws of 1854, ch. 240.

12. An act to authorize the agent and warden of Sing Sing prison to let by contract the labor and services of convicts in that prison, to the business of quarrying, splitting, sawing and removing stone, for a term of years. Passed April 12, 1855.

Laws of 1855, ch. 334.

13. An act to provide for insane criminals. Passed April 13, 1855.

Laws of 1855, ch. 456.

14. An act to amend the several acts in relation to state prisons. Passed April 19, 1855.

Laws of 1855, ch. 552.

15. An act to amend the several acts in relation to state prisons. Passed March 10, 1857.

Laws of 1857, ch. 94.

16. An act appropriating money for making provisions for insane convicts. Passed March 20, 1857.

Laws of 1857, ch. 144.

17. Sections ten, eleven and twelve of an act to organize the state lunatic asylum for insane convicts. Passed April 8, 1858.

Laws of 1858, ch. 130.

18. An act authorizing the reports of the male and female departments of state prisons to be made separately. Passed April 12, 1860.

Laws of 1860, ch. 283.

19. An act to amend the several acts in relation to state prisons. Passed April 14, 1860.

Laws of 1860, ch. 399.

20. An act to increase the compensation of assistant matrons of the Sing Sing female prison. Passed April 16, 1860.

Laws of 1860, ch. 458.

21. An act to increase the duties and compensation of the physicians respectively at the Auburn, Sing Sing and Clinton prisons. Passed April 21, 1862.

Laws of 1862, ch. 403.

22. An act to alter the term for which criminals may be sentenced to state prison, and to provide for their earning a commutation of sentence and an increase of the amount to be paid them on their discharge. Passed April 22, 1862.

Laws of 1862, ch. 417.

23. An act to amend the act to organize the state lunatic asylum for insane convicts, passed April 8, 1858. Passed April 17, 1863.

Laws of 1863, ch. 139.

24. An act to amend section first of chapter four hundred and seventeen of the Laws of 1862.

Laws of 1863, ch. 415.

25. An act in relation to contracts and labor at the state prisons of the state. Passed May 5, 1863.

Laws of 1863, ch. 465.

26. An act in relation to the compensation of the several officers of state prisons. Passed April 23, 1864.

Laws of 1864, ch. 300.

27. An act to amend section second of chapter four hundred and fifteen of the Laws of 1863. Passed April 23, 1864.

Laws of 1864, ch. 321.

The provisions of the statutes in force prior to December, 1847, were embraced in the general act, *Laws of* 1847, ch. 460; and the former statutes themselves repealed by section 160 of that act. That section is as follows:

"This act shall take effect on the first day of January, one thousand eight hundred and forty-eight, and from that time the acts and parts of acts hereinafter enumerated, except such provisions therein as are temporary in their nature, and have not yet been fully executed, shall be and are hereby repealed: the whole of chapter third in the fourth part of the Revised Statutes; 'an act concerning convicts under the age of seventeen years,' passed April 16, 1830; 'an act relative to the state prisons,' passed April 20, 1830; 'an act for the erection of state prison buildings for female convicts,' passed April 20, 1835; 'an act in relation to the state prisons,' passed May 11, 1835; 'an act to authorize the formation of a militia company for the protection of the Mount Pleasant state prison,' passed April 24, 1835; 'an act in relation to Geneva college,' passed April 20, 1836; 'an act relative to state prisons,' passed April 23, 1836; an act relative to the state prisons of the state of New York,' passed March 20, 1837; 'an act in relation to state prisons,' passed April 25, 1832; 'an act for the better regulation of the state prisons at Auburn and Mount Pleasant,' passed May 4, 1840; 'an act concerning the state prison at Mount Pleasant," passed March 8, 1832; 'an act in relation to the state prisons,' passed May 20, 1841; 'an act supplementary to an act entitled 'an act to authorize the formation of the militia company for the protection of the Mount Pleasant state prison,' passed April 24, 1835,' passed April 7, 1842; 'an act in relation to convict labor in the state prisons,' passed April 9, 1842; 'an act in relation to state prisons,' passed May 1, 1844; 'an act in relation to the trial of convicts in county and state prisons,' passed January 31, 1846; 'an act to amend an act entitled 'an act in relation to the trial of convicts in county and state prisons,' passed February 3, 1847; the first six sections and the eleventh section of an act entitled 'an act to amend an act in relation to state prisons,' passed April 16, 1845; the second section of an act entitled 'an act authorizing the establishment of a medical faculty in the University of the city of New York,' passed February 11, 1837; the fourth section of chapter eighty-six in the laws of the first session of 1847, and the third, fourth and fifth sections of an act entitled 'an act making an appropriation for the relief of the Mount Pleasant state prison,' and for other purposes, passed May 13, 1846; and from the same time all other acts and parts of acts that are inconsistent with the provisions of this law or that are embraced therein, shall be and are hereby repealed."

Time when Code takes effect.

§ 1071. This Code shall take effect on the day of 186 .

APPENDIX.

APPENDIX A.

A

BRIEF ACCOUNT

OF THE

PRINCIPAL PENAL CODES

OF

CONTINENTAL EUROPE.

The statements of this article are, for the most part, drawn from an official report upon the subject, made in 1853, by H. S. Sanford, formerly chargé d'affairs of the U. S., at Paris, to the President of the United States. They are believed to be substantially accurate down to the date of that report; but the time at the disposal of the commissioners has not admitted of a close inquiry for modifications which may have been introduced since that time in the penal law of the countries to which reference is made.

It should be added that in the present article no mention is made of Codes, or parts of Codes, which relate to matters of Procedure.

PENAL CODE OF FRANCE. (*Code Pénal.*)

The earliest systematic penal law in France was the ordinance of 1539. It was almost wholly occupied with regulations of procedure, and the forms introduced by it were arbitrary and barbarous. In 1670, Louis XIV published an ordinance which mitigated the severity of that of 1539, and increased the independence of the criminal courts. The criminal law continued, as thus established, until the revolution of 1789.

One of the principal reforms wrought by that revolution was in penal legislation. A new Code embracing important principles of criminal law, and not merely regulations of procedure, was promulgated in 1791. This formed the basis of a Code adopted, after long discussion and deliberation, under the government of Napoleon I, and which took effect in 1811. It continued in force, with few changes, until 1832, when a new Code was published, by the government of Louis Philippe. The alterations were, however, but limited; the principal object of the new Code being to assuage the severity of some punishments; to abolish certain others, *e. g.*, the pillory, which were considered inconsistent with the spirit of the times; to reduce other penalties, *e. g.*, banishment, to narrow limits; and, lastly, to mitigate the surveillance of the police. An additional mitigation was introduced in 1835, by the adoption of the rule by which the jury may find a verdict of guilty under "extenuating circumstances;" which qualification of the verdict entitles the accused to a mitigation of punishment.

The *Code Pénal* thus dates from 1832; but it is substantially founded upon that of 1791. It is divided into four books, to which is prefixed a short introduction. The first book treats of punishments and their consequences; the second, of persons who are punishable, excusable, or responsible for crimes or misdemeanors; the third, of crimes and misdemeanors themselves, and their punishments; the fourth, of police infractions and their punishments.

All prohibited actions are divided into: *Contraventions*, *Délits*, or misdemeanors, and *Crimes*. These grades of offense are not defined, but are classified according to their degrees of punishment. Contraventions, which are lowest in the scale, and which come within the jurisdiction of the *Tribunal de Police*, are punishable by a fine not exceeding fifteen francs, or imprisonment not exceeding five days. Misdemeanors are those offenses made punishable with upwards of fifteen francs fine, or five days imprisonment; they fall within the jurisdiction of the *Tribunal Correctionnel*. The last and highest grade, *crime*, is judged by the *Cour d'Assizes*, and is subject to an "afflictive" or "infamous" punishment.

This division of offenses forms the basis of the jurisdiction of the French tribunals. They are of three grades. A single officer, either a justice of the peace (*Juge de paix*) or mayor (*Maire*), is judge of the *Tribunal de Police*. The *Tribunal Correctionnel*, which passes judgment upon misdemeanors, is composed of three members of the tribunal judging in first instance, (*Tribunal de Première instance*,) which is also the tribunal for civil cases of the first category. The *Cour d' Assizes*, which has the jurisdiction of crimes, is composed of three members of the Court of Appeal (*Cour d'Appel*), and has a jury.

Appeal from the decision of the *Tribunal Correctionnel* can be made to the correctional chamber of the Court of Appeal. Persons condemned for *contraventions* may appeal to the *Tribunal Correctionnel;*

but no appeal is allowed for a punishment of less than three francs. There is no appeal from a sentence of the *Cour d'Assizes;* but in case of a formal or material violation of the law, recourse can be had to the court of cassation; and a new trial must follow before another Court of Assizes.

To complete the description of the organization of the tribunals of France, and the connection of its judicial hierarchy with the administrative division of its territory, it may be proper here to remark, that France is divided into eighty-six departments, each department being governed by a Prefect with a council, and subdivided, according to the size of the department, into *arrondissements*, governed by Sub-Prefects. The *arrondissements* are divided in turn into *cantons*, which are subdivided into *communes*.

Each canton has a *Juge de paix;* and, consequently, a *Tribunal de police*. Each *arrondissement* has a Court of First Instance (*Tribunal de Première Instance*) divided into civil and correctional chambers. Each department has a *Cour d'Assizes* composed of members of the *Cour d'Appel.*

At the head of all is the *Cour de Cassation*, the seat of which is at Paris. This consists of three chambers, of which two are for civil affairs, and the third for criminal cases.

There is a public prosecutor connected with every court. At the police court he is the commissary of police; at the Tribunal of first instance he is the "*Procureur Imperial;*" at the court of appeal he is the "*Procureur Général.*" The chief of the whole body of prosecutors is the *Procureur Général* of the Court of Cassation.

The following is an analysis of the *Code Pénal:*

BOOK I: PUNISHMENTS AND THEIR CONSEQUENCES.

The *Code Pénal* differs from most existing codes, in commencing with the punishment, instead of the description of offenses. Instead of definitions of offenses, their nature is indicated by the punishments which follow them.

Punishments of CRIMES are either "afflictive and infamous," or simply "infamous." Punishments of MISDEMEANORS are "afflictive," without being degrading. There are also certain punishments which are common to both crimes and misdemeanors.

A defect in the system is, that the infamy results, not from the intrinsic nature of the crime, but from the accidental nature of the punishment.

The following are the punishments prescribed, for CRIMES:

Capital punishment. The crimes punishable with death are:

High treason.

Exciting to civil war.

Seducing the troops from their duty.

Usurpation of any of the rights of the executive.

Conspiracy of public functionaries against the internal safety of the state.

Blows or wounds inflicted on a public agent (with intent to kill) when he is in the performance of his duties.

Murder; Parricide; and Infanticide.

Sequestration of any person, accompanied by physical torture.

Perjury or bribery of witnesses, when it results in a sentence of death.

Arson, when it consists in burning an inhabited or habitable building.

The jury may declare the existence of extenuating circumstances, in which case the punishment is commuted.

The mode of capital punishment is decapitation. In case of parricide, the punishment is aggravated by the criminal being compelled to walk barefooted to the scaffold, clothed only in a shirt, with a black veil over his head, and being exposed on the scaffold while the sentence of condemnation is read.

The execution is public, and takes place in one of the public squares.

The family of a criminal who has been condemned to death can claim his body after execution, but upon the express condition that it be buried without ceremony.

Imprisonment and hard labor for life. The crimes subject to this punishment are:

Counterfeiting gold or silver coin.

Passing the same.

Counterfeiting the seal of the state, bank bills, or state bonds with the government stamp.

Counterfeiting on the part of a public officer in the exercise of his functions, whether by false signatures, or by alteration of acts, writings, or signatures, or by substituting the names of persons in public documents (whether by additions or interpolations), after such documents have been completed; or by altering or interlining public records in any way.

The fraudulent distortion of the substance or details of any official paper on the part of the functionary who draws it up, whether the fraud consists in writing agreements other than those which have been dictated to him by the parties, or in stating as true facts, which are false, or in falsely certifying as to facts agreed upon by the parties to the instrument.

The commission of violence, resulting in death, against a public agent or functionary, while in the performance of his duties.

The furnishing of arms by a prison officer to a prisoner to assist him in his escape.

Homicide, when neither preceded, accompanied, nor followed by another crime; and also when it had for its object either to prepare, facilitate, or commit a misdemeanor, or to assure the safety of the authors or accomplices in a misdemeanor.*

Premeditated corporeal injury, resulting in immediate death, or fatal wounds, when this injury is inflicted upon a legitimate or illegitimate father or mother, or upon other legitimate ascendants, and when the injury, if committed by another, would be punished with hard labor for a term of years.

Violation of a child under fifteen years of age, accompanied by personal injury, and when the guilty person has a certain authority over the child, whether that of parent, teacher, priest, or public functionary, and when the criminal has been aided by one or more persons.

The detaining or sequestration of a person against his will for more than a month.

The exposure and abandoning of a child, when death follows such exposure.

False witness against any one accused of crime, when followed by sentence to hard labor for life—in which case, the false witness is subjected to the same punishment.

Bribery of witnesses is a similar case, and is followed by similar results.

Robbery, attended by the following circumstances: if committed in the night; if committed by two or more persons; if the criminal or either of his accomplices was armed, secretly or openly; if committed in an inhabited house, apartment, chamber, lodging, or any place serving for a habitation, or any outhouses belonging thereto, by means of false keys, or scaling the walls, or the use of any external violence; when the criminal takes the title of a public functionary, or of any civil or military authority; when committed by corporeal violence, or threat of arms; and when the criminal inflicts personal wounds, or leaves marks of contusion.

Fraudulent bankruptcy by exchange agents and brokers.

Arson committed under certain circumstances.

Transportation has been employed as a punishment for political offenders; but only to a limited extent.

Imprisonment and hard labor for a term of years. This punishment is very common. The duration of it is not less than five, nor more than twenty years. It is applied to the following offenses:

Counterfeiting or altering the copper coins of French or foreign currency, or passing or assisting in the circulation of counterfeit copper coin.

---

* In this last case as in the one preceding, however, the punishment may be death.

Counterfeiting the common stamp of the state, or the gold and silver stamp, or the timber mark.

The forgery of legal documents, or of commercial or banking paper, whether by counterfeiting or altering the writing or signature, or by the writing of false articles of contract, or false provisions to legal documents, or false indictments, or false codicils, or the alteration of clauses, depositions or statements of which any legal document is composed, or assisting in the execution of, or in any way practising such forgeries.

The giving of a passport, on the part of a public officer, made out in a name, which he knows to be false.

The embezzlement or purloining, on the part of a clerk, receiver, public depositary or accountant, of public or private money, or current bills, or documents, or titles, or movable effects, which may be in his possession by virtue of his functions, provided the value is over 3,000 francs; and no matter what may be the value of the embezzled or purloined property, if this property exceeds or equals a third of the whole receipts or deposits in the offender's possession; or if it consists of money, or documents received or deposited as security; or if it is a receipt or deposit attached to a place requiring security; or if, lastly, it is a third of the common product of the receipts for one month, or a receipt composed of successive entries not subject to security.

The destruction, suppression, embezzlement, or intentional mislaying, by any judge, administrator, or public officer, or functionary or clerk (whether of government or of any public depositary), of acts or documents, of which he is, in his official capacity, the depositary, or which have been confided or communicated to him in his official capacity.

Rebellion, when more than twenty armed persons are engaged in it;

Favoring the escape of a person condemned to death or to hard labor for life, whether by the guardian of the prison or persons who have corrupted him.

Breaking of seals.

The forming or commanding of bands before any crime has resulted from their organization.

Wounds given with premeditation, or lying in wait.

The suggestion or application of means of abortion by physicians, when followed by the effect intended.

Violation of a child under twelve years of age.

Bigamy.

Sequestration of a person without the order of the proper authorities, except, in those cases provided for by law.

Exposure of a child.

Abduction of a girl under sixteen years old.

Perjury for money.

Aggravated theft.

Misdemeanors of constructors or purveyors.

Those who in these numerous cases have been condemned to hard labor are employed at the severest kind of work. Each one has a chain and ball attached to his foot. When the nature of the work permits it they are chained together in couples. Women and girls condemned to hard labor, are employed in the interior of the prisons. The men, generally, work in the open air.

Those who are condemned to hard labor and confinement are exposed, for one hour, on a public place. A writing placed over the head gives, in large legible letters, the name, profession, domicile, crime, and punishment of the criminal. This punishment cannot be pronounced against minors under eighteen years of age, or septuagenarians. The court of assizes can also, when the condemnation is not for life, and when it is the first offense of the criminal, direct that it be dispensed with.

The Penal Code of 1832 substituted for the pillory, public exposure. The only mitigation of the severity of this kind of punishment is in the power given to the court of assizes of dispensing with it, which is frequently done.

Another consequence of this punishment, as well as of *réclusion*, *détention*, and banishment, is civil degradation, which involves the being placed under the *surveillance* of the high police, and deprivation of all civil rights.

A brief abstract of the sentence is printed and posted in the chief town of the department, or in the city where it was pronounced; in the *commune* of the place where the offense was committed; in that where the sentence is executed; and in that of the domicile of the criminal.

Dètention. Those who are sentenced to this punishment are confined in some one of the fortifications in continental France. The prisoners communicate with the persons in and out of the fortifications, according to a police regulation established by an ordinance of the executive power.

This punishment cannot be pronounced for less than three nor more than twenty years. It is applicable to:

Conspiracy, when not followed by an over act.

Design upon the life of any member of the reigning family, when formed by one person alone, and followed by some overt act towards its execution.

The irregular celebration of a marriage by a priest who has not first satisfied himself, by presentation of the *acte civil*, that the marriage has been regularly contracted, and who has been already punished twice for a similar omission. In explanation of this provision it may be remarked, that the civil code recognizes no other marriage than the *mariage civil*, which must be performed before a civil magistrate, according to certain prescribed forms — a regulation provided by Napoleon, in order to diminish the influence of the clergy.

Writing a direct provocation to the disobedience of the laws, or to any act of the public authorities, or which has a tendency to excite citizens to take arms.

Réclusion. This consists of imprisonment in a penitentiary, in which the prisoners have a choice of labor in several trades. The duration of this punishment is not less than five or more than ten years. A decree of 25th of February, 1852, regulates the work in the prisons. The prisoners who are not directly employed by the administration in works destined to the service of the prisons, or to the public service, can be employed in works of private industry, under certain conditions, determined on by particular regulations. In virtue of this decree, the minister of the interior has issued a regulation, by which the employment at different works, which may be exercised in the *maisons centrales* and prisons of the Seine, is fixed by contract and by public competition.

With the consent of the administration, the manufacturers in the prisons can make experiments, which may be introduced at a later period in their establishments.

The minister of the interior fixes the minimum and the maximum of the number of prisoners who can be employed at each trade.

This penalty is inflicted for:

Counterfeiting, under certain circumstances, whether of money or documents.

Bribery of a judge or jury in criminal affairs.

Abuse of authority in certain cases, or aiding or abetting the same, when against the commonwealth.

Rebellion without arms, when more than thirty persons are engaged in it, or with arms, when it consists of from three to twenty persons.

Premeditated violence against public functionaries, or their agents, when it causes wounds, sickness, or the shedding of blood.

Favoring the evasion or escape of a prisoner.

Breaking the seals of public documents, or taking them away from public depositories.

Lending any assistance to a band or association of malefactors, formed against persons or property; or knowingly and voluntarily furnishing weapons, munitions, instruments of crime, lodging, retreat, or place of meeting, to any such band, or to any portion of it.

The commission, on the part of a beggar or vagrant, of any act of violence for which, owing to the peculiar circumstances, other and severer punishments have not been provided.

Using of false certificates, passes or passports by beggars or vagrants.

Assault and battery, causing wounds or sickness, or leading to inability to work for twenty days; or committed against a parent or grandparent.

Furnishing the means for producing abortion in a pregnant woman, when by the use of the same there results sickness, or inability to labor for more than twenty days.

An indecent assault, attempted or committed, without violence, on the person of a child of either sex, under eleven years of age, or any such assault on a person over fifteen years of age.

The abduction of a child; the concealment or denying the existence of a child; the substitution of one child for another; or the passing off of a strange child as the child of a woman who has never been delivered.

The abduction of minors, or enticing them away from their proper guardians.

Perjury, without bribery, in a trial for misdemeanor, or a simple police case.

Banishment. Persons who are condemned to banishment, are conducted to the frontiers of the State, under order of the government, and there set at liberty.

This punishment, which dates back to the Roman law, was abolished by the code of 1791, but re-enacted by the code of 1810.

In case the banished person returns to the country before the expiration of his term, he is condemned, on the simple evidence of his identity, to imprisonment for a term of years at least equal to, but never more than double, his unexpired term of banishment.

Civil Degradation. This is rather an accessory than an independent punishment, being the result of a condemnation to *détention*, *réclusion*, or banishment.

The punishments of hard labor for life, of transportation, and of death, involve also civil disability, or, as it is sometimes called, civil death, the chief characteristics of which are, the loss of all property on the part of the condemned; the opening of a new succession in favor of his legal heirs; incapacity to dispose in any way of his property, in whole or in part; incompetency to perform any civil act; and, finally, so far as its civil effects are concerned, dissolution of marriage.

The results of civil degradation are:

Forfeiture of all political, but not civil rights.

Dismissal from public functions or employments.

Deprivation of the right of voting, or of being elected to any office.

Incapacity to give evidence in public affairs, or to be a juryman or an official appraiser or surveyor.

Exclusion from acting as a tutor or guardian, &c.

Deprivation of the right to bear arms, to belong to the national guard, to serve in the army, to keep school, or to be employed in any educational institution.

The only instances of civil degradation without previous punishments are for:

Fraud at elections, such as fraudulently taking away or altering ballots.

The infringement on the personal liberty of a citizen by the arbitrary action of a public officer.

Willful resignation of a public office for the purpose of preventing or suspending the administration of justice, or of any public affairs.

The usurpation, on the part of a judge, of legislative or administrative functions which do not belong to him.

The taking of pay by a public officer, for doing his duty, when no pay is allowed by the law.

Insult offered to a judge in court, or to a priest while in the exercise of his functions.

The bribery of witnesses in a case before the correctional police. Perjury in civil procedure, is provided for in the same way.

The punishments for misdemeanors are as follows:

Temporary imprisonment. This is not for less than six days, nor more than five years, except in case of repetition of an offense, when the judge, in view of aggravating circumstances, can increase the punishment. Persons sentenced to imprisonment are confined in a house of correction, where they have the privilege of choosing some kind of labor. The product of their labor is applied partly to the expenses of the prison, partly where it is merited, to procure some alleviation of the lot of the prisoners, and partly to form a reserved fund, which is given to the prisoner on the expiration of his sentence.

Temporary forfeiture of certain political and social rights. The rights which in case of civil degradation are completely annulled, are in this case merely suspended.

Fine. This punishment is either pronounced separately, or in addition to imprisonment. In the system of fines imposed, no allowance is made for the difference of property of offenders.

Damages and surveillance. In addition to the above described punishments, the law allows, in certain cases, both in crimes and misdemeanors, that pecuniary damages should be awarded to the party injured by the crime; and, also, that an offender should be placed under the "surveillance" of the high police. This surveillance is a punishment which was much mitigated by the Code of 1832. By the original penal code, persons who incurred it had to give bonds for good behaviour, on leaving prison, and were compelled, besides, to reside in some place appointed by the magistrate. In the code of 1832, this provision was abolished, and the government allowed only to designate certain places to which the criminal should *not* go.

At the expiration of his term of imprisonment, the criminal must declare where he intends to reside, and is furnished with a passport to that place, by which he must regulate his route, and from which he is not to deviate. This passport indicates also the time he can rest in each place on the route.

Within twenty-four hours after his arrival, he must present himself at the mayor's office, and not leave it till he has received a new passport. In case of violation of either of these provisions, he is liable to imprisonment for a term not exceeding five years.

Police punishments. To this lowest class of penalties belong imprisonment and fine, and the confiscation of certain objects seized by the authorities.

The penalty of imprisonment pronounced by the police courts cannot be less than one day, or more than five days, according to the distinction and classes laid down by law. One day's imprisonment is a term of twenty-four hours.

The fine can be from one to fifteen francs, inclusive, and is also pronounced according to the different classes and distinctions of the law. Fines are applied to the benefit of the commune where the offense was committed.

In certain cases fixed by law, the police court can pronounce the confiscation, either of the object seized, or the materials or instruments which have served, or were destined to commit the offense.

BOOK II. CONCERNING PERSONS PUNISHABLE, EXCUSABLE, OR RESPONSIBLE FOR CRIMES OR MISDEMEANORS.

This book contains general provisions concerning the personal effects of a punishable action; and rules concerning participation in a punishable action. It is divided into two parts; the first treating of the consequences of the participation of several persons in the same crime or misdemeanor; the second, defining the circumstances which make the act of an individual punishable. The judge and jury are not limited in their decisions in the last respect, as they have in every case to determine whether there is impunity, and to what extent. The law gives merely the general grounds which are demanded by equity and morality, without ever making the application to a single case. Complicity differs therefore from culpability as a principle, in so far that, in what regards the first, the law defines clearly and fully its nature and consequences; while in what regards the second, all the circumstances which constitute an offense are not positively defined, but only negatively; and there are some exceptions in which a complete or partial exercise of judicial discretion is allowed.

Complicity. By complicity in its widest sense is understood the action of a person who has participated in the preparation, execution, or consummation of a crime. It is of a two-fold nature—material and moral. The material participation consists in furnishing the means of execution; the moral participation consists in the direct or indirect provocation to crime by means which are particularly defined by the law. In article 60 every case of complicity is detailed.

According to this article, there are punished as accomplices:

Those who have excited to crime, or aided and abetted in it by gifts, promises, threats, abuse of authority or of power, machinations, or guilty artifices.

Those who may have furnished arms, instruments, or any other means which may have served in the commission of the offense, knowing that they were to be so used.

Those who have knowingly aided and abetted the author or authors of a crime by any acts which may have prepared or facilitated its execution.

This is without prejudice to the punishment specially prescribed against the authors of *complots*, or of provocation against the exterior or interior security of the state, even in the case when the contemplated crime of the conspirators has not been committed.

In order to better understand this last provision, it must be remarked that a very important distinction exists between "complicity" and "complots." Both are alike in this, that in both there exists a co-operation of several; the difference between them is, that complicity is in general the participation of several, whilst the complot is either alone a particular offense on account of the object of the association; or with the complot the grade of the offense, and the quantum of the punishment, in certain cases designated by the law, are augumented. In other words, in case of complicity, the participation in the case of each individual is examined separately, and the fact of the co-operation of several is regarded as accidental and without influence. In case of complot this distinction of the particular participation is not established, and the fact of the association or conspiracy is alone the ground of the punishment.

In the *Code Pénal*, complot, in this last signification, is treated of in articles 265 to 268. "Complot" is, in article 265, called a crime against public peace, and is defined as "every association of malefactors against personal property."

The article following shows clearly the nature of a complot as has been described. According to it, the complot exists by the fact alone of the organization of bands, or correspondences between bands and their chiefs and commanders, or by the fact of covenant, even agreeing to render account, or to make peculiar divisions of the products of the misdeed. The members of these bands are punishable by temporary hard labor; and those who are not members of the band, but have knowingly co-operated with the same, are punished by *réclusion.*

Under the term "complicity," those persons are punished as accomplices who, knowing the criminal intentions of malefactors proposing robbery, or violence against the security of the state, the public peace, persons, or property, furnish them habitually lodging, or places of retreat, or of meeting; and also those who have knowingly received and secreted objects taken away, embezzled, or obtained by means of any crime or misdemeanor.

The accomplices in a crime or misdemeanor are subject to the same penalty as the authors, except in a few cases where the law has provided otherwise, and except that the judge has power to prescribe a different measure of punishment, by graduating it according to the degree of the offense, and act within the limit of punishment prescribed.

It has been decided by the court of cassation, that when the punishment must be more rigorous, in consequence of the repetition of the crime, this aggravation does not touch the accomplice, because the repetition is a personal matter, and does not affect the nature of the crime itself.

It has been also decided, that an accomplice can be prosecuted and punished, even when the principal cannot be prosecuted — for example, in case of flight or death of the latter.

In the treatment of the subject of complicity, striking differences are observable, between the French Penal Code and the codes of other continental nations.

Persons excusable from punishment. Article 64, of the Penal Code, contains most important provisions, to the effect that neither a crime nor a misdemeanor exists when the accused is in a state of mental alienation at the time of the commission of the act, or when he is constrained by a force which he cannot resist.

The laconicism of the French code on this subject is not to be found in most of the other codes, where want of intelligence or free will are specified. Some codes go so far in this respect, that they enumerate the cases of mental alienation — one might almost say medically. For example, the code of Oldenburgh, which speaks even of melancholy as a ground of impunity.

Other codes speak specially of the deaf and dumb, and make a special distinction between those who by their education have reached such a degree of intelligence, that it is to be supposed they can distinguish good from evil; and those whose mental and moral incapacity is as unfortunate as their incapacity for hearing and speaking. Many codes treat of very old age, and declare those persons who have reached their second childhood to be irresponsible.

The French code has established a general formula, under which all these particular cases fall, and has thereby a great advantage over other codes, for the greatest controversies always arise in the settlement of individual and exceptional cases, concerning which the other codes are always insufficient and defective.

The judge or jury must seek in every particular case to know if the offender was exposed to influences or impulses which he was incapable of resisting; if he was a responsible being in the full exercise of free will and mental capacity; or if, in the absence of those mental and physical qualities which distinguish rational men from lunatics and idiots, he had not ceased to be an accountable being. Lastly, when there is full possession of the mental faculties, an offense may be committed under circumstances which could not have been resisted, as, for example, when the husband kills the adulterer whom he surprises *in flagrante delicto*, he may be said to have been impelled by an irresistible force. If he kills the adulterer some time after the adultery has been committed, then it cannot be said that he acted under the influence of irresistible force, for it is to be supposed that in the interval his reason had resumed its sway.

The French code contains not one word about drunkenness, and it is only necessary to know if a man in that condition was so far clouded in his faculties as to have been impelled by a force which such a state of mind made him unable to resist. The court of cassation, however, has repeatedly decided, that drunkenness was no ground for excuse or impunity.

The Penal Code does not speak of self-defense in the general part of the second book, but only in the special part of the third book, in which the different crimes and misdemeanors are treated of. Homicide, wounds, or blows, necessitated by legitimate self-defense, constitute neither crimes nor misdemeanors. This legitimate defense exists: 1st. When the homicide is committed, or the wounds or blows given result from repelling an attempt to break into enclosures, over walls, or into the entries of a dwelling house, or inhabited apartment; 2d. When committed in defending one's self against robbers or persons engaged in pillage by means of violence.

In some cases, the French law declares an offender excusable in manslaughter. For instance, wounds and blows, when provoked by wounds or violence against the person, or when committed in repelling a breaking into an inhabited house during the day; the killing of an adulterous wife or her accomplices when caught in the act; and even the crime of castration, when it is provoked by a violent indecent assault. In these cases, the excusability does not imply complete impunity, but the ordinary punishment is greatly diminished.

Concerning youth, the French code decides that when the accused is less than sixteen years of age he shall be acquitted, provided it is ascertained that he acted without discernment. But in that case he is either given over to his parents or put into a house of correction, in order to be educated and reformed. In the latter case he is detained as long as the sentence of the court determines, which time, however, cannot extend beyond the epoch at which he shall have completed his twentieth year. If it is decided that he committed the offense with discernment—that is, with a knowledge of its character—he is punished, but with a milder punishment than in ordinary cases. Thus, instead of punishment of death he is sentenced to imprisonment and hard labor for life. Instead of transportation, he is condemned to imprisonment from ten to twenty years in a house of correction. Instead of imprisonment and hard labor for a term of years with *détention* or *réclusion*, he is condemned to confinement for a term equal to one-third at least, and one-half at most, of the term fixed by law. Instead of civil degradation and banishment, he is condemned to confinement in a house of correction for from one to five years.

A child under sixteen years of age, and having no accomplices older than himself, who is accused of a crime other than that which the law punishes with death, imprisonment and hard labor for life, transportation, or *détention*, is not judged by the court of assizes but by the *tribunal correctionnel*, and according to the rules which have been given above.

In all cases, when the minor, under sixteen years of age, has committed only a simple misdemeanor, the punishment pronounced against him cannot exceed the half of the punishment which he would have been sentenced to had he reached sixteen years.

"*Extenuating Circumstances.*"—A general principle of the French code is, that no crime or misdemeanor can be excused, except in those cases especially provided for by law. In a similar manner, there can be no mitigations of punishments, except in cases provided for by particular provisions. There is one case only, that of parricide, where no extenuating circumstances or palliation is allowed. In all other crimes and misdemeanors, the punishment can be mitigated, when extenuating circumstances are shown to have existed.

The code of 1832 set forth an entirely new theory on this point; according to which, whenever there are extenuating circumstances, the punishment is changed and graduated, according to a given scale. The existence of extenuating circumstances is decided in each case by the jury. The correctional courts can also decide on this subject. In this theory the French code stands alone; in the other codes extenuating circumstances have only this effect, that the judge chooses within the minimum and maximum of the punishments fixed by law, and, according to his judgment, pronounces either the minimum or an appropriate quantum. The peculiarity of the provisions of the French law can be explained, when it is understood that the legislator wished to give the judge the power to make in every case an exception to the rule, in favor of the accused, for whom the general punishment seemed too severe. The most prominent writers on criminal law, and more especially Fautin-Hélie, in his excellent work on French penal legislation, criticise this system, on the ground that the judge wields too great a power, and that by admitting an exception to every rule, in the end no general rule can remain.

The punishment of imprisonment and hard labor for life, of transportation, and of imprisonment and hard labor for a term of years, cannot be pronounced against any person over seventy years of age. These punishments are replaced in each case in the following manner: Transportation is changed to imprisonment for life; hard labor to confinement. Also, when a person condemned to imprisonment and hard labor reaches seventy years before the expiration of his sentence, he is freed from that punishment and confined in a *maison de force* for the remainder of his term of punishment.

Second offenses. Whoever has committed a crime, and on this account is condemned to an afflictive or infamous punishment, is, on the commission of a second crime, which has for its punishment civil degradation, condemned to banishment. When the penalty for the second crime is banishment, he is condemned to *détention*. When the penalty in the second instance is *réclusion*, he is condemned to imprisonment and hard labor for a term of years. When it is *détention*, he is condemned to the maximum of the same punishment, which, in certain cases, can be doubled. When it is hard labor and imprisonment for a term of years, he is condemned to a maximum of this punishment, which can also, in certain cases, be doubled. If it is transportation, he is condmned to imprisonment and hard labor for life. And, when it is imprisonment and hard labor for life, he can be condemned to death.

Whoever, after having been punished for a crime, commits afterwards a misdemeanor, which is liable to correctional punishment, is condemned to the maximum of this penalty, which can also, in certain cases, be doubled.

Whoever has already been punished for a misdemeanor by imprisonment of over one year, is condemned to the maximum of the punishment provided for the new offense, which can also be doubled, and is also placed under the surveillance of the high police, during not less than five, nor more than ten years.

In its provisions touching the repetition of offenses, the French code differs from all others in this respect, that the increased severity of a punishment, on account of a former condemnation, does not depend on the identity of the two offenses, but on the nature of the punishment to which the criminal was before condemned. This theory is logical with the whole system by which crimes and misdemeanors are not separately defined, but depend upon the punishments which are attached to them.

Condemnation for imprisonment of less than one year has no influence on the sentence for a second misdemeanor.

For *contraventions*, the second offense involves increased severity of punishment only when it occurs within a twelve month of the first offense, and within the jurisdiction of the same police court.

Cases of repetition of offense have also the peculiarity, that the punishment cannot be mitigated on account of extenuating circumstances, excepting at the correctional courts, and then only in the case of the punishments of imprisonment or fine. In this last case, when there are extenuating circumstances, the imprisonment can be reduced to less than six days, and the fine to less than sixteen francs. The correctional courts can even pronounce these penalties separately, and in certain cases substitute fine for imprisonment; without, however, pronouncing a penalty less than that of the police court.

A jury, although it always decides in a matter of extenuating circumstances, has no decision in the matter of second offenses. The consideration of these belongs exclusively to the judge, who, on the basis of the verdict of the jury, applies the law and determines the punishment.

Duration of punishment. A punishment ends not only by the expiration of its term, but also for other legal reasons. It has already been shown that the punishment of imprisonment and hard labor ceases at seventy years of age. A more general case than this is the extinction of a punishment by limitation, *préscription.*

The Penal Code does not treat of this subject; its principles, however, are laid down in the Code of Criminal Procedure. According to these principles, limitation of a punishment for crime takes place in twenty years, counting from the date of the sentence; for misdemeanors, in five years after date of sentence; for contraventions, in two years after date of sentence. Prosecution on account of a crime punishable by an afflictive or infamous punishment, cannot be instituted after a lapse of ten years from the day when the crime was committed, if within this period no prosecution has been entered. A misdemeanor cannot be prosecuted after three years have elapsed from the date when it was committed, nor a simple contravention after one year.

Limitations of the period for prosecution, as well as of the period of punishment, are found in all European codes. The necessity and

54

justice of such limitations in these respects, is placed on the ground that, after the expiration of a long period of time, the traces of a crime become effaced, and at the trial the accused might easily be sacrificed on vague and insufficient evidence.

BOOK III. CRIMES, MISDEMEANORS, AND THEIR PUNISHMENTS.

This book enumerates the crimes and misdemeanors in particular, and gives the punishments attached to them; it exhibits the application of the general principles set forth in the two previous books. It commences with the divisions of crimes and misdemeanors.

These are divided into two classes, those against the state, and those against individuals.

Crimes and misdemeanors against the State. These are divided into: 1. Those which compromise the security of the state; 2. Those which are in violation of the constitution; and, 3. Those which disturb public tranquillity.

In the first class are those offenses which, by means of communication with a foreign enemy, affect the external safety of the state, in which case the punishment is death; those which affect its internal safety by a criminal attempt against the executive power, or his family, also punishable with death; or by crimes tending to trouble the state; by civil war; by the employment of armed force; or by public devastation and pillage; in which cases also, when the execution of the crime has been commenced, the punishment is death.

In the second class are offenses which refer to the exercise of civil rights at political elections, attempts upon the liberty of citizens by the arbitrary acts of public officers, and encroachments on administrative and judicial authority.

In the third class are, counterfeiting; malfeasance by public functionaries in the exercise of their duties; troubles caused to public order by the ministers of the different religions in the exercise of their functions; resistance to, or disobedience of, public authorities; associations of malefactors; vagabondage and mendicity; misdemeanors by writings, images, or engravings, distributed without the name of the author engraved or printed on the same; lastly, prohibited associations or meetings.

Counterfeiting consists either in the preparing of false money (the falsification of silver money being more severely punished than that of copper money); or the counterfeiting of the seal of the state, or of bank notes, public papers, stamps, *timbres*, and marks; or the counterfeiting of public and authentic acts; or of commercial or banking paper; or of private documents; or lastly, the counterfeiting of passports, traveling papers, or certificates.

The offenses by public functionaries in the exercise of their functions, are the embezzlement by a public depositary of objects confided to him; taking bribes; the demanding or taking by a public officer, in the exercise of his functions, of money or taxes which are not due; taking some part in commerce or in affairs incompatible with the office; the corrupting of public officers; the abuse of authority in regard to individuals, *e. g.*, the violation of the secrecy of letters; or in respect to the state, *e. g.*, misdemeanors concerning the keeping the registers of births, marriages, and deaths; and lastly, in the exercise of public authority illegally anticipated or prolonged.

Troubles to public order by ministers of religion, in the exercise of their ministry, are either acts tending to compromise the social relations, *e. g.*, performing the religious ceremonies of a marriage before the marriage has been duly celebrated as prescribed by the Civil Code; or criticisms, censures, or provocation, directed against public authority in a sermon publicly pronounced, or a pastoral writing; or correspondence on religious affairs by the ministers of religion, with foreign courts or powers, without having authorization for the same from the minister charged with the surveillance of religion.

Resistance, disobedience, and other like offenses against public authority, are, rebellion, that is, forcible attack, or violent resistance to a public officer in the exercise of his functions; violence or outrage against the depositaries of the government, when committed by words tending to inculpate the officers; the refusal of a service legally due (under which head falls the refusal of service by a commandant, officer, or sub-officer of the public peace, and the case of a juryman or a witness alleging a false excuse); promoting the escape of prisoners, and concealing criminals (the guardians of a prison, in case of an escape, being punished according to the grade of punishment to which the prisoner was condemned); the breaking of seals, or removing of documents from the public departments; the defacing or mutilation of public monuments; the usurpation of titles and functions; and hindrance offered to the free exercise of religion.

To the category of associations of malefactors, vagrancy, and mendicity, belong associations of malefactors against persons and property; and the vagrancy of persons who have no fixed domicile nor means of subsistence, and who exercise habitually no trade or profession; and the asking of alms in any place where there is a poor house.

Misdemeanors committed by writings, images, or engravings distributed without the name of the author printed or engraven on the same. This category explains itself. By a law of 10th December, 1831, no writings on political subjects can be publicly posted or distributed in the public streets or squares.

Forbidden associations are those which, composed of more than twenty members, assemble at fixed times for the discussion of religious, political, or literary subjects, without having obtained the authorization of the government.

Crimes and misdemeanors against Individuals. These are divided into 1. Those against persons; and, 2. Those against property.

In the first class are:

Murder, or voluntary manslaughter.

Assassination, or murder with premeditation and lying in wait.

Threatening, by anonymous or signed letters or writings, to commit assassination, poisoning, or any crime against others, punishable with death, hard labor and imprisonment for life, or transportation. The penalty for such menace is imprisonment and hard labor for a term of years, in case the threat is accompanied by an attempt at extortion, such as ordering the deposit of a sum of money in a particular place, or any requirement of the kind.

Voluntary wounds or blows, without intention to kill, or any other voluntary crimes named in the laws, such as the fabrication of prohibited arms, castration, abortion, or sale of adulterated liquors containing mixtures injurious to the health.

Involuntary homicide—that is, homicide resulting from imprudence or negligence; also wounds and blows inflicted under the same circumstances.

Attempts against morals, including violation of the person; corrupt ing and debauching of persons under twenty-one years of age; adultery on the side of the wife, which can only be denounced before the law by the husband; and on the side of the husband, but only in case of his keeping a concubine in the conjugal residence; and bigamy.

The illegal arrest and sequestration of persons.

Crimes and misdemeanors tending to interfere with or destroy the civil and social condition of a child, or to compromise its existence; the abduction of minors; and infraction of the laws concerning inhumation.

Perjury, calumny, injury, and revelation of secrets. The last misdemeanor is liable to be committed by physicians, surgeons, and other officers of health; by apothecaries, midwives, and all other persons who by their calling or profession, are intrusted with individual or family secrets.

In the second class are:

Robbery; that is, the fraudulent taking away of an object which does not belong to the person taking it. Robbery is either simple or "qualified." Qualified robbery is that which is accompanied by aggravating circumstances, such as have been before stated.

Fraudulent bankruptcy; swindling; breach of trust; contravention of the regulations concerning gambling houses, pawnbrokers' shops and lotteries, which, since 1830, have been prohibited, unless they have had for their object the encouragement of art or charity; hindrance to the freedom and honesty of public auctions; violation of the regulations relative to manufacturers, commerce, or art, to which class belong strikes of workmen for higher wages, and lastly, misdemeanors of quartermasters-general, and other agents of the government for the purchase and distribution of provisions, forage, &c.

Destruction of property, or injuries to the same, to which class belongs incendiarism.

BOOK IV. POLICE OFFENSES AND THEIR PUNISHMENTS.

In contraventions, the *animus* or criminal intention is not considered; the punishment is regulated solely by the nature of the act and its results.

The code divides contraventions into three classes: the first being punishable with a fine of from one to five francs, inclusive; the second by one of from six to ten francs; and the third by one of from eleven to fifteen francs.

Imprisonment can also be imposed for a term not exceeding five days, according to circumstances.

PENAL CODE OF PRUSSIA. (*Straf-Gesetzbuch.*

The remarkable code lately promulgated in Prussia, although founded on the French *Code Pénal*, differs from it in many important particulars. The Prussian code has been in force only since the 1st of July, 1851. It is the product of twenty-five years of legislative labor. Six complete and elaborated projects were presented and discussed in the years 1827, 1830, 1843, 1845, 1847, and 1851. If the desired goal was not sooner arrived at, it was not for want of profound investigation, sixty commentaries and criticisms having been written on one single project, that of 1830. The reason of this delay is to be found partly in the slow movements of the legislative bodies, and partly in the long-continued differences on the question, whether a new code should be made, or whether the former laws should be revised.

The criminal law of Prussia, before the reform, was contained in the general Prussian law of 1794, the *Landrecht.* By a cabinet order of the king, dated 28th January, 1826, the revision of the penal laws was decreed; and on this occasion it was expressly remarked that no new body of laws was intended, but that it was only meant to give the former laws a thorough examination, and, according to the result, to improve and complete the existing system. The minister of justice, Graf Von Danckelmann, protested against this plan of revision, and declared that the general *Landrecht* could be revised in all its parts, except the criminal law, for which a new code was required. The king yielded to this opinion, and decreed by a cabinet order of 14th November, 1826, the plan purposed by the minister, that a commission should be appointed to prepare a new penal code for the whole State of Prussia.*

In order to hasten its preparation, a second commission was appointed in 1838, called *Immediat Commission*, consisting of the ministers of justice and of the interior, and of several members of the council of State. The proceedings of this commission were to be more prompt than those of the ordinary commission, and it was to stand in immediate relation with the *plenum*, or general assembly.

The project of the year 1843, the revised project of 1845 (the latter under the direction of the celebrated Savigny, then minister of justice), and the project of the year 1847, were the result of the labors of this commission. The last project was laid before the legislative chambers on their first meeting, under the celebrated *patent* of the 3d February, 1847. It was discussed during twenty-six sittings, in a committee of ninety-nine members, named for the purpose, and a report made to the assembly. The general discussion commenced on the 17th January, 1848, and was interrupted in the sitting of the 6th March, by the revolution.

In the year 1850, the project, remodeled by the minister of justice, Herr Simons, was again taken up, with alterations rendered necessary by the reformed organization of the judiciary. In the first and second chambers the project was adopted without discussion, and promulgated as law the 14th April, 1851, to take effect the 1st July following.

Of all the German penal codes, that of Prussia most resembles the French, both in form and principle. It consists of three hundred and forty-nine articles, or rather paragraphs, and is divided into three parts, preceded by introductory prescriptions. These last are founded on the preliminary provisions of the penal code of France, and are almost a literal translation of them. Offenses are divided into crimes, misdemeanors and contraventions. A crime is punishable with death, hard labor, or "confinement" for more than five years. A misdemeanor, with confinement for less than five years, "imprisonment" for more than six weeks, or a fine of more than fifty thalers. A contravention, with imprisonment for a term of less than six weeks, or a fine not exceeding fifty thalers.

---

* In the Rhenish provinces the French penal code was in force till the adoption of the new Prussian code. The commission had great difficulty in satisfying these provinces, in which, besides, the French system of penal procedure was also in force.

PART I. GENERAL PRINCIPLES CONCERNING PUNISHABLE ACTS.

The Prussian code recognizes but five kinds of punishment: death, hard labor, confinement, imprisonment and fine. Civil death is abolished, and civil degradation is pronounced only in very grave cases.

Death is inflicted by decapitation. The execution is private and in an enclosed space. Two members of the court judging in first instance, the public prosecutor, or his substitute, a clerk, and one of the superior officers of the prison, must be present. Notice of the execution must be given to the municipal council of the place where the execution is to take place. This body must send twelve persons of consideration to act as witnesses. A member of the same religion with the condemned, and his counsel, must be admitted. Other persons can obtain admission only on particular grounds; the law, however, neither gives those grounds, nor does it name the magistrate by whom the permission is granted.

Hard Labor is imposed either for life or for a term of from two to twenty years. Those condemned to it are employed, as in the *bagnes* in France, at such labor as is fixed by law in the prisons prepared for this purpose. They are not capable during their term of punishment of performing any civil act; and, in case of holding property, a *curator* is named for them who administers their affairs. They are deprived of their civil rights, by which is understood the following: loss of right to wear the Prussian national cockade; incapacity to maintain or receive public office, honors, titles, orders, or decorations; loss of nobility; incapacity to be a juryman or elector, or to perform any other political act; incapacity to make oath as a witness or appraiser, to serve as witness to a public document, to be guardian or member of a family council, with the exception of guardianship of the offender's own children, with the approval of the family council, or other council of guardianship; and lastly, the loss of right to bear arms or to enter the army.

Confinement. This punishment is incarceration in fortresses, or other places named for the purpose, with employment at different trades, for the most part chosen by the prisoners. It cannot exceed twenty years.

Imprisonment. Those condemned to this punishment are confined in a prison, and are employed according to their capacities and circumstances. Its duration is from one day to five years.

Fines. A fine of less than one thaler cannot be levied. In case of insolvency of the condemned, the judge can change the fine to imprisonment; a fine of from one to three thalers counting as one day's imprisonment. Under such circumstances, it can never exceed four years.

The Prussian code, like the French, does not prescribe general confiscation of property as a punishment, but only a special one of those objects which are the fruits of the crime or misdemeanor, or which were used, or intended to be used, for the commission of the offense.

Besides the entire privation of civil rights, there is a temporary interdiction of them of from one to ten years, with the effects before mentioned. The temporary interdiction of the right of holding public office, however, cannot exceed five years.

The *surveillance* of the police, introduced into this code, has also been adopted from the French. The residence in certain places can be interdicted to a convict; and he is subjected to visits from the police as often as they deem it advisable. Those who are punished and placed under the *surveillance* of the police on account of theft, robbery, or of receiving stolen goods, are not allowed to leave by night either their domicile or lodging, without permission of the police. A foreigner, instead of being placed under the *surveillance* of the police, is ejected from the Prussian territory.

All condemnations to death, hard labor, or confinement for more than five years, must be published in the official organ of the government, in the district in which the punishment is pronounced.

Offenses receive a much milder punishment by the Prussian, than by the French code; and the principal difference of the effects of punishment is, that the system of penalties dishonoring the person is not adopted in the former, and that only in certain very grave cases deprivation of civil rights and consideration is pronounced. Capital punishment appears in much fewer cases; the punishments of civil death, exile, transportation, and *détention*, do not exist.

Attempts (*Versuch*). The second chapter treats of attempts to commit crimes or misdemeanors, and establishes a theory which is almost literally copied from the French Penal Code. An attempt is only punishable when the same is manifested by acts which constitute a commencement of execution, and when the consummation is hindered only by circumstances independent of the will of the author. The attempt to commit a crime is punished in the same manner as the crime itself, except that the judge, in fixing the measure of punishment which is within the limits allowed him by the law, is permitted to take into consideration that the crime was not consummated. The only other exception to the rule is, in case of an attempt to commit a crime, which, if perpetrated, would be punishable by capital punishment or hard labor for life; in which case the penalty must be changed to hard labor for at least ten years, with *surveillance* of the police. The attempt at a misdemeanor is only punished in the cases specified by the laws; the punishment is, in such cases, the same as for the misdemeanor itself, with the above mentioned modification in respect to judicial discretion.

Complicity. The third chapter treats of the participation in a crime or misdemeanor. The following questions are decided:

Who shall be punished as author or accomplice of a crime or misdemeanor?

What punishment must be pronounced in the different cases?

How is he to be punished who takes part in a punishable action after the same has been committed?

The following persons are punishable as the accomplices of a crime or misdemeanor:

Whoever excites, seduces, or persuades the doer, by gifts or promises; by threats, abuse of authority or power; by intentional provocation or other means.

Whoever has advised the commission of a crime or misdemeanor; or has procured weapons, instruments, or other means, which have served for the deed, knowing that they were to serve in the perpetration of a punishable action; or has, knowingly, given aid in the acts which have either prepared, facilitated, or completed the offense. The punishment is, in this case, whether the offense is consummated, or only attempted, the same for both the principal and accomplice; but the judge can, in applying the law, have regard to the degree of the co-operation. In the case of capital punishment, or hard labor for life, when the part taken was not essential to the accomplishment of the crime, hard labor for a term of years must replace these penalties, and when, besides, extenuating circumstances exist, the punishment is imprisonment of from two to ten years.

Whoever excites to a crime or misdemeanor, by speeches at public places or meetings, or by writings, prints, or other publications, which are sold, distributed, propagated, exposed or posted, is considered and punished as an accomplice, when the instigation has resulted in a crime or misdemeanor, or a punishable attempt at either. If no result has followed these provocations, imprisonment of at most one year is generally pronounced.

A person who, after the perpetration of a crime or misdemeanor, knowingly assists the perpetrator to escape punishment, or to secure the advantage of the offense, is punishable by a fine of at most 200 thalers, or imprisonment of at the utmost one year. When a person does this with the intention of saving a blood relative, either ascendant or descendant, brother, sister, or spouse, from punishment, he incurs no penalty. Nevertheless, in the case when this assistance is given in consequence of an agreement made before the commission of the offense, a common *Complicität* exists, even for a relation of the grade just mentioned.

The third chapter closes with a provision which is not found in many other codes. Whoever has received notice of a project of high treason, counterfeiting of money, murder, robbery, kidnapping, or a crime dangerous to the life of man, when the hindering of the same is still possible, and fails to denounce the fact to the authorities, or to the person threatened, is punishable with imprisonment for a term which can be extended to five years, when the crime is committed or attempted.

Exemption from or mitigation of punishment. In the fourth chapter, which, logically, is connected with the first on punishments, are enumerated the grounds which exclude or mitigate punishments. In the three following cases, there is neither a crime nor misdemeanor committed, although the external conditions of one exist: 1st. When the author at the moment of the deed, is insane or idiotic, or when the freedom of the will is hindered by force or menace; 2d. When the deed is an act of legitimate defense, to repulse an attack on one's self, or on another, even in cases when, from terror, fright, or horror, the limits of defense are exceeded; 3d. When the author has not completed his sixteenth year, and it is proved that he has acted without discrimination. In this latter case the judge decides whether he shall be intrusted to his family, or sent to a house of correction. If sent to the latter, he remains there as long as the administrators deem it necessary, but not beyond his 20th year. When a youth, under 16 years, has committed a crime, and it is shown that he acted with discernment, no other punishment but imprisonment can be pronounced against him. If the crime is punished in ordinary cases with death or hard labor for life, the penalty is changed to imprisonment from three to fifteen years. In all other cases the judge is authorized to diminish the *minimum* of the ordinary punishments; he can never exceed the half of the ordinary *maximum*. The imprisonment for such young persons is in separated wards within the ordinary prisons.

Limitation. The prosecution of crimes and misdemeanors is subject to limitation. The limitation for crimes punishable with death is thirty years; for those crimes whose punishment is loss of liberty for more than ten years, the limitation is twenty years; and for those of which the penalty is a milder punishment, the period is ten years. Those misdemeanors which are punishable with more than three months' imprisonment as a *maximum*, cannot be prosecuted after five years, nor others after three years.

The term of limitation begins with the day that the crime or misdemeanor is committed. A crime or misdemeanor which can only be punished on the complaint of a private individual—for example, theft from a near relative—cannot be prosecuted after the lapse of three months, which commences with the time of knowledge of the offense. When it is interrupted by a judicial examination which leads to no result, a new term of limitation commences with the latter judicial act. Whoever escapes by flight from the examining magistrate cannot avail himself of the new limitation. The law defines precisely the interruption of the limitation, and embraces therein every motion or other act of the public prosecutor, as well as every decision and every other act of the judicial magistrate, concerning the opening, continuation or termination of the investigation or incarceration of the accused. No limitation is admitted for punishments pronounced by a definitive judgment.

When the culpability of an action depends either on matters peculiar to the person of the offender, or to the one against whom the action is directed, or, in particular circumstances, such action is not to be counted as a crime or misdemeanor, when the doer at the time of the deed was ignorant of such relations.

Cumulation and repetition of offenses. The first part closes with the 5th chapter, concerning the cumulation of several offenses, and the repetition of offenses. The first occurs when the same action includes the characteristics of several crimes or misdemeanors, in which case that law is applied which inflicts the severest punishment, or when, by several independent actions, several crimes or misdemeanors are committed. In the last case, all punishments to which the criminal is subjected are to be cumulated in one, with the following modifications: When there are several punishments of loss of liberty for a less term than for life, the term cannot, for crime, exceed twenty years, and for misdemeanors ten years. If the punishments are of different kinds, the severest is to be pronounced, and the milder are, by a fixed rule, reduced to the same kind. One year's imprisonment counts as eight months' confinement, and one year's confinement for eight months' at hard labor. In case of the cumulation, imprisonment, which by law cannot in ordinary cases exceed five years, can be extended to ten years.

Punishment is aggravated in case of the perpetration of a crime or misdemeanor for which an individual has been already condemned by a Prussian court of justice. In such case, the maximum of the ordinary punishment is increased, but by not more than one-half, and it cannot exceed incarceration for twenty years. The term of five years for imprisonment can, in this case, be augmented. This augmentation does not occur when ten years have elapsed since the time when the punishment of the crime last committed has been inflicted or remitted. When the deed, in the first or last case, or in both, consists merely in being accessory to a crime or misdemeanor, or to the attempt to commit the same, the same augmentation of severity of punishment is to be observed.

PART II. CRIMES, MISDEMEANORS, AND THEIR PUNISHMENTS.

This part contains very numerous special provisions concerning the nature and the mode of prosecution of punishable actions, excepting offenses against the police regulations. The offenses considered are the following:

High Treason. High treason is an undertaking against the king, tending to kill, imprison, or deliver him to the enemy, or to render him incapable of governing, or forcibly to alter the succession to the throne or the constitution, or to incorporate the territory of Prussia, in whole or in part, with a foreign state, or to wrest a portion of its territory from the kingdom. The punishment in these cases is death. If the action is only prepared, and not commenced, its punishment is hard labor; or, when there are mitigating circumstances, confinement.

A Prussian who excites a foreign government to war against Prussia, suffers, if war follows the same, capital punishment and civil degradation. The giving assistance by a Prussian citizen to the enemy during a war with Prussia is punished with hard labor.

Insult to the King. Insult to the king is either by words or deeds; the latter is punished with death, or, in certain cases, with hard labor for from ten to twenty years.

An offense committed against one of the members of the royal family is punished with hard labor for from five to twenty years.

The manifesting of a want of reverence for the king, by words, writings, prints, or drawings, is punished with hard labor for from five to twenty years. If against a member of the royal family, with imprisonment for from one month to three years.

Acts against Allies. A Prussian, in or out of Prussia, or a foreigner during his stay in Prussia, who commits an action against one of the German States or rulers, which, if exercised against Prussia or its king, would be high treason, is punished with hard labor of from two to ten years. The same punishment is pronounced when the action is directed against another state with which reciprocity in such cases is guaranteed by law or treaty.

The insulting by words the sovereign of a German State, or of another state, when reciprocity is assured for such cases, is punished with imprisonment of from one month to two years. The prosecution in the last case is made on the proposition of the foreign government.

The insulting the foreign agent accredited to the Prussian courts is punished with from one month to one year's imprisonment.

Offenses to Political Rights. An offense against the exercise of political rights is committed by the undertaking forcibly to dissolve the representative body, to obtain the adoption of a resolution, or forcibly to eject or exclude a member of the chambers, or to prevent his going to the same, or voting, or to falsify an electoral act. The punishment is hard labor or imprisonment.

The buying or selling a vote is punished with imprisonment of from three months to two years.

Resistance to Legal Authorities. By resistance to the authorities is understood the provoking another to disobey the laws or orders of the magistrates; the exciting a soldier to breach of discipline; the justifying a crime or misdemeanor; the attack on a magistrate, or resistance to the same in the exercise of his functions; lastly, the forcing a magistrate to do or omit an official act. The punishment is fine or imprisonment. The law includes, under this head, the favoring the escape of a prisoner, and the conspiracy of prisoners; in the latter case imprisonment must be pronounced.

Offenses against Public Order. By an offense against public order is understood the illegal formation of armed bodies; the taking part in a secret association, or associating to prevent the execution of the laws; the exciting citizens to hatred and contempt for each other, or for the institutions of the state, or for the orders of the authorities; the insulting a person while in the exercise of a political or religious right; the usurpation of a public office, uniform, decoration, or title; the destroying or removing of public ordinances which are posted in public places; the breaking official seals; the false accusation of a witness or juror; emigration without permission, when thereby the person seeks to avoid military service, or practicing the profession of inducing to emigrate; the seducing Prussian soldiers to desert, or seeking to induce Prussian subjects to enlist in a foreign army; vagrancy, or the wandering over the country without having, or attempting legitimately to obtain the means of subsistence; beggary, when with threats, force, weapons, or false representations; and the making beggars of children, or persons who are intrusted to the care or authority of the persons so doing; the leading a life of drunkenness, gambling, and idleness, which prevents the person from giving support to those who are dependent on him; the refusal by one who receives support from a public establishment for the poor, to perform the labor suitable to his strength which is allotted him. The case of a person who, after the loss of his means of support, has, within a term fixed by the police, procured no other means of subsistence, and cannot prove that, after taking all necessary pains, he has not been able to procure the same, is also included in this title. In all these cases the punishment is imprisonment; or, in rare cases, fine; or both.

Counterfeiting Money. By counterfeiting money, is understood the imitating of the coin or paper money of Prussia, or of any foreign state;

or the altering of moneys in order to give them the appearance of higher value, or to give to uncurrent money the appearance of current. This crime is punished with hard labor of from five to fifteen years, and with surveillance of the police.

The same punishment is incurred by him who procures false or falsified money, and either imports the same or puts it in circulation; whoever receives such money, and, after recognizing its spuriousness, passes it, or seeks to pass it, as genuine, is punished with imprisonment of not more than three months, or fine not to exceed 100 thalers.

Perjury. Perjury is committed by him who knowingly swears falsely in civil or criminal suits. The punishment is more severe in the latter than in the former case, as the penalty of hard labor for a term of twenty years can be pronounced for perjury in a criminal suit.

An appraiser who knowingly confirms a false statement with an oath, is punished as a false witness.

Testimony on oath, is not required for the members of those religious societies where the oath is forbidden, or for those who have already in the same suit made oath, or when a sworn magistrate gives official affirmation, making appeal to his oath of office. Whoever gives knowingly to a public officer a false affirmation, which is received instead of an oath, is punished with imprisonment of from three months to one year, and the judge can even pronounce temporary interdiction of civil rights. Subornation of perjury is punished with condemnation to hard labor, which can extend to five years.

This chapter closes with a prescription not to be found in any other code: Whoever, through negligence, makes a false oath, can be condemned to imprisonment for one year. This punishment is not pronounced when the individual revokes, formally, his false testimony before he has been denounced or prosecuted, and before any injurious consequences have resulted from it.

False Informing. Whoever addresses to the public authorities a denunciation against a person on account of a punishable action is, if the denunciation is made falsely, and with intent, punished with imprisonment of not less than three months, and according to the discretion of the judge, with temporary interdiction of civic rights. In this case the sentence is copied from the records, and published in a journal designated by the judge.

Offenses against Religion. Offenses against religion are public blasphemy, or the calumniating of a Christian church, or of another authorized religious society; mockery of their doctrines, institutions, or customs, or contempt of the same; misbehavior in church; and injury to objects destined to the service of religion. The offender can be condemned to imprisonment of at most three years.

Whoever takes from the guardianship of those entitled to it, the body or part of the same of a deceased person, or disturb graves or tombs, or dishonors them, is punished with imprisonment of from one month to two years; and when this is done with a view to gain, the interdiction of civic rights is pronounced in addition.

Offenses in regard to Civil Rights. Whoever substitutes, or intentionally changes, a child, or in other ways changes or suppresses the fact of the birth, marriage, or death of a person, is punished with hard labor not to exceed ten years.

Offenses against Good Morals. Offenses against good morals, are bigamy, adultery, incest, bestiality and sodomy, rape, seduction effected through false representations, professional prostitution contrary to police regulations, pimping, seduction of a girl between fourteen and sixteen years, public indecency, the sale, distribution, or propagation of immoral writings, prints, pictures or images.

Bigamy is punished with hard labor, which cannot exceed five years. The same punishment is pronounced against the person who knowingly marries one already married, and the priest or magistrate who performs the ceremony of marriage for them.

Adultery is only punished when divorce ensues on account of such offense, by imprisonment from four weeks to six months, which reaches equally the accomplice. The plaintiff can, during the suit for divorce or the criminal process, desist from the prosecution, in which case the accomplice is also set free.

Incest between parent and child is punished, in the former by hard labor, which cannot exceed five years, and in the latter, after the age of sixteen years, with imprisonment from three months to two years. Incest between parents-in-law and children-in-law, between brothers and sisters, or half-brothers and sisters, is punished with imprisonment from three months to two years; and, when there are aggravating circumstances, with temporary interdiction of the exercise of civil rights. Step-children are exempt from punishment when under sixteen years.

Tutors, ministers of religion, and teachers who are guilty of indecent actions towards those minors who are intrusted to their charge; magistrates who are guilty of the same conduct towards persons against whom they are directing prosecutions, or who are committed to their surveillance, and officers, physicians, or surgeons who are employed in prisons or public hospitals, guilty of the same offense towards those under their charge, are punished with hard labor, not to exceed five years.

Bestiality and sodomy, are punished with imprisonment from six months to four years, and with temporary interdiction of civil rights.

Rape, is a forcible satisfaction of lust on another without will or intelligence, or on a child under fourteen years. If death follows, the punishment is hard labor for life; otherwise, for a term not exceeding twenty years.

The seduction of a female by false representations is punished with hard labor for five years.

A common prostitute, if unlicensed, is punished with imprisonment which cannot exceed six weeks, and, if a foreigner, can be expelled from the kingdom. The judge can order that the person so sentenced be put in a house of correction, where she remains so long as the local police judge necessary, for a term not exceeding one year.

Pimping, or the habitual or professional pandering, whether for gain or not, by mediation, or providing opportunities, is punished with imprisonment for not less than six months, and the being placed under the surveillance of the police. In aggravated circumstances, the imprisonment is changed to hard labor, which can be extended to five years.

The seduction of a child of from fourteen to sixteen years, is punished, on the complaint of the parents or tutor of the child, with imprisonment of from three months to one year.

Public indecency is punished with imprisonment from three months to three years, and, if the judge thinks fit, with temporary interdiction of civic rights.

The sale, distribution, or propagation of indecent writings, prints, or representations, is punished by a fine of from ten to one hundred thalers, or with imprisonment from fourteen days to six months, and the confiscation of the *corpus delicti.*

Slander and Libel. Whoever publicly or by writing insults another, is punished by fine, which can amount to three hundred thalers, or to imprisonment, not to exceed six months. When a person insulted replies immediately with insults, the judge is empowered to pronounce a milder punishment against one or both, or he can acquit them.

Criticisms, blaming scientific or artistic works, warning superiors against their subordinates, and denunciations of official acts, or sentences of a magistrate, and analogous cases, are punishable when it appears from the form or circumstances that there was an intention to do injury.

Physicians, and all persons who betray secrets which were confided to them on account of their position, are punished by a fine which can amount to 500 thalers, or imprisonment of at most three months.

Calumny is the asserting or spreading false imformation concerning another, which may expose the same to the hate or contempt of the public. If the calumny is public, the punishment is imprisonment from one week to one year. When, however, the defendant proves the truth of his assertions, which he has the right to do, by all means that are admitted for criminal cases, he is not punished, except when it appears from the form or circumstances that he had the intention to do injury.

The punishment for libel and calumny is only pronounced on the demand of the injured party, who can renounce his accusation at any moment. This complaint can be instituted by husbands in the name of their wives, and by fathers in the name of their children. In all these cases, the sentence of condemnation is published at the cost of the person condemned.

Dueling. The principals in a duel, and the person who carries the challenge, are punished. The seconds, witnesses, physicians, and surgeons are not punishable, and are not bound to denounce the duel to the authorities. The punishment for dueling is confinement from two months to twenty years, according to the consequences of the duel and the circumstances of the case. The bearers of the challenge are acquitted when they have earnestly endeavored to prevent the duel.

Offenses against Life. An action by which the life of a person is taken is a murder, when performed with intent to kill, and with premeditation; when without premeditation, but with intent, it is manslaughter. Murder is punished by death, manslaughter by hard labor for life. The last is punished with death when committed on a parent or grandparent, or when committed in order to overcome resistance to the commission of a crime or misdemeanor already commenced, or to escape from being taken in the act of committing a crime or misdemeanor. The punishment is changed to imprisonment of not less than two years, if the crime is committed under the influence of excitement caused by grave insult to the person or to his relations.

A mother who kills her illegitimate child during or immediately after birth, is punished with hard labor from five to twenty years. All others who participate in this crime are punished according to the general rules concerning murder or manslaughter.

A mother who intentionally procures abortion is punished by hard labor of not more than five years, and the accomplices receive equal punishment.

The exposure of a child under seven years, or an infirm person, or the abandoning of such persons by those who are intrusted with them, is punished with imprisonment of not less than three months, and hard labor of not more than ten years, in case death ensues from it.

Negligence, which has for result the death of another, is punished with imprisonment from two months to two years. When the author of such negligence is bound by his trade or profession to particular care and prudence, he may, besides the above punishment, be deprived of the exercise of such trade or profession.

The interring or removing of a dead body, without notice to the authorities, is punished by a fine of at least 200 thalers, or imprisonment of at most six months. The mother who inters or removes her illegitimate new-born child, without giving notice to the authorities, is punished with imprisonment which can reach two years.

Corporeal Injuries. The code distinguishes between light and severe injuries inflicted on another. The first are punished by imprisonment of at most two years, and when with premeditation, the imprisonment may be increased to three years. "Severe injuries" are such as cause sickness or incapacity to work for more than twenty days, or mutilation, or privation of speech, sight, hearing, generative power, or intelligence. In such cases, hard labor for fifteen years can be pronounced against the author, and when the death of the injured person follows, the punishment can be increased to twenty years.

Corporeal injuries, inflicted through negligence, are punished by fine of from 10 to 100 thalers, or imprisonment of at most one year, on the complaint of the injured person; or, in case of a grave injury, on the demand of the public prosecutor.

Whoever undertakes the care of an internal or external malady, or to perform the functions of a midwife, without being legally authorized to do so, for money, or contrary to a prohibition of the police, is punished with a fine of from five to fifty thalers, or imprisonment for at most six months. This punishment is not applied, when, in a case of urgent necessity, the assistance of a duly licensed physician is impossible. These last who, in case of imminent danger, refuse their assistance without sufficient ground, are punished by a fine of from 20 to 500 thalers. The midwife who omits to call in a physician, in case of a dangerous delivery, is punished by a fine of not more than 50 thalers, or imprisonment of not more than three months.

Architects who, in the erection of a building, endanger the lives of persons entering or passing, by negligence or ignorance of the rules of their profession, are punished with imprisonment from six weeks to six months, or a fine of from 50 to 300 thalers. In case of repetition, they may be deprived of the right of exercising their profession.

Offenses against Personal Freedom. A crime or misdemeanor against personal freedom, is man-stealing, or the artful or forcible abduction of a person in order to put such person in a helpless condition, or to carry the same into slavery or bondage, or into foreign service on land or sea. The punishment for this is hard labor from five to twenty years.

The artful or forcible abduction of a person under sixteen years, for gain or lust, is punished by hard labor from two to fifteen years; when committed without such intention, if of a minor, with imprisonment of not less than one year, if of a woman, for cohabitation or marriage, hard labor from two to ten years; in case of consent of the female, she being unmarried and a minor, but without the consent of her parents or tutor, with imprisonment from three months to two years.

The sequestration of a person, or the deprivation of personal freedom, is punished with imprisonment from three months to five years; it is changed to hard labor from two to fifteen years when the action has for result grave personal injuries, when the loss of liberty has been for more than a month, or when against a parent or grandparent. The provisional detention of a person, in case of the commission of a crime, or of grounded suspicion of the same, immediately after the commission, is not regarded as sequestration; so, also, of the confinement of a person on account of insanity.

The compelling, or seeking to compel, to the commission of a crime or misdemeanor, by threats, in words or writing, is punished by imprisonment for not more than one year.

Theft and Embezzlement. Theft is the taking the personal property of another, with the intention of appropriating the same unjustly. The punishment is imprisonment of not less than one month, and temporary interdiction of the exercise of civil rights. In case of extenuating circumstances, the imprisonment can be reduced to one week; and, in case of aggravating circumstances, the condemned can be placed under the surveillance of the police.

A more severe punishment—not less than three months' imprisonment—is pronounced in the following cases:

When agricultural instruments and animals employed in agriculture, or gathered crops, are stolen from fields, meadows or gardens; when wood, prepared for burning or for building purposes, is stolen from the forest, or from the place of deposit; when a person who serves for wages, or for board, steals in the house, or a workman steals in the shop of the master; lastly, when a tavern keeper, or servant of the same, steals the effects of a lodger, or when the lodger steals while in the house.

The highest punishment—hard labor, not to exceed ten years, and surveillance of the police—is pronounced in the following cases:

When objects destined to the service of religion are stolen; when theft is committed, either by night, or by two or more persons in an inhabited house; when theft is committed in a building or enclosed place, by means of breaking in, or climbing over, or when false keys are employed to enter; when traveling effects, or objects which are destined to be transported, are stolen on a public street, or in a building of the post or railroad, by cutting away or loosening the objects serving to secure the same, or by the use of false keys; when objects are stolen from a weak-minded person, or child under twelve years; when the thief, or one of the accomplices is armed; when two or more persons co-operate as instigators or participators, who have associated for the continued exercise of robbery or theft; lastly, when objects exposed to loss at a fire or inundation are stolen.

Whoever has already been condemned twice or oftener on account of theft or robbery, is, in case of conviction for simple theft, condemned to hard labor of at most fifteen years, and in case of an aggravated theft, it can reach twenty years. This augmentation of punishment is not applicable when ten years have elapsed since the time when the punishment of the crime or misdemeanor last committed is expiated or remitted.

Embezzlement is the alienation, pawning, consumption, or removal of the personal property of another by those to whom the same is intrusted with the obligation of restitution, or by those who have found or accidentally become in possession of the same. Embezzlement to the prejudice of children or spouse is not punished. A theft or embezzlement from parent or grandparent, stepparents or stepchildren, brother and sister, adoptive parents, tutors, or guardians, are only prosecuted on the complaint of the injured party.

Robbery and Extortion. A robbery is a theft accompanied by force, or violence exercised by a thief seized immediately after the act, in order to save the stolen objects. It is punished in ordinary cases by hard labor from five to fifteen years, and surveillance of the police; if there are aggravating circumstances, the punishment is from ten to twenty years, or for life. Those which subject the author to the first punishment, are the bearing arms, the co-operation of several persons, as originators or assistants, and the committing the crime on a public place or road. The severest punishment is incurred when the robber has been already sentenced by a Prussian court on account of this crime; when a person is tortured or mutilated, or deprived of an organ, or deprived by ill treatment of ability to labor for a longer term than twenty days.

The punishment of extortion is imprisonment for not more than three months, and temporary interdiction of civic rights; surveillance of the police can also be added. The imprisonment is changed to hard labor from two to five years, when the threatened crime is murder, arson, or causing inundation. This offense is regarded as robbery when the menace is accompanied with danger to life or limb, or with violence.

Receiving Stolen Goods. The purchase, taking in pawn, or secreting of objects known to be stolen, embezzled, or procured by means of another crime or misdemeanor, or the favoring, for gain, of persons who have committed such offenses, is punished by imprisonment of not more than one month; if there are extenuating circumstances, it can be reduced to one week, and temporary interdiction of the exercise of civil rights. The judge can also condemn to the surveillance of the police. The receiving of goods obtained by robbery, or the protection afforded to robbers, is punished by hard labor from two to ten years, and the being placed under the surveillance of the police.

Professional receiving is punished by hard labor from two to fifteen years, which penalty is also pronounced against those who have been condemned, once or oftener, for the same crime by a Prussian court.

Fraud. The fraud criminally punishable is the injury to the property of another, with intent to gain, by leading into error, by making false allegations, or disguising, or concealing the truth. The punishment for this crime, and for the attempt, is a fine from 50 to 1,000 thalers, imprisonment from one month to five years, and temporary interdiction of the exercise of civic rights. When there are extenuating circumstances, the penalty can be reduced to one week's imprisonment, or to a fine of five thalers; if there are aggravating circumstances, provided for by the laws, the minimum of imprisonment is three months. The severest aggravation (which can be punished by hard labor from two to ten years, and by fine of from 100 to 2,000 thalers), is the setting fire to insured property,* or the wrecking a ship to gain the insurance on it or its cargo.

Breach of Trust. A breach of trust is punishable, where tutors, guardians, administrators of charitable institutions cause injury, intentionally, to the persons confided to them, and when brokers, or any of those persons who have a particular license from the authorities to carry on their business, knowingly do injury to those whose affairs they have charge of in the business confided to them. The punishment is imprisonment of not less than three months, and temporary interdiction of the exercise of civil rights; in case of its being done for gain, a fine of from 50 to 1,000 thalers is added.

Counterfeiting Documents. Whoever falsifies a document, or counterfeits one, and makes use of the same to deceive, is punished by hard labor of at most five years, and a fine from 50 to 1,000 thalers.

The same punishment is awarded against him who, contrary to the will of the signer, makes a declaration or obligation over a signature with intent to cause him prejudice, and against him who knowingly makes use of a false or counterfeit document. If there are aggravating circumstances, such as the falsification of public papers, acts or registers, wills, and bills of exchange, the penalty is hard labor from two to ten years, and fine from 100 to 2,000 thalers.

The falsifying or counterfeiting of stamped paper, or postage stamps, is punished by imprisonment from three months to five years.

The falsifying or counterfeiting a passport is punished by imprisonment from one week to three months, and, of an official certificate, by imprisonment from two weeks to six months.

---

* The Prussian code differs from other codes in the appreciation of this offense, which by them is declared a separate crime — arson.

Bankruptcy. Fraudulent bankruptcy is the suspension of payment by merchants and tradesmen, ship-owners, and manufacturers, when they have secreted or set aside the whole or a part of their fortune; when they have declared debts and engagements which do not exist; when they have failed to keep their commercial books, with the intention of doing injury to their creditors; or when, for the same purpose, they have secreted or destroyed their books. The punishment is hard labor from two to fifteen years; when there are extenuating circumstances, it is reduced to imprisonment for not less than three months.

Simple bankrupty is punished with imprisonment not to exceed two years. It consists in extreme negligence in conducting business, and in the manner of living; without, as in fraudulent bankruptcy, the intention to deceive.

Punishable selfishness. Punishable selfishness includes a long list of offenses, of which the principal are: usury; professional pawnbrokery; professional gambling; the keeping gambling houses; the undertaking a lottery without permission of the authorities; fishing in the waters of another; hunting or shooting on the grounds or district of another; lastly, the opening of sealed letters, or documents, without having the right to do so.

In all these various cases, the penalties are imprisonment or fine.

Injuries to another's property. Whoever intentionally and unjustly injures or deranges the property of another, is punished with imprisonment, not to exceed two years; and if there are extenuating circumstances, by a fine not to exceed 50 thalers. When there are aggravating circumstances, on account of the nature of the damaged objects, the minimum of the imprisonment is fourteen days, and in some cases, a maximum of two months. When several persons are associated for this purpose, they are punished by hard labor from two to fifteen years.

Offenses of a generally dangerous character. Crimes and misdemeanors of a generally dangerous character are: arson; the destruction of buildings by the use of powder, or other explosive substances; the causing an inundation; injuries to railroads, telegraphs, or other means of communication; the poisoning of springs, &c., &c.

In all these cases, if loss of life is a consequence, the punishment of death is pronounced; when not, the penalty is hard labor for life, or for a term of years; when without criminal intention, the punishment is imprisonment.

To this kind of offense belongs the non-fulfilling, in time of war, of an engagement to deliver subsistence for the army, or of provisions for relieving distress, in times of scarcity. The punishment for which is imprisonment for not less than six months; and, in cases of simple negligence only, not to exceed two years.

Offenses by public officers. A public officer who receives a bribe or other advantage, or who stipulates to violate the duties of his office, or perform an act which he is duly bound to perform gratuitously, is punished in the first case by hard labor from two to ten years; or if there are extenuating circumstances, by imprisonment for not less than six months, and temporary interdiction of civil rights; in the latter cases, by imprisonment of not more than six months, or fine. The officer can also be temporarily suspended from his office.

Besides the case of bribery, there are other high grades of abuse of authority; the intentional injustice of a judge; the employing of coercive measures against an accused in penal procedure, in order to provoke a confession or declaration; the execution of a punishment which is contrary to the laws; the misuse, or falsification of public documents, by those who give authenticity to the same. In all other cases, imprisonment alone is pronounced.

PART III. CONTRAVENTIONS.

This last part of the Prussian code is divided into four chapters. The first treats of the punishment of contraventions in general. The second treats of contraventions in respect to the security of the State, and public order. The third, of contraventions in respect to personal security, honor, and freedom; and lastly, the fourth chapter treats of offenses of this denomination against property.

In general only such actions are to be punished as contraventions which are so declared by the laws, or the regulations of the authorities. The legal punishments are: the *police imprisonment*, which consists in simple deprivation of liberty of not less than one day or more than six weeks; and *fine* from ten silbergroschen* to fifty thalers, and the confiscation of certain objects. In case of insolvency of the offender, the fine is changed to imprisonment; one day counting for from ten silver groschen to two thalers.

The attempt at a contravention is not punishable.

The limitation for contraventions is in three months, with the exception of the case of insult, which extends to six months.

Contraventions in respect to the security of the State, and of public order, are punished by fine or imprisonment. To this class belongs a long list of offenses, which consist in actions without criminal intention, which threaten the well-being of the State; such as the secretly collecting of arms or munitions, the founding of certain associations without the assent of the authorities; the refusal of assistance in case of public danger or necessity; the disturbance of Sunday and religious or public holiday; the making indecent noises in the streets; the public ill treat-

* Twenty-three cents—Thirty silbergroschen make one thaler.

ment of animals; lastly the carrying on of games of chance on the public places. The same punishment is pronounced for beggary, and against the person who compels children to beg; whoever remains in a tavern or place of public amusement longer than is allowed by the laws, after being directed to leave by the proprietor or police officer, is punished by a fine not exceeding five thalers. The landlord is punished with a fine, not to exceed twenty thalers, or imprisonment, not to exceed fourteen days, when he does not seek to hinder his guests from keeping late hours.

Insult is punished, on the complaint of the person insulted, with a fine, not exceeding fifty thalers, or imprisonment, not exceeding six weeks; in the cases of disturbing security, convenience, cleanliness, and quiet in the public streets or squares; in cases where the danger to public security is great, as in the case of the preparing or sale of poisons or medicaments; the manufacture and having in possession inflammable or explosive substances, the opening of cellars, pits, or cisterns on the public streets without taking the proper precautionary measures; the non-observance of the public regulations respecting the reparation or destruction of dilapidated buildings. The same punishment is pronounced against the person who enters the dwelling of another without right, and refuses to depart when summoned to do so; him who sets dogs on persons, who throw stones or other hard or foul objects at others.

Whoever, by an action without criminal intention, injures or threatens to injure the property of another is punished with a fine, not exceeding twenty thalers, or imprisonment, not exceeding fourteen days; in particularly aggravating circumstances the maximum of fifty thalers or imprisonment for six weeks can be pronounced.

FEUERBACH'S PENAL CODE FOR BAVARIA.
(*Strafgesetbuch.*)

Bavaria, in common with other German states, was for a long time governed, as to its law of crimes and criminal procedure, by the celebrated statutes of Chas. V, known as the *Carolina Criminalis.* The preparation of this system of law was commenced in 1498, and the system itself was completed and adopted as law in 1532. This code was not so much devoted to criminal law as to procedure, being called, in its preface, "a simple instruction for unlearned judges to teach them how to proceed in criminal cases." It, however, gave definitions of the graver crimes, and prescribed their punishment.

The *Carolina Criminalis* continued in force for a long time. Modifications were, however, introduced, differing in the different states composing the empire, until at last a great number of penal codes grew into existence, even the smallest states having codes of their own. The *Carolina Criminalis*, the source and origin of all, has thus, though never formally repealed, become virtually abolished.

The most important of the German codes which are above described as having grown up to replace the *Carolina Criminalis*, is a code prepared for Bavaria by the famous German jurist, Feuerbach. It was originally promulgated in 1813. It is no longer in force in its original form; but as it became the parent of many systems of penal law adopted in the neighboring states, it is here described as it originally stood, disregarding the subsequent modifications of penal law which have been made in, but are peculiar to, Bavaria.

A distinguishing feature of Feuerbach's code is the distinctness of his definitions of crimes. He arranged in distinct classes all kinds of criminal actions, distinguished each class from others by fixed definitions, marked strict boundaries to the sphere of each crime, and employed language which is simple and free from ambiguity. Some of the codes framed in other states upon the basis of Feuerbach's, are, however, regarded as superior to his in execution, having less the style of a compendium than his, and being composed in language more appropriate to a law.

Another peculiar feature is the theory of punishment adopted. The principle which underlies the system is, that punishment ought to be more severe in proportion as the temptation to commit the offense was powerful; so that in general the punishment shall involve a greater evil than the offender would have experienced by resisting the temptation. This view leads to some results which, to those trained under a different system, appear unadvisable; thus, for example, a thief who had a powerful and preponderating temptation to steal, is more severely punished than a parricide who acted without such inducements and temptations as influenced the thief.

The Bavarian code (of Feuerbach) is divided into two parts; the first treats of crimes and misdemeanors; the second of procedure.

Part I is divided into three books.

The first book is divided into five chapters, and gives the general provisions concerning crimes and misdemeanors. The topics of these chapters are: Punishable actions, and their various degrees of punishment; the perpetration of crimes, criminal intention, and the authorship of crimes; criminal attempts, criminal participation, and crimes resulting from culpable negligence; rules for proportioning of the punishment to the crime and its attendant circumstances of extenuation or aggravation; and the grounds for remitting punishment.

The second book treats of crimes and their punishments, in detail. They are classified as crimes against individuals and crimes against the State. In the first class are: crimes against human life; personal injuries and maltreatment; theft, embezzlement, robbery and extortion; injuries done to property; fraud; and breach of trust. In the second are high treason, offenses against the king or the royal family, and other crimes against the security or existence of the State.

The third book treats of misdemeanors both against persons and the State, and of the punishments which are provided for them. To misdemeanors against individuals belong the lighter offenses against the person; and such as theft, embezzlement, personal injuries under certain circumstances and certain lower grades of breach of trust. To misdemeanors against the State belong offenses compromising the honor of the State; resistance to authorities; offenses against public peace; against public credit, and against public property; and lastly, the particular misdemeanors of public officers.

In this code, as in the French *Code Pénal*, punishable actions are either crimes, misdemeanors, or contraventions. Crimes are all offenses, which, by their nature and gravity, incur the penalties of death, confinement in irons, hard labor of the first or second degree, imprisonment in a fortress, deprivation of public office, or declaration of incapacity for all offices or honors of State or trust. Misdemeanors are all offenses, committed with or without criminal intention, which are punishable with imprisonment, flogging, fine, and other lighter punishments. Contraventions are actions or omissions, which, although not causing injury to the rights of the State or the subject, are prohibited or commanded under certain penalties, because they endanger public order, and compromise public security. Lighter offenses, which are referred by particular laws to the examination of the police authorities, who also have the punishment of them, come likewise under this head.

From these definitions, it is easy to perceive that the legislator recognizes an offense as punishable only when it is in violation of an essential right of the individual or the State. The later codes have, however, abandoned this fundamental principle of the Bavarian code.

The punishment of death is either simple or aggravated. The mode is decapitation. In the first case, the criminal is led to the place of execution, clad in a grey blouse, and bare headed, with a tablet on the back and breast, inscribed with the name of the crime. In the second, the criminal, dressed and labeled in the same way, is exposed for half an hour in the pillory.

Confinement in irons is for life, and is accompanied by civil death. The labor of the prisoner is determined by the State. The prisoner is fastened by a chain to a heavy iron ball.

The punishment of hard labor, of the first degree, is either for a definite term of from eight to twenty years, or for a term not fixed by the sentence, in which case, after ten years, on evidence of repentance or improvement, the punishment is remitted. A judge can never sentence to hard labor *for life*. The second degree of hard labor consists of the prisoner being confined in another and separate establishment, where he is treated in a milder manner, and his punishment is less laborious than in the first.

Imprisonment in a fortress is of three kinds. The first is substituted in particular cases for imprisonment in irons; the second, for hard labor of the first degree; and the third for hard labor of the second degree. The first and second degrees of this punishment, as well as of other punishments, may be augmented by confinement in dark dungeons, diminution of food, flogging, and exposure in the pillory.

In case of flogging, the number of lashes is named in the sentence, and cannot exceed fifty; and they can only be given on the declaration of a physician that they will not endanger the criminal's life.

Imprisonment for not exceeding two years takes place in a local prison, or in a fortress, where there is no compulsory labor, but where the quantity of food can be diminished.

Whoever causes the condemnation of a criminal to be made a reproach to his relatives, may be subjected to a penalty of from eight to fourteen days' imprisonment.

Those persons are considered as authors of a crime who assist in its execution by direct bodily strength of exertion; who render an assistance without which the crime could not have been consummated; or who excite and provoke other persons to its commission.

A "complot" is different from these cases, and consists in two or more persons joining with another, for a common interest, in the commission of a crime; and who bind themselves, by promises of mutual assistance, to co-operate in its execution.

Participation in the execution of a crime incurs the same penalty as the crime itself, although the ringleaders receive the severest punishment.

An accomplice is he who knowingly and intentionally participates in a crime resolved on by another, whether by words, acts, or omissions to act, and even when such participation was not so necessary but the crime could have been committed without it. The law recognizes and determines three grades of complicity, according as the co-operation or participation is of more or less importance in the commission of a crime. The punishment of an accomplice is regulated by that of the perpetrator. In the third grade of the crime of complicity, we observe one of the peculiarities of the theory of Feuerbach. The persons who are included in this grade, and who are liable to its penalty, are those who fail to denounce a crime or a misdemeanor, of which they have knowledge, and who, though not public officers, do not hinder or prevent a crime so far as is possible, even by the use of physical force. The receiving of stolen goods, or the favoring of the escape of a criminal, is also punished as a second degree of complicity.

Criminal attempt consists in having the intention to commit a crime, and having done anything in preparation or towards the perpetration of the same. It is either proximate, distant, or aggravated. A proximate attempt is when the criminal is present, and is taken at the commencement of the action by which the crime or misdemeanor would have been immediately consummated. A distant attempt is when the offender has only assisted in certain acts which are regarded as merely preparatory to the crime. An aggravated attempt is when the attempt constitutes in itself a crime or misdemeanor. The punishment in this case is more severe than the punishment of a proximate attempt, or of the crime independently, even when the punishment for this last is more severe than that laid down for attempt. Criminal attempt of the two first grades is not punished, as in the French code, with the same penalty which is attached to the crime itself; but it is increased or diminished in proportion as it is distant or proximate to the actual commission of the crime.

As has been already stated, a leading peculiarity of Feuerbach's system is his theory as to the meting out of punishments.

When the law has not defined the precise grade of punishment, it must be determined by the judge, always in observance of the following principles: The punishment must be increased in proportion as the reasons for obeying the law are numerous and important; as the obligations violated by the offender are great and serious; as the criminal is in a condition clearly to know his motives for the commission of the crime; as the hindrances to the commission of the crime were great, or as the criminal was instigated by his own impulses, or by external circumstances; as the offender, by the continued practice of bad manners, and the performance of loose actions, has become intractable and disposed to crime; and as the lusts and passions manifested in the commission of the crime were dangerous and malicious. On the other hand, the punishments are decreased when the offender, having an opportunity to commit a greater crime, restrained himself voluntarily to a smaller one; when he takes pains to prevent the consequences of the crime, or voluntarily to repair the injury done; when he voluntarily delivers himself up to justice; when at the first or second examination he confesses his crime; or lastly, when he has led to the detection of other criminals, or furnished means or opportunity for their seizure.

Though the crime is *proven* against the accused, nevertheless, if in an important matter of fact, there is an essential point of the evidence defective, a milder punishment than that prescribed by law is inflicted.

The commission at the same time of several crimes is punished by an accumulation of the penalties of all.

Repetition of a crime or misdemeanor is punished more severely than the original offense. It exists when a person, after having undergone a punishment, repeats an offense similar to that for which he was sentenced.

No punishment is pronounced against children under eight years of age, insane persons, idiots, or persons who, from melancholy or other grave mental affection, have lost the use of their judgment; those who cannot judge of the consequences of their actions, nor be sensible that a penalty is attached to them; those who, by reason of weakness caused by old age, have lost the use of their judgment; deaf and dumb persons, so far as they are not regularly instructed in their duties; those who are in incurable ignorance, and have, therefore, regarded their actions as allowable and not criminal; those who have committed a criminal action under the influence of physical force which they could not resist, or of bodily fear, such as menace against life; and, finally, those who have resolved on committing a crime, and have executed it, while in a confused state of mind or senses for which they were not answerable.

No crime exists for defending one's self, nor for those who have assisted in such defense. The law provides for, and affixes penalties to, those cases where the limits of legitimate defense are exceeded.

In general there is no limitation to punishments. If, however, the criminal has not been prosecuted within a period fixed by the law, and if, meanwhile, he has conducted himself irreproachably, he is declared exempt from punishment.

The second part of this code is devoted to criminal procedure.

PENAL CODE OF SAXE-WEIMAR.

The penal code of the grand duchy of Saxe-Weimer dates from the year 1838.

There were no great difficulties to the introduction of this code, nor any important parliamentary discussions on the subject, it having been founded on the codes of the other German states, which immediately preceded it, and on the Prussian project. It is not without interest to remark, that the code of this state, which numbers the population of a second-rate city of the United States, commences with principles of international law. It proclaims that not only the inhabitants of this grand duchy, but also that the *Saxe-Weimarers* who have, in foreign parts, committed an action which is high treason against the grand duchy, or the ducal family, or on account of an action which is committed without the limits of the state, in order to defraud the laws of the same, are subject to the prescriptions of this code.

A very original prescription of this body of laws is, that the punishments are pronounced not only on account of violation of the *letter*, but also on account of violation of the *spirit* of the law. All other existing codes forbid analogy in the interpretation of penal law, and admit only the strict application of the text.

The punishments admissible in Saxe-Weimar, are: Death; confinement in irons; hard labor of first and second degrees; confinement in a fortress; infamy and degradation; flogging; imprisonment in a fortress; fine. In the execution of these punishments, the same regulations are observed as in the Bavarian code, already described. The provisions of this code are so far copied from the Bavarian, throughout, as to render further details unnecessary.

PENAL CODE OF BADEN.

This code was promulgated March 6th, 1845. It is divided into two parts: the first treats of offenses and their punishments in general; the second, of individual offenses and their penalties.

The division of offenses into crimes, misdemeanors, and contraventions, employed in the *Code Pénal*, and most of the other codes of Europe, is not adopted in that of Baden. Offenses are neither defined nor graduated. The first article merely bears the title "*punishable actions*," and provides that the commission or omission of an action is only punishable when the law prescribes a penalty for the same.

There are two classes of punishments; criminal and civil.

The criminal punishments are: Capital punishment; hard labor for life; hard labor for a term of not less than three nor more than twenty years, and deprivation of office. The citizens of Baden who are sentenced to hard labor, and those who are particularly dangerous to public security, may, on coming out of prison, be placed under the surveillance of the police for a term of from one to five years. An individual receiving this punishment cannot leave his house, or place of residence given to him by the authorities, over night, and is subjected to house-searchings at the discretion of the police or judicial authorities.

The civil punishments are: Confinement in a house of correction or fortification, from six months to two years; imprisonment; removal from office with the capability of being restored again after three years; loss of license to exercise certain professions; fine not to exceed, as a rule, 1,000 guildens;* confiscation of certain objects, and judicial admonition. Imprisonment can be aggravated in certain grave cases,

* The guilden is forty cents.

by solitary confinement of not more than two months duration; by confinement in the dark, not to exceed four days; short diet, of bread and water, or bread and warm gruel, not longer than seven days, which cannot be consecutive; lastly, by being put in chains for a period not to exceed four weeks.

Attempts to commit crimes receive a milder punishment than complete perpetration; and a distinction is observed between different classes of attempts. If all has been accomplished necessary to the consummation of the offense, which, however, has been impeded by some circumstance independent of the will of the criminal, the punishment is considerably more severe than when this is not the case.

The originators of an offense are not alone those who have accomplished it by deeds, but those who have decided on, or incited to the same. When the perpetration of the offense does not depend on the influence of the counselor, however, he is punished less severely than the perpetrator, but receives the same penalty as the accomplice.

An accomplice is he who knowingly facilitates or furthers the offense of another. The punishment for this grade of guilt is less than for the originator or perpetrator; the punishment of death is changed to hard labor for life, or for a term of years; in all other cases the minimum of the punishments inflicted on the ringleader, or the next lower grade of penalty, is incurred. Rendering aid and comfort to a criminal after the act, is punishable, regard being had in adjusting the penalty to the importance and motives of the principal crime.

The system of aggravating and extenuating circumstances, which is according to Feuerbach's theory, is interesting. The punishment is *aggravated* in proportion as the reasons for committing the offense were more numerous and important; as the obstacles and dangers in the way of the execution were great; as the external incentives to the offense were small or insignificant; and as the offender by his former manner of living had manifested immorality and perversity. The punishment is *mitigated* when the offender was not aware of the result of the act or the extent of the punishment of the same; when led to commit the offense either by necessity, persuasion, deceit, seduction, order, or menace; when he was in a state of great mental excitement; when he has led an irreproachable life; when, under the influence of repentance, he has sought to hinder the injurious consequences of the punishable action; and when he has himself given information of his offense to the authorities.

There is no punishment for an offense committed when the exercise of a free will or the knowledge of the penalty of the offense was wanting, or when in ignorance of the facts which make an action punishable, or which increase the penalty of the same. Children under twelve years old are not held accountable for offenses; those from twelve to sixteen years old are only punished when they have acted with discernment, and then with a milder penalty than that inflicted on those of riper years.

Self-defense, in case of imminent danger to one's life, or to one's property, or defense of a near relation whose life is in danger, is not punished when thereby an action is committed which in other cases would receive punishment.

When several offenses are committed by the same party, the severest of the punishments incurred is inflicted, with augmentation in proportion to the nature and number of the offenses.

The term of limitation for those offenses which incur capital punishment, or hard labor, is twenty years; for other offenses ten years; for those offenses which are prosecuted on the demand of the injured party, two years.

PENAL CODE OF AUSTRIA.

This code was promulgated by imperial patent, May 27, 1852. It applies to all the states of the monarchy, with the exception of the military frontiers. It was accompanied by laws defining the jurisdiction of courts, and regulating some matters of procedure; also, by a proclamation of the emperor, laying down principles to govern the application of the penal code and accompanying laws. Provision was made that from the day when the code should take effect, no offenses should be prosecuted, other than such as were defined in the code; except that for actions committed before that time, the code should only be applied when the punishments prescribed by it were not severer than those of the former law.

A great difference, both in system and classification, is to be remarked between this and the other codes which have been given. The Austrian code does not commence with preliminary and general principles, but is divided into two parts, which contain the special laws on punishable actions, and their penalties. The first part treats of crimes; the second part of misdemeanors and contraventions. The Austrian code has thus adopted the classification of offenses employed in that of France, although this classification is not recognized by any special article.

PART I. CRIMES.

This part is divided into twenty-nine chapters, of the contents of which the following is a compend:

Crime generally. The first thing to be sought for to prove the existence of a crime is criminal intention; it exists, not only when, before or during the commission of the crime, the injury, which is the consequence of the crime, was intended; but also when, owing to another evil intention, something was undertaken or omitted, in which the injury caused by the same has resulted, or can easily result, as a consequence of the action. No crime, therefore, exists when the actor is totally deprived of reason, or when he commits the deed in a moment of temporary insanity; when he is in a condition of complete drunkenness, or any other confusion of the senses; when he is under fourteen years old; when, through error, he cannot see a crime in the action; when the evil consequences have resulted from accident, negligence or ignorance; or, lastly, when the act resulted from compulsion by superior force, or in the exercise of self-defense. The plea of self-defense is only to be admitted when it is to be supposed, in taking into account the person, time, place, kind of attack, or other circumstances, that only the necessary means of defense were used, in order to repel an unjust attack on life, liberty or property; or, that the bounds of self-defense were exceeded under the influence of intimidation or fear.

No one can plead ignorance of this code.

The immediate criminal is not alone guilty of a crime, but also he who, by command, counsel, instruction, or praise, prepares the offense, or intentionally has rendered assistance towards the execution of the same, or towards removing the obstacles to its commission; lastly, he who has stipulated with the offender beforehand to give him criminal assistance after the deed, or to participate with him in the gain arising therefrom. Whoever, *after* the commission of the crime, and without preliminary stipulation, gives assistance to the criminal, or divides the spoils with him, is not equally guilty, but by those acts becomes guilty of another and special crime. When the law on the press is violated, the author, the translator, the publisher, and in case the offending publication is periodical, the editor, and generally all persons who *have co-operated to print or spread* such publication, are guilty of the same crime.

Criminal attempt is punishable when the criminal has committed an action leading to the commission of a crime, which crime, however, was hindered by some circumstances independent of the will of the author. The punishment of attempt is, in all cases in which the law establishes no particular exception, the same as for the consummated crime, in which case, nevertheless, those extenuating circumstances allowed in the law are admitted. An attempt exists, also, when a person endeavors to persuade another to a crime which he does not commit.

Crimes of the press, on the part of the author, translator, editor, and publisher, date from the delivering the manuscript to be printed.

No one is answerable for his *thoughts* or internal resolutions, when no external criminal action is undertaken, or nothing laid down in the laws is omitted.

Punishment of crimes. These are the following:

Death—this is inflicted by hanging.

Confinement in a dungeon—"*Kerker.*" There are two grades of this punishment—the simple and the aggravated.

Simple *Kerker*, consists in confinement in a small space, without being put in irons, and in subordination to the regulations introduced for punishments. In aggravated *Kerker*, the criminal is chained by the foot; and conversation with others than his keepers is only allowed under particular and important circumstances. The punishment of the *Kerker* is inflicted either for life or for a term of years. The term commences only from the moment when no appeal from the sentence is possible. The punishment can be aggravated by diminution of food, deprivation of bed, isolation (for not longer than one month uninterruptedly), and solitary confinement in a dark cell (for not longer than three days uninterruptedly).

Flogging with rods or whips. The flogging for youths, under eighteen years old, and for *women*, is with the whip; for men, with rods. The operation can only be executed after an opinion of the surgeon on the power of endurance of the criminal. Nevertheless, this punishment can never exceed thirty blows, which cannot be given in public.

Lastly, banishment after the expiration of the term of punishment.

The legal consequences of every punishment on account of crime are, deprivation of all foreign and national decorations; the loss of all public titles and academical honors; exclusion from the responsible publication of a periodical magazine or paper; loss of every public office or service; if a minister of religion, deprivation of titles; loss of judicial dignity of office, or profession of notary public, lawyer, attorney, or barrister; and, lastly, loss of all pensions.

The surveillance of the high police is regulated by special laws. The loss of nobility is connected with the punishment of death, and of aggravated *Kerker*. To the latter also, is annexed incapacity, during the term of punishment, to perform any legal act.

When a criminal has committed different crimes, which are the objects of the same prosecution, he can only be punished for that crime which has for penalty the severest punishment, regard being had, however, to the other crimes.

When an Austrian commits a crime in a foreign land, he is, nevertheless, punished according to the prescriptions of this code; and when he has been already punished where the crime was committed, he receives, if that punishment was less than laid down in the laws of Austria, the additional punishment on his return.

The crime of high treason, or of counterfeiting the obligations, bank notes, or coins of Austria, by a foreigner, receives the punishment laid down in the code, when even committed in another country.

Aggravating circumstances. This code has here followed very closely the theory of Feuerbach. The crime is greater in proportion as the preparations to the same were more premeditated; as the injury caused, or the danger connected with, the crime was greater; or more obligations were broken, and less precaution could have been taken against the same. Besides these general aggravating circumstances, there are the following special ones: When several crimes of different natures are committed, or the same crime be repeated; when the criminal has already been punished on account of a similar crime; when he has seduced others to the crime; when he has been the exciter, ringleader, or author of a crime committed by several persons; lastly, when the accused seeks to deceive the judge by making false allegations.

Extenuating circumstances. These depend upon the person of the criminal or on the nature of the offense. Those depending on the person of the criminal, are as follows: When he is less than twenty years old; when he is of weak intellect or grossly ignorant; when he has led an irreproachable life before the commission of the crime; when he has been induced to commit the crime by another, or has committed the same under the influence of fear, or intimidation; when he has been urged to the commission of the crime by violent mental excitement, "growing out of the ordinary feelings of man;" when he has been tempted, by good opportunity, to the commission of a crime suggested by the imprudence of another; when he has been under the influence of extreme poverty; when he has sought to repair the injury caused by the crime, or to prevent further injurious consequences; when, at the time of its perpetration, he could easily have escaped, or remained undiscovered, and yet has informed against himself, and confessed the crime; when he has led to the detection of other criminals, and has furnished opportunity and means for their seizure; lastly, when he has been imprisoned for a long term on account of unusual delay of the preliminary proceedings for which he was not to blame.

The extenuating circumstances on account of the nature of the crime are the three following: When the contemplated crime is not consummated; when the crime is perpetrated with voluntary abstention from the commission of greater injuries, for which there was opportunity; and, lastly, when the damage resulting from the crime is small, or when the injured person has received full reparation.

Application of aggravating and extenuating circumstances in determining the punishments. Aggravating circumstances are only taken into account, in so far as they are not accompanied by extenuating circumstances; just as extenuating circumstances are considered only in as far as they are not accompanied by aggravating circumstances.

In case of aggravation, the nature of the punishment provided by the law cannot be altered, nor the *maximum* penalty increased.

There is no aggravation of the punishment of death, or of imprisonment for life.

In case of extenuating circumstances, for the crimes of which the duration of punishment is not fixed by law at more than five years, the confinement can be modified to a milder grade, and the legal duration of the term can be reduced. This mitigation can even be pronounced in favor of a guiltless family, when by a longer duration of the punishment it might experience serious diminution of its means of subsistence.

Different kinds of crime. Crimes affect either the common security, in the unity of the state and in the public confidence, or they affect the security of the individual in his person or in his property, liberty, or other rights.

Without entering into the details of the different classes of crimes, some peculiarities may be remarked.

High treason. The crime of high treason is committed when any one injures or endangers the person of the Emperor, in body, health, or freedom; or when a violent change in the form of government is attempted; or when the separation of a part of the empire, or an insurrection or civil war is aimed at.

High treason is committed when these actions are directed against the existence, integrity, or security of the constitution of the German confederation. The punishment for these crimes is death, which is executed upon the authors, ringleaders, and accomplices; and which is also incurred in case of an attack on the person of the Emperor, when the result sought for is not attained. The intentional omission to inform of a conspiracy, for this object, is punished with aggravated *Kerker* from five to ten years, unless the information was withheld by reason of near relationship to the criminal.

Whoever has become concerned in an association of persons guilty of high treason, but who, nevertheless, through penitence, informs against the members of the same, and exposes their statutes, intentions, and undertakings, at a time when they are still secret, and when the injury can be prevented, is not punished; and his secrecy is not violated.

Offenses against the sovereign. Offenses against the sovereign are committed in cases of personal insult, public invectives, defamation or derision, by prints or writings, or pictorial representations. The punishment in these cases is aggravated *Kerker* from one to five years. When these offenses are committed against any other members of the imperial house, the punishment is simple *Kerker* from one to five years.

Disturbance of the public peace. The crime of disturbance of the public peace is committed by provoking others, by means of printing, writings, or pictorial representations, to contempt or hatred against the person of the Emperor, the unity of the empire, the form of government, or the administration of the state; by the provoking, in like manner, to disobedience, resistance, or insurrection against the laws, ordinances, sentences of the courts, or orders of other public authorities; by the refusal to pay taxes; and where it is sought to induce to participation in these actions, or to take part in the same in any manner. The punishment of these crimes is aggravated *Kerker* from one to five years.

The same punishment is inflicted when the action which constitutes high treason is undertaken against any state of the German confederacy, or the sovereign of the same; or against another foreign state, or its chief, when, by law, or by particular conventions, this reciprocity is guaranteed and legally published in the empire of Austria. In this last case, when there are aggravating circumstances, the punishment of aggravated *Kerker* from five to ten years can be inflicted.

Whoever seeks to discover circumstances in the military defense of the state, or in the army, with the intention of giving information of the same to the enemy; or whoever, in time of peace, discovers and betrays the operations which the state has made for its security, is punished as a spy, according to special military laws.

Sedition and riot. Sedition is the uniting of several persons with the intention of offering resistance to the authorities. The criminal, in such cases, is equally guilty, whether he takes part in the conspiracy from the beginning, or afterwards. The punishment is *Kerker*, which can reach twenty years. When, by such a conspiracy, resistance is made to the authorities which requires extraordinary measures to restore peace and good order, it is called *riot.* When, in this case, martial law is proclaimed, the punishment of death is pronounced against the rioters; in other cases the ringleaders and those exciting to the riot are punished with aggravated *Kerker* from ten to twenty years, and this punishment is also applied in case of a great degree of malice and danger to life. The other rioters are punished with aggravated *Kerker* from one to five years, and, when there are aggravating circumstances, from five to ten years.

Counterfeiting. The crime of counterfeiting the bonds of the state, or other public securities, or bank notes, is punished, for principals and accomplices, with aggravated *Kerker* from ten to twenty years. The counterfeiting of coins is punished with aggravated *Kerker* from five to ten years, and when there is particular danger or injury, from ten to twenty years. When, nevertheless, the counterfeiting was obvious to every one, the punishment is from one to five years.

Crimes against religion. Among the cases of crimes against religion are the inducing a Christian to renounce his religion, and the spreading doctrines contrary to the Christian religion. The punishment for these offenses is aggravated *Kerker* from one to five years, and when there are aggravating circumstances, from five to ten years.

Bigamy. The punishment of bigamy is simple *Kerker* from one to five years.

Extinction of crimes and punishments. A crime is extinguished, either: By the death of the criminal; or, by his having undergone the punishment of the same, with the reservation of the further consequences which have been before mentioned; or, by pardon; or, by limitation. The limitation for crimes punishable with *Kerker* for life takes place after twenty years; for crimes punishable with *Kerker* from ten to twenty years, after ten years; for all other crimes, after five years. The limitation is only admitted when the criminal no longer possesses any advantage from his crime; when he has, as far as possible, made restitution; when he has not fled from the country; and, lastly, when during the period of limitation he has committed no new crimes which have death for penalty. After a lapse of twenty years, aggravated *Kerker* from ten to twenty years can only be pronounced.

PART II. MISDEMEANORS AND CONTRAVENTIONS.

Punishments. The punishments for misdemeanors and contraventions, by the Austrian code, are: Fine; Confiscation of certain objects; loss of certain rights and privileges; imprisonment; arrest; flogging; banishment from certain places; banishment from one of the crownlands of the empire; banishment from the monarchy.

The punishment of imprisonment is of two grades; by the first the prisoner is confined in a prison without being put in irons, in which case he can provide his own food, and can choose the labor in which he is to be employed. The imprisonment of the second grade is called aggravated. The prisoner in this case is not put in irons, but is only subjected to the ordinary regulations of the prison concerning food and labor. Besides these two grades of imprisonment, there is a so-called "house arrest," which consists in the obligation, on the part of the person so condemned, not to leave his house under any pretext, under penalty of expiating the remainder of his term of "house arrest" in a public prison. The court can order a sentry to be placed before the house. The *Arrest* is from twenty-four hours to six months.

Flogging of youths under eighteen years, and women, is inflicted with whips; of others, with rods. The number of the blows cannot exceed twenty for misdemeanors and contraventions.

Banishment from the monarchy can only be pronounced against

foreigners. Banishment from a town or state is pronounced for a fixed or uncertain time.

Imprisonment can be aggravated by diminution of food; hard labor; deprivation of bedding, not oftener than twice a week; isolation, not longer than fifteen days; solitary confinement in a dark cell, not longer than twenty-four hours. Flogging is only permitted in case of repetition of offenses.

In general a penalty provided by the law cannot be changed—with the exception that when the fine is beyond the resources of the person condemned, or when, by the duration of the imprisonment, the property of the prisoner or of his family can receive serious injury, in the first case the fine can be changed to a proportional imprisonment; in the second case the term of the imprisonment can be reduced to less than the *minimum* term.

Circumstances which aggravate a misdemeanor or a contravention. These are: Continuation of the punishable action for a long period; repetition; serious danger to others resulting from the act; damage caused by the same; relationship between the guilty person and the one injured; seduction of youth or other honest persons; giving pernicious example to one's family; causing public scandal; the making preparations for the criminal action, or removing obstacles to the execution of the same; authorship or ringleadership of a punishable action committed by several persons; committing of several misdemeanors or contraventions of different kinds; deceiving the judge by false statements on the part of the accused; and, lastly, misdemeanors or contraventions committed against public decency, by a well educated or "accomplished" person.

Circumstances which extenuate. These are chiefly the following: Youth; weakness of intellect, and neglected education; former good behavior; seduction; fright, or false idea of dignity; violent excitement of mind; extreme poverty; non-consummation of the action; taking less advantage than might have been taken from the action; the voluntary abstention from causing greater damage; reparation of the injury done; voluntarily bringing to light of the deed, and exposing the accomplices to the same.

When several of these extenuating circumstances occur for the same misdemeanor or contravention, and when there is reason to anticipate an improvement of the guilty person, the imprisonment can be mitigated and the time diminished.

Classification. Misdemeanors and contraventions are either against public society, public establishments, measures for public safety, or the functions of public officers, or against the security of individuals, in life, health, body, property, honor, and reputation, or other rights; and, lastly, against public decency.

Extinction of Misdemeanors and Contraventions. For those misdemeanors and contraventions which have for maximum punishment *arrest* of the first degree, without aggravation, or a fine not exceeding fifty guilders, the time of limitation is three months; when *arrest* of the first degree, with aggravation, or a fine not exceeding two hundred guilders, it is six months; and for all other misdemeanors and contraventions, as well as all cases where loss of rights and privileges are included in the punishment, the period of limitation is one year.

PENAL CODES OF SWITZERLAND.

The best Swiss codes, among those which nearly every canton possesses are: In the canton of Lucerne, the code of 1836; in Turgau, that of 1841 (this code is copied from that of Baden); in Zurich, that of 1835; in Vaud, that of 1843; in Basle, that of 1821; in Berne, that of 1843. The oldest codes of Switzerland as those of Argua, of 1804; and the two codes of Saint Gallen; the *Code Correctionnel* of 1800, and the *Code Criminel* of 1817; lastly, that of Tessin, of 1816.

These codes are founded, for the most part, on the penal code of France, with modifications of the German jurists.

Most of the cantons have also codified their system of penal procedure. The punishments are milder, the penalty of degradation being almost unknown.

PENAL CODE OF SARDINIA.

The penal legislation of this state is based on the French *Code Pénal*. In 1839 the penal code now in force in Sardinia was promulgated, the code of civil laws having been in force since 1837. The object of its authors was, says the king, in the proclamation which accompanies it, "the composition of a penal code which should be equal for all, and based on certain principles which should furnish the magistrate the rules suitable for his guidance in the application of the punishments; in according to him, nevertheless, a discretionary power needed in numerous circumstances which the law cannot provide for."

Like the *Code Pénal* of France, a preliminary chapter precedes the first book, which treats of punishments and general rules for their execution.

The second book treats of crimes and misdemeanors.

The third book treats of contraventions and their punishments.

It is in the system of punishments that it differs most from the French code, the penalties of civil death and ignominy not being retained; the interdiction of holding a public office being the only degrading punishment. There are two new kinds of correctional punishments, the *Con-*

fino and local exile. There is also a simple detention for offenders of tender years, or having little discernment.

The *Confino* consists in the obligation imposed on the delinquent to dwell in a designated commune, distant one and a half *myriametres* at least from the place of the commission of the misdemeanor, or from the commune where the injured party resides.

By local exile, is understood the banishment from the commune in which the person resides, for a distance of three *myriametres* from the commune where the offense was committed, and from the domicile of the injured party.

There is in this code a special category of accessory punishments, not to be found in the French code; they are, the pillory; the apology; the interdiction, or suspension of the exercise of an employment or profession, business or art; the surveillance of the police; the submission and the admonition.

The apology consists in the avowal of his culpability made by the delinquent before the judge, and the praying for forgiveness, and the promising not to commit another offense.

The submission consists in the promise made before the judge either not to commit again the action for which he is to be punished, or to conform himself to what has been prescribed to him.

By the admonition is understood the censure of the judge pronounced against a person, on account of illegal actions, words, or writings, and the warning, that in case of repetition he will incur the severest punishment laid down in the law.

There are some modifications of the French law in regard to *complicity* and *attempt.*

The perpetrators and the accomplices, without whose co-operation the offense could not have been committed, receive the same punishment; whilst the other accomplices incur penalties two or three degrees lighter.

The *attempt* does not receive the same punishment as the consummated offense, but the punishment is diminished from two to three degrees according as the execution was more or less distant. This principle is observed for crimes and *misdemeanors.*

When several crimes or misdemeanors are committed by the same person, the principle is observed of accumulating all the punishments when possible.

It is a peculiarity of this code, that it admits of no limitation for a large number of crimes, such as high treason, parricide, poisoning, homicide in certain cases, robbery accompanied by murder, and arson. When, however, an individual guilty of any of these crimes, excepting the two first, is arrested twenty years after the commission of the same, the punishment for it is diminished by one degree. There is no limitation after condemnation to death, or hard labor for life.

These are the principal points of difference between the penal codes of Sardinia and of France. The special part resembles too nearly the French code to require an analysis of it.

PENAL CODE OF RUSSIA.

In Russia the oldest collection of penal laws is contained in the "*Prawda Russkaja*" of the year 1020. This law continued in force till the general code, which was promulgated in 1649, by Alexis Michaelovitch, and called the "*Uloschenie*." As but a small portion of this code was devoted to penal law, and that portion consisting of most arbitrary prescriptions, a commission was named, about the beginning of the year 1700, to prepare a radical reform of the criminal law, which, under Peter the Great, was employed with great activity on this work.

The emperor promulgated on the 1st of May, 1846, the existing penal code. The spirit of this code may be seen by the following extract from the imperial proclamation that announced its promulgation. "It was necessary to introduce order and clearness in the laws, in order to guarantee the security and rights of my well-beloved subjects. For this reason, We have caused general laws to be prepared, by which operation, without leaving the fundamental cases of the national legislation, the existing laws are completed and brought into conformity with the social condition of the people, and the exigencies of usage; so that all infractions may be specified in a more precise and satisfactory manner than is done in the existing laws, without omitting their different modifications or their aggravating and extenuating circumstances; in short, that each misdemeanor shall have a fixed penalty or repression analogous to its nature, and proportioned to its culpability, in order to interdict, as far as is possible, arbitrariness in the judgment, and to place the criminal under the direct action of the law alone.

"The penal code has been discussed and amended in a special committee, composed of the ministers of justice, the senators and attorney-general, rectified after observations from all the other ministries and administration, and finally examined by a commission taken from the council of the empire, preparatory to being brought definitively before the general assembly."

This code, called "Code of Capital and Correctional Punishments," holds the middle ground between a systematic code of penal law, and a simple revised collection of the laws and statutes which had theretofore existed.

Arrangement of the Russian code. It is divided into chapters. The first chapter of this code treats of general principles. In this the co-operation of the German jurists, who were intrusted by the emperor with the labor, is very evident. The second chapter is devoted to offenses against religion. The third treats of high treason and political crimes. The fourth treats of resistance against the constituted authorities. The fifth treats of prevarication of public functionaries. The sixth treats of contraventions against the regulations concerning the collection of taxes, and the military service. The seventh treats of contraventions and transgressions against public order and the general weal. The eighth treats of contraventions and misdemeanors against life, health, honor and individual freedom. The ninth treats of contraventions against the fundamental principles and laws of family. The tenth treats of contraventions and misdemeanors against property.

Punishments. These are either capital or correctional. Capital punishments are those which admit of no possibility of amendment, or of recovering the former social position. They are either privileged or non-privileged. The first are only applied to the higher classes of subjects.

The *privileged* capital punishments are death, hard labor, "colonizing" in Siberia, and colonizing beyond the Caucasus. For the *non-privileged* class, the first and fourth punishments are adopted equally; but the second and third punishments are aggravated by flogging and branding.

The correctional punishments for the privileged classes are two: 1st. Temporary local exile in Siberia; for the non-privileged classes, temporary incorporation in a disciplinary regiment; 2d. For the privileged classes, temporary local exile to other parts than Siberia; for the non-privileged, confinement in a prison, with compulsory labor. The third punishment is confinement in a fortress. The fourth, imprisonment in a house of correction. The fifth, imprisonment in a jail. The sixth, arrest for a short term. The seventh, reprimand by the judge, and fine.

These punishments admit of various gradations. Thiss, a celebrated Russian jurist, makes out from this code no less than forty-one kinds of punishment.

Consequences of punishments. These are, either civil death, which affect not only the criminal, but also his family; deprivation of particular privileged rights belonging to the condemned, according to the class to which he belongs; lastly, loss of rights, which can only be executed at a late period, such as the right to be elector or elected. Besides these, there are certain accessory punishments, which can in every case be inflicted in connection with the principal punishments, religious expiation, confiscation, publication of the sentence, banishment, surveillance of the police, and, lastly, solicitation for pardon

By an imperial ukase of the month of April, 1846, the punishment of the knout was abolished and replaced by the whip. Thirty lashes count as ten blows of the knout, and ten to twenty blows of the knout are replaced by fifty lashes.

The great rigor of this penal system lays in the power given the judge to accumulate various punishments for the same case.

PENAL CODE OF TURKEY.

Another absolute State, Turkey, has also a code which was promulgated before the one just spoken of. It is one of the most curious that exists, containing in fourteen small articles all the dispositions of penal law for that country. It depends upon a kind of constitution or charter called "*Hatti Sheriff.*" The present sultan accords in this act equality before the law, without any particular parliamentary right.

The code, which is the continuation of it, commences with the recognition of the equality of all before the law. Besides this there are no general principles laid down, the fourteen articles containing fourteen special cases of punishable actions with their penalties. These are the following: Capital crimes; high treason; libel; theft; bribery (two articles); infidelity of officers and agents of government; refusal of imposts; assault; want of respect to the government and its agents; highway robbery and violence; conduct of masters towards their subordinates; article 13 gives exemplary punishments of superior officers of state who are guilty of abuse of their functions, and forbids their being concerned in other business; and article 14 forms the conclusion of the code, and contains the maxim that all subjects are equal before the law.

This code distinguishes two kinds of offenses, those of words and those of deeds.

He who excites by words to revolt is punished with death;

He who by words or deeds injures another, is judged by the council of justice in Constantinople, and the local councils in the provinces, and punished with imprisonment, of long or short duration.

Theft is punished "because his Highness the Sultan has abstained from stealing." The punishment of theft is restitution of the stolen object, exile for a year, and, when the thief is a functionary of the government, removal from office.

The accepting a bribe by a public officer is forbidden, because, as the law adds, "all officers are sufficiently remunerated." The punishment is removal from office and hard labor for three years. If the officer is employed by the government, he is sentenced to the galleys; and, if an officer of finance, is punished with five years at hard labor.

The persons who are charged with the receipts and payments of the empire must render an account yearly, which must be revised by the council of justice. In case of a deficit, the officer is compelled to refund the same, and loses his office.

There are three kinds of authority: justice, exercised by the court; *Imans*, police, exercised by the *Mochirs*, charged with the preservation of good order; and the authority of the *Mouhassits*, charged to levy the imposts and to send them, at proper periods, to the minister of finance at Constantinople. These three authorities must harmonize with each other. In case of discord "the one in the wrong shall be punished."

Those who refuse to pay the taxes on their property, are punished with imprisonment; those who resist with weapons are punished with hard labor for three years; if a wound is caused thereby, with hard labor for five years, and to payment of the costs of healing the person; if he dies, capital punishment is inflicted.

He who attacks another with weapons is punished with hard labor for a year; if a wound is given, the penalty is hard labor for three years, and if death follows, capital punishment is inflicted.

Robbery is punished with seven years hard labor.

Immodesty and insubordination are punished with "a penalty corresponding to the offense."

Certain high officers, like the *Mouhassits*, the *Hakims*, and the military governors, receive "exemplary punishments" when guilty of infraction of these laws.

This code is, as will have been observed, for officers of the government rather than for individual subjects. As may be imagined, the old usages and system of punishment continue in force with it. The whole substance of it has been given.

PENAL CODE OF BELGIUM.

In Belgium, in 1848, a commission was named by the minister of justice, which was charged with the preparation of a new penal code. In the following year a commission was named for revising the code of penal procedure. The first named commission prepared a project, consisting of two books, the one general, the other special, which was laid before the chambers, and a commission named by them made a report on the same, in the sitting of the 2d of July, 1851. The discussion was adjourned to the next session, when the amended project was adopted. A report on the same was laid, in 1852, before the senate, prepared by the commission named by that body, which proposed some unimportant modifications.

These reports, which include only the general principles of criminal law, being the first book, differ from the French code, in respect to the principles of the punishments and their effects, and also in respect to criminal attempts, repetition, and accumulation of offenses and crimes.

They proposed the abolition of penalties of transportation, branding, general confiscation, pillory, banishment, civic degradation, and mutilation, in case of parricide; also the punishment of death for political offenses, imprisonment in a fortress for twenty years taking its place.

Punishments. The following are the punishments proposed: Death; hard labor for life, or for a term of from ten to fifteen, or fifteen to twenty years; imprisonment in a fortress from five to ten or from ten to fifteen years; confinement from five to ten years.

These four penalties are regarded as "criminal punishments."

The punishments which are not so termed are: Confinement for at least eight days, and for police offenses not more than seven days; fine, for crimes and misdemeanors, at least twenty-six francs; and for contraventions, from one to twenty-five francs; the special confiscation of objects which have been used in the commission of an offense or have been produced by the same.

Punishments which are common to correctional and criminal offenses, are: Interdiction of certain civil and political rights, and the special surveillance of the police, the effects of which are entirely analogous to those of the French code of 1832.

The last modification of this report in the system of punishments, is the introduction of the cellular system for those condemned to hard labor and confinement in prisons, called *maisons de force* and *maisons de réclusion.*

Attempt. An attempt, according to these reports, exists when the "resolution to commit a crime or misdemeanor has been manifested by any external acts, which form a commencement of execution of the crime or misdemeanor, and which have only been suspended, or failed in their effect, owing to circumstances independent of the will of the author."

It is seen by this, that the law, unlike nearly all other systems, recognizes only one kind of attempt, and makes no difference between those which are direct or indirect attempts.

The Belgian law, unlike the French, does not inflict the penalty of the consummated offense, but with the "punishment immediately inferior to that inflicted for the crime itself." Nevertheless, for misdemeanors, the rule of the French code is observed, the punishment being inflicted only in cases specially laid down in the law.

Accumulation of different offenses. In respect to accumulation of different offenses, the Belgian legislation has introduced the principle of the Roman law, that the greater punishment suspends the lesser (*pœna major absorbet minorem*), nevertheless, this principle is only applicable to crimes; for in cases of several contraventions, the punishment is pronounced for each; in case of cumulation of misdemeanors, with one or more contraventions, the fine is paid for each, and the punishment of correctional confinement absorbs that of police imprisonment. In case of several misdemeanors, the punishments are inflicted for each; nevertheless, without exceeding the double of the maximum of the severest penalty. When, however, a crime, and one or several misdemeanors or contraventions, are committed, the punishment for the crime alone is inflicted.

The report to the senate proposed, as an amendment to this, that the punishment pronounced for several crimes can be increased for five years over the ordinary term of punishment, when one of these crimes has for penalty hard labor, or confinement or *réclusion.* By "severest penalty" is understood that of which the duration is the longest; when they are for the same term, that of hard labor and reclusion are regarded as severer than confinement in a fortress.

Complicity. Touching *complicity*, there are some important changes. The accomplice to a crime being punished with a penalty immediately inferior to the punishment which would have been pronounced if he were the perpetrator of the same. The punishment for complicity to a misdemeanor can never exceed two-thirds of the punishment of the perpetrator. The following, however, are considered as accomplices to a crime or misdemeanor: Those who have given instructions to commit the same; those who have procured weapons, instruments, or other means which have served for the offense, knowing that they were to serve for the same; those who knowingly have aided or assisted the author or authors of the crime or misdemeanor in the actions which have prepared, or facilitated, or consummated the deed.

Repetition of offenses. Concerning repetition, there are but few modifications from the French system. The punishment for the repetition of an offense is pronounced in case of a previous criminal or correctional punishment. Whoever has been condemned to a criminal punishment, or to a correctional imprisonment of more than six months, and commits afterwards a misdemeanor, can be punished by a penalty double to the maximum of the punishment of the misdemeanor. He can also be condemned to surveillance of the police from five to ten years.

THE PENAL CODE OF SPAIN.

Spain has had a penal code since the year 1848. Before that time the penal legislation in this country was in a very confused state. The oldest monument of Spanish jurisprudence is the so-called "*Fuero Juzgo*," of the 8th century. This was followed by a compilation published in the year 1265 — "*Las Siete Partidas,*" and in 1556, a new collection of Spanish laws was given out, entitled "*Recopilacion de las Leyes de Espana.*" This new penal code contains the principles laid down in these compilations, expressed carefully and laconically; the last compilation of the year 1808 being more particularly the basis of it.

The circumstances which aggravate or extenuate a crime are especially enumerated in this code, which is a peculiarity of it worthy of particular remark — the aggravating circumstances depend generally on grounds personal to the criminal. The judge, when these occur, can condemn to a punishment *equal to* the maximum, but not over, as in the French code.

Circumstances which Aggravate an Offense. These are the following: When the offender is an ascendant, descendant, brother, or sister, or of the same grade of relationship by marriage, or spouse of the injured person; when the offense has been committed in consequence of bribe, promise, or recompense; when with premeditation, craft, fraud, or disguise; when with abuse of power or trust, or employment of means to render the injured person helpless; when with usurpation of the character of a public officer, if in order to commit another offense; when committed on the occasion of a fire, shipwreck or other calamity; when with the help of armed men, or of those who can assure impunity for the time being; when by night, or in isolated places; when with offense against the authorities or their residences, or in a house of worship, or consecrated place; when with contempt for the consideration due to the injured persons, on account of their dignities, age, or sex, or in their house; when by means of force, false keys, or escalade, or with prohibited weapons. Lastly, circumstances analogous to the above named are included in this category.

Extenuating Circumstances. These are the following: When the guilty person is under eighteen years of age; when he had not the intention to cause *all* the evil which he has produced; when he was provoked or menaced by the injured party; when he avenges an injury or insult to him or his relations; when in a state of inebriation which is not habitual to him, and which does not date from before the project to commit the offense; when in a state of anger or great mental excitement.

Cases where no Punishment Occurs. From these cases are to be distinguished those in which there is no punishment.

Are not punished: children under nine years of age; children between the ages of nine and fifteen years, who have acted without discernment; those who are attacked in their honor, property, or relations, and defend the same. The condition in this last case is, that the attack be unprovoked, and that the limits of defense be not exceeded; those who are excited to the same by an irresistible power peculiar to themselves, or by an invincible fear of a great injury; and whoever performs a duty or executes a legal order.

Punishments. The punishments of this code are: death; loss of liberty; degradation; fine.

The endeavor to render the punishments divisible, according to the theory of Bentham, and, where the nature of the punishment allows, to establish as many grades as possible, is characteristic to this code.

Capital punishment is executed in public on a day which is neither a feast day of the church nor of the nation. The criminal is clad in a black mantle, and drawn in a cart to the place of execution, accompanied by a public crier, who repeats the sentence in a loud voice; the manner of execution is by the *garotte*, or strangulation by means of the tightening of an iron band, which passes around the neck; it is aggravated for the parricide and for the regicide; in the last case the criminal is mounted on an ass, and led to the place of execution; he is clad in a yellow mantle and cap, both spotted with red. The execution of the regicide takes place at the same hour of the day as the commission of the crime. After the execution, the body is exposed till one hour before nightfall. The body is given to the family, but not to the wife of the criminal, if she is with child — nor, in such case, is the sentence even communicated to her.

The fine must correspond to the means of the person condemned. In case of insolvency, one *duro* (dollar) counts as one day of imprisonment.

Attempt. Criminal attempt is a direct commencement of execution, by external acts, the realization of which is hindered by causes independent of the will of the author; the punishment is two degrees inferior to that of the perpetrator.

Complicity. Accomplices are those who co-operate in the execution of a punishable action, by acts simultaneous or anterior to the offense; and those who give asylum to a criminal, or co-operation to his flight, when he is not a relation. In these last two cases an exemption is admitted in favor of near relatives of the criminal. The punishment of the accomplice is one grade lighter than that of the principal offender.

Political crimes. By an ordinance of the month of April, 1852, the provisions of the penal code concerning political crimes, and concerning the competency of courts for the trial of offenses of the press, were altered. The jury is abolished for all kinds of political offenses, and the correctional courts decide on the same in *first instance*, and the royal court of appeals in *second instance*. Exceptionally, a jury decide in affairs of the press, but it is a newly organized jury, which is composed of the notables, and those paying the greatest taxes. Misdemeanors against the king are punished with imprisonment from one to six years, and with fine of from 20,000 to 60,000 reals. The person condemned for the same is declared incapable of holding office, or of wearing a decoration. A misdemeanor against the royal family is punished with imprisonment from six months to two years, and fine from 10,000 to 30,000 reals, and with temporary suppression of functions, honors, and decorations. Misdemeanors against the security of the state, or public order, are punished with imprisonment from one month to three years, and with fine from 5,000 to 25,000 reals. Misdemeanors against the king, the royal family, religion, and the security of the state, and against foreign sovereigns, are judged by the supreme court, which consists of at least nine members.

Want of space has preventea the commissioners from giving in this place, what seems desirable to complete this account of foreign codes, viz, an analysis of the more complete of the systems of statute law of crimes, which are in force in other American States and in England. Brief notices of the principal statute books containing these, are, however, to be found in the next following appendix.

APPENDIX B.

A CATALOGUE

OF

AUTHORITIES.

No attempt is here made to give anything like a complete bibliography either of the law of crimes, or of prison discipline. The object of the article is to indicate the sources from which the views embodied in the Code were drawn; and, with the exception of a few works upon prison discipline for which the inquiry made by the commissioners was unsuccessful, it embraces only books in the library of one of the members of the board, which were actually consulted and used in the compilation of the work.

It will be observed that only works specially devoted to subjects connected with crimes and punishments are mentioned. It is scarcely necessary to say that in addition to these the great body of English and American reports and statutes have been extensively examined, upon almost every portion of the Code; and that many treatises not reckoned among books of the criminal law have also been consulted upon collateral topics.

Addington (William).

An Abridgment of Penal Statutes; which exhibits at one view the offenses and the punishments or penalties in consequence of those offenses, the mode of recovering and application of the penalties, the number of the witnesses and the jurisdiction necessary to the several convictions, and the chapters and sections of the enacting statutes. Third edition, London, 1786.

The text of this work consists of the various penal clauses of the British statutes, abridged, and classified under alphabetic titles. Foot notes present the adjudications turning upon the statutes.

The work was never more than a copious index to the criminal statutes; and its value in that respect is greatly lessened by the extensive modifications which have been made in the statute law of crimes since its date.

There is a later edition than that above mentioned.

Adshead (Joseph).

Prisons and Prisoners. With illustrations. London, 1845.

Alabama.

The Code of. Prepared by John J. Ormond, Arthur P. Bagly, George Goldthwaite. With head notes and index by Henry C. Temple. Published in pursuance of an act of the general assembly, approved Feb. 5, 1852. Montgomery, 1852.

This Code repealed all former laws "of a public nature designed to operate on all the people of the state," not embraced in the Code; and it constituted a complete system of statute law for the state, at the time of its passage. Part IV, entitled "Of crimes and their punishment, proceedings in criminal cases, jails and penitentiary," forms, therefore, the criminal Code of the state; and as such has been consulted by the commissioners.

Albany County Penitentiary.

Account of. Albany, 1848.

Reports of, for 1850, 1851, 1852, 1853, 1854, 1855, 1856, 1857, 1858.

Archbold. See *Waterman*.

Arkansas.

A Digest of the Statutes of Arkansas; embracing all laws of a general and permanent character in force at the close of the general assembly of 1846. Together with notes of the decisions of the supreme court upon the statutes. By E. H. English. Little Rock, 1848.

An official compilation of the statute law of the state. Chapter 51, occupying about sixty pages, entitled "Criminal law," contains a system of law upon crimes; but is not full enough to suggest many additions to the present law of our own state.

Arkley (Patrick).

Reports of Cases before the High Court and Circuit Courts of Justiciary in Scotland, during 1846–48. Edinburgh, 1849.

One of the standard volumes of Scotch criminal reports.

Articles in Reviews, &c.

American Quarterly. Articles on prison discipline, in vol. 14, p. 228; vol. 18, p. 451.

Blackwood's Magazine. On prisons of France, in vol. 42, p. 145.

Childs' National Almanac. Contains brief summaries of prison statistics for the leading American States.

Christian Examiner. Articles on prison discipline:

By L. Tappen, in vol. 3, p. 203.
L. A. Elliott, in vol. 10, p. 15.
F. W. P. Greenwood, in vol. 16, p. 251.
R. C. Waterston, in vol. 26, p. 54.
F. Parkman, in vol. 27, p. 381.
C. Sumner, in vol. 40, p. 122.
J. H. Morrison, in vol. 44, p. 273.

Democratic Review. On prison discipline, in vol. 19, p. 129, and vol. 20, p. 172.

Eclectic Review. On prison discipline, in vol. 4, p. 568.

On prison reform abroad, in vol. 22, p. 455.

On London prisons, in vol. 27, p. 280.

Edinburgh Review. On prison discipline. By F. Jeffrey; in vol. 30, p. 463; vol. 36, p. 353, and vol. 64, p. 169.

On punishment of untried prisoners. By Sidney Smith; in vol. 39, p. 229.

On prisons. By Sidney Smith; in vol. 35, p. 286.

On prisons. By Neild; in vol. 22, p. 385.

Foreign Quarterly Review. On prison discipline, in vol. 12, p. 49, and vol. 27, p. 283.

London Times. See various articles in this journal, mentioned in preface to Adshead's Prisons and Prisoners.

Monthly Review. On prison discipline, in vol. 97, p. 427; vol. 130. p. 421.

On prisons, in vol. 106, p. 311, and vol. 89, p. 119.

North American Review. On prison discipline:

By Edward Everett, in vol. 37, p. 117.
Geo. S. Hilliard, in vol. 47, p. 452.
Francis Wayland, in vol. 49, p. 1.
Francis Bowen, in vol. 66, p. 145.

Princeton Review. On prison discipline, in vol. 21, p. 331.

U. S. Literary Gazette. On prisons, in vol. 4, p. 176.

Westminster Review. On prison discipline, in vol. 3, p. 420.

Barbour (Oliver Lorenzo).

A Treatise on the Criminal Law of the State of New York, and upon the jurisdiction, duty and authority of justices of the peace, and incidentally of the power and duty of sheriffs, constables, &c., in criminal cases. Second edition, Albany, 1852.

This volume, being expressly founded upon the law of our own state, and coming down to a quite recent date, has been of indispensable service, as a manual of, and index to our existing law, as found in our statutes and reports.

Beaumont (G. de).

Penitentiary System of the United States, and its application in France; translated from the French, with introduction, &c. By F. Lieber. Philadelphia, 1833.

Beck (Theodoric Romeyn and John B.)
Elements of Medical Jurisprudence. Tenth edition. 2 vols. Albany, 1850.

This work maintains the highest rank among treatises upon its subject; and although that subject is only collaterally connected with the task of compiling the Penal Code, the book has been frequently of service in its preparation.

The work had reached its twelfth edition in 1858.

Bennett (Edmund H.) & Heard (Franklin Fiske).
A Selection of Leading Cases in Criminal Law, with notes. 2 vols. Boston, 1856.

The cases in these volumes are to be found in the original reports. But it has been very convenient to consult them collected together in the compass of two volumes. The notes are, in many instances, extensive and useful.

Bentham (Jeremy).
Considerations on Prisons; with plans for their better regulation. 1812.

Bishop (Joel Prentiss).
Commentaries on the Criminal Law. Second edition. 2 vols. Boston, 1858.

The first volume contains the general principles of responsibility and punishment for crime. Its usefulness for purposes so purely practical as those of the commissioners, is somewhat qualified by the introduction of topics belonging quite outside the domain of penal law. The second volume, containing a discussion of the American Law of Crimes, arranged in alphabetic order, has been of the highest utility.

Blackstone (Sir William).
Commentaries on the Law of England. In four books. Book fourth. Of Public Wrongs.

Blackstone's definitions of crimes are frequently made the basis of those employed in the Penal Code. The commissioners have availed themselves of four of the numerous editions of this work: Tucker's, Chitty's, Wendell's and Sharswood's; having found Sharswood's, however, which is the most recent, the most satisfactory.

Boston.
Reports of the Houses of Industry and Reformation in,—for 1838–52.

British Crown Cases.
Crown Cases reserved for consideration and decided by the

twelve judges of England, from the year 1799 to 1851. 6 vols. Philadelphia, 1839–53.

This is a reprint of the standard English reports of Crown cases during the period above described, and embraces the reports of Russell and Ryan, Moody, Jebb, Denison, and Denison & Pearce. These reports have, of course, been of indispensable service.

Britton.

Containing the antient Pleas of the Crown. Translated and illustrated with references, notes and antient records. By Robert Kelham. London, 1762.

This work shows the criminal law of England as it stood in the beginning of the reign of King Edward the First; the "English Justinian;" and has been of service whenever the original rules of the common law required to be reviewed.

Broun (Archibald).

Reports of Cases before the High Court and Circuit Courts of Justiciary in Scotland, during 1842–45. 2 vols. Edinburg, 1844, 1846.

One of the series of standard reports of Scotch criminal cases.

Bucknill (John Chas.) and Tuke (Daniel H).

A Manual of Psychological Medicine; containing the history, nosology, description, &c., of Insanity. With an appendix of cases. Philadelphia, 1858.

Valuable as an aid to the discussion of questions connected with the effect of different kinds of insanity upon criminal responsibility.

Burke (Peter).

Celebrated Trials, connected with the aristocracy in the relations of private life. London, 1849.

—— Celebrated Trials, connected with the upper classes of society in the relations of private life. London, 1851.

These two volumes exclude, for the most part, trials of a political character; and they are, therefore, the more instructive to the reader of the criminal law.

Burr (Aaron).

Trial of—on an indictment for treason. Before the Circuit Court of the United States, held in Richmond, Va., May 7, 1807. Taken in short hand by T. Carpenter. 2 vols. Washington City, 1808.

Burrill (Alex. M.)

A Treatise on the nature, principles and rules of Circumstantial Evidence, especially that of the presumptive kind, in criminal cases. New York, 1856.

A valuable work; and one which touches topics so nearly connected with those embraced within the Penal Code, as to have been of service.

Buxton (Sir Thos. Fowell).

Inquiry whether crime and misery are produced or prevented by our present system of prison discipline; with J. J. Gurney's Notes on a visit made to some of the prisons in Scotland and the north of England. London, 1818.

Canada.

Consolidated Statutes of. Proclaimed and published under the authority of the act of 22 Vict., cap., 29; A. D. 1859. Toronto, 1859.

This system of laws is to be distinguished from that enacted in 1859, entitled Consolidated Statutes of *Upper* Canada; and from that enacted in 1860, entitled the Consolidated Statutes of *Lower* Canada. Those volumes contain laws applicable in one or the other province only; while in the Consolidated Statutes of *Canada* are contained laws of a general application throughout both provinces. In the latter is found a series of chapters, Nos. 90 to 98 inclusive, filling about sixty royal octavo pages, which comprise a system of penal law recently framed, and quite comprehensive and complete. Its provisions are, however, almost all taken from previous acts of parliament; and in general, where a section has been made the basis of a provision of the present code—which has been done in several instances—it has been thought better to consult and make reference to the original act, as more likely to be accessible to the profession in this state, than to cite the Consolidated Statutes.

Carey (Matthew).

Thoughts on Penitentiaries and Prison Discipline. 1831.

Celebrated Trials;

And Remarkable Cases in Criminal Jurisprudence from the earliest records to the year 1825. 6 vols. London, 1825.

These reports, of interesting trials, are prepared more with a view to attract the general reader than to serve the purposes of the criminal lawyer. They are not without utility, however, to the lawyer, in exhibiting the modes of procedure and rules of evidence which obtained, upon criminal trials, at an early date; and in furnishing attendant details respecting cases which are also found in books of technical law. A review of these cases has brought to mind some crimes of rare but not impossible occurrence, against which it was proper that provisions should somewhere be made, in a code aiming to embody all offenses.

Chandler (Peleg W.)
American Criminal Trials. 2 vols. Boston, 1841.

The trials collected in these volumes are of greater interest to the general reader than to those engaged in an examination of the criminal law.

Chitty (J.)
A Practical Treatise on Medical Jurisprudence; with so much of anatomy, physiology, pathology, and the practice of medicine and surgery as are essential to be known by members of parliament, lawyers, coroners, magistrates, &c., and all the law relating to medical practitioners, with explanatory plates. Second American edition. Philadelphia, 1836.

So far as there has been occasion to consult treatises on medical jurisprudence, those of Beck, Dean, and Wharton and Stillè have been found more serviceable than this work.

City Hall Recorder. See *Rogers*.

Coke (Edward).
The third part of the Institutes of the Laws of England, concerning high treason, and other pleas of the crown, and criminal causes. London, 1797.

Is of leading value as an authority on the state of the English criminal law during the time of Lord Coke.

Cole (W. R.)
On criminal informations, and informations in the nature of *quo warranto*. London, 1843.

Connecticut.
The Statutes of. To which are prefixed the Declaration of Independence, &c. Compiled and published by authority of the general assembly. New Haven, 1854.

This is the volume known as the "Compilation of 1854." Less than forty pages are devoted to the law of crimes, strictly considered; and the system there embodied is too brief and inadequate, when compared with our own existing statute law, to furnish many materials towards its amendment.

Cox (Edward W.)
A Digest of all the cases decided, relating to the Criminal Law, from 1850 to 1862. London, 1862.

Has been used as an index to the English cases decided during the period indicated.

—— Reports of Cases in Criminal Law, argued and determined in all the courts in England and Ireland, 1843 to 1862. Vols. 1 to 8, and 7 parts of vol. 9. London, 1846–62.

A valuable collection of recent adjudications in criminal cases.

Crown and Circuit Companion.

First American edition, into which has been incorporated the Crown and Circuit Assistant. Both works carefully revised. New York, 1816.

This is a book of forms appropriate to criminal proceedings, to which are appended brief statements of the leading rules of law governing their use. There are later editions than the above; but the work has not been of any important service.

Dagge (Henry).

Considerations on Criminal Law. London, 1772.

Was anonymously published in the first edition in 1772, but was in 1774 republished, enlarged, and under the author's name. It has, however, been superseded by later publications, and is no longer of importance.

Davis (Daniel).

A Practical Treatise upon the authority and duty of Justices of the Peace in Criminal Prosecutions. Third edition. Revised and greatly enlarged by F. F. Heard. Boston, 1853.

Davis (James Edward).

The Criminal Law Consolidated Statutes of the 24th and 25th of Victoria, chapter 94–100. Edited with notes. London, 1861.

A reprint of the acts referred to, with brief notes. These acts are described under the title *Greaves.*

Dean (Amos).

Principles of Medical Jurisprudence, designed for the professions of law and medicine. Albany, 1850.

A valuable work. In so far as questions pertaining to medical jurisprudence have come up for consideration in preparing the Penal Code, this volume has been of considerable service.

Delaware.

Revised Statutes of—to 1852, inclusive. Published by the authority of the General Assembly. Dover, 1852.

Contains a brief title, of twenty-three pages, of "crimes and punishments," inadequate to aid materially in the present task.

Denison. See *British Crown Cases.*

District of Columbia.

The Revised Code of. Prepared under the authority of the act of Congress of March 3, 1855. Washington, 1857.

Contains a comparatively brief title upon "crimes and the punishment thereof;" which has, however, been only of secondary service.

Dix (Miss D. L.)
Remarks on Prisons and Prison Discipline. Boston, 1845.

East (Edward Hyde).
Treatise of the Pleas of the Crown. 2 vols. London, 1803.

There are later editions of this work than that above mentioned. It is well known as a standard authority in English criminal law, and has been of constant service to the commissioners, especially in ascertaining the common law definitions of the various crimes.

English Commissioners.
Reports of, on the Criminal Law. 2 vols. Comprising eight successive reports.

—— Reports of, on Revising and Consolidating the Criminal Law. 1 vol. Comprising five reports.

These reports show the history and progress of the efforts so long continued in Great Britain, by the ablest jurists of the realm, to accomplish the codification or at least the systematic consolidation of the criminal law. They abound in information upon the defects of the former statute law of Great Britain, and in suggestions for its improvement; and though not easily used, for want of the systematic arrangement, and the indexes, common in professional manuals, but not easily available in legislative reports of this character, they well repay one who studies the law with a view to its amendment, for the labor required for their examination.

English Statutes.

The Consolidated Statutes of 1861, are elsewhere described. See *Greaves*. The earlier acts relative to crimes, have, however, been extensively consulted, in the statutes at large; which now exist in upwards of eighty volumes.

Florida.
A Manual or Digest of the Statute Law of—of a general and public character, in force Jan. 6, 1847. Digested and arranged under an act of assembly approved Dec. 10, 1845. By Leslie A. Thompson. Boston, 1847.

Contains about 30 pages devoted to crimes and misdemeanors. The common law of England, except as relates to the mode and degree of punishment, is preserved, and offenses known to the common law and not expressly provided for otherwise, are made punishable by a fine not exceeding $100, or imprisonment not exceeding 12 months, at the discretion of the *jury*. Very few offenses known by distinct names to the English law, are defined, but punishments are simply affixed to them by their names, the courts being left to the common law authorities to ascertain the acts intended to be punished. Such a system of laws can aid the preparation of a true code, only by suggesting specific offenses that might otherwise be overlooked.

Field (J.)

The Advantages of the Separate System of Imprisonment, as established in the new county gaol of Reading, with a description of the former prisons, and a detailed account of the discipline now pursued. London, 1846.

—— Prison Discipline, or the Advantages of the Separate System of imprisonment. 2 vols. London, 1848.

Foster (Sir Michael).

Crown Law. A Report of some proceedings on the Commission for the Trial of the Rebels in the year 1746, in the county of Surry, and other Crown Cases; to which are added Discourses upon a few branches of the crown law. Second edition with additional notes and references, by Michael Dodson. London, 1791.

This work was not intended as a systematic treatise on criminal law. It has, however, attained a rank nearly equal to that of the best of the earlier English treatises, as respects the subjects treated in the "discourses," which are chiefly Treason, Homicide and Accomplices. There has been, however, but little necessity for relying on this work in the preparation of the Code.

Foulke (W. P.)

Remarks on the Penal System of Pennsylvania, particularly with reference to county prisons. Philadelphia, 1855.

—— On Cellular Separation. Philadelphia, 1861.

French Codes.

Les Codes Francais, conformes aux textes officiels, avec la conférence des articles entre eux: contenant les lois, decrets, ordonances, avis du conceil d'etat, circulaires qui expliquent, completent, modifient on abrogert certaines dispositions des Codes: les lois de la presse, les tariffs en matière civil et criminelle, l'enregistrement, le timbre, les hypotheques etc. Specialement tous les textes donnés comme matières de thèses par les facultés des droit. Nouvelle édition entirement refondue; précédée d'une table chronologique et suivie d'une table alphabetique. Par M. P. Royer Collard. aveè la collaboration de M. Mourlon. Paris, 1858.

—— Codes de la legislation Francaise, avec des annotations sur les lois les plus ussuelles, la definition et explication des termes de droit. &c., par M. Napoleon Bacqua. Edition nouvelle 're partie pour l'audience, les fcnctionnaires publics et les écoles de droit. Code Politique,—Code Napoleon—Code de procedure Civile—Code de Commerce,—Code d'instruction criminelle,—Code Penal—Code des frais—Code forestier. Paris, 1860.

Gabbett (Joseph).

A Treatise on Criminal Law. Comprehending all crimes and misdemeanors punishable by indictment, and all offenses cognizable summarily by magistrates; with the modes of proceeding upon each. 2 vols. bound in 3. Dublin 1843.

A very full and conveniently arranged statement of the modern criminal law of the United Kingdom as it existed subsequent to "Peel's acts," so called, and before the important statutes known as Lord "Campbell's acts," and the "Consolidation acts" of 24 and 25 Vict. It was designed chiefly for use in Ireland, but contains information on the English law where that differs from the law of Ireland.

Georgia.

A Codification of the Statute Law of—including the English Statutes of force, in four parts. Compiled, &c., by William A. Hotchkiss, by authority of the Legislature. Second edition. Augusta, 1848.

Part IV of this compilation contains about seventy pages devoted to the law of crimes. The system here presented approaches to the comprehensiveness and completeness desired in a code. Rules of criminal responsibility are prescribed; and the various crimes are defined, and the definitions given are in general lucid and well framed. No express provision has been noticed excluding the application of the common law of offenses to crimes not provided for by the statute; but the evident object is to prevent a necessity for recurrence to the common law. The definitions of this act have aided the commissioners in several instances; though chiefly by way of confirming those already in use in the authorities recognized in this state. The act is not sufficiently recent in date to be relied on as likely to point out deficiencies in our law.

Gray (F. C.)

Prison Discipline in America. Boston, 1847.

Greaves (Chas. Sprengel).

Lord Campbell's Acts for the further improving the administration of criminal justice, and the better prevention of offenses, together with the act for the better protection of apprentices and servants, and the act for amending the law relating to the expenses of prosecutions. With notes, observations and indictments. London, 1851.

The important provisions of Lord Campbell's acts, upon subjects which fall within the scope of the present Penal Code, were repealed by the acts passed in the 24th and 25th Vict., substituted enactments being therein given. In general, therefore, the later provisions have been consulted in preference to the earlier and repealed ones.

—— The Criminal Law Consolidation and Amendment Acts of the 24 and 25 Vict., with notes, observations and forms for summary proceedings. Second edition. London, 1862.

The series of acts republished in this volume must be recognized as of the highest importance in their bearing upon the reform of criminal law, wherever the influence of the English law of crimes and punishments is felt. The series does not attempt to embody in form a complete code of criminal law. The preparation of such a code seems to have been contemplated in the original appointment of the Criminal Law Commissioners in 1833; but the statutes now under consideration, and which are known as the "Criminal Law Consolidation Acts," are distinct acts, each intended rather as a consolidation of the existing statute law upon the subject to which the act relates, than as a codification of the yet unwritten law. The scope of the series, however, is so extensive that it covers the leading and important portions of the law of crimes, and approaches practically to the completeness, if it does not aim at the symmetry, of a code.

The acts in question are seven in number; their subjects, arranging them in the order in which they stand in Mr. Greaves' work, being the following:

1. An act to consolidate and amend the Statute Law of England and Ireland, relating to Accessories and Abettors of Indictable offenses. 24 and 25 Vict., ch. 94. Contains eleven sections.

2. An act to consolidate and amend the Statute Law of England and Ireland, relating to Offenses against the Person. 24 and 25 Vict., ch. 100. Contains seventy-nine sections.

3. An act to consolidate and amend the Statute Law of England and Ireland, relating to Larceny and other similar offenses. 24 and 25 Vict., ch. 96. Contains one hundred and twenty-three sections.

4. An act to consolidate and amend the Statute Law of England and Ireland, relating to Malicious Injuries to Property. 24 and 25 Vict., ch. 97. Contains seventy-nine sections.

5. An act to consolidate and amend the Statute Law of England and Ireland, relating to Indictable offenses by Forgery. 24 and 25 Vict., ch 98. Contains fifty-six sections.

6. An act to consolidate and amend the Statute Law of the United Kingdoms against offenses relating to the Crown. 24 and 25 Vict. Contains forty-three sections.

7. An act to repeal certain enactments which have been consolidated in several acts of the present session, relating to indictable offenses and other matters. 24 and 25 Vict. Contains four sections, and a lengthy schedule, enumerating in detail the acts and parts of acts repealed.

Frequent reference has been made in the preparation of the Penal Code to these English statutes; and they have been the source from which many of the additions to our existing law, embodied in the Code, have been drawn.

The present volume contains, not only the Consolidation Acts themselves, but also an elaborate introduction, and many annotations by Mr. Greaves, who had himself a principal share in the preparation of the statutes. This introduction and these notes have been of essential service in the preparation of the Penal Code.

Hale (Sir Matthew).
History of the Pleas of the Crown, with notes by Solom Emlyn. First American edition, with notes, &c., by W. A. Stokes and E. Ingersoll. 2 vols. Philadelphia, 1847.

The value and authority of this work as a standard one in English criminal law is too well known to require any extended comment. It has been resorted to, in common with the works of East, Hawkins, and others, whenever questions as to the earlier English law of crimes have arisen.

Hawkins (William).
A Treatise of the Pleas of the Crown; or a system of the principal matters relating to that subject, digested under proper heads. 7th edition, by Thomas Leach. London, 1795. 4 vols.

The merits of this volume, like those of that last mentioned, are well known. As a compend of the earlier English law of crimes, it is more full and comprehensive than the works of East and Hale. Although, in the progress of jurisprudence, all works of this class have become of secondary value to the practitioner, resort to the treatise of Sergeant Hawkins is frequently necessary by those who, having in charge the amendment of the law, require to trace its history in the progress of its development.

The classification of crimes framed by Hawkins, as remodelled by Blackstone in the fourth part of the commentaries, has been more closely followed than any other one system, in the Penal Code. In Hawkins' work the leading principle is, that offenses are classified by the person against whom they are committed. His order is: 1. Offenses which are more immediately against God, or against religion and the established church; 2. Those more immediately against the king, under which head are included many offenses which among us are considered as offenses aimed peculiarly against the state; 3. Offenses more immediately against the subject; being those against the life of a man—those against his goods—those against his habitation—and those against the public justice, revenue, trade, funds, credit, health, peace, &c. There are some difficulties in the attempt to classify crimes accurately upon this principle; but it has been so widely adopted and approved as a basis of later works, and is so far superior, in a philosophic point of view, to the method adopted in our own Revised Statutes, of classifying crimes by the measure of punishment awarded: 1. Crimes punishable by death; 2. Crimes punishable by imprisonment in a state prison—subdivided into offenses against the person, offenses against property, and offenses against public peace, &c.; and, 3. Offenses punishable by imprisonment in a county jail and by fine—that it has been preferred as the governing principle in the arrangement of subjects in the Code.

Hayes (Edmund).

Crimes and Punishments; or a Digest of the Criminal Statute Law of Ireland. Second edition. Dublin, 1842–43.

The extensive changes in the statute law, which have been made since the date of this work, have deprived it of much of its usefulness.

Haynes (Gideon).

See his report as warden of Massachusetts state prison, Charlestown, for 1861—in which he contrasts the results of the Auburn or congregated plan of prison discipline with its opposite, and gives statistics for 30 years of Charlestown prison and Eastern Penitentiary, Pennsylvania.

These statistics are summed up in Child's National Almanac for 1863, p. 377, 378.

Hill (Frederick).

Crime; Its Amount, Causes and Remedies. London, 1855.

Holford (George).

Account of the general penitentiary at Milbank. London, 1828.

Holland (Laws of).

Institutes of the Laws of Holland. By Johannes van der Linden, LL. D.; translated by J. Henry. London, 1828.

Includes a view of the criminal law of Holland.

Holtzendorf.

The Irish Convict System. London, 1860.

Howard (John).

State of the Prisons in England and Wales. Fourth edition. London, 1789–92. 2 vols.

Howell (T. B. and T. J.)

Cobbett's Complete Collection of State Trials and Proceedings for High Treason and other crimes and misdemeanors, from the earliest period to the present time. London, 1809–11. 10 vols. Vols. 11 to 21, in continuation, compiled by T. B. Howell, London, 1811–16; and a continuation from the year 1783 to 1820, by Thomas J. Howell, in 12 vols., being vols. 22 to 33 of the entire series, London, 1817–26; with a General Index by David Jardine, London, 1828, entitled "State Trials, vol. 34." 34 vols. in all.

Among the original sources of the English Criminal Law, these volumes have a high place. In tracing the history of the law of the more common and familiar crimes, for the purposes of the Code, frequent reference to the series has been needful.

Hubbell (G. B.)

State Prison Discipline. Remarks in N. Y. Assembly, 1859. Albany, 1859.

Hume (David).

Commentaries on the Law of Scotland, respecting crimes; with a supplement by Benj. Robert Bell. 2 vols. 4to. Edinburgh, 1844.

A standard authority in the criminal law of Scotland.

Illinois.

A Compilation of the Statutes of—Of a general nature, in force Jan. 1, 1856, collated with reference to decisions of the Supreme Court, and prior laws. By N. H. Purple. 2 vols. Chicago, 1856.

Contains a systematic penal statute of 1845, with provisions of later laws appended. The act of 1845 is similar in general character, and in many of its provisions to that of Georgia, elsewhere described.

Indiana.

Statutes of the State of—containing the Revised Statutes of 1852, with the amendments thereto and the subsequent legislation, with notes, &c. Edited by James Gavin and Oscar B. Hord. 2 vols. Indianapolis, 1812.

Contains a brief statute on crimes, amounting to but little more than a regular system of punishments for crimes recognized as already known to the common law, with the addition of penalties imposed for some other specific acts.

Indian Penal Code.

Return to an order of the House of Commons dated 30 July, 1838, for a copy of the Penal Code prepared by the Indian Law

Commissioners and published by command of the Governor General of India in council. Ordered by the House of Commons to be printed, 3d August, 1838.

This is the Commissioners' draft of the statute enacted for India many years later, under the following title:

—— The Indian Penal Code (Act XLV of 1860) with notes by W. Morgan and A. G. Macpherson, barristers-at-law. London, 1861.

This code was originally prepared by the Indian Law Commissioners when Lord Macaulay was the president of that body, and was laid before the Governor-General of India in council, in the year 1837. It was enacted in 1860. The present volume contains the act as passed, with extensive notes explaining its meaning and application.

The provisions of the Indian Code have suggested several amendments of our own law, embodied in the Penal Code.

Jameson (Mrs.).

Sisters of Charity and Communion of Labor. Containing articles on Prisons and Penitentiaries, &c. London, 1859.

Jardine (David).

A Reading on the use of Torture in the Criminal Law of England, previously to the Commonwealth. London, 1837.

An interesting tract on a topic quite unimportant to the practical amendment of the criminal law of New York.

—— Criminal Trials, supplying copious illustrations of important periods of English history. 2 vols. London, 1846–47.

The remark elsewhere made relative to the similar collection of trials by Chandler, applies to these volumes.

Jebb. See *British Crown Cases*.

Kentucky.

Revised Statutes of—in force from July 1, 1852, with all the amendments subsequently enacted, and notes of decision; and an appendix containing all the enactments passed during 1859 and 1860, by Richard H. Stanton. 2 vols. Cincinnati, 1860.

The remark above made upon the statute law of *Indiana* applies to the brief chapter on criminal law contained in this compilation.

Leach (Thomas).

Cases in Crown Law, determined by the Twelve Judges, by the Court of King's Bench, and by Commissioners of Oyer and Terminer and General Gaol Delivery, from 4 Geo. II (1730) to 55 Geo. III (1815). Fourth edition. London, 1815. 2 vols.

A general and valuable collection of English decisions.

Leading Criminal Cases. See *Bennett.*

Letters.

On the comparative merits of the Pennsylvania and New York systems of penitentiary discipline By a Massachusetts man. Boston, 1836. 8 vo.

Lewin (Sir Gregory A.)

A Report of Cases determined on the Crown side on the Northern Circuit, commencing 1822 and ending 1833. London, 1834.

Not arranged like an ordinary volume of reports, but partaking the character of a digest, in so far as that the points of the various cases are classified under their appropriate titles, alphabetically arranged.

Lieber (Francis).

A Popular Essay on subjects of Penal Law, and on Uninterrupted Solitary Confinement at Labor, as contradistinguished to solitary confinement at night, and joint labor by day; in a letter to John Bacon. Philadelphia, 1838.

Livingston (Edward).

Letter to Robert Vaux on the Pennsylvania system of prison discipline. Philadelphia, 1828.

—— A System of Penal Law for the State of Louisiana. Consisting of: a code of crimes and punishments; a code of procedure; a code of evidence; a code of reform and prison discipline; a book of definitions. Prepared under the authority of a law of the said state. To which are prefixed a preliminary report on the plan of a penal code, and introductory reports to the several codes embraced in the system of Penal Law. Philadelphia and Pittsburgh, 1833.

One of the most famous essays towards law amendment, in our language. Very complete, accurate, philosophic and suggestive. In style it partakes too much of the character of a treatise, too little of that of a statute to be fully adapted for enactment; but the substance of many of its provisions has been embodied in provisions of this code.

—— A system of penal law for the United States of America. Consisting of: a code of crimes and punishments; a code of procedure in criminal cases; a code of prison discipline, and a book of definitions. Prepared and presented to the house of representatives of the United States, by Edward Livingston. Printed by order of the house. Folio. Washington, 1828.

Louisiana.

A Digest of the penal law of the State of Louisiana, analytically arranged. By authority. By M. M. Robinson. New Orleans, 1841.

Has been of only secondary service.

Luckey (Rev. John).

Prison Sketches. By a Chaplain. Edited by D. P. Kidder. New York, 1849.

McLeod (Alexander).

Trial of—for the murder of Amos Durfee.

This trial has been famous in American jurisprudence, and acquires renewed importance at the present day, from its bearing upon questions of public law. The alleged offense was committed in 1837. The Caroline was a small steamer, owned in Buffalo and plying as a ferry boat between that city and Navy island, on which a band of insurgents were posted with the intention of invading Canada for the overthrow of its government. While lying at Schlosser, a short distance above Niagara Falls and within the State of New York, she was, on the night of the 29th of December, 1837, boarded by an armed body from the Canadian shore, seventy or eighty strong. One person was mortally wounded, others were shot and seriously injured, and twelve others, missing, were supposed to have perished in the steamer, which was cut loose, set on fire and sent over the Falls.

In 1839, Alexander McLeod, of Upper Canada, was arrested at Lewiston, in New York State, on a charge of murder and arson in this affair of the Caroline. This arrest excited much feeling, both in this country and in England, and very soon a demand was made by the British government for McLeod's liberation under the avowal that the proceedings in which he took part were under its sanction. This was refused. The trial however, ended in the acquittal of the accused on the ground of an *alibi*.

MacNally (Leonard).

Rules of Evidence on Pleas of the Crown, illustrated from printed and manuscript trials and cases. 2 vols. Philadelphia, 1804.

A reprint of an Irish work of considerable merit.

McNeil (D. B.)

Laws of the State of New York, relating to State prisons and the State Lunatic Asylum for insane convicts, passed since the adoption of the Constitution of 1846. Compiled from and compared with the original laws on file in the office of the Secretary of State. Albany, 1864.

A reprint of the statute laws. The same matter may be found scattered throughout the annual volumes of session laws; but it is exceedingly convenient to the student of the particular subject, to have them collected in this form. Had the work been received by the commissioners before title XIX of the Code was prepared, it would have materially assisted their labors upon that part of the work.

Maine.

Revised Statutes of the State of—passed April 7, 1857. Portland and Hallowell, 1857.

The leading features of the statute law of crimes in Maine, are borrowed from that of Massachusetts; and the more recent compilation in the latter State has rendered recourse to the statutes of Maine comparatively infrequent.

Maryland.

The Maryland Code. Public General Laws. Compiled by Otho Scott and Hiram McCullough, commissioners. Adopted by the Legislature, January, 1860. With an Index by Henry C. Machall. 1 vol. Baltimore, 1860.

One article of this compilation treats of the criminal law, somewhat fully, as respects the number of offenses provided for; but without any such completeness in regard to the definitions of offenses, as to give the work fully the character of a code, properly so-called. A supplement, issued in 1862, was received too late to be of service.

—— Rules and Regulations of the Maryland Penitentiary. Enlarged edition. Baltimore, 1853.

Massachusetts.

The General Statutes of the Commonwealth of. Revised by commissioners, amended by the Legislature, and passed Dec. 28, 1859. Edited and published under authority of resolves of 1859. Boston, 1861.

If it be the best policy to forego a code, and to rely, in the administration of the criminal law, upon a system of statutes covering, by express provisions, the leading and more common crimes, and upon a reserved power in the courts to apply general principles of unwritten law to new developments of misconduct and to cases suggesting nice distinctions, it is difficult to see how the work of penal legislation could be better done, having reference to the wants of the particular State, than in Title I of Part IV of this compilation. Not all crimes are defined; nor are common law offenses excluded; but the definitions, when given, are lucid and easily applied, the language is compact and concise, and the whole construction of the act, practical, and adapted for easy and just administration. The provisions fill about thirty-six royal octavo pages, more closely printed than many like compilations. They have been frequently consulted in the preparation of the Penal Code, and always with advantage.

—— Report of the Penal Code of—prepared under a resolve of the Legislature, passed February 10, 1837. Boston, 1844.

This work is an inchoate undertaking similar in character and design to the draft of the present Penal Code. It only purports to exhibit the method upon which the Massachusetts commissioners appointed to codify the criminal law of that State, proposed to proceed in the execution of their task. It forms, however, a full sized volume, and treats quite comprehensively and suggestively of the leading offenses. Some aid has been derived from it in framing the analysis and some of the definitions given in the Penal Code.

—— Report of the Joint Standing Committee on Prisons, to inquire what change is necessary, if any, in the discipline at the State Prison. Mass. House of Rep., May, 1857.

—— Laws of the Mass. State Prison, 1829. Charlestown, 1830.

Matthews (James M.)

Digest of the Laws of Virginia of a criminal nature, illustrated by judicial decisions. Richmond, 1861.

Has been of occasional service.

Mechanics' State Convention.

Proceeding of the, at Utica, 1834, on the effect produced on the trades by the system of state prison discipline.

Michigan.

Compiled Laws of the State of. Published by authority. Compared and arranged by Thos. M. Cooley. 2 vols. Lansing, 1857.

Contains a tolerably complete title, filling sixty pages, upon crimes and the punishment thereof.

Minnesota.

The Public Statutes of the State of—1849–1858. Compiled by Messrs. Sherburne and Wm. Hollinshead, commissioners. Published by State authority. St. Paul, 1859.

The provisions on crimes in this collection of laws follow too closely the existing statutes of New York to be of much aid in amending them.

Missouri.

Revised Statutes of the State of. Revised and digested by the 18th general assembly during 1854 and 1855. Charles H. Hardin, commissioner. Published by authority of law. 2 vols. Jefferson, 1856.

Contains a chapter upon crimes, which is tolerably full, but has not been of any essential service.

Moody. See *British Crown Cases.*

Morgan. See *Indian Penal Code.*

New Hampshire.

The Compiled Statutes of the State of; to which are prefixed the Constitution, &c. Published by order of the legislature. Second edition. Concord, 1854.

The provisions upon crimes in this volume are too brief to have been of any material service.

New Jersey.

A Digest of the Laws of. By Lucius Elmer. Third edition, containing all the laws of general application, now in force, from 1709 to 1861, inclusive, with the rules and decisions of the courts. By John T. Nixon. Published under the patronage of the legislature. Bridgeton and Trenton, 1861.

Several provisions of the Penal Code have been suggested by the New Jersey statutes presented in the above work.

—— Statistics of the state prison of New Jersey from 1799 to 1845. Trenton, 1846.

—— Reports on the condition of the state prison, 1856, 1857, 1858.

New York.

Auburn state prison. Reports of inspectors between 1829 and 1847.

—— Clinton state prison. Annual reports, 1845, 1846, 1847.

—— Mount Pleasant state prison. Annual reports between 1832 and 1848.

—— Report of select committee of the assembly on the condition of the state prisons. 1852.

—— Annual reports of the inspectors of state prisons since 1849.

—— State of New York. No. 98. In Senate, March 18, 1846. Report of the Secretary of State, of abstracts of convictions for criminal offenses, and of the returns of sheriffs respecting the persons convicted.

—— Statutes of.

The most cursory glance at the Code will show that the Revised Statutes and Session Laws of our own State have been its principal basis. Indeed, as already explained in the preliminary note, the general rule has been to take the provision of the Code from the existing statute, if there was one, upon the subject under consideration, and to introduce a new enactment only in cases when there was none at all, or where the present law was believed to be in some way defective or objectionable.

North Carolina.

Revised Code of—enacted by the general assembly at the session of 1854, together with other acts of a public and general nature, passed at the same session, &c. Prepared under acts of the general assembly, passed at the sessions of 1850 and 1854. By Bartholomew T. Moore and Asa Biggs. Boston, 1855.

The remark made relative to the provisions of the Maryland Code, applies equally to this volume.

Ohio.

Special Report of the warden (L. Dewey) of the Ohio penitentiary, on prisons and prison discipline. Columbus, 1851.

—— Report of the directors and warden (J. Ewing) for 1856. Columbus, 1856.

—— The Revised Statutes of—of a general nature, in force, August 1st, 1860. Collected by Jos. R. Swan, with notes by Leander J. Critchfield. 2 vols. Cincinnati, 1860.

A very well arranged and digested compilation of a somewhat heterogeneous collection of statutes, passed at various dates during the last thirty years.

Packard (F. A.)

Inquiry into the alleged tendency of the Separation of Convicts, one from the other, to produce disease and derangement. By a citizen of Pennsylvania. Philadelphia, 1849.

—— Memoir of a late visit to Auburn penitentiary. Philadelphia, 1841.

—— Vindication of the separate system of prison discipline from the misrepresentations of the North American Review, July, 1839. Philadelphia.

Parker (Amasa J.)

Reports of Decisions in Criminal Cases made at term, at chambers, and in the courts of oyer and terminer of the State of New York. 4 vols. Albany, 1855–1856.

These volumes are important to one who would acquaint himself fully with the criminal jurisprudence of New York State, and they have been, of course, frequently referred to in the preparation of the Code. A majority of the cases are not elsewhere reported, and many of them are of recent date and contain authoritative decisions of important questions.

Paris (J. A.) and Fonblanque (J. S. M.)

Medical Jurisprudence. 3 vols. London, 1823.

A leading work in its day. The preparation of the Code has not required, however, very extended researches in medical jurisprudence; and upon the questions which have arisen, the more recent works of Beck, Dean, and Wharton & Stillé have been found more convenient than this one, eminent as it is.

Partidas.

The laws of Las Siete Partidas, which are still in force in the State of Louisiana. Translated from the Spanish by L. Morean Lislet and Henry Carleton. New Orleans, 1820.

Was of service in perfecting the analysis of the Code.

Pennsylvania.

History of the Eastern Penitentiary of. Philadelphia, 1852.

—— Journal of Prison Discipline and Philanthropy. Published quarterly under the direction of the Philadelphia Society for the alleviation of the miseries of public prisons. From 1845 onward.

—— Reports of the Eastern Penitentiary of. From 1846 onward.

Philadelphia Society.

Sketches of the Principal Transactions of the Philadelphia Society for the alleviation of the miseries of public prisons, from its origin. Philadelphia, 1859.

Pitcairn (Robert).

Criminal Trials in Scotland, from A. D. 1488, to A. D. 1624; embracing the entire reigns of James IV and V, and Mary Queen of Scots, and James VI; compiled from the original Records and MSS.; with Historical Notes and Illustrations. 3 vols. Edinburgh, 1833.

Powers (Gershom).

Letter to Edward Livingston in relation to Auburn State Prison. 1829.

—— A brief account of the Auburn State Prison. Auburn, 1826.

Prison Association.

Nineteenth Annual Report of the Executive Committee of the Prison Association of New York. Transmitted by the Legislature, Jan. 29, 1864. Albany, 1864.

Gives the results of the visits of inspection made by the committees of the association during 1863, to the State prisons and county jails and penitentiaries of the State. Abounds in valuable information upon the present condition of the institutions visited, and in important suggestions towards their improved management.

Pulton (Ferdinando).

De Pace Regis et Regni, viz: A Treatise declaring which be the great and generale offences of the Realme, and the chiefe impediments of the peace of the King and the Kingdome, as Menaces, Assaults, Batteries, Treasons, Homicides and Felonies, Ryots, Routs, Vnlawful assemblies, &c., &c., which being reformed, or duly checked, *Florebit pax Regis et Regni.* Collected out of the Reports of the Common Lawes of the Realme, and of the Statutes in force, and out of the painful workes of the Reverend Judges, Sir Anthony Fitzherbert, &c., &c. 1 vol. folio. London, 1609.

A leading authority upon the common law in its early condition, and as such, very serviceable.

Ray (J.)
A treatise on the Medical Jurisprudence of Insanity. Fourth edition, with additions. Boston, 1860.

A recent and somewhat enlarged edition of a work, always highly respected upon the special topic to which it relates. Upon the important topic of the amenability of persons laboring under mental diseases, to criminal punishment for their acts, Dr. Ray is of opinion that the rules of the English and American law originated at a time when the philosophy of disease of the mind was not well understood, and that the courts of law have not kept pace with the progress of science on this subject; that under the usual legal definitions, many persons are held liable to punishment who, upon views more in accordance with the facts of mental derangement, would be deemed excused; and that the protection of society against the acts of the insane ought to be sought more through efforts for their guardianship and restoration, and less through the administration of criminal punishment, than is done at present. These views are advocated throughout his volume with great ability. The questions connected with this subject have been considered with much care in the preparation of the provisions of the code which bear upon the criminal responsibility of the insane, and the views above indicated, as advocated by Dr. Ray and others no less entitled to respect, have been attentively considered. But while the commissioners regard the subject as one of great difficulty, a majority of them have considered it wiser to maintain the rule of legal responsibility, as it has been declared by the later adjudications of the courts. The rule has been so declared in sections 16 and 18 of the Code.

Rhode Island.
The Revised Statutes of the State of Rhode Island and Providence Plantations. Published by authority of the General Assembly. Providence, 1857.

Contains a title of about 25 pages "Of crimes and punishments," which has been several times useful.

Rogers (Daniel).
The New York City Hall Recorder. Containing reports of the most interesting trials and decisions which have arisen in the various courts of judicature for the trial of jury causes in the hall

during those years, particularly in the court of sessions. 6 vols. bound in 3. 1816–1821. New York, 1817–22.

This was a species of law magazine, being published in monthly numbers, from Jan., 1816, to Dec., 1821. It is chiefly devoted to criminal cases tried at the New York City Hall during the period of its publication. It contains, however, some notices of cases in other states. Not many of the cases reported in these volumes contain decisions of points of law which now have much authority. The work embodies, however, an interesting, if not a very useful, exhibit of the earlier criminal jurisprudence of our State, as administered in the city of New York.

Roscoe (Henry).

A Digest of the Law of Evidence in Criminal Cases. Second edition, with considerable additions by T. C. Granger. With notes and references by George Sharswood. Philadelphia, 1840.

A well known and very valuable manual.

Russell (William Oldnall).

A Treatise on Crimes and Indictable Misdemeanors. With additional notes of decisions in the American courts, by Daniel Davis. Second American from the second English edition, with additional references, by Theron Metcalf. Philadelphia, 1831.

Well known as the leading work on the English criminal law as it existed prior to the recent sweeping statutory changes. A new edition of Russell is understood to be in preparation by Mr. Chas. S. Greaves, in which form the work will doubtless resume its former place at the head of the manuals of the criminal law.

Russell and Ryan. See *British Crown Cases.*

Sampson (M. B.)

Rationale of Crime, and its Appropriate Treatment; being a treatise on Criminal Jurisprudence, considered in relation to Cerebral Organization. With notes and illustrations by E. W. Farnham. 12 mo. New York, 1846.

Sanford (H. S.)

The different systems of Penal Codes in Europe; also a report on the administrative changes in France, since the Revolution of 1848. 33d Congress, 1 sess. Ex. doc. No. 68. Washington, 1854.

So much of this volume as relates to the penal codes of Europe, forms the basis of Appendix A which follows the text of this Code in the present volume. It will be seen by referring to that paper, that the work has been of essential service.

Saunders (T. W.) and Cox (Edward W.)

The Criminal Law Consolidation Acts, 1861; the other new criminal statutes and parts of statutes of the sessions 1861 and 1862; together with a digest of the criminal cases from 1848 to 1862. Second edition. London, 1862.

The criminal law consolidation acts are elsewhere described. See *Greaves*. The present volume contains one or two later acts, which are comparatively unimportant. The digest is substantially the same with that already described. See *Cox*.

Shaw (John).

Reports of Cases before the High Court and Circuit Courts of Justiciary in Scotland, during 1848–1852. Edinburgh, 1853.

One of the series of standard reports in the criminal law of Scotland.

Smith (John Gordon).

The Principles of Forensic Medicine systematically arranged and applied to British practice. Second edition. London, 1824.

The remark made upon *Chitty's Medical Jurisprudence* applies equally to this work.

Smith (G. W.)

A Defense of the System of Solitary Confinement of prisoners in Pennsylvania. Philadelphia, 1838.

Spanish Civil Law.

Institutes of the Civil Law of Spain. Translated from the Spanish, with notes, &c., by Lewis F. C. Johnston. London, 1825.

Two of the titles of this volume—titles 19 and 20, of Book II—treat of criminal law, and were examined in preparing the analysis; both for the purpose of perfecting the classification, and to ascertain offenses which ought to be included.

Starkie (Thomas).

Treatise on Criminal Pleading; with precedents of indictments, special pleas, &c. First American from the last London edition. 1 vol. Exeter, 1824.

Staundeforde (Guilliaulme).

Les Plees del Coron, diuisees in plusors titles and comon lieux, 1574.

Has been occasionally consulted on questions relative to the early rules of the common law.

Stephen (Henry J.)

Summary of the Criminal Law. Philadelphia, 1840.

A reprint of an English work, formerly much esteemed. There is a later edition.

Swinton (Archibald).

Reports of Cases before the High Court and Circuit Courts of Justiciary in Scotland from 1835 to 1841. 2 vols. Edinburgh, 1838, 1842.

One of the standard series of Scotch criminal reports.

Tellkampf (J. L.)

Essays on Law Reform, Penitentiaries, &c., in Great Britain and the United States. London, 1859.

Thacher (Peter O.)

Reports of Criminal Cases tried in the criminal court of the city of Boston, before Peter Oxenbridge Thacher, judge of that court, from 1823 to 1843. Edited by Horatio Woodman. Boston, 1845.

Townsend (William C.)

Modern State Trials; revised and illustrated with essays and notes. 2 vols. London, 1850.

Contains a number of interesting English trials of comparatively recent date, and important bearing on the law of crimes.

Tomlins (Harold Nuttall).

A Digested Index to the Common Law; containing all the points relating to criminal matters, comprehended in the reports of Blackstone, Burrow, Cowper, Douglas, Leach's C. L., Lord Raymond, Salkeld, Strange, Wilson, and the Term Reports, &c. Second edition. Revised, corrected and enlarged with the addition of such cases as have been decided since the first publication of the work. London, 1820.

A convenient index to the criminal cases in the reports above mentioned.

Tremaine (John).

Placita Coronæ; or Pleas of the Crown, in matters criminal and civil, containing a large collection of modern precedents. In the Savoy. Folio (London), 1723.

United States Digest.

Of Decisions in Criminal Cases contained in the Reports of the Courts of the United States and the several State Courts. By John L. Hanes. New York, 1856.

A very convenient index to American cases on criminal law, decided prior to 1856.

Van Leeuwen (Simon).

Commentaries on the Roman Dutch Law. Translated from the Dutch. London, 1820.

Embraces the subject of penal law.

Vermont.

The Compiled Statutes of the State of; being such of the Revised Staütes, and of the public acts, and laws passed since, as are now in force. To which are prefixed the Constitution, &c. Compiled in pursuance of an act of the legislature. By Chas. L. Williams. Burlington, 1851.

The remark made relative to the New Hampshire statutes applies also to this collection.

Voorhies (Albert).

A Treatise on the Criminal Jurisprudence of Louisiana. 2 vols. bound in 1. New Orleans, 1860.

Virginia.

The Code of—with the Declaration of Independence, &c. Published pursuant to an act of the general assembly of Virginia, passed August 15, 1849. Richmond, 1849.

The remark made relative to the Maryland Code applies equally to this compilation.

Washington Territory.

Statutes of. Tenth annual session held at Olympia, 1862. Also containing the Territorial Organic Act, &c. Olympia, 1863.

Contains "an act relative to crimes and punishments," &c., eleven chapters of which are occupied with a tolerably comprehensive system of penal law. This volume was not received until after the Penal Code was substantially completed.

Waterman's (Thomas W.) Archbold.

A Complete Practical Treatise on Criminal Procedure, Pleading and Evidence, in indictable cases, with minute directions and forms, for every case that can arise, either at common law, under the English statute, or under the statutes of the several states; comprising the "new system of criminal procedure, pleading, and evidence," by Mr. Archbold, and also the fourteenth and last London edition of "Archbold's pleading and evidence in criminal cases," by Messrs. Jervis & Welsby; with comprehensive notes containing all of the American and English decisions to the date of publication. Seventh edition. 2 vols. New York, 1860.

A work well known to the American practitioner. Although its discussions of the nature of crimes are incidental to its main purpose—the elucidation of procedure and evidence—it has been found of frequent service as an aid in collating the recent American decisions and statutes.

Wharton (Francis).

Treatise on the Criminal Law of the United States, comprising a general view of the criminal jurisprudence of the common and civil law, and a digest of the penal statutes of the general government, and of Massachusetts, New York, Pennsylvania, Virginia and Ohio, with the decisions or cases arising upon those statutes. Fifth revised edition. 2 vols. Philadelphia, 1861.

A very comprehensive and valuable work.

—— Treatise on the Law of Homicide in the United States; to which is appended a series of leading cases on homicide, now out of print, or existing only in manuscript. Philadelphia, 1855.

—— Precedents of Indictments and Pleas adapted to the use both of the courts of the United States and those of all the several States. With notes on criminal pleading and practice. Second and revised edition. Philadelphia, 1857.

—— State Trials of the United States during the administrations of Washington and Adams. Philadelphia, 1849.

Wharton (Francis) & Stillè (Morton).
Treatise on Medical Jurisprudence. Philadelphia, 1855.

This work is rich in information of the recent progress of medical jurisprudence on the continent of Europe. Has been of material service upon the few questions connected with this science, which have arisen in the preparation of the Code.

Wheeler (Jacob D.)
Criminal Law Cases, with notes and references; containing also a view of the Criminal Laws of the United States from September, 1822 to 1824. 3 vols. New York, 1823–1825.

The first volume of this series contains, principally, reports of criminal trials in the courts of the city of New York. The second and third volume contain cases from courts of other States, besides a tolerably systematic review of the criminal law. The work is, however, comparatively unimportant at the present day.

Wills (William).
An Essay on the Rationale of Circumstantial Evidence. Illustrated by numerous cases. Philadelphia, 1843.

A reprint of an English work. The volume contains an interesting discussion of the force and effect of circumstantial evidence, with narratives of leading English cases illustrative of the subject. Although the subject of evidence is excluded from the Penal Code, yet on some questions relative to presumptions and the burden of proof, which have arisen collaterally in framing definitions of offenses, this work has been useful.

Wisconsin.
The Revised Statutes of the State of—passed and approved, 1858, to which is prefixed the Declaration of Independence, &c. Printed and published pursuant to law, under the superintendence of one of the revisers. Chicago, 1858.

The remark made relative to the statutes of Minnesota applies also to this collection.

APPENDIX C.

TABLE OF STATUTES

SHOWING THE PROPOSED EFFECT OF THE CODE UPON THE EXISTING LAW.

In this table are mentioned the important provisions of the original Revised Statutes and subsequent acts of the Legislature, which affect subjects within the scope of the Penal Code, and are of a public or general character,* and are still in force.

If the Penal Code contains any provision corresponding to a given statute, reference is made in the table to the section of the Code covering the statute. In this class of cases, it is to be understood that although the previous statute *should not be repealed*, section 2 of the Code will prevent any prosecution under it, as to offenses commenced after the Code takes effect. (See section 2, and note to section 786.) Such offenses are only punishable so far as the Code permits.

If the statute, though apparently within the scope of the Code, is one of those which, by sections 783–786, is to remain unaffected—so that, notwithstanding the passage of the Code, proceedings may be taken under such statute—or if it is one of those relating to prisons, which are repealed by the express provisions of section 1070—reference is made to those sections respectively.

If the statute, although within the scope of the Code, has been designedly omitted, in preparing it—so that after the passage of the latter there will be no provision of law really corresponding to it—the reason why it is omitted is briefly indicated.

Acts that have heretofore been repealed are, in general, not mentioned in this table, unless there are provisions in the Code corresponding to them in substance. This is often the case where a statute was repealed by a later one which contained similar provisions.

* Acts operative within particular municipal corporations only, are continued in force by section 786, subd. 1. But to save space, these are not enumerated in this table.

The Revised Statutes.

1 *Rev. Stat.*, 121, § 31, imposing penalty for acting as officer without oath or bond.

Covered by section 96 of the Penal Code.

1 *Rev. Stat.*, 124, § 50, relative to refusal of public officer to deliver books, &c., to his successor.

Covered by section 111.

1 *Rev. Stat.*, 149, §§ 1, 2, relative to perjury at elections.

Covered by sections 150, 162.

1 *Rev. Stat.*, 154, §§ 12–15, relative to powers of legislature to punish, &c.

Preserved by sections 784, 785.

2 *Rev. Stat.*, 199, § 15, imposing punishment for making false return of survey.

Covered by section 223.

1 *Rev. Stat.*, 206, § 54, relative to former owner of lands sold by surveyor-general, returning to resettle upon them.

Covered by the more general provision of section 493.

1 *Rev. Stat.*, 235, §§ 94, 95, relative to drawing water from the canals.

Covered by section 515.

1 *Rev. Stat.*, 241, § 125, punishing delivery of false bill of lading on canal.

Covered by section 511.

1 *Rev. Stat.*, 248, §§ 179, 180, relative to abusing canals.

Covered by section 514.

1 *Rev. Stat.*, 311, § 29, relative to contempt of court martial.

All laws of this kind are preserved by section 785.

1 *Rev. Stat.*, 312, §§ 1–11, authorizing military fines and penalties.

All laws of this kind are preserved by section 785.

1 *Rev. Stat.*, 350, § 15, relative to county clerk omitting to return names of constables.

Covered by section 223.

1 *Rev. Stat.*, 421, § 15, relative to omission of duty by certain public officers.

Covered by section 215.

1 *Rev. Stat.*, 422–455, containing chapter 14 of part I, entitled "Of the Public Health."

The commissioners have contemplated the revision of the Health Laws as a separate body of laws from either of the Codes (See either of the Codes (see note to section 786). The more important offenses connected with quarantine are, however, covered by sections 435–439; and obstructions or violations of the health laws are made punishable by sections 440–441.

1 *Rev. Stat.*, 525, §§ 128, 129, relative to injuries to mile stones, &c.

Covered by section 694.

1 *Rev. Stat.*, 527, § 7, relative to violating recognizance to keep a ferry.

Covered by section 460.

1 *Rev. Stat.*, 529, §§ 1–40, relative to offenses connected with auction sales.

This subject is covered by sections 502–510.

1 *Rev. Stat.*, 536, §§ 1–199, relating to the inspection of provisions, produce and merchandize.

The commissioners have contemplated the revision of the Inspection Laws as a separate body of laws from either of the Codes (see section 786, note); which is the reason why the penal provisions of the existing statutes are not incorporated in the Code.

1 *Rev. Stat.*, 589, §§ 1–31, relative to acts of directors of corporations.

The penal provisions of these sections, with others of greater stringency, are embodied in sections 645–658.

1 *Rev. Stat.*, 635, § 11, relative to confinement of insane persons.

Covered by section 425.

1 *Rev. Stat.*, 658, §§ 8–12, relative to selling or exporting persons as slaves.

Provisions upon this subject are given in sections 272–276.

1 *Rev. Stat.*, 662, §§ 11–13, relative to betting and gaming.

Covered by sections 388–390.

1 *Rev. Stat.*, 664, § 21, allowing certain offenders to be discharged.

Omitted, for reasons stated in note to section 391.

1 *Rev. Stat.*, 665, §§ 22–37, relative to lotteries.

More stringent provisions are contained in sections 370–384.

1 *Rev. Stat.*, 671, § 53, relative to forgery of lottery tickets.

Omitted, for reasons stated in note to section 371.

1 *Rev. Stat.*, 672, § 55; relative to racing for stakes.

Covered by section 400.

1 *Rev. Stat.*, 673, § 59, relative to racing in New Utrecht.

Omitted; the general provisions of sections 207, 400 and 472, on the subject of racing, being deemed sufficient.

1 *Rev. Stat.*, 673 and 674, §§ 61–63, relative to profane swearing.
Covered by sections 34–37.

1 *Rev. Stat.*, 674, § 64, relative to disturbing religious meetings.
Covered by sections 55 and 56.

1 *Rev. Stat.*, 675, §§ 69–72, relative to observance of Sunday.
Covered by sections 38–52.

1 *Rev. Stat.*, 682, § 25, punishing offenses against the provisions relative to excise.

See provisions on this subject in sections 723–728.

1 *Rev. Stat.*, 684, § 9, and 685, § 11, relative to management of steamboats.

See section 729.

1 *Rev. Stat.*, 694, §§ 25, 26, relative to taking or defacing marks upon wrecked property.

Covered by sections 597 and 420.

1 *Rev. Stat.*, 695, § 4, relative to running horses on highways.
Covered by section 472.

1 *Rev. Stat.*, 696, § 1, and 697, § 3, relative to fires in the woods.
Covered by sections 456, 457.

1 *Rev. Stat.*, 699, § 10, relative to defacing marks upon lumber.
Covered by section 421.

1 *Rev. Stat.*, 711, § 9, relative to pawnbrokers.
Covered by sections 401–403.

1 *Rev. Stat.*, 762, § 35, relative to false acknowledgments of deeds, &c.

This offense is left to the operation of the general principles embodied in sections 215, 216, 223.

1 *Rev. Stat.*, 766, § 19, relative to frauds in affairs of limited partnership.

Covered by section 423.

2 *Rev. Stat.*, 44, § 16, relative to officers suffering escapes.

The criminal punishment is embraced within section 172; and the civil penalty is preserved by section 783.

2 *Rev. Stat.*, 140, § 12, relative to solemnizing improper marriages.

Covered by section 424.

2 *Rev. Stat.*, 149, § 7, relative to removing or secreting child to evade habeas corpus.

Omitted for reasons stated in note to section 429.

2 *Rev. Stat.*, 267, § 234, relative to constables receiving rewards.
See sections 171–174 and 215.

2 *Rev. Stat.*, 267, §§ 235, 236, relative to buying demands, &c., by justices and constables.

Covered by sections 195, 196.

2 *Rev. Stat.*, 278, §§ 10–15, relative to punishment for contempt. The power of the court to punish by attachment is preserved by section 785. Punishment upon conviction on indictment is provided for by section 201. And see sections 740, 741.

2 *Rev. Stat.*, 287, §§ 68–74, relative to certain offenses by attorneys.

Covered by sections 209, 210 and 194–198.

2 *Rev. Stat.*, 288, §§ 75–82, relative to evidence of buying demands illegally.

See section 200, and note.

2 *Rev. Stat.*, 291, § 95, relative to selling liquor in court houses.

Covered by section 208.

2 *Rev. Stat.*, 428, § 11, relative to certain violations of duty by sheriffs.

The right to recover damages here conferred is preserved by section 783 of the Code; but the provision for criminal punishment is omitted as unnecessary in view of sections 215 and 216.

2 *Rev. Stat.*, 431, § 29, relative to sale of liquor in jails.

See section 208.

2 *Rev. Stat.*, 438, § 65, relative to voluntary escapes.

Covered by section 172.

2 *Rev. Stat.*, 534, §§ 1–37, relative to contempt of court.

Preserved by section 785. Punishment of contempts upon conviction on indictment is provided for by section 201. See also sections 740, 741.

2 *Rev. Stat.*, 550, § 1, relative to unauthorized suits.

See section 219.

2 *Rev. Stat.*, 571, §§ 60–64, of violations of habeas corpus act.

See sections 426–429.

2 *Rev. Stat.*, 650, §§ 5–7, relative to taking excessive fees.

Covered by sections 102, 104.

2 *Rev. Stat.*, 656, § 1, enumerating crimes punishable with death. Covered by sections 60, 247 and 539.

2 *Rev. Stat.*, 656, § 2, defining "treason."

Covered by sections 57–59.

2 *Rev. Stat.*, 656, § 3, relative to outlawry for treason.

Omitted, for reason stated in note to section 59.

2 *Rev. Stat.*, 656, §§ 4–7, relative to murder.

Covered by sections 236, 241, 246, 738 and 739.

2 *Rev. Stat.*, 657, § 8, abolishing petit treason.
See section 239.

2 *Rev. Stat.*, 657, §§ 9 and 10, defining arson in first degree.
Covered by sections 532, 533.

2 *Rev. Stat.*, 660, §§ 2–4, defining justifiable and excusable homicide.

Covered by sections 260–262.

2 *Rev. Stat.*, 661, § 5, prescribing verdict in cases of justifiable and excusable homicide.

Omitted, as belonging to procedure.

2 *Rev. Stat.*, 661–663, §§ 7–21, relative to manslaughter.
Covered by sections 234, 248–259.

2 *Rev. Stat.*, 663, §§ 22–26, relative to rape, abduction, &c.
Covered by sections 319–329.

2 *Rev. Stat.*, 664, § 27, relative to mayhem.
Covered by sections 263–271.

2 *Rev. Stat.*, 664, §§ 28–32, relative to kidnapping.
Covered by sections 272–274.

2 *Rev. Stat.*, 665, § 33, relative to place of trial for kidnapping.
Omitted as belonging to procedure. See *Code of Cr. Pro.*, § 134.

2 *Rev. Stat.*, 665, §§ 34, 35, relative to decoying and abandoning children.

Covered by sections 337 and 332 respectively.

2 *Rev. Stat.*, 665, § 36, relative to certain assaults.
Covered by sections 278 and 290.

2 *Rev. Stat.*, 665, §§ 37, 38, relative to poisoning.
Covered by sections 277–405.

2 *Rev. Stat.*, 666, § 39, relative to assaults with intent, &c.
See sections 279–291.

2 *Rev. Stat.*, 666, 667, §§ 1–9, of arson.
This subject is provided for by sections 521–539. See also, section 703.

2 *Rev. Stat.*, 668, §§ 10–21, of burglary.
This offense is provided for by sections 540–552.

2 *Rev. Stat.*, 670, §§ 22–47, of forgery.
These provisions, with some additional ones, are embodied in sections 553–583.

2 *Rev. Stat.*, 676, §§ 48–54, relative to false personations and cheats.

Covered by sections 620–627, and 212, 213, except that section 49 of the Rev. Stat. is omitted as appertaining to procedure.

2 *Rev. Stat.*, 677, §§ 55–57, of robbery.

Covered, with some additional provisions, by sections 280, 289.

2 *Rev. Stat.*, 678, § 58, relative to threatening letters.

See section 618.

2 *Rev. Stat.*, 678, §§ 59–62, of embezzlement.

More extensive provisions, in which these are included, are contained in sections 601–612.

2 *Rev. Stat.*, 679, §§ 63–66, of grand larceny.

Covered by sections 587, 589, 591, 593.

2 *Rev. Stat.*, 679, § 67, of stealing lottery tickets.

Omitted for reasons stated in note to section 594.

2 *Rev. Stat.*, 680, § 68, relative to severing parts of the realty.

See section 596.

2 *Rev. Stat.*, 680, §§ 69, 70, relative to stealing records.

Covered by sections 147, 148.

2 *Rev. Stat.*, 680, § 71, of receiving stolen goods.

Covered by section 598.

2 *Rev. Stat.*, 680, § 72, relative to prosecutions for receiving.

Omitted for reasons stated in the note to section 598.

2 *Rev. Stat.*, 682, §§ 9–12, of bribery, &c.,

See sections 98, 99, 120, 121, 125–131.

2 *Rev. Stat.*, 681, §§ 1–7, of perjury.

These provisions, with some additional ones, are contained in sections 150–164.

2 *Rev. Stat.*, 681, § 8, of attempting to suborn a witness.

See section 170.

2 *Rev. Stat.*, 684, §§ 13–24, relative to escapes, &c.

See sections 136–146, 172, 173, 215.

2 *Rev. Stat.*, 686, §§ 1–7, of dueling.

Covered by sections 294–297, 301–303, except section 7, which pertains to procedure.

2 *Rev. Stat.*, 687, §§ 8–12, of bigamy, &c.

Covered by sections 338–342, except section 10, which is omitted as belonging to procedure. See *Rep. Code Cr. Pr.*, § 135.

2 *Rev. Stat.*, 688, §§ 13–15, relative to disinterment, &c.

More comprehensive provisions are contained in sections 345–362.

2 *Rev. Stat.*, 689, § 16, relative to poisoning animals.

Covered by section 698.

2 *Rev. Stat.*, 689, §§ 17, 18, relative to compounding felonies.

Covered by section 183.

2 *Rev. Stat.*, 689, § 20, of sodomy.
Covered by section 343.

2 *Rev. Stat.*, 690, § 1, relative to petit larceny.
See sections 586–590.

2 *Rev. Stat.*, 690, § 2, of attempts at extortion.
See section 619.

2 *Rev. Stat.*, 690, § 3, of fraudulent assignments.
Covered by section 641.

2 *Rev. Stat.*, 691, § 4, of concealments of property by insolvents.
Covered by section 206.

2 *Rev. Stat.*, 691, §§ 5–7, of buying lands in suit, &c.
Covered by sections 187–189.

2 *Rev. Stat.*, 691, §§ 8, 10, of conspiracy.
Covered by sections 224 and 226, except that section 9 is omitted for reasons stated at the end of note to section 224.

2 *Rev. Stat.*, 692, § 11, relative to false arrests.
Covered by section 175.

2 *Rev. Stat.*, 692, § 12, relative to compounding misdemeanors.
Covered by section 183.

2 *Rev. Stat.*, 692, § 13, relative to racing near a court.
Covered by section 207.

2 *Rev. Stat.*, 692, § 14, prescribing punishment for criminal contempts.
Covered by section 201.

2 *Rev. Stat.*, 693, § 15, relative to certain trespasses.
See section 707.

2 *Rev. Stat.*, 693, § 16, relative to corrupting jurors, &c.
See section 131.

2 *Rev. Stat.*, 693, § 17, relative to misconduct of jurors.
Covered by section 128.

2 *Rev. Stat.*, 693, § 18, relative to misconduct in drawing jurors.
Covered by section 132.

2 *Rev. Stat.*, 694, § 20, relative to posting for refusing a challenge.
Covered by section 300.

2 *Rev. Stat.*, 694, § 22, relative to acts of intoxicated physicians.
Covered by section 404.

2 *Rev. Stat.*, 694, § 23, relative to selling poisons.
See provisions on this subject in sections 445–448.

2 *Rev. Stat.*, 694, § 24, relative to overloading vessels.
Covered by section 406.

2 *Rev. Stat.*, 694, § 25, relative to negligence in management of steamboats.

Covered by section 407.

2 *Rev. Stat.*, 695, § 26, relative to cruelty to animals.

Covered by section 699.

2 *Rev. Stat.*, 695, §§ 27–29, relative to opening sealed letters.

Sections 27 and 28, are covered by sections 717 and 718 of the Code. Section 29 is omitted, and the cases contemplated are left to the operation of sections 738 and 739.

2 *Rev. Stat.*, 695, § 30, relative to destroying bridges, &c.

Covered by section 693.

2 *Rev. Stat.*, 695, § 31, relative to destroying dams, &c.

Covered by section 711.

2 *Rev. Stat.*, 695, § 32, relative to removing land marks.

Covered by section 709.

2 *Rev. Stat.*, 696, § 33, relative to injuring mile stones, &c.

Covered by section 694.

2 *Rev. Stat.*, 696, § 34, relative to auctioneers omitting to render account.

Covered by section 509.

2 *Rev. Stat.*, 696, §§ 35–37, relative to selling offices.

Covered by sections 106–109.

2 *Rev. Stat.*, 696, § 38, relative to willful neglect of official duty.

Covered by section 215.

2 *Rev. Stat.*, 696, § 39, declaring performance of prohibited act a misdemeanor.

Covered by section 216.

2 *Rev. Stat.*, 696, § 40, prescribing a general punishment for misdemeanors.

See section 14.

2 *Rev. Stat.*, 697, § 2, exempting insane persons.

See section 16, subd. 4.

2 *Rev. Stat.*, 698, § 3, relative to attempts.

See sections 745–747.

2 *Rev. Stat.*, 698, § 4, relative to stealing in another State.

See section 15, subd. 2, and note.

2 *Rev. Stat.*, 698, § 5, relative to former acquittal abroad.

See sections 738, 739.

2 *Rev. Stat.*, 698, §§ 6, 7, relative to principals and accessories.

See sections 26–30.

2 *Rev. Stat.*, 698, §§ 8–11, relative to second offenses.
See sections 748–753.

2 *Rev. Stat.*, 700, § 12, relative to imprisonment for life.
Covered by section 753.

2 *Rev. Stat.*, 700, § 13, authorizing fines.
Covered by section 756.

2 *Rev. Stat.*, 701, §§ 19–22, relative to effect of convictions.
See sections 757–760.

2 *Rev. Stat.*, 702, § 26, relative to attempts.

See section 745.

2 *Rev. Stat.*, 702, § 29, avoiding lease of house let for a bawdy house.

See a more stringent provision in section 369 of the Code.

2 *Rev. Stat.*, 702, §§ 30–32, defining "felony," "infamous crime," and "crime" or "offense."

See sections 3–6.

2 *Rev. Stat.*, 702, §§ 33 and 34, defining "property" and "personal property."

See sections 774–776.

2 *Rev. Stat.*, 703, § 35, relative to term "person"
See section 778.

2 *Rev. Stat.*, 703, § 36, relative to intent to defraud.
See section 782.

2 *Rev. Stat.*, 735, § 18, relative to rape and crime against nature.
Covered by sections 321 and 344.

Laws of 1829, ch. 94.

An act to create a fund for the benefit of the creditors of certain moneyed corporations, and for other purposes. Passed April 2, 1829.

Section 29 provides a penalty for false statements relative to affairs of moneyed corporations. Its provisions, somewhat extended, are covered by sections 646 and 656 of the Code.

Laws of 1829, ch. 139.

An act directing the manner of choosing electors of president and vice-president. Passed April 15, 1829.

As to the offenses designated in sections 16 and 17, see sections 716, and sections 215 and 216, of the Penal Code.

Laws of 1829, ch. 270.

An act for the prevention of masquerades. Passed April 25, 1829.

See section 480.

Laws of 1829, ch. 313.

An act to incorporate the president, directors and company of the Merchants' and Mechanics' Bank in the city of Troy. Passed April 29, 1829.

Section 19 declares false swearing in the affidavit required by the act, that the requisite capital has been paid in, to be perjury. This is covered by the more general provision of section 150 of the Code.

Substantially the same provision occurs, again and again, in subsequent acts relative to moneyed corporations. To save space these acts are not enumerated in the table. The general principle upon which acts of this character are embraced in one general section, is fully explained in the note to section 150.

Laws of 1829, ch. 368.

An act in relation to the appraisal of damages on the canals and for other purposes. Passed May 4, 1829.

So much of section 1, as declares certain false swearing perjury, is covered by the more general provision of section 150 of the Code.

Laws of 1829, ch. 373.

An act to preserve the purity of elections. Passed May 5, 1829.

See sections 65 and 66.

Laws of 1830, ch. 320.

An act to amend certain provisions of the Revised Statutes, and in addition thereto. Passed April 20, 1830.

As to section 58, relative to manslaughter by causing death of woman or child in attempting to procure miscarriage, see the more stringent provision of section 250 of the Code.

Laws of 1832, ch. 51.

An act in relation to the Troy Water Works Company, and for insuring to the city of Troy a supply of water for the extinguishment of fires and other purposes. Passed March 20, 1832.

As to section 6, making it a misdemeanor to injure certain water-works, see the more general provisions of section 722 of the Code.

Laws of 1832, ch. 162.

An act to incorporate the New York and Albany Railroad Company. Passed April 17, 1832.

Section 13 makes it a misdemeanor to injure buildings, &c., of the company. This offense is covered by the more general provisions of sections 690, 695 of the Code.

Substantially the same provision, with section 13, above mentioned, occurs in a number of later acts relative to railway and other public works owned and operated by corporations. To save space these provisions are not enumerated in this table.

Laws of 1833, ch. 170.

An act to regulate sales at auction in the village of Canandaigua. Passed April 19, 1833.

Section 3, requires sales, except of books and prints to be in the day. In section 508 of the Code the commissioners have embodied this principle, applying it to such localities as seemed to them judicious.

Laws of 1833, ch. 230.

An act to prevent the introduction of foreign convicts. Passed April 25, 1833.

Covered by section 214.

Laws of 1833, ch. 260.

An act relative to the forgery of foreign bank bills. Passed April 29, 1833.

See section 559.

Laws of 1833, ch. 281.

An act to prevent persons from transacting business under fictitious names. Passed April 29, 1833.

Covered by section 409.

Laws of 1834, ch. 201.

An act respecting the salt springs in the county of Onondaga, and regulating the manufacture of salt therein. Passed April 28, 1834.

Section 7, declaring certain false swearing to be perjury, is covered by section 150 of the Code.

Laws of 1834, ch. 281.

An act to provide for the public security. Passed May 5, 1834.
Covered by section 519.

Laws of 1835, ch. 62.

An act to amend part first, title first of chapter seventeenth of the Revised Statutes, entitled "Of the regulation of trade in certain cases." Passed April 11, 1835.

The subject of the act is auction sales; as to which see sections 502 and 510 of the Code.

Laws of 1835, ch. 110.

An act to prohibit the sale of ardent spirits to the St. Regis Indians. Passed April 20, 1835.

Covered by the more general provisions of section 724.

Laws of 1835, ch. 304.

An act to amend the act relating to the militia and public defense. Passed May 11, 1835.

The penalties authorized by this act are preserved by section 785.

Laws of 1836, ch. 171.

An act relative to state prisons. Passed April 23, 1836.

The act itself was repealed by Laws of 1847, ch. 460, § 160. See note to section 1070 of the Code. The rule relative to sentences prescribed by section 6 of the act is, however, continued, in a form modified to correspond with later statutes, by section 754 of the Code.

Laws of 1837, ch. 150.

An act authorizing a loan of certain moneys belonging to the United States, deposited with the State of New York for safe keeping. Passed April 4, 1837.

Section 42, of the act declaring certain false swearing perjury, is covered by section 150 of the Code.

Laws of 1837, ch. 184.

An act for the licensing and government of the pilots of the port of New York, by the way of Sandy Hook. Passed April 12, 1837.

So much of the act as punishes unlicensed piloting, is covered by section 442.

The provisions of the act which authorize a pilot to be deprived of his license, with other portions of the act, remain unaffected by the Code.

Laws of 1837, ch. 235.

An act to regulate the distribution of bank stock. Passed April 22, 1837.

The provision of section 7, declaring certain false swearing perjury, is covered by section 150 of the Code.

Laws of 1837, ch. 430.

An act to prevent usury. Passed May 15, 1837.

Section 6, of the act declaring the receipt of usury a misdemeanor, is covered by section 426 of the Code; the punishment being modified.

So much of section 8 as makes false swearing, upon an examination under the act, perjury, is covered by section 150.

Laws of 1837, ch. 457.

An act to amend the Revised Statutes in relation to escapes from prisons, and assisting therein. Passed May 16, 1837.

On this subject, see sections 130–146.

Laws of 1838, ch. 52.

An act authorizing any citizen of the State of New York to become an auctioneer. Passed February 28, 1838.

The system of provisions recommended by the commissioners relative to offenses peculiar to the vocation of auctioneers will be found in sections 502–510.

Laws of 1838, ch. 160.

An act to punish willful injuries to railroads. Passed April 6, 1838.

Covered by sections 690, 691.

Laws of 1839, ch. 112.

An act to protect Hudson and Poughkeepsie from fires from steamboats. Passed March 29, 1839.

Covered by section 729.

Laws of 1839, ch. 153.

An act to incorporate the Long Island Rural Cemetery. Passed April 10, 1838.

Section 10 of the act declares it a misdemeanor to destroy, &c., monuments, plants, &c., within the cemetery of the company. For provisions on this subject equally applicable to all cemeteries, see sections 361, 696, 702, 707, 720.

Substantially the same provision with section 10, above mentioned, occurs in some later acts incorporating cemetery companies. To save space these provisions are not enumerated in this table.

Laws of 1839, ch. 355.

An act concerning foreign bank notes. Passed May 7, 1839.

Preserved by section 786, subd. 3.

Laws of 1840, ch. 225.

An act to extend the right of trial by jury. Passed May 6, 1840.

As to several offenses corresponding to various sections of this act, see sections 105, 271, 276, and 427–429.

Laws of 1840, ch. 363.

An act to amend the act entitled "an act to authorize the business of banking." Passed May 14, 1840.

Preserved by section 786, subd. 4.

Laws of 1841, ch. 183.

An act in relation to the Onondaga and Montezuma Salt Springs. Passed May 10, 1841.

It seems so probable that this act was intended to be superseded by Laws of 1859, ch. 346, that the commissioners have made no special provision corresponding with section 16. But see section 224, subd. 5.

Laws of 1841, ch. 292.

An act to prevent fraudulent practices in the management of moneyed incorporations, and to provide for a prompt replenishing of the safety fund. Passed May 26, 1840.

As to the offenses provided for by sections 1–4 of the act, see sections 651–653 of the Code.

Laws of 1841, ch. 301.

An act concerning elections in cities other than New York. Passed May 26, 1841.

Section 9 of the act, declaring certain false swearing perjury, is covered by section 150 of the Code.

Laws of 1842, ch. 130.

An act respecting elections other than for militia and town officers. Passed April 5, 1842.

This act contains a number of penal provisions looking towards the protection of the purity of elections. Most of them are embodied, with such modifications as seemed advisable in sections 61–95 of the Code. Section 18 of title VII of the act, is covered by section 716.

Laws of 1842, ch. 215.

An act in relation to burying grounds. Passed April 11, 1842.

Provisions deemed sufficient to protect burying grounds from disturbance are embraced in sections 350, 351 and 355–361.

Laws of 1842, ch. 247.

An act to provide for the prompt redemption of the circulating notes of insolvent safety fund banks; to restrict the liability of the safety fund, and for other purposes. Passed April 12, 1842.

Sections 10 and 11 of the act relative to certain dealings by bank officers, are covered by sections 651 and 652 of the Code.

Laws of 1843, ch. 57.

An act to prohibit members of common councils of cities, towns, trustees of villages and supervisors of towns to be interested in certain contracts. Passed March 20, 1843.

See as to sections 1–3 of this act, section 501 of the Code; as to section 4, section 150.

Laws of 1845, ch. 3.

An act to prevent persons appearing disguised and armed. Passed February 28, 1845.

Section 1, declaring certain persons vagrants, is expressly preserved by section 785 of the Code.

Sections 2, 3 and 5, relate to procedure and are unaffected by the Code.

Section 4 is deemed covered, so far as is expedient, by sections 177 and 178 of the Code.

Section 6 is the basis of section 478 of the Code.

As to section 7, see section 475 of the Code, subd. 3.

Laws of 1845, ch. 69.

An act to enforce the laws and preserve order. Passed April 15, 1845.

Section 17 declares it a misdemeanor to resist the execution of process. For provisions upon this offense see sections 100, 101, 177, 178, 201, subds. 4 and 5, 214, subd. 5.

Section 18, of the act declaring a penalty for resisting execution of process after proclamation by the governor, is covered by section 179 of the Code.

Laws of 1845, ch. 201.

An act to preserve certain waters from the effects of gas tar and refuse of gas houses and factories. Passed May 13, 1845.

Covered by the more general provisions of section 434.

Laws of 1845, ch. 228.

An act to prevent the disturbance of evening schools in the several school district houses of this state. Passed May 13, 1845.

A severe penalty is denounced for this species of offense, by the more general provision of section 473.

Laws of 1845, ch. 260.

An act to punish the procurement of abortion, and for other purposes. Passed May 14, 1845.

For provisions corresponding to the various sections of this act, but more stringent in some details, see sections 250, 334, 335, 336 and 749.

Laws of 1846, ch. 22.

An act to amend the "act to punish the procurement of abortion, and for other purposes," passed May 13, 1845. Passed March 4, 1846.

See section 250.

Laws of 1846, ch. 62.

An act in relation to duties on goods sold at public auction, and to the bonds of auctioneers. Passed April 11, 1846.

As to offenses by auctioneers, such as are designated by section 8 of the act, see section 502 of the Code.

Laws of 1846, ch. 120.

An act in relation to district attorneys, and to prevent their law partners from acting as counsel in certain cases. Passed April 30, 1846.

Covered by sections 730, 731.

Laws of 1846, ch. 241.

An act in relation to the keeping of gunpowder, saltpetre, and certain other substances, in the city of New York. Passed May 13, 1846.

Violations of this act, and of laws or ordinances relative to gunpowder affecting other places than New York city, are made punishable by sections 258 and 433.

Laws of 1846, ch. 300.

An act concerning quarantine, and regulations in the nature of quarantine, at the port of New York. Passed May 13, 1846.

The commissioners have contemplated the revision of the Health Laws as a separate body of laws from either of the Codes (see note to section 786). The more important offenses connected with quarantine are, however, covered by sections 435–439; and obstructing the execution of or violating the Health Laws as they may exist from time to time, is made punishable by sections 440, 441

Laws of 1846, ch. 324.

An act in relation to the Clinton State Prison. Passed May 13, 1846.

This act made provision for insane convicts. A different system, conformable to more recent legislation, is embodied in sections 1048–1057.

Laws of 1847, ch. 69.

An act concerning the pilots of the channel of the East river, commonly called Hellgate. Passed April 15, 1847.

As to piloting through Hellgate channel, without license, declared misdemeanor by section 8 of the act, see section 442 of the Code.

Laws of 1847, ch. 86.

An act to authorize the agent of the state prison at Auburn to build an armory for the use of the Auburn Guards; to sell certain lands belonging to the state; to inclose the state land adjoining the prison; to lay a walk, and for other purposes. Passed April 19, 1847.

Section 4 of the act relating to inquiry to be made into former trade or business of criminals, upon conviction, was repealed by section 160 of Laws of 1847, ch. 460; but the same principle was continued in section 70 of the latter act, which is embodied in section 991 of the Code; but should be transferred to the Code of Criminal Procedure.

Laws of 1847, ch. 133.

An act authorizing the incorporation of rural cemetery associations. Passed April 27, 1847.

Section 8 of the act declares it a misdemeanor to destroy monuments, plants, &c., within cemeteries. For provisions on this subject, see sections 361, 696, 702, 707, 720.

Laws of 1847, ch. 205.

An act for the organization of the first division of the New York State militia. Passed May 6, 1847.

The organization of the militia is now chiefly regulated by later laws. As to such offenses as are indicated by section 16 of this act, see sections 519 and 696 of the Code.

As to neglect of duty by civil officers, such as is designated in section 38 of the act, see section 215 of the Code.

All existing laws authorizing military penalties are preserved by section 785.

Laws of 1847, ch. 207.

An act in relation to the sale of bottles used by the manufacturers of mineral waters and others. Passed May 7, 1847.

Provisions relative to refilling stamped bottles, corresponding to Laws of 1860, ch. 117, are given in sections 417–419 of the Code.

Laws of 1847, ch. 240.

An act to amend the act entitled, "an act respecting elections other than for militia and town officers," passed April 5, 1842. Passed May 8, 1842.

As to sections 15 and 16 of the act, relative to unauthorized voting, see sections 74 and 89 of the Code.

Laws of 1847, ch. 280.

An act in relation to the judiciary. Passed May 12, 1847.

As to section 79, declaring certain false swearing perjury, see section 150 of the Code.

Laws of 1847, ch. 290.

An act to provide for the enrollment of the militia and to encourage the formation of uniform companies, excepting the first military division of this state. Passed May 13, 1847.

The organization of the militia is now chiefly regulated by later laws. As to such offenses as are indicated by section 36 of this act, see sections 519 and 696 of the Code.

All existing laws authorizing military penalties are preserved by section 785.

Laws of 1847, ch. 365.

An act to amend the act for the protection and improvement of the Seneca Indians residing on the Cattaraugus and Allegany reservations in this state. Passed November 15, 1847.

All existing laws relative to Indians are preserved by section 785 of the Code.

As to section 16 of the act, declaring certain false swearing perjury, see sections 150, 162 of the Code.

Laws of 1847, ch. 432.

An act in relation to the fees and compensation of certain officers in the city and county of New York. Passed December 10, 1847.

Existing laws relative to municipal corporations are preserved by section 786 of the Code, subd. 1.

As to a public officer neglecting to account for fees, provided for by section 12 of the act, see sections 215 and 497, 498 of the Code.

Laws of 1847, ch. 460.

An act for the better regulation of the county and state prisons of the state, and consolidating and amending the existing laws in relation thereto. Passed December 14, 1847.

This act forms the basis of title XIX of the Code. The provisions of the later acts on the same subject, together with such amendments of the laws as the commissioners have thought it well to suggest, are incorporated with the provisions of the act of 1847 still in force, and a new arrangement of the whole, presented in that title. The act itself is repealed by section 1070, subd. 1.

Laws of 1847, ch. 462.

An act to authorize parties in civil suits, at their election, to obtain the testimony of the adverse party. Passed December 14, 1847.

As to section 4 of the act declaring certain false swearing perjury, see section 150 of the Code.

Laws of 1847, ch. 470.

An act to amend an act entitled "an act in relation to the judiciary." Passed May 12, 1847.

As to section 47 of the act, extending provisions of law relative to buying of claims by attorneys, to persons who prosecute in person, see section 199 of the Code.

Laws of 1847, ch. 497.

An act in relation to the transportation of convicts to the state prisons and houses of refuge.

See different provisions of this subject in 792–796. The act is repealed by section 1070, subd. 2.

Laws of 1848, ch. 105.

An act to punish abduction as a crime. Passed March 20, 1848. See section 328.

Laws of 1848, ch. 111.

An act to punish seduction as a crime. Passed March 22, 1848. See sections 330, 331.

Laws of 1848, ch. 154.

An act to incorporate the Utica water works company. Passed March 31, 1848.

As to section 17 making it a misdemeanor to injure certain water works, see the more general provisions of sections 696, 712 and 722 of the Code.

Laws of 1848, ch. 219.

An act for the protection of emigrants arriving in the State ot New York. Passed April 11, 1848.

All acts relating to emigrants, &c., are preserved by section 786, subd. 2.

Laws of 1848, ch. 229.

An act in relation to the court of sessions of the county of Jefferson.

This act, which confirms certain sentences to imprisonment in Clinton state prison, is unaffected by the Code.

Laws of 1848, ch. 265.

An act to provide for the incorporation and regulation of telegraph companies. Passed April 12, 1848.

As to section 7 of the act making it misdemeanor to injure telegraph property, see sections 695, 696 of the Code.

Laws of 1848, ch. 294.

An act to amend the act for the better regulation of the county and state prisons of the state.

This act relates to insane convicts. See provisions as to their custody, conformable to later laws, in sections 1048–1058 of the Code. The act of 1848 referred to, is repealed by section 1070 of the Code, subd. 3.

Laws of 1849, ch. 115.

An act to make the clerk's office of Erie county a salaried office. Passed March 21, 1849.

As to section 19 of the act, declaring certain false swearing perjury, see section 150 of the Code.

Laws of 1849, ch. 123.

An act fixing the fees of sheriffs for transporting convicts to the state prisons. Passed March 22, 1849.

See section 792.

Laws of 1849, ch. 132.

An act in relation to the removal of convicts from one state prison to another. Passed March 26, 1849.

Covered by section 797.

Laws of 1849, ch. 133.

An act authorizing the inspectors of state prisons to administer oaths and take affidavits in certain cases. Passed March 26, 1849.

See sections 842 and 843.

Laws of 1849, ch. 141.

An act in relation to Sing Sing prison. Passed March 27, 1849.

The act is repealed by section 1070, subd. 4. The subjects covered by sections 2 and 5 and 6 of the act, the only ones deemed of a permanent character, are provided for by section 2, section 789 of the Code; section 5 of the act by sections 847, subd. 7, and 947 of the Code; and section 6 of the act by section 854 of the Code, subd. 14.

Laws of 1849, ch. 254.

An act to amend "an act for the organization of the first division of the New York State militia." Passed April 7, 1849.

The organization of the militia is now chiefly regulated by later laws. As to such offenses as are indicated by section 24 of this act, see sections 519 and 696 of the Code.

As to the various neglects of duty by civil officers, see section 215.

All existing laws authorizing military penalties are preserved by section 785.

Laws of 1849, ch. 278.

An act to prevent the manufacture, use and sale of slung shot. Passed April 7, 1849.

Covered by sections 453, 454.

Laws of 1849, ch. 280.

An act making appropriations for Clinton prison. Passed April 7, 1849.

Unaffected by the Code.

Laws of 1849, ch. 282.

An act to protect the woodlands in Suffolk county against destruction by fire. Passed April 7, 1849.

The general provision of section 456 is deemed broad enough upon this subject, so far as the criminal remedy is concerned. The remedy by damages given by section 2 of the act, is unaffected by the Code. See section 783.

Laws of 1849, ch. 321.

An act to amend an act entitled "an act for the protection of emigrants arriving in the State of New York," passed April 11, 1848.

All existing laws relating to emigrants, &c., are preserved by section 786, subd. 2.

Laws of 1849, ch. 331.

An act to amend "An act for the better regulation of the county and state prisons of the state, and consolidating and amending the existing laws in relation thereto," passed December 14, 1847. Passed April 10, 1849.

This act is repealed by section 1070 of the Code, subd. 8. The provisions of section 2 of the act, are embodied in section 1046.

Laws of 1849, ch. 426.

An act to incorporate the Watertown Waterworks company. Passed April 11, 1849.

Section 17 of the act, declaring malicious injury to works of the company a misdemeanor, is covered by the general provisions of section 722 of the Code.

Substantially the same provision occurs in later acts incorporating aqueduct companies. To save space, these acts are not enumerated in this table.

Laws of 1850, ch. 24.

An act in relation to juvenile delinquents. Passed February 26, 1850.

Section 2 is repealed by section 1070, subd. 9, of the Code. Its provisions are embodied in section 801.

Laws of 1850, ch. 123.

An act to amend an act passed May 14, 1845, entitled "An act to punish and prevent frauds in the use of false stamps and labels." Passed April 1, 1850.

This act was repealed by Laws of 1862, ch. 306; but the subject is covered by sections 410–416 of the Code.

Laws of 1850, ch. 140.

An act to authorize the formation of railroad corporations, and to regulate the same. Passed April 2, 1850.

Sections 38, 41 and 42 of the act are covered, respectively, by sections 463, 462 and 461 of the Code.

Laws of 1850, ch. 251.

An act to amend the act entitled "An act to amend the act entitled an act to authorize the business of banking," passed May 14, 1840. Passed April 10, 1850.

Preserved by section 786, subd. 5.

Laws of 1850, ch. 306.

An act making an appropriation for Clinton prison. Passed April 10, 1850.

As to section 3 of the act, see section 900 of the Code.

Laws of 1850, ch. 324.

An act for the preservation of the public health. Passed April 10, 1850.

The commissioners have contemplated the revision of the Health Laws as a separate body of laws from either of the Codes. (See section 786, note.) A general provision punishing violations of these laws, is contained in section 441.

Laws of 1850, ch. 338.

An act in relation to the penitentiary in the county of Onondaga. Passed April 10, 1850.

Unaffected by the Code.

Laws of 1850, ch. 32.

An act relative to the penitentiary of Onondaga county. Passed March 11, 1851.

Unaffected by the Code.

Laws of 1851, ch. 102.

An act to preserve the purity of certain streams used to supply the city of Albany with water. Passed April 8, 1851.

This act is deemed sufficiently covered by the more general provisions of sections 430–434. The special power conferred on the common council of Albany by section 3 of the act, is however, preserved by section 786 of the Code, subd. 1.

Laws of 1851, ch. 144.

An act amending the Revised Statutes in relation to obtaining money under false pretenses. Passed April 11, 1851.

See section 624.

Laws of 1851, ch. 180.

An act for the enrollment of the militia, to abolish militia fines in certain cases, and exempt members of uniformed companies from working on highways and serving on juries. Passed April 16, 1851.

As to such neglect of official duty as is defined in section 14 of the act, see section 215 of the Code.

Laws of 1851, ch. 182.

An act to amend title six, chapter one, part four of the Revised Statutes, entitled "Of offenses punishable by imprisonment in a county jail and by fines." Passed April 16, 1851.

See section 707, subd. 4 and 5.

Laws of 1851, ch. 259.

An act making appropriations for the Clinton state prison, and amendatory of section six of chapter seventy of the Laws of 1845. Passed June 20, 1851.

As to section 4 of the act, see section 808 of the Code.

Laws of 1851, ch. 388.

An act to incorporate the Buffalo Suspension Bridge company. Passed July 3, 1851.

As to section 11 of the act, relative to injuries to the bridge, &c., of the company, see sections 692, 696 of the Code.

Substantially the same provision occurs in later acts incorporating bridge companies. To save space, these acts are not enumerated in this table.

Laws of 1851, ch. 504.

An act more effectually to suppress gambling. Passed July 10, 1851.

See sections 392–399.

Laws of 1852, ch. 165.

An act in relation to indictments for libel, and the trial thereof. Passed April 7, 1852.

Omitted, as belonging to procedure.

Laws of 1853, ch. 138.

An act to punish gross frauds and to suppress mock auctions. Passed April 9, 1853.

As to section 2 of the act, see sections 627 and 737.

Laws of 1853, ch. 183.

An act requiring the police justices in the city of New York to file records of all convictions of vagrancy. Passed April 12, 1853.

Preserved by section 786, subd. 6.

Laws of 1853, ch. 185.

An act to provide for the care and instruction of idle and truant children. Passed April 12, 1853.

Preserved by section 786, subd. 7.

Laws of 1853, ch. 223.

An act to amend an act entitled "an act concerning foreign bank notes." Passed April 13, 1853.

Preserved by section 786, subd. 8.

Laws of 1853, 279.

An act for the construction of a workhouse in the county of Monroe. Passed May 27, 1853.

Section 12 of the act relative to escapes from the workhouse, is embraced in the more general provisions of sections 139–146 of the Code.

Laws of 1853, ch. 539

An act to amend the existing law relating to bribery. Passed July 18, 1853.

This act treats of the bribery of all classes of officers together. In the Code the provisions relative to bribery of various officers are stated in connection with provisions on other subjects, relative to the officers respectively. See sections 61, 98, 99, 120, 121, 125–131, 170, 172.

Laws of 1853, ch. 573.

An act for the more effectual prevention of wanton and malicious mischief. Passed July 18, 1853.

The criminal remedy herein given is embraced in section 720 of the Code. See also sections 696, 697. The civil remedy is preserved by section 783.

Laws of 1853, ch. 629.

An act for the protection of birds in public cemeteries. Passed July 21, 1853.

Covered by section 702.

Laws of 1854, ch. 58.

An act to amend the Revised Statutes in relation to agents of state prisons. Passed March 13, 1854.

This act is repealed by section 1070, subd. 10. The substance of its provisions, as amended by Laws of 1860, ch. 48, is embodied in section 863 of the Code.

Laws of 1854, ch. 74.

An act to provide for the punishment of assaults with dangerous weapons. Passed March 23, 1854.

Covered by section 308.

Laws of 1854, ch. 109.

An act for the protection of gas-light companies. Passed April 1, 1854.

Covered by section 599.

Laws of 1854, ch. 130.

An act in relation to libel. Passed April 1, 1854.

Covered by sections 315, 316.

Laws of 1854, ch. 175.

An act to prevent the destruction of timber on the lands of the Tuscarora Indians, and to regulate the highway labor among said Indians. Passed April 7, 1854.

All existing laws relative to Indians are preserved by section 785.

Laws of 1854, ch. 223.

An act to appoint commissioners to investigate and examine into the pecuniary affairs and condition of the several state prisons of this state, and to report thereon, and also such laws as they may deem proper for the better regulation and discipline of said prisons, to the Legislature of this state. Passed April 14, 1854.

Unaffected by the Code.

Laws of 1854, ch. 232.

An act for the incorporation of companies formed to navigate the lakes and rivers. Passed April 15, 1854.

As to officer of corporation refusing to exhibit its books to stockholders, provided for by section 23 of the act, see section 658 of the Code.

Laws of 1854, ch. 240.

An act to amend the several acts in relation to state prisons, and making appropriations for the Clinton, Auburn and Sing Sing prisons. Passed April 15, 1854.

This act is repealed by section 1070. So far as its provisions are deemed important to be continued, they are embodied in title XIX.

Laws of 1854, ch. 332.

An act prescribing regulations in regard to the management of the canals, and for other purposes. Passed April 15, 1854.

Section 8 of the act, declaring certain false swearing perjury, is covered by section 150 of the Code.

Laws of 1854, ch. 398.

An act to provide for the enrollment of the militia and the organization of uniformed corps, and the discipline of the military forces of the state. Passed April 17, 1854.

Cases of false swearing such as are embraced within section 6 of title III of the act, are covered by the general provision of section 150 of the Code.

Neglects of duty by civil officers such as are made punishable by the act, are covered by section 215.

All existing laws authorizing military penalties, are preserved by section 785.

Laws of 1855, ch. 20.

An act to enable the common council of the city of New York to take testimony, in matters referred for investigation or inquiry. Passed February 8, 1855.

All existing laws authorizing punishment for contempts are preserved by section 785.

As to so much of the act as declares certain false swearing perjury, see section 150 of the Code.

Laws of 1855, ch. 155.

An act to provide for the punishment of the fraudulent and

unauthorized issue and transfer of the stock and bonds of corporations and joint stock companies. Passed April 5, 1855.

Covered by section 566.

Laws of 1855, ch. 199.

An act in relation to the property and money taken from persons arrested and accused of crimes in the city of New York and Brooklyn. Passed April 9, 1855.

Preserved by section 786, subd. 9.

Laws of 1855, ch. 214.

An act to amend an act entitled "An act for the more effectual suppression of gambling," passed July 10, 1851. Passed April 9, 1855.

Covered by section 393.

Laws of 1855, ch. 231.

An act for the prevention of intemperance, pauperism and crime. Passed April 9, 1855.

Omitted, because repealed by Laws of 1857, ch. 628, § 33; its leading principle having been pronounced unconstitutional. See People *v.* Toynbee, 20 *Barb.*, 168; People *v.* Berberrich, *Id.*, 168, 224; 2 *Park. Cr.*, 329; 11 *How. Pr.*, 289; People *v.* Quant, 2 *Park. Cr.*, 410; 12 *How. Pr.*, 83; Wynehammer *v.* People, 13 *N. Y.*, 378.

Laws of 1855, ch. 334.

An act to authorize the agent and warden of Sing Sing prison to let by contract the labor and services of convicts in that prison, to the business of quarrying, splitting, sawing and removing stone, for a term of years. Passed April 12, 1855.

Repealed by section 1070. Its provisions are embodied in sections 1015–1017.

Laws of 1855, ch. 427.

An act in relation to the collection of taxes on lands of non-residents, and to provide for the sale of such lands for unpaid taxes. Passed April 13, 1855.

Neglects of duty by public officers, such as are designated by section 88 of the act, are covered by section 215 of the Code.

Laws of 1855.

An act to provide for insane criminals. Passed April 13, 1855.

Repealed by section 1070. Provisions in relation to insane convicts are given in sections 1048–1058.

Laws of 1855, ch. 499.

An act in relation to stealing and forging of railroad tickets. Passed April 14, 1855.

As to forging of railroad tickets, see section 571.

As to larceny, see sections 594, 595.

Laws of 1855, ch. 501.

An act to provide for the payment of the debts of the several state prisons, and for other purposes. Passed April 14, 1855.

Unaffected by the Code.

Laws of 1855, ch. 531.

An act for the prevention of frauds upon the canal revenues. Passed April 14, 1855.

Laws authorizing forfeitures are preserved by section 783.

Section 4 of the act relative to officers concealing frauds upon the canal revenues, is covered by section 513 of the Code.

Laws of 1855, ch. 536.

An act in relation to the first division and fifth brigade, of the New York State militia. Passed April 14, 1855.

This act was repealed by Laws of 1862, ch. 476, § 319.

Neglects of duty by civil officers, such as are designated by the act, are covered by section 215.

As to injuries to state property, see sections 519 and 696.

All existing laws relative to military punishments are preserved by section 785.

Laws of 1855, ch. 552.

An act to amend the several acts in relation to state prisons. Passed April 19, 1855.

This act is repealed by section 1070. In provisions, so far as they are deemed important to be continued, are embodied in title XIX.

Laws of 1855, ch. 564

An act to amend an act entitled "An act for the protection of birds in public cemeteries," passed July 21, 1853. Passed April 19, 1855.

The amendment here made, is deemed too stringent. The provisions of the original act only are presented. See section 702 of the Code.

Laws of 1856, ch. 34.

An act making appropriation for rebuilding the prison building at Sing Sing. Passed March 11, 1856.

Unaffected by the Code.

Laws of 1856, ch. 147.

An act relative to public health and quarantine, and regulations in the nature of quarantine at the port of New York, and to the Marine Hospital. Passed April 9, 1856.

The commissioners have contemplated the revision of the Health Laws as a separate body of laws. (See section 786, note.) Provisions for their enforcement, embodying many of the sections of the above act, are found in sections 435–441.

Laws of 1856, ch. 158.

An act in relation to the punishment of crimes in certain cases. Passed April 11, 1856.

See section 755 of the Code.

Laws of 1857, ch. 43.

An act for the more effectual prevention and punishment of vagrancy and crime in the county of Washington. Passed February 19, 1857.

Unaffected by the Code.

Laws of 1857, ch. 94.

An act to amend the several acts in relation to state prisons. Passed March 10, 1857.

This act is repealed by section 1070, subd. 15. Its provisions, so far as they are deemed important to be continued, are embodied in title XIX.

Laws of 1857, ch. 144.

An act appropriating money for making provisions for insane convicts. Passed March 20, 1857.

This act, except the provisions of sections 1 and 2, which are temporary in their nature, is repealed by section 1070, subd. 16.

As to section 3 of the act, relative to insane convicts, see sections 1048–1058; and note to section 1048.

Laws of 1857, ch. 181.

An act to amend "An act regulating highways and bridges in the counties of Suffolk, Queens and Kings," passed February 23, 1830. Passed March 26, 1857.

As to the offense of injuring trees, &c, on highways, mentioned in section 22 of the act, see sections 696 and 720 of the Code.

Laws of 1857, ch. 193.

An act to regulate the business of purchasing rags, rope and metals in the city of Albany. Passed March 28, 1857.

Preserved by section 786, subd. 10.

Laws of 1857, ch. 199.

An act to authorize the formation of a railroad corporation in place of the Northern Railroad Company, dissolved, and to empower said railroad company to execute a mortgage upon its property. Passed March 31, 1857.

Cases of misapplication of corporate property by officers, such as are specified in section 6 of the act, are deemed sufficiently covered by the provisions on embezzlement, (sections 601–612), and on frauds in management of corporations, (sections 645–668).

Laws of 1857, ch. 243.

An act to amend the Pilot Laws, passed June 28, 1853. Passed April 3, 1857.

Unlicensed piloting is covered by section 442.

Laws of 1857, ch. 255.

An act to provide for straightening and working the highway leading from Losee's Corner to the village of Sing Sing, in the town of Ossining. Passed April 6, 1857.

Unaffected by the Code.

Laws of 1857, ch. 348.

An act to make the office of supervisor in Albany county a salaried office, and to regulate the compensation of the clerk of the board of supervisors in said county. Passed April 13, 1857.

A violation of the first clause of section 3 of the act will be punishable as a misdemeanor under section 215 of the Code.

Laws of 1857, ch. 396.

An act to punish nuisances and malicious trespasses on lands. Passed April 13, 1857.

Section 1 of the act is covered by section 494 of the Code.

Laws of 1857, ch. 437.

An act for the better regulation of the firemen of the city of Buffalo. Passed April 14, 1857.

The offense of personating a fireman, designated in section 16 of the act, is covered by section 622 of the Code.

Laws of 1857, ch. 470.

An act to prevent frauds in the sale of tickets to passengers upon railroads, steamboats and steamships. Passed April 15, 1857.

More stringent provisions upon this subject, founded upon the more recent act, Laws of 1860, ch. 103, are presented in sections 669–682 of the Code.

Laws of 1857, ch. 569.

An act to establish a metropolitan police district and provide for the government thereof. Passed April 15, 1857.

Preserved by section 786, subd. 11.

Laws of 1857, ch. 628.

An act to suppress intemperance and to regulate the sale ot intoxicating liquors. Passed April 16, 1857.

As to the various offenses declared by this act, see sections 728-733.

Laws of 1857, ch. 659.

An act to provide for the preservation of timber and stone on the lands of Onondaga Indian Reservation. Passed April 16, 1857.

Preserved by section 786, subd. 12.

Laws of 1857, ch. 671.

An act to establish regulations for the port of New York. Passed April 16, 1857.

Preserved by section 786, subd. 13.

Laws of 1858, ch. 130.

An act to organize the State Lunatic Asylum for insane convicts.

Sections 10, 11 and 12 of the act, relating to the custody of insane convicts, are repealed by section 1070, subd. 17.

The remaining provisions, which relate to the organization and management of the asylum, are unaffected by the Code.

Laws of 1858, ch. 139.

An act authorizing the imprisonment of persons convicted of certain crimes in the counties of Montgomery and Oneida, in the Albany County Penitentiary. Passed April 12, 1858.

Unaffected by the Code.

Laws of 1858, ch. 322.

An act in relation to jurors and to the appointment and the duties of a commissioner of jurors in the county of Kings. Passed April 17, 1858.

Preserved by section 786, subd. 14.

Laws of 1858, ch. 326.

An act to prevent the issue of false receipts and to punish fraudulent transfers of property by warehousemen, wharfingers and others. Passed April 17, 1858.

This act is the basis of sections 683–689.

Laws of 1858, ch. 330.

An act to amend "An act to extend the jurisdiction of the courts of general and special sessions of the peace, in and for the city and county of New York," passed April 12, 1855. Passed April 17, 1858.

Omitted as relating to procedure.

Laws of 1858, ch. 359.

An act to amend an act entitled "An act for the prevention of masquerades," passed April 25, 1829. Passed April 19, 1858.

Covered by section 480.

Laws of 1859, ch. 36.

An act to enable agricultural and horticultural societies to extend a more perfect protection to their property, and the property of exhibitors at fairs, and to allow the board of managers to appoint a police for that purpose. Passed March 7, 1859.

Malicious injuries to property, such as are designated by the act, are covered by sections 696 and 721 of the Code.

The gaining admission to the grounds improperly, is not deemed to require criminal punishment except as it may fall within general provisions relative to disturbance of the public peace. The provisions of the act in this respect are anomalous.

Laws of 1859, ch. 37.

An act to prevent and punish prize fighting. Passed March 7, 1859.

See sections 485–491.

Laws of 1859, ch. 82.

An act to provide for the organization and government of the police force of the city of Albany. Passed March 31, 1859.

Preserved by section 786, subd. 15.

Laws of 1859, ch. 137.

An act to incorporate the Kane Monument Association in the city of New York. Passed April 5, 1859.

Misappropriation of corporate property, by officers of the corporation, such as is designated by section 6 of the act, is deemed sufficiently covered by the provisions of the Code on embezzlement (see sections 601–612), and on frauds in management of corporations. (See sections 645–658.)

Injuries to monuments are covered by sections 361 and 696 of the Code.

Laws of 1859, ch. 249.

An act to authorize the agent and warden of the Auburn prison to sell certain lands belonging to the state. Passed April 12, 1859.

Unaffected by the Code.

Laws of 1859, ch. 254.

An act empowering the boards of supervisors in the respective counties of this state to fix and determine the compensation to be allowed for the conveyance of juvenile delinquents to houses of refuge, and insane criminals to insane asylums. Passed April 12, 1859.

Unaffected by the Code.

Laws of 1859, ch. 289.

An act to extend the provisions of "An act authorizing the imprisonment of persons convicted of certain crimes in the counties of Montgomery and Oneida, in the Albany County Penitentiary," passed April 12, 1858, to all the counties in this state. Passed April 13, 1859.

Unaffected by the Code.

Laws of 1859, ch. 311.

An act to provide for the inspection and sealing of gas meters, and for the protection of consumers of illuminating gas. Passed April 14, 1859.

The frauds upon gas companies designated by section 11 of the act, are covered by section 599 of the Code.

Laws of 1859, ch. 346.

An act concerning the salt springs and the manufacture of salt. Passed April 15, 1859.

Section 62 of the act, relating to injuries to salt works, is embodied in section 518 of the Code.

Laws of 1859, ch. 349.

An act to amend an act entitled "An act for the regulation and government of the Central Park in the city of New York," passed April 17, 1857, and further to provide for the maintenance and government of said park. Passed April 15, 1859.

Preserved by section 786, subd. 16.

Laws of 1859, ch. 350.

An act vesting the control of the piers, booms and dams, on Salmon river, in the commissioners for improving said river. Passed April 15, 1859.

Section 2, relative to interfering with piers, &c., on Salmon river, is covered by the more general provision of section 710.

Laws of 1859, ch. 353.

An act to amend the act entitled "An act to prevent the issue of false receipts, and to punish fraudulent transfers of property by warehousemen, wharfingers and others," passed April 17, 1858. Passed April 15, 1859.

See sections 683–689; and note to section 686.

Laws of 1859, ch. 380.

An act for ascertaining by proper proofs the citizens who shall be entitled to the right of suffrage, and to prevent fraudulent voting. Passed April 15, 1859.

The provision of section 5, relative to false statements on applying to be registered as an elector, is covered by the more general provision of section 77 of the Code.

As to section 14 of the act, see sections 75, 76 and 150.

Laws of 1859, ch. 453.

An act for the enlargement of the Clinton, Auburn and Sing Sing prisons, and for other purposes. Passed April 18, 1859.

Unaffected by the Code.

Laws of 1859, ch. 470.

An act providing for the sale of certain lands belonging to the state, and appropriating the moneys arising therefrom. Passed April 18, 1859.

Unaffected by the Code. Such cases of false swearing as are provided for by section 7, are, however, covered by section 150 of the Code.

Laws of 1859, ch. 491.

An act in relation to the court of special sessions in the city and county of New York, and the powers of police justices. Passed April 19, 1859.

Preserved by section 786, subd. 17.

Laws of 1860, ch. 20.

An act in relation to the cutting of ice in the Hudson river. Passed February 11, 1860.

More extended provisions are given in sections 464–466.

Laws of 1860, ch. 27.

An act to authorize the agent and warden of the state prison at Sing Sing to purchase certain land. Passed February 11, 1860.

Unaffected by the Code.

Laws of 1860, ch. 39.

An act to compel the attendance of witnesses before committees of common councils of cities, and to punish false swearing by such witnesses. Passed February 18, 1860.

Section 1 of this act, declaring false swearing before committee perjury, is covered by section 150 of the Code.

Section 3, allowing punishment for contempt, is preserved by section 785.

Laws of 1860, ch. 103.

An act to prevent frauds in the sale of tickets upon steamboats, steamships and other vessels. Passed March 23, 1860.

The provisions of this act are the basis of sections 669–682 of the Code.

Laws of 1860, ch. 117.

An act to amend an act entitled "An act in relation to the sale of bottles used by the manufacturers of mineral waters and others," passed May 7, 1847. Passed March 24, 1860.

The provisions of this act are the basis of sections 417–419.

Laws of 1860, ch. 141.

An act to amend an act entitled "An act to prevent and punish prize fighting," passed March 7, 1859. Passed March 31, 1860.

Covered by section 496.

Laws of 1860, ch. 155.

An act in relation to bale hay and hay scales. Passed April 3, 1860.

Covered by sections 449, 450.

Laws of 1860, ch. 172.

An act to incorporate the Westfield gas company. Passed April 6, 1860.

Section 7, relative to injuring gas pipes of the company is covered by section 722 of the Code.

Laws of 1860, ch. 213.

An act to provide the means for the completion of the canals of this state, and fully supply them with water, and for other purposes. Passed April 9, 1860.

Section 5, relative to certain offenses affecting the canals, is covered by sections 516, 517 of the Code.

Laws of 1860, ch. 259.

An act to amend an act entitled "An act to establish a metro politan police district, and to provide for the government thereof;" passed April 15, 1857. Passed April 10, 1860.

Continued in force by section 786, subd. 18.

As to section 25 of the act, see note to section 150 of the Code.

Laws of 1860, ch. 265.

An act to provide for the manner of holding elections on the Cattaraugus and Allegany reservations in this state. Passed April 11, 1860.

Section 7 of the act, relative to corrupt practices at Indian elections is preserved by section 785 of the Code.

Laws of 1860, ch. 283.

An act authorizing the reports of the male and female departments of state prisons to be made separately. Passed April 12, 1860.

Covered by section 791

Laws of 1860, ch. 337.

An act requiring the justices of the peace in the several towns of Monroe and Niagara counties, and the police justice of the city of Rochester, to pay over to the county treasurer all fines received by them, and to report annually to the board of supervisors. Passed April 12, 1860.

Section 4 of the act, relative to omissions of duty by certain officers, is covered by the more general provisions of section 215 of the Code.

Laws of 1860, ch. 373.

An act to incorporate the Orange county milk association. Passed April 14, 1860.

Section 11, relative to selling adulterated milk, is covered by the more general provisions of section 451 of the Code.

Laws of 1860, ch. 399.

An act to amend the several acts in relation to state prisons. Passed April 14, 1860.

The various provisions of this act are covered by sections 844, 849, 850, 864, 869, 874, 878, 997–1007.

Laws of 1860, ch. 410.

An act in relation to capital punishment, and to provide for the more certain punishment of the crime of murder. Passed April 14, 1860.

See note to section 241, for reasons why this act is omitted.

Laws of 1860, ch. 442.

An act to regulate the sale of poisons. Passed April 16, 1860.

Covered by sections 446 and 448; except section 3 of the act, which is omitted for reasons stated in note to section 448 of the Code.

Laws of 1860, ch. 458.

An act to increase the compensation of assistant matrons of the Sing Sing female prison. Passed April 16, 1860.

Laws of 1860, ch. 465.

An act for ascertaining and collecting the damages caused by the destruction of the marine hospitals and other buildings and property at Quarantine. Passed April 16, 1860.

The provision of section 4, declaring false swearing perjury, is covered by section 150.

Laws of 1860, ch. 488.

An act to lay out a public park and a parade ground for the city of Brooklyn, and to alter the commissioner's map of said city Passed April 17, 1860.

Continued in force, by section 786, subd. 19.

Laws of 1860, ch. 501.

An act to preserve the public peace and order on the first day of the week, commonly called Sunday. Passed April 17, 1860.

Continued in force, by section 786, subd. 20.

Laws of 1860, ch. 508.

An act in relation to police and courts in the city of New York. Passed April 17, 1860.

So much of this act as relates to disorderly persons is expressly preserved by section 785. Other portions are not within the scope of the Code, and are, of course, unaffected by it, except sections 18, 33 and 34; as to which, see sections 550 and 587, and note.

Laws of 1861, ch. 63.

An act for the removal of insane convicts from the state lunatic asylum at Utica, to the state lunatic asylum for insane convicts at Auburn. Passed March 21, 1861.

Unaffected by the Code.

Laws of 1861, ch. 124.

An act concerning the navigation of the canals and the collection of tolls. Passed April 3, 1861.

Section 4 is covered by section 512 of the Code, and section 5 by section 515.

Laws of 1861, ch. 282.

An act to supply Sing Sing prison with Croton water, and for the sale of certain lands of the state. Passed April 17, 1861.

Unaffected by the Code.

Laws of 1861, ch. 283.

An act for the protection and improvement of the Tonawanda band of Seneca Indians, residing on the Tonawanda reservation in this state. Passed April 17, 1861.

Section 15, which declares false swearing in certain cases to be perjury, is covered by section 150 of the Code.

Laws of 1861, ch. 303.

An act in relation to cases of murder, and of arson in the first degree, occurring previously to the fourth day of May, in the year one thousand eight hundred and sixty. Passed April 17, 1861.

For the punishment for arson and murder prescribed by the Code, see sections 241, note, 247 and 539.

Laws of 1861, ch. 306.

An act to amend the act passed May eighth, eighteen hundred and forty-six, entitled "An act to authorize the establishment of the House of Refuge for juvenile delinquents in western New York." Passed April 17, 1861.

Unaffected by the Code.

Laws of 1861, ch. 340.

An act to amend an act entitled "An act to lay out a public park and a parade ground in the city of Brooklyn, and to alter the commissioner's map of said city;" passed April 17, 1860. Passed May 2, 1861.

Continued in force by section 786, subd. 21.

Laws of 1862, ch. 197.

An act to repeal chapter four hundred and ten, passed April 14, 1860, and chapter three hundred and three, passed April 17, 1861, and to divide the crime of murder into two degrees, and to prescribe the punishment of arson. Passed April 12, 1862.

As to so much of this act as relates to degrees in murder, see note to section 241 of the Code. Sections 7 and 8, punishing arson, are covered by section 539.

Laws of 1862, ch. 198.

An act to amend an act entitled "An act to supply Sing Sing prison with Croton water, and for the sale of certain lands of the state," passed April 17, 1861. Passed April 12, 1862.

Unaffected by the Code.

Laws of 1862, ch. 235.

An act to enable the people of this state to acquire certain lands situated in the town of Ossining, in the county of Westchester, for the use of the Sing Sing prison. Passed March 15, 1862.

Unaffected by the Code.

Laws of 1862, ch. 273.

An act to amend an act entitled "An act to regulate the sale of poisons," passed April 16, 1860. Passed April 17, 1862.

Covered by sections 446–448.

Laws of 1862, ch. 281.

An act to regulate places of public amusement in the cities and incorporated villages of this state. Passed April 17, 1862.

Continued in force by section 786, subd. 22.

Laws of 1862, ch. 285.

An act to amend chapter four hundred and twenty-seven of the Laws of 1855. Passed April 17, 1862.

Section 2, prohibiting the comptroller to be interested in any tax sales, is covered by section 499.

Laws of 1862, ch. 306.

An act to prevent and punish fraud in the use of false stamps, brands, labels, or trade marks. Passed April 17, 1862.

See the provisions on this subject in sections 410—416 of the Code.

Laws of 1862, ch. 356.

An act to provide for the regulation and inspection of buildings, the more effectual prevention of fires, and the better preservation of life and property in the city of New York. Passed April 19, 1862.

Continued in force by section 786, subd. 1.

Laws of 1862, ch. 374.

An act to prevent attempts to commit burglaries and other crimes. Passed April 19, 1862.

Section 1 of the act is covered so far as the commissioners have thought advisable, by sections 549 and 550 of the Code; section 2 by section 587, subd. 2; and section 3 is omitted for the reason stated in the note to section 587 of the Code.

Laws of 1862, ch. 378.

An act to amend an act entitled, "An act in relation to jurors and to the appointment and the duties of a commissioner of jurors in the county of Kings," passed April 17, 1858. Passed April 21, 1862.

The only penal provision is that of section 4, relative to misconduct in drawing jurors in Kings county. The commissioners perceive no reason why a special rule on this subject should be prescribed for a particular county; and they have omitted this statute, leaving the case contemplated to the operation of sections 103, 132 and 215 of the Code.

Laws of 1862, ch. 403.

An act to increase the duties and compensation of the physicians respectively, at the Auburn, Sing Sing and Clinton Prisons. Passed April 21, 1862.

This act is doubtless impliedly repealed by Laws of 1864, ch. 300; but as that act contains no repealing clause, the act of 1862 is enumerated among the acts repealed by section 1070 of the Code. (See subd. 21.)

Laws of 1862, ch. 417.

An act to alter the term for which criminals may be sentenced to state prison, and to provide for their earning a commutation of sentence, and an increase of the amount to be paid them on their discharge. Passed April 22, 1862.

As to section 1 of the act, see section 753 of the Code. As to sections 2–4, relative to commutation of sentences, see sections 1018–1023. As to section 5, permitting sums received from visitors to be applied to the use of discharged convicts, see section 870, last clause.

Laws of 1862, ch. 467.

An act to prevent the adulteration of milk, and prevent the traffic in impure and unwholesome milk. Passed April 23, 1862.

Sections 451 and 452 of the Code, are believed to be practically adequate to accomplish the object of this act.

Laws of 1862, ch. 474.

An act for the preservation of moose, wild deer, birds and fresh water fish. Passed April 23, 1862.

Preserved by section 786, subd. 23.

Laws of 1862, ch. 477.

An act to provide for the enrollment of the militia, the organization and discipline of the National Guard of the State of New York, and for the public defense. Passed April 23, 1862.

Section 11 of the act, declaring certain false swearing perjury, is covered by section 150 of the Code.

Sections 19, 294 and 296, relative to neglect of duty by certain officers, by section 215.

Section 314, relative to the retaining of military property by a person belonging to the military forces, contrary to orders, is deemed anomalous in its present form. So far as public property of a military character requires protection from the wrongdoers, irrespective of their membership in the military force, the general provisions relative to larceny, embezzlement, &c., and the provisions of sections 517, 519, 696, &c., are deemed sufficient. In so far as the offense consists in the disobedience to a military order, a military punishment seems more appropriate.

The various military punishments authorized by the act, are preserved by section 785.

Laws of 1862, ch. 484.

An act in relation to the courts in the city and county of New York. Passed April 24, 1862.

Laws of 1863, ch. 15.

An act to authorize the levying of a tax upon the taxable property of the different counties and towns in this state, to repay moneys borrowed for, or expended in the payment of bounties to volunteers, or for the expenses of their enlistment, or for aid to their families, or to pay any liability incurred therefor. Passed February 21, 1863.

So much of section 11 of the act as relates to omission of duty by supervisors, is covered by section 215 of the Code.

Laws of 1863, ch. 51.

An act to amend the Revised Statutes in relation to misdemeanors. Passed March 25, 1863.

Covered by sections 106–109.

Laws of 1863, ch. 139.

An act to amend the act to organize the State Lunatic Asylum for insane convicts, passed April 8, 1858. Passed April 17, 1863.

See sections 1048–1053, and notes.

Laws of 1863, ch. 174.

An act in relation to the detention of prisoners in the county of Kings. Passed April 17, 1863.

See sections 174 and 215.

Laws of 1863, ch. 192.

An act for the protection of the skating pond upon the Byram river. Passed April 20, 1863.

Omitted, for the reason that a statute penalty recoverable by civil action would be a more appropriate mode of protecting a merely local interest, like that referred to, than to create a new criminal offense.

Laws of 1863, ch. 209.

An act to amend the act entitled, "An act to prevent and punish fraud in the use of false stamps, brands, labels, or trade marks," passed April 17, 1862. Passed April 23, 1863.

See the provisions on this subject, in sections 410–416 of the Code.

Laws of 1863, ch. 244.

An act to amend section seventeen of article two of title three of chapter one of part four of the Revised Statutes, entitled "Of Burglary." Passed April 29, 1863.

See section 545.

Laws of 1863, ch. 291.

An act appropriating certain waters to the use of the Clinton state prison, and to make compensation therefor. Passed April 29, 1863.

Unaffected by the Code.

Laws of 1863, ch. 358.

An act establishing a Quarantine and defining the qualifications, duties, and powers of the health officer for the harbor and port of New York. Passed April 29, 1863.

The commissioners have contemplated the revision of the Health Laws as a separate body of laws. (See section 786, note.) Provisions for their enforcement, embodying many of the sections of the above act, are found in sections 435–441.

Laws of 1863, ch. 415.

An act to amend section first of chapter four hundred and seventeen of the Laws of eighteen hundred and sixty-two. Passed May 4, 1863.

This act relates to the earning of commutations of sentence by convicts in the state prisons. See provisions on that subject in sections 1018–1023.

Laws of 1863, ch. 465.

An act in relation to contracts and labor at the state prisons of the state. Passed May 5, 1863.

Sections 1–3 of the act are embodied in sections 1008–1110 of the Code; section 4 in section 848; and section 5 in section 852, subd. 3.

Laws of 1864, ch. 2.

An act to amend section three of chapter one hundred and eighty-four of the Laws of 1863, entitled "An act to promote the re-enlistment of volunteers now in the service of the United States, and the enlistment of persons into regiments and corps now in said service, and hereafter to be organized." Passed April 17, 1863. Passed January 29, 1864.

Continued in force by section 786, subd. 28.

Laws of 1864, ch. 142.

An act to revise and amend an act entitled "An act to authorize the formation of a railroad corporation in place of the Northern railroad company, dissolved, and to empower said corporation to execute a mortgage upon its property." Passed March 31, 1857. Passed April 8, 1864.

The offense contemplated by section 4, amending section 6 of the original act, is deemed sufficiently covered by the more general provisions of sections 601–612.

Laws of 1864, ch. 196.

An act for the better regulation and discipline of the New York State Inebriate Asylum. Passed April 15, 1864.

Preserved by section 786, subd. 24.

Laws of 1864, ch. 253.

An act to enable the qualified electors of this state, absent therefrom in the military service of the United States, in the army and navy thereof, to vote. Passed April 21, 1864.

Preserved by section 786, subd. 28.

Laws of 1864, ch. 276.

An act in relation to the sale, use and disposition of butts, hogsheads, barrels, casks, or kegs used by the manufacturers of malt liquors. Passed April 22, 1864.

Preserved by section 786, subd. 25.

Laws of 1864, ch. 300.

An act in relation to the compensation of the several officers of state prisons. Passed April 23, 1864.

Is the basis of section 854.

Laws of 1864, ch. 321.

An act to amend section second of chapter four hundred and fifteen of the Laws of 1863. Passed April 23, 1864.

Relates to earning commutations of sentence by convicts in state prisons. See provisions on that subject in sections 1018–1023.

Laws of 1864, ch. 390.

An act to amend section seven of the act entitled "An act to authorize the levying of a tax upon the taxable property of the different counties and towns in the state, to repay moneys borrowed for, or expended in the payment of bounties to volunteers, or for the expenses of their enlistment, or for aid to their families, or to pay any liability incurred therefor, or that may hereafter be incurred, and to amend section one of chapter five hundred and fourteen of the Laws of 1863." Passed February 9, 1864. Passed April 25, 1864.

This act was promulgated after the Code was so far completed, that the act could not be made the basis of any distinct sections in the body of the work; and in so far as it declares new misdemeanors it is deemed too obscure and uncertain to be continued in force in its present form, as authorizing criminal prosecutions. It is therefore disregarded. Violations of the act falling within sections 215 and 216 of the Code, will, however, be punishable under those sections.

Laws of 1864, ch. 391.

An act to prevent the swindling of persons enlisting into the military or naval service of the United States, and to make such offenses felony, and to punish the use of certain means to procure enlistments. Passed April 25, 1864.

Preserved by section 786, subd. 28.

Laws of 1864, ch. 403.

An act to amend an act entitled "An act to establish a Metropolitan police district, and to provide for the government thereof," Passed April 15, 1857. Passed April 10, 1860. Passed April 25, 1864.

Preserved by section 786, subd. 26.

Laws of 1864, ch. 451.

An act to incorporate the Long Island City Water Company. Passed April 30, 1864.

Section 17 of the act, making it a misdemeanor to injure the works or property of the company, is deemed sufficiently covered by sectious 696 and 722.

Laws of 1864, ch. 452.

An act to incorporate the Cambridge Valley Water Company. Passed April 30, 1864.

Section 17 of the act making it a misdemeanor to injure the works or property of the company, is deemed sufficiently covered by sections 696 and 722.

Laws of 1864, ch. 544.

An act to amend chapter four hundred and sixty-seven of the Laws of 1862, entitled "An act to prevent the adulteration of milk, and to prevent the traffic in impure and unwholesome milk." Passed May 2, 1864.

See the act amended, in its place in this table. The amendatory act was promulgated after the Code was too nearly completed to admit of its being made the basis of provisions in the body of the work.

Laws of 1864, ch. 555.

An act to revise and consolidate the general acts relating to public instruction. Passed May 2, 1864.

Preserved by section 786, subd. 27.

INDEX

TO THE PENAL CODE,

INCLUDING THE NOTES.

[N. B. The figures refer to the page.]

C

D

E

G

H.

I.

O